marketing communications

theory and applications

John R Rossiter and Steven Bellman

PEARSON

Prentice
Hall

Copyright © Pearson Education Australia (a division of Pearson Australia Group Pty Ltd) 2005

Pearson Education Australia
Unit 4, Level 2
14 Aquatic Drive
Frenchs Forest NSW 2086

www.pearsoned.com.au

Senior Acquisitions Editor: Sonia Wilson
Senior Project Editor: Carolyn Robson
Editorial Coordinator: Liz Male
Copy Editor: Annie Chandler
Proofreader: Jennifer Coombs
Indexer: Russell Brooks
Cover and internal design by Natalie Bowra
Cover image courtesy of Abbott Mead Vickers BBDO
Typeset by Midland Typesetters, Maryborough, Vic.

Printed in Malaysia, VVP

2 3 4 5 09 08 07 06 05

National Library of Australia
Cataloguing-in-Publication Data

Rossiter, John R.
Marketing communications: theory and applications.

Includes index.
ISBN 1 74103 269 5.

1. Communication in marketing. 2. Positioning (Advertising). I. Bellman, Steven. II. Title.

658.8

An imprint of Pearson Education Australia
(a division of Pearson Australia Group Pty Ltd)

about the authors

John R. Rossiter is Research Professor of Marketing at the University of Wollongong, Australia. Internationally, he is the most-cited Australian marketing academic. He is also permanent Visiting Professor of Marketing at the Rotterdam School of Management, The Netherlands, where he is based for two months each year. John gained his Ph.D. — in Communications — at the University of Pennsylvania and was Assistant Professor at Wharton and Associate Professor at Columbia University's Graduate School of Business, before returning to Australia, to the University of Technology, Sydney, then the Australian Graduate School of Management, then to Australia's "city of innovation," Wollongong, which hosts the University of Wollongong. He travels widely, and teaches and consults widely. In recent years, John's research has covered marketing (and marcoms) knowledge, brain research in advertising, and measurement, with articles in *Marketing Theory*, the *Journal of Consumer Research*, the *Journal of Advertising Research*, and the *International Journal of Research in Marketing*.

Steven Bellman is Senior Lecturer in Marketing at the University of Western Australia and by the time this book is published will be Research Leadership Fellow at the Interactive Television Research Institute, Murdoch University, Perth, Australia. Steve is a new generation, e-marketing-savvy, fast-tracking young academic who had his first job as an advertising art director and copywriter. (I wrote this copy, as Steve's too modest — JRR.) Steve's Ph.D. is from the Australian Graduate School of Management and he did his postdoctoral research at Wharton with Eric Johnston and Jerry Lohse, while working with data from the Media Metrix panel of Internet consumers and the Wharton Test Market panel. Steve and partner Deryn were recently blessed with their first child, Zak. Steve is also co-owner of a Sydney-based Web consultancy. Steve's research has appeared in *Management Science*, the *Journal of Marketing*, *Marketing Letters*, and the *Journal of Interactive Marketing*.

brief contents

	Preface	**xvii**
	Acknowledgments	**xix**
PART I	**MARCOMS AND BRAND POSITIONING**	**1**
1	Marcoms and the brand	3
2	How marcoms work and an overview of marcoms campaign planning	24
3	Brand positioning: T-C-B positioning model	42
4	Benefit positioning: I-D-U benefit analysis and the a-b-e benefit claim model	62
PART II	**MARCOMS CAMPAIGN OBJECTIVES**	**79**
5	Campaign target audience selection and action objectives	81
6	Campaign communication objectives	102
PART III	**ADVERTISING — CREATIVE STRATEGY**	**121**
7	Creative idea generation and selection	123
8	Brand awareness and brand preference (grid) tactics	151
9	Attention tactics	188
10	Pre-testing rough ads	212
PART IV	**ADVERTISING — MEDIA STRATEGY**	**233**
11	Media-type selection and the reach pattern	235
12	Effective frequency and strategic rules for implementation of the media plan	259
PART V	**BUDGET AND TRACKING**	**295**
13	Setting the campaign budget	297
14	Campaign tracking	312
PART VI	**OTHER MARCOMS**	**345**
15	Sales promotions	347
16	Corporate image advertising, sponsorships, and PR	375
17	Personal selling: direct selling and telemarketing	401
18	Social marketing campaigns	430
	Glossary	**471**
	Index	**491**

contents

Preface   **xvii**

Acknowledgments   **xix**

PART 1   **MARCOMS AND BRAND POSITIONING**   **1**

CHAPTER 1   MARCOMS AND THE BRAND   3

Marcoms defined   **6**

Advertising   6

Promotions   7

Marcoms media expenditures and use   **7**

Overall expenditures   7

Media use by individual advertisers   10

Sales effects   **11**

Advertising and sales   11

Promotions and sales   16

Brand equity   **18**

Corporate brand equity   18

Brand-item equity   19

Summary   **21**

Discussion questions   **22**

Notes   **22**

CHAPTER 2   HOW MARCOMS WORK AND AN OVERVIEW OF MARCOMS CAMPAIGN PLANNING   24

Customer decision stages   **24**

Brand communication effects   **25**

Acquisition   26

Choice   28

Ad or promotion processing   **28**

Operation of the three levels of effects   **29**

Customer response steps   **30**

Marcoms planning stages   **32**

Brand positioning   32

Campaign objectives   33
Creative strategy   34
Promotion strategy   35
Media strategy   35
Campaign management   35
The steps in action   **36**
Brand positioning   36
Campaign objectives   36
Creative strategy   37
Promotion strategy   37
Media strategy   38
Campaign management   38
Summary   **39**
Discussion questions   **40**
Notes   **41**

CHAPTER **3**   BRAND POSITIONING: T-C-B POSITIONING MODEL   42
The T-C-B positioning model   **43**
Always do positioning first   44
Research and judgment   44
T-C-B positioning model: overview   44
The target customer (T) positioning decision   **45**
The end-customer target   45
Campaign-level targets   46
The category need (C) positioning decision   **46**
Present versus intended category need   48
Target customer and category positioning   48
The key benefit (B) positioning decision   **49**
Central versus differentiated positioning   50
Emphasized benefit   51
Entry-ticket benefits   56
Inferior benefit   56
Brand architecture and positioning   **57**
Summary   **58**
Discussion questions   **59**
Notes   **59**

CHAPTER **4**   BENEFIT POSITIONING: I-D-U BENEFIT
     ANALYSIS AND THE A-B-E BENEFIT CLAIM MODEL   62
I-D-U benefit analysis   **62**
Importance or desirability (in the category)   63
Delivery (by each brand)   64

Uniqueness (between brands)	64
Example of I-D-U analysis for archetypes	65
Example of I-D-U analysis for functional benefits	67
I-D-U strategy options	**68**
What-ifs that anticipate competitive reactions	69
A word or three about terminology	70
The a-b-e benefit claim model	**71**
Integrated marcoms and positioning	**72**
The positioning statement	**73**
Long-form positioning statement	73
Short positioning statement	73
Summary	**74**
Discussion questions	**75**
Notes	**76**

PART II	**MARCOMS CAMPAIGN OBJECTIVES**	**79**
CHAPTER 5	CAMPAIGN TARGET AUDIENCE SELECTION AND ACTION OBJECTIVES	81

Customer targeting using brand loyalty segmentation	**82**
Brand loyals (BLs)	83
Favorable brand switchers (FBSs)	84
Other-brand switchers (OBSs)	85
Other-brand loyals (OBLs)	86
New category users (NCUs)	86
Brand loyalty groups and subgroups classification	**87**
Selecting the target audience	**88**
Sales maintenance	88
Sales growth	89
Assessing target audience potential via leverage	89
Action objectives	**90**
Pre-purchase behaviors	90
Purchase behaviors	91
Post-purchase behaviors	92
Action objectives as goals	92
Media target	**93**
Creative target	**94**
Behavioral sequence model	**95**
Summary	**97**
Discussion questions	**99**
Notes	**100**

CHAPTER **6**   CAMPAIGN COMMUNICATION OBJECTIVES   102

(1) Category need   **102**
Category motives – how to sell category need   105
(2) Brand awareness   **107**
Brand recognition   108
Brand recall   109
Brand-recall-boosted brand recognition   110
(3) Brand preference   **110**
(4) Brand action intention   **114**
(5) Purchase facilitation   **116**
Summary   **117**
Discussion questions   **117**
Notes   **118**

PART III   **ADVERTISING — CREATIVE STRATEGY**   **121**

CHAPTER **7**   CREATIVE IDEA GENERATION AND SELECTION   123

Components of an ad   **124**
1. The key benefit claim   124
2. The creative idea   125
3. Brand awareness and brand preference tactics   126
4. Attention tactics for ads in various media   126
The creative brief   **126**
Key benefit claim   **130**
The creative idea: the remote conveyer model   **131**
Properties of the conveyer   133
Conveyer types   135
Conveyer brainstorming (I-G-I method)   137
Conveyer screening and selection   137
What about the ad agency's creative ideas?   142
Postmodernism as the creative idea   **143**
Summary   **146**
Discussion questions   **147**
Notes   **147**

CHAPTER **8**   BRAND AWARENESS AND BRAND PREFERENCE
          (GRID) TACTICS   151
Rossiter-Percy-Bellman grid   **151**
Brand awareness tactics   **153**
Brand recognition   153
Brand recall   157
Brand-recall-boosted brand recognition   159

Brand preference tactics	**160**
Low-involvement/informational	160
Low-involvement/transformational	164
High-involvement/informational	168
High-involvement/transformational	173
Presenters	**177**
Executional integration tactics	**180**
Summary	**181**
Discussion questions	**183**
Notes	**183**

CHAPTER 9	ATTENTION TACTICS		188
	TV commercials		**188**
	Length		190
	Fast cuts		190
	Interest pattern		190
	Mystery ads		192
	Independent functioning of video and audio		192
	Radio commercials		**192**
	Length		193
	Format		193
	Style		194
	Newspaper ads		**194**
	Size and color		194
	Placement		196
	Structure		196
	Magazine ads		**198**
	Consumer and general business magazine ads: size and color		199
	Industrial magazine ads: size and color		200
	Structure		200
	Yellow Pages/directory ads		**201**
	Size		201
	Structure		202
	Outdoor ads		**203**
	Location		203
	Structure		204
	Online ads		**204**
	Email ads		206
	Web banner ads		206
	Websites		206
	Web TV ads		206
	Summary		**207**

Discussion questions		**208**
Notes		**208**

CHAPTER 10	PRE-TESTING ROUGH ADS	212
	Management judgment ad test	**212**
	Why the MJAT is necessary	213
	Rough ads	214
	MJAT methodology	216
	Examples of MJAT questionnaires	218
	Customer response ad test	**221**
	CRAT method	222
	Measures for the CRAT	225
	Overall scoring in the CRAT	228
	Summary	**230**
	Discussion questions	**231**
	Notes	**231**

PART IV	**ADVERTISING — MEDIA STRATEGY**	**233**

CHAPTER 11	MEDIA-TYPE SELECTION AND THE REACH PATTERN	235
	Primary and secondary media-type selection	**236**
	Primary medium	236
	Secondary media	237
	Primary medium selection	**239**
	Large-audience advertisers (B-to-C and B-to-B)	239
	Small-audience local retail advertisers	241
	Small-audience B-to-B advertisers	242
	Direct-response advertisers	243
	Secondary point-of-decision (P-O-D) media	**243**
	The reach pattern	**244**
	Reach patterns for new products	**244**
	Blitz pattern	245
	Wedge pattern	246
	Reverse-wedge/PI pattern	247
	Short fad pattern	248
	Reach patterns for established products	**248**
	Impact-schedule pattern	249
	Awareness pattern	252
	Shifting reach pattern	253
	Seasonal priming pattern	254
	Combining reach patterns	**255**
	The right perspective on the reach pattern decision	256

Summary	**256**
Discussion questions	**257**
Notes	**257**

CHAPTER 12 EFFECTIVE FREQUENCY AND STRATEGIC RULES FOR IMPLEMENTATION OF THE MEDIA PLAN **259**

Effective frequency	**260**
Insertions and exposures	260
Disposition to purchase (or act)	261
Minimum and maximum effective frequency	262
Minimum effective frequency (MEF/c) estimation formula	**265**
Examples of MEF/c calculations	268
No adjustment necessary for carryover	269
Ad unit adjustments to MEF/c	**269**
MEF/c and MaxEF/c for direct-response ads and promotions	271
Wedge and reverse-wedge changes to MEF/c	272
Retailer support	272
Short-term tactical adjustments in frequency to assist promotions	272
Very short-term scheduling	273
Media data, duplications and strategic rules	**274**
Duplication within and between vehicles	275
Strategic rules for selecting the vehicles	278
Implementing and optimizing the media schedule	**280**
Media models	280
Media Mania's models	280
Model example of reach and frequency strategies	281
Media budget setting	286
Summary	**288**
Discussion questions	**289**
Notes	**291**

PART V **BUDGET AND TRACKING** **295**

CHAPTER 13 SETTING THE CAMPAIGN BUDGET **297**

The total marcoms allocation	**297**
Total adspend	297
Purposeful adjustments in total adspend	301
Adspend policy in an industry recession	302
Adspend set and a competitor attacks	303
Campaign budget-setting	**303**
The task method	303
Schroer's method	307

Summary   **309**
Discussion questions   **310**
Notes   **311**

CHAPTER 14   CAMPAIGN TRACKING   312

Customer tracking survey   **312**
Measures used in tracking   **313**
Exposure measures   313
Ad processing measures   314
Brand communication effects measures   317
Target audience action measures   317
The customer tracking survey sample   318
Sales and market share measures   318
Brand equity and profit measures   319
Methodologies for tracking surveys   **319**
Customer tracking survey methodology   319
Customer tracking survey interview methods   321
Order of measures in the customer tracking survey   322
Analysis of campaign tracking results   **327**
Causal analysis   328
Quasi-causal analysis   328
Exposure-to-sales analysis   329
Tracking and campaign management   **329**
Determining why the campaign is or is not working   330
Adjusting the budget   330
Adjusting the media plan   330
Adjusting the exposure ratio of individual ads in the pool   330
Making minor improvements in ads   330
How often to track   **331**
Campaign initiation   331
Major change   332
Maintenance tracking   333
Campaign wearout   **333**
First audit: the marketing plan   334
Second audit: the media plan   336
Final audit: the ads themselves   338
Summary   **341**
Discussion questions   **342**
Notes   **343**

PART VI   **OTHER MARCOMS**   **345**

CHAPTER 15   SALES PROMOTIONS   347
    Manufacturer's trial promotions to retailers   **347**
    Introductory price allowance   349
    Returns   349
    New line fee   349
    Manufacturer's trial promotions to end-customers   **349**
    Product or service sampling   350
    Rebates   351
    Bonus packs   351
    Direct price-offs   352
    Warranties   352
    Premiums   353
    Coupons (for FMCG products and services)   353
    Manufacturer's repeat-purchase promotions to end-customers **354**
    Direct price-offs   354
    Sweepstakes or contests   355
    Multi-purchase premiums   355
    Packaging   356
    Retailer's promotions   **357**
    Store layout   **359**
    Retail atmosphere   **360**
    Color   360
    Music   360
    Olfactory cues   361
    Credit card stickers   361
    Retail feature ads   **362**
    Point-of-purchase displays   **363**
    Price-off promotions   363
    Price-off wording   365
    Monetary or percentage savings   366
    Price-endings   366
    Limited time or purchase amount   366
    Store brands   **367**
    Card-based loyalty programs   **367**
    Home shopping   **368**
    Summary   **369**
    Discussion questions   **371**
    Notes   **372**

CHAPTER 16   CORPORATE IMAGE ADVERTISING, SPONSORSHIPS,
                      AND PR   375
Sponsorships, PR, and product placements   **378**
Will it work – creatively   378
Target audience effective reach and reach pattern   384
Measuring the effects of sponsorship, PR, or product placement   385
Corporate image advertising   **387**
Communication objectives of corporate image advertising   389
Taglines (slogans)   393
Action objectives of corporate image advertising   395
Summary   **395**
Discussion questions   **397**
Notes   **398**

CHAPTER 17   PERSONAL SELLING: DIRECT SELLING
                      AND TELEMARKETING   401
Salesperson factors by type of selling   **402**
Regular retail selling   403
Small business selling   406
Trade selling   406
Telemarketing   407
High-end retail selling   411
Technical selling   413
Stages of selling and message tactics   **414**
Prospecting (optional)   416
Approach   416
Benefit presentation   418
De-resistance   422
Closing the sale   422
Follow-up   423
Summary   **424**
Discussion questions   **426**
Notes   **426**

CHAPTER 18   SOCIAL MARKETING CAMPAIGNS   430
Target audiences in social marketing   **432**
Stage 1: Segmentation by brand loyalty   432
Stage 2: Segmentation by personality and perhaps by gender,
         ethnicity, or literacy   434
Brand positioning in social marketing   **435**
Persuasion in social marcoms   **438**

An ethical alternative   440
Personality traits and perhaps gender – and persuasion   441
Media strategy in social marcoms campaigns   **447**
Media type selection   447
Reach pattern selection   449
Minimum effective frequency per advertising cycle   449
Media vehicle selection and use of the media model   450
Research in social marketing   **450**
The ethics of marketing communications: our view   **452**
Lying can be justified if and only if the truth would cause harm   454
Summary   **457**
Discussion questions   **459**
Notes   **460**

Glossary   **471**

Index   **491**

preface

Marketing communications – marcoms – are broadening and evolving, even as you read this, which poses a challenge to us as authors to identify the substantial and the worthwhile from among the many recent trends. The broadening and evolving marcoms options also pose a challenge to you, the present or future marketing manager, because they make it increasingly difficult to make intelligent decisions in planning a marcoms campaign. In the increasingly complex world of marcoms, there is greater need than ever for a comprehensive but workable planning system for marcoms management. This book provides such a system.

In composing this book, Steve and I have tried to evaluate and reconcile the best of the offerings of academic and practitioner researchers. Complicating the task of writing this book, and indeed any book in the field of marketing today, is the academic–practitioner divide. Academics (and the principal authors are both academics) love to do research on the major type of marcoms – advertisements – but the published work of most of these academics (and here we exclude ourselves) all too often indicates that they have never had to plan and implement a real advertising campaign. Most academic studies are conducted in forced-attention situations, with non-behavioral outcome measures, and show effects so small that they would be overwhelmed in a real campaign; notable for these faults are the many studies using the Elaboration Likelihood Model, the ELM, the most popular theoretical model among academics in advertising. Advertising practitioners ignore this research. Actually, they rarely see it because few academics place their research in practitioner publications and practitioners do not read our academic publications – the possible exception is the U.S.-based *Journal of Advertising Research*. But even if practitioners did see this academic research, in most cases they would be correct to ignore it because it is too difficult for them to decide what is useful from the academic studies. It is difficult enough for us – and we straddle the academic–practitioner fence! Practitioners' work, on the other hand – which consists of theory as well as valuable real-world empirical findings – is not sought out by academics. Citations in other textbooks and in U.S. academic journals to the British practitioner journal *Admap*, for instance, which is easily as useful as *JAR*, are close to zero. Practitioners are not without their own faults; the most annoying is reinvention of theory under some new label – for instance, Heath's "new" theory of Low Involvement Processing, which has been given extensive coverage in *Admap*. The practitioner-oriented journals, and *JAR* and *Admap* are both guilty here, should insist that authors acknowledge the origin of the ideas they promote. That said, there are a lot of genuinely new ideas coming out of the practitioner literature. This can't be said of the academic literature, which has remained straitjacketed in terms of marcoms ideas for at least 10 years and has pursued trivial sameness with just a few exceptions. Academic researchers, particularly in advertising, must learn to get real.

Some readers may be curious about the bloodline and gestation of this new book, to use a metaphor from horse-racing. It builds on – but adds greatly to – the influential earlier books written by Rossiter and his colleague Larry Percy. That partnership reached the peak of its life cycle with the Rossiter and Percy (1997) book. Steve Bellman is new generation, and the new book reflects this perspective. What is new about this book? We (Steve and I) nominate eight new and unique content features:

- Brand planning as well as planning for specific brand-items
- Expanded coverage of visual advertising as more campaigns go global
- Hyper-emphasis on attention tactics for ads as media become more cluttered
- Emphasis on emotional positioning as the most relevant for brands, and as an alternative to functional benefit positioning for brand-items
- New creative tactics for the six-cell advertising planning grid
- Analysis of the merits of postmodern advertising for the young-adult consumer audience
- Clear advice on how to integrate the marcoms campaign (IMC)
- Consistent approach carried through to other marcoms – sales promotion; personal selling and telemarketing; sponsorships, PR, and corporate image advertising; and social marketing campaigns

The book's style is also new and unique. Special terms, bold initially for the glossary, are then emphasized with initial capitals when that term would be emphasized orally in a lecture. This may make your reading a bit bumpier than usual (unless you read German, whence came English, which capitalizes nouns) but it will raise your understanding because many of the special terms are made up of common words such as "brand" and "recall" that together – Brand Recall – have a specific meaning that we want the reader to acknowledge. By this stylistic device we hope to overcome the biggest problem in marcoms management which is, ironically, communications – vague buzzwords that Postmodernly, everyone understands, but differently!

The book has a Website <www.pearsoned.com.au/rossiter> on which readers can locate many of the marcoms campaigns that we discuss.

Note that all monetary amounts in the book are in U.S. dollars unless, occasionally, specified otherwise.

We hope you will appreciate and enjoy the theory we have put into this book. The theory is presented as more authoritative than it really is but we have found that it produces superior applications and we fully expect that you will, too.

JOHN R. ROSSITER
STEVEN BELLMAN

acknowledgments

Preparation of this book was assisted in various ways by the following people. Marilyn Yatras, one of Rossiter's two first-class administrative assistants, coped admirably with the details of the several drafts of this long manuscript, always responding gracefully to requests for changes that must have seemed fastidious. Priscilla Kendall, the other, masterminded the visual exhibits of figures and even some ads! Deryn Alpers, Steve's partner, we both thank for her tolerance and support. Larry Percy, co-author with John of the forerunner to this book, was intellectually instrumental in helping us decide which frameworks to retain and which to modify or add and his contribution is gratefully acknowledged. We should add a promotion here for Larry's new book with Richard Elliott, *Advertising Strategy*, published by Oxford University Press, which, as planned, is a briefer version of the previous Rossiter and Percy textbook with some contemporary additions. Max Sutherland, who also has his own book, *Advertising and the Mind of the Consumer*, published by Independent Publishers Group, and is a lifelong colleague of John's, warrants special thanks for drawing attention to the really important issues in advertising management through his regular column in the Australian advertising trade newspaper, *AdNews*. Ale Smidts, Professor of Marketing at the Rotterdam School of Management, challenged and helped to test some of the frameworks in our book such as the Rossiter-Percy-Bellman Grid and the CESLIP Presenter Model. Sandra Jones, Associate Professor at the Health and Productivity Research Centre, University of Wollongong, kindly checked the facts in the social marcoms chapter without always endorsing our interpretations. Joëlle Vanhamme, Assistant Professor of Marketing at the Rotterdam School of Management, gave generous and valuable feedback on early drafts of the chapters and assisted greatly by testing them in class. France Leclerc, Professor of Marketing at the University of Chicago, also kindly class-tested the chapters. John's students in Marketing Communications at the University of Wollongong must also be thanked for their helpful feedback in this respect. Stewart York Rossiter, John's son and research assistant, served as a contemporary critic and corrector of his dad's work.

Cath Godfrey, Paul Petrulis and Sonia Wilson at Pearson Education Australia got the book conceived initially. Carolyn Robson at Pearson creatively and encouragingly kept the authors and the book on track (toughest job). Liz Male, Annie Chandler, Jennifer Coombs, Marji Backer, and Louise Burke most capably handled special aspects of the book's production. Thanks too to Natalie Bowra for the great design and layout.

The front cover illustration was generously provided by Guinness Plc and Abbott Mead Vickers BBDO advertising agency (it is an extract from Guinness' "Surfers" TV commercial). The illustration is wow on attention and a nice metaphor for what the book is about.

PART I

marcoms and brand

positioning

CHAPTER ONE
Marcoms and the brand 3

CHAPTER TWO
How marcoms work and an overview of
marcoms campaign planning 24

CHAPTER THREE
Brand positioning: T-C-B positioning
model 42

CHAPTER FOUR
Benefit positioning: I-D-U benefit analysis
and the a-b-e benefit claim model 62

CHAPTER 1

Marcoms and the brand

Marketing communications (marcoms) mean advertising – and much more. In modern marcoms, all possible "contact points" with potential and current customers are regarded as opportunities to communicate about the brand. Figure 1.1 shows a contemporary encircling list of brand contact points.[1] (The brand here could be the "brand name" of an entire company or organization, a specific "brand-item" of a product or service offered by the company, or a "brand" in social marketing promoted by a government organization, such as quitting drugs or getting regular exercise.) Consumers and business customers encounter, and sometimes actively seek, communications about brands from numerous sources. These prospects see or hear brand communications while they are commuting – via billboards, posters or on the car radio; while in the office – reading business newspapers or business magazines, or when opening direct mail or "spam" emails; while at home – watching TV, reading a newspaper, magazine or a mailed brochure, listening to the radio, handling food and beverage packages, looking at a calendar, or using a computer, or a pen; while attending sports events, concerts, plays, and movies – on tickets, in the program brochure, on the field, on the screen, on clothing; and, of course, while shopping in all types of stores – which could be actual stores or virtual (Internet) stores, and often before they enter the store as well as inside the store. And these are just some of the many marcoms contact opportunities in the traditional media. Then there are the new media, which are sometimes bizarre, and intrusive – ads on toilet walls, ads graffiti-style on sidewalks (the launch of Xbox in Sydney), and, in London, ads semi-permanently tattooed on university students' foreheads (the student is paid about $10 to wear the ad for three hours).[2] In social marketing, various brands of "good behaviors" are presented in government- or charity-sponsored political or health communications, while the competing brands of "bad behaviors" tempt most of us in everyday life. Marcoms – advertising especially – may reflect everyday life (slice-of-life ads), make an ironic comment about everyday life (postmodern ads), try to change our everyday life (public service ads), or temporarily deliver us from everyday life into a fantasy world of aspirations (see one of the ads from Smirnoff vodka's "Pure thrill" campaign in Figure 1.2. These days, marcoms contact us in all aspects of our life – real life and imagined life – influencing what we buy and what we want to be.

Marketing managers, including specialized brand managers and marketing communications managers, require useful planning frameworks and procedures to effectively navigate and select from the maze of modern marketing communications. In this book, we introduce a **six-step marcoms planning approach**. The parts of the book are organized sequentially in accordance with the six steps. The six steps, in abbreviated form, are: brand positioning, campaign objectives, creative strategy, promotion strategy, media strategy, and campaign management. We will revisit the six steps in more detail in Chapter 2 after we have explained, in that chapter, how marketing communications work.

FIGURE 1.1 *Brand contact points of marcoms.*

SOURCE: Adapted, with additions, from Donaghey and Williamson, 2003, p. 24, reference in note 1. This figure is reproduced and adapted with the permission of *Admap*. For more details go to <www.warc.com/admap>.

FIGURE 1.2 *One of the ads in Smirnoff vodka's long-running "Pure thrill" campaign. The ad is attention-getting and, most important, it efficiently communicates the elements of brand positioning (the key schema). The category need (alcohol) is signaled by the clear bottle; the brand identity (Smirnoff) correctly follows for brand recall; the key benefit (making the mundane thrilling) is communicated visually and reinforced in the tagline.*

SOURCE: Reproduced by kind permission of Diageo Plc. © 1993.

In this introductory chapter, a definition of Marketing Communications is presented first, accompanied by a classification of the major types of marketing communications. Second, we consider the effectiveness of the two main types of marketing communications – Advertising and Promotions – in generating Sales, which is the main measure of immediate success. Third, we consider Brand Equity – regarded by most as the principal measure of marketing communications' long-run success.

MARCOMS DEFINED

Marketing Communications – Marcoms – consist of what appear to be diverse activities (see Figure 1.1). However, marcoms activities share a common factor in that they are all concerned with marketing – that is, they try to *sell* the brand. Another common factor is that they do this by communicating *about* the brand, even when confronting the customer directly with the brand as in packaging and point-of-sale. The communications part comes from the Latin word *communicus*, which means "common" and refers in the marcoms context to the establishment of a commonality or identity between the marketer's intended communication message and the customer's inter-preted communication message: more particularly, between the marketer's intended positioning of the brand and the customer's perceived positioning of the brand. (The goal of commonality should suggest immediately why the pre-testing and also post-testing of ads and promotions, in the form of campaign tracking, are so important.)

Marcoms, therefore, are defined as *marketer-originated messages, placed in various media, their purpose being to sell the brand by showing it, saying things about it, or both, in a manner that establishes the marketer's desired position for the brand in the minds of target customers.*

Two major forms of marcoms are *advertising* and *promotions*. (The third is *PR* and the fourth is *personal selling*, but these are usually managed separately from advertising and promotions. They are included in this book in extra chapters, though presented from a perspective consistent with our marcoms planning approach.) There are, of course, various types of advertising and promotions, as we now describe.

Advertising

Advertising comes from the Latin verb *advertere*, which means "to turn toward," indicating that the purpose of advertising is to "turn the mind" of the prospective customer "toward" the brand.

The main types of advertising (and the public refers to all these things as "advertising" even though managers would use their more specialized names) include:

- **Brand advertising**, also called **awareness advertising**, which means advertising that is placed in mass media such as TV, radio, cinema, newspapers, magazines, and outdoor, and that is "mind turning," not direct-response, in its purpose.

- **Direct-response advertising**, which may be placed in mass media or in narrower, direct-to-customer media (the telephone, that is, telemarketing, being by far the biggest direct-response medium, followed by direct mail, and then Websites, still small as a direct-response medium but growing quite rapidly, particularly in business-to-business marketing) and attempts to be *"immediately* mind turning" so as to produce a sales inquiry, retail visit, or direct purchase.

- **Corporate image advertising**, **sponsorships**, and – in theory despite its typically separate management – **public relations (PR)**, all of which advertise the branded company or organiz-ation or the flagship brand, rather than specific brand-items.

All of these marcoms activities are advertising in the broad sense in that they aim to turn the prospective customer's mind toward consideration of the brand. Direct-Response Advertising additionally has the "act now" characteristic of a promotion, although it is never called a promotion.

Promotions

Promotions, the word, comes from the Latin verb *promovere*, which means "to move forward or advance," indicating that the aim of promotions is to produce immediate purchase of the brand (or to produce some other immediate action that will increase the opportunity for purchase of that brand, such as store visits or online inquiries). Promotions offer an *incentive to act now.* In practice, promotions are often included *in* advertisements and the most effective promotions are those that take the opportunity to communicate about the brand.

Promotions can be classified by who *originates* them: manufacturers, retailers or either of these two types of marketers (direct marketing promotions):

- *Manufacturers* originate **salesforce promotions**, such as sales commissions, frequent-flyer points rewards, and other non-cash bonuses; **trade promotions**, which are nearly always monetary incentives offered to wholesalers (in some cases) and retailers (in almost all cases) to carry and sell the manufacturer's products or services; and manufacturers' **direct-to-customer trial promotions**, such as product or service sampling, manufacturers' warranties, and rebates, and also **repeat-purchase promotions**, such as multiple-purchase coupons and bonus offers.

- *Retailers*, too, originate promotions. These include physical **store layout** (and *Website* layout) chosen to facilitate the flow of customer traffic; psychological **store atmosphere** stimuli such as lighting, color, and music; **retail feature ads**, which advertise promotions on the products offered by the retailer, and are placed in mass media or narrower media such as direct mail; in-store **point-of-sale (POS) displays** and **price-off promotions**; the retailer's **own brand(s)**; and, in some cases, **TV or PC interactive shopping**, in retail outlets or at home. Retail feature ads and in-store promotions are in most cases *cooperative* (in terms of paying the cost) with manufacturers, who regard them as forms of trade promotions. The other types of retailer's promotions are paid for by the retailer.

- *Manufacturers* and *retailers* originate **direct-marketing promotions**. The most effective direct-marketing promotions make use of **database marketing** to direct introductory offers to new prospects and to reward, via a **loyalty program**, those customers who make repeat purchases.

We also regard two other forms of marcoms – **personal selling** (face-to-face selling) and **telemarketing** (selling by telephone) – as promotions rather than as advertising as their emphasis is on persuading prospects to act now. Actually, personal selling and telemarketing are very much like direct-response *advertising* because there is mind-turning involved before the push to action. The public, also, would see these as "promotions."

MARCOMS MEDIA EXPENDITURES AND USE

Overall expenditures

The U.S.A. accounts for about 45% of world advertising expenditures and that country's figures are the most readily available. In Table 1.1, U.S. marcoms expenditure figures, by medium, are shown for 2003, the most recent year of complete information at the time of writing.[3] There are some interesting aspects:

- Telemarketing is the largest marcoms medium in the U.S.A., although it is dropping by about a third as we write this, to the approximate level of Direct Mail, as the result of a new "do not call" registry opened in June 2003. In the European Union "outbound," that is, unsolicited, telephone selling is prohibited. (Personal Selling, i.e., face-to-face selling, is not shown in the table but is a major form of marcoms. Estimates of expenditure on personal selling in the U.S.A. range from a conservative $145 billion cited in Kotler's leading textbook, to $500 billion, and we believe the larger figure is closer to the truth because every employee is essentially a salesperson for the company or organization.[4])

- Direct Mail, another direct-response advertising medium, and just as much a "mass" medium in terms of reach as other print media, is now the second largest medium of advertising and with restrictions on telemarketing will soon become the largest.

- Altogether, Print Advertising – direct mail, newspapers (over 80% of the ads are local), magazines, directories such as the Yellow Pages (also over 80% local ads), outdoor, business publications, most "miscellaneous," such as flyers and calendars, *and* the Web – makes up about *two-thirds* of all mass-media advertising.

- TV Advertising, both free-to-air and pay TV, is about *one-quarter* of mass media advertising by expenditure and is the only medium that achieves close to universal reach. Pay TV (cable in the U.S.A., cable or satellite elsewhere) advertising is growing fast. However, at present, pay TV penetration is much higher in the U.S.A. (reaching about 65% of households) than in other Western countries (20 to 30%). Cinema Advertising (TV commercials preceding movies) has just been reintroduced in the U.S.A. whereas the rest of the world has always had it.

- Internet Advertising, consisting of Web banner ads and Websites, is a small but substantial 1.9% of mass media expenditure, with recent tremendous growth up to 2002 but just 5% or so annual growth at present.

- Outdoor Advertising, similar in expenditure to Internet Advertising, has also increased greatly in recent years – in acknowledgment of the increasingly mobile and longer-commuting population.

- Sponsorships – both ongoing and for special events – are a very large, and growing, marcoms medium. Sponsorship attracts budgets similar to those of Magazine Advertising.

- Trade Shows are the main medium for *industrial* business-to-business, or B-to-B, advertisers. Trade shows, of course, are an opportunity for face-to-face selling.

For advertising, in the overall sense, what should strike you is that the major portion – about 60% – depends on classic, time-honored *copywriting skill*. This is vital in the newest medium, Internet advertising, too, and there is clearly a major and growing demand for creatives in agencies who can "sell off-the-page" as in long-copy direct mail ads. At the same time, the 40% or so of ads in the brief but high reach and salient media – TV, Outdoor and Sponsorships – increasingly demand the *visual communication skill* of movie directors, many of whom now consult to ad agencies, for production values and often for a postmodern slant. The upshot is two very big and very different types of effective advertising.

TABLE 1.1 *Estimated expenditure on marketing communications: U.S.A., 2003.*

MARKETING COMMUNICATIONS MEDIUM	EXPENDITURE PROJECTED FOR 2003 ($ BILLIONS[a]) AND GEOGRAPHIC BREAKOUT (WHERE APPLICABLE)	%
Telemarketing	67.0[b]	21.1
Direct mail	49.1	15.5
Newspapers	45.7 (national 7.2, local 38.5)	14.4
TV (free-to-air)	43.1 (national networks 15.6, major markets 14.1, local 13.4)	13.6
Miscellaneous media	30.0	9.4
Radio	19.7 (major markets 4.3, local 15.4)	6.2
Yellow Pages	14.0 (national 2.1, local 11.9)	4.4
Pay (cable, satellite) TV	13.3	4.2
Magazines	11.8	3.7
Sponsorships, events	9.2	2.9
Internet (Web)	5.1	1.6
Outdoor	5.1	1.6
Business publications	4.5	1.4
Trade shows	1.1	0.3
Total	**317.7**	**100.0**

[a] The first entry above, for instance, is $67 billion in U.S. and now virtually worldwide terminology, that is, $67 thousand millions, whereas the previous British "billion" was a million millions.

[b] Telemarketing expenditure is likely to have declined to about $45 billion by now (see text).

SOURCES: Universal McCann, New York, Insider's Report by Robert J. Coen, June 17, 2003, for mass (measured) media; and estimates for other marcoms published in *Advertising Age*, June 28, 2002, on this trade paper's Website.

No really reliable figures are available for expenditures on Promotions, and wildly varying estimates appear in trade publications (and in textbooks). It is commonly believed that promotions' expenditures now exceed advertising expenditures for the U.S. economy as a whole, but this is impossible to substantiate because of the increased use of *integrated* communications, in which promotions are *also* ads. (So-called Free-Standing Inserts, or FSIs, which appear in newspapers in the U.S.A. and in shopper magazines in other countries, are a good example of ads that mostly, but not 100% of the time, include a promotion.[5]) Although it has long been true that sales promotion costs exceed advertising costs for some types of marketers, notably manufacturers of fast-moving consumer goods (FMCG) who offer trade promotions as well as consumer promotions, we estimate that the overall ratio of advertising expenditure to sales promotions expenditure for the *U.S. economy as a whole* is something like 75% advertising and 25% promotions. We estimate also that this is about the ratio that consumers and customers *see and hear*: approximately 75% advertising-alone messages and 25% promotion offers, including in-store promotions. In other Western economies, we estimate that the ratio is a little higher in favor of advertising, but not a lot!

Media use by individual advertisers

Looking at the choice of marketing communications from the individual advertisers' perspective rather than from the aggregated perspective reveals another interesting fact. From Figure 1.1 earlier, it is easy to gain the impression that all advertisers use all forms of marcoms. Such a misconception is easy to believe because marcoms textbooks and popular marketing publications often highlight "multi-media" campaigns. In reality, individual advertisers usually concentrate their expenditures on one *primary* medium of advertising and supplement this with just one or two secondary media. Table 1.2 shows a rarely seen tabulation by *individual advertisers*, in this instance from the Australian economy.[6] (The same tabulation for the U.S. economy was not readily available; however, Australia, though smaller, has a similar overall pattern to the U.S.A.) The figures are for national advertisers and do not include allocations by smaller, regional or local advertisers, but the inclusion of figures for them would only strengthen the already apparent conclusion, which is that individual advertisers use only a few media.

TABLE 1.2 *Individual advertisers' use of marcoms media: Australian National Advertisers, 2002.*

MARCOMS MEDIUM	USE (%)	USE MOST (%)
TV (free-to-air)	92	61
Newspapers	84	21
Magazines	84	5
Radio	79	3
Internet (Web)	77	0
Outdoor	61	1
Exhibitions, trade shows	55	1
Catalogs	52	5
Cinema (movie theater ads)	39	0
Pay (cable, satellite) TV	38	2
Direct marketing	2	0
Sponsorship	2	0

SOURCE: Starcom Worldwide, *Media Future Report 2003*, survey of national advertising in Australia.

As the table reveals, the traditional mass media of TV, newspapers, magazines, and radio are used by about 80% or more of national advertisers in Australia, with TV highest at 92%, although this means that there are 8% of national advertisers who do not use TV at all. TV dominates with 61% of national advertisers using it as their *primary* medium. However, another 21% put their primary advertising in newspapers. After that, small percentages of individual advertisers use another medium as their primary medium: magazines are used as primary by 5% of advertisers; catalogs by 5%; radio by 3%; pay TV by 2%; with another 1% of individual advertisers concentrating on outdoor advertising and 1% concentrating on exhibitions and trade shows. What is also interesting is which media are *not* primary media. Internet advertising (Web banner ads and company or brand Websites) is used by 77% of Australian advertisers, but no advertiser uses Internet advertising as the primary medium. Cinema (movie theater) advertising is used as a medium by a surprisingly large proportion of advertisers, 39%, although none use cinema advertising as the primary medium. The total incidence of use of direct marketing (mainly telemarketing and direct mail) and of sponsorship, at 2% each, is much lower than in the U.S.A., and no national advertisers in Australia use direct marketing or sponsorship as their primary medium.

What determines the choice by a national advertiser of a particular primary medium such as TV, newspapers, or, say, catalogs? In the chapters on media strategy, it will be seen that, *assuming* that the medium has the capacity to carry all the communication objectives for the brand, the main selection criterion for the primary medium is *target customer reach*. There is an additional consideration of a sufficient rate of frequency, but this can be achieved quite well, even in low-frequency media such as monthly magazines, by multiple ad placements per issue, known as *impact scheduling*.

SALES EFFECTS

We hope to further motivate you to read this book by showing you what marketing communications *can* do, at their very best, and also caution you – another reason for reading this book – by considering what marketing communications usually *do* do. For marketing communications we will keep the dichotomy between Advertising (meaning media advertising) and Promotions (meaning price promotions) because these two types of marcoms have very different effects on sales. We consider here advertising's short-run effect on sales and its one-year effect on sales. For price promotions, we consider the short-run effect on sales. Sales increases are the effects that excite managers most but we will see in the next section of the chapter that what they should be focusing on is not just sales but rather Brand Equity, because that is what produces long-run profit.

Advertising and sales

What *sales effect* can the manager expect, on average, from an advertising campaign? Table 1.3 provides a summary answer to this question based on a major meta-analysis study (a study that calculates the average results over numerous previous studies) of "advertising elasticity."[7] Advertising elasticity, as *we* use the term, is the percentage increase in the brand-item's sales (in sales units) that can be expected from a 10% increase in the brand-item's advertising spending (adspend). Although elasticities are usually reported based on 1% increases, we use 10% because this is a more typical amount of increase in adspend from month to month or year to year (or a 10% decrease, in which case reverse the signs in the table).[8] Also note that these are advertising elasticities for the "normal operating range" of changes in adspend and would be different if changes were made at the extremes outside the normal operating range; for example, a 10% increase in the current budget would have the effect shown, but a 10% increase on top of a previous 90% increase in the budget would understandably have much less effect (a lower elasticity figure). In the table, because these differ considerably, we show the advertising elasticities separately for fast-moving consumer goods (FMCG) and for high-priced products (consumer durables and industrial products); for the brand-item's adspend considered in isolation (absolute) and alternatively as "share of voice" (relative), that is, share of total category adspend; and for the short term (10-week sales effect of one week's adspend) and long term (one-year sales effect of one year's adspend).

According to the original study, and quite unexpectedly, advertising elasticities do *not* differ for new brand-items (introduction and growth stages) versus established brand-items (maturity stage of brand-item life cycle). However, *price* elasticity does differ, being much lower for new brand-items than for mature brand-items. We will see when discussing Brand Equity at the end of this chapter that a price-related purpose of advertising is to reduce the brand-item's price elasticity, that is, reduce consumers' price sensitivity, but only for its own price increases. The other price-related purpose of advertising is to *increase* the brand-item's price elasticity for its own price cuts.

TABLE 1.3 *Average % change in unit sales of a brand-item that can be expected from a 10% increase in adspend for FMCG products and for durables, by absolute and relative adspend, short-term and long-term.*

| | SALES UNITS INCREASE (%) | |
| | 10-WEEK | 1-YEAR |
FAST-MOVING CONSUMER GOODS (FMCG)	PERIOD	PERIOD
Adspend increased by 10% for one week (10-week effect) or over the year (1-year effect)	+ 0.3	+ 1.4
Relative adspend (SOV) increased by 10% for one week (10-week effect) or over the year (1-year effect)	+ 0.4	+ 2.0

| | SALES UNITS INCREASE (%) | |
| | 10-WEEK | 1-YEAR |
DURABLES (CONSUMER DURABLES AND INDUSTRIAL PRODUCTS)	PERIOD	PERIOD
Adspend increased by 10% for one week (10-week effect) or over the year (1-year effect)	+ 0.8	+ 3.6
Relative adspend (SOV) increased by 10% for one week (10-week effect) or over the year (1-year effect)	+ 1.1	+ 5.2

SOURCE: Estimates adjusted from elasticities and adjustment factors in R. Sethuraman and G.J. Tellis, 1991, reference in note 7.

FMCG advertising elasticity

Looking at the first row in the table, we see that, for FMCG products, on average, a 10% absolute increase in the brand-item's adspend for one week will produce a 0.3% (that's three-tenths of one percent) increase in the brand-item's *unit* sales over 10 weeks (we use a 10-week period for sales effects as this is how long the sales effect of a one-week burst of advertising typically lasts, although most of the effect occurs in the first week or two.[9]) Over a year, if adspend has been increased by 10%, the unit sales increase will be 1.4%, on average. Note that a 1.4% sales return for a 10% increase in advertising does not necessarily mean a loss, because the 10% increase in advertising is on a much smaller base amount than the dollar base of sales. For instance, if the adspend budget is $10 million, a 10% increase in the budget would be (an additional cost of) $1 million. If the advertising expenditure as a percentage of dollar sales, that is, the advertising-to-sales ratio, is 5%, a fairly typical adspend ratio, then dollar sales would be $200 million, and a 1.4% increase would produce (additional revenue of) $2.8 million. In this case, the extra sales revenue would easily cover the advertising cost. But whether this would be *profitable* depends on the product's unit profit margin. This sales increase would yield a profit only if the unit profit margin is at least 36% ($2.8 million $\times$ .36 = $1.01 million, an amount which is just higher than the advertising cost, that is, above "break-even").

Durables advertising elasticity

Looking now at the first row in the second panel of the table, which shows the short-term and long-term advertising elasticities for durables (high-priced consumer products and industrial products), it can be seen that durables respond more than twice as strongly to advertising than do FMCG products. A one-week increase of 10% in adspend for durables will produce, on average, an increase in sales over the next 10 weeks of 0.8%, and the yearly increase in adspend of 10% will produce a 3.6% increase in sales for the year. High-priced consumer products and high-priced business and industrial products generally have very large dollar sales (the price per unit is high) so that the advertising cost as a percentage of sales dollars is quite low in these cases, usually to the order of 1% or 2%. Whereas this may imply that the increases shown in the table would always be profitable, the authors of the meta-analysis are careful to point out that advertising for durables usually has to be supported by extra salesforce time and perhaps extra salespeople, as well as, for many products, additional technical assistance and service support – which adds substantially to the total marketing communications cost.

In terms of *profit*, based on their consultancy's analysis of more than a decade of advertising campaigns, for consumer *and* business products and services, Clancy and Krieg estimate that most (68%) have produced a return on investment, an ROI, of just 1% to 4% which, as they note, is a worse return than putting the money in a bank's interest-earning account! The top 16% have a 5% to 20% ROI; the bottom 16%, zero or a loss.[10]

Competitive advertising

A lot of the time during the brand-item's advertising campaign competitors are also advertising. The second row of advertising elasticities in each panel of the table shows what can be expected if the advertising for the brand-item can be scheduled so as to represent a 10% increase in *relative* adspend in the product category, that is, a 10% increase in "share of voice" (SOV), which may or may not represent a change in absolute adspend. When our advertising achieves an increase of 10% in SOV, the effect on sales is about 25% higher than if "just adspend" had been increased by 10%.

Advertising quality

The advertising elasticity figures shown in the table are estimates of the sales effect that managers can expect if their ad campaign is of *average* quality – more specifically, average in terms of achieving Brand Awareness and Brand Preference. (We will draw attention to special terms in marcoms by using initial capitals. This means that the term or concept is important *and* that you should use our definition of it.) The fact is, however, that the quality of the advertising campaign has an enormous effect on sales. The next table, Table 1.4, shows the advertising elasticities estimated from the same meta-analysis but this time with the quality of the advertising campaign factored in. We see that if the 10% increase in adspend is spent on ads of high quality – ads that strongly generate Brand Awareness and Brand Preference – the sales effects increase by an average of 175%. We see that, with high-quality advertising, managers of FMCG brand-items can expect a short-term sales increase of 0.8% and a long-term sales increase of 3.9%, for a 10% increase in adspend. For durables, the sales increases are 2.2% and 10.0%, respectively. If the change in adspend represents a 10% increase in SOV, then the sales increases in both cases are about 40% higher than that. Note, however, that the advertising quality factor works both ways. Increasing adspend with *low*-quality ads can actually cause the brand-item's sales to go *down*, as we shall see next.

TABLE 1.4 *Advertising quality: sales effects of increases in adspend when the quality of the advertising campaign is factored in.*

FAST-MOVING CONSUMER GOODS (FMCG)	SALES UNITS INCREASE (%)	
	10-WEEK PERIOD	1-YEAR PERIOD
Adspend increased by 10% for one week (10-week effect) or over the year (1-year effect)	+ 0.8	+ 3.9
Relative adspend (SOV) increased by 10% for one week (10-week effect) or over the year (1-year effect)	+ 1.1	+ 5.5

DURABLES (CONSUMER DURABLES AND INDUSTRIAL PRODUCTS)	SALES UNITS INCREASE (%)	
	10-WEEK PERIOD	1-YEAR PERIOD
Adspend increased by 10% for one week (10-week effect) or over the year (1-year effect)	+ 2.2	+ 10.0
Relative adspend (SOV) increased by 10% for one week (10-week effect) or over the year (1-year effect)	+ 3.0	+ 14.4

SOURCE: Estimates adjusted from elasticities and adjustment factors in R. Sethuraman and G.J. Tellis, 1991, reference in note 7.

Jones' data on TV ad quality

Data from an analysis by Jones[11] show that high-quality TV ads (the top 30% of TV ads in the U.S.A. and the top 20% elsewhere) can have an enormous sales effect and that low-quality TV ads (the worst 30% in any country) can actually hurt the brand-item's sales. Jones' results are shown in Table 1.5 for TV ads analyzed in three different countries. The ad campaigns in each country were divided into deciles in terms of their short-term sales effectiveness – weekly sales in Jones' analysis. Weekly sales effectiveness of an ad is defined as the increase or decrease in unit purchases of the advertised brand-item in *those households* exposed to the ad in that week compared with unit purchases of the brand-item in those households not exposed to the ad that week. (The figures in the table do not represent the increase in sales across all households. To calculate the overall sales effect, we would need to know *how many* households were exposed to the ad that week. Thus, for instance, the figure of +24% for the average campaign in the U.S.A. indicates that there was a 24% sales increase contributed by those who saw the ad; only if all households saw the ad that week, a rather unlikely event, would the sales increase be 24% overall.)

TABLE 1.5 *Short-term sales effects of TV ad campaigns by range (deciles) of effectiveness in three countries. Entries in table are percentage changes in weekly sales units among those households that saw the ad that week, relative to normal sales among those households that did not. Campaign effects measured over 52 weeks. N = number of brands (brand-items) and thus number of ad campaigns in each country studied.*

| | SALES INCREASE (AMONG EXPOSED HOUSEHOLDS) IN % | | |
DECILES OF AD EFFECTIVENESS	U.S.A. (N = 78)	ENGLAND (N = 67)	GERMANY (N = 28)
Top 10% of campaigns	+ 136	+ 84	+ 54
2nd 10%	+ 64	+ 29	+ 27
3rd 10%	+ 39	+ 19	+ 16
4th 10%	+ 21	+ 14	+ 8
5th 10%	+ 16	+ 10	+ 6
6th 10%	+ 8	+ 7	+ 1
7th 10%	+ 3	+ 2	0
8th 10%	− 3	− 2	− 2
9th 10%	− 11	− 7	− 8
Bottom 10%	− 27	− 27	− 17
Average campaign	+ 24	+ 13	+ 8

SOURCE: J.P. Jones, 2002, reference in note 11, p. 23. © 2002 by Sage Publications, Inc. Reprinted by permission of Sage Publications, Inc.

The top 10% of ad campaigns in the U.S.A., as shown in the table, produced a weekly sales increase, among households reached, of 136%. In the U.K. and Germany, two countries in which quantitative pre-testing of ads is much less often employed, the sales increases for the top 10% of ads were 84% and 54%, respectively. However, the bad news is that in each of the three countries, the worst 30% of ads caused the brand-item's sales rate to go *down*. This is not necessarily, as Jones is careful to point out, because these ads turn consumers off the brand (although this could happen if the ad changed to a different Key Benefit Claim that made otherwise-loyal buyers defect) but rather that these ads are not good enough to protect against the effectiveness of *other brands'* ads seen by those households during that week. Note that these negative effects on sales, like the positive effects, are against a *no advertising* control. The implication of Jones' data is that it is better not to advertise than to advertise with low-quality ads.

A principal reason for a TV ad's failure to protect is when it does not clearly identify the brand and thus fails to generate Brand Awareness. In the U.S.A., McCollum Spielman company's pre-test data suggest that 45% of TV ads may have this problem.[12] When consumers are asked approximately 10 minutes after seeing the ad to name the brand that was advertised, about 35% of TV ads are "nameless" to consumers and 10% are attributed to a competitor! In the U.K., a recent estimate is that 52% of TV ads do not get the brand across.[13] For print ads, we note, the reader "has control," and the mis-branding incidence for print ads that are noticed in the first place is only about 14%.[14]

The most important objective for the manager is to make sure that only ads that are highly likely to be effective (ads can be checked by valid pre-testing) are used in the ad campaign. "Effective" means the ad gets Attention, generates correct Brand Awareness, and creates, increases, or reinforces Brand Preference.

Promotions and sales

Promotions – and here we are talking about *price promotions*, which are by far the most prevalent type of promotion – produce large, immediate sales effects ("immediate," here means within four weeks of the initial price reduction). On average, a 10% price reduction will produce a 17% increase immediately in unit sales.[15] Durable products show a greater sales response to price cuts than do FMCG products. As shown in Table 1.6, first row, FMCG products show an average 16.4% rise in sales when their price is reduced by 10% whereas durable products show a 21.4% rise in sales. As we will see shortly, these sales increases are not likely to be profitable unless the brand-item has a very large unit profit margin (50% or higher margin). This is because price reductions are a direct cost; a 10% increase in advertising is on the base of the advertising budget, but a 10% reduction in price comes out of total sales revenue.

TABLE 1.6 *Average % change in unit sales of a brand-item that can be expected from a 10% price reduction for FMCG products and for durables. The table shows the direct price-off effect and the larger effect when the price reduction is "announced" via a promotion and accompanied by high-quality advertising (immediate sales effect within one month of the price reduction).*

	SALES UNIT INCREASE (%)	
	FMCG	DURABLES
10% price reduction by direct price-off	+ 16.4	+ 21.4
10% price reduction in a promotion and with high-quality advertising	+ 32.6	+ 42.6

SOURCE: Estimates adjusted from elasticities and adjustment factors in R. Sethuraman and G.J. Tellis, 1991, reference in note 7.

In the second row of the table, we have estimated, from the data provided in the original meta-analysis, the sales effects of a 10% price reduction when the price reduction is "announced" by a promotion rather than being a simple price-off and when it is accompanied by (ideally, *immediately preceded by*) high-quality advertising for the brand-item. When these two events occur, the sales increase from the 10% price reduction is approximately doubled: a 32.6% sales increase for FMCG products, on average, and a 42.6% sales increase for durable products. Yet sales increases of these magnitudes still may not be profitable.

The next table, Table 1.7, shows *why* price reductions may not make a profit. For a 50% increase in sales to be profitable at a 10% lower price, the profit margin on the item (before the price-off) has to be more than 30%. At unit profit margins of 30% or less, a 50% increase in sales from a 10% price cut is a loss. The truth is that price-off promotions have to sell a lot of extra volume to be profitable. Big sales increases are easy to achieve with deep price cuts (as the price elasticity norms show), which may make the manager look good – but, you have to ask, what is the effect on profit?

TABLE 1.7 *Extra % sales units needed from price-off promotions to break even at various unit profit margins.*[a]

UNIT PROFIT MARGIN (AT NORMAL PRICE)	SALES INCREASE (%) NEEDED AT PRICE-OFF AMOUNT OF				
	5%	10%	15%	20%	25%
5%	(loss)	(loss)	(loss)	(loss)	(loss)
10%	100	(loss)	(loss)	(loss)	(loss)
15%	50	200	(loss)	(loss)	(loss)
20%	33	100	300	(loss)	(loss)
25%	25	67	150	400	(loss)
30%	20	50	100	200	500
35%	17	40	75	133	250
40%	14	33	60	100	167

[a] Calculated by solving for V, where V is the percent unit sales increase needed to break even, in the equation V = 100 [normal profit margin/(normal profit margin – discount)] – 100. For example, for the first column, second entry: V = 100 [10%/(10% – 5%)] – 100 = 100%. Note that if the price-off is equal to or greater than the normal profit margin, no amount of extra sales could increase gross profit, hence (loss) in table.

However, we do not want to give the impression that price-off promotions serve no purpose. Promotions are very useful when:

- they attract *new triers* to the brand-item and the triers then purchase the brand-item repeatedly afterwards at its full price

- they are used to promote an established brand-item to encourage consumers to *stock up* during the launch of a competing brand-item so that consumers' trial of the new item is delayed, for some consumers, or may never happen

- they are used tactically to follow bursts of equity-building advertising

This last point leads us to consider next the long-run purpose of marcoms, which is to enhance brand equity.

BRAND EQUITY

Brand equity, in the sense of "brand value," has emerged as the most popular bottom-line measure of marketing – including marcoms – effectiveness. Brand Equity applies to the corporate brand and to brand-items, but differently.

Corporate brand equity

Interbrand's **brand valuation** procedure for measuring *corporate brand* equity has emerged as world-leading because its valuations are accepted by the world's leading stock markets. Interbrand's corporate brand valuation procedure is based on expert assessment of seven main marketing characteristics of the brand, weighted as follows: leadership 25%; internationality 25%; stability 15%; market strength 10%; market trend 10%; support 10%; and protection 5%. The brand's score on these factors, with each factor consisting of about four sub-factors which are not listed here, is converted to a single monetary value figure. According to Interbrand, the world's 10 most valuable brands in 2002 were: Coca-Cola $70 billion; Microsoft $64 billion; IBM $51 billion; General Electric (GE) $41 billion; Intel $31 billion; Nokia $30 billion; Disney $29 billion; McDonald's $26 billion; Marlboro $24 billion; and Mercedes $21 billion.[16]

Contrary to the popular impression, corporate brand valuations cannot be taken for granted in the long term and show surprising volatility even on an annual basis. For instance, Samsung gained 30% in brand value from 2001 to 2002, from $6.4 billion to $8.3 billion; and the Nivea, Harley-Davidson, Dell, and Starbucks brands each gained over 10% in value. On the other hand, Ericsson lost 49%, almost half, of its brand value in the same period, from $7.1 billion down to $3.6 billion; and Ford, AT&T, Boeing, and Merrill Lynch each lost 25% or more of their brand value over the same period. As Interbrand makes clear, it is not just marketing communications but marketing activities overall that cause the changes in a brand's value. For instance, Merrill Lynch, a loser over the year, had a well-publicized conflict of interest. Dell, a winner, relies mainly on its built-to-order production rather than its advertising, although its advertising – particularly on its Website and in newspaper inserts – has been very good. On the other hand, Samsung's spectacular growth in brand value over the year has been largely the result of its new advertising campaign, a campaign that repositions Samsung as a leader and as a more upscale and stylish brand. The cost of Samsung's advertising campaign is not reported but some indication is provided by the fact that it spent $200 million on advertising during the following year, 2003, to reinforce its new positioning.

Corporate brand valuations such as these are probably of most interest to corporate accountants and industry investors. Some companies, such as Procter & Gamble and Simplot, do not have a corporate brand for their products but instead use many different brand names, such as Tide and Head & Shoulders in P&G's case and Birds Eye and Four 'N' Twenty (a famous brand of Aussie meat pies!) in Simplot's case, and these brands are not individually large enough to be valued by Interbrand's method. So what does P&G do, since it too must be attractive to the stock market? It indulges in large advertising budgets for its products and lets this be known to the financial community (an unconfirmed rumor heard from a leading marketing scientist is that P&G spends 110% of its net profit on advertising). As a study by Joshi and Hanssens demonstrates, even if a company's product advertising is not very effective, investors will pay a premium for a company that is an aggressive advertiser.[17]

Brand-item equity

Marketing managers should be concerned with the equity of specific *brand-items*. To measure and track Brand Equity for a specific *brand-item*, Moran's method is best.[18] Moran's method is based on tracking the brand-item's price elasticity of demand, which was discussed earlier as one of the performance factors that marcoms can influence. Moran's insightful contribution is to separate price elasticity of demand into "upside elasticity" and "downside elasticity." This produces two types of brand-item equity:

1. The brand-item's **value equity** is indicated by its upside elasticity. High value Equity means that the brand-item's sales go up sharply in response to even a small price cut because the brand-item is seen as better value at this price, where value is benefits received for the price paid.

2. The brand-item's **uniqueness equity** is indicated by its downside elasticity. High uniqueness of the brand-item is indicated by *low* downside elasticity; that is, sales do not go down much, if at all, when the brand-item's price is raised or when competitors lower their prices. Lack of sales fall-off means that customers see the brand-item as relatively *unique* (non-substitutable) and therefore do not switch to the (now) relatively lower-priced brands when the brand's relative price is increased.

An illustration of Moran's dual price-elasticity of demand method will help. A hypothetical illustration, based on actual but disguised data, is shown in Figure 1.3. This particular brand-item shown in the diagram has one good aspect – high Value Equity, which is shown by the sharp sales rises when its price falls below the category average price. On the other hand, it reveals a bad aspect – this brand-item has almost no Uniqueness Equity, as shown by the fact that whenever its relative price rises above the category average its sales fall off sharply.

Moran's method requires tracking of unit sales, week by week, and of relative price in comparison with the category average price. We will return to this method in Chapter 14, which covers Campaign Tracking.

Moran goes on to consider strategy based on the results from his method. There are four main scenarios that can eventuate for brand-item equity. These, and the implications for the brand-item's marcoms, are listed below.

- *High value, high uniqueness*: This is the most desirable position. Use bursts of advertising to remind customers of the good value of the brand-item, each burst followed immediately by a promotion, as sales will respond sharply to a very small price reduction. Promoting on the back of an advertising burst is known as the **ratcheting strategy**.

- *High value, low uniqueness*: Good, but could be better. Try to find or develop a unique benefit for the brand-item, and advertise this, emphasizing perceived uniqueness.

- *Low value, high uniqueness*: Good, but could be better. Try to broaden distribution of the brand-item and also raise its price, within reason. Continue to emphasize perceived uniqueness in the advertising.

- *Low value, low uniqueness*: This is the undesirable position. Almost certainly, a product problem precedes the marcoms problem. Use R&D to find a benefit that adds value and *also* differentiates the brand. The brand-item's advertising then has to advertise both value, via the new benefit, and uniqueness compared with other brand-items.

Both types of brand-item equity (Value Equity and Uniqueness Equity) contribute to the ultimate marketing objective at the brand-item level, which is long-run profit. Value Equity sells units of the product at a faster rate when there is an actual or *de facto* price cut, thus preserving overall profit. Uniqueness Equity helps maintain profit by protecting against loss of sales rate when there is a *de facto* price increase and by directly increasing profit, even at a slightly reduced sales rate, when there is a real price increase.

Identifying valuable and unique benefits is an important prelude to brand and brand-item positioning, as we will see in Chapters 3 and 4. Before that, however, in Chapter 2, we need to explain how marcoms work.

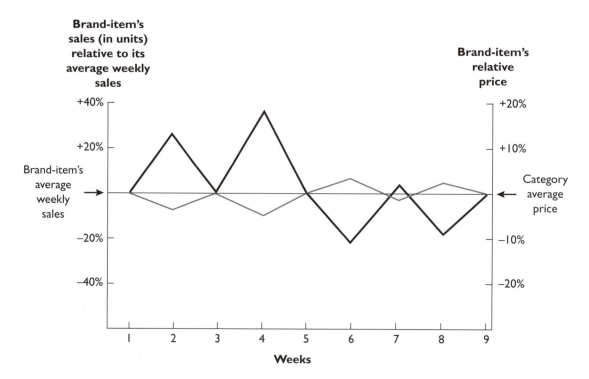

FIGURE 1.3 *Sales changes (heavy line) in response to changes in relative price (thin line): hypothetical example. This brand-item has high value equity, as indicated by the large sales increases when the price is below the category average, but low uniqueness equity, because when its relative price is above average, its sales decline substantially.*

SUMMARY

Marcoms – marketing communications – are everywhere, including a lot of new places. Although limited a little by privacy legislation in some countries, marketers regard almost all of our daily activities as possible "brand contact points." To the public, marcoms – especially advertising and promotions – *are* marketing and, for most marketing managers too, marcoms planning and implementation are most of what they do as marketing. Today more than ever the marketing manager requires a good planning system of frameworks and procedures, which this book is designed to provide.

In this introductory chapter, we introduced the reader to the wide variety of marcoms and specifically to the different types of advertising and promotions; there is a later chapter on corporate marcoms that includes PR and a later chapter on personal selling, as these marcoms are usually managed separately from advertising and promotions.

An important finding regarding advertising is that, despite the multiplicity of media options available, individual advertisers typically use just one primary medium and perhaps one or two secondary media. Later it will be seen that we endorse this focus because although the use of many media can increase the reach of a campaign, such a practice is prohibitively expensive and is not very efficient for achieving the frequency and, when needed, continuity that most brands require.

We then looked at what managers can expect in terms of the sales effectiveness of advertising and of promotions, on average. On average, a 10% increase in adspend produces a cumulative sales increase over the year of 3.6% for industrial products and consumer durables and 1.4% for fast-moving consumer goods (FMCG). These sales increases may be profitable because they are percentaged on a larger monetary amount – total sales revenue – which is typically about 20 times larger than the monetary amount of the advertising budget. We further saw that the sales increases are about three times greater than average if the ads employed in the campaign are of high quality (meaning that they generate Brand Awareness and create, increase, or reinforce Brand Preference).

Promotions, and here we considered price promotions, have very large short-term (four-weekly in our data) effects on sales; for example, a 10% price reduction produces, on average, a 21.4% increase in unit sales for durables and a 16.4% increase in unit sales for FMCG products. If the price promotion is coupled with (i.e., immediately preceded by) high-quality advertising, the sales effects are doubled. However, products or services sold with a price promotion are sold, of course, at a lower price, and the sales increase in units has to be very large for the promotion to be profitable. For instance, as we showed in Table 1.7, if the unit profit margin on the item is 15%, and the price reduction is 10%, then 200% more units have to be sold just to break even. Introductory promotions, however, can be very profitable if they attract new buyers to the brand-item and if those buyers repeat purchase of the item at its normal price.

The long-run measure of marcoms success is not sales as such, but rather Brand Equity, which delivers profit from those sales. We discussed corporate brand equity, which is of most interest to investors. Then we discussed brand equity for the specific brand-item, drawing attention to Moran's excellent method of measuring this in terms of Value Equity (upside price elasticity) and Uniqueness Equity (downside price elasticity). Brand or brand-item positioning, examined in the next part of the book, is largely focused on developing Value Equity and Uniqueness Equity.

DISCUSSION QUESTIONS

1.1 Review the definition of Advertising and the definition of Promotion in the chapter and then find an ad (the local newspaper is a good place to look) that appears to use a fairly equal mix of both. Explain how you arrived at this assessment.

1.2 Suppose that you wish to sell your car but do not want to go to the expense of placing an ad in any sort of paid media. What would be some effective "contact points" at which to place your message?

1.3 Go to Coca-Cola's Website and find out what major Sponsorships the brand Coke is currently engaged in. Select one of these and explain whether you believe it to be a good choice for Coke.

1.4 Why do you think individual advertisers do not use more than one or two media when there are so many options available?

1.5 Talk to a local retailer with whom you are on good terms and find out the retailer's percentage profit margin on just one item. Using the table in the book, calculate the estimated sales increase that would be needed if the retailer were to offer that item at a 10% Price Off. Discuss your estimate with the retailer and write a brief report.

1.6 For the same retailer and the same item (but you don't need to visit this time): how could the retailer *increase* the sales effect of the price-off promotion?

1.7 How does the concept of Brand-Item Equity differ from the concept of Corporate Brand Equity?

NOTES

1. B. Donaghey and M. Williamson, Thinking through "through-the-line," *Admap*, 2003, April, 24–26.

2. Ads on heads, footpaths; pushing the limits in marketing, *Professional Marketing,* March/April, 2003, p. 6.

3. The references are in the sources note in the table.

4. The $145 billion estimate for personal selling is cited in the 2000 edition of P. Kotler's *Marketing Management* textbook; the $500 billion estimate, also approximately for the year 2000 and just for face-to-face selling, not telemarketing, is cited in A.A. Zoltners and S.E. Lorimer, Sales territory alignment: an overlooked productivity tool, *Journal of Personal Selling & Sales Management*, 2000, 20(3), pp. 139–150.

5. See F. LeClerc and J.D.C. Little, Can advertising copy make FSI coupons more effective?, *Journal of Marketing Research*, 1997, 34(4) pp. 473–484. In Chapter 8, we generalize their important findings in an advertising tactic.

6. Starcom, *Media Future Report 2003,* survey of national advertisers in Australia.

7. Estimates adjusted from elasticities and adjustment factors in R. Sethuraman and G.J. Tellis, An analysis of the tradeoff between advertising and price discounting, *Journal of Marketing Research*, 1991, 28(2), pp. 160–174.

8. Typical U.K. figures for 2000 to 2003, for example, show that while 50% to 60% of companies (the proportion changes by year) keep their annual adspend constant the rest revise adspend quarterly, with changes averaging about plus-or-minus 10%, Bellwether report, *Admap,* September 2003, Adstats section, p. 3.

9. S. Broadbent, *When to Advertise,* Oxfordshire, U.K.: Admap Publications, 1999.

10. K.J. Clancy and P.C. Krieg, *Counterintuitive Marketing,* New York: The Free Press, 2000. The 68% comes from taking one standard deviation (34% of cases) either side of the mean of a normal curve and the 16% in each tail are more than one s.d. out from the mean.

11. J.P. Jones, *The Ultimate Secrets of Advertising*, Thousand Oaks, CA: Sage, 2002.

12. These normative findings come from tests with over 22,000 TV commercials conducted by McCollum Spielman Worldwide, a research company in Great Neck, NY. The test ad is embedded in a half-hour program with six other ads for non-competing products. At the end of the program, viewers, who have watched the program in an invited central-location setting, are asked "What brands were advertised in the program you just saw?" Post-test tracking studies overstate correct branding because they base it on those who have recalled the ad.

13. S. Brook, Consumers left dumbstruck by local campaigns, *The Australian*, Media section, September 19–25, 2002, p. 3.

14. This finding is based on thousands of magazine ads, in consumer and business publications, analyzed by the Starch/INRA Hooper (now Roper Starch) research service. The norms for one-page, color consumer magazine ads, for instance, are 49% for noticing the ad in the first place and 42% for noticing the advertiser's brand name or logo. See J.R. Rossiter, The increase in magazine ad readership, *Journal of Advertising Research*, 1988, 28(5), pp. 35–39.

15. R. Sethuraman and G.J. Tellis, 1991, same reference as in note 7.

16. G. Khermouch, The best global brands, *Business Week*, August 5, 2002, pp. 92–99.

17. W.T. Moran, Insights from pricing research, 1976; The advertising–promotion balance, 1978; and Marketplace measurement of brand equity, *Journal of Brand Management*, 1994, 1(5), pp. 272–282. The two early papers by leading marketing consultant William T. Moran were published in conference proceedings (by The Conference Board and the Association of National Advertisers, respectively, in the years shown) and are somewhat difficult to obtain but they are well worth reading before his 1994 journal article. The two early papers explain his concepts of "upside" and "downside" price elasticity of demand (related later to brand equity) and associated brand strategies as summarized in our chapter. The 1994 article, we should note, refers to upside elasticity as "relative price" and downside (in)elasticity as "durability."

18. A. Joshi and D. Hanssens, Advertising spending and market capitalization, paper presented at the INFORMS Marketing Science conference, College Park, MD: University of Maryland, June 2003.

19. W.T. Moran, 1976, 1978, references in note 17.

CHAPTER 2

How marcoms work and an overview of marcoms campaign planning

In the first chapter, we looked at what marketing communications can *do* for the brand but not *how* they do it. It is important to consider how marketing communications work because of widespread confusion about "the" hierarchy of effects, which is a misleading oversimplification. A proper understanding of *levels* of effects is a prerequisite for marcoms campaign planning and these levels are explained in the first part of the chapter. A summary sequence of customer response steps is then identified for the purpose of campaign planning. The marcoms campaign planning stages are explained in the second part of the chapter.

The confusion over how marcoms work has emerged because marcoms theorists have not made it sufficiently clear that there are *three levels* of effects going on simultaneously during marketing communications. The three levels of effects are:

1. Ad or promotion processing
2. Brand communication effects
3. Customer decision stages

These three levels of effects relate to one another as shown in Figure 2.1. The diagram may look complicated but it's quite easy to understand when you work your way through it. It's easiest to explain by starting at the right-hand side (level 3, the customer decision stages) and working back.

CUSTOMER DECISION STAGES

For any given product or service category, at any given time, the potential customer is in *one* of the customer decision stages (level 3). The customer is either **not in the market** at present for the

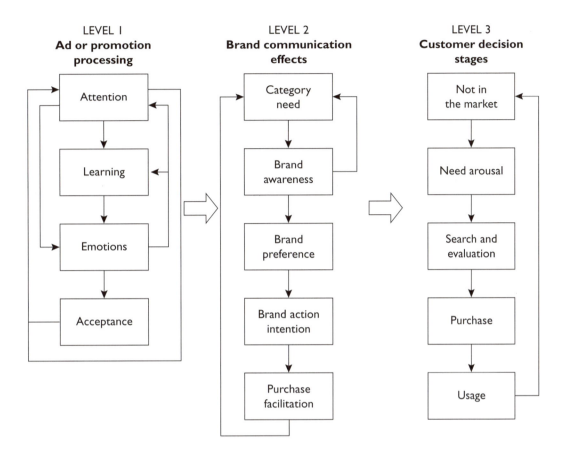

FIGURE 2.1 *Three simultaneous levels of marcoms effects.*

product or service category, or is experiencing **need arousal**, or is **searching and evaluating** brand-item alternatives, or **purchasing**, or **using** the product or service. These decision stages are usually hierarchical in occurrence ("fixed sequential" is a more accurate description but the term "hierarchical," which refers to superiority or rank rather than time order, has become common). There are occasional exceptions such as when Search and Evaluation continues during Usage (making a trial of a free sample or participating in a service demonstration would have this characteristic). But in most cases each stage is completed before the next – so, yes, there is a hierarchy of effects at the customer decision stage level. When considering a *repeat* Purchase in the category, the customer cycles back through the stages after being out of the market for a while, as shown by the right-hand arrow.

BRAND COMMUNICATION EFFECTS

Feeding into these customer decision stages are communication effects for each brand (level 2). Actually, they are for each *brand-item*, but we will use the broader term "brand" for easier discussion. We will examine brand communication effects in detail in Chapter 6, but introduce them now. The brand communication effects are:

1. **Category need** – really a category communication effect but regarded as a brand communication effect *in that* the particular brand has to be connected to the customer's need for the product or service category to produce the next communication effect, Brand Awareness; also, a particular brand, usually the market leader, may attempt to grow the category.

2. **Brand awareness** – which is necessary in order that the brand can be considered for purchase – the brand either has to be recognized as an item of that category (Brand Recognition) or recalled as an item when the category need arises (Brand Recall) in the decision process.

3. **Brand preference** – which is, absolutely, a favorable *attitude* toward the brand and, relatively, *preference* for it over other brands.

4. **Brand action intention** – usually *Purchase* Intention, which must occur consciously as a self-instruction to act if choice of the brand is a high-risk decision.

5. **Purchase facilitation** – a communication effect that is necessary in some cases so that the customer can act on the Brand Action Intention.

Now, let us consider the acquisition of these communication effects, as distinct from the utilization of these communication effects when making a brand choice.

Acquisition

The six brand communication effects do *not*, from the brand's marcoms, have to be *acquired* hierarchically. For instance, the customer's Category Need may arise *after* he or she has become aware of the brand and learned a preference for it (e.g., you may be well aware of, and prefer, Huggies diapers but not need to buy them until you have a baby[1]); this order is shown by the loop on the right-hand side of the first and second communication effects. Brand Awareness and Brand Preference, the second and third communication effects, are usually acquired *simultaneously*. An ad usually attempts to make people aware of the brand, or regenerate their awareness of the brand, *and* create, increase, or reinforce preference for it. The exception might appear to be with a "teaser" ad campaign – a campaign that attempts to build Brand Awareness first, then to reinforce awareness and establish Brand Preference in the main campaign (see, e.g., the teaser ad for the launch of the Chrysler Crossfire automobile, in Figure 2.2). We would suggest, however, that a teaser campaign also begins to create Brand Preference, even if the preference is vague at first (with the Crossfire teaser ad, you would have to feel some attraction to the particular automobile shown or, more precisely, partly shown, before you would be among "the first to find out" by going to the Website).

The next two communication effects, Brand Action Intention and Purchase Facilitation, are usually acquired in that order, following Brand Preference, although even here it is possible to know where to buy the brand and its approximate price (Purchase Facilitation) without at the time having the Brand Action Intention to purchase it. Also, if choice of the brand is "low involvement" (low purchase-risk), these last two communication effects are not necessary and are bypassed; this

FIGURE 2.2 *Teaser ad for the launch of the Chrysler Crossfire automobile in Australia.*

SOURCE: Image is courtesy of DaimlerChrysler Australia/Pacific Pty Ltd (ABN 23 004 411 410). © DaimlerChrysler Corporation. Chrysler is a registered trademark of DaimlerChrysler Corporation.

path is shown in the diagram by the loop back to Category Need after Brand Preference. Direct-Response Ads, called in the U.K. simply Response Ads, attempt to achieve *all five* communication effects, or certainly all four after Category Need if the need is already present, in a *single* exposure. Awareness Ads, called in the U.K. Brand Ads or Brand-Building Ads, in contrast to Direct-Response Ads, usually require *multiple* exposures to build Brand Awareness and Brand Preference.

The "building" idea suggests that they are not expected to work in just one exposure. Brand ads loop round and round the processing boxes and the results pop out into the brand communication effects boxes – but this is much too complicated to draw in the diagram!

The main point is, as you can see by the "short circuit" loops at level 2, that there is hardly ever a strict hierarchy of *acquisition* of brand communication effects. The big mistake in the hierarchy of effects account of brand communication effects is the notion, repeated in many textbooks and believed by many students and quite a few managers, that marketing communications have to *instill* the brand communication effects *in sequence* – for instance, that an ad campaign has to generate Category Need before it can generate Brand Awareness, and generate Brand Awareness before it can generate Brand Preference, and so forth. An ad campaign or promotion campaign does not work by instilling one communication effect at a time, in a hierarchy. Think instead of the brand communication effects as "mental boxes to be filled or topped up" in the *one* campaign. They start filling together and may be topped up with one exposure or only after several.

Choice

A likelier instance of a hierarchy of effects is found during *choice*. During choice of a brand, the previously acquired brand communication effects "go into action." The communication effects become mental *outputs* that input to, and influence, choice of the brand. During choice, the five brand communication effects usually *do* operate as a hierarchy. That is, the prospective customer experiences the Category Need first, then Recalls or Recognizes alternative brands, together with his or her intensity of Preference for each – although, note, Brand Recognition often *precedes* Category Need – then Intends to purchase one of them and may have to have that intended purchase Facilitated. The process of choice, then, pretty much is based on a hierarchy of the brand's communication effects.

AD OR PROMOTION PROCESSING

Feeding into the brand's communication effects are *short-term responses* to individual ads and promotion offers for the brand. These short-term, and immediate, responses to the ad or promotion (level 1) are given the collective name **processing**. The processing responses occur – or, to be more correct, the advertiser *hopes* they will occur – during exposure to each ad or promotion offer and again if the same ad or promotion offer is seen or heard again. We avoid the usual label of "information processing" because it doesn't do justice to emotional responses to ads or offers (e.g., responses to the typical Benetton ad or Coke ad, or a child's responses to a toy offer in a Coco Pops box). We could have added *sales presentation* processing here, as in face-to-face selling or telemarketing. We will leave that until Chapter 17, as the two-way communication complicates matters, although the four key processing responses are exactly the same.

Ad processing, or promotion processing, then, is a collective description of four diverse responses that can be made during exposure. These responses are Attention responses, Learning responses, Emotion responses, and Acceptance responses. They occur in *many different permutations* (hence the many arrows in the level 1 diagram):

- **Attention** precedes the other three responses – indeed, *repeated* Attention responses, either actual or imagined, are necessary for the prospective customer to fully process an ad or offer.

- After Attention, **learning** may occur, and that might be the end of processing (e.g., you learn from the ad that Orange is a telephone company, and that it is "contemporary," and that's all).

- Alternatively, after Attention, only an **emotion** response might be made in processing (e.g., you may hate the ad and *never* learn which brand it advertises; or you might simply experience a positive emotion in conjunction with the brand, which alone may be sufficient for later preference of it).

- **Acceptance**, technically, is a combination of Learning and Emotion (Acceptance is the result of learned Benefit Beliefs subjectively perceived as "true" of the brand, which are positively emotionally weighted). Acceptance responses in processing, indicated by the prospective customer's *net positive* "cognitive responses," are necessary when advertising a brand to customers for whom its purchase is *high risk*, or when making a *promotion* offer.

The effects in Processing are more accurately described as *polyarchical* – from the Greek word meaning "many" – because they can occur in many different permutations. They are never hierarchical, because of the looping back of Attention and also the possible Attention-to-Emotion "short" circuit or Attention-to-Learning "short" circuit.

OPERATION OF THE THREE LEVELS OF EFFECTS

Now look at Figure 2.1 again and try to see how there are three levels of effects going on at once.

The whole customer response process is triggered by exposure to an ad or promotion offer, or by exposure to the brand itself during Usage, producing responses at level 1, the Processing level. This exposure could be to an ad for the brand, with this ad seen or heard for the first time. However, Processing would also be triggered by the customer's second exposure to the same ad, seen or heard for the second time. Or it could be triggered by exposure to an ad for *another* brand, seen or heard for the first time, or the second time, etc. Alternatively, exposure to a promotion for the brand, or for the other brand, would likewise trigger Processing, as would exposure to the brand during Usage, the usage being by you *or* someone else.

Processing of the ad for the brand, at level 1, will initiate – or increase, or reinforce – Brand Communication Effects for the brand, at level 2. The prospective customer might never have heard of the brand before, in which case the first ad will be initiating communication effects for it. On the other hand, the prospective customer may be well aware of the brand and may even have purchased it before, in which case Processing of the ad would be "topping up" or reinforcing Brand Awareness and Brand Preference. Also, if the ad includes a promotion offer, it may be attempting to stimulate an immediate Brand Purchase Intention. Subsequent exposures to the same ad for the brand or to different ads in the same campaign for the brand will similarly contribute to the brand's communication effects at level 2.

Processing of ads or offers from *other* brands will, in turn, initiate or top up brand communication effects for *them*, also, at level 2. These marcoms for other brands competing for the same Category Need might *interfere* with the communication effects established for the first brand.

For instance, the prospective customer may have preferred the first brand until seeing a competitor's ad that raises the customer's preference for *that* brand higher than for the first. The phenomenon of competitive interference in advertising is severe, as we saw in Chapter 1, unless the brand runs only high-quality ads.

The prospective customer now has communication effects for perhaps several brands lodged in his or her mind. These Brand Communication Effects may become activated in the Customer Decision Stages at level 3. For instance, an ad for a brand may promote the Category Need (a communication effect at level 2) which in turn moves the prospective customer from the stage of being Not in the Market for the category to the next stage, Need Arousal (at level 3). Communication effects for brands are most relevantly activated during the Search and Evaluation stage of the customer decision process (level 3) but they can and might be activated at *any* stage.

A **considered purchase** goes through the levels but in a slow and back-and-forth manner. The process of buying a new car, for example, might extend over weeks or months. During this time, the prospective customer is likely to be exposed to many ads and promotion offers for a number of brands, and perhaps see the cars on the street, though will pay Attention, mostly, to ads for those cars in the particular category or of the particular type that he or she is interested in (level 1). These ads or promotion offers and, of course, there may also be other marketing communications in the form of Website visits or dealer visits, will add to the prospective customer's mental database of brand communication effects (level 2). These brand communication effects will be elicited during the Search and Evaluation stage and will influence the Purchase stage (level 3). Also, if you are typical, you will continue to pay Attention to ads for the car you have just bought, during the Usage stage![2] This cognitive-dissonance-reducing phenomenon serves to reassure the new owner, of, say, a new Nissan Z car, that he or she has made the right choice.

In contrast, a so-called **impulse purchase** provides an interesting demonstration of how the three levels can operate *simultaneously*. Ad Processing (level 1) is caused by the package and its display at the point of purchase (the package works like an ad). You have never seen this item before. The communication effects for it – the whole five, Category Need through to Purchase Facilitation – get acquired in one exposure, or, if you have seen the item before, then communication effects 1, 4 and 5 get acquired in one exposure and 2 and 3 get reinforced (level 2). Before you know it, you are in the Purchase stage of the customer decision sequence (level 3).

What all the foregoing has led up to is the conclusion that there are three levels of effects that the manager must take into account in marcoms planning. The third level, the Customer Decision Stages, usually occurs as a hierarchy of effects. The effects at the first level – Ad or Promotion Processing – however, are polyarchical, and can occur in any order following repeated attention. The effects at the second level – Brand Communication Effects – can be acquired simultaneously and do not require waiting for a hierarchy to develop (this is the main practical implication for the marcoms manager) even though they usually are mentally *outputted* as a hierarchy during choice.

CUSTOMER RESPONSE STEPS

Having presented our account of what's really going on regarding levels of the effects of marcoms, we are now going to simplify by identifying in a very broad manner the **customer response steps** that a marcoms campaign aims for. The customer response steps begin with a step that does not appear in any of the levels in Figure 2.1 earlier – Exposure. Providing the *opportunity* for exposure is a step taken not by the customer but by the campaign manager: the manager has to get the ads and offers exposed to the target audience customers, and exposed often enough, via the media schedule. Whereas it is true that customers sometimes deliberately seek out ads (e.g., Yellow Pages ads or Website ads) and promotions (e.g., bargain hunters or coupon collectors seek out promotions), the manager still has to *place* the ads or offers in the media so that they are *there* to be sought. In any event, it is accurate to label the first customer response step prior to processing as *Exposure,* whether this be deliberate on the part of the customer or incidental, and despite the fact that it is the manager who provides the exposure opportunity.

We then short-cut *across* the levels of effects as follows, in four steps: (1) Exposure → (2) Ad or Promotion Processing → (3) Brand Communication Effects → (4) Target Audience Action. For convenience of reference, the customer response steps are shown in Figure 2.3. As we have explained in the first part of the chapter, there is a lot more going on at each step than these summary labels reveal, but these are the essential steps that the campaign aims to achieve and must achieve if marcoms are going to produce sales (or behavior change on a large scale in the case of a social marketing campaign). The four customer response steps also indicate the types of measures to be taken in Campaign *Tracking* (see Chapter 14).

Two further steps – executed by the company, not the customer – can be added as objectives of *planning:* (5) Sales and Market Share and (6) Brand Equity. We argued in Chapter 1 that brand equity is the main determinant of profit, and achievement of the sixth step implies long-run profitability.

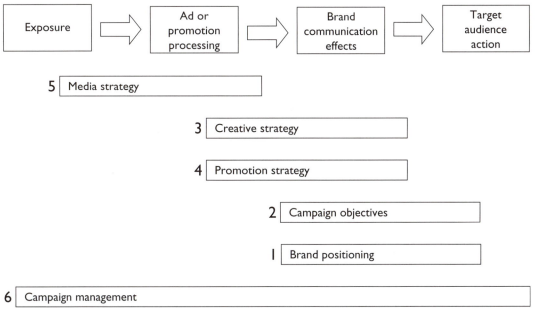

FIGURE 2.3 *Customer response steps. Manager's approximately corresponding planning stages are indicated under the response steps, with their planning order numbered.*

The customer response steps indicate roughly in reverse the *stages* taken by the *manager*, in marcoms planning, which we explain next. In Figure 2.3, we have approximately aligned the planning stages with the customer response steps. The planning stages are explained next.

MARCOMS PLANNING STAGES

The six stages of marcoms planning are listed in Table 2.1. The six stages are Brand Positioning, Campaign Objectives, Creative Strategy, Promotion Strategy, Media Strategy, and Campaign Management. Their main sub-stages are listed. We briefly explain each stage below and conclude with an instructive example of the stages in action.

TABLE 2.1 *The six marcoms planning stages (with their sub-stages summarized).*

STAGE	SUMMARY LABEL	SUB-STAGES OF PLANNING
1	Brand positioning	• T-C-B positioning model • I-D-U benefit analysis • Integrated marcoms
2	Campaign objectives	• Campaign target audience selection and action objectives • Campaign communication objectives
3	Creative strategy	• Key benefit claim • Creative idea • Brand awareness and brand preference (grid) tactics • Attention tactics by medium
4	Promotion strategy	• Sales promotions • Personal selling and telemarketing
5	Media strategy	• Media-type selection • Reach pattern • Minimum effective frequency estimation • Media plan implementation
6	Campaign management	• Campaign budget • Tracking measures and analysis • Diagnosing and preventing wearout

Brand positioning

Marcoms planning begins or *should* begin with Brand Positioning. In our marcoms consulting work, and we'll bet you that this applies in the consulting work of others as well, the issue to be settled first is *always* the issue of brand positioning. Before the manager can make a reasonable decision about where the brand should be headed via its marcoms, the manager first has to decide – to change, if necessary, or to shore up and reconfirm – the brand's positioning. This means, as we will see in the chapters on positioning, deciding who (the Target Customer within stakeholder audiences) the brand should be targeted towards; identifying the customer's Category Need for which the brand can best compete; and selecting the Key Benefit the brand should emphasize. This we call the T-C-B (target-category-benefit) model of positioning and it leads to the *positioning statement* for the brand. The positioning statement is completed after the next sub-stage. In the next sub-stage of positioning, I-D-U (importance-delivery-uniqueness) analysis is used to select the Key Benefit, Entry-Ticket Benefits, and traded-off or omitted Inferior Benefits, if any.

Brand Positioning has to be agreed on by management (and positioning statements prepared) for the brand as a whole, for its sub-brands if sub-brands are part of the brand's "architecture," and for the specific brand-items. That is, the company's entire product or service portfolio must be armed with brand positioning statements.

Campaign objectives

Marcoms campaigns, at any one time, apply to any one of the above brand entities. The manager could, for instance, be preparing an Awareness advertising campaign for the brand or for a sub-brand and also a Response (direct-response) advertising campaign to advertise and promote a particular brand-item. The campaigns could be aimed at one or more Target Customer types identified in the brand's, sub-brand's, or brand-item's positioning statement.

Leverage calculations are used to select the target customer group or groups for the campaign, collectively called the Target Audience. Target Audience **action objectives** – for pre-purchase behaviors, such as Visits and Inquiries, or actual purchase behaviors, such as Trial and Repeat Purchase – are also established. Additional useful support for setting the action objectives is the construction of a BSM (Behavioral Sequence Model). This model is also instrumental in identifying the Creative Target for the campaign and for revealing potential *media contact points* for the campaign's media strategy.

As we explained above, marcoms work, via the ads or promotions constituting the campaign, by creating, increasing, or reinforcing *communication effects* for the brand. Once more, we will refer to the "brand" here, recognizing that the campaign could be about a sub-brand or a specific brand-item. Via ads or promotions, brand communication effects are initiated at level 1 (ad or promotion offer processing) but achieve their impact at level 2, that is, at the level of the brand (brand communication effects). As we saw, there are five communication effects that must necessarily be present in the Target Customer's *mind* before the customer will take Action, which is overt *behavior*. However, some of these brand communication effects may *already be present* in the target customer's mind, thereby highlighting the difference between communication effects and campaign **communication objectives**. If a campaign is launching the brand as the pioneer brand in a new product or service category, or if the brand campaign is attempting to grow the category, then all five communication effects may be objectives for the campaign. If the campaign is for an established brand, then either the second and third communication effects, if the purchase decision is low risk, or the second, third, fourth, and perhaps fifth if the purchase decision is high risk, will be objectives for the campaign. For each of the five communication effects, the manager must decide whether or not it is to be an objective for the campaign and then nominate the objective (for instance, Category Need is nominated as either to be omitted, and therefore not an objective, or to be reminded via the campaign, or to be "sold" via the campaign). The five *potential* communication objectives, again, are: Category Need, Brand Awareness, Brand Preference, Brand Action Intention, and Purchase Facilitation.

The campaign communication objectives specify "what" the campaign should achieve by way of mental effects for the brand in the target customer's mind, though not "how." The how is the focus of the next planning stage, creative strategy.

Creative strategy

The **creative strategy** planning stage commences with the preparation, by the manager, of the *creative brief*. The creative brief is quite a difficult document to prepare because it has to *be* brief yet include the brand's Positioning Statement as well as the campaign's Target Audience Action Objectives and Communication Objectives. In our planning framework, the creative brief goes one important step further: management should decide and include in the brief the *Key Benefit Claim*. Usually, the creative brief is sent to the advertising agency and the manager sees nothing from the agency until the agency presents the proposed rough ads or the proposed promotion offer in outline, for approval. In our planning approach, however, the manager or management team can take an active role in deciding creative strategy. An active role is necessary if the creative (the ads or promotions) is to be prepared in-house or, for many readers of this book, prepared as part of a marcoms class project. But we believe just as strongly that the manager should be involved in deciding creative strategy even when using the services of an advertising agency. The agency can make a crucial contribution to creative strategy: the Creative Idea. We show how, alternatively, the management team can make this contribution. Such a contribution is, we note, not always welcomed by the agency, but we see a strong reason for managers to be more proactive in creative strategy, which is that they will *then* get ads or offers that are *on strategy*, which is a summary label certifying that the ad or offer positions the brand as intended and completely addresses the communication and action objectives. Off-strategy ads and offers submitted by the agency are a big time-waster.

The planning of Creative Strategy consists of four sub-stages. First, the **key benefit claim** for the brand (for this campaign and foreseeable future campaigns) has to be carefully *crafted* from possible alternatives. Second, the **creative idea** that will *dramatize* this claim has to be generated and selected – in the most important sense, the creative idea *is* the ad. Third, in-ad **creative tactics** have to be chosen for achieving the two universal campaign communication objectives of Brand Awareness and Brand Preference. Last is the choice of in-ad **attention tactics**, for each of the types of ad in the main marcoms media, that will be most likely to gain the Target Customer's attention and maintain interest in processing the message. If an advertising agency has been employed to construct the ads or promotions, ratings of the properties of the creative ideas and a checklist of the in-ad tactics should be used by the management team to decide which ads or promotions to approve for the campaign as being *on strategy*. The same ratings and checklist – called a Management Judgment Ad Test, or MJAT, are used if you do the creative yourself or in-house.

Creative Strategy, and Promotion Strategy, below, address the link between Ad or Promotion Processing (level 1) and Brand Communication Effects (level 2) in the overall model of how marcoms work.

Promotion strategy

The marcoms campaign may include, or even be focused on, one or several other types of promotion other than advertising – sales promotions, personal selling, or telemarketing. Each has the aim of generating immediate purchase and can therefore be regarded as a promotion. If so, the **promotion strategy** stage of planning will be required.

The promotion strategy stage is needed for manufacturer's promotions if you are a manufacturer marketer, and for retailer's promotions if you are a retailer. Note that we include *Personal Selling* as a form of promotion practiced by both manufacturers and retailers, as we do, in countries where it is permitted, *Telemarketing*.

The most important aspect of promotion strategy is to design promotions so that they are **customer franchise-building** (CFB), which means that they will contribute to Brand Awareness and Brand Preference and not just induce temporary Action. The second most important aspect is timing – if advertising is used – which is really part of media strategy to make sure that Awareness advertising precedes the promotion offer.

Media strategy

The **Media Strategy** planning stage applies no matter what form of marcoms is to be employed in the campaign. Media provide the "contacts" that enable the ads or promotion offers to be processed by target customers (level 1). The contacts may be made by mass media, point-of-sale or point-of-use media, personal selling, or telemarketing, as was shown in Chapter 1, Figure 1.1.

Media Strategy planning consists of four sub-stages. First, the **media-type selection** has to be confirmed in terms of a Primary Medium and possible Secondary Media for the campaign; in the actual sequence of planning, this decision will have already been made, based on the Behavioral Sequence Model for the particular target group or groups chosen earlier for the campaign and the medium or media to be used will have been specified in the *creative brief*. Second, a **reach pattern** for the media schedule must be decided (basically, whether we want to advertise with a Blitz, or a decelerating pattern or an accelerating one, or to reach as many prospects as we can just once or twice). Third, the required **minimum effective frequency** has to be estimated for each of the advertising cycles in the reach pattern and Effective Reach goals set for the media-months in the schedule. Finally, the **media schedule** is implemented in a manner that best represents the media strategy for the campaign, within the **media budget** allocated for it.

Campaign management

The last stage in marcoms campaign planning is campaign management. Finalization of the campaign Media Budget is the first sub-stage; whereas the overall budget limit, in reality, will have been indicated much earlier by top management, the precise planned expenditure can only be determined after the media plan has been cost-quoted. Before the campaign launch, tracking measures have to be put in place and continued throughout the campaign. As we will see, these measures can range from **aggregate tracking** to individual-level **customer survey tracking**. The latter is necessary for the very last sub-stage of campaign management, which is to diagnose and prevent campaign wearout.

THE STEPS IN ACTION

The descriptions of the five marcoms planning stages above were necessarily quite abstract and it might be helpful to outline a concrete example. We take as our example a case history report on the marcoms campaign by Skoda U.K. to re-launch the Skoda Fabia, the Czechoslovakian brand of car owned by Volkswagen AG of Germany, in the U.K. market.[3]

Brand positioning

By February 2000, Skoda had experienced about 10 years of poor sales in the U.K., attaining only 0.8% share of that market. The Skoda brand was positioned – by prospective new car owners, not by the company – as a small car in the low-end price category, built in Communist Czechoslovakia and therefore pretty much "worthless." Skoda was the butt of British jokes such as, "How do you double the value of a Skoda? Fill it with gas." Obviously, if Skoda U.K. was going to increase sales, the brand's positioning – on the Key Benefit factor – had to be greatly improved. Skoda U.K. knew it had a good product (when Volkswagen AG bought the nationalized Czechoslovakian car company in 1991 it gave Skoda vehicles a complete makeover and, in the rest of Europe, the Skoda Fabia won a number of "best in class" car awards and drew accolades from motoring journalists). The Skoda product line, of which the Fabia was the front runner, was to be targeted (T) at prospective customers who resemble current Skoda owners in the U.K., who are not demographically distinctive but are characterized *attitudinally* by seeing themselves as "rational" car buyers; category-positioned (C) in the small economy-car category where it naturally belongs; and benefit-positioned (B) not in terms of the Skoda Fabia's excellent functional features but rather the car's *smart appearance.* The T-C-B positioning incorporated an I-D-U benefit strategy in which the Skoda Fabia's smart appearance was selected as the Key Benefit to be *emphasized*, its Entry-Ticket Benefits of low price and very good fuel economy were to be *mentioned*, and the engineering-based functional benefits of the car itself were to be *omitted*.

Campaign objectives

In March 2000, a new hatchback version of the Fabia was ready to be launched in a campaign that would also re-launch the Skoda brand. The campaign had a limited budget of (in U.S. dollars) $7 million against competitors spending two or three times as much. Because of the limited budget, the marcoms of Sponsorships and Event Marketing, which are popular with managers in the U.K. for the launch of new cars, were eliminated from consideration and the campaign focused on TV advertising, PR, and Direct Mail advertising.

For the TV advertising component of the Fabia campaign, the Target Audience was identified as "Skoda rejectors," who in our terminology would be Other-Brand Switchers and Other-Brand Loyals, a very large target group, rather than current Skoda owners, a very small group. The Action objective of the TV campaign was to have Skoda rejectors test drive a Skoda Fabia (a *pre-purchase* Action objective). The campaign communication objectives, though not spelled out in the case history we are describing, were probably Brand Recall (necessary to prompt a Visit to a dealer), Brand Preference increase (from a negative preference to at least a moderate and hopefully strong preference), and Brand Action Intention (to Visit a Skoda dealership, necessary for taking a test drive).

The PR component of the campaign was aimed at motoring journalists and particularly those the advertiser believed to be more independent and open-minded (representing the U.K. newspapers *The Guardian* and *The Spectator*). The *action* objective of the PR was, as might be expected, to encourage journalists to write favorably about the Skoda Fabia.

The direct mail campaign, which began after the other two marcoms components, was targeted at two groups: Skoda rejectors who attitudinally resembled current Skoda owners (who presumably are Favorable Brand Switchers) and current, that is, previous-model, Skoda owners (who presumably will continue to be Brand Loyals). The *action* objective of the Direct Mail campaign was, like that of the TV campaign, to encourage recipients to Visit and test drive the new Skoda Fabia.

Creative strategy

The Key Benefit Claim for the Skoda Fabia was "Smart appearance." This wording (as is often the case) was not itself employed in the creative but rather was the likely *prompt* used by the creative team to brainstorm the Creative Idea for the campaign. The Creative Idea was hit upon by Skoda U.K.'s advertising agency, the London office of Fallon Worldwide. The Creative Idea, which dramatized the Key Benefit Claim of "Smart appearance," was to show people in situations in which, because the car looks so good, they can't believe it's a Skoda. We do not know what type of brainstorming was used by the agency to generate this creative idea or what type of screening by management was used to select it, but it turned out to be a very good one! Several TV commercials (a *poolout*, since a single commercial used throughout the campaign would be likely to wear out) were produced based on this creative idea. One TV ad, for instance, shows a distraught parking attendant accompanying a man back to the man's car, a Skoda Fabia, saying, "I'm afraid some little vandal has stuck a Skoda badge on the front of your car." The TV ad ends with the voice-over conclusion, "It's a Skoda. Honest." So that the journalists targeted in the PR component of the campaign would be in tune with the creative idea, Skoda gave them a preview of the ads before they went on air and also lent the select journalists Skodas to drive – an apparent use of the *reciprocity principle* that we will discuss in conjunction with sales promotion (Chapter 15) and personal selling (Chapter 17). The Creative Idea was further integrated into the Direct Mail campaign with the same touch of humor as in the TV campaign. One mailing piece, for instance, enclosed a (very nice) cardboard replica Skoda badge and asked potential buyers to carry the badge with them for a while and show it to their friends, and then a second mailing piece invited them to come into the dealership for a test drive – the two-step mailing resembling a personal selling tactic known as *foot-in-the-door*.

Promotion strategy

Skoda U.K. did not employ any Price-Off Promotions in the Skoda Fabia campaign. Even in the Direct Mail component, there was no price-off offer. Rather, the car was sold at its normal price subject, of course, to individual buyers' negotiations.

Media strategy

Skoda U.K. selected TV as the Primary Medium for the campaign, spending 75% of the budget in that medium and the remainder on PR and Direct Mail. The Target Customer, it will be recalled, was "Skoda rejectors," and this included nearly all adults in the U.K. as the broad Media Target. TV was necessary, as opposed to, say, Radio advertising, because the creative executions had to show the car and also people's reaction to it. We do not know the actual media strategy used for the campaign in terms of reach and frequency, but it is likely that a Wedge reach pattern was used which consists of several large bursts of TV advertising in which the reach is kept very high and the frequency is decelerated from a very high down to a moderate level. The PR component of the campaign coincided with the initial burst of TV, as far as we can tell, and the Direct Mail component of the campaign, sent to 100,000 prospects nationwide in England, probably followed two or three bursts of the TV advertising so that prospective buyers were fully primed with the brand's and the brand-item's communication effects.

Campaign management

As is usual for a major campaign such as this, Skoda U.K. carefully tracked the campaign through a series of weekly consumer surveys, a research methodology known as *continuous tracking*. The Skoda Fabia ads collectively achieved 55% *advertising* awareness at their peak, ahead of the 44% advertising awareness achieved by its nearest rival's ads, for the Fiat Punto. The research firm that conducted the tracking research, Millward Brown, uses the Brand-Prompted Ad Recall measure of advertising awareness; randomly selected adults are asked whether they have seen or heard "any advertising, recently, for the Skoda Fabia". We do not know, however, whether the 55% figure for advertising awareness is a good achievement because to judge this we would have to know the Effective Reach of the media schedule. For instance, if the TV campaign reached, say, 90% of adults enough times for them to remember the advertising, then the 55% figure would not be so good; however, if the campaign's Effective Reach, at its peak, was more like 60% or even 65%, then the 55% advertising awareness for the Skoda Fabia would be regarded as very satisfactory. We also do not know the three Conversion Ratios (how many people visited a dealer after seeing the TV ads, or the newspaper and magazine PR articles, or after the Direct Mail component of the campaign), though it is likely that Skoda U.K. assessed these figures carefully. In any event, the combined marcoms campaign was judged by Skoda's management as highly successful.

One of the crucial communication effects for the brand, Brand Preference operationalized as the proportion of prospective car buyers who "would consider" buying a Skoda, increased from 14% before the campaign to 21% after the first year and, whereas these percentages may not seem absolutely large, the increase represents one million potential new customers. Skoda's sales during that year, 2001, grew by 23.2% in comparison with a total new car sales increase of 10.5%, and Skoda's market share almost doubled from its previous 0.8% to 1.5%. Less formally, but very important for word-of-mouth, it is reported that you don't hear Skoda jokes in the U.K. anymore!

This recent case history illustrates the six marcoms planning stages – from brand positioning (repositioning in this case) through to campaign management. As full details were not available in the report from which we took the case, we have had to infer in some instances what we think the marketer and the agency would have done – realizing, too, that they could not have read this book and anticipated how we would analyze the case! That said, they appear to have done most things right. There is, however, much more to the planning stages than can be illustrated with one case history. You will find more details throughout the book.

You will also find that we have emphasized *advertising* planning in the next series of chapters because this is the main form of marcoms and it can stand alone in many cases. We cover corporate image advertising, sponsorships, and PR, related as corporate advertising, later (Chapter 16). We cover promotion strategy in two later chapters (Chapter 15 on sales promotions and Chapter 17 on personal selling and telemarketing). We cover social marcoms campaigns and, for all marcoms, we present our views on ethics, in the concluding Chapter 18.

SUMMARY

It is important, obviously, that the manager understand, overall, how marcoms work before commencing the stages involved in marcoms campaign planning. In order to work, ads, promotion offers and other types of marcoms must successfully pass through three levels of effects: ad or promotion processing, brand communication effects and customer decision stages. Each level has a number of effects (responses to be made by the prospective customer) in it. Ad or promotion processing (level 1) includes Attention, Learning, Emotions, and Acceptance. The alternative permutations of these responses make them polyarchical, not hierarchical, at this first level. Brand communication effects (level 2) consist of potentially five mental responses, made by the prospective customer, connected with the brand: Category Need, Brand Awareness, Brand Preference, Brand Action Intention, and Purchase Facilitation. The brand communication effects can be acquired in any order, often with some acquired together. In a Direct-Response advertising campaign, the whole six communication effects are acquired simultaneously. In an Awareness or Brand advertising campaign, the respective communication effects may be created, increased, or reinforced during multiple exposures to the brand's ad or ads. In the prospective customer's mind, communication effects for competing brands are mentally outputted during the customer decision stages (level 3). At the level of the product or service category, the prospective customer goes through the stages of Not in the Market, then Need Arousal, Search and Evaluation, Purchase, and Usage. These customer decision stages are what the brand's marcoms must favorably influence. The customer decision stages are experienced usually in the above sequence, that is, as a hierarchy of effects. The prospective customer passes through all five stages for the first purchase in the product or service category but restarts at the second stage, Need Arousal, for Repeat Purchase.

For the purpose of campaign planning, we simplify these levels of effects into four customer response steps that the campaign must achieve: exposure → ad or promotion processing → brand communication effects → target audience action.

Marcoms campaign planning consists of six stages for creating marcoms that work, and for making them work. Stage 1 is Brand Positioning, because planning of a marcoms campaign depends on clear, agreed positioning of the brand, sub-brand, or brand-item up front. Stage 2 is the establishment of Campaign Objectives: target audience action objectives, and campaign communication objectives. Stage 3 is Creative Strategy – the generation and selection of a key benefit claim and dramatic creative idea for the campaign, and execution of the creative idea in an ad or ads to be employed in the campaign. Stage 4 is Promotion Strategy, which is used if the campaign includes, or is based on, sales promotions, personal selling, or telemarketing. Stage 5 is Media Strategy, which concerns the selection and scheduling of the ads or promotion offers in media vehicles that together will reach the target audience in sufficient numbers, and sufficiently often, to meet the sales goal for the campaign. Stage 6 is Campaign Management, which requires deciding the media budget, tracking the effects of the campaign as they emerge, and detecting and correcting for wearout during the campaign. Also, there is learning from the campaign to be consolidated for next time.

DISCUSSION QUESTIONS

2.1 What is meant by levels of effects in explaining how marcoms work?

2.2 In explaining how a Direct-Response Ad works, it is common to refer to the hierarchy of effects known as AIDA (awareness → interest → desire → action). Analyze these responses by comparing them with the more specific responses in our three-levels model and thereby identify which responses, at which levels, must occur for a Direct-Response ad to work.

2.3 Awareness Ads, that is, Brand Ads that do not attempt to generate an immediate Purchase response, usually require multiple exposures to achieve their intended effects. Look at Nike's "Streaker" TV commercial (on the Website) and write a one-page account explaining how this ad would successfully pass through the three levels of effects.

2.4 What does "polyarchical" mean and why is this a more accurate description than "hierarchical" for describing the Processing responses a prospective customer makes? Find a Web banner ad and record your responses to it. Provide the text of the ad (or reproduce it) prior to summarizing and labeling your Processing responses.

2.5 What are the Customer Response Steps and why do we use this simplified representation of the levels of effects?

2.6 Why do the marcoms campaign planning stages begin with Brand Positioning?

2.7 The Campaign Objectives stage involves a selection and two types of objectives. What is this selection and how do the two types of objectives differ? Exemplify your answer with reference to the managers of Pepsi-Cola considering a Sponsorship campaign of an international soccer tournament.

NOTES

1. If you read "About the Authors," you'd see that Steve and Deryn had the category need for diapers arise recently, but were certainly aware of various brands of diapers before that.

2. D. Ehrlich, I. Guttman, P. Schonbach, and J. Mills, Post decision exposure to relevant information, *Journal of Abnormal and Social Psychology*, 1957, 54, pp. 90–102. Also see M.L. Ritchins and P.H. Bloch, After the new wears off: the temporal context of product involvement, *Journal of Consumer Research*, 1986, 13(2), pp. 280–287. We have interpreted the "nonrecent buyer of cars group" in their study as being like future buyers.

3. D. James, Skoda is taken from trash to treasure: TV campaign boosts car's brand mileage, *Marketing News*, February 18, 2002, pp. 4–5.

CHAPTER 3

Brand positioning: T-C-B positioning model

In this chapter and the next chapter, a three-level procedure for positioning is presented (see Figure 3.1). In this chapter, we explain the first level: the T-C-B Positioning Model. In Chapter 4, we explain the second level, I-D-U Benefit Analysis, and the final, most specific level of positioning, the a-b-e Benefit Claim Model.

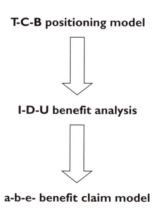

T-C-B positioning model

I-D-U benefit analysis

a-b-e- benefit claim model

FIGURE 3.1 *The three levels of positioning.*

Brand positioning is an attempt to create and maintain a unique representation of the brand in customers' minds, a representation that is expected to stimulate choice of that brand. The representation has three nodes emanating from the central node of Brand Identity: the Category

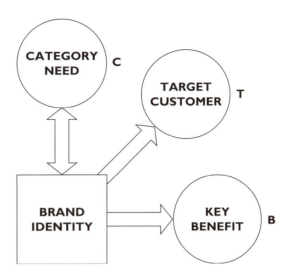

FIGURE 3.2 *The T-C-B positioning model. The brand associations are shown here in the order they occur to the target customer, that is, the category need usually arises first and suggests the brand (or vice versa); "For me?" asks the target customer and, if "Yes," the target customer then asks "What does it offer?" as its key benefit. The manager, however, makes the brand positioning decisions in the T-C-B order.*

Need, the Target Customer the brand is for, and its Key Benefit (see Figure 3.2). Children acquire large numbers of brand associations as they are socialized into the consumer world.[1] By the time the consumer is an adult, he or she may have as many as 10,000 brand representations stored in the brain[2], though not all will have the three necessary associations completely formed.

THE T-C-B POSITIONING MODEL

The T-C-B model of positioning requires the manager to choose a position for the brand in terms of three factors:

1. The *Target Customer* for the brand (T factor)

2. The *Category Need* into which the brand is to be positioned (C factor)

3. The *Key Benefit* offered by the brand (B factor)

These three decisions constitute the **T-C-B positioning model**. The brand's Positioning Statement will be of the form: "To the target customer (T), Brand X is the brand of category need (C) that offers the key benefit (B)." The brand must be positioned and then, if the company's product or service mix uses *sub-brands* or *brand-items* that differ on T, C, or B, these must be positioned as well.

Always do positioning first

Positioning decisions have to be made for new brands, of course, and for an existing brand or brand-item when repositioning it. But even for well-established brands, the manager should revisit the Positioning Statement prior to the commencement of a marketing communications campaign. In our experience, the managers of a surprising number of brands, even "well-known" brands, cannot readily answer the basic questions about the brand's positioning: Who is our Target Customer? Which Category Need are we competing in? What Key Benefit do we offer?

Markets change and customers' perceptions of our brand's benefits may have changed or drifted, especially if our brand's recent marcoms have been nonexistent, poorly executed, or not well integrated. Answering the above three questions requires market and customer research and always requires careful decisions to be made by the brand manager, decisions that will commit the brand, sub-brands, and brand-items for their foreseeable marketing futures.

Research and judgment

Customer research helps in deciding which target customers will be most "leveragable" in a marcoms campaign for the brand. Customer research and open-minded consideration of the true competitive market are usually necessary to decide exactly what the Category Need is (it is rarely adequately summarized by just naming the physical product or obvious service category). Customer research helps the manager, too, to make decisions at the I-D-U level of positioning – to determine which emotional or functional benefit should be emphasized by the brand and which other benefits are "entry tickets" that the brand has to mention in its communications.

The most useful types of research for positioning are:

1. *Marcoms Situation Audit* Conduct or commission an electronic search of the main brands' marketing strategies and their ads. Information about brands' marketing strategies is surprisingly plentiful in trade publications such as *Forbes*, *Business Week*, and *Advertising Age* or equivalent publications in your own country. Once you have these brands' ads, "reverse engineer" the typical ad for each brand, to infer the T-C-B positioning that the brand appears to be employing.

2. *Qualitative Research (Individual "Depth" Interviews)* Ask the questions marked off in italics in this and the next two chapters to determine the Category Need, Benefits sought, and the Purchase Decision Process.

However, research, though vital, will not give you direct answers to positioning decisions. The manager has to evaluate the *alternative positioning options suggested by the research and make judgments.*

T-C-B positioning model: overview

The T-C-B model of brand positioning is shown in Figure 3.1 in the order that the positioning questions are likely to arise in the *potential customer's* mind: What is it? Who's it for? What does it offer? The *manager*, however, makes the positioning decisions in the T, C, then B order, and that is the order that will appear in the brand's Positioning Statement. First, the manager has to decide who is intended to be the broad **target customer** for the brand; the brand's positioning must answer the question of "Who's it for?" Second, the manager has to decide the precise **category need**, the customer-need category, in which the brand is *intended* to compete; in everyday terms, the brand's positioning must answer the question of "What is it?" Third, the manager has to decide the **key benefit** (emotional or functional) that the brand will emphasize to its target customers, in answer to their question of "What does it offer?" (To answer this question, the manager actually has to do the I-D-U Benefit Analysis and then loop back and insert the benefits that the brand's positioning will emphasize, mention, and possibly trade off or omit – see Chapter 4.)

Each of the T, C and B positioning decisions is considerably more complex than suggested in the summary diagram in Figure 3.2 earlier. It is essential to make these decisions as carefully and correctly as possible because the positioning statement for the brand (or sub-brand or brand-item) will guide its total marcoms strategy. We now examine these three decisions in detail.

THE TARGET CUSTOMER (T) POSITIONING DECISION

Who is the brand (or sub-brand or brand-item) for? The macro answer is that it is for different *types* of customer known as **stakeholders**. Whereas the brand is obviously "for" its End-Customers – business users or consumers – it is also for Suppliers, Distributors, Investors, Regulators, and prospective and current Employees of the company or organization. (Dowling, in his recent book on corporate reputation[3], which we strongly recommend, provides a more comprehensive list of types of stakeholder, but these are the main types.) A Positioning Statement should be prepared for *each* of these stakeholder target customers. Each stakeholder target may see the brand as being in quite a different category than the End-Customer does. Investors, for instance, may regard the brand as being in one of the well-known BCG categories – a "cash cow" or a "star," for instance. Retailers may regard the brand – the company really – as being in the "dependable, easy to deal with" category, for instance, or as being in the "hard-bargaining" category. As we will explain in the next section, the Category Need, from a customer-need perspective, is no less psychological for these types of customer than it is for end-customers. Likewise, the Key Benefits are likely to differ between stakeholder Target Customer types. What the Investor wants in a brand, for instance, is not the same as what the Retailer wants, nor what the End-Customer wants, and Regulators probably want something *very* different. The Positioning Statements will differ for the different stakeholders.

The end-customer target

Of major (but by no means sole) importance for marcoms planning is the End-Customer who is the target for the brand – or sub-brand or brand-item. We will concentrate on this decision. By illustrating the end-customer decision, the choice of Target Customer for the *other* stakeholder types should be quite easy to carry out.

The key is to define the End-Customer target for brand positioning as broadly as possible – to include not only current but all *potential* and actual buyers and users of the brand, with a reasonably realistic but not too narrow interpretation of "potential." For example, and we emphasize that this is hypothetical, for Citibank Corporate Services, the End-Customer target might reasonably be defined as "all businesses that could or do use a financial service." For Birds

Eye Vegetables, the Target Customer (End-Customer) might be reasonably defined as "consumers of frozen vegetables" or, if Birds Eye's management is ambitiously planning to bring new users into the "frozen" category, then "consumers of vegetables."

What you do not want to do is mistakenly fuse into the definition of the target customer (T) the customer-need category (C) or the brand benefit (B). This mistake is made too often. One sees, for example, positioning statements that identify the target customer (T) in terms such as "seekers of high-quality frozen vegetables (the C factor) who want a brand name they trust (the B factor)." Well, in this purely hypothetical example, that would rule out many customers who *could* buy Birds Eye Vegetables as well as many who do *now*. Only if the manager knows, from market research, that actual or *potential* buyers of Birds Eye Vegetables *never* buy "low-quality frozen vegetables" or *never* buy "unknown" brands would the above target customer definition be correct. This is not likely. The target customer (T) should be defined to include *all realistic potential and actual* buyers and users of the brand. The same applies for sub-brands and brand-items.

Campaign-level targets

As outlined below the target customer section in Figure 3.3, what the manager has to do further for a marcoms *campaign* is distinguish a **target audience** – the target customer group or groups to whom the marcoms *campaign* is directed. For a specific marcoms campaign, there will also be a Media Target and a Creative Target. The selection of these three campaign-specific targets is covered in Chapter 5.

THE CATEGORY NEED (C) POSITIONING DECISION

Brands, sub-brands, and brand-items compete, not in a category as product manufacturers or service providers regard categories, but rather to meet a customer *need*. It is vital to identify and describe the Category Need in customer language. A common mistake, indicative of what marketing guru Ted Levitt called "marketing myopia," which still affects many companies, is to describe the product or service category from the manufacturer's or service provider's point of view rather than to look at the truly competing alternatives the way the *customer* sees them. As Levitt observed, businesses and households need "energy" rather than electricity or oil or gas in particular and, in a futuristic comment, he observed that people want "entertainment" rather than movies or TV or, more recently, videos or DVDs.[4] Levitt was among the first to point out that customers usually have a generic need to be filled, rather than a specific need for a particular item. IBM, for example, positions its Master Brand in the category of "business solutions," not computers as such. Charles Revson, founder of Revlon, is reported to have said, "In the factory we make fragrances, in the store we sell hope," thereby indicating the *customer-need* category that the Revlon brand (again, more precisely, its Master Brand) competes in. Freddy Heineken, grandson of the founder of the Heineken brewery in Holland and the family executive responsible for taking Heineken beer worldwide, said, "I do not sell beer, but gaiety."[5] Of course, "business solutions," "hope," or "gaiety" are not quite full enough descriptions of the category in any of these cases but they do illustrate the idea of identifying the category as a *customer need*.

Because companies commonly receive their sales and market share data in terms of industry-defined product or service categories, it is very easy to misidentify the customer-defined category

Target customer: defined broadly to include all potential and actual customers within each stakeholder type

POSITIONING STATEMENT

- End-customer (business or consumer)
- Suppliers
- Distributors
- Investors
- Regulators
- Prospective and current employees

Target audience

CAMPAIGN

- New category users
- Other-brand loyals
- Other-brand switchers
- Favorable brand switchers
- Brand loyals

Media target

CAMPAIGN

Creative target

CAMPAIGN

FIGURE 3.3 *Customer targeting distinctions.*

– and thus the true market for the brand or brand-item – unless consumers or customers have been consulted.

> The best way to identify a category, expressed as a customer need, is to recruit a small sample of broad-category customers, say 20 to 30, and ask them individually: (1) "What need, purpose, or end-use did you, or would you, have in mind when choosing that particular brand-item?" (for more "psychological" products or services, the interviewer will need to ladder-probe "And why that purpose?" to uncover the real need) and (2) "What alternatives or substitutes did you consider or would you find acceptable?"

Some good examples of Category Need labels defined by customer need are given in the pioneering study by Loken and Ward[6] of the determinants of brand typicality for its product category. For instance, for all restaurants considered together, the Category Need is "Good food," whereas for fast-food restaurants as a sub-category, it is "Quick and convenient food." For footwear in general, the Category Need, according to their study, is "Stylish-looking footwear," whereas for athletic shoes as a sub-category, it is "Comfortable footwear for sports."

Present versus intended category need

In specifying the Category Need in the Positioning Statement for the brand, the manager has to think about not only customers' conceptualization of this need but also the strategic marketing issue of *which customer need it would be most advantageous* for the brand to be competing for. The manager may attempt to expand the brand's category, narrow it, or reposition the brand into a different category.

For example, Spam canned ham competes in the "convenient meats" category with other brands of canned meats such as Plumrose and with brands of packaged, sliced meats. But the strategy might be to position Spam to compete not just with other convenient meats but with tuna, cheese and other products that are readily available for a quick sandwich lunch or snack. The manager would then define the Category Need, for positioning purposes, as "Convenient lunches" rather than "Convenient meats." This is an example of category *expansion.*

Some brands intend to position themselves in a *narrower* category. Some brands of bank, for example, have chosen to specialize in meeting a customer need for low-interest loans, whereas others have tried to position themselves as financial service investment advisers.

Another example, this time an example of repositioning into a *different* category, is that of automobile service stations. Most of them have abandoned automobile service altogether. They are now food mini-markets where you can conveniently shop or eat, after you, yourself, have put petrol or gas in your car. The category reference, "Just stopping into the gas station," could mean that you are going there to buy almost anything, except get service on your car! A further example of positioning the brand in a different category is Hallmark, the U.S. greeting card company, which successfully entered the flower delivery category by regarding their Category Need as "Showing you care."[7]

The brand's *present* category, of course, may be the one it should be positioned in. For the brand's Positioning Statement, this still requires the manager to *name* the Category Need. *Asking a sample of target customers what* they *call what they need when they are buying your and close competitors' brands will produce the right name.*

Target customer and category positioning

The Target Customer – the first factor in positioning – quite obviously has to be taken into account when making the category positioning decision. What has to be taken into account, specifically, is the customer's "mindset" when making the choice. The Category Need, from the Target Customer's viewpoint, is reflected in his or her **consideration set**, the set of brand-items that are seriously considered as alternatives for purchase.

The consideration set is best understood by recognizing that when making a brand-item choice, the consumer or customer will have already mentally *partitioned* the overall product or service category. An example of customer-perspective category partitioning for automobiles in the U.S. consumer market is shown in Figure 3.4. The Target Customer in this example mentally partitions the total category of automobiles by type, then make, then size, and finally price. This partitioning "tree" leads to this customer group's serious consideration set of Chevrolet Monte Carlo, Ford Focus, and Chrysler Sebring. This group's Category Need is evidently for a medium-priced, mid-size, American sedan. The desired attribute "American" makes it clear that the Category Need is psychological rather than merely mechanical.

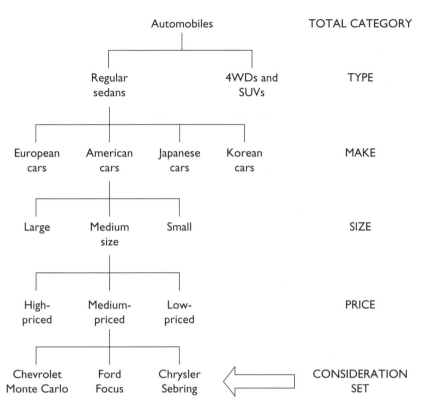

FIGURE 3.4 *Example of how a prospect group of U.S. consumers might mentally partition the automobile category to arrive at their consideration set.*

The most important research step is to interview potential category customers to find out exactly what need they have in mind during the choice process and what products they see as close substitutes.

The set of acceptable substitutes is the correct definition of a "market" and the substitutes' attributes collectively provide the reason for customers' regard of this set as the "category." Find out what they – the customers – call the category. If a broader, or different, or even a narrower category looks to be an attractive opportunity for the brand to increase its sales or raise its profit margin, the interviews should be with customers who buy the acceptable substitutes in the "new" category.

THE KEY BENEFIT (B) POSITIONING DECISION

The third factor in the brand's positioning is the Key Benefit (B) decision. As outlined in Figure 3.5, this is in fact several decisions:

• Central versus differentiated benefit positioning

• Emphasized benefit: instinctual, archetypal, emotional, or rational

- Entry-ticket benefits
- Inferior benefit: trade off versus omit

These decisions are explained below.

Benefit positioning within the category
- Central
- Differentiated
- Central me-too

Emphasized benefit type
- ISP (instinctual selling proposition)
- ASP (archetypal selling proposition)
- ESP (emotional selling proposition)
- RSP (rational selling proposition)

Other benefits
- Entry-ticket benefits (mentioned)
- Inferior benefits (traded off or omitted)

FIGURE 3.5 *Benefit positioning decisions.*

Central versus differentiated positioning

The **market leader** can elect to adopt **central positioning** within the category, because the market leader's key benefit is usually that it delivers best on the *set* of benefits that meet the category need, in other words, that it is the "best of its kind" in the category. For instance, Coca-Cola can claim that it is the best cola (its advertised benefit claims over the years have often done this, such as "Coca-Cola is it" and "The real thing"). IBM can claim that it is the best general-purpose desktop computer. Kleenex can claim that it is the best facial tissue. Budweiser can claim that it is the best of (U.S.) beers. We will introduce in the next chapter, Chapter 4, a more specific model and procedure for selecting the brand's Key Benefit and will see that a central brand's uniqueness comes from the *combined* benefits that it offers and, indeed, it may not have a differentiated superiority on any single benefit!

Follower brands – which means *most* brands – have to adopt **differentiated positioning** on at least one important benefit. For instance, Pepsi differentiates on a user-as-hero benefit by claiming it is "For those who think young" ("The Pepsi Generation"). Dr. Pepper, on the other hand, is functionally different (a cherry-flavored cola) and its user target is "Individualists." In the PC category, Apple Computer[8] claims to be easiest to use and its slogan is "Think different." Hewlett-Packard (H-P) computers are "For technophiles" and at present this brand is employing very high-tech and unconventional, perhaps even postmodern, advertising executions. In the facial tissues category in the U.S. market, where Kleenex is the central brand, Sorbent claims to be "Softest." Miller beer in the U.S.A. claims to be the ideal brand to relax with after a hard day's work ("It's Miller time").

There is one other option, called **central me-too positioning**, which is available mainly to **store brands** (the store's private labels or own-name brand). Store brands offer the same benefits as the central brand at a substantial price saving. In 70% of supermarket product categories, the retailer's store brand is among the top three sellers and, overall, store brands account for about 20% of retailers' unit sales. Almost always, the store brand's benefit positioning mimics that of the leading national brand.[9] A good-quality, low-cost manufacturer's brand could also adopt central me-too positioning.

Emphasized benefit

The benefit to be emphasized is the Key Benefit and it may be instinctual, archetypal, emotional, or rational. To explain the manager's options here, we turn to brain-levels theory.

The world of marketing and the choices that customers make is becoming more globally oriented and perceptually faster. Recent research into processing by the human brain (more technically known as neuro-imaging[10]) supports the theory that decisions between alternatives – especially between alternative brands but also, in quite a number of product and service categories, between specific brand-items – will be made much faster, in a matter of seconds, if the decision is made by one of the lower levels of customers' brain systems.[11] To use an analogy, you are more likely to catch the ball if you use a lower-level perceptual brain process rather than attempt to forecast its parabolic arc by differential calculus! Other highly respected marketing researchers to buy into brain-levels theory are Gordon in the U.K.[12] and Zaltman in the U.S.A.[13] Table 3.1 provides an overview of brain-levels theory. Figure 3.6 shows where most of the brain regions referred to in the theory are located – not that this matters, strictly speaking, for the *theory*.

TABLE 3.1 *Brain-levels theory and modes of persuasion.*

BRAIN REGION	PROCESSING MODE	PERSUASION LABEL
Prefrontal cortex ("new" or higher brain, or neocortex, with memory and learning input from the hippocampal system)	Judgment and reasoning	RSP (rational selling proposition)
Limbic system (mid-brain, comprising the thalamus, hypothalamus, amygdala, and periaqueductal grey area, and associative areas of cortex)	Emotions; and imprinted Archetypal schemas	ESP (emotional selling proposition) ASP (archetypal selling proposition)
Reptilian level ("old" or lower brain, comprising the lower brainstem cerebellum, medulla, and olfactory lobes)	Instincts	ISP (instinctual selling proposition)

SOURCE: Adapted from J. Wilson, 2002, reference in note 11, with some added anatomical detail from J. Panksepp, 2000, reference in note 15.

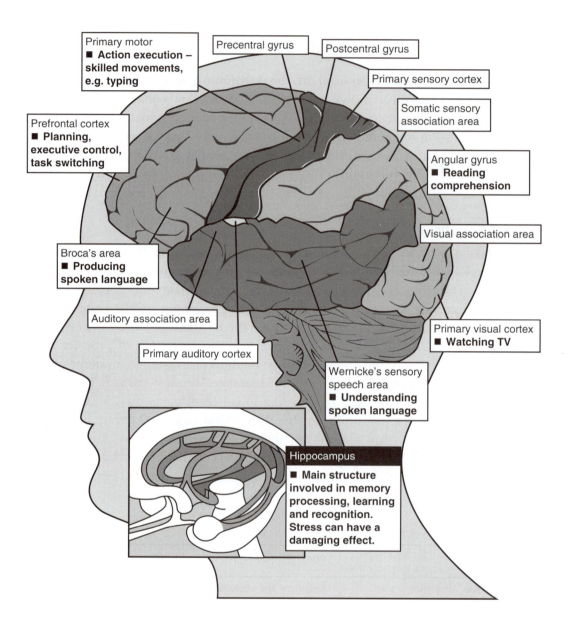

FIGURE 3.6 *Functional regions of the human brain.*

SOURCE: Based on T. Smith (Ed.), *The Human Body*, Penguin Books, 1995.

The levels are discussed below, starting with the lowest or most primitive level and working up. We have attached an appropriate label to the type of *selling proposition* (Key Benefit type) that the levels imply. We must point out before reviewing the levels that it is not possible for all brands to benefit-position themselves successfully at a lower level – though we are convinced that it is worth a try. Nor is it advisable for *brand-items* to do so in categories where *functional* benefits are the main basis of item choice. However, even a functionally based item may encourage preference by borrowing from, or leveraging on, its brand or sub-brand *name* that *has* been successfully positioned at a lower, deeper level.

ISP (instinctual selling proposition)

The early psychologist McDougall defined an **instinct** as "an inherited or innate psychophysical disposition which determines its possessor to perceive, and to pay attention to, objects of a certain class, to experience an emotional excitement of a particular quality upon perceiving such an object, and to act in regard to it in a particular manner, or, at least, to experience an impulse to such action."[14] This definition still fits well today. Although his final list of 18 instincts overstated the number of instincts that initiate human behaviors, there is no doubt that there are about 10 innate basic drives that we share with the animal kingdom, hence the "reptilian" brain location of these.[15]

Negative instinctive drives are *anger*, which initiates aggressive behavior (fight); *fear of the unknown*, which initiates withdrawal behavior (flight); and *panic*, or fear of separation, which initiates affiliative behaviors (seeking social contact). These drives may be relevant in social marketing in campaigns with the objective of *de-marketing* – which involves repositioning – undesirable "brands" such as dangerous driving and road-rage (defusing anger); smoking and illicit drug use (associating these *with* fear of the unknown); and too much TV watching (interestingly, by defusing fear of separation).[16]

Positive instinctive drives that initiate approach behaviors, and thus are relevant in commercial marketing, are the *sex drive*[17] (lust); *nurturance* (a natural tendency to care for others); *affiliation* (usually an urge arising from reaction to the negative instinctive drive of fear of separation); *curiosity* (innate interest in novel stimuli); *play* (a natural tendency to engage in rough-and-tumble activity, producing the emotion of joy); and *dominance*, or power-seeking (which is positive for the seeker though not for the subordinates).

The positive drives can be triggered, as can negative drives, by **subliminal affective priming**[18], that is, by stimuli too subtle to be consciously noticed. However, we hold subliminal triggering to be unethical (see Chapter 18) and, anyway, instincts can be triggered by *conscious* stimuli.

Brands may be able to uniquely tap into positive instincts or, if appropriate, negative instincts, and use an ISP. (However, *brand-items*, which require sharper differentiation than brands, will be more likely to position at one of the two uppermost levels, using an emotional ESP or a rational RSP.) Some apparent examples of ISPs for *brands* are, for the Red Cross and McDonald's – *nurturance*; for IBM and Nike – *dominance*; for Coke and for Red Bull energy drink – *play*; for Gucci Rush perfume and for Haagen-Daz icecream – *lust*; and for Fisher-Price toys – *curiosity*. The launch ad for Gucci Rush perfume from several years ago was ground-breaking because of its blatant depiction of lust; the ad showed the facial expression of a young woman experiencing an orgasm or a "rush" induced by heroin[19]. However, most instincts can be tapped into with simple primitive symbols in the ad. Some examples are sketched in Figure 3.7.

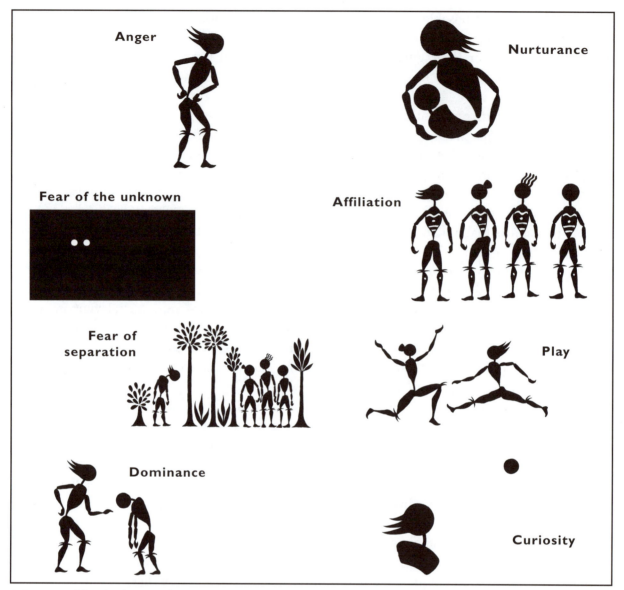

FIGURE 3.7 *Most instincts can be tapped into by using primitive visual symbols in the ad, as illustrated here.*

SOURCE: Illustrations by Boris Silvestri.

ASP (archetypal selling proposition)

The next level invokes primarily the mid-brain region of emotional processing. Distinguished within this level is a lower level where "imprinting" of emotionally laden universal personality characters – called **archetypes** – is, in theory, believed to reside. The leading advocate of archetypal theory was the psychoanalyst and experimental psychologist Jung[20], whose catalog of story-character stereotypes which appear in almost every known culture is experiencing new interest.[21] These archetypal schemas – patterns that are imprinted or overlearned early in childhood if not innately passed on from generation to generation in the "collective unconscious" as Jung believed – are processed (recognized) very quickly. There is fast access in the brain to patterns that resemble a well-learned schema.[22]

Some fairly obvious examples of brands that have successfully tapped into Archetypal Selling Propositions, ASPs, are Richard Branson and the Virgin brand as *The Outlaw* (also known as *The Anti-Hero*); American Express as *The Hero*; Nature's Way vitamins as *The Earth Mother*; and Disney as *The Little Trickster*.

Archetypal characters are processed very quickly. They depend for their effectiveness on "knowing the story," so it doesn't have to be told in full. Knowing the story is at the next level up from instincts but still, in theory, involves only basic pattern recognition rather than higher cortical associations. A brand can "borrow" the traits of the archetypal character. An archetypal character is one type of Conveyer (which is the best form of creative idea) as we will see in Chapter 7.

ESP (emotional selling proposition)

Still at the fast-processed, mid-brain level but mostly requiring the additional upper-brain step of cognitive labeling are the Emotions. Recent theory posits that there are two types of emotion. **Type 1 emotions** consist of Arousal, Positive Affect, and Negative Affect, which do *not* require the person to mentally label them, that is, consciously acknowledge their occurrence. **Type 2 emotions** consist of the more complex human emotions such as Ecstasy, Delight, Nostalgia, Pity, Empathy, and perhaps 30 or so others, which *are thought about* as they occur.[23] The type 1 emotions of Arousal and Positive and Negative Affect are very important for the effective processing of marcoms stimuli (notably ads), and type 1 Positive Affect or Negative Affect that becomes attached to the *brand* can automatically motivate approach or avoidance behavior – in this sense acting like an *instinct*.[24] In the U.K., for young leisure flyers, for instance, Virgin is reactively perceived as good and approachable, whereas British Airways is bad and avoided.[25]

A brand's or brand-item's Emotional Selling Proposition, however, is much more likely to use a *type 2* emotion. State Farm, the U.S. insurance company, for instance, uses a strong appeal to the feeling of being Reassured (a quite common motivating emotion for customers of service providers) as evidenced by its long-running slogan, "Like a good neighbor, State Farm is there." Kodak in its many campaigns over the years for its film and camera products has appealed to Nostalgia; in a recent variation on the nostalgia theme, Kodak's ads tug at the *negative* emotion of the Regret that you feel if you realize that you did not take those family snapshots years ago. Coke's marcoms usually intend to generate the strong positive emotion of Excitement or the even stronger positive emotion of Elation.

RSP (rational selling proposition)

The **rational approach** to identifying a Key Benefit focuses on a functional performance benefit. For high-risk products or services, this may be a *set* of functional benefits. A Rational Selling Proposition, or RSP, is the conventional approach and it is the right one for an *Informationally* motivated choice between brand-items (see Chapter 8). Federal Express courier service promises Speedy Delivery via its RSP, "When it absolutely, positively has to be there overnight." Crest toothpaste (in the U.S.A.) and Colgate Fluorigard toothpaste (outside the U.S.A.) both focus on the functional key benefit of Protection Against Dental Cavities. Colgate's ad agency, then called Ted Bates, and its legendary copywriter, Rosser Reeves, invented the USP – unique selling proposition – which is a brand-differentiating RSP. Reeves' original USP for Colgate toothpaste was, "Cleans your breath while it cleans your teeth."[26] Later, cavity prevention became more important in the toothpaste category. Indeed, it became an Entry-Ticket Benefit, as explained next.

Entry-ticket benefits

There may be **entry-ticket benefits** – usually functional benefits but in some cases emotional benefits – that have to be *mentioned* in the marketing communications for a *brand-item.* These are benefits that the target customer expects the brand-item to have as "par for the course" in that category, but needs to be explicitly shown or told that it *does* have. In more technical terminology, in paying attention to entry-ticket benefits, the target customer is executing a *conjunctive* choice rule ("must meet my standards on all the important benefits") to screen the items that will form his or her consideration set.[27]

A new brand-item that is entering the category has to mention Entry-Ticket Benefits for a while. For example, new diet drinks have to state that they are "Sugar-free." New pain remedies have to tell consumers, until everyone knows the brand, whether they are paracetamol-based or aspirin-based. So also do brand-items in categories of products or services that people buy *infrequently* – to remind customers that the item has these basic benefits.

Also, a benefit that is an *Entry-Ticket* Benefit for *all other* brand-items in the category could be used by *one* brand-item as a *differentiating* benefit (a Key Benefit) *if* the brand can offer superior delivery on that benefit *and* provided that enough potential customers desire more-than-acceptable delivery on the benefit. Crest and Colgate Fluorigard toothpastes are examples of this with the benefit of Cavity Prevention. Another example is the Volvo automobile brand; in most markets, Volvo emphasizes its historical key benefit of "Safety," a reasonable level of which is an *entry-ticket* for most other brands.

Inferior benefit

Finally, the brand-item may be perceived as having *inferior delivery* on a particular, important benefit. Usually, thankfully, there is just one **inferior benefit** and there may be none. An Inferior Benefit is a problem if the benefit is *important* to the target customer. In such cases, the inferior benefit can be *traded off* in the brand-item's positioning by compensating for poor performance on the inferior benefit with superior performance on another benefit (to use this tactic, you have to be sure that customers use a *Compensatory* choice rule). The most typical example of this is when a brand-item with *otherwise unacceptably* moderate delivery on the overall quality benefit trades this off by offering a substantially lower price (it is positioned as a "value" brand). The Central Me-Too positioning adopted by most store-brand products is an example, although value positioning can certainly be used for "brand name" brand-items as well. Another quite common example is a retailer (as a brand) with inferior location convenience, who must then offer superior quality, a wider range or very good prices to compensate. For example, the internationally expanding German supermarket chain, Aldi, trades off limited item selection with very low prices.

Alternatively, can an important but inferior-delivered benefit be *omitted*? If the product or service brand-item is frequently bought, the Inferior Benefit cannot be omitted because it will quickly be "found out" and repeat purchase will suffer. Therefore, in the *frequent-purchase* case, the Inferior Benefit has to be *traded off*. However, with one-off or infrequently-purchased products and services, the temptation for the marketer may be to omit any reference to the Inferior Benefit. Whereas no law requires an ad to state *everything* about the brand, omission of a *material* benefit is ethically wrong (see Chapter 18) and will usually be found out in the long run. Financial services and insurance products are two categories that face the issue of disclosing inferior benefits and some companies in these industries often stretch the limit of *caveat emptor* and make it necessary for the industry or government to impose regulations or for customers to employ an expert adviser.

BRAND ARCHITECTURE AND POSITIONING

A company that wishes to "leverage" its brand name or one of the brand names that the company owns to assist preference for particular product items or service items that it sells has to ensure that the brand-items' positionings are consistent with – meaning that they reflect rather than restate – the Master Brand's positioning, or the Sub-Brand's positioning if a Sub-Brand is used. Examples of Master Brands are Birds Eye in FMCG products, and CitiBank in business and consumer services. Examples of Sub-Brands, corresponding, are Birds Eye Vegetables (the company also makes Birds Eye Fish as a Sub-Brand) and CitiBank Corporate Services (as distinct from CitiBank Consumer Services).

Brand architecture is the contemporary term given to the process of ensuring that the *master-brand or sub-brand positioning* comes across in the positioning of particular *brand-items*, while at the same time distinguishing each of the brand-items within the product or service line. Without this differentiation, cannibalization of the company's own products and service items will become a real problem.

Tait, a brand consultant, provides an excellent framework for Brand Architecture.[28] We have adapted his framework to fit our terminology, as shown in Figure 3.8. An example of a Sub-Brand that differs on the category-need factor (C) of positioning from the Birds Eye master brand is Birds Eye Create-a-Meal. An example of a Sub-Brand that differs on the target customer factor (T) of positioning from the Lee Jeans master brand is Lee Dungarees, aimed at 17–22 year-olds. Tait's framework for master brands, sub-brands, and new master brands makes a lot of sense. In the figure, we have translated his ideas into our terminology based on the T-C-B positioning model.

As we noted earlier in discussing brain-levels theory, the manager of the *brand*, that is, of the Master Brand, should investigate deeper benefit positioning using an emotional selling proposition (ESP), archetypal selling proposition (ASP), or even an instinctual selling proposition (ISP). In the jargon of contemporary brand consultancies, **branding** "is about adding . . . emotional meaning to a product or service . . . a strong layer of emotional affinity, or identification, between brand and constituent [target customer]."[29] This can be achieved by using one of these deeper levels of positioning.

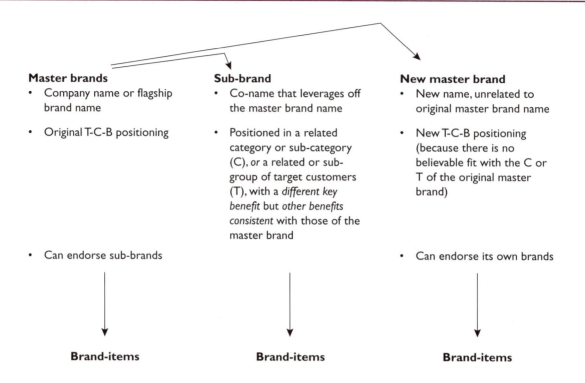

Master brands
- Company name or flagship brand name
- Original T-C-B positioning
- Can endorse sub-brands

Sub-brand
- Co-name that leverages off the master brand name
- Positioned in a related category or sub-category (C), *or* a related or sub-group of target customers (T), with a *different key benefit* but *other benefits consistent* with those of the master brand

New master brand
- New name, unrelated to original master brand name
- New T-C-B positioning (because there is no believable fit with the C or T of the original master brand)
- Can endorse its own brands

Brand-items   **Brand-items**   **Brand-items**

FIGURE 3.8 *Brand architecture positioning.*

SOURCE: Adapted from B. Tait, Do gaps in marketing theory make new brands fail?, *Admap*, 2001, June, pp. 40–43. This figure is reproduced with the permission of *Admap*. For more details go to <www.warc.com/admap>.

SUMMARY

Brand Positioning aims to create a unique representation of the brand in customers' minds (a schema in the brain). Based on the T-C-B Positioning Model, this representation should link the brand to a category need (C), signal the type of customer the brand is targeted towards (T), and link the brand to its key benefit (B). The manager makes the second decision first, hence the order for the manager is T, C, then B. Brand Positioning applies for the Master Brand, Sub-Brands if used, and particular Brand-Items.

The target customer (T) positioning for the master brand, sub-brand, or brand-item should identify the stakeholder target customer type (Suppliers, Distributors, Investors, Regulators, Employees, or End-Customers). Subsequently, for a marcoms *campaign*, the Target Audience has to be identified, as does the Media Target and the Creative Target. At the macro positioning level, however, the target customer is defined as the broad group of realistic potential and actual buyers of the category, within the stakeholder type.

The category positioning (C) for the master brand, sub-brand, or brand-item should be defined in terms of the Target Customer's Category Need and it can be defined broadly, narrowly, or differently to reflect where the manager realistically would *like* the brand to be competing, or defined as it currently is, if that is the best category positioning for it.

The key benefit (B) positioning for the brand requires several decisions. Central versus Central Me-Too versus Differentiated benefit positioning has to be decided; the Key Benefit itself – emotional (at an ISP, ASP, or ESP level) versus functional (RSP) – has to be emphasised; and any necessary Entry-Ticket Benefits mentioned. Also, when an inferior-delivered benefit is present, a decision has to be made as to whether to trade it off or omit it. The I-D-U Model, covered in the next chapter, is essential for making good decisions about benefit selection.

Brand Architecture is how the positioning statements of the master brand, sub-brands (if used), and brand-items *fit together*. Going from general to specific, the C and T factors should remain related but the B – the *Key Benefit* – will often be different.

DISCUSSION QUESTIONS

3.1 What are the three factors in terms of which the brand should be positioned? How does clear representation of the brand on these three factors facilitate choice?

3.2 A marcoms Situation Audit is recommended as one of the two most useful types of research for positioning. In the Situation Audit, what should you do with competing brands' ads? Collect three magazine ads (for different but competing brands) from the men's or women's fragrances category and do the recommended analysis.

3.3 Does the Category-Need description of "fast food" adequately describe where McDonald's is now trying to position its restaurants?

3.4 Construct a Category Partitioning Diagram for soft drinks leading to your personal Consideration Set of them.

3.5 Explain the difference between the Target Customer and the Target Audience. Exemplify your answer with reference to (the sub-brand) Dell desktop computers.

3.6 What is Central Positioning, which brands in the category should use it, and why?

3.7 Explain why, for a Master Brand, an Instinctual Selling Proposition or an Archetypal Selling Proposition is worth trying. An Emotional Selling Proposition, for a master brand, will not be quite as effective – why not?

NOTES

1. J.U. McNeal and M.F. Ji, Children's visual memory of packaging, *Journal of Consumer Marketing*, 2003, 20(5), pp. 400–427.

2. This obviously ballpark estimate is reported in W. Gordon and S. Ford-Hutchinson, Brains and brands: re-thinking the consumer, *Admap*, 2002, January, pp. 47–50.

3. Dowling categorizes stakeholder types as normative (government, regulatory agencies, trade associations, professional societies, stockholders, board of directors); functional (employees, unions, suppliers, distributors, service providers); diffuse (journalists, special interest groups, community members); and customers (end-customer segments). See G. Dowling, *Creating Corporate Reputations*, Oxford, U.K.: Oxford University Press, 2001, chapter 2.

4. T. Levitt, Marketing myopia, *Harvard Business Review*, 1960, 38, July–August, pp. 45–56.

5. *The Times*, Obituary of Alfred (Freddy) Heineken, reprinted in Brewer with global vision, *The Australian*, January 7, 2002, p. 12.

6. B. Loken and J. Ward, Alternative approaches to understanding the determinants of typicality, *Journal of Consumer Research*, 1990, 17(2), pp. 111–126. Also see M. Viswanathan and T.L. Childers, Understanding how product attributes influence product categorization: development and validation of fuzzy set-based measures of gradedness in product categories, *Journal of Marketing Research*, 1999, 36(1), pp. 75–94.

7. D. Rhodes, Get creative: become agencies for new ideas, *The Australian*, Media section, April 10–16, 2003, p. 11.

8. We give the brand its full name. In 1981, Apple Computer was sued by The Beatles' company, Apple Corps, for theft of the name, and settled for an agreement never to enter the music business. It now has entered the music business, with its sub-branded iPod portable music player and iTunes Music Store on the Web (positioning in a different category, see earlier in the chapter). Apple Corps is suing Apple Computer again. D. Frith, PowerBook sales languish, *The Australian*, IT Section, September 23, 2003, p. 4. See iPod's striking outdoor ads in Chapter 9.

9. S. Sayman, S.J. Hoch, and J.S. Raju, Positioning of store brands, *Marketing Science*, 2002, 21(4), pp. 378–397.

10. A. Smidts, Kijken in het brain, *ERIM Report*, Rotterdam School of Management, Erasmus University, The Netherlands, October 2002, provides a recent comprehensive review of brain functions and decision-making.

11. J. Wilson, Whole-brain branding, *Admap*, 2002, September, pp. 47–49. For evidence that affective (emotional benefits) processing is faster than cognitive (rational benefits) processing, see M.T. Pham, J.B. Cohen, J.W. Pracejus and G.D. Hughes, *Journal of Consumer Research*, 2001, 28(2), pp. 167–188.

12. See W. Gordon and S. Ford-Hutchinson, same reference as note 2.

13. J. Olson and G. Zaltman's ZMET qualitative research method is based on brain-level theory. See G. Zaltman, Rethinking marketing research: putting people back in, *Journal of Marketing Research*, 1997, 34(3), pp. 424–437; and G. Zaltman, *How Customers Think*, Boston, MA: Harvard Business School Press, 2003.

14. The definition of an instinct is from W. McDougall, *An Introduction to Social Psychology*, London: Methuen, 1908, p. 30. McDougall's final theory of instincts listed 18 instincts: in the avoidance category, disgust, fear, submission, and rest or sleep; in the approach category, food-seeking, sex, curiosity, anger, self-assertion, appeal, protective or parental propensity, acquisitive propensity (cf. materialism), constructive propensity, laughter, comfort, migratory propensity (cf. population mobility) and bodily needs (breathing, coughing, sneezing, elimination). See W. McDougall, *The Energies of Men: A Study of the Fundamentals of Dynamic Psychology*, London: Methuen, 1932. McDougall argued that instincts are the primary motivators of behavior and, most interesting, that pleasure and pain are themselves non-motivational, serving as mere cues that instincts are successfully or unsuccessfully running their course. See G.W. Allport, The historical background of social psychology, in G. Kindzey and E. Aronson (Eds), *Handbook of Social Psychology*, *Vol. 1*, New York: Random House, 1985, chapter 1.

15. The modern theory of "basic emotions," that is, instincts, is from J. Panksepp, Emotions as natural kinds within the mammalian brain, in M. Lewis and J.M. Haviland-Jones (Eds), *Handbook of Emotions*, 2nd edn, New York: Guilford, 2000, chapter 9.

16. The complex motives underlying most "brands" in social marketing are discussed in our Chapter 18.

17. D. Zillmann, Coition as emotion, in D. Byrne and K. Kelley (Eds), *Alternative Approaches to the Study of Sexual Behavior*, Hillsdale, NJ: Erlbaum, 1986, pp. 173–199, shows that sex is a basic drive, like anger and fear.

18. For recent demonstrations of subliminal affective priming, see S. Sohlberg and A. Birgegard, Persistent complex subliminal activation effects: first experimental observations, *Journal of Personality and Social Psychology*, 2003, 85(2), pp. 302–316. Subliminal priming works in Web pages, too; see N. Mandel and E.J. Johnson, When web pages influence choice: effects of visual primes on experts and novices, *Journal of Consumer Research*, 2002, 29(2), pp. 235–254.

19. Though this is not such a far-fetched comparison; a recent study by M. Holstege at the University of Groningen in The Netherlands using neuro-imaging found that, during sex, an orgasm has the same effect on the brain as a dose of heroin. See: Sex on the brain in Dutch study, *The Australian*, October 24, 2003, p. 12.

20. C.G. Jung, *Collected Papers on Analytic Psychology*, 2nd edn, translated London: Balliére, Tindall, and Cox, 1922.

21. And earning big consulting bucks. For instance, G. Clotaire Rapaille, of the Florida-based company Archetype Discoveries Worldwide, charges about $225,000 per qualitative study (at least four times the usual fee) and delivers only an oral report! Olson and Zaltman's ZMET is lucrative too. Both ADW and ZMET have some *very* major clients. See M. Wells, In search of the buy button, *Forbes Global*, September 1, 2003, pp. 34–35, 38–40.

22. Memories of an object or event are recalled as a group – as a schema – rather than as simple unrelated associations; see S.T. Fiske and P.W. Linville, What does the schema concept buy us?, *Personality and Social Psychology Bulletin*, 1980, 6(4), pp. 543–557.

23. J.A. Russell, Core affect and the psychological construction of emotion, *Psychological Review*, 2003, 110(1), pp. 145–172. For an excellent analysis of what we call type 2 emotions, see A. Ben-Ze'ev, *The Subtlety of Emotions*, Cambridge, MA: MIT Press, 2000. For a classic study of type 2 emotions perceived from photos of facial expressions (as might be used in ads), see H. Schlosberg, The description of facial expressions in two dimensions, *Journal of Experimental Psychology*, 1952, 44, pp. 229–237.

24. M. Chen and J.A. Bargh, Consequences of automatic evaluation: immediate behavioral predispositions to approach or avoid the stimulus, *Personality and Social Psychology Bulletin*, 1999, 25(2), pp. 215–224.

25. W. Gordon and S. Ford-Hutchinson, same reference as note 2. See also M. Chen and J.A. Bargh, Consequences of automatic evaluation: immediate behavioral predispositions to approach or avoid the stimulus, *Personality and Social Psychology Bulletin*, 1999, 25(2), pp. 215–224.

26. See M. Mayer, *Madison Avenue U.S.A.*, Harmondsworth, England: Penguin, 1958. And here's a USP: this is the most insightful book ever written about the ad agency business. And the business, almost 50 years on from Mayer's classic book, has not changed but merely invented new buzzwords for old concepts periodically, such as "account planners" for those who used to be the agency's market research managers.

27. M. Laroche, Selected issues in modeling consumer brand choice: the extended competitive vulnerability model, in A.G. Woodside and E.M. Moore (Eds), *Essays by Distinguished Marketing Scholars of the Society for Marketing Advances*, Vol. 11, Amentan: JAI/Elsevier, 2002, pp. 115–138. See also T.J. Gilbride and G.M. Allenby, A choice model with conjunctive, disjunctive and compensatory screening rules, paper presented at the Marketing Science conference (INFORMS), University of Maryland, June 2003.

28. B. Tait, Do gaps in marketing theory make new brands fail?, *Admap*, 2002, June, pp. 40–43.

29. A. Bergstrom, D. Blumenthal, and S. Crothers, Why internal branding matters: the case of Saab, *Corporate Reputation Review*, 2002, 5(2,3), pp. 133–142. The quotation is from p. 134.

CHAPTER 4

Benefit positioning: I-D-U benefit analysis and the a-b-e benefit claim model

An essential input to brand positioning is **benefit positioning**, especially of the Key Benefit. The Key Benefit, as explained in the previous chapter, could be an instinct, archetype, strong emotion, emotional benefit, or functional benefit. The manager has to *select* a Key Benefit (usually a single benefit but sometimes a set of several benefits) that is:

1. Important or motivating to target customers (I factor)

2. Deliverable by the brand (D factor)

3. Unique to the brand (U factor)

The strategy for the brand's marcoms is to *emphasize* the brand's Key Benefit (important, deliverable, *and* unique); mention any required Entry-Ticket Benefits (important, but deliverable by all brands in the category); and *trade off* or *omit* any Inferior Benefits (important and delivered poorly by the brand), of which there is quite often just one.

I-D-U Benefit Analysis applies to positioning of the master brand, the sub-brand (if used), and brand-items. For convenience of exposition, we will refer to each as "the brand".

I-D-U BENEFIT ANALYSIS

To decide which benefits are important, which benefits our brand is enabled to deliver well on, and whether such delivery is perceived as unique, the manager has to evaluate the potential of multiple benefits, using what is called a **multiattribute model**. Although the model refers to "attributes," this model is readily adapted to include Instincts, Archetypes, Strong Emotions, benefits that are intrinsically Emotional, or benefits that are Functional. We call our multiattribute model the **I-D-U model** and base the analysis on this model.

We must explain, before examining the I-D-U Model, that this is a strategy model for use by the *manager.* The model is not meant to imply that customers actually perform the sort of mental calculation that we are about to describe every time they make a choice of a brand, although sometimes they perform calculations *like* these if the choice is to be made from a high-risk, new (for them) product or service category. Most times, however, they are much more likely to base their choice on a simpler "heuristic," a short-cut choice rule, that focuses only on, what is for *them,* the Key Benefit (the "lexicographic" choice rule) or, even simpler, on *previously formed* Brand Preference (the "affect-referral" choice rule).[1] Although choice is only sometimes computed in the multiattribute manner, a good case can be made that customers' brand preferences are *formed,* in other words *acquired,* through a process that mimics the multiattribute model, the I-D-U Model, and this is what makes it valuable to the manager as a tool for deciding benefit positioning strategy. The I-D-U Model is a model for use by the *manager* to find an effective "way in" to creating, increasing or maintaining the target customer's Brand Preference.

Importance or desirability (in the category)

In order to select a Key Benefit to emphasize for the brand, the manager first has to know which benefits are *important or desirable* to consumers in the *category.*

The best way to identify the important customer benefits in a product or service category, as well as to reveal whether the weighting or evaluation of the benefits differs by category need, is to commission qualitative research in which about 10 users of each of the major brands are interviewed by asking them why they use the brand that they do and why they would avoid buying the other major brands. Although group interviews (focus groups) appear to be efficient for this, the identification of benefits is usually faster in individual interviews. Show the users the competing packages (for services, show the brand logos) and competing ads for the brands. These stimuli will help to identify emotional benefits, in addition to the functional benefits, that will be missed if only an abstract prompt (the brand name) is used. Emotions that can be associated with the brand include descriptions, by users, of other users as "rugged," "sexy," "cool," "fun," "exciting."

Each person is asked to first place himself or herself into his or her *Category Need mindset,* and then to rate the desirability of each benefit on a nine-point bipolar scale of desirability, as follows:[2]

+ 4	Extremely desirable	− 1	Slightly undesirable
+ 3	Very desirable	− 2	Somewhat undesirable
+ 2	Somewhat desirable	− 3	Very undesirable
+ 1	Slightly desirable	− 4	Extremely undesirable
0	Neither desirable nor undesirable		

It is vital to remember that the Key Benefit is not the *only* benefit that customers in the segment want. They want the Entry-Ticket Benefits *as well*.

Delivery (by each brand)

The next step is to determine how well each competing brand, confining the analysis to the major brands of interest to our target customers, is perceived to *deliver* on the various benefits in the category currently. Depending on the I-D-U strategy that we select, we will then have to nominate *intended* delivery levels for our brand on some of these benefits – targets.

> To see how customers perceive each of the major brands in terms of "delivery" on the important benefits, interview the same large random sample who provided the desirability ratings, and provide them with a list of the major brands (not the packages or ads this time), and then, for each brand in turn, ask them to rate how well it performs (delivers) on each of the important benefits. For low purchase-risk product or service categories, a five-point rating scale of 1 = poor, 2 = fair, 3 = good, 4 = very good, 5 = excellent provides sufficient discrimination of consumer beliefs or perceptions about brands. For high purchase-risk products or services, an 11-point rating scale from 0 = not at all, to 10 = excellent brand-item delivery is used because consumers or customers make finer discriminations for these riskier product or service choices.[3]

Uniqueness (between brands)

Uniqueness is relevant in key-benefit selection because, as we saw in conjunction with uniqueness equity in Chapter 1, uniqueness serves to protect the brand against competition. Uniqueness is *differentially superior delivery*.

Differentially superior delivery is the main way (but not the only way, as we shall see under I-D-U strategies) of raising Brand Preference. In a now-classic analysis based on consumer goods in the PIMS database, Boulding, Lee and Staelin[4] show further that uniqueness must be perceived in the *message* about the benefit (what we will later call the Key Benefit Claim). Message-*perceived* superior benefit delivery is what reduces downside price elasticity, enhancing the brand's uniqueness equity.

The degree of advantage can be estimated by computing an overall Brand Preference score from I-D-U ratings (actually, just the I and D ratings are needed for this). To calculate the Brand Preference score for a given brand, multiply its delivery rating by the importance weight (its desirability rating) for each benefit and then sum them. Algebraically, the formula for calculating brand preference (the same as for preference of sub-brands or brand-items) is

$$BPREF_b = \sum_{i=1}^{n} (D_{bi} \times I_i)$$

where $BPREF_b$ is the brand preference score for brand b; D_{bi} is brand b's delivery rating on a particular benefit, i; I_i is the importance or desirability of benefit i; n is the number of benefits;

and Σ is the sum of the importance-weighted delivery ratings. An expanded I-D formula applies if an instinct, archetype, or strong emotion is attached to the brand, b. The expanded formula is

$$\mathrm{BPREF_b} = \left[\sum_{j=1}^{m} (D_{bj} \times E_j) \right] w_1 + \left[\sum_{i=1}^{n} (D_{bi} \times I_i) \right] w_2$$

where the second expression on the right-hand side refers to benefits, as in the basic formula, and the first expression on the right-hand side refers to the deeper *emotional* basis of brand preference, which may be an Instinct, an Archetype, or a Strong Emotion. In the first expression, an *evaluative response* to the emotion j, E_j, appears instead of importance. Also, for any one brand, b, there will be only *one* Instinct on which it delivers – its ratings on any other instincts in the category should be zero. If the brand is successfully associated with an Archetype, then the j's are the (few) salient traits elicited by the archetype, with the j's differing if other brands use other archetypes. The same interpretation of the j's applies to strong emotions. The w_1 and w_2 are weights which sum to 1.0. If emotional branding – an ISP, ASP or ESP – is *not* used, then w_1 is 0, w_2 is 1.0, and the formula reduces to the basic benefits formula. Do not let the appearance of the formula(s) put you off – it is really quite simple arithmetic to do. This will be seen in the I-D-U examples that follow.

Example of I-D-U analysis for archetypes

Recently, Howard-Spink[5] has shown how a suitable Archetypal Selling Proposition can be selected for the brand. Implicitly, his method uses the I-D-U model. Howard-Spink's method begins with Pearson's[6] simplified but generally sufficient typology of 12 **master archetypes** (there is a larger number of possible archetypes – see the references in Chapter 3) which are shown in Figure 4.1. What is useful about this typology, which we have modified slightly from Pearson's original, is that it classifies the archetypes loosely but reasonably in terms of whether the brand's best option for benefit positioning is to make it be seen as an "order keeper" versus a "change agent" (the vertical dimension) and, cutting across this dimension, as "self-oriented" versus "group-connected" (the horizontal dimension). *Everyman*, for instance, is a group-connector who leans toward order-keeping. *Explorer* is the opposite, a self-orienter who leans toward change.

Archetypes are personality profiles in the sense that each is represented by a distinct *set* of personality traits. For instance, the *Champion* is "tough," "courageous," "ambitious," and "persistent." The *Outlaw* is "iconoclastic," "crusading," "rebellious," and "charismatic." If a brand fits an archetype (has strong delivery, D_{bj}, where j is an Archetype), it will automatically elicit in the consumer's mind the traits that define the archetype.[7] To estimate the relevance or motivating potential (the E_j) of each archetype, we need only rate the *archetype*, not the traits. We use the desirability scale given earlier (–4 to +4) to rate how desirable each archetype is for the brands of products or services in the *category*.

We will now give an example of archetypal-fit ratings. Table 4.1 shows a hypothetical example of brands in a category where four archetypes could potentially apply although one, *Jester*, is negatively evaluated. Brands A, B, and C *already* deliver variously well on these archetypes, so we do not show target ratings. However, unlike the later I-D-U applications, archetypal application is *not* compensatory: in other words, a brand cannot pick up brand preference points by trying to belong to more than *one* archetype. Brand A could do well by adopting the *Champion* archetype.

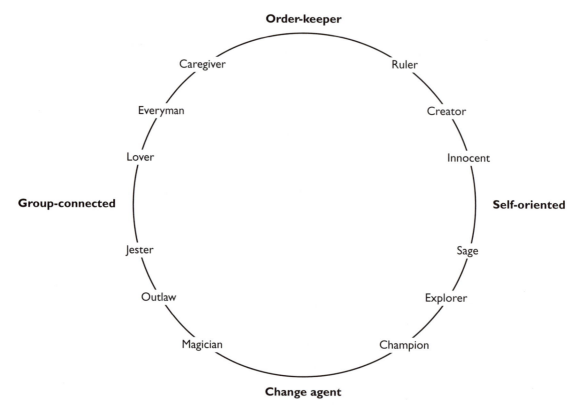

FIGURE 4.1 *Pearson's typology of the 12 master archetypes in relation to two underlying dimensions. Slightly modified from the original in the labels of the dimensions and the order of the archetypes.*

TABLE 4.1 *I-D-U model applied to archetypes (hypothetical example).*

| | PERCEIVED FIT (0 TO 10) | | | |
ARCHETYPE	BRAND A	BRAND B	BRAND C	DESIRABILITY (−4 TO +4)
Champion	10	8	7	(+4)
Magician	3	9	5	(+4)
Outlaw	8	2	10	(+2)
Jester	6	8	2	(−1)

Brand A as "Champion" = 10 x (+4) = 40 points
Brand B as "Magician" = 9 x (+4) = 36 points
Brand C as "Outlaw" = 10 x (+2) = 20 points

Brand B could do well, a little better even, by adopting the *Magician* archetype. Brand C could do best by adopting the *Outlaw* archetype. Although *not* the examples we had in mind, which were purely hypothetical, one might see, in the personal computing category, IBM as the *Champion*, Apple as the *Magician*, and Dell as the (innovative but for-the-people) *Outlaw*. Uniqueness (the U factor in the I-D-U Model) enters by default in that it is not advisable for competing brands to try to own the same archetype.

Example of I-D-U analysis for functional benefits

We show in Table 4.2 an I-D-U Matrix, with hypothetical numbers, for the category of frozen peas in the Australian household consumer market. Consumers in this category – about 70% of Australian households buy frozen peas – are mostly Routinized Favorable Brand Switchers (see Chapter 5) for the three competitive brands shown. They make their choice on each purchase occasion – a very quick choice, taking only a few seconds – in terms of three important benefits: Product Pack-Photo Appeal, Brand Reputation, and Low Price within the category. Brand Reputation here is a "surrogate indicator," or "discriminative stimulus" in operant learning terminology, that consumers have learned as a signal for the product *attributes* of consistent size of the peas and good texture, that is, not soft and at the other extreme, not dry and crinkly. We have estimated the importance weights (the I_i's), using the –4 to +4 scale of Desirability, which in effect becomes a unipolar 0 to +4 scale of Importance, as Product Pack-Photo Appeal, +4; Brand Reputation, +3; and Low Price, +2. All are important benefits but Product Pack-Photo Appeal is *essential* (consumers won't consider the brand-item further if the photo isn't appealing – a rating of 4.0, minimum, on brand delivery D_{bi}) and Reputation is *compensatory* (i.e., consumers will give up a little reputation for a lower price).

TABLE 4.2 *I-D-U matrix for frozen packaged peas (hypothetical data). Birds Eye's target (post-campaign) positioning ratings are shown in bold.*

BENEFIT (i)	BRAND BENEFIT DELIVERY (D_{bi}) MEAN RATINGS ON 1–5 SCALE			IMPORTANCE (I_i) ON –4 TO +4 DESIRABILITY SCALE
	BIRDS EYE	HEINZ	STORE BRAND	
Product pack-photo appeal	4.5→**4.9**	4.5	4.0	+4
Brand reputation	5.0	4.5	2.0	+3
Low price	1.5→**2.0**	1.5	5.0	+2

$$BPREF_b = \sum_{i=1}^{n} (D_{bi} \times I_i)$$

$BPREF_{Birds\ Eye\ (Pre)}$ = 4.5 (+4) + 5.0 (+3) + 1.5 (+2) = 36.0 = 80%

$BPREF_{Heinz}$ = 4.5 (+4) + 4.5 (+3) + 1.5 (+2) = 34.5 = 77%

$BPREF_{Store\ Brand}$ = 4.0 (+4) + 2.0 (+3) + 5.0 (+2) = 32.0 = 71%

$BPREF_{Ideal\ Brand}$ = 5.0 (+4) + 5.0 (+3) + 5.0 (+2) = 45.0 = 100%

$BPREF_{Birds\ Eye\ (Post)}$ = **4.9** (+4) + 5.0 (+3) + **2.0** (+2) = 38.6 = **86%**

Brand Benefit belief ratings – Delivery ratings – are shown for three brands: Birds Eye, Heinz, and "the" Store Brand, here considering all labels of store brands as one. The Brand Benefit Delivery ratings are on a 1 to 5 scale, used for low-risk products, where 1 = poor, 2 = fair, 3 = good, 4 = very good, and 5 = excellent. Mean ratings (across consumers) are shown. Towards the bottom of the table are ratings for the "Ideal Brand"; this would score 5s on all benefits and, with the importance weights the same, produce a brand preference score ($BPREF_{Ideal\ Brand}$) of 45.0. The worked examples of BPREF indicate that Birds Eye Peas have an overall BPREF score of 36.0, which can be interpreted as 80% of ideal (36.0/45.0 = 80%); Heinz Peas, 34.5, or 77%; and the typical Store Brand Peas, 32.0, or 71% of ideal. We note that it would hardly be financially profitable for a major brand such as Birds Eye or Heinz to continuously offer the Lowest Price and thus come very close to the "Ideal Brand"; not only that, but *too* low a price would be suspect. However, these two brands still have *some* "room to move" by considering other I-D-U strategies. Either brand, for instance, could try to find the perfect Product Photo for its pack, which would add 2.0 points. Heinz could advertise to improve its Brand Reputation and gain 0.5 points, which would take its BPREF score to the same as Birds Eye's. The particular Store Brand also has room to move upward on delivery of the Photo benefit and the Brand Reputation benefit.

In bold is an example of a potential I-D-U strategy for Birds Eye. Suppose the manager believes a new Product Photo can be produced that has an appeal rating of 4.9 and that the manager decides to *slightly* lower the Price of Birds Eye to a rating of 2.0 (i.e., better delivery on low price), which would be effective if Birds Eye Peas has high upside elasticity (Value Equity). The estimated revised $BPREF_{Birds\ Eye}$ score with these two moves, shown in the worked example in the bottom row of the table, would be 38.6, or 86% of ideal, and probably successful.

There are other I-D-U strategies that could be tried for the brand, as we will see in the next section. Also, as you may have realized from the examples, there is an art rather than just a science side of I-D-U analysis. Much of the *art* is in stating emotional benefits and functional benefits in *consumer language* so that the wording is, on the one hand, not so dry that it would never motivate anyone and, on the other, not so flowery that it would only ever appear as advertising copy in a specific ad. Also requiring art is the realization from qualitative research that desirability or importance weights should *not always be taken at face value* when obtained directly from consumers.

I-D-U STRATEGY OPTIONS

Having worked through two examples of I-D-U analysis, it is now appropriate to summarize the strategic options that are available to the manager for increasing the brand's market share via key-benefit positioning. There are five main options, and they are listed from first to last *in order of ease of implementation*:

1. *Increase our brand's perceived delivery on an important benefit* – a benefit which is, or could be, unique to our brand. (For a Centrally positioned brand, the uniqueness comes from combined superior delivery on the *set* of important benefits and not necessarily on any one benefit.) This was the strategy in the Birds Eye example.

2. *Increase the perceived importance* of a benefit on which our brand already delivers uniquely. (Importance would be "desirability" when the I-D-U is on instincts, archetypes, emotions, or emotional benefits.) In the archetypes example, for example, it would be advantageous for Brand C to increase the desirability of the Outlaw archetype, if possible.

3. Attempt to *decrease a competitor's perceived delivery* on an important benefit (comparative advertising). In the Birds Eye example, for example, *Heinz* could use a comparative ad to attack Birds Eye's Brand Reputation by demonstrating equal quality of the physical products. Here "our brand" would be Heinz.

4. *Add a new benefit* – if technically feasible – on which our brand delivers uniquely (preferably a benefit that is difficult to imitate or to imitate quickly). In the Birds Eye example, for example, Birds Eye might find a way to add more Vitamins C and D to its peas.

5. Attempt to *change the choice rule* used by customers in favor of our brand (this is equivalent to a severe manipulation of the importance weights, an extension of the second strategy above, and it is rarely feasible).

By far the majority of marcoms campaigns use strategy 1 – attempting to increase their brand's perceived delivery on an important benefit (sometimes on two or three if the product or service category is high in purchase risk, or on the whole set if adopting a Central Positioning strategy). Strategy 2 is probably the next most used and indeed implementation of 1, increased delivery, will often have the secondary effect of increasing the importance, at least slightly, of the emphasized benefit. Strategy 3, the Comparative Approach, is quite usual in the U.S.A. but is prohibited by law or by self-regulatory advertising codes in many other countries although *implicit comparative* advertising, which does not name the competitor, may be permitted. Strategy 4, adding a new benefit, is effective to the extent that it is both technically feasible and difficult to imitate; the new benefit is usually based on a new attribute built in or added to the product or service, or it could be a "discovered" new emotional benefit (a strategy used quite often in the beer category, not surprisingly). Strategy 5, attempting to change the customer's choice rule to favor choice of your brand, is the most difficult because it amounts to "teaching" the customer how to choose differently within the whole *category*; in effect, it attempts to change the importance weights that customers have previously assigned to the benefits (e.g., a change from the normal linear compensatory additive rule, the "Σ" in the formula, to a lexicographic rule in which customers are urged to choose on just *one* benefit – that on which our brand wins in terms of delivery – is equivalent to assigning a weight of +4 to that benefit and a weight of zero to the other benefits).

What-ifs that anticipate competitive reactions

To decide on the best strategic option for key-benefit emphasis – whether to use strategy 1, 2, 3, 4 or 5 above and for which benefit or benefits – the manager, or management team, should perform various "what-if" simulations based on the I-D-U Matrix, calculating what the expected Brand-Preference *returns* would be if the target ratings were successfully implemented.[8] It is important to also consider practical reality, which usually means answering two questions: Is it technically feasible for us to offer (more of) this benefit if an *attribute* is involved? How much of a change in perceptions or importances can we realistically achieve *via* marcoms?

Also to be considered before deciding on the key-benefit strategy is how competitors – often just the leading competitor is threat enough – might react.

To do this, we adopt Armstrong's suggestion to employ role-playing.[9] Several managers should each "be a brand" and debate what they would do if our brand, also role-played by a manager, were to make the "what-if" change.

The most likely competitive reactions should themselves be factored into the I-D-U table and the expected outcome for our brand recalculated for the new "marketplace." Through role-playing and recalculation it is possible to avoid selecting a strategy that is too easily countered and may even prove fatal – and there are many that have failed in the real marketplace – and instead select a safer though still effective strategy.

Interestingly, Armstrong himself has mounted convincing evidence that companies (including brands) should concentrate on their own betterment and not "drive via the side mirrors" by adopting a competitive, market share focus.[10] While mainly true, it would be naïve to take your eye off the competition completely.

A word or three about terminology

The multiattribute model formulation underlies the I-D-U Model. If you come across this model in textbooks or journal articles, you will find three major streams of terminology. *Consumer behavior* theorists in marketing tend to use the terminology of "beliefs" (delivery), "evaluation" or "desirability" of attributes (importance), and refer to the results of the mental computation leading to brand choice as "overall brand attitude." Writers with more of a quantitative *marketing science* background refer to brand delivery as "perceptions" rather than "beliefs"; they refer to "benefit importances," "benefit utilities," or, somewhat confusingly, "benefit preferences"; and they are most likely to use the term "brand preference" rather than "brand attitude." Furthermore, *economists* studying decision-making talk about "probability" (p) rather than "delivery," and "value" (v) rather than "importance," with the outcome of p × v representing a "prospect," which is the same as a "brand preference" score. It is helpful to keep these differences in terminology in mind because otherwise you might think that you are reading about different models when they are one and the same: the multiattribute model.

Also note that "attributes" and "benefits" and "emotions" have been used interchangeably when referring to the *multiattribute* model. Shortly, with the a-b-e model, we will distinguish them.

A further observation is that some managers are visually oriented and prefer to see brand delivery data such as those shown in the previous tables represented as a "perceptual map." We do *not* recommend the use of perceptual maps. One problem, in nearly all cases, is that researchers plot only the first two important attributes. Other attributes are usually neglected. Perceptual maps, when confined to two attributes, do not provide a complete picture except for rare cases in which there *are* only two important benefits. A second problem is that the attributes are invariably plotted as though they were of equal importance. There is no way of representing benefit importance in perceptual maps. Thus, we prefer the numerical representation, as in the I-D-U Model.

THE a-b-e BENEFIT CLAIM MODEL

The a-b-e Model represents the final, executional stage of positioning at the level of *Benefit Claims* in marketing communications. Benefit-claim positioning is added here, rather than in the chapter on advertising execution factors, because brands and brand-items are in fact benefit-positioned by a benefit *claim* rather than the benefit itself. From the I-D-U analysis, perceived benefit delivery is accomplished by a Benefit Claim and so, too, is perceived uniqueness – especially, we have to say, when other brands offer objectively the same benefit! (A British chain of pubs recently got sprung – by an employee, not by patrons – for serving the same beer under several different labels from different taps at different prices![11])

> Benefit *Claims*, rather than benefits as such, are where the action is in advertising. They are also where the action is in the other forms of marketing communications such as *planted* publicity and *announced* price promotions (e.g., "Now slashed by 20%"). Paradoxically, this is because benefit claims are concrete (real) whereas the benefits they represent are abstract (inferred)!

Think about what we've just said here. Sophisticated market researchers such as Moskowitz and Rabino[12] actually conduct the benefit importance identification procedure described for the I-D-U Model earlier by asking consumers to rate the personal relevance of *specific extracts* from actual advertising claims, claims on packages, video clips from the brand's TV commercials or illustrations from its print ads – that is, they use the Benefit *Claims* to represent the underlying benefits. After all, these are what customers see or hear in the real world of advertising and marketing communications.

The a-b-e Benefit Claim Model looks at the *structure* of benefit claims. The modality of benefit claims can be visual, written, or auditory. In terms of the content of benefit claims, the a-b-e Model distinguishes between *attributes* (a), which are what the product or service *has* – that is, contains or offers – objectively; *benefits* (b), which are, subjectively, "what the customer *wants*," that is, a benefit in the everyday meaning of the word; and *emotions* (e), which refer to the antecedent *or* consequent "feelings" experienced by the customer in conjunction with delivery of a benefit, or to feelings elicited *directly* by the brand. Many permutations of a, b, and e are possible although there are six most common ones as indicated in Figure 4.2.

The "support," also known as the "proof," in benefit-claim positioning is provided by the a-b-e *chain* employed in the execution of the ad (or other item of marketing communications). Whereas the combinations of a's, b's and e's are potentially unlimited, ads for **informationally motivated** products and services (see Chapter 8) tend to use either an $e^- \rightarrow b$ ("Problem-solution") or $a \rightarrow b$ ("Here's how") benefit chain. Ads for **transformationally motivated** products and services (again see Chapter 8), on the other hand, tend to use either a single-step "chain" focusing on the benefit, b, or a $b \rightarrow e^+$ chain (called "end-benefit" focus), or sometimes purely a positive emotional focus, e^+.[13] The Smirnoff vodka ad from the brand's famous "Pure thrill" campaign, shown in Chapter 1, Figure 1.2, comes pretty close to pure e^+ (actually, it's more precisely $b \rightarrow e^{++}$, to use the symbols we'll move to in Chapter 6 on creative). Although a Benefit Claim is usually *composed* of a's, b's and e's, the requirement of a composite – that it is smooth to process – makes it quite difficult to distinguish the a, b and e elements after the fact.[14]

> Although there are some theoretical considerations such as Informational versus Trans-formational purchase motivations that should favor one type of a-b-e chain over another, the

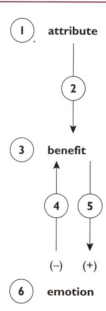

FIGURE 4.2 *The a-b-e model of benefit claim structure. Focus may be on the level itself (1, 3, 6) or on a sequential path ending at the level (2, 4, 5).*

most effective a-b-e chain (combinations of a, b or e, with the e being a negative emotion as an antecedent, e⁻, or a positive emotion as a consequence, e⁺) is best decided by *testing of potential Benefit Claims with prospective customers.* Depending on the stimuli that are likely to be used in the advertising campaign, the test can be conducted with verbal claims – actual copy written by the advertising agency; or with *visually executed* claims – in the form of print ad illustrations or video clips; or with *sound-effect executed* claims – for TV and radio ads.[15]

The a-b-e Benefit Claim Model of positioning therefore operates at the most specific – concrete – level. This "micro" level of positioning can be, and usually *is*, delegated to the advertising agency (the creative team) to decide. However, our view is that the *brand manager* should take a keen interest in this topic of "how advertising *specifically* works" and be involved in this decision. In Chapters 7 and 8, on the creative idea and advertising execution tactics, we will meet the a-b-e Benefit Claim Model again, with examples.

INTEGRATED MARCOMS AND POSITIONING

The Positioning Statements for the Master Brand, Sub-Brands and brand-items within either – if these various distinctions of Brand Architecture are employed in the marketer's branding – will differ somewhat at the macro level (T-C-B), markedly at the middle level (I-D-U), and often completely at the micro level (a-b-e). How, then, should their marcoms messages be *integrated* – to show that they are related brands? The answer is **cosmetic integration** – which is at the most superficial level of all, the surface level, which is pre-macro! That is, the ads and promotion offers across the entire line should share the "same look and feel."[16] A variation of cosmetic integration is integration by *brand personality,* of which an archetypal character is an application. We will discuss

Cosmetic Integration along with advertising execution tactics in Chapter 8 but it won't hurt to preview the principle here: When cosmetic integration is employed in marcoms executions, the target customer must see (or hear) immediately that the ad or offer is *from* Brand X but this realization must stop at this point to be replaced by curiosity that it is a *new message* for Brand X.

THE POSITIONING STATEMENT

Long-form positioning statement

A useful format for the **long-form positioning statement** is provided in Table 4.3. You will see that the format incorporates the decisions made from the T-C-B positioning model, I-D-U benefit analysis, and the a-b-e benefit claim model (this last decision can be delegated to the ad agency but the *result* of that decision should be entered in the positioning statement). The following table, Table 4.4, provides a Campaign Positioning Statement that fits the example discussed in the chapter for the Birds Eye Peas brand-item.

Short positioning statement

The long-form format is very structured. After it is filled out, the positioning decisions can be extracted and stated more simply in the *T-C-B format*. For the Birds Eye Peas brand-item campaign (omitting the a-b-e details here), the **short positioning statement** is: "To buyers of frozen peas who switch between several brands including Birds Eye (T), Birds Eye Peas is the brand of frozen peas (C) that emphasizes pack-photo appeal, mentions brand reputation, and trades off its higher price with its brand reputation (B)."

TABLE 4.3 *Long-form positioning statement format. Starred (*) entries are used for a campaign only.*

BRAND (OR SUB-BRAND OR BRAND-ITEM) _____

TARGET CUSTOMER

1. Target customer type (retail, consumer, business users, etc.) and description that includes all realistic potential and actual buyers: _____
2.* Campaign target audience: _____
3.* Media target: _____
4.* Creative target (targeted decision role): _____

CATEGORY NEED

1. Customer need: _____
2.* Alternative brands (or brand-items) that the target audience considers (including ours if target customer considers or uses it now): _____   _____
   _____   _____

BENEFITS

1. Key benefit (or key benefit combination) to be emphasized: _____
   _____
2.* Key benefit claim chain (the specific a's, b's or e's and their sequence): _____
   _____
3.* Entry-ticket benefit, or benefits, to be mentioned: _____
   _____
4.* Inferior benefit (or purchase barrier) _____ to be traded off with _____ benefit, or deliberately omitted (note here why omission is a feasible option _____)

TABLE 4.4 *Hypothetical campaign positioning statement for the Birds Eye Peas brand-item.*

BRAND (OR SUB-BRAND OR BRAND-ITEM) *BIRDS EYE PEAS*

TARGET CUSTOMER

1.   Target customer type (retail, consumer, business users, etc.) and description that includes all realistic potential and actual buyers: *CONSUMERS – BUYERS OF FROZEN PEAS*

2.*   Campaign target audience: *ROUTINIZED FBSs – BUYERS OF FROZEN PEAS WHO SWITCH BETWEEN SEVERAL BRANDS INCLUDING BIRDS EYE*

3.*   Media target: *HOUSEHOLD GROCERY SHOPPERS*

4.*   Creative target (targeted decision role): *MEAL PLANNER (DECIDER)*

CATEGORY NEED

1.   Customer need: *FROZEN PEAS*

2.*   Alternative brands (or brand-items) that the target audience considers (including ours if target customer considers or uses it now): *BIRDS EYE*   *HEINZ*   *STORE BRAND*

BENEFITS

1.   Key benefit (or key benefit combination) to be emphasized: *BIRDS EYE PACK-PHOTO APPEAL*

2.*   Key benefit claim chain (the specific a's, b's or e's and their sequence): *a's → b → e+: PHOTO OF PLUMP, CLEAN, MEDIUM-GREEN PEAS (ATTRIBUTES) → LOOK WHOLESOME (BENEFIT) → ANTICIPATORY SENSORY EXPERIENCE OF "DELICIOUS" (POSITIVE EMOTION)*

3.*   Entry-ticket benefit, or benefits, to be mentioned: *BRAND REPUTATION*

4.*   Inferior benefit (or purchase barrier) *HIGHER PRICE THAN STORE BRAND* to be traded off with *BIRDS EYE'S BRAND REPUTATION* benefit

SUMMARY

This chapter *elaborates* on Key Benefit selection (B) for the T-C-B brand positioning decision. Key Benefit selection is accomplished by conducting an I-D-U Benefit Analysis of competing brands in the category. For our brand, the manager then evaluates the feasibility and effectiveness of alternative I-D-U *strategies* and selects *target I-D-U ratings* to be achieved by the campaign.

I stands for importance or desirability (of benefits in the category), D stands for delivery (perceived delivery by each of the brands), and U stands for uniqueness (differentially superior delivery on one or more benefits by our brand). In the brand's marcoms, the manager should *emphasize* the brand's Key Benefit (unique benefit), *mention* any necessary Entry-Ticket Benefits, and *trade off or omit* any Inferior Benefits, of which there is rarely more than one.

I-D-U analysis can be applied to Instincts (though measurement at this level is difficult), Archetypes, Strong Emotions, Emotional Benefits, or Functional Benefits. An I-D-U formula is provided whereby Brand Preference is defined as the weighted sum of the brand's Emotional associations (any of the first three listed above) and Brand Benefit Beliefs (emotional *benefits* or functional benefits). For the benefit positioning of Master Brands and Sub-Brands, the Emotions component will usually have the most weight, whereas for the benefit positioning of brand-items, Benefits (which can be emotionally charged or of the more functional type) assume more weight.

Emotions and Benefits produce the communication effect of Brand Preference. There are five possible I-D-U strategies for improving Brand Preference: increase perceived delivery on a benefit that is important and can be delivered uniquely by our brand; increase the perceived importance of a benefit on which our brand already delivers uniquely; attempt to decrease a competitor's perceived delivery on an important benefit; add a new benefit on which our brand delivers uniquely; or attempt to change the customer's choice rule in the category in favor of our brand. The I-D-U analysis allows "what if" simulations to estimate the effect of these alternative strategies to select one that will be feasible and effective.

The benefit-positioning "battle" is actually fought at the level of Benefit Claims, rather than benefits. The a-b-e model of benefit claim structure is useful here. This model distinguishes attributes (objective), benefits (subjective), and emotions (antecedent or consequent feelings) and shows how chains of them can be constructed to achieve most effectively the targeted benefit positioning for the brand. Integrated benefit positioning is completely the opposite: it's pre-macro (cosmetic).

At the end of the chapter is the long-form Positioning Statement format, incorporating the T-C-B model from the previous chapter, the I-D-U model from the present chapter, and the a-b-e model from the present chapter. The short-form Positioning Statement format is based on the T-C-B model.

DISCUSSION QUESTIONS

4.1 Some people won't understand the I-D-U Model properly and will get the impression that there are three different types of benefits, namely, important benefits, deliverable benefits, and unique benefits. Explain why this impression does not reflect a proper understanding of the model.

4.2 In theory, a brand can develop an *archetypal* personality and this may be advantageous for business (e.g., Virgin as the *Outlaw*, appealing to customers who don't want to go along with the establishment). Take three major brands (brand names) in the oral hygiene category, such as Colgate (but take Crest in the U.S.A.), Aqua-Fresh, and Oral-B and, for each, discuss which of the Archetypes in Figure 4.1 in the chapter could be effectively used by that brand.

4.3 Suppose you are the marketing manager for BMW cars. The main competing makes are Mercedes and Audi. Examine possible I-D-U strategies by "what if" simulation and choose a likely strategy for improving Brand Preference for BMW. Explain why you think your strategy would be achievable and estimate its Brand Preference effect using the I-D-U formula.

4.4 Conduct individual depth interviews with five or six women who are acquaintances of yours about their choice of hair salon. From these interviews, identify and describe the several most important benefits and assign numerical weights to them using the +4 to −4 scale of desirability. Then take two of the salons that were mentioned and infer deliverability ratings for them, thereby arriving at an I-D-U Matrix. For the *less*-preferred salon, outline a feasible and effective I-D-U benefit strategy.

4.5 Two benefits that are often important in choosing fashion clothing are Brand Reputation and Country of Manufacture. Suppose that your brand's strongest benefit is Brand Reputation and that the quality reputation of the Country in which your brand's clothing is manufactured is an inferior benefit. Check some of the big-name brands of fashion clothing in stores and discuss how you would handle the positioning decision.

4.6 What are the advantages of the numerical I-D-U model over a perceptual map? Select an example of a perceptual map from any convenient marketing textbook and criticize it in I-D-U terms.

4.7 Study the a-b-e Benefit Claim Model in Figure 4.2. What might be the most effective level *or* chain for: (a) a cold remedy, (b) the latest CD from the country music band, The Dixie Chicks, and look the band up on its Website if you have to, and (c) the Palm Pilot hand-held computer with keyboard.

NOTES

1. The classic and still the best reference for choice rules is P.L. Wright, Consumer choice strategies: simplifying vs. optimizing, *Journal of Marketing Research*, 1975, 12(1), pp. 60–67.

2. From K.J. Clancy and P.C. Krieg, *Counterintuitive Marketing*, New York: The Free Press, 2000, chapter 8.

3. J.R. Rossiter, The C-OAR-SE procedure for scale development in marketing, *International Journal of Research in Marketing*, 2002, 19(4), pp. 303–335.

4. W. Boulding, E. Lee, and R. Staelin, Mastering the mix: do advertising, promotion and salesforce actitivies lead to differentiation?, *Journal of Marketing Research*, 1994, 31(2), pp. 159–172.

5. J. Howard-Spink, Who is your brand? And what is its story?, *Admap*, 2003, October, pp. 15–17.

6. C. Pearson, *Awakening the Heroes Within: Twelve Archetypes to Help Us Find Ourselves and Transform the World*, San Francisco: Harper, 1998.

7. Because an archetype is supposed to function like a schema and tell the whole story at once, it could be argued that archetypal fit should be measured holistically as we have done here.

8. For a quantitative method of estimating the monetary return for attribute improvements, see E. Ofek and V. Srinivasan, How much does the market value an improvement in a product attribute?, *Marketing Science*, 2002, 21(4), pp. 398–411.

9. J.S. Armstrong, Role playing: a method to forecast decisions, in J.S. Armstrong (Ed.), *Principles of Forecasting*, Boston: Kluwer, 2001, pp. 15–30. However, this method can be used only for functional benefits. Emotional benefits are "felt" but cannot be weighed in terms of money. For an excellent discussion of emotional benefits, see the recent article that appropriately acknowledges the great Ernest Dichter and develops a dynamic Gestalt theory of emotional benefits, by D. Ziems, The morphological approach for unconscious consumer motivation research, *Journal of Advertising Research*, 2004, 44(2), pp. 210–215.

10. J.S. Armstrong and F. Collopy, Competitor orientation: effects of objectives and information on managerial decisions and profitability, *Journal of Marketing Research*, 1996, 33(2), pp. 188–199.

11. "Lucifer," Jottings, *Admap*, 2004, April, p. 50.

12. S. Rabino and H.R. Moskowitz, Cross-national concept development/optimization using principles of concept-response segmentation, *Journal of Targeting, Measurement and Analysis for Marketing*, 1998, 7(1), pp. 59–81. Also see their Website, IdeaMap.net.

13. J.R. Rossiter and L. Percy, The a-b-e model of benefit focus in advertising, in T.J. Reynolds and J.C. Olson (Eds), *Understanding Consumer Decision Making*, Mahwah, NJ: Lawrence Erlbaum Associates, 2000, pp. 183–214.

14. Notably, even trained judges cannot reliably identify how many different "sales points" there are in a typical ad; see D.W. Stewart and D.H. Furse, *Effective Television Advertising: A Study of 1000 Commercials*, Lexington, MA: Lexington Books, 1986. This is probably because of benefit

claim structure; for instance, an attribute supporting one benefit might be wrongly counted as two sales points instead of one, or a benefit and its emotional consequence wrongly counted as two sales points.

15. An innovative and extremely interesting study of sound effects that connote the image of "luxury" was reported recently by T. Lageat, S. Czellar, and G. Laurent, Engineering hedonic attributes to generate perceptions of luxury: consumer perception of an everyday sound, *Marketing Letters*, 2003, 14(2), pp. 97–109.

16. L. Percy, J.R. Rossiter, and R. Elliott, *Strategic Advertising Management*, Oxford, U.K.: Oxford University Press, 2001, chapter 13. The "same look and feel" is Larry Percy's apt description of cosmetic integration.

PART II

marcoms campaign

objectives

CHAPTER FIVE
Campaign target audience selection and action objectives 81

CHAPTER SIX
Campaign communication objectives 102

Campaign target audience selection and action objectives

The T factor in the T-C-B positioning model requires the manager to select the *Target Customer* for the brand or brand-item. At this macro level of positioning, target customers are described broadly – firstly as one of the types of stakeholders and then, within the stakeholder type, as all those with reasonable potential to "buy" and current "buyers" of the brand. We use "buy" here to stand for *any relevant action by stakeholders*, such as investing, supplying, supporting – or in social marketing – doing. Customer targeting for a marketing communications *campaign* for a master brand, sub-brand, or brand-item is more specific. The manager will be required to specify a group or groups – known as the Target Audience – from within the broad group of potential and actual buyers. The Target Audience is the group or groups from whom most of the *Action* attributable to the campaign is expected to come. Also to be specified are the *Media Target* (unless the Direct Matching method is used to select media), and the *Creative Target*, which is the *decision role-player* to whom the marcoms messages (e.g., ads or promotions) in the campaign are addressed.

For a specific campaign, Action Objectives then have to be chosen for the target audience group(s). Actions are observable, physical *behaviors* that occur in the real world. (They are distinct from unobservable, mental, *communication effects*, which occur in customers' *minds*, and which cause the behaviors. See Chapter 6.) The Action Objectives most often chosen for marcoms campaigns are the *Purchase Behaviors* of Trial and Repeat Purchase. However, *Pre-Purchase Behaviors* that lead to trial, such as Store Visits or telephone or On-Line Inquiries, may also be used as action objectives, as may *Post-Purchase Behaviors*, such as Display, that lead to repeat purchase or that encourage others to buy. Sales, in aggregate, are made up of the actions of single Purchases, or Trial purchases and Repeat Purchases, by individual customers. The measurement of Purchase or Trial *incidence* and Repeat-Purchase *rates* is essential for using the recommended *Task Method* of budget-setting, as discussed in Chapter 13.

In this chapter, we show how to select a Target Audience Group or Groups for the campaign and how to specify Action Objectives for them or, preferably, Action *Goals*. We then show how to identify the Media Target (using business and consumer demographics). Lastly, we show how to identify the Creative Target.

CUSTOMER TARGETING USING BRAND LOYALTY SEGMENTATION

The purchase of a brand-item is caused mainly by awareness of it and preference for it. (As we will see in the next chapter, Brand Awareness and Brand Preference are the two *necessary* communication objectives for all campaigns.) It is therefore best to assess the total potential market for the brand-item on the basis of prospective customers' current (or, for durables, intended) purchase behavior toward the brand-item *and* the awareness and preference states of mind that cause their behavior. Awareness of and preference for the category as a whole and for the competing brand-items have to be taken into account.

To define the potential target audience groups, we use **brand loyalty segmentation**, where "loyalty" is defined as the propensity to choose the brand-item *caused by* awareness of it and preference for it (rather than by the customer not having any real option to buy some other brand-item in the category). Brand Loyalty as a propensity can completely determine purchase for some customers. For instance, Campo, Gijsbrechts and Nisol[1] found in a recent purchase panel study that for breakfast cereals, 56% of consumers did not buy in the category that day if their favorite brand-item was out of stock and, for margarine, 39% did not buy if their favorite brand-item was out of stock. It should be remembered that there is only about a 1% chance in big stores or 5% chance in small stores that the brand-item will be out of stock, but these figures suggest substantial-sized loyal groups when that does happen and presumably this loyal preference guides their choice when the brand-item *is* in stock. Identification of potential target audiences has to be based on *their degree of brand loyalty* – to our brand or to another.

Brand Loyalty Segmentation can be achieved by considering the total potential market to consist of *five groups* in terms of their buyer behavior toward our brand, which are further divided into *13 subgroups* when awareness and preference are considered. These potential target audience groups and subgroups are listed in Table 5.1. We now consider the five potential target audience groups, and their subgroups, in greater detail.

TABLE 5.1 *Potential target audience groups and subgroups according to brand loyalty segmentation.*

Brand loyals (BLs)

  1. Single-brand loyals

  2. Multi-brand loyals

Favorable brand switchers (FBSs)

  3. Experimental favorable brand switchers

  4. Routinized favorable brand switchers

       } OUR BRAND'S CURRENT CUSTOMERS

Other-brand switchers (OBSs)

  5. Favorable other-brand switchers

  6. Neutral other-brand switchers

  7. Unfavorable other-brand switchers

Other-brand loyals (OBLs)

  8. Favorable other-brand loyals

  9. Neutral other-brand loyals

10. Unfavorable other-brand loyals

       } OTHER BRANDS' CUSTOMERS – WHO COULD TRY OR RE-TRY OUR BRAND

New category users (NCUs)

11. Positive new category users

12. Unaware new category users

13. Negative new category users

       } NON-USERS OF THE CATEGORY – WHO COULD TRY OR RE-TRY THE CATEGORY VIA OUR BRAND

Brand loyals (BLs)

Brand loyals (BLs) – in some product categories, depending on survey results – can be divided into *Single-Brand Loyals* and *Multi-Brand Loyals*, who are loyal to two or three brands.

Single-brand loyals (single-BLs) can be found in every category. They buy our brand on most purchase occasions, although the incidence of Single-Brand Loyals depends on the exact cutoff used to operationalize "most occasions." In studies of FMCG shoppers' store loyalty, for instance, *Single-Store Loyals* are typically defined as those consumers who do 80% or more of their shopping at the one grocery store (the U.S. term for supermarket). We will revisit store loyalty in Chapter 15 on sales promotion, under retailers' promotions. In the U.S.A., 28% of grocery shoppers are Single-Store Loyals.[2] The 80%-or-more criterion is also widely accepted for defining Single-*Brand* Loyalty at the product level. Single-Brand Loyals are a large group – about 40% to 50% of all customers – in *personal use* FMCG categories, such as bath soap, shampoo, and toothpaste.[3] Single-Brand Loyals also make up a particularly high incidence in so-called *subscription* product and service categories, such as bank credit cards and telephone services, and in many *specialized industrial supply* categories where it is not easy or not convenient to switch brands.[4]

Multi-brand loyals (multi-BLs), in contrast, buy and *prefer* two or three brands, including ours, in the category. Why do they prefer more than one brand? The usual reasons are for variety, or for slightly different end-uses.[5] Potato chips and other snack and dessert foods have a high prevalence of Multi-BLs. But so too do most industrial product and service categories because most industrial buyers expect that service would suffer or the price would rise if they were loyal to just one supplier. With Multi-Brand Loyals, household and also business customer surveys indicate that usually the several brands that the customer buys will not be equally bought in terms of *share of requirements (SOR)* but rather there will be a first favorite, second favorite, and perhaps third favorite, which together make up virtually 100% of their purchases.

The only factor that distinguishes Multi-BLs from the next group, Favorable Brand Switchers, FBSs, is *Brand Preference strength*. The Brand Preferences of Multi-BLs are strongly held and it is consequently much more difficult for a marketer to induce them to switch to a brand outside their "repertoire" of favorites. However, *within* the repertoire, there is a realistic opportunity for a marketer to try to increase, over a period of several years, the proportion of purchases (SOR) that our brand-item attains, so that it becomes the first favorite of Multi-BLs.[6]

Favorable brand switchers (FBSs)

Switchers, in contrast to Multi-Brand Loyals, have only *moderate* preferences for the brands that they buy. To **favorable brand switchers**, **FBSs**, our brand is one of several acceptable brands, rather than one of two or three preferred brands (see the target audience classification questionnaire described shortly). For *future* purchasing of our brand, then, FBSs are merely *considerers* in that they have not definitely decided beforehand to buy it.

There are two groups into which Favorable Brand Switchers can be divided for target audience consideration. Early in the product *category* life cycle, customers will tend to try several new brands and then they will settle on the several that they find acceptable, becoming Multi-Brand Loyals, or, if they find only one brand acceptable, they will become Single-Brand Loyals. Early in the life cycle, they are **experimental favorable brand switchers (experimental FBSs)**.

Later in the product category life cycle, when there are few or no new triers of the category, Favorable Brand Switchers will have developed their switching into a "routine," based still on just *moderate* preferences. They are **routinized favorable brand switchers (routinized FBSs)** because their switching behavior can be expected to persist. The action objective is to maintain our brand-item in their consideration set and to try to get these customers to increase their repeat-purchase rate of it, that is, the percentage of occasions on which our brand-item is purchased. Routinized Favorable Brand Switchers, as contrasted with Multi-Brand *Loyals*, are "vulnerable" to switching *out* from our brand.[7] It is relatively easier – using promotions – for us to induce greater switching to our brand but also for others to induce switching *from* our brand. Advertising aimed at Routinized FBSs tries to keep them aware of our brand and to reinforce preference for it (Value Equity) *and* make them more resistant to competitive promotions (Uniqueness Equity). These dual brand-equity concepts were discussed in Chapter 1.

Measurement of potential customers' *Brand Preferences* is essential for determining whether they are Multi-Brand Loyals or Favorable Brand Switchers. Measurement of their Purchase behavior alone will not do it. Consider, for instance, the Maxwell House brand of instant coffee in the U.S. market. One survey at a particular time period, a time period that is immaterial to the point we are making, showed that, of Maxwell House's total customers, 38% bought it just once a year, 16% twice a year, 11% three times a year, 8% four times a year, 7% five times a year, and 20% bought it six or more times a year. These 20% heavy buyers of Maxwell House accounted for approximately 50% of the brand's sales volume.[8] However, we cannot tell from these behavioral data alone whether these 20%, comprising half the brand's franchise, are Single-Brand Loyals, Multi-Brand Loyals, or Routinized Favorable Brand Switchers. If you were the manager of Maxwell House trying to protect heavy buyers of your brand, or if you were the manager of another brand trying to attract the heavy buyers of Maxwell House to switch to *your* brand, then you would have to know their preference strength to make the correct target group classification.

Moreover, measurement of Purchase behavior alone is inadequate for identifying the loyalty group (any group, not just FBSs) for durables – *infrequently purchased* products or services. To classify new car prospects, for instance, you have to measure prospects' awareness of and preferences for the various brand-models in the category in which you are competing, that is, the consideration set, with regard to the *next* purchase, that is, the future purchase that they are going to make. FBSs, in this case Experimental FBSs are those car-buyer prospects who would favorably *consider* buying, say, a Chrysler Crossfire as their next purchase.

Other-brand switchers (OBSs)

Other-Brand Switchers (OBSs) do not include our brand in their switching behavior. The manager has to survey the awareness and preferences of other-brand switchers to determine why they are not buying our brand. Their Brand Awareness and Brand Preference status will enable their classification into one of three subgroups: **favorable other-brand switchers (favorable OBSs)**, who would consider switching to our brand; **neutral other-brand switchers (neutral OBSs)**, who have not heard of our brand and therefore cannot recognize it or recall it; and **unfavorable other-brand switchers (unfavorable OBSs)**, who may have tried our brand in the past and disliked it, or may dislike it just on the basis of its advertising or its packaging. Unappealing ads or "blah" packaging can turn prospects off a brand just as surely as an unsatisfactory trial.

Quite evidently, from the description of these three subgroups of Other-Brand Switchers, the likelihood of being able to persuade them to try, or re-try, *our* brand will be in descending order of probability. Re-trial of our brand by Unfavorable OBSs who have tried and rejected it probably will not be achievable without a repositioning of the brand so as to remove or substantially reduce their objection to it. On the other hand, trial inhibition by Unfavorable OBSs could be due to our ads or package appearance. In both cases, whether to make a change depends on the potential for increased sales from OBSs compared with sales to our current customers. More precisely, as we will explain in the next section, it depends on the relative *leverage* of the two groups.

Other-brand loyals (OBLs)

Other-brand loyals (OBLs) have exactly the same subgroups classification as Other-Brand Switchers, except that they are strongly loyal to at least one other brand. (Technically, there are Single-Other and Multi-Other OBLs, but it is not worth distinguishing them because in *both* cases we have to break loyalty to a major other brand.) The subgroups are **favorable other-brand loyals (favorable OBLs)**, who would consider trying our brand; **neutral other-brand loyals (neutral OBLs)**, who have not heard of it or know nothing about it; and **unfavorable other-brand loyals (unfavorable OBLs)**, who have probably previously tried the brand or dislike it for other reasons. All three subgroups, because of their loyalty to a current other major brand, will be very difficult to persuade to try or re-try our brand.

However, there is a significant realization about Other-Brand Loyals, or at least Neutral OBLs and Favorable OBLs, that makes them worth assessing as a marcoms customer target. If we can get them to try or re-try our brand and its benefit delivery proves satisfactory, they will be likely to transfer their *entire* loyalty to our brand – in the form of heavy buying of it. That is, if we can get them to switch, they will be likely to join our valuable group of Single-Brand Loyals. This is because, in many product categories, many consumers deliberately develop loyalty (usually Single-BL behavior) as a means of efficiently "shopping the category."

New category users (NCUs)

New category users (NCUs) are at present non-users of the category but we assess their potential as *new* users. Take, as an example, the current craze in the U.S.A. for low-carb (low carbohydrate) foods.[9] Early in 2004, industry surveys indicated that 40% of U.S. consumers were "watching" their carbohydrate intake, up from just 11% the previous year. **Positive new category users (positive NCUs)** have heard about the category and are favorably disposed toward it but have not yet made a Trial Purchase of any low-carb product. Low-carb products are marketed by Unilever, Heinz, and Hershey, among others, and there is also a new low-carb beer, Michelob Ultra, marketed by Anheuser-Busch.

Unaware new category users (unaware NCUs) are the most naïve subgroup in that they have not heard of the category and it is important to realize that, once they do hear about it, these potential customers will be *reclassified* as Positive New Category Users or Negative New Category Users depending on their overall attitude (preference) toward the product or service *category*. At the time of writing, the low-carb craze had not yet reached Australia, so all consumers here are, or were at the time, Unaware NCUs.

Negative new category users (negative NCUs) have heard about the category and are uninterested, unimpressed, or actively dislike the category. Obviously, people holding a negative attitude toward the entire category have very low potential for purchase of any brand-item in the category. A word of advice is that you *should* be a Negative NCU for the low-carb category; going on a low-carbohydrate diet would mean not eating bread, pasta, or fruit, which, long term, would be dangerous to your health unless you are one of the very few who are allergic to gluten.[10]

BRAND LOYALTY GROUPS AND SUBGROUPS CLASSIFICATION

How can the manager accurately make the classification of the total potential market into these 13 brand loyalty subgroups?

In Table 5.2, we provide a questionnaire to achieve the classification. The questions can be asked of a random sample of people for any product or service category. By using a fairly large random sample (a sample size of 200 or 300 would be adequate for most categories) a fairly good estimate of the incidence or prevalence – the size – of each brand loyalty group and subgroup can be obtained.

TABLE 5.2 *Questionnaire for classifying customers into the 13 brand-loyalty subgroups.*

1. (NON USERS OF THE CATEGORY) How would you classify yourself with regard to this product (or service) category?
   - ☐ Never heard of it (→ Unaware new category user)
   - ☐ Aware of, never used, and would not try this category under any circumstances (→ Negative new category user)
   - ☐ Used this category in the past, no longer use it, and would not use this category under any circumstances (→ Negative new category user)
   - ☐ Used this category in the past, no longer use it, but might re-try this category (→ Positive new category user)
   - ☐ Aware of, never tried, but might try this category (→ Positive new category user)

2. (CATEGORY USERS) How would you classify yourself with regard to brands (brand-items) in this product or service category? CHECK ONE BOX PER BRAND, DOWN THE PAGE.

	Our brand	Comp. A	Comp. B	Comp. C
a. Not aware of it	☐	☐	☐	☐
b. Aware, never used, and would not try it	☐	☐	☐	☐
c. Aware, never used, might try it	☐	☐	☐	☐
d. Aware, used before, would not re-try it	☐	☐	☐	☐
e. Aware, used before, might re-try it	☐	☐	☐	☐
f. One of several that I buy – but I'm not strongly committed to it	☐	☐	☐	☐
g. One of several strongly preferred brands that I buy	☐	☐	☐	☐
h. The one brand that I strongly prefer and always or nearly always buy	☐	☐	☐	☐

CODING FOR Q. 2:

a for our brand + f for other brands → Neutral other-brand switcher

c or e for our brand + f for other brands → Favorable other-brand switcher

b or d for our brand + f for other brands → Unfavorable other-brand switcher

a for our brand + g or h for other brands → Neutral other-brand loyal

c or e for our brand + g or h for other brands →Favorable other-brand loyal

b or d for our brand + g or h for other brands → Unfavorable other-brand loyal

f for our brand → Experimental (early in product life cycle) or Routinized (maturity stage of product life cycle) favorable brand switcher

g for our brand → Multi-brand loyal

h for our brand → Single-brand loyal

SELECTING THE TARGET AUDIENCE

The Target Audience for a marcoms campaign will consist of one or several of the 13 brand-loyalty subgroups. (In the Positioning Statement for a specific campaign, the brand-loyalty subgroup or subgroups targeted must be spelled out in *everyday, category-specific language*. For example, "Instant coffee buyers who switch between several brands, not including Maxwell House, but are willing to try or re-try Maxwell House" describes Favorable OBSs in plain, everyday, category-specific language.)

Target audience selection depends on the *Sales* Objective of the campaign. (We say the *sales* objective recognizing that all marcoms campaigns should also have a *brand equity* objective, namely to maintain or increase Value Equity, i.e., sales response to price cuts, and maintain or increase Uniqueness Equity, i.e., maintain or *decrease* sales falloff when our price increases or competitors cut their prices.) The straightforward metric of Sales (in units) is sufficient for choosing which type of target audience to emphasize. There are two possible sales objectives: sales *maintenance* and sales *growth*. These two objectives have different implications for target audience emphasis, as explained next.

Sales maintenance

If the purpose is to maintain the brand-item's sales at the current rate, which is a perfectly acceptable objective for an established brand-item in a category that is itself stable, then the primary target audience for the brand-item's marcoms would be *Favorable Brand Switchers* and the secondary target would be *Brand Loyals*. The priority is based on the assumption that more effort is needed to retain the brand-item's brand switchers than to retain its loyals and that the communications appeal that will work for brand-switchers will also work for loyals, whereas an appeal that is sufficient to hold loyals may not be strong enough to also keep switchers attracted. Remember, FBSs have only moderate preference for our brand and if you are not to bribe some of them with promotions and price cuts – ill-advised for most brands in the long run – then your ads have to get their Brand Preference *up*: you have to *keep* pushing it up, in fact, just to hold them as current FBSs. This point is addressed again later, in Chapter 10 on media strategy.

FMCG sales maintenance

The action objective for FBSs and BLs under a sales maintenance plan for FMCG products and services is to maintain their current rate of *Repeat Purchase* of our brand-item. For instance, if Favorable Brand Switchers of Maxwell House instant coffee buy the brand between one and five times a year, say an average of three times a year, then that would be the repeat-purchase rate *goal* to be achieved for the next campaign. (A **goal** is an **objective** made specific as to magnitude and time period.) Similarly, if Brand Loyals buy Maxwell House six or more times a year, say an *average* of eight times a year, then that would be the goal for this secondary customer target group.

Durables sales maintenance

For consumer durables and major industrial products, where the category purchase cycle is long and thus the potential repeat-purchase interval may extend over several years, a modified interpretation of "repeat-purchase rates" is required. *Here, you have to survey each group's Intentions to purchase or repeat the purchase of our brand-item when, in the future, the category need arises again.* New car marketers, for instance, use the forecast incidence of Intended Repeat Purchase together with Intended Switch-In Purchase to set action goals for next year's sales.

Sales growth

If, on the other hand, the objective of the marcoms campaign is to substantially *increase* sales, then the primary customer target will have to be one or more of the subgroups *other than our own present customers*. Sales growth will be the objective for a new brand-item in a growing category, or a struggling brand-item in an established category.

In FMCG categories, to give the typical figures, about 60% of sales *growth* comes from attracting new customers to the brand-item via Trial and subsequent Repeat Purchase and 40% from inducing current customers to increase their *rate* of Repeat Purchase. A recent study of FMCG products covering 21 product categories and 353 brand-items in the Canadian national market found that, over a five-year period, approximately *one-third* of the brand-items experienced market share changes (which would be equivalent to unit *sales* changes in these mature categories) of 50% or more, that is, *large* loss or *large* growth. Market share *growth* was, on average, accomplished by about 60% new trial (or re-trial) and subsequent repeating, and 40% by increased *rate* of repeating among those who already buy the brand-item.[11] The increased repeat-purchase rate would occur mainly among FBSs and Favorable *OBSs*, the moderate-preference groups who have "room to move," rather than among BLs, who are already buying the brand-item at a very high rate (high share-of-requirements). Given that the advertising elasticity is much the same for consumer durables and industrial products as for FMCG products, as stated in Chapter 1, we would expect – although we do not know exactly – that sales growth for *consumer durables and industrial products* would also be in the approximate proportion of 60% trial or re-trial and 40% increased repeat purchase, over a longer purchase cycle for individual customers, of course.

Sales growth may also come from attracting New Category Users, most of whom will be Neutral or Positive NCUs. For instance, Red Bull, whose current customers are mostly 14- to 28-year-olds, is trying to attract older sportsmen – golfers – into the energy drink category.[12]

Assessing target audience potential via leverage

Target audience potential has to be assessed via **leverage calculations**. For FMCG, 11 subgroups, *other than* FBSs and BLs, are potential targets for *Trial* of the brand; FBSs and BLs are potential targets for *Repeat Purchase* of the brand-item. For durables, all 13 subgroups – potentially – are targets for *Purchase* of the brand-item. The manager has to (1) estimate the size of the group in the product or service category; multiply this number by (2) the increase in *dollar* purchases per capita if the group could be persuaded to try, re-try, or continue to repeat-purchase the brand-item, where in the repeat-purchase case the "increase" is the manager's estimate of the *loss* of purchases *without* advertising; and (3) subtract from this increased sales estimate the cost of the marcoms campaign that would be needed to achieve it:

Leverage = [Number in subgroup × Per capita increase in sales dollars] – Cost of campaign

The more negative the group's preference toward our brand, the greater the marcoms cost will be to induce them to try it, presuming that a message can be found that will do so. The manager of a new brand-item in a growing category will probably find that Positive NCUs provide the highest leverage. A new brand-item in an established category will have to increase sales by taking them from the competitors, and thus Favorable OBSs and perhaps Favorable OBLs will have the highest leverage.

ACTION OBJECTIVES

Action Objectives now have to be set for the target audience group or groups selected for the campaign. Action is *behavior,* and the question that has to be answered here is: what do we expect the Target Audience to *do* as a result of seeing or hearing our marcoms?

At a general level, the answer to this question will depend on the type of *stakeholder* to which the campaign is directed. All *stakeholder* action objectives can be regarded as some sort of Trial behavior or Repeat behavior. If targeting Suppliers, for instance, the action objective may be for the supplier to start supplying materials, products or services to us, or to continue to do so. If targeting Investors, the action objective may be for them to start investing in our stocks or to raise their investment if they are already our customers. If we are targeting Potential Employees, the action objective would be a "trial purchase" in the form of an inquiry for a recruitment interview or the filling out of a job application; whereas, if targeting our Current Employees, a "repeat-purchase" objective of employee retention would be appropriate. If we are targeting government or industry Regulators, the action objective may be for them to pass legislation in our favor or, alternatively, for them to amend or abandon legislation that inhibits our business. For many businesses, legislators are from time to time a serious stakeholder target. A topical example of this at the time of writing is the proposal by the World Health Organization (WHO) to ban the advertising of allegedly fattening foods and beverages in children's media. The U.S. government has refused to go along with this proposal, citing a complete absence of causal evidence that such advertising contributes to weight problems among children, a stance which keeps all the U.S. food and beverage companies who market these products happy.[13] In Chapter 16 on corporate communications we discuss these stakeholder action objectives again.

Most marcoms campaigns, however, are aimed at End-Customers, business or consumer, and these are the stakeholders we will concentrate on. Action objectives for End-Customers can be categorized as Pre-Purchase, Purchase, or Post-Purchase. A listing of the most typical behaviors under these three headings is provided in Table 5.3.

Pre-purchase behaviors

The action objective is usually a *pre-purchase* behavior if the purchase itself needs to be "closed" by Personal Selling. The *advertising* is expected to cause a sales Inquiry, a retail Visit, a Website Visit, or some form of pre-purchase trial of the product or service by Sampling (such as taking a test drive, attending a product or service demonstration, or commissioning a feasibility study). The advertising campaign will have done its job behaviorally if it achieves the Pre-Purchase action objective.

TABLE 5.3 *The main types of action objectives.*

PRE-PURCHASE ACTIONS (USED MAINLY WHEN PURCHASE IS "CLOSED" BY PERSONAL SELLING)	PURCHASE ACTIONS	POST-PURCHASE ACTIONS
• Retail visit (or Website visit)	• Purchase (durables) • Trial (FMCG, including category trial if NCU target)	• Display the item (especially if retailer target but also possibly consumers)
• Inquiry (by phone, fax, online, mail or in person)	• Re-trial	• Recommend (retail and consumer)
• Enter contest or sweepstakes where prize is the desired purchase	• Repeat purchase	• Recruit other prospects
• Sampling trial (including, e.g., test drive, demonstration, feasibility study)	• Purchase amount per occasion • Purchasing timing	• Use (more, more often, extend; use correctly; use less)

Purchase behaviors

For an *FMCG* product or service, the First Purchase is indeed a *trial* purchase – you don't have to buy the product or service again if you aren't satisfied. For FMCG, then, state the first-purchase action objective as Trial. For *durables*, however – a house, a car, clothing, electronics – the first purchase is *the* purchase, not a trial, unless the vendor has an amazingly liberal return policy! For durables, with a long purchase cycle, state the first-purchase action objective simply as Purchase.

For target audiences who have bought the brand-item previously but have stopped buying it, the current contemplated purchase will be a Re-trial and should be labeled as such because the communication objectives to achieve re-trial will usually be different than if it were the first trial.

Repeat Purchase is the action objective for our current buyers – Favorable Brand Switchers and Brand Loyals. In particular, the objective is usually to increase (for FBSs) or maintain (for BLs) their *rate* of repeat purchase, that is, purchase of our brand-item per time period, such as weekly, monthly, or yearly.

Two supplementary types of purchase-action objectives are relevant for some marcoms campaigns, for any of the target audience groups. Purchase Amount (per purchase occasion) may be an action objective for promotion campaigns – bonus offers are an obvious example. In social marketing, *limiting* the amount purchased per occasion may be an objective, such as during periods of energy shortages or water restrictions or national emergencies. Purchase Timing may also be an action objective supplementary to purchase itself. Accelerated timing is a fairly common objective for promotion campaigns – end-of-season price discounts to clear stock are an obvious example. On the other hand, *delayed* timing may sometimes be a supplementary objective, as in loan repayments to increase the vendor's revenue from interest, or in social marketing campaigns in which deferral of consumption has a welfare rationale.

Post-purchase behaviors

Beyond purchase, trial, and repeat purchase, the marketer may also derive an advantage from particular Post-Purchase actions such as Display, Recommendation, or Usage.

Display is a relevant action objective when targeting Distributors and is an action objective of most trade promotions by manufacturers. Display might also be a supplementary action objective for End-Customers where social influence, in the form "word-of-eye," plays a role in encouraging purchase by *others*. Automobiles are a category where consumer display is relevant, as is designer apparel. In this sense, display overlaps with the next category, by serving as an implicit recommendation.

Recommendation – "word-of-mouth" – is a frequent action objective beyond purchase. Manufacturers solicit Recommendations from retail clerks and salespeople and many pay "push money" to help get recommended. Further, unsolicited Recommendations from *satisfied customers* are an important supplementary action objective in many product and service categories. Indeed, marketers might *explicitly factor in* Recommendations as objectives of a marcoms campaign (diffusion models of buyer behavior, for instance, have a Personal Influence coefficient in them and we will see this used in one of the Reach Patterns in media planning, in Chapter 11).

A final type of Post-Purchase action objective is *Usage*. This can take several forms. As a follow-on from the action objective of an increased purchase amount, the marketer may aim for increased, more frequent, or extended *uses* of the product or service (see the interesting research on this by Wansinck and colleagues[14]). Social marketers, on the other hand, or commercial marketers selling complex or dangerous products, may have to add a "use properly" action objective. Social marketers, and, sometimes, commercial utilities marketers, pursue a "use less" action objective, which is not always very believable in the case of commercial utilities.

In summary, the type of target audience and the nature of the product or service will usually quite straightforwardly indicate the appropriate Action Objective for the marcoms campaign. The behaviors in Table 5.3 may help as a reminder of the main options. The construction of a Behavioral Sequence Model, BSM, will refine the choice exactly, as shown in the final part of this chapter.

Action objectives as goals

The manager should not just nominate action objectives but should specify these as *goals*. Goals are objectives that are *numeric* and *time-bound* (e.g., "To gain four million purchasers in the first three months of the campaign and a cumulative total of six million purchasers by the end of the year"). Likewise, for a repeat-purchase action objective, the rate should be specified as a goal that is numeric and time-bound (e.g., "To increase the repeat-purchase rate by favorable brand switchers from an average of 3.0 purchases of the brand-item per year to an average of 4.0 purchases per year").

The setting of realistic goals depends on the manager having available good survey data. In the absence of good data, which is really inexcusable with the relatively low cost of telephone or Internet surveys, the manager can nevertheless set *directional* objectives (e.g., "increase," "maintain," or, for social marketing campaigns aimed at reducing "bad" behaviors, "decrease") and may nominate the time period as for a goal.

We will revisit Action Goals in Chapter 13 – in conjunction with setting the marcoms campaign *Budget*. In setting the Budget, you are forced to be numeric and time-bound!

MEDIA TARGET

The manager also has to identify a **media target** for the marcoms campaign. We will discuss this decision here because we recommend that the media target be included in the brand-item's campaign Positioning Statement (the long-form statement) and not left until just before the media are bought. The description of the Media Target has to be sent to the media agency or advertising agency so that the agency will know which advertising media and perhaps promotions media to purchase for the campaign. The Media Target must cover the target audience groups or subgroups and preferably should do so with not much wastage on non-target customers.

If the *Direct Matching* survey method is used, the Media Target will be exactly the *same* as the *Target Audience*. **Direct matching** is explained in Chapter 11 and its measurement is exemplified in Chapter 14.

If Direct Matching is *not* used – it should be used but far too often is not – the Media Target is identified by **demographic proxy**. "Proxy" is a contraction of "an approximation." A typical demographic (actually buyergraphic) media target description for FMCG campaigns, for instance, is: the household Grocery Buyer. This gives a better target than the demographic variables of gender and age. Most media owners conduct their own surveys – for prospective advertisers – which report the number of Grocery Buyers watching their programs, listening to their radio station timeslots, or reading their print vehicles. For industrial products, companies' **corpographic proxies** (an identical but less-used term is *Firmagraphic*) are used for describing the Media Target. The most-used corpographic for industrial products is Industry Type, which is a proxy for Category Need.

One sees some ridiculously narrow *demographic* media targets identified in consumer marcoms media plans (and in marketing plans). Usually, these reflect a false stereotype of those who the manager *assumes* are most likely to buy the product or service. Washing machines are a case in point. The usual demographic guess is women aged 21 to 39, because they are most likely to be starting a family, but, in fact, only about one-quarter of washing machine sales are made to this demographic group.[15] False stereotypes may apply in business marcoms too. In one study that the first author conducted for a manufacturer of personal computers, conventional management thinking was that business buyers of PCs would be most efficiently found by placing ads in computer magazines and in computer sections of weekly newspapers. They overlooked the fact that company purchasers of personal computers are also everyday consumers as far as their media habits are concerned, and most of them do *not* especially read about computers. A Direct Matching survey conducted for the PC manufacturer resulted in a shift of approximately 50% of the media purchases into general rather than specialized publications, with greatly increased sales results.

Notice that we do *not* recommend corpographic, demographic, or, though we didn't exemplify this, psychographic, *segmentation*. Such segmentation is relevant *only* when a company decides that there is an unmet gap or need that could be met by designing a *new product or service* that would appeal to buyers *because of* their particular corpographics or demographics (e.g., accounting software for owners of small grocery stores, or large-print reissues of non-fiction and fiction books for older readers). Within the corpographic or demographic group, the company can *then* identify New Category Users, Other-Brand Loyals, and so forth. Indeed, if you nominate a Media Target described by corpographics, demographics or psychographics, what you will most likely get is the total group of Category Users, undifferentiated by their brand loyalty status. A better way is to use brand loyalty status *directly* as the media target description, which requires a Direct Matching survey (see Chapters 11 and 14).

CREATIVE TARGET

The best creative writers write "to an individual"; that is, they imagine themselves in a one-on-one situation telling a person about the product or service.[16] The person that they imagine talking to is the **creative target**. More specifically, the Creative Target is an individual in a particular *decision role*. There are five main decision roles and each role has a specific action objective for the marcoms to aim for. The decision roles and specific action objectives are shown in Table 5.4.

TABLE 5.4 *Main decision roles (potential creative targets) and their action objectives.*

ROLE (POTENTIAL CREATIVE TARGET)	ACTION OBJECTIVE
1. Initiator	Propose category need
2. Influencer (may be a product or service consultant or specialist)	Favor criteria on which our brand rates well and recommend our brand
3. Decider	Choose our brand
4. Purchaser	Buy our brand
5. User	Use our brand

For instance, the writer of an ad for one of Disney's Disneyland theme parks would most likely open by addressing individuals, who would most likely be children, in the *Initiator* role. The ad would then move on to address the *Decider* role, a role played by parents, giving reasons why Disneyland should be the brand of choice within the theme park category. Or, for instance, the writer of an ad in the U.S.A. for men's fashion clothing might choose to address women in the *Influencer* role, in view of the well-known statistic that about two-thirds of men's clothing choices are influenced by women partners, or even the *Purchaser* role, since about two-thirds of clothes worn by *married* men are *purchased* by women. Hagar, a men's clothing brand, has pursued women in both roles as the Creative Target, placing about half of its advertising in women's magazines. Writers of ads for FMCG products usually address consumers in the *Decider* role, but we do see and hear ads that alternatively address partners or children as *Influencers*. Also, some FMCG product ads address the consumer in the *User* role, by suggesting new ways to prepare or serve the product or, for condiments and the like, reminding the user to add them.

The key question to ask when nominating the Creative Target for a marcoms campaign is: *What stage of decision-making must I influence with my message?* The answer to this question will pinpoint the target role-player, that is, the Creative Target. To help answer it, the construction of a Behavioral Sequence Model, or BSM, is essential.

BEHAVIORAL SEQUENCE MODEL

The *buyer behavior* basis of marcoms strategy – "who we should talk to" and also "where" and "when" – is illuminated by the construction of a **behavioral sequence model (BSM)**.

The BSM is most easily constructed from a particular type of qualitative research called Individual Depth Interviews (sometimes abbreviated as IDIs, as distinguished from GDIs, or Group Depth Interviews, which are also known as Focus Groups). In the IDI procedure, the researcher recruits a sample of about 10 or 12 individuals per target customer subgroup (whichever these may be, such as Multi-BLs, Unfavorable OBLs, or Positive NCUs). Each participant, individually interviewed, is asked to mentally walk through and think aloud about the last purchase he or she made in the category, from the customer decision stages of Not-in-the-Market through to Usage. For New Category Users (non-users as yet) the questioning must be slightly different, asking them if they have ever heard of the category, investigated any alternative brands, and so forth. For consumer durables, couples can be interviewed together if joint decision-making is prevalent. For business products and services, the members of the "buying center" are interviewed, not together, but in IDIs, otherwise you will get a biased BSM. The interview answers are put together to construct a common picture of the target customer's decision process in the category.

The BSM identifies:

1. The *main stages of the decision* (this corresponds to Customer Decision Stages, level 3 of the three levels of effects introduced in Chapter 2, and the stages must be *customized to suit the category*[17]).

2. Who the *role-players* are at each stage (the individual person could play *all five* roles, as in an "impulse" purchase, or a *particular* role, such as Influencer, at one or more stages of the decision process).

3. *Where* the decision stages took place (the "where" information is very useful for the media planner, suggesting possible *contact points* with the customer).

4. Over what *time intervals* and at what *times* the decision stages took place (these indicate the *purchase cycle interval* and potential *media vehicles*).

5. *How* the decision at each stage was achieved (this difficult-to-write but vital row of boxes summarizes how the Creative Target can be persuaded!).

In Figure 5.1, we provide a hypothetical example of a BSM for consumer choice of children's video games.[18] In Figure 5.2, we provide a hypothetical example of a BSM for corporate choice of a travel agent for employee air travel.[19] We do *not* discuss either example, because the BSM has to be *self-explanatory* – that's the whole idea of a BSM!

(1) WHAT (decision stages)	Need arousal ⟶	Information search and evaluation of alternatives ⟶	Store choice and purchase ⟶	Usage
(2) WHO (roles)	• Child (initiator)	• Child (decider) • Children's TV presenters (influencer) • Children's magazines, e.g., K-Zone (influencer) • Friends (influencer)	• Mother (final decider and purchaser)	• Child (user)
(3) WHERE (location)		• Children's TV – home • Children's magazines – home or school • Friends – school	• Games store • Discount department store, e.g., K-Mart	
(4) WHEN (time and timing)	t_1 = anytime	t_2 = approx. 4 weeks from launch of game	t_3 = approx. 6 weeeks from launch of game	t_4 = approx. months usage period
(5) HOW (decision process)	• Currently played video games nearing end of interest life cycle	• New "adventure" game for Gameboy Advance • Characters currently popular, e.g., Zelda, Harry Potter, new-series Pokemon or Digimon	• Must be G rated not M (15+) • If price is above $30, wait until discounters stock the game	• Child asks Mum to buy link cable so child can "battle" with a friend (encouraged in most game videos)

FIGURE 5.1 *BSM for children's video games. Here, "children" refers to "tweenagers" (ages 7 to 14).*

It is important to note that, if more than one Target Audience *subgroup* is involved in the marcoms campaign, *a separate BSM should be constructed for each.* As these BSMs are likely to overlap in many respects, *the differences should be highlighted.*

Also, the BSM does not point to the Creative Target automatically. This is still a decision that has to be made by the manager: the *best-opportunity* stage and role have to be selected. The stage and role can be selected by reviewing the Individual Depth Interview research and asking: *Where is our brand-item "missing out"?* Are we too often missing out on "getting on the *Initiator's* shopping list" in the first place? Are we not getting recommended strongly enough by *Influencers?* Are our benefit claims not appealing enough to make our brand-item the preferred choice of the *Decider?* Are we losing sales with the *Purchaser,* at the point of purchase? Is our brand-item bought but not selected in-home or in-office often enough by the *User?*

Similarly, the "where" boxes of the BSM indicate potential *contact points* for marcoms messages to reach the *Media Target.* And the "when" boxes indicate the timing, especially the information search and evaluation "window" period, and perhaps particular times of day or week, relevant to media vehicle selection and scheduling.

As should be evident, the BSM is a very useful piece of research information. It provides valuable input to both the Creative Brief and the Media Brief. In preparing these, you, the manager, must show *how you made use of the information* from the BSM.

(1) WHAT (decision stages)	Need arousal and preliminary evaluation of proposal →	Personal sales visit →	Negotiate and sign contract →	Usage and evaluation of service →	Contract renewal
(2) WHO (roles)	• Travel agency (initiator) • Referrals from current customers (influencer) • CEO (decider) • Financial controller (decider)	• Senior travel agency rep (influencer) • Financial controller (decider)	• Senior travel agency rep (influencer) • Financial controller (decider and purchaser)	• Personal secretaries (indirect users) • Employees individually (direct users)	• CEO (decider) • Financial controller (decider)
(3) WHERE (location)	• Proposal letter received by CEO and FC in office	• In office	• In office	• Secretaries: in office • Employees: from home, at airports, at hotels	• In office
(4) WHEN (time and timing)	• June or December (peak months for contract renewal)	• Same month	• Same month	• 12 months of usage period	• June or December (12 months after initial contract)
(5) HOW (decision process)	• Good price offer (e.g., net plus 5%) • Promise of personalized service • Check on referrals	• Establishment of personal trust	• Key is avoidance of "rip off" perception that plagues travel agent industry	• Personalized (same agent every time) • Same-day replies to email orders • Instant access by phone when an in-transit difficulty arises or change of plan needed	• Letter reminder from travel agent to important, valued customer (often with gift)

FIGURE 5.2 *BSM for corporate choice of travel agent for employee air travel.*

SUMMARY

We are now planning for a specific marcoms *campaign*. The campaign will be directed to *one* of the stakeholder customer types. From within the customer type, the manager now has to select a *Target Audience* for the campaign. When the Target Audience is selected, the manager then has to nominate appropriate Action Objectives for that audience for the campaign.

The best method of selecting a Target Audience is not through business or consumer demographics or psychographics or other indirect indicators, but rather by realizing, logically, that the total set of potential customers from whom sales must come consists of *five groups* defined in terms of their *brand loyalty status* with regard to the product or service category: New (currently non) Category Users, Other-Brand Loyals, Other-Brand Switchers, (our) Favorable Brand Switchers, and (our) Brand Loyals. Whereas the names of these groups, abbreviated NCUs, OBLs, OBSs, FBSs, and BLs, may suggest that the groups are distinguished purely behaviorally, in fact they are distinguished by *Brand Awareness and Brand Preference* with respect to the *next* purchase decision in the category. Favorable Brand Switchers, FBSs, for instance, are those who are favorably *considering* our brand or brand-item for the next purchase. To define the target audience precisely, you need to measure individuals' Brand Awareness, Brand Preference, and current brand Purchase behavior, if any. The combination of these three factors leads to 13 *potential* target audience subgroups. For example, New Category Users, NCUs, are identified as either Negative NCUs, Unaware NCUs, or Positive NCUs, depending on their awareness of, and disposition toward, the *category* (and thus all brands in it). At the other end of the spectrum are Brand Loyals, BLs, who in most categories can be further divided into Multi-BLs and Single-BLs.

In the Campaign Positioning Statement, the primary and, if used, secondary target audience must be described in *plain language* suited to the category, rather than referred to only by their technical labels. An example of the primary target audience for the Saab 9.5 automobile might be: "Positive NCUs – prospective car buyers who have not previously owned a prestige import car but are favorably disposed toward buying one."

The manager chooses *one or more* of these brand loyalty subgroups as a target audience for the campaign by making an assessment of each subgroup's *leverage*. Leverage is here measured as the size of the subgroup multiplied by the estimated increase in monetary sales per capita, assuming a successful campaign, and subtracting the approximate cost of the campaign. While not precise, of course, the leverage estimates will be different enough to indicate which subgroup or subgroups offer the best potential for future sales, considering cost. Usually, one *primary* target audience will be nominated, from whom most of the future sales are expected to come, and one *secondary* target audience, which will usually be the brand's own Brand Loyals if they were not the primary target.

A questionnaire covering status with regard to the category and status with regard to our brand and major competing brands is provided in the chapter to enable classification of everyone into the 13 subgroups.

Action Objectives – consisting of measurable behaviors – must then be set for the subgroup or subgroups in the target audience. Assuming that the target audience is End-Customers, either business or consumer, the action objective will be a Pre-Purchase behavior (such as a sales inquiry or a retail store visit), a Purchase behavior (such as purchase itself in the case of durables; or trial, re-trial, or repeat purchase in the case of FMCG products and services), or a Post-Purchase behavior (such as a referral recommendation or a usage recommendation). Ideally, and necessarily if the Task Method of budget-setting is to be used, action objectives should be specified as *goals*, by forecasting the degree of behavior expected and the time period within which it is expected to occur.

In addition to identifying the target audience for the campaign, the manager also has to identify a *Media Target* (usually by means of profiling the brand-loyalty-defined target audience in terms of significant corpographic, demographic, or sometimes psychographic descriptor variables, although these are not necessary if the Direct Matching method of media vehicle selection is used) and also a *Creative Target* (the key role-player to whom the marcoms campaign will be principally directed). To assist with these last two decisions, and also with the determination of precise action objectives, it is highly advisable to construct a *Behavioral Sequence Model (BSM)*. The BSM is based on small-scale qualitative research, consisting of either individual depth interviews or dyadic interviews if decision-making in the category is truly joint, in which the interviewer asks potential and actual customers to mentally "walk through" and talk through the entire decision process, and then formulates a one-page summary of the main elements (only) of *buyer behavior* in the category. The BSM specifies the Decision Stages, the main Role-Players at each stage, the physical Location of each stage, the Time and Timing of each stage, and, very important, a capsule description of the Hows – the decision factors that are of prime influence at each stage.

This completes the target audience and action step of campaign planning.

DISCUSSION QUESTIONS

5.1 Your company is about to launch a new brand of rice-based breakfast cereal. You have to prepare a marcoms campaign directed at Consumers. Your marketing assistant suggests that the best target audience would be "Female grocery buyers between the ages of 18 and 49." Why is this not a good definition of the Target Audience? Specify a better definition of the target audience.

5.2 Using the questionnaire for classifying Target Audience Subgroups provided in the chapter, interview and classify 20 people regarding their use of the instant coffee category and brands. Then suppose that you are about to introduce a new brand into the instant coffee category. Even though your survey is limited in terms of sample size and cross-section, use the results to estimate the target audience *leverage* of, firstly, the five broad potential target audience groups. Next – for the group or groups that show the most potential – estimate the leverage of the *subgroups*. Then select a *primary* target audience and a *secondary* target audience from among the subgroups and justify your selections. Also, set Action Objectives (don't worry about goals) for the two subgroups that you have selected.

5.3 Suppose you are the marketing manager for the brand-item, Vanilla Coke, in Thailand. You are preparing an advertising campaign targeting Routinized FBSs, that is, consumers who buy Vanilla Coke regularly but also other soft drinks. Would they in fact be Routinized FBSs, or would they be better described as Multi-BLs (how can you tell)? How would you go about establishing a Repeat-Purchase *goal*, rather than just an objective, for this target audience?

5.4 Name three different types of product for which Post-Purchase Usage action objectives could be set. Describe the usage exactly.

5.5 How is a Media Target described and what is the main limitation of the traditional method of describing the Media Target?

5.6 Apple Computer might describe its Media Target psychographically as "People who prefer things that are different" ("Think different" is its corporate brand's key benefit claim). As a media consultant, how might you be able to identify and implement this media target? Next, *infer* Apple's media target for its iPod sub-brand of products and explain how you might implement that.

5.7 You are the marketing manager for a major bank for business development loans. You see an opportunity to increase your market share in the small business sector. Describe the likely Target Audience, construct a BSM for this target audience, set an appropriate Action Objective, and identify the likely Creative Target.

NOTES

1. K. Campo, E. Gijsbrechts, and P. Nisol, The impact of retailer stockouts on whether, how much and what to buy, *International Journal of Research in Marketing,* 2003, 20(3), pp. 273–286.

2. E.J. Fox and S. Hoch, Cherry pickers, switchers, and store loyals, paper presented at the INFORMS Marketing Science Conference, College Park, MD, University of Maryland, June 17–20, 2003.

3. Roper survey results reported in H. Charpa, Ripe old age, *Advertising Age,* May 13, 2002, p. 16.

4. B. Sharp, M. Wright, and G. Goodhart, Purchase loyalty is polarised into either repertoire or subscription patterns, *Australasian Marketing Journal,* 2002, 10(3), pp. 7–20. For instance, in a U.S. national survey in 1997 it was found that only 6% of adults in the last six months had switched banks for their checking account, although 18% had switched to another long-distance telephone provider in this more competitive category; see R. Sant, Did he jump or was he pushed?, *Marketing News*, May 12, 1997, p. 2.

5. H.C.M. van Trijp, W.D. Hoyer, and J.J. Inman, Why switch? Product category-level explanations for true variety-seeking behavior, *Journal of Marketing Research,* 1996, 33(3), pp. 281–292.

6. A.L. Baldinger and J. Rubinson, The jeopardy in double jeopardy, *Journal of Advertising Research,* 1997, 37(6), pp. 37–49.

7. J. Hofmeyr and B. Rice, *Commitment-Led Marketing,* Chichester, UK: Wiley, 2000; M. Laroche, Selected issues in modeling consumer brand choice: the extended competitive vulnerability model, in A.G. Woodside and E.M. Moore (Eds), *Essays by Distinguished Marketing Scholars of the Society for Marketing Advances,* Vol. 11, Amsterdam, The Netherlands: JAI/Elsevier, 2002, pp. 115–138.

8. MRCA panel data analyzed in A.S.C. Ehrenberg, Buyer behaviour and NBD, working paper, London Business School, 1987.

9. S. Thompson, Low-carb craze blitzes food biz, *Advertising Age,* January 5, 2004, pp. 1, 22.

10. Not surprisingly, but commendably, other weight-loss mega-brands – weight loss is the category need here – Jenny Craig and Weight Watchers International, are running TV commercials and direct-mail campaigns to educate consumers about the dangers of a low-carb diet, and promote their own weight-loss plans, of course. See S. Thompson, Weight-loss programs counter low-carb diets, *Advertising Age,* January 5, 2004, p. 22.

11. A.L. Baldinger, E. Blair, and R. Echambadi, Why brands grow, *Journal of Advertising Research,* 2002, 42(1), pp. 7–14.

12. H. Karp, Red Bull aims at an older crowd – golfers, *The Wall Street Journal Europe,* June 4–6, 2004, p. A7.

13. Fat chance, says U.S., to anti-obesity plan, *The Australian,* January 22, 2004, p. 10. We note that this is an extremely complicated issue, both empirically to investigate and ethically to interpret. In the U.S.A., free speech for legally marketed products is likely to continue to win out (although there are restrictions on liquor and tobacco advertising in that country) even if, as is sure to be the case, studies show these ads do increase children's *and parents'* choice of these products.

14. B. Wansinck, Can package size accelerate usage volume?, *Journal of Marketing*, 1996, 60(3), pp. 1–14.

15. Roy Morgan Research Pty Ltd, Australia, proprietary figures.

16. A.J. Kover, Copywriters' implicit theories of communication: an exploration, *Journal of Consumer Research*, 1995, 21(4), pp. 596–611.

17. Useful examples of decision stages for health and safety behaviors are provided in R. Donovan and N. Henley, *Social Marketing Principles and Practice*, Melbourne, Australia: IP Communications, 2003.

18. Sandra Jones and her children, Austin and Lincoln, helped with this example – thanks!

19. We thank Sandra Pelekanakis, Managing Director of Kingsford Travel, Australia, for her assistance with this example.

CHAPTER 6

Campaign communication objectives

We saw in Chapter 2 that level 2 of "how marcoms work" consists of brand or brand-item **communication effects**, in the prospective customer's mind. The five communication effects are: (1) Category Need, (2) Brand Awareness, (3) Brand Preference, (4) Brand Action Intention, and (5) Purchase Facilitation. These are shown in relation to the key schema (see back cover) in Figure 6.1.

Communication Objectives for a particular marcoms *campaign* must be selected from among these communication effects. For each of the communication effects, there are *options* that the manager can select as communication *objectives*. The five communication effects and their options as objectives for the marcoms campaign are defined and explained next, accompanied by the best way to measure each of them.

(1) CATEGORY NEED

Quite obviously, target customers will buy the brand-item only if they have the *Category Need* for it. The Category Need may arise as an effect in the customer's mind by naturally-occurring business or consumer circumstances (e.g., the business has to re-order supplies, or the consumer has run out of soda in the home refrigerator or is simply thirsty when away from home). In such cases, the manager can *omit* Category Need as a communication objective.

The need for some types of product or service is sometimes forgotten or neglected by the customer and he or she can usefully be *reminded* in marcoms to the marketer's advantage. Examples of Category Need reminders can be found in ads for automobile servicing, medical and dental checkups, and overindulgence remedies, as in Alka Seltzer's long-running campaign headlined "Will

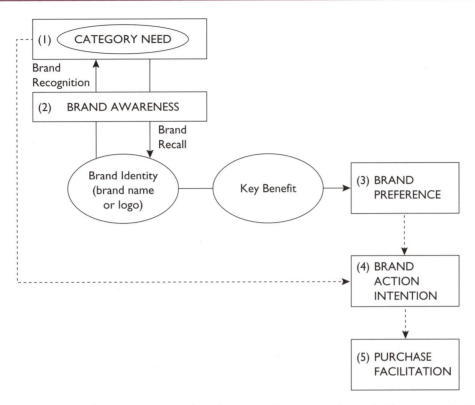

FIGURE 6.1 *Communication effects to be achieved in the prospective customer's mind. The communication effects are capitalized. Concepts in the customer's mind are circled – the concepts have to be connected by marcoms and form our key schema (see back cover). Processes are in normal type. Solid arrows: relations that apply in all cases. Dashed arrows: additional for high-involvement choices.*

it be there when you need it?" A very topical Category Need reminder ad for Scholl's travel stockings is shown in Figure 6.2.

Alternatively, and more complex to achieve, when targeting New Category Users, the Category Need has to be *sold* via marcoms – the marcoms of any brand-item that is trying to attract new users into the category. NCUs, obviously, are the target for new categories of products and services. However, the manager of a *high market share* brand could also decide that NCUs, most likely Positive NCUs, are a high-leverage target group and then attempt, through marcoms, to "grow the category," since a leading brand will benefit most if category growth is achieved (this will be the market leader or another high-share brand). For example, personal digital assistant (PDA) category sales are now flat, due to competition from Internet-enabled mobile phones (cell phones), so the PDA market leader, Palm Pilot, would have a vested interest in trying to re-grow the category.[1]

The *sell* objective is also employed when the brand-item *is* a category itself and is declining within the larger category. For example, red meat consumption has declined by over half in Western countries over the last 30 years and the red meat industry promotes the category of red meat as a "brand" in the superordinate category of "main dishes" from time to time to try to counter this trend.

FIGURE 6.2 *Ad for Scholl's travel stockings – a topical reminder of category need.*

SOURCE: Courtesy of Scholl.

For Category Need as a campaign communication objective, therefore, the manager must select one of the options of omitting, reminding, or selling. These options, and the corresponding Target Customer's prior state of mind, are summarized in Table 6.1.

TABLE 6.1 *Managerial options with regard to category need as a communication objective.*

TARGET CUSTOMER'S PRIOR STATE OF MIND	COMMUNICATION OBJECTIVE
Category need already present	Category need can be *omitted* as an objective of the advertising or promotion
Latent category need	Category need has only to be *mentioned* to *remind* the buyer of a previously established need
No or weak category need	Category need must be "*sold*" using *category* communication effects

The buyer's mental state with regard to Category Need can most precisely be determined from the Behavioral Sequence Model, the BSM, which was explained in the previous chapter. When targeting New Category Users, NCUs, the marcoms message has to *sell* the category need. All other target groups already use the category, so the only decision here is whether they have to be *reminded* of the category need, via marcoms, or whether it can be assumed to be already present, in which case it is *omitted* as a communication objective.

Category motives – how to sell category need

Category *Need* is a motivating communication effect. Category Need gets the entire sequence of customer decision stages going by energizing the stage of Need Arousal (level 3 of overall effects – see Chapter 2). Category Need motivates customers via a perceived negative *or* positive discrepancy, a departure, from the customer's normal state of equilibrium. Category Need as a communication effect is *defined* as the target customer's acceptance that the category (the product or service) is necessary to remove or satisfy a perceived discrepancy between the customer's current motivational state and his or her desired motivational state.[2]

A census of customer behaviors would show that a majority, perhaps two-thirds, of products and services are bought, at a *category* level, through *negatively originated* motives. We will see shortly that this is not necessarily the case for *brand* or *brand-item* choice. The energizing here originates from a perceived problem of some type and the product or service category offers a solution to the problem. The negatively originated motives are:

1. *Problem Removal* The target customer experiences a *current* problem and seeks a product or service that will *solve* the problem.

2. *Problem Avoidance* The target customer anticipates or fears a *future* problem and seeks a product or service that will *prevent* the problem.

3. *Incomplete Satisfaction* The target customer is *not satisfied* with the current product or service and is motivated to *search* for a better product or service.

4. *Mixed Approach-Avoidance* The target customer likes some things about the product or service but dislikes other things about it, thus experiencing an approach-avoidance conflict, and is motivated to find an alternative product or service that will *resolve* the conflict.

5. *Normal Depletion* The target customer is out of stock or running low and seeks to *maintain* a regular supply of the product or service (this motive cannot be used to instigate purchase of the category, that is, to generate category need; it can only motivate purchase of the *item* by its own brand loyals).

Category Need for other product and service categories is generated by *positive-ending* motives. Consumer life, and life in general, would be rather grim if our motives were all negatively originated. Positive-ending motives energize Need Arousal by offering hope of a *positive* discrepancy from the customer's normal state of equilibrium. The positive-ending motives are:

6. *Sensory Gratification* The target customer seeks extra (physiological) stimulation to *enjoy* the product or service.

7. *Intellectual Stimulation and Mastery* The target customer seeks extra (psychological) stimulation to *explore and master* the product or service.

8. *Social Approval* The target customer sees an opportunity for *personal recognition from others* (social reference groups or reference individuals) through use of the product or service.

To generate Category Need in a particular marcoms campaign, the message has to appeal to at least one (and usually only one) of these motives. The appeal is made through a *specific manifestation* of the motive rather than by the generic labels in the list above. For instance, a campaign for Brand "X" extra-strength pain reliever might claim to relieve "migraine headaches," as an instance of the Problem Removal motive. Brand "Y" CD player might appeal in its marcoms with a claim such as "hear *your* music like you've never heard it before," as a specific instance of the Sensory Gratification motive. That is, the underlying mechanism for Category Need is one of the eight motives but the application is category-specific.

Brand or brand-item preference motives may differ

We will be discussing the Brand Preference communication effect later but it is important to emphasize here that the motive for preferring the brand or brand-item may differ from the motive that energizes the Category Need. Brand-items in categories that are based on negatively originated motives often employ a Key Benefit that is based on the same motive as that of the category. For instance, Brand "X" extra-strength pain reliever may claim that it is the *most effective* product for stopping migraine headaches and thus Category Need and Brand Preference are based on the same motive of Problem Removal. This does not mean that all brand-items in the category should follow this approach and, indeed, as we saw in the T-C-B positioning model in Chapter 3, each should differentiate on its key benefit. For instance, Brand "Z" extra-strength pain reliever might mention the Category Benefit of relief of migraine headaches and then differentiate on the Brand Benefit that it is *also* gentle to the stomach (the standard claim for Paracetamol-based pain relievers versus aspirin-based pain relievers) and thus appeal to, not the category motive of Problem Removal, but the motive of Mixed Approach-Avoidance for target customers who want a pain reliever that works but one that avoids stomach upset. A brand-item of pain reliever for children that has as an Entry-Ticket Benefit that it tastes nice would also be appealing to the Mixed Approach-Avoidance motive (conflict removal) but in a very different manifestation of this motive.

Similarly, for brands or brand-items in product or service categories that have their Category Need generated by a positive-ending motive, a particular brand or brand-item – often the market leader or "central" brand – usually will go with the flow and promise to be the best in delivering (the appropriate category-specific manifestation of) Sensory Gratification, Intellectual Stimulation and Mastery, or Social Approval. Differentiation of the Key Benefit for *other* brands or brand-items, however, might advantageously cross to a Key Benefit that taps into a completely different motive. A well-known example of this is the positioning for Burger King hamburgers. Hamburgers as a category are principally sold via the Sensory Gratification motive; however, Burger King appeals to the Incomplete Satisfaction motive, as it has done in campaigns such as "Have it your way," "The burgers are bigger at Burger King," and recently "The burgers are better at Burger King."

Thus, when the campaign communication objective is to *sell* the Category Need, the message appeal as far as Category Need is concerned will be to the *category* purchase motive, even though the purchase motive for the brand or brand-item, in the rest of the message, may be quite different.

(2) BRAND AWARENESS

Brand Awareness is one of two universal campaign communication objectives. Brand Preference is the other. Every marcoms campaign must aim at Brand Awareness and Brand Preference, even if it has no other communication objectives.

But don't some brands seem to already have 100% Brand Awareness? While it may be contended that some big brands such as Coke, McDonald's, or IBM already have maximum awareness, the fact is that they would not run an *unbranded* ad or promotion. Also, many individual target customers – especially those who are not Brand Loyals or Favorable Brand Switchers – may fail to recall even a well-known brand or may pass by its logo or package without noticing it. The safest conclusion is that *all* marcoms campaigns must have Brand Awareness as a communication objective.

There are two *types* of Brand Awareness: *Brand Recognition* and *Brand Recall*. Both types require the target customer to associate the Brand Identity (the way the brand is identified – by name, pack, or logo) with the Category Need. For Brand Recognition, the directional association required is: Brand Identity → Category Need. For Brand Recall, it is the reverse as the Category Need arises *first* in the choice process, thus: Category Need → Brand Identity. Check this distinction in previous Figure 6.1 and make sure you understand the two types of Brand Awareness!

There are three options for the Brand Awareness communication *objective*: Brand Recognition, Brand Recall, and Brand-Recall-Boosted Brand Recognition. The appropriate Brand Awareness objective can be determined from the BSM, the Behavioral Sequence Model, which describes how the typical customer arrives at his or her choice. The appropriate Brand Awareness objective depends on the target customer's mental environment *at the time of brand-item choice*. (This theoretical point is missed, still, by most academic advertising researchers and most advertising research practitioners, even though it has been emphasized for almost 20 years by Rossiter and Percy.[4] For instance, the first author had just returned at the time of writing from an international advertising conference at which a leading academic and, in another presentation, a well-known practitioner, chose whichever brand awareness measure produced the best score for their brand! Make sure *you* don't make this common mistake.) The differences are identified in Table 6.2, which lists the options for the Brand Awareness communication objective, and they are explained next.

TABLE 6.2 *Managerial options with regard to brand awareness as a communication objective. (Note that an "increase" objective is assumed for each option.)*

BRAND CHOICE MADE	COMMUNICATION OBJECTIVE
At point of purchase	Brand *recognition*
Prior to purchase	Brand *recall*
Intended brand choice made prior to purchase but *then* brand must be identified at point of purchase	*Both* brand recall and brand recognition (brand-recall-boosted brand recognition)

Brand recognition

Look at the Behavioral Sequence Model (BSM) that you have constructed. If the target customer delays formation or finalization of his or her "consideration set" of brand-items until he or she is *at* the point of purchase, then the appropriate objective is **brand recognition**. From a message standpoint, what the marcoms have to achieve for Brand Recognition is to teach the target customer what the brand-item's *package* or *logo* looks like. This is a matter of *visual "iconic" recognition learning*[5] in Processing (level 1). There is, however, the occasional BSM situation where auditory "echoic" recognition learning is necessary. This occurs if the names of the brand-items at the point of purchase are presented *verbally* rather than visually. For instance, if you ask a waiter "Which imported beers do you have?" you will get a spoken list of brand-items and you have to *echoically recognize* those in your consideration set.

Brand Recognition is the easiest type of Brand Awareness to achieve in marcoms. The main branding tactic for Brand Recognition, as discussed in Chapter 7, is to show the pack or visual brand mark (alternative types of Brand Identity) clearly. Many a mistake is made in this regard in TV commercials because creatives dislike taking up video time with "boring pack shots"; you, as the manager, have to insist on them. Remember the appalling incidence of mis-branded TV ads: 45%! The brand mark (and here we include retail store signage and corporate stationery and signage) must act like the original ad – it is, essentially, a last-minute ad at the point of purchase. Brand Recognition at the point of purchase continues to be a major problem for a very large number of brand-items. This is mainly because the brand-item's *pre-purchase* marcoms have not properly taught customers how to recognize it.

There is an additional requirement for the Brand Recognition objective in a marcoms campaign which launches a *new brand-item*. Because it is new, the message has to show brand recognition *in the context of the category*. To give an extreme example, familiar to Western consumers who travel widely, have you ever tried to buy beer from one of those all-purpose vending machines in Japan? Which cans are the beer? Unless you have visually learned to associate a label such as Kirin with the category of beer, you may find yourself drinking a can of iced coffee! This, of course, is an extreme example but with the thousands of new FMCG brand-items launched each year, you must, in your ads and promotions, show consumers which *category* your new item belongs to. Even though brand-items may be helpfully arranged in product categories at the point of purchase, foreknowledge via marcoms *speeds recognition* of the new item.

The necessity of including the Category Need on the package or logo of a *new* brand-item is supported by recent research that importantly modifies the previously accepted "encoding specificity" principle. Recognition of new visual stimuli (such as a new pack or logo) is reduced markedly if the semantic context (the verbal label of what it "is") in which it appears is changed from it was learned to when it has to be recognized. Thus, absence of the Category Need at the time of *learning* (during marcoms processing) would make the brand-item very difficult to recognize at the point of purchase (with the category need now present as a new context). To achieve Brand Recognition of a *new* brand-item, therefore, *the Category Need should be clearly shown or stated in the marcoms message*. This is not the case for familiar visual stimuli, however. Recognition of a familiar visual stimulus (such as an established brand-item's pack or logo) is unaffected by the context in which it later appears, presumably because people have learned much earlier what its category need (context) is.[6]

Brand recall

Look again at the Behavioral Sequence Model that you have constructed for the target customer. Where is he or she likely to *be* when generating the "consideration set" of brand-items from which to purchase? If the target customer is (1) away from the point of purchase or (2) *not* looking at or listening to a *direct-response* ad, then the target customer has to *recall* brand-items in the consideration set.

To achieve **brand recall** reliably, the marcoms message must *associate* the Category Need and the Brand Identity. In situations requiring Brand Recall, the Brand Identity is the brand-item's *name* or its logo that *gives* its name. The two main message tactics to increase Brand Recall are *association of the brand name with the category need* and *repetition of the association*, either in the message or by repeating the message in the media schedule or in both. Brand Recall is a matter of *verbal paired-associates learning* at the level of Processing (review the effects levels in Chapter 2). However, paired-associates learning is *asymmetric*. The association Brand Mark → Category Need (Brand Recognition) is *easy* to learn because there are few or no competing responses (there are few or no other category needs that are trying to attach themselves to the brand). The association Category Need → Brand Name (Brand Recall) is *difficult* to learn and retain because of verbal interference – other brand names are also attaching, or have previously attached, themselves to the same category need! If their attachments are stronger than ours, the customer will be less likely to recall our brand.

One purpose of a **tagline** (the older and more political term is **slogan**) is to teach Brand Recall (the alternative purpose is to teach the brand's Key Benefit). Examples of taglines in which the Brand Name and the Category Need are associated for Brand Recall are: "Which bank? The

Commonwealth Bank" (Australia); "Beanz means Heinz" (U.K.); "Weekends were made for Michelob" (U.S.A.). We will take a further look at effective and ineffective taglines in Chapter 16 on corporate marcoms.

Brand-recall-boosted brand recognition

There is a third option for Brand Awareness that is the *most* difficult to achieve in marcoms. This goes by the long label of **brand-recall-boosted brand recognition**. It applies in situations (again, check the BSM that you have constructed) where the target customer must recall the brand *prior* to the point of purchase and then later recognize it so as to find it *at* the point of purchase. This circumstance increasingly describes the crowded product displays in the hyperstores and hypermarkets of today. Take, for instance, the new product Birds Eye Oven Roast. You see the ad, and oven-roasted potatoes and oven-roasted vegetables in convenient-to-prepare form seem like a very good idea so you make a mental note – and subsequently you recall – to buy these new Birds Eye items when next at the supermarket. When next at the supermarket, you come to the giant freezer case. Where is Birds Eye Oven Roast? If the marcoms have taught you to recall the brand-item but have not taught you to recognize the pack, and if the pack is not eye-poppingly distinctive on its own, Birds Eye will lose the sale.

Marcoms messages for Brand-Recall-Boosted Brand Recognition are the most difficult because they have to achieve *twin* Brand Awareness objectives: the message has to teach the customer to recall the brand-item and also to recognize it. This requires verbal recall tactics and visual recognition tactics in *the one ad*. We emphasize that this twin brand-awareness objective is not an option to be chosen casually in the hope of "covering both bases" of brand awareness. Only in some circumstances are both needed and then you have to take the extra step of insisting that the creative incorporate *both* sets of tactics.

> How does the manager test for Brand Recall and Brand Recognition in Ad Testing and in Campaign Tracking? To measure *Brand Recall*, the survey participant is provided only with the Category-Need description and is asked which Brand Names come to mind. To measure *Brand Recognition*, the participant, in a face-to-face or online interview, is shown a picture of a typical category display and asked to call out, in the normal time it takes to make a choice, the brand-items that he or she *notices*. A *verbal list of brand names* is not suitable for testing Brand Recognition *unless* the customer (in the BSM) has to make an auditory recognition from a spoken list. To measure *Brand-Recall-Boosted Brand Recognition*, apply the Brand Recall test face-to-face or online and then test for Brand Recognition for only those brands that the participant has recalled.

(3) BRAND PREFERENCE

The other universal campaign communication objective, besides Brand Awareness, is Brand Preference. Just as it would be pointless to run a marcoms campaign that does not increase or maintain Brand Awareness, so the marcoms campaign must also attempt to increase (or, in the case of our brand-loyal target customers, reinforce) Brand Preference.

Brand Preference is a more precise term for the communication effect that is otherwise known as Brand Attitude, which consumer behavior researchers denote as A_b, which stands for "Attitude toward brand 'b'," and which we denote as $BPREF_b$ (we introduced this notation in Chapter 4). Brand Preference is the *better* term because it more accurately describes what the marcoms campaign is trying to achieve: we are trying to develop the target customer's *preference* for our brand, over competing brands, rather than merely a favorable attitude toward it.

The manager has to select *one of four options* for Brand Preference as a campaign communication *objective*. The relevant option depends on the Target Customer's *prior* (pre-campaign) state of preference for our brand. These pre-campaign preference states and the Brand Preference communication objective for each, that is, the Brand Preference objective to be achieved by the campaign, are summarized in Table 6.3. If the Target Customer has a *negative* preference (a negative attitude) toward our brand, then the objective will be: *moderate preference*. If the Target Customer is *unaware* of our brand or – the same result – has heard of it or seen it but *knows nothing about it*, then the objective is: *strong preference*. If the target customer already has *moderate* preference for our brand, then the objective, again, is: *strong preference*. Lastly, if the target customer already has a *strong* preference for our brand, then the objective is: *reinforce strong preference*.

TABLE 6.3 *Managerial options with regard to brand preference as a communication objective. (Also see usual target subgroup alignment with brand preference objectives – in text.)*

TARGET CUSTOMER'S PRIOR STATE OF PREFERENCE	COMMUNICATION OBJECTIVE
Negative preference	Moderate preference (change to)
Unaware	Strong preference (create)
Moderate preference	Strong preference (increase)
Strong preference	Strong preference (reinforce)

The alternative Brand Preference objectives align closely with the Target Customer Subgroups that were presented earlier in the previous chapter. For Negative NCUs, Unfavorable OBSs, and Unfavorable OBLs, the brand preference objective will be: *change to moderate preference*. This objective frequently has to be used in social marketing campaigns when targeting behavioral "offenders," such as speeders, people who are dangerously overweight, people who use illicit drugs, or people who over-use legal drugs (alcohol, cigarettes, medications). In business and consumer marketing, the (change to) moderate preference objective is mainly employed when a marketer sees potential in being able to encourage non-users who dislike the category to change their minds and try it. A notable example is the yoghurt category, usage of which doubled with the introduction of better-tasting flavored yoghurt. Another example is the "reluctant user" segment of personal computer converts. Attitudinally they are still Negative NCUs and they probably hold only a moderate preference for (any brand of) personal computers. Thus, when attitude or preference *change* is required, a post-preference that is *moderately* positive is usually the realistic objective. However, if you believe your marcoms can achieve an even greater change, then substitute this with the objective of *change to strong preference*, which is not shown as an option in the (summary) table.

For Unaware NCUs, Neutral OBSs, and Neutral OBLs, the objective is *create strong preference*. These groups presently feel neutral toward our brand, so there is no negative attitude to overcome. Creation of strong preference is therefore a realistic objective.

The objective of *create strong preference* also applies to Experimental FBSs because, being experimental, there is a good opportunity to do this. However, it applies to Routinized FBSs only if their "routine" can be broken by them developing a strong preference for our brand (for highly routinized customers, strong preference should always be the *aim* of the brand's advertising, even when a price promotion is additionally needed to increase their rate of repeat purchase of our brand). For buyers of other brands who are favorable to our brand, that is, Favorable OBSs and Favorable OBLs, the *increase* to strong preference objective applies.

Our own BLs, either our Multi-BLs or Single-BLs, *already* have a strong preference for our brand. The objective for these target groups is to *reinforce strong preference*. Whereas we could have used the word "maintain" here, an effective marcoms campaign actually achieves maintenance by re-increasing – that is, "reinforcing" – their strong brand preference. Practically considered, BLs are usually a secondary target group, exposed to the same marcoms message that is trying to create strong preference among the primary target group, so BLs will in fact receive a reinforcement message.

How does the manager measure Brand Preference in a marcoms Pre-Test, and in Campaign Tracking? In a Pre-Test of the ad or promotion offer, brand preference is often measured directly, behaviorally, by asking target customers to make a choice of a brand-item from a set of brand-items pre-exposure, and then to make another choice between the brand-items post-exposure. In categories where customers usually choose just one brand-item per purchase occasion, they are asked to choose just one item each time. If several brand-items are typically purchased on one purchase occasion, such as with, say, frozen vegetables, soft drinks, or snack products, a typical procedure is to allow them to choose up to 10 brand-items pre- and post-exposure, selecting as many or as few of each as they wish.

This pre-post choice procedure, known as "persuasion-shift" testing, using the method of direct behavioral choice described here, is not possible to implement in Campaign Tracking, which is usually conducted by an Internet, telephone, or shopping-mall interview where the products are not present. Sometimes in pre-testing, and nearly always in campaign tracking, therefore, an *attitudinal* measure of brand preference is taken. The most comprehensive measure of brand preference is the measure that we introduced at the end of Chapter 5 to classify the brand loyalty target groups. This measure covers all brand-items considered. An efficient version of it is:

☐ My single preferred brand
☐ One of my several preferred brands
☐ An acceptable brand that I would buy only if it is "on special"
☐ A brand that I would not buy under any circumstances
☐ I do not know enough about this brand to consider buying it

Strong Preference *and* Uniqueness Equity is indicated by a "top box" rating; Multi-BLs are more likely to choose a "second box" rating, indicating high Value Equity but not Uniqueness.

Moderate brand preference is indicated by a "third box" rating. Negative Preference is indicated by a "fourth box" rating. Neutral Preference is indicated by a "fifth box" rating. The success of the ad or promotion offer – or, in tracking, the entire marcoms campaign – is gauged by the proportion of target customers who, *given* that they are *aware* of the brand, by Brand Recognition or Brand Recall or both if appropriate, shift up to the moderate or, respectively, Strong Preference level or, if reinforcement is the objective, the proportion who stay at the Strong Preference level.

Brand preference scores, BPREFb, from the I-D-U analysis can also be related to ratings on the above scale (I-D-U analysis is used in strategy development, of course, not in pre-testing or tracking). The "percent of ideal" score provides an Absolute brand preference rating, that is, a Brand Attitude rating, and also indicates the brand's Value Equity. Percent-of-ideal, described in Chapter 4, is the brand's preference score as a percentage of the preference score that would be obtained by the ideal brand (which has maximum delivery ratings but the importances or desirabilities stay constant). Comparison of the percent-of-ideal scores across competing brands in the category easily reveals whether a brand is "single preferred" or "one of several preferred," although the remaining box ratings cannot be readily inferred. Differences between percent-of-ideal scores indicate Uniqueness Equity.

The box ratings have a further important advantage for diagnostic purposes. Comparison of the "Acceptable" box ratings between brands enables the manager to detect what proportion of our brand's customers are *vulnerable* to competitive brands' overtures. By the same measure (the "Acceptable" box, indicating a Moderate Preference), the manager can assess what proportion of other brand's customers might be *available* if we were to position our brand to appeal to them.[7]

Where do brand benefit beliefs and brand emotions come in?

The Brand Benefit Belief(s) and Brand Emotion(s) for the brand are identified in the *I-D-U analysis*. It is possible to regard Brand Benefit Beliefs and Brand Emotions as communication objectives for a particular ad or promotion offer and perhaps for the overall campaign – in that these mental (and in the case of emotions, bodily) responses are the presumed *means* of achieving the *Brand Preference* objective. We do not include them among the five communication effects because they are content-specific – not general to all campaigns like the other five. Instead, the specifically-targeted Brand Benefit Belief(s) and Brand Emotion(s) are included as communication objectives when *pre-testing* the ad or offer (in the MJAT, and, if employed, the CRAT, as explained in Chapter 10) and when *tracking* the campaign (as explained in Chapter 14). In pre-testing, Brand Benefit Beliefs and Brand Emotions have the same status as creative tactics (Chapter 8) and attention tactics (Chapter 9): they must be measured for the specific ad or offer. In tracking, though, they do not necessarily have to be remembered as they should have done their job during ad processing. The exception is the belief about the brand's *Key Benefit*, which target customers should be able to remember at all times.

A Low-Involvement purchase (Low Risk) brand-item's communication objectives can stop with Brand Preference. However, for products or services that are perceived as High-Risk purchases – or for target groups who perceive the trial or re-trial of a brand-item as high risk in an otherwise low-risk category, that is, so it becomes a High-Involvement choice – the next, fourth, communication effect is additionally necessary as an objective, as is, often, the fifth.

(4) BRAND ACTION INTENTION

Whenever the target customer is contemplating a High-Involvement purchase or action, it is necessary that the prospective customer form a *conscious action intention* as a result of the brand-item's marcoms. This is literally an inner voice, a self-instruction to act (e.g., "I'd like to test drive a Nissan Z car," or "I *will* buy myself a Hugo Boss suit," or "I will *stop* drinking so much alcohol on weekends"). The definition of Brand Action Intention as a *self-instruction* to act comes from the attitude theory developed by Triandis.[8] Further, Bagozzi[9] has shown that for action based on High-Involvement brand attitude, Intention is a necessary mediator in the causal path from Attitude, or Preference, to Behavior. Ouellette and Wood[10], in their meta-analysis, a comprehensive summary of many studies, have shown that decisions about frequent, routine behaviors are mediated mostly by Habit (previously established brand awareness plus brand preference). But they showed decisions about infrequent, more important behaviors are mediated mainly by Intention formation.

The *action* in an Action Intention must correspond to the *action objective* for the target audience. For FMCG products and services, the action is most often Purchase, either Trial or Repeat. For durables, however, it may be a behavior that is a first step toward purchase (a Test Drive, an Inquiry, and so forth). For social marketing, the *behavior itself* (there may be no purchase in the usual sense) is the action; an intention to perform it, or to cease to perform it as the case may be, must be generated.

Whether Brand Action Intention should be a campaign communication objective is therefore dependent on whether the target customer regards purchase of the particular brand-item as having a low-risk outcome or a high-risk outcome (the perceived risk could be the "functional" risks of product failure or monetary loss, or the "emotional" risks of loss of prestige or loss of self-esteem).[11] Perceived risk places the customer in a state of Low or High Involvement about the decision. We define **involvement** as the perceived risk of choosing *this brand* (or brand-item) on the *next* occasion. Involvement is *brand-choice involvement* – not to be confused with product category interest or being interested in an advertisement, which are other meanings of "involvement" that you will sometimes come across. From the customer's perspective, involvement is *dichotomous*: prospective customers either decide that it is worth investing time and effort to search and verify brand-item information, or that it is not.[12]

Table 6.4 summarizes the options for Brand Action Intention as a campaign communication objective. For campaigns aimed at stimulating a Low-Involvement purchase, brand action intention can be deliberately *omitted*. For campaigns aimed at stimulating a High-Involvement purchase – and note that the inclusion of a Promotion Offer requires the generation of a "self-instruction" to take advantage of the offer, even for an otherwise low-risk product or service – the objective is to *generate* brand action intention.

TABLE 6.4 *Managerial options with regard to brand action intention as a communication objective. See our definition of "involvement," in text.*

TARGET CUSTOMER'S STATE OF MIND	COMMUNICATION OBJECTIVE
Low-involvement decision	*Omit* brand action intention
High-involvement decision (which includes the situation of a promotion offer on an otherwise low-involvement item)	*Generate* brand action intention

How can the manager measure Brand Action Intention? Because the action intention has to arise spontaneously and consciously, it is most validly measured in *pre-testing* of the ads or promotion offers by a questioning technique called *Cognitive Response*[13] measurement, which is more accurately called *Cognitive and Emotional Responses* measurement. In this technique, the target customer is asked to report, immediately after being exposed to the ad or offer, the "thoughts, feelings, or images that ran through your mind" while watching, reading, or listening to the ad or offer. These conscious processing responses, which are usually tape-recorded or quickly written down by the interviewer, are then content-analyzed for spontaneous mention of a purchase intention. Note that this could be a "purchase-related" intention such as to visit a dealership or, in social marketing campaigns, to visit a doctor or counselor, rather than a final intention to purchase. Spontaneous generation is a very strict measure of action intention. However, it is the best measure to use when *pre-testing* marcoms campaigns aimed at achieving High-Involvement customer choices.

A different method is used to measure Brand Action Intention in *campaign tracking*. In the tracking interview situation, of course, target customers have *not* just a minute or so ago been exposed to the ad or offer, so they would not have a spontaneous intention in mind. An intention scale prompts it. Again, action intention measurement is necessary only for High-Involvement purchases or behaviors, and for Promotion Offers if the promotion offer is well-publicized and ongoing. For instance, BMW automobiles had a long-running promotion offer for which air travelers had to turn in their boarding pass to enter a sweepstakes to win a new BMW. Intention to enter the sweepstakes would be appropriate to track.

In the measure for tracking Brand Action Intention, a distinction has to be made between a high-risk purchase for the target customers in an otherwise low-risk product or service category, and a high-risk purchase in a category that is itself high risk. In the first case – an example of which might be a campaign that attempts to persuade women prospects to try a new brand of hair coloring for home use – a four-point intention scale is best, here worded for purchase intention:

☐ Definitely will buy
☐ Probably will buy
☐ Might buy
☐ Will not buy

To calculate the *predicted incidence* of actual purchase, the purchase intention scores are weighted as follows: would not buy, 0; might buy, .1; probably will buy, .4; definitely will buy, .9, indicating that approximately 0%, 10%, 40%, and 90% of target customers checking the respective scale points will actually buy the product.[14]

For high-risk purchases in high-risk categories, the Juster 11-point scale of intention is best. This is a numerically and verbally labeled scale as follows:

☐ Certain or practically certain (99% chance)
☐ Almost sure (90%)
☐ Very probable (80%)
☐ Probable (70%)
☐ Good possibility (60%)
☐ Fairly good possibility (50%)
☐ Fair possibility (40%)
☐ Some possibility (30%)
☐ Slight possibility (20%)
☐ Very slight possibility (10%)
☐ No chance or almost no chance (0%)

Note, however, that the parenthesized numbers in the scale are *not* the weights for predicting the incidence of purchase. Ideally, the weights should be calibrated for the particular product or service category by the manager. However, in the absence of this information, a fairly accurate general set of weights for high-risk choices is to start with .05 for the zero end of the scale and step up in increments of .05 so that the 99% end receives a weight of .55. If the Juster scale is used for a high-risk choice in an otherwise low-risk category, the scale is re-weighted as follows: certain or practically certain, .99; almost sure down to probable, .76; good possibility down to some possibility, .4; slight possibility down to no chance or almost no chance, .06. The .06 weight at the lower end is because high-risk purchase intentions are more *indefinite* than zero, in that some customers who said no on the interview will later change their minds and purchase the item.

(5) PURCHASE FACILITATION

The fifth potential campaign communication objective is Purchase Facilitation.[15] This is *brand* purchase facilitation but that should be obvious and we use the shorter term. Purchase Facilitation is mainly relevant in marcoms campaigns by Retailers (bricks-and-mortar retailers or online retailers). The purpose is to let the target customer know where the brand-item can be purchased (e.g., "dealer tags" at the conclusion of TV and radio commercials or at the bottom of print ads); how to get to the nearest retail outlet (if it is not an online retailer); and how it can be paid for (credit card, debit card, check, or cash only). Although this error seems unforgivable, because it imposes on the prospective customer an unreasonable burden of search, one quite often sees ads and promotion offers that neglect facilitation of action.

The manager's options for Purchase Facilitation as a campaign communication objective are summarized in Table 6.5. If purchase facilitation is not needed – as it won't be for frequently purchased FMCG products and widely available services – it can be *omitted*. Otherwise, mainly for categories that are rarely shopped for by the target customer, purchase facilitation must be *incorporated* in the marcoms for the brand-item.

TABLE 6.5 *Managerial options with regard to purchase facilitation as a communication objective.*

TARGET CUSTOMER'S STATE OF MIND	COMMUNICATION OBJECTIVE
Target customer knows where to buy the product or service, how to find the retail outlet, and how they may pay for it	*Omit* purchase facilitation
Any or all not obvious: where to buy, how to find the retailer, how to pay	*Incorporate* purchase facilitation content in the marcoms as appropriate

When Purchase Facilitation is an objective, it can be measured in Pre-Testing and in Campaign Tracking by asking the sample of target customers to answer the appropriate question or questions: "Where is this item available?", "How do you get there?" (a question that could be asked for online retailers to make sure target customers have the correct URL), and "By what methods can customers pay for it?"

The manager has now positioned the brand and brand-item. The manager has now selected the primary target audience and perhaps a secondary target audience for the marcoms campaign (including, from the BSM, the creative target role-player). Action objectives (behavioral, and preferably goals) and communication objectives (mental states to be achieved by the campaign, expected to cause action) have been set for the campaign. In other words, we know the what, the who, and the why. The next decision is *how*; this is the question of Creative Strategy.

SUMMARY

To induce individual prospective customers to take action, that is, to make a trial purchase or to repeat the purchase of the brand-item, the marcoms campaign must install from zero or otherwise "top up" *communication effects* for the brand-item, in the minds of prospective customers. There are five potential communication effects: (1) Category Need, (2) Brand Awareness, (3) Brand Preference, (4) Brand Action Intention, and (5) Purchase Facilitation. The first and last of these communication effects, Category Need and Purchase Facilitation, may be present in the customer's mind *before* the campaign and therefore will not have to be addressed in the campaign. Those communication effects that have to be addressed – created or topped up – become campaign communication *objectives*. These always include (2) Brand Awareness (Brand Recall or Brand Recognition) and (3) Brand Preference, and, if the brand-item choice for the target customer is high risk – that is, the purchase decision is *high involvement* – then it is also necessary to include (4) Brand Action Intention as an objective and often (5) Purchase Facilitation.

DISCUSSION QUESTIONS

6.1   Category Need is obviously a communication objective whenever a new product category is advertised or promoted. But "selling the category" also may be an objective for *established* products. Under what circumstances is this true?

6.2 How might the brand-item purchase motive differ from the overall category purchase motive? Select and discuss an example where the two are identical and another example in which they differ.

6.3 Brand awareness responses can take the form of Brand Recognition or Brand Recall or sometimes Brand-Recall-Boosted Brand Recognition. Which form of brand awareness response do you think would be most relevant for brands in the following product categories, and why? (a) Airlines that fly to Australia; (b) shampoo; (c) gasoline service stations; (d) department stores, such as Saks, located mainly in shopping malls.

6.4 Brand Preference can be interpreted both on an absolute basis and on a relative basis. What is the meaning of these two interpretations as far as the success of the brand's marcoms is concerned?

6.5 Two communication effects are universally objectives in every campaign. Which are they and why are they necessarily communication objectives? Discuss too the special case of "teaser" ads, which we discussed in Chapter 2 (the Chrysler Crossfire ad, for example). Also, some of our more naïve colleagues have argued that the consumer can acquire a preference without being aware of the preferred object; while that is true, why is it incorrect to conclude, as they have, that brand preference could be an objective without brand awareness as a prior objective?

6.6 Skim through a magazine in which there are a number of ads for New Cars. Select two ads for which your Brand Action Intention reaction, as defined in this chapter, differs. Discuss how and why your reactions differed.

6.7 Select a Direct-Response Ad that you think is particularly complete and effective for the Purchase Facilitation communication objective. Justify your selection.

NOTES

1. *The Economist*, Have PDAs had their day?, reprinted in *The Australian*, IT Business section, October 28, 2003, p. 5. The article notes that the Palm Source company licenses the Palm operating system to manufacturers of PDAs *and* phones. Worldwide sales of PDAs are flat at 11 million units per year; total mobile phone sales are 460 million p.a. of which "smart" phones are 12 million and rising fast. By comparison, PCs (desktop and laptop) sell at 130 million units a year, a big but also pretty flat category. In the longer run, PDAs and cell phones will probably be the one product.

2. J.R. Rossiter and L. Percy, *Advertising Communications & Promotion Management*, New York: McGraw-Hill, 1997, chapter 5.

3. R. Thomaselli, Reebok's strategy: play up vector logo, *Advertising Age*, August 25, 2003, p. 6.

4. J.R. Rossiter and L. Percy, *Advertising and Promotion Management*, New York: McGraw-Hill, 1987, especially p. 141. Ten years later, and no doubt still today, *none* of 100 managers could give the correct definition of brand awareness; see E. MacDonald and B. Sharp, Management perceptions of the importance of brand awareness as an indication of advertising effectiveness, *Marketing Research On-Line*, 1996, 1(1), pp. 1–15.

5. J.R. Rossiter and L. Percy, Visual communication in advertising, in R.J. Harris (Ed.), *Information Processing Research in Advertising*, Hillsdale, NJ: Lawrence Erlbaum Associates, pp. 83–125.

6. P. Dalton, The role of stimulus familiarity in context-dependent recognition, *Memory & Cognition*, 1993, 21(2), pp. 223–234; R. Russo, G. Ward, H. Geurts, and A. Scheres, When unfamiliarity matters: changing environmental context between study and test affects recognition memory

for unfamiliar stimuli, *Journal of Experimental Psychology: Learning, Memory and Cognition*, 1999, 25(2), pp. 488–499.

7. J. Hofmeyr and B. Rice, *Commitment-Led Marketing*, Chichester, England: Wiley, 2000.

8. H.C. Triandis, Values, attitudes, and interpersonal behavior, in H.E. Howe and M.M. Page (Eds), *Nebraska Symposium on Motivation: 1979*, Lincoln, NE: University of Nebraska Press, 1980, pp. 195–259.

9. R.P. Bagozzi, J. Baumgartner, and Y. Yi, An investigation into the role of intentions as mediators of the attitude-behavior relationship, *Journal of Economic Psychology*, 1989, 10(1), pp. 35–62. Intention was originally proposed as a necessary mediator by Fishbein and Ajzen in their attitude model but it turns out only to be necessary for high-involvement choices. See M. Fishbein and I. Ajzen, *Belief, Attitude, Intention, and Behavior*, Reading, MA: Addison-Wesley, 1975.

10. J.A. Ouellette and W. Wood, Habit and Intention in everyday life: the multiple processes by which past behavior predicts future behavior, *Psychological Bulletin*, 1998, 124(1), pp. 54–74.

11. The best references on sources of perceived risk are R.A. Bauer and D.F. Cox, Rational vs. emotional communications: a new approach, in D.F. Cox (Ed.), *Risk Taking and Information Handling in Consumer Behaviour*, Cambridge, MA: Harvard University Press, 1967, pp. 469–486; P.E. Nelson, Information and consumer behavior, *Journal of Political Economy*, 1970, 78(2), pp. 311–329; and J.P. Peter and L.X. Tarpey, A comparative analysis of three consumer decision strategies, *Journal of Consumer Research*, 1975, 2(1), pp. 29–37.

12. Academic researchers may note that the ELM also regards involvement as next-action risk and as dichotomous (low or high) although in several recent papers ELM theorists have also referred to moderate involvement, making it a trichotomy. Based on years of research experience investigating customer choice, we are convinced that the dichotomous concept of involvement is correct.

13. Cognitive Response measurement was originated by the Yale Group (C.I. Hovland and colleagues) in the late 1940s as a human counterpart of C.L. Hull's concept of the "fractional antedating goal response," an anticipatory response to the goal; for instance, a rat runs faster, salivates and so forth when it expects a food reward at the end of the laboratory runway device. In humans, these "little $r_g \rightarrow s_g$ connections" anticipate attitude (preference) strengthening, or weakening if they are predominantly negative. Keen students of learning theory, which is still the most relevant body of theory for advertising – by far – might profit from tracking down Hull's original writings, following his theory through the work of the Yale group and also the work of R.F. Weiss. If you look really hard, you'll see where our five communication effects came from.

14. The source of the four-point intention scale weights for low-risk categories is G.L. Urban and J.R. Hauser, *Design and Marketing of New Products*, 2nd edition, Englewood Cliffs, NJ: Prentice Hall, 1993, chapter 12, in which they review purchase intent-to-behavior translation studies. For the 11-point high-risk intention scale, see T.F. Juster, Consumer buying intentions and purchase probability: an experiment in survey design, *Journal of the American Statistical Association*, 1966, 61(3), pp. 658–696 and D.G. Morrison, Purchase intentions and purchase behavior, *Journal of Marketing*, 1979, 43(2), pp. 65–74. The scale of weights is inferred from Juster's study with automobiles and is identically represented by Morrison in a later study with automobiles and closely confirmed by a later study by Infosino on the adoption of a new telephone service; see W.J. Infosino, Forecasting new product sales from likelihood of purchase ratings, *Marketing Science*, 1986, 5(4), pp. 372–384. The weights for translating the 11-point Juster scale down to the four-point low-risk purchase intention scale come from A. Gruber, Purchase intent and purchase probability, *Journal of Advertising Research*, 1970, 10(1), pp. 23–27. For evidence that low-involvement intentions are basically dichotomous (by far the greatest weight is given to the top box) and high-involvement intentions gradated, see M.U. Kalwani and A.J. Silk, On the reliability and predictive validity of purchase intention measures, *Marketing Science*, 1983, 1(3), pp. 243–286.

15. Purchase facilitation also is derived from Triandis' model, which in turn is based on Hull's earlier model in which facilitation was reversed as inhibition and subtracted from action tendency, which is brand action intention in our model.

PART III

advertising –

creative strategy

CHAPTER SEVEN
Creative idea generation
and selection 123

CHAPTER EIGHT
Brand awareness and brand preference
(grid) tactics 151

CHAPTER NINE
Attention tactics 188

CHAPTER TEN
Pre-testing rough ads 212

CHAPTER 7

Creative idea generation
and selection

The **creative** – used as a collective noun, not the adjective – is the marcoms term for advertisements and also for the materials used to support promotion offers. In this chapter, we will refer to *ads* as "the Creative", while you should remember that this term also applies to promotion offers. The Creative is usually brainstormed and produced by "the Creatives" – a plural noun this time – the artists and writers in an advertising agency, or sometimes in a media agency, or in the company or organization itself in the case of in-house preparation of ads.

How can the marketing manager or brand manager ensure that he or she gets *effective* Creative from the agency, or from the in-house creative department, before a couple of hundreds of thousands or, for bigger advertisers, tens of millions of dollars are spent behind the Creative in the next campaign? Think again about the campaign success statistics that we provided in Chapter 1: these statistics underscore the importance of running *only high-quality ads*. Recall the figures for FMCG products (for consumer durables and industrial products the effects are greater but so are the supplementary selling costs). For a 10% increase in Adspend over a year, the average ad campaign produces a 1.4% increase in unit Sales. This is an average increase; you might do worse than this, and even an average increase may not deliver any Profit from sales once the advertising cost is taken into account. With high-quality Creative, the Sales effect can be increased to 3.9%, which means that high-quality Creative, on a relative basis, is 178% more sales-effective than average-quality creative and almost certainly will be a big Profit generator. Similarly, for TV advertising for FMCG products, Jones' data for short-term (weekly) sales effects indicate that *only about 30%* of U.S. TV ads are clearly profitable in terms of large sales increases when they are on air (the figure is *about 20%* of TV ads in other countries, probably because in those countries they do less pre-testing of ads). About 40% of U.S. TV ads (50% elsewhere) do little more than "hold" sales and may not pay back their media expenditure, or not by much. In *all* countries surveyed, the *worst 30%* of TV ad campaigns actually cause weekly sales to go *down*, mainly because they fail to protect against better campaigns by competitors seen that week.

Creative strategy occupies Chapters 7 through 10 and is the longest part of the book – justifiably, because while it is important to get positioning, targeting and then media right, without high-quality Creative you have nothing, because the campaign will not work. This chapter is about how to write a Creative Brief for the advertising agency and how to brainstorm and select effective Creative Ideas. Chapter 8 is about effective Brand Awareness tactics and effective Brand Preference tactics. Chapter 9 covers the vital topic of Attention tactics for ads in the various media. Chapter 10, the concluding chapter on creative strategy, explains Pre-Testing – how to design and conduct a Management Judgment Ad Test, and, when necessary, a Customer Response Ad Test.

To make this division of creative strategy meaningful, we must begin by defining the *components* of an ad – that is, "the things that go in to" it. These things also go into a promotion offer, but it is easier to focus on ads.

COMPONENTS OF AN AD

An advertisement is a deeply complex piece of communication! This realization is true no matter whether we are talking about a multi-million dollar TV commercial, or a local advertiser's TV commercial made for just a few thousand dollars; a one-page newspaper or magazine ad; an announcer-read radio commercial for a local retailer; a two-line classified ad that you place by yourself on the Internet, or in a newspaper or magazine; or a corporate annual report, which is, after all, an ad for the company. If effective ads were not complex, then we would not need advertising agencies. In fact, much retail advertising, directory advertising, most classified ads, and many ads by small business firms are in-house "do-it-yourself" efforts, some of which, by a costly trial-and-error process over the years to acquire the right components, have become very effective.

On the "surface", an ad is just some combination of pictures, words, and, if it is a broadcast ad, music or sound effects. Analysis of an ad's "deep structure," however, reveals *four* components. These are summarized for reference in Figure 7.1 and discussed below.

1. The key benefit claim

The Key Benefit Claim, or KBC, is a *unique statement* of the key benefit. The Key Benefit *Claim* is unique to the brand (or sub-brand or brand-item) whereas the Benefit underlying the claim in many cases is *not* unique. The Key Benefit Claim may be explicitly stated as the campaign's headline or tagline (called strapline in the U.K.). On the other hand, and this is important to understand, the Key Benefit Claim may be explicitly stated *only* for the purpose of generating a Creative Idea (component 2) and then *implied* in the campaign (e.g., the KBC "You too can be sexy in private" is not *stated* in Victoria's Secret ads). The Key Benefit Claim is the first thing that needs to be "created." *One* KBC has to be selected. This involves members of the management team, individually, each nominating the best wording and then a management team judgment to select the one to be used.

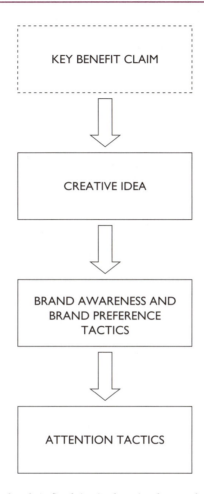

FIGURE 7.1 *Components of an ad. The key benefit claim is the stimulus used to generate the creative idea but may not necessarily appear in the ad (hence the dashed box).*

2. The creative idea

The Creative Idea dramatizes the Key Benefit Claim. The ad is *built around* this component.[1] Essentially, the ad *is* the Creative Idea – take the Creative Idea out of the ad and the message could look or sound the same for every brand-item in the category! The creative idea is so influential that – sometimes – it can *change* the Key Benefit originally selected! The agency, while brainstorming creative ideas, may discover a Creative Idea that suggests a *better way of selling* the brand or brand-item than the way suggested by the Key Benefit Claim. Actually, this happens most often when the agency has *not* been provided with a Key Benefit Claim in the brief; the agency then has to *invent* one, and what they come up with may tap into a *different benefit*.[2] If the agency happens to hit upon what *appears to be* a more persuasive Key Benefit Claim, do the following. Have the creative team also brainstorm several Creative Ideas that clearly dramatize the original Key Benefit Claim – assuming you provided one – but also include *their* Creative Ideas based on *their* Key Benefit Claim. In this test of the Creative Ideas, their Key Benefit Claim may prove to be better. If it *is* better, rewrite the Key Benefit in the Positioning Statement and rewrite the Key Benefit Claim.

3. Brand awareness and brand preference tactics

The ad must include appropriate **brand awareness tactics**, which execute or "structure" the brand awareness message content to achieve Brand Recognition, Brand Recall, or both. Also, the ad must include **brand preference tactics** – the brand emotions and brand benefits needed to achieve the Brand Preference communication objective. See Chapter 8.

4. Attention tactics for ads in various media

An ad has first to gain, and then hold, the Attention of Target Customers. Until a few years ago with the emergence of multiple TV channels worldwide and already-available remote control handsets, Attention was hardly a problem for TV commercials; but it is now. *Attention is the biggest problem facing ads in all media, TV included* – no Attention means no Processing and therefore no Communication Effects. Attention Tactics are, surprisingly enough, mainly *structural* factors such as ad duration or size, picture size, form of headline, brand-identity placement and, for TV and radio ads, the "interest pattern" that the commercial can employ. See Chapter 9.

Our purpose in the *present* chapter is to explain the components of the Creative that have the biggest effect, components 1 and 2. We begin with a *pro forma* for the Creative Brief, from which the creative strategy proceeds. The creative process itself starts with generation of, and agreement on, the Key Benefit Claim. Then we explain how to generate and select potential Creative Ideas that will dramatize the claim.

THE CREATIVE BRIEF

The **creative brief** is absolutely the most vital piece of communication to pass from the management team to the creative team. What the brief communicates to the Creatives on the account will influence the entire creative strategy and be the cause of the ads you will get.[3] The Creative Brief provided to the advertising agency creatives or to DIY creatives consists of *five sections*. The brief must be stated on *no more than two pages*:

1. Behavioral Sequence Model, after which the key role-player – the Creative Target for the campaign – is identified and the Primary Medium for the campaign is specified together with the Media Target.

2. Campaign Action Objectives.

3. Campaign Communication Objectives.

4. Brand or brand-item's *Campaign* Positioning Statement, which nominates the Target Audience for the campaign (T); the Category Need in which the brand-item is intended

to compete (C); and, from the I-D-U analysis, the benefits (B), consisting of the Key Benefit (and the *Key Benefit Claim*), together with Entry-Ticket Benefits, and any benefit to be traded off or omitted.

5. Mandatory content (if any).

The Creative Brief should be quite an easy document to compose if you follow our approach because it summarizes the research and strategic decisions that have been made previously. If this groundwork hasn't been done, or done properly, you will be issuing an inadequate Creative Brief and thereby delegating the major decisions about the brand's Positioning and Target Audience selection to the agency! We comment here that some clients favor a very brief brief which states just the brand name and the sales objective. Agencies favor this too, because it gives them total freedom to, in effect, position the brand, choose the target audience, and decide the key benefit; not only does the brand become the agency's responsibility when a brief brief is given, it usually means more income for the agency, since most now charge an hourly fee.[4] The enormous variety of "creative solutions" that a brief brief will bring if given to different agencies, as happens in an account pitch, was the main observation that led to our Theory of *Random* Creativity, discussed later in the chapter. The first author collects case histories of agencies' responses to the same brief because the randomness is so startling. This is not evident in the real world of advertising because we see only the *one* creative solution that gets to air or to print. Here is an example that proves the point. In 1993, the Church of England asked five leading U.K. agencies to pitch, *pro bono*, as is common for charities, a campaign "To swell the Church of England's congregations" (that was the brief brief). In Britain, at the time, only a fifth of the population went to (any) church regularly, that is, monthly or more often. The results were published in the U.K. newspaper, *The Weekend Guardian*, April 10, 1993, pp. 6–9, 11. The headline alone of each campaign will reveal the diversity of approaches taken. Two, quite by chance, are similar. Most employ a play on words (pun) which is the British way.

- "Who does your child think is the most powerful force in the universe?" (Gold Greenless Trott)

- "You never know where you might find yourself." Tagline: "The experience of a lifetime, every week. The Church of England." (Grey)

- "Wouldn't it be wonderful if life had a pause button." Tagline: "Church. This Sunday. An hour's refreshment." (McCann-Erickson)

- "Why? God only knows." Tagline: "The Church of England. You'll never really know until you go." (TWBA)

- "You could soon find yourself here." Tagline: "The Church of England. Open Sundays for better values." (Social Service Advertising)

The startling thing is that not only are the Creative Ideas different (well, four of them are) but so too is the *Key Benefit* that they rely on: "Children's moral guidance," "Self-discovery and implied contentment" (twice), "Spiritual self-restoration," and "The promise of finding answers to life's big questions." The variety of *Creative Ideas* will still be very large with a structured brief like ours but the Key Benefit will be consistent.

We provide two *hypothetical examples* of a Creative Brief – in our format – in Table 7.1, for a typical business service and a typical FMCG product. In the DHL example, we have not attempted to choose the Key Benefit Claim (a task which is discussed next). In the Heineken example, we have taken the Key Benefit Claim to be the campaign's tagline, "It's all about the beer."

TABLE 7.1 *Creative briefs – hypothetical – for a typical business service, DHL Worldwide Express couriers (panel A), and a typical FMCG product, Heineken beer (panel B).*

(A) DHL WORLDWIDE EXPRESS COURIER SERVICE – GLOBAL MARKET

1. BSM

	Need arousal →	Information search →	Choice →	Usage →	Re-order
Who	Business executive (initiator)	Business executive (negative influencer) Personal assistant (influencer)	Personal assistant (decider and purchaser)	Personal assistant (the contact user) Business executive (the service user)	Personal assistant (redecider)
Where	Office or when traveling	Internal (business executive, for any vetoes) External (personal assistant, approved list)	PA's office	PA's office	PA's office
When	Business hours	On the spot	Several minutes later	1–3 days	4th day or soon after
How	Need arises to send package locally, or interstate, or overseas to some part of the world	BE vetoes any specific couriers with recent bad experience for that destination; PA considers prompt response from availables	PA makes final choice from among prompt responders on low price	PA tracks if delay	Brand remains in consideration set if last experience satisfactory

Creative target: Personal assistants (PAs)

Media: SPAM emails or faxes

Media target: Companies with 10 or more employees

2. Action objective

Increased rate of placement with DHL Worldwide Express (share of requirements) among all companies with 10 or more employees, especially for overseas destinations. Goal: 10% increase on current unit market share, by end of financial year

3. Communication objectives

Category need: Remind of remote destination difficulties

Brand awareness: Brand recall

Brand preference: Increase to strong preference

Brand action intention: Generate intention by PA to call DHL Worldwide Express courier first

Purchase facilitation: 24/7 phone or email contact and pickup

TABLE 7.1 *Continued*

4. Positioning statement for campaign

To all PAs in larger companies who order couriers, DHL Worldwide Express is the brand of courier for all destinations, local to remote, that has the best knowledge of remote destinations and also offers prompt pickup, reasonable delivery duration by destination, 24/7 tracking, at "competitive" prices by destination

Key benefit: Remote destinations knowledge (key benefit claim and a-b-e support not decided)

Entry-ticket benefits: Prompt pickup, tracking, competitive price

Tradeoff or omit: None

5. Mandatory content

Web address, toll-free phone number

(B) HEINEKEN BEER – INTERNATIONAL MARKET

1. BSM

	Need arousal $\rightarrow$	Information search $\rightarrow$	Choice $\rightarrow$	Usage
Who	Self (initiator) Peers (influencers)	Self (influencer) Peers (influencers)	Self (decider)	Self (user)
Where	Pub	Internal (from previous media exposure)	Pub	Pub
	Restaurant Liquor store	External (peers' brand choices)	Restaurant Liquor store	Restaurant Home
When	Weekends mainly	At point of decision	Instant	Instant or over ensuing week
How	Need arises for beer as beverage	What do I like? What are influentials drinking?	"Wise" choice or socially approved choice	Ego reinforcement or social reinforcement

Creative target: The beer drinker (decider) himself or herself

Media: TV, suitable special-event sponsorships

Media target: Men 18–35, upper-middle class

2. Action objective

Trial of Heineken (for FBSs who haven't tried) and then high repeat-purchase share of requirements (all FBSs). Long-run goal: 80% SOR among FBSs after first three months of campaign

Continues

TABLE 7.1 *Continued*

3. Communication objectives

Category need: Remind

Brand awareness: Brand recall

Brand preference: Increase to strong preference

Brand action intention: Omit

Purchase facilitation: Omit

4. Positioning statement for campaign

To favorable-brand-switcher beer drinkers, Heineken is the brand of premium, "upmarket" beer that is the wisest choice because it is the best product in the category

Key benefit: Best premium beer (key benefit claim: "It's all about the beer")

Support: It must be, because users insist on it, even beyond social niceties, which is $e^- \rightarrow b$ (incomplete satisfaction) with e^+ (self-reward, wise choice) end-emotion

Entry-ticket benefit: Premium, upmarket beer – shown by setting in ads

Tradeoff or omit: Omit price

5. Mandatory content

Safe-drinking warning in countries where required

KEY BENEFIT CLAIM

From the Creative Brief, the first task is to generate alternative wordings of the Key Benefit Claim, and then agree on *one*. The management team should do this. If they are briefing an external advertising or media agency, the Key Benefit Claim must be included in the brief that goes to them (see "THE CREATIVE BRIEF," earlier). The Key Benefit Claim is the actual *stimulus* from which the creative team will brainstorm Creative Ideas, that is, ideas for the creative executions of the ads.

The Key Benefit Claim, or KBC, is defined as: an accurate, persuasively sufficient, succinct statement of the key benefit.[5] For a *brand* or *sub-brand*, the Key Benefit Claim might be a selling proposition based on an Instinct (ISP), an Archetype (ASP), or a Strong type 2 Emotion (ESP) rather than, as for a *brand-item*, an Emotional Benefit Claim (also an ESP), or a Functional Benefit Claim (an RSP). With any type of benefit claim, it will be difficult to arrive at the right *wording*, which is why alternatives must be examined. Moreover, even if the Key Benefit Claim will not appear literally in the ad, although often it will as a tagline, the claim must still be *stated in words* for the purpose of brainstorming. What does the definition of a KBC mean? By "accurate" we mean that the claim must describe the benefit that the management team selected as the key benefit from the I-D-U analysis, without suggesting or bringing in any other benefit. By "persuasively sufficient" we mean that the claim has to include just enough a, b or e content to answer the marketing manager's question: "How are we going to persuade them?", "we" being management and "them" being the target customers.[6] The references to a, b and e in the following examples help to illustrate this. By "succinct" we mean one to four words. It is essential that the KBC be as short as possible because the creative team – or you as the creative person if you are doing it yourself – cannot brainstorm effectively from a complicated stimulus. To give some examples, the Key Benefit Claim from which to brainstorm might be worded as follows (the a's, b's and e's, parenthesized, are from the a-b-e benefit claim structure model introduced in Chapter 4):

- For the McDonald's brand, "sustenance" (an instinct, which is an $e^- \rightarrow b$ chain – we suggest this approach, but at present McDonald's is using the *emotional* benefit claim "I'm lovin' it," which is a transformational $b \rightarrow e^{++}$ chain[7])

- For the Nike brand, "The Hero" (an archetype, which is a schema-set of b's)

- For the sub-brand Volvo Cars, historically, "Safety," and more recently "Performance with safety" (the first is b focus and meets the problem-avoidance motive; the second has two b's which usually conflict and thus it meets the mixed approach-avoidance motive)

- For the sub-brand American Express Card, "Prestige" (this is b focus and addresses the social approval motive)

- For the sub-brand American Express Gold Card, "Quiet clout" (we have to admit that we have shortened this, as the actual key benefit claim used by the agency Ogilvy & Mather for brainstorming, but not in the ads, was President Truman's dictum, "Walk softly but carry a big stick"; both claims are $b \rightarrow e^{++}$ chains appealing to the intellectual stimulation and mastery motive)

- For Shell Optimax gasoline, "Better acceleration" (an $a \rightarrow b$ chain, where Optimax is a "magic ingredient" attribute, addressing the incomplete-satisfaction motive; Shell has used the magic ingredient approach in the past for its sub-brands, one long-running claim being "Shell X-100 – with platformate")

- For Wisk laundry detergent, "Enzymes remove tough stains" (an $a \rightarrow b$ chain, addressing the problem-removal motive)

- For Guinness Stout, "Refreshment worth waiting for" (b focus, addressing, by promising to overcome, the motive of incomplete satisfaction)

> The Key Benefit Claim must be agreed upon *first*. To do this, each member of the management team (who may also be the creative team if you are doing the creative in-house) should, individually, look at the Key Benefit in the brand's or brand-item's Positioning Statement and then write his or her nomination for the most persuasive statement of it – which must also be accurate and succinct (up to four words). Then, as a group, discuss the nominations and decide on the best statement for the KBC.

THE CREATIVE IDEA: THE REMOTE CONVEYER MODEL

The second component of an ad is The Creative Idea – which *dramatizes the key benefit claim*. To generate potential creative ideas, we use one of our theoretical frameworks, the Remote Conveyer Model. The **remote conveyer model**[8], which we will sometimes abbreviate as the **RC model**, works as shown in Figure 7.2. There are three elements: the Conveyer, the Product or Service

Representation, and the Key Benefit Prompt. As an example, look at the ad for Volkswagen brand cars in Figure 7.3. A *straight ad* would be just the *right-hand page* of this ad; it would include just the last two elements, the Product or Service Representation (the picture of the VW car) and the Key Benefit Prompt (the lower-placed headline, which is also the tagline). The picture of the car, an object that is quite conventional, would be processed in the right hemisphere of the brain.[9] The headline, and perhaps the car's license plate, would be processed in the left hemisphere. On the other hand, the *conveyer ad* is the whole *two pages*. The woman on the left-hand page, in this case with some explanatory "second headline" copy next to her, is the *Conveyer.*

A **conveyer** increases the effectiveness of an ad by starting in motion a sequence of four steps. (1) The Conveyer should be chosen and executed to be eye-catching and therefore increase *Attention* to the ad. (2) The Conveyer, because it is incongruous – remote in relation to the type of product or service that it advertises – should produce a state of *Curiosity* in the target customer's mind. A picture discrepancy, as in the Volkswagen ad, causes the right "vigilator" hemisphere of the brain to engage the left "comparator" hemisphere, the verbally specialized hemisphere, to interpret what's going on (more technically, to extract the semantic meaning of the whole scene). (3) To satisfy the curiosity, the brain is energized to *Search* the message for the Key Benefit, a search that is often aided by a Key Benefit Prompt. (4) A successful search provides *Resolution* by identifying the Key Benefit that is being conveyed and further provides a quick mental *reward*

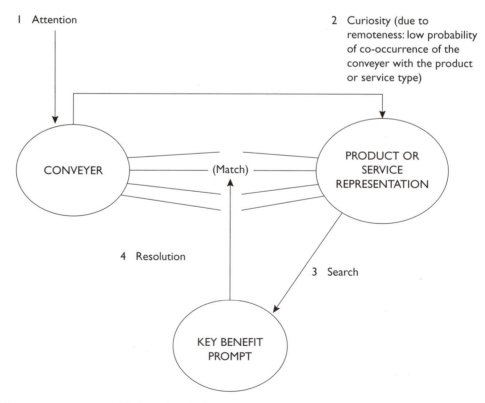

FIGURE 7.2 *The remote conveyer model. Steps 1 to 4 of conveyer processing are explained in the text.*

FIGURE 7.3 *Volkswagen car ad using conveyer (the girl in the bathing suit trying to reach a missed patch on her back).*

SOURCE: Supplied by Volkswagen Group Australia.

when resolution is achieved. In the VW ad, the Key Benefit Prompt is the tagline "If only everything in life was made like a Volkswagen" and the detailed copy on the left explains that each VW car has its body protected with over 90 square meters of paint, which protects not only against rust but also UV radiation, with none of the car's entire surface being missed. Now you understand the ad.

A *Conveyer Ad* thus gets the KBC across *indirectly* – purposefully indirectly – in contrast with the direct-to-the-KBC method of a Straight ad.

Properties of the conveyer

The Conveyer's remoteness alone can make the ad creative. But it also has to be *effective* – by persuasively communicating the key benefit. This is the fourth of five essential properties that an effective conveyer must have.

The five essential properties of an effective Conveyer are:

I. Attention-getting

The Conveyer increases customers' Attention by *reflexive* means – that is, it *elicits* an orienting response because it, the Conveyer, at first seems *out of context*. A Straight ad, in contrast, has to rely on customers' *selective* attention and this selective attention response will be made only by the few who have the Category Need right now!

2. Correctly labeled by the target customer

The Conveyer has to be *quickly and correctly identified* by the target customer – as the object, person, character, animal, situation or story, or product or user distortion that it is (see *conveyer types* below). Remote Conveyers that are too vague to be quickly identified will not work.

3. Perceived as remote

Remoteness refers to a *low probability of co-occurrence in the real world* and, it should be added, in the world of advertising, a world that encompasses fantasy and reality, between the Conveyer and the Product or Service advertised. Generally, the more remote, the better (as this will increase curiosity). However, there is an essential qualification regarding remoteness. If the Key Benefit Claim depends on *Visual Sensory Gratification* or on *Social Approval* (two of the positive-ending motives discussed previously), then the conveyer should be only *moderately* remote. Too much exaggeration in ads for food products (visual sensory gratification), for example, or for luxury or prestige products or services (social approval), will risk violating the fifth property below, through conflicting associations.

4. High association of the key benefit when prompted

The Key Benefit must be a *high associate* of, that is, an obvious attribute of, the Conveyer, at least when prompted. This is the most difficult property for the conveyer to achieve. It is quite easy to find a conveyer that is attention-getting, correctly labeled, and remote from the product or service. But the conveyer also must get the Key Benefit across – in a dramatic manner. Some Conveyers can be effective *without* the Key Benefit Prompt; it is immediately obvious, once the target customer thinks about it briefly, which Key Benefit is being conveyed. Some of Volvo's ads are good examples; one famous print ad that reportedly tracked very well in campaign evaluation research showed a drawing of a large, open safety pin shaped like a car with just the word "Volvo" as the copy (see Figure 7.4). Usually, however, a Key Benefit Prompt in the headline, slogan, tagline or copy will be necessary because the conveyer will tend to have multiple associations, so that the customer has to be guided to the correct one. This is especially the case for new products or new benefit positioning for an existing product and we note that the Volvo ad follows existing positioning for that brand. Anyway, even with the prompt, the Key Benefit must emerge as a *now-obvious high associate* of the Conveyer.

5. No high-incidence conflicting associations

A remote Conveyer usually elicits at least several associations, one of which may be a conflicting – negative or contradictory – association for at least *some* target customers. Toyota Camry Station Wagon, for instance, ran an infamous print ad in Australia to demonstrate its Key Benefit of "Wide-bodied" in which the Conveyer was a naked, pregnant woman who showed, obviously, a wide body. It was not until this ad was post-tested in campaign tracking that it was discovered that a substantial proportion of target customers could not envision how the pregnant woman could safely wear a seatbelt, a thought that interfered with thinking about the "wide-bodied" benefit, and some believed the nakedness was also exploitative. The client decided that the prevalence of conflicting associations was too high and stopped the campaign. The rule of thumb in the Conveyer Screening Test (see below) is that if the median rating on the "free of conflicting associations" property is below 2.5 the potential Conveyer should be dropped from further consideration. Many Conveyers in actual ad campaigns trip and fall, and thus fail, on this final property.

VOLVO

FIGURE 7.4 *Volvo's "safety pin" conveyer ad.*

SOURCE: Courtesy of Volvo Car Australia.

Conveyer types

Conveyers are metaphors – they dramatize the Key Benefit by likening the product or service to another object that has that benefit even more strongly. As with any metaphor, a Conveyer can be portrayed visually *or* stated in words. For instance, an ad for a sports watch could show a *picture of a dolphin* – a visual metaphor for its Key Benefit Claim of "Waterproof." Or the ad could state the same metaphor *verbally*: "Prio sportswatch is like a dolphin."[10] A **visual conveyer** should be used – for three reasons.[11] First, a verbal conveyer depends for its effectiveness on *visual imagery* from the meaning of the word(s), but a visual conveyer ensures that this imagery is accurate.[12] Second, in real-world advertising exposure conditions, visual conveyers are more effective than non-conveyer visuals, that is, the product or user visuals in a straight ad, probably due to their superior attention-getting capacity, whereas verbal conveyers seem to be more effective than non-conveyer verbals only in unrealistic forced-exposure experiments.[13] Finally, visual conveyers can be used internationally or even globally, whereas most verbal conveyers cannot. If you want to extend a visual conveyer to a non-visual medium – here we have in mind radio, but tele-marketing, where allowed, would also be such a medium – it is better to *verbally describe the visual conveyer* than to introduce a new verbal conveyer because an additional conveyer runs the risk of introducing a shift in the perceived Key Benefit Claim.

The Conveyer can be:

(a) *another object* that exaggeratedly possesses the key benefit

(b) an *animal* or *bird* that exaggeratedly possesses the key benefit

(c) a person or character who is an *expert user* of the product or service, an expert with regard to the key benefit

(d) a *situation*, which can be extended to a *story*[14] for a TV or radio campaign's creative idea, that dramatically demonstrates the key benefit

(e) a *benefit-illustrating distortion* of the product, or of the product or service user[15]

We deliberately put the Distortion classification, class (e), last because it should be brainstormed last, as a last resort. Benefit-Illustrating Distortions are not a true conveyer type because they do not involve a remote object as a metaphor and therefore do not produce the curiosity, search, and resolution steps. But they do increase Attention and can dramatize the Key Benefit (so they meet the definition of a *creative idea*). The Cole Haan women's shoes ad in Figure 7.5, from the agency Lloyd & Co. New York, is an example (in this case, of size distortion to show off the fine details of the shoe). This ad doesn't have the problem, but Distortions can too easily violate the fifth property of a conveyer, which is *freedom from conflicting associations*.

For a particular product or service item, one or more of these Conveyer types *might be ruled out from the start*. For instance, if the Brand of the item is already very well known, it may be decided that a famous person or character is not necessary. Conveyers used for *competing* brand-items also have to be taken into account. For instance, some companies already use animals in their advertising, such as Budweiser Beer, which uses talking frogs and lizards in its domestic U.S. campaign. Competitors in the same market would not normally use the same type of conveyer, although they may in other markets; for example, Löwenbrau Beer periodically uses a Lion symbol, from which its name is derived ("Löwe" is German for "lion"), in Europe, so Budweiser does not use animal symbols in Europe, or we've never seen Bud do so.

FIGURE 7.5 *Ad for Cole Haan women's shoes using size distortion.*

SOURCE: Photo courtesy of Cole Haan © 2004 Cole Haan. Cole Haan is a trademark of Cole Haan and is used with permission.

The best method is to conduct separate, but brief, brainstorming sessions on *each* of the Conveyer types that are judged *viable* for the brand.

We now describe the Conveyer Generation (brainstorming) procedure, called the I-G-I method, which includes Conveyer Screening and Selection.

Conveyer brainstorming (I-G-I method)

The best method of Conveyer Generation, or brainstorming, is the **individual-group-individual (I-G-I) method**.[16] This is conducted in the steps below.

(1) Select about four to six Individuals as brainstormers. The brainstormers do not have to be especially "creative" individuals. I-G-I brainstorming will work for any individual who is averagely fluent and flexible in thinking up associations. Studies of creativity have shown that typical professional creative people are no more "creative" than the typical business manager – the difference is that professional creatives have greater executional expertise.[17] Fluency and Flexibility of ideas are guaranteed by using multiple independent brainstormers. *Unusualness* – an essential component of creativity – is pretty much the result of the number (fluency) of different ideas (flexibility).[18]

(2) Provide the brainstormers with the *key benefit claim* – which must be an accurate and succinct statement. The individuals are then given five minutes to complete each brainstorming task, with a required *minimum* of three ideas to be suggested for each task. The tasks are to think of, respectively: (a) objects; (b) animals or birds; (c) people or characters who would be expert users; and (d) situations (dramatic stories for TV or radio commercials) that come rapidly to mind for the key benefit *claim*. Product or service distortions are not brainstormed until later, if at all, as a last resort or for fine-tuning of the attention-getting property. The process is thus:

Key benefit → Conveyer 1, Conveyer 2, Conveyer 3, etc.

This direction of associations is known as "typicality," in that you want to generate conveyers that *typify* the key benefit.[19]

(3) Write everyone's conveyer ideas in random order but not identified by individual, on a whiteboard, flip chart, or PC screen for the Group phase, of conveyer development.

(4) As a Group, the creative team now takes the opportunity to consider each idea – across all types together, hence the random order – and to improve it if it needs improving. Ideas that are redundant with an idea that has already been suggested are eliminated. The goal is to produce a reduced set of candidate ideas for screening and selection. Write the improved ideas down – this is the candidate list of conveyers.

Conveyer screening and selection

The Conveyer Screening and Selection procedure continues in the next steps.

(5) The judges Individually, not as a group, rate each conveyer idea as either "not remote," "moderately remote," or "very remote." If the purchase motivation underlying the Key Benefit is either *Visual Sensory Gratification* or *Social Approval*, you want only *moderate* remoteness for the conveyer. Other than these two cases, you want *very remote* conveyers. Tally the ratings. Apply a strict criterion of no more than one judge rating the idea as falling outside the relevant

rating category of remoteness. While strict, this criterion is practical in that you will still have many creative ideas retained for further consideration.

How many surviving creative ideas (conveyers) do you need? The answer to this important question depends on the probability of achieving a successful campaign in the category and on how confident the manager wants to be that there will be at least one successful idea among those generated, according to the **theory of random creativity**[20]. Here we will assume, not unreasonably, that the use of four or more brainstormers generating ideas independently has doubled the creative ability of the creative team and thus the number of ideas normally required is halved. Using the binomial theorem from the Theory of Random Creativity to calculate the probability of *failing* to observe a success in n tries, setting p (success) = .3 for the typical risky situation and confidence = 99%, we need to solve for n the expression $(1-.3)^n < (1-.99)$, or $(.7)^n < (.01)$. The value of n is 13, and halving this, rounding up, is *seven* ideas. Taking an easier, less risky situation, say for durables, with large market value, if p (success) = .5 and keeping confidence near certainty at 99%, we solve for n the expression $(1-.5)^n < (1-.99)$, or $(.5)^n < .01$. The value of n in this situation is 7, and halving this, rounding up, is *four ideas*.

If the number of surviving ideas, from step 6 below, is fewer than the number needed, you must repeat steps 1 to 5 until the number is attained.

(6) "Back-test" each of the four or more conveyer ideas for its strength in suggesting the key benefit claim. The question asked of the judges is to write down the first three things that the conveyer suggests (its spontaneous associates). The process is thus:

Conveyer 1 → associate 1, associate 2, associate 3, etc.

This direction of associations is known as "dominance," in that you want the key benefit to be a *dominant* associate of the conveyer.

The rule of thumb that we use is that a Close Paraphrase of the key benefit claim should be listed among the Top Three Associates by All But One judge.

The high-associate (dominance) test will always eliminate a large proportion of the creative ideas (the potential conveyers) and this is a tough – but essential – test to pass. If none of the conveyers passes, either repeat steps 1 to 6, that is, go through the whole procedure again, which is the best solution, or go to the last resort: individually brainstorm Distortions of the product or service representation that exaggerate the key benefit (e.g., a giant cereal box if size is the key benefit, or a highly delighted user of a service).

(7) Assuming you are going to use a *visual* conveyer, the surviving conveyers, which have been described only verbally until now, must be rendered into sketched drawings. The creative team member with the best artistic skills can do this but the drawings do not have to be highly professional – just easy to understand. Each Conveyer Drawing will be of an object, an animal, a famous person or character, a situation or several frames of a "storyboard" for a TV commercial (which would be described as a dramatic story for the radio commercial version, if radio ads are used).

To each drawing, add a *Product or Service Representation*. The representation can be a picture of the product, if it needs to be shown, a picture of the service in use, or simply the brand-item's word mark or visual brand mark. The Volvo ad, earlier, was a *brand* ad and used the Volvo word mark only, without a product picture.

Lastly, think up and add to the drawing the *Key Benefit Prompt* – in the form of a headline or tagline (or strapline in U.K. terminology) or as a single key benefit claim written as copy, that is, body copy or audio for broadcast ads. For over-learned brands, the brand name alone may serve as the Key Benefit Prompt (such as in the Volvo ad). For a new brand, however, the ad will need the Key Benefit Prompt spelled out. Its wording should be sufficient to make the Key Benefit clear and thus "resolve" the curiosity generated by the remote conveyer.[21] The verbal prompt must *complement* the conveyer picture. It must not be used to explain or otherwise correct the picture[22]; if you have to explain the picture, then you have made an inadequate drawing of it and will have to re-do it.

Now, and this is extra but necessary work, the team assists the artistic member of the team to produce a *second drawing* for each of the conveyers. The reason for this Second Drawing – a second *execution*, in effect – is that the conveyer must be "campaignable." The campaign should not use a conveyer that depends entirely for its effectiveness on one execution, no matter how brilliant the conveyer in the first execution. Don't say this to the team before they try, but it sometimes happens that a conveyer is a one-off, with restricted executional possibilities. If the team can't think of a good second execution, then cancel the conveyer. In general, you cannot count on one execution to carry the whole campaign, as the likelihood of wearout is too great.

(8) Now comes the final screening test that leads to conveyer *selection*. There are five properties that an effective conveyer must have and these are measured in a *Management Judgment Conveyer Screening Test*. We will label this the MJCST to distinguish it from another management judgment test, the MJAT, later. The MJCST uses as stimuli the rough ad executions, each of which has a Conveyer drawing, a branded Product or Service Representation, and the Key Benefit Prompt. The two executions of each conveyer are tested together.

The screening ratings must be done Individually by the judges, not as a group.

A three-point rating scale for each property of the conveyer is sufficient. The set of rating scales for the MJCST is provided in Table 7.2. Note the alternative scoring for the remoteness property when a *moderately* remote conveyer is sought, to give moderateness the highest score.

TABLE 7.2 *The management judgment conveyer screening test (MJCST) for rating the five essential properties of the conveyer.*

CONVEYER:	EXECUTION:		
PROPERTY	NO	MODERATELY	DEFINITELY
Attention-getting	1	2	3
Correctly labeled	1	2	3
Remote in relation to the product (*when seeking a moderate conveyer, scored 1–3–1*)	1	2	3
Key benefit conveyed	1	2	3
Free of conflicting associations	1	2	3

The criteria for selecting suitable conveyers are (a) a median rating, across judges, of at least 2.5 on all five properties and (b) both executions must pass. In the case of an execution that achieves a very close median score on one or maybe two properties, it is fair to allow one attempt to improve the conveyer to a passing score. The execution should be returned to all judges for them to try this independently, then re-rated.

The goal is to identify *at least two conveyers*, each represented by *two executions*. You need the second conveyer ready to substitute in the campaign if the first one does not meet its goals in campaign tracking, for whatever reason.

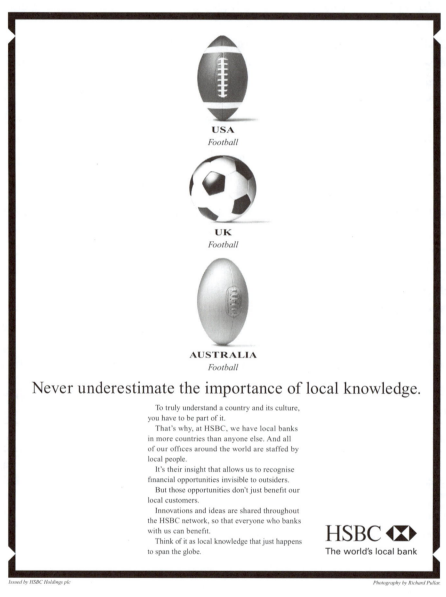

FIGURE 7.6 *HSBC Bank ad using the "football" conveyer, which appeared in the global business magazine,* The Economist.

SOURCE: Courtesy of HSBC. Photography by Richard Pullar.

FIGURE 7.7 *Another execution of the same creative idea and key benefit claim for HSBC Bank, this time using the "protection" conveyer, which appeared in* Forbes *magazine.*

SOURCE: Courtesy of HSBC. Photography by Richard Pullar.

Here are a couple of examples of ad campaigns that use a Conveyer. The first example (on page 140) is a business magazine ad for the fast-expanding global bank, HSBC, in Figure 7.6. The "Football" conveyer nicely dramatizes HSBC's key benefit represented by its tagline: "The world's local bank." This was probably the four-word key benefit claim used initially to brainstorm the conveyer. Is this creative idea "campaignable" into several executions? A second execution, "Protection," is shown in Figure 7.7.

The second example of a conveyer ad is much more subtle – bordering on an Instinctual Selling Proposition, or ISP (see Chapter 3). Look carefully at the magazine ad for Coke in its "contour" bottle in Figure 7.8. The conveyer appears to be a female torso with the navel (belly button) as the focal point and above it a vague image of ribs and the underside of the breast. This conveyer would probably not rate well on "correctly labeled" but that is probably deliberate by the art director. It is probably just moderately remote but even if regarded as very remote, that is okay for a sensory-gratification product (the bottle, not the drink) that is not primarily visual (it is Tactile Sensory Gratification). It surely conveys the key benefit, "sensuality" well. And for the younger target audience at least, there would be no conflicting associations. Not exactly "Classic," but well done, Coke!

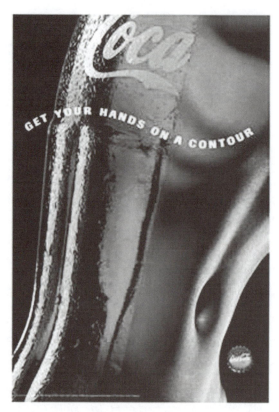

FIGURE 7.8 *A subtle conveyer is employed in this ad for Coke in its "contour" bottle. This ad appeared in British Airways' flight magazine reaching an international audience. And it's an ISP (see text).*

SOURCE: Trade marks of The Coca-Cola Company are used with permission. The Coca-Cola Company is not the producer of this guide, nor does it endorse the contents.

What about the ad agency's creative ideas?

In presenting the Remote Conveyer Model, the RC Model, we have assumed that you – the management team – are going to come up with the creative idea, and also the reserve creative idea, for the campaign. As we commented before, you can be just as creative as the agency's creatives team, so why not? Also, small businesses who prepare the creative in-house, as well as business-student teams doing a marcoms campaign project, need a model and procedure like ours, because brainstorming effective creative ideas is too difficult otherwise.

However, what if you decide to stay with the usual practice of requesting creative ideas, in the form of rough ads, from professionals – from your advertising agency? Well, 99 times out of 100, what the agency will come up with is one or more Conveyers! Peruse any advertising trade magazine or advertising industry Website and look at the award-winning campaigns. We will bet you that they all use a Conveyer, and nearly always a Visual Conveyer.[23] Therefore, if you want to rely on your agency – and they *do* have the advantage of professional executional expertise – then fine. And despite our firm belief backed by many case histories now that any team of individuals can use the RC Model to generate a terrific ad, we don't really expect to change the almost magical faith that marketing managers (and CEOs) have in advertising agencies. Most of their campaigns are *not* successful; as we have seen, only 20% to 30%, depending on the country, produce a clearly profitable return, assuming that the media plan is adequate. But it's those giant successes that occur occasionally that reinforce the faith (in learning-theory terminology, this is partial or intermittent reinforcement, which makes the response very resistant to extinction). But very important: ask to see "n" ideas (from the binomial formula earlier) and run the agency's creative ideas through the five-properties Conveyer Screening Test (the MJCST). The agency's ideas are no less subject to random creativity – and to having to meet the conveyer properties – than yours would be.

We also comment that advertising agencies' proprietary in-house procedures for generating creative ideas, when such procedures are formally applied, usually resemble the RC Model's procedure. Although it is a matter of professional pride for creatives not to admit that they use any sort of "structured" procedure, we know first-hand of several agencies who acknowledge that, in its essential details, they use the RC procedure. And they should. Applied with the random creativity number, success is virtually assured.

POSTMODERNISM AS THE CREATIVE IDEA

Postmodern creative is a recent and growing trend in advertising. We define a **Postmodern ad** as an ad whose script or style of presentation departs radically from the "ad schema" that is conventional for ads in that product or service category.[24] Postmodern ads do not use product attribute metaphors and thus they are not Conveyer ads.[25] Although Conveyer ads contain unconventional content via the incongruity or remoteness of the Conveyer from the Product, they nevertheless follow a well-accepted script (broadcast ads) or format (print ads). Postmodern ads either don't follow the script or format (e.g., Hewlett Packard's recent print campaign) or else they invoke the script in an obviously tongue-in-cheek style as if to say "this is what you usually get" (e.g., the Pepsi Max launch campaign of about 10 years ago that used somewhat "dorky" and laid-back presenters rather than the usual attractive, enthusiastic, 20-something presenters). Therefore what some might regard as the first famous Postmodern ad, Apple Macintosh's "1984" TV commercial that was shown only once in the U.S. telecast of the January 1984 Superbowl football match, we would not classify as Postmodern because it was clearly a TV commercial by its script;

it merely – though very effectively – used a remote conveyer in which a world populated by drones, implicitly symbolizing users of IBM computers, was freed by a young woman who symbolized the Macintosh computer. (A 20-years-later, 2004, update of this commercial, now featuring Apple iPod, can be viewed at AdAge.com, Qwikfind AAP26U.) Instead, we would regard the Nike Shox TV commercial by Wieden & Kennedy, U.K., which appeared early in 2003, as the first indisputably Postmodern TV commercial (see the excerpts in Figure 7.9). This commercial employs a schema (script) departure. In what appears to be an interruption to an ongoing football game, a male streaker is caught live on camera, with ad-libbed comments by the football commentators while he is chased by police. When he's captured, the streaker is shown to be wearing only a scarf and a pair of running shoes, which the ending super (on-screen writing) identifies to be Nike Shox.

A further recent example is the Australian campaign created by Clemenger BBDO Sydney in 2003 for Canadian Club & Cola, a pre-mixed rye whiskey drink, which, like the campaign for Pepsi Max much earlier, spoofed the "macho young guys" stereotype often used in beverage ads (this was a multi-media campaign – one of its outdoor ads is shown in Figure 7.10). This campaign resulted in a sales increase of 156% over six months among the 18 to 24 year-old male target market.[26]

Two of the top 10 overall creativity award-show winners for 2004 based on results tallied just before our book was published were strikingly Postmodern and many readers will remember them: Sony PlayStation's "People Mountain" TV commercial for its PS2 game, by the agency

FIGURE 7.9 *Excerpts from the Nike Shox postmodern "Streaker" TV commercial.*

SOURCE: Courtesy of Nike Australia.

FIGURE 7.10 *Outdoor ad from the postmodern campaign for Canadian Club & Cola in Australia.*

SOURCE: Courtesy of Allied Domecq Spirits and Wines (Aust.) Pty Ltd.

TWBA, London, and Honda Motor Co.'s "Cog" TV commercial for its Honda Accord car, by, again, Wieden & Kennedy, U.K.[27]

Postmodern *print* ads break the expected schema by placing *unexpected* content in the *whole* ad (we have called this "format" for want of a better term). For example, a recent magazine ad for Diesel casualwear, created by the agency Kesselkramer, Amsterdam, shows a young woman sprawled on a crosswalk (wearing Diesel gear) with the shadow of a pigeon that is approaching from above. The tagline is "Acid pigs fly over me." Not a usual picture or headline for a fashion clothing ad! The Key Benefit Claim is implicit but clear: "Supercool streetwear."

It is reasonable to expect that Postmodern *ads* will work best among Postmodern *consumers*, which approximately refers to those in the age group 18 to 34, or so-called Generation Y (18–23) and Generation X (24–34) consumers.[28] Eighteen year-olds are old enough to have developed a keen sense of "advertising literacy."[29] Through this age range, the Postmodern consumer is held to be skeptical about conventional advertising and possibly more receptive to "different" approaches.[30] A major caution, however, is that if *younger* consumers, under age 18, are in your target audience, they may not understand the ad; nor may *older* consumers, over age 35, who are presumably less advertising literate or at least less tolerant of the "alliteracy" that Postmodern ads employ. For these younger and older age groups, it is essential that the stories in the ad "hang together."[31] However, if the target audience for the brand is mostly within the media target age group of 18 to 34, Postmodernism as the Creative Idea is definitely worth a try among this reputedly hard-to-reach and hard-to-persuade age group.

Postmodern ads allegedly work with this age group because they slip through the defensive guard that young adults use to screen out conventional ads. However, although this remains to be tested, we suspect they work primarily because the Parody in a Postmodern ad (e.g., hyperhard sell or offbeat humor) makes the audience think of its *opposite*, so that the postmodern consumer actually *rehearses the Key Benefit Claim.*

SUMMARY

High-quality Creative (the ads or promotion offers) is the most important ingredient for a successful marcoms campaign.

Creative strategy proceeds from a Creative Brief and we provide a suggested format for this vital document. The Creative Brief summarizes research and decisions made previously and has five sections: (1) Behavioral Sequence Model, (2) Action Objective, (3) Communication Objectives, (4) Positioning Statement for the campaign, and (5) Mandatory content elements, if any. The Creative Brief should be no more than two pages.

The creative strategy itself has to be approached by considering the "deep structure" components of an ad. These components are there but they are not always obvious on the surface. Careful analysis will reveal, however, that even the simplest ad is a deeply complex piece of communication. The four components are the Key Benefit Claim, the Creative Idea, Brand Awareness and Brand Preference tactics, and Attention tactics. This chapter has covered the Key Benefit Claim and the Creative Idea – how to generate and select both.

The Key Benefit Claim is the stimulus from which potential Creative Ideas are brainstormed. In order for it to be used as a brainstorming cue, the Key Benefit Claim *must be stated in words*, even if an Instinctual, Archetypal, Emotional or Rational selling proposition is sought. The Key Benefit Claim must be *accurate*, *persuasively sufficient*, and *succinct*. Several alternative wordings should be examined and one should be agreed on by the management team.

In our theory of effective creativity, Creative Ideas are either Conveyers or, for the 18 to 34 age group, Postmodern-scripted or Postmodern-formatted ads, which do *not* use a Conveyer. For this age group, Postmodernism is worth a try because the group is hard to reach and cynical about ads. In all other cases, the ad should use a Conveyer. The Conveyer functions according to the Remote Conveyer Model (the RC Model). The RC Model's procedure requires Individual brainstorming to generate potential Conveyers, followed by Group improvement of the unique ones, and Individual screening judgments to select the candidate set of Conveyers. The whole procedure, described in the chapter, is called the I-G-I method of brainstorming. An effective Conveyer must have *five properties*: Attention-getting, Correctly labeled, Remote (or moderately remote if the brand or brand-item's purchase motive is based on Visual Sensory Gratification or Social Approval), Key-benefit association, and be Free of Conflicting associations. These properties are evaluated in the Management Judgment Conveyer Screening Test (the MJCST). Calculations from another of our models, the Theory of Random Creativity, indicate that you will need between four and seven candidate Conveyers to go into this Conveyer-properties test, with two rough executions of each. You want the two executions of *two* Conveyers to survive this test, in case replacement of the first choice is necessary during the campaign.

If creative ideas are sought from an advertising agency, insist on a number of ideas being presented equal to the estimated binomial theorem number, and put each of the ideas through the MJCST of conveyer properties.

We now move on to the other two components of an ad – Brand Awareness and Brand Preference tactics, and Attention tactics – in the following two chapters.

DISCUSSION QUESTIONS

7.1   Coke, the brand-item, has employed many different Key Benefit Claims over its more than 100-year history and sometimes returns to very early ones (e.g., "Enjoy," "Refreshing," and more recently "Real"). For each of Coke's Key Benefit Claims below, write a brief analysis of what the claim appears to be attempting in terms of the I-D-U model of benefit positioning (review it in Chapter 4): (a) "The real thing"; (b) "A Coke and a smile"; (c) "Coke is it"; (d) "Always"; (e) "Life tastes good"; and (f) which of the foregoing would best counteract Pepsi's new (January '04) slogan, "Pepsi – it's *the* Cola"?

7.2   The Key Benefit Claim is very difficult, and very important, to get right – why?

7.3   A Presenter (see next chapter for more details) is a type of Conveyer. In terms of the five conveyer properties, evaluate (a) Nicole Kidman as a presenter for Chanel fragrances and (b) the typical real-person presenter shown in ads for "wonder diet" plans. Note that you will have to *infer* the key benefit, if not the key benefit claim, in both cases.

7.4   Find two examples of ads for the same category of Social Approval (e.g., prestige) products, one that employs a *very remote* Conveyer and another that employs a *moderately remote* Conveyer. Which degree of remoteness is most suitable and why?

7.5   An alternative to a Conveyer as the creative idea is Postmodern scripting (broadcast ads) or formatting (print ads). For whom are Postmodern ads likely to be most effective and why? Look through some magazines targeted at the "whom" and find two Postmodern print ads to use as examples in your answer.

7.6   The hypothesis that successful Creative Ideas are the result of a random process does not sit well with creatives at ad agencies. Therefore, write a convincing explanation of why they, and the client, will be better off to use the random creativity number from the binomial theorem as the target number of creative ideas to be generated.

7.7   Discuss several situations in which a Straight ad might be more effective than a Conveyer ad. That is, when might a conveyer be a risky distraction or possibly lead to a negative evaluation of the product? How can you avoid these problems? Of course, one could always argue that the creative idea is, in fact, to "go straight," which would actually be Postmodern if most other ads in the category are "far out."

NOTES

1. Research evidence that "creative" ads work better than "straight" ads is relatively recent. Creative award-winning TV commercials have a much higher success rate in increasing sales (about 86.5% of winners increase sales) than TV commercials in general (about 50%); see the careful survey by D. Gunn, reported in J Aitcheson, *Cutting Edge Commercials*, Singapore: Prentice Hall, 2001, pp. 448–451.

2. Briefs without a key benefit claim are far more prevalent than we have let on here. The prevalence of cases of agencies selecting not only the key benefit claim but also the key benefit, and thus superseding the I-D-U analysis, is very high – we estimate that at least 50% of campaigns are created this way. For instance, in their otherwise very useful book, Morrison, Haley, Sheehan and Taylor *recommend* that the key benefit claim be decided by the agency's account planner. We think the management team – the client – should decide it.

See M.A. Morrison, E. Haley, K.B. Sheehan, and R.E. Taylor, *Using Qualitative Research in Advertising*, Thousand Oaks, CA: Sage, 2002, chapter 7.

3. In view of the pivotal influence exerted by the creative brief, it is surprising how little agreement there is in the advertising literature and in the advertising world about its form and especially its content. Most commentators emphasize that it must be brief but then recommend content that is inadequately brief or else so much content that it can't be brief. All briefs have the problem of jargon. We recommend a brief here that uses our clearly defined terms, fits our approach, and includes only the essentials.

4. In Australia, the main reason currently given for a client to change its advertising agency, is that "the agency's strategic planning is not adequate"; this reveals a scandalous lack of effort by Australian marketers, in our opinion. The reason that "the advertising is not creative enough," which is the only *good* reason to change, has dropped to number five in importance. See *Ad News*, January 16, 2004, p. 20.

5. A popular but typically vague other name for the key benefit claim, associated with the emergence of agency account planners in the U.K. and now everywhere, is the "key consumer insight." See, for instance, M.A. Morrison, *et al.*, same reference as in note 2. But an "insight" could refer to anything. We define what the insight has to be: the key benefit claim.

6. We first isolated this question in the 1997 Rossiter and Percy book. It was worded more colloquially as "How're ya gonna persuade 'em?" (p. 180) and for that reason its importance may not have been fully appreciated. However, there it was posed as the question that has to be answered by the creative idea (the conveyer), whereas now we realize that applies directly to the key benefit claim (a concept that was not explicitly identified in R&P). "How are we going to persuade them?" is the meaningful question that the creatives ask *themselves* when they receive a brief. Here, we ask management to answer that question.

7. "I'm lovin' it" was predicted by noted U.S. advertising critic Bob Garfield to be a monumental flop for McDonald's. We disagreed, arguing that "I'm lovin' it" would prove to be a clever way of "positivizing" the product lines of more nutritious menu items that McDonald's has introduced, such as diet platters and salads, which are not items that people usually love to eat. See R. Garfield, Ad Review: I'm loathin' it, *Advertising Age*, September 8, 2003, pp. 1, 95. We were right: McDonald's restaurants have reported double-digit sales gains since the "I'm lovin' it" campaign began, and half the sales gains are due to the new low-fat items. See K. MacArthur, Fast-feeders ditch buns to lure dieters, *Advertising Age*, January 12, 2004, pp. 3, 39; K. MacArthur, Rivals not lovin' McD's comeback, *Advertising Age*, July 26, 2004, pp. 1, 28.

8. The Remote Conveyer Model, previously called the RAM-Conveyor Model, has its origin in the theory of visual persuasion in advertising due to the brilliant German marketing professor and consultant Werner Kroeber-Riel (1933–1993). This was as a result of several invited visits that the first author, Rossiter, made during the period 1985–1993 to Kroeber-Riel's Institute for Consumer and Behavioral Research at the University of the Saarland. Further contributions were made by Lawrence Ang, then my doctoral student at the Australian Graduate School of Management; Frank Winter, in translating key principles of Kroeber-Riel's work from the German; and discussions with Franz-Rudolph Esch, then Kroeber-Riel's doctoral student, and Tobias Langner, later Esch's doctoral student. See J.R. Rossiter, The RAM-Conveyor theory of creative strengtheners in ads, in Forschungsgruppe Konsum und Verhalten, *Konsumentenforschung*, Munich: Vahlen, 1994, pp. 119–138, and J.R. Rossiter and L. Percy, *Advertising Communications & Promotion Management*, New York: McGraw-Hill, chapter 7.

9. D. Zaidel, Different organization of concepts and meaning systems in the two cerebral hemispheres, *The Psychology of Learning and Motivation*, 2001, 40(1), pp. 1–21. We thank Max Sutherland for bringing Zaidel's work to our attention; the descriptions of the right hemisphere as the "vigilator" and the left hemisphere as the "comparator" are his.

10. This verbal conveyer is from an experiment by Hitchon and Churchill, in which it was found that verbal conveyers produced greater brand preference than a basic non-conveyer claim, in this example "Prio Sportswatch is waterproof." They further showed that conveyers do *not* depend on valence or "affect transfer," because the metaphor "Prio sportswatch is a shark" worked just as well as the dolphin. See J.C. Hitchon and G.A. Churchill, To be or what to be: an empirical investigation of metaphor's persuasive effects in advertising communications, working paper, School of Journalism and Mass Communication, University of Wisconsin, 1992.

11. Also see the extremely insightful article which appeared at the same time as Kroeber-Riel's and Rossiter's early work on conveyers and was apparently independent although it uses as an example one of Kroeber-Riel's

conveyers (for Volksbanken Raiffeisenbanken) by A.L. Biel and J. Lannon, Steel bullet in a velvet glove? Harnessing "visual metaphor" in brand building, *Admap*, 1993, April, pp. 15–18.

12. M. Marschark and R.R. Hunt, On memory for metaphor, *Memory & Cognition*, 1985, 13(5), pp. 413–424. Technically, a visual conveyer does not actually require imagery, in the sense of a self-generated visual image, as to a concrete word, because it *is* the iconic image. See especially J.R. Rossiter and L. Percy, Visual communication in advertising, in R.J. Harris (Ed.), *Information Processing Research in Advertising*, Hillsdale, NJ: Erlbaum, 1983, chapter 4, and more directly S.M. Kosslyn and W.L. Thompson, When is early visual cortex activated during visual mental imagery?, *Psychological Bulletin*, 2003, 129(5), pp. 723–746.

13. E.F. McQuarrie and D.G. Mick, Visual and verbal rhetorical figures under directed processing versus incidental exposure, *Journal of Consumer Research*, 2003, 29(4), pp. 579–587.

14. The story should be a "classic drama" (character or characters with a problem, which gets resolved at the end, in an engaging but easy-to-follow story line) rather than a slice-of-life "vignette" (someone doing or using something). See W. Wells, Lectures and dramas, in P. Cafferata and A. Tybout (Eds), *Cognitive and Affective Responses to Advertising*, Lexington, MA: Lexington Books, 1989, pp. 13–20; and J.E. Escalas and B.B. Stern, Sympathy and empathy; emotional responses to advertising dramas, *Journal of Consumer Research*, 2003, 29(4), pp. 566–579.

15. J.R. Rossiter, T. Langner, and L. Ang, Visual creativity in advertising: a functional typology, Australian and New Zealand Marketing Academy (ANZMAC) Conference Proceedings, 2003, electronic document.

16. J.R. Rossiter and G. Lilien, New "brainstorming" principles, *Australian Journal of Management*, 1994, 19(1), pp. 61–72.

17. R. Houland, G.B. Wilcox, and T. Hoffman, An exploratory study identifying characteristics of advertising creatives: the creative quotient test, in J.D. Leckenby (Ed.), *American Academic of Advertising Proceedings*, 1988, RC-142 to RC-143.

18. The joint criteria for an idea to be regarded as "creative" are that it is *unusual* and *useful*. Note "unusual" not "original" as it may not be original! The "usefulness" criterion is represented in the RC Model by Conveyer requirement number 4 – *key benefit conveyed*.

19. The distinction between typicality and, later in the procedure, dominance was proposed by P.H. Farquar, P.M. Herr, and R.H. Fazio, in M.E. Goldberg, G. Gorn, and R.W. Pollay (Eds), A relational model for category extension of brands, *Advances in Consumer Research*, 1990, 17, pp. 856–860.

20. This is a simplified account of the Theory of Random Creativity originated by I. Gross, The creative aspects of advertising, *Sloan Management Review*, 1972, 14(1), pp. 83–109, and developed by J.R. Rossiter and P. Saintilan, Advertising agencies' attitudes toward competing for creative assignments, *Australian Journal of Market Research*, 1993, 1(1), pp. 15–17. See also B.G. Van den Bergh, L.N. Reid, and G.A. Schorin, How many creative alternatives to generate?, *Journal of Advertising*, 1983, 12(4), pp. 46–49, and G.C. O'Connor, T.R. Willemain, and J. MacLachlan, The value of competition among agencies in developing ad campaigns: revisiting Gross's model, *Journal of Advertising*, 1996, 25(1), pp. 51–62.

21. B.J. Phillips, The impact of verbal anchoring on consumer response to image ads, *Journal of Advertising*, 2000, 29(1), pp. 15–24.

22. W. Kroeber-Riel, *Bildkommunikation*, Munich: Vahlen, 1993.

23. See the theoretical analysis of creative ideas in J. Goldenberg and D. Mazursky, *Creativity in Product Innovation*, Cambridge, U.K.: Cambridge University Press, 2002.

24. For the concept of an ad schema, see J.R. Rossiter and S. Bellman, A proposed model for explaining and measuring Web ad effectiveness, *Journal of Current Issues and Research in Advertising*, 1999, 21(1), pp. 13–31. According to one definition, postmodern ads (a) hint at the benefit rather than stating it, (b) often lack a clear story line, (c) often borrow content from other well-known "texts," such as the stereotyped text of *modern* ads, and (d) often have a feminist, or non-macho, slant; see S. Proctor, T. Proctor, and I. Papasolomou-Doukakis, A post-modern perspective on advertisements and their analysis, *Journal of Marketing Communications*, 2002, 8(1), pp. 31–44.

25. This criterion rules out several studies that have been conducted using incongruent pictures in ads, most of which depict an *irrelevant* attribute or benefit. Postmodern ads always depict a *relevant* benefit, even though it may be difficult to detect at first. We thus dismissed from consideration otherwise interesting studies by Houston,

Childers, and Heckler (1987), Heckler and Childers (1992), Goodstein (1993), Lee and Mason (1999), and Arias-Bolzmann, Chakraborty, and Mowen (2000); we don't provide the references for these as we think they are not helpful, but academics in advertising will know them. The only study that we could find that clearly manipulates postmodernism was by T.F. Stafford and M.R. Stafford, The advantages of atypical advertisements for stereotyped product categories, *Journal of Current Issues and Research in Advertising*, 2002, 24(1), pp. 25–37. This study found a small and not very impressive advantage on brand attitude for postmodern versus conventional ads for car dealers. Unfortunately, the experiment was confounded in that the benefits differed between the postmodern and the conventional commercials and also the age group of the sample, average age 34, was older than the age group for which we expect postmodern ads to be most effective.

26. Creative awards data compiled by *Creativity* magazine and reported in B. Garfield, Award winners' edge: that's entertainment, *Advertising Age*, August 9, 2004, pp. 16–17.

27. A. Sophocleous, Case study: Canadian Club, *Ad News*, March 24, 2000, p. 28.

28. S.M. Noble and C.D. Schewe, Cohort segmentation: an exploration of its validity, *Journal of Business Research*, 2003, 56(12) pp. 979–987. Researchers should use qualitative methodology to examine generation or cohort differences in information processing and priority of values, which are undoubtedly valid differences; see the chilling discussion of false conclusions emerging from quantitative research across age groups by N. Schwarz, Self-reports in consumer research: the challenge of comparing cohorts and cultures, *Journal of Consumer Research*, 2003, 29(4), pp. 588–594.

29. E.F. McQuarrie and D.G. Mick, Visual rhetoric in advertising: text-interpretative, experimental, and reader-response analyses, *Journal of Consumer Research*, 1999, 26(1), pp. 37–54.

30. A.F. Firat and C.J. Schultz, Preliminary metric investigations into the nature of the "postmodern" consumer, *Marketing Letters*, 2001, 12(2), pp. 189–203.

31. A.J. Kover, S.M. Goldberg, and W.L. James, Creativity vs. effectiveness? An integrating classification for advertising, *Journal of Advertising Research*, 1995, 35(6), pp. 29–40.

CHAPTER 8

Brand awareness and brand preference (grid) tactics

With the Key Benefit Claim and Creative Idea decided, we now move on to the third component of an ad: Brand Awareness tactics and Brand Preference tactics. To organize these tactics, we introduce the Rossiter-Percy-Bellman Grid.

ROSSITER-PERCY-BELLMAN GRID

Brand Awareness and Brand Preference *tactics* differ based on where the brand or brand-item (not the product or service category as a whole) is located in the **Rossiter-Percy-Bellman grid**.[1] The grid is a six-cell grid, consisting of *two* types of Brand Awareness and *four* types of Brand Preference, as shown in Figure 8.1.

The Rossiter-Percy-Bellman Grid focuses on the mental state, for purchase of *Our* brand or brand-item, of the *Target Audience* for whom the marcoms campaign is intended. This means that *other* brands or brand-items, or *other* people who are not in the target audience for the campaign, might be located elsewhere in the grid.

Based on research (qualitative research for the BSM will do), the manager has to locate our brand or brand-item in one of the two brand-awareness boxes *and* in one of the four brand-preference boxes. (There are therefore $2 \times 4 = 8$ possible locations for a brand or brand-item in the total grid.)

At the head of the grid, the campaign for the brand or brand-item will have either Brand Recognition or Brand Recall as the brand awareness objective (see Chapter 6). In the rare case of Brand-Recall-Boosted Brand Recognition, we also provide a set of combined tactics.

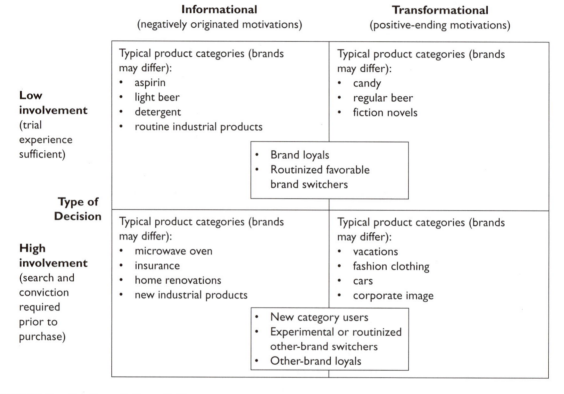

FIGURE 8.1 *Rossiter-Percy-Bellman Grid.*

In the body of the grid, the Brand Preference typology has two dimensions: type of decision (Low Involvement or High Involvement) and type of purchase motive (Informational or Transformational). The decision by the target audience customer to purchase *our* brand or brand-item on the *next* purchase occasion is classified as **low involvement** if only a small economic or psychosocial loss is at stake should the customer make a poor choice. In other words, the target customer is quite willing to pay his or her money to find out what the brand or brand-item is like and, indeed, may already know what it is like. The classification of Low Involvement depends not only on the type of product or service but also on the target group. In general, people who have bought our brand or brand-item before and are satisfied with it – (our) Brand Loyals and

Favorable Brand Switchers – will be making a low-risk decision to buy it again. On the other hand, for those people who have not bought our brand or brand-item before or not bought in the category for a long time, and especially those who have previously been loyal to another brand or brand-item, the decision is classified as **high involvement**. (You have to determine this from research with Target Group Customers and, in marginal or split cases, the correct classification is to be conservative and assume a *high*-involvement choice.) The second dimension of Brand Preference typology is the type of purchase motive, which can be either **informational** (negatively originated) or **transformational** (positive-ending). This distinction of motives was explained in Chapter 6 in conjunction with category motives, which also apply at the brand or brand-item level. "Informational" and "Transformational" actually refer to the marcoms *messages* that correspond with negatively originated and positive-ending motives, respectively. This is based on which of the two types of motive the *Key Benefit Claim* for the brand or brand-item is tapping into. Whereas Rossiter and Percy[2] previously stated that the conservative decision in split cases is to assume an Informational motive, extensive use of the grid in actual campaigns has now convinced us that this decision cannot be split and that the major motive type *for the Key Benefit* must be correctly identified in advance (the a-b-e chain employed for the Key Benefit Claim will reveal this). The most usual difficulty occurs in the High-Involvement/Transformational cell of brand preference, as these types of products and services often have to provide *Informational* benefits to "close the sale." We have anticipated this in the brand preference tactics for that cell.

In the following sections of the chapter, we explain the Brand Awareness tactics and the Brand Preference tactics. It will help if you keep this organizing image handy or in mind when reviewing the tactics:

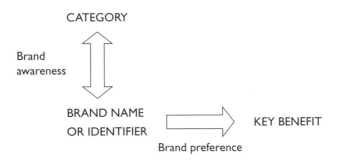

BRAND AWARENESS TACTICS

Brand recognition

The creative tactics for Brand Recognition are listed in Table 8.1.

Realism curved
The first tactic for Brand Recognition (BRGN) comes from the important study of *visual* brand logos – also called the *brand mark* – by Henderson and Cote[3], in which they identified properties that promote high recognizability and uniqueness (potential new logos or modifications to an

TABLE 8.1 *Advertising tactics for brand recognition.*

BRGN-1	Use a logo or pack shot that is realistic (represents a real object), has some natural curvature in it, is highly but not perfectly symmetrical and balanced, and has some internal repetition – and features a distinctive color
BRGN-2	Ensure sufficient exposure of the logo or pack-shot, and the brand-item name, in the ad (and hold for at least two seconds in a broadcast commercial)
BRGN-3	The category need should be mentioned or portrayed (unless it's immediately obvious)

existing logo can easily be rated by a sample of about 30 judges in accordance with these properties). The same properties apply to pack shots – a photo or drawing of the product used for packaged goods where the customer cannot otherwise see the contents and where the appeal of the contents is an important part of the brand-item's appeal, such as food products and products of all types that are sold in kits for assembly by the buyer. **Realism curved** is a summary label for visuals that (1) are *realistic*, that is, they depict a namable everyday object (although this affects Brand Preference rather than Brand Recognition, the object, if a logo, should be a *Conveyer* for the brand's Key Benefit – e.g., Merrill Lynch's bull, Travelers Insurance's umbrella[4]); (2) have *some natural curvature* (what Henderson and Cote call "organic"); (3) are *highly* – but not perfectly – *symmetrical and balanced,* and (4) contain *some internal repetition.* It seems that logos and – note – pack shots must have at least three of the four properties to produce high recognition (without spending millions of dollars to establish them). Figure 8.2 shows some prospective logos rated on these properties. Though we can't show this, it really helps to (5) feature a distinctive *color.*

The two most widely known Brand Marks globally are undoubtedly McDonald's "Golden Arches" and Nike's "Swoosh." The "Golden Arches" logo fits three of the four properties (it is too perfectly balanced). The "Swoosh" logo fits only one of the high-recognition properties – natural curvature (it is not a real object, is not high in symmetry and balance, and has only quasi-repetition in that the top line of the "Swoosh" partly repeats the bottom line). Brand Marks that are not intrinsically high recognition can only be made recognizable with a great deal of media spend, which was certainly the case with McDonald's and Nike. In many Nike ads the "Swoosh" is used without the word mark of the brand name, Nike. Reebok, trailing Nike's 35% market share of the sports footwear and apparel market with 18% share, now wants the same and is spending an estimated U.S.$50 million on a global advertising campaign to promote its "Vector" brand mark.[5]

Exposure two seconds

The second Brand Recognition tactic is to expose the Brand Identity for long enough (for two seconds at least in TV commercials or repeat it in total for two seconds in radio commercials if auditory brand recognition is the objective) and make sure it is clear to see (all visual media). Brand Recognition requires *visual iconic learning*[6] or *auditory echoic learning*, and each is a function of exposure time.[7] The critical minimum time for focusing on a new visual stimulus so that it will be recognized later is about two seconds. The creative team usually does not like to "waste time"

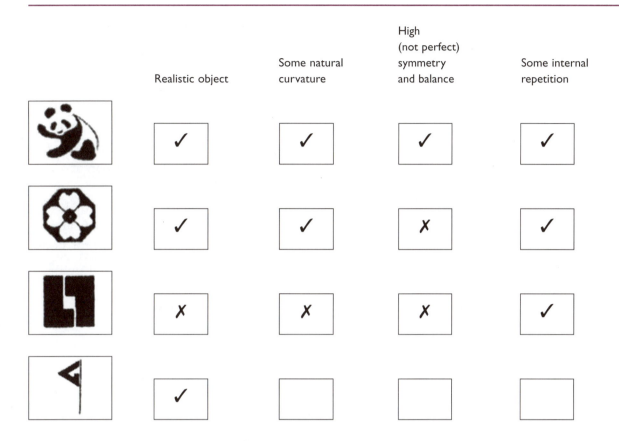

	Realistic object	Some natural curvature	High (not perfect) symmetry and balance	Some internal repetition
🐼	✓	✓	✓	✓
❀	✓	✓	✗	✓
⊔	✗	✗	✗	✓
⚑	✓			

FIGURE 8.2 *Hypothetical visual logos (or brand marks) that do or do not have the Henderson and Cote properties for high recognizability and uniqueness. High-recognition and unique logos should have at least three of the four properties.*

SOURCE: Based on P.H. Henderson and J.A. Cote, 1998, reference in note 3.

on pack shots or logos – but, if Brand Recognition is the objective, they must be instructed to do so. Visual brand recognition of the pack or logo must be taught via the ad. Consider a category such as children's breakfast cereals. In their U.S. study, McNeal and Ji[8] observed that there were 50 children's brands available, out of 93 total cereal brands! This competition at the point of purchase means that visual brand recognition is essential to enable choice. A pack that has not been sufficiently exposed in its ads hardly stands a chance of being noticed.[9] The **two-second exposure rule** is essential to apply to new products or services, of course, but it *applies equally to established products and services* because you do not want to risk having your ads or promotion offers go unbranded or mis-branded by customers – a frequent occurrence. For print ads, the logo or brand package should be clearly visible, although it does not have to be grossly prominent. In a print ad, the reader will very likely search for the Brand Identity anyway, so as long as it is clear, this is sufficient.[10] For a radio ad, two seconds, total, of *name repetition* should be sufficient to ensure auditory recognition; in practice, this means mentioning the name twice.

Category need explicit

The third Brand Recognition tactic is called **category need explicit**: the Category Need should be *mentioned or portrayed* in the ad *unless* it is immediately obvious. When choice is by Brand Recognition, the brand is noticed first and the category-need *question* comes after – "What is it?" Mentioning or portraying the Category Need is especially important for *new* brand-items whose category-need positioning (the C factor in the T-C-B model of positioning) is going to be established by the launch marcoms. Remember the example we gave in Chapter 6. You see a can of something, a bottle of something, a package of something, or even some sort of apparently new service advertised – but what is it? Target customers have to learn to associate the brand with the correct Category Need. In applying the Explicit Category Need tactic, it is best to make the reading (or listening) sequence correspond with the direction of the association necessary for Brand Recognition, that is, Brand Name (or Brand Mark) → Category Need. The ad for Booth Signs – indeed, the company's name itself – does this.

FIGURE 8.3 *Ad for Booth Signs company that explicitly tells the consumer that the brand (Booth) is a company that makes signs (category need). It employs the correct brand name → category need sequence for brand recognition – or, more precisely, for cognition now and recognition next time.*

SOURCE: Courtesy of Mr. Arthur Booth, managing director, Booth Signs, Wollongong, Australia.

Brand recall

For Brand Recall, the mental events are in the reverse order of those for Brand Recognition. The Category Need arises first and then the customer must mentally recall one or more brands – the question here is "What brands *are* there?" This sequence is detectable from the BSM. Moreover, the manager may believe there is a good chance of "forcing" choice of the brand-item if the target customer recalls it prior to the point of purchase in what would *otherwise* be a *Brand Recognition* situation. In both cases, the brand awareness objective will be Brand Recall.

Associate and repeat

As explained in Chapter 6, Brand Recall is by *verbal paired-associates learning*. The essential association for the target customer to learn is: Category Need → Brand (or brand-item) Name. The association must be learned in *that* direction.[11] The first two Brand Recall (BRCL) tactics listed in Table 8.2 address this learning process. First, the Category Need and the Brand Name have to be associated in the ad (the usual way of doing this is through the wording of the headline or tagline, although it is also possible for this to be done visually if it can be shown through pre-testing that the target customer "reads" the category need and the brand name from a visual presentation of them; this is very likely because people automatically "label" pictures of real objects[12] as in the Stingose ad in Figure 8.4, which portrays the Category Need visually and the Brand Name visually (as a word mark)). The second tactic is to repeat the *association* – both in the ad and by repeating the ad itself. Brand Recall is basically a result of rote learning, and repetition is far and away the most effective tactic to ensure this learning. Note that repetition of the brand name *alone*, the sheer number of brand name mentions, has no effect on Brand Recall.[13] You have to repeat the Category Need and Brand Name as a *pairing*. We summarize this tactic as **associate and repeat**.

TABLE 8.2 *Advertising tactics for brand recall.*

BRCL-1	Associate the category need and the brand name in the main copy line (or ensure that these two elements are automatically "read" from the visuals) in the sequence: category need → brand name
BRCL-2	Repeat the association (not just the brand name)
BRCL-3	Encourage a personal connection with the brand *or*
BRCL-4	Use a celebrity presenter *or*
BRCL-5	Use a mnemonic device: interactive picture for TV or print ads, or a catchy tagline or jingle for broadcast ads
BRCL-6	(If you have this option) choose a recallable brand or brand-item

Whereas the association and repetition-of-the-association tactics are the most important for Brand Recall, there are several other tactics that may also be tried which are discussed next, and note that they are *alternatives*, hence "or" in the table.

Personalization

One additional Brand Recall tactic is **personalization:** *encourage a personal connection with the brand* – a straightforward matter of using personal words in the tagline. Examples: "At McDonald's, we do it all for *you*" (second-person wording); "Take me away, P&O," (first-person pronoun wording) for the cruise ship company P&O; and "Stay where you are New Zealand, I'm coming over" (first-person wording), the tagline for a very successful tourism campaign for that country.[14]

Celebrity presenter

Another Brand Recall tactic is to employ a presenter who is a *Celebrity*, at least in the eyes of the target group. The executional essential here, which can be detected by pre-testing, is to make sure that the naturally high attention to the special presenter transfers to the brand name. Holman and Hecker provide ample evidence from campaign tracking that a **celebrity presenter** will almost always increase Brand Recall – and by a large degree – over competing brands.[15]

Mnemonic device

Yet another tactic to try is a **mnemonic device** – a prompt to rehearse the Category Need → Brand Name association. There are two such devices, visual or verbal. One is a visual brand logo *that depicts the category*.[16] Well-known examples are the logo for Mobil oil company in which the "o" is a car's petrol tank aperture and the logo for McDonald's in which the brand name is superimposed over the yellow "M", which resembles french fries. The other, in broadcast ads, is a catchy slogan or jingle that mentions the category and the brand name. The best example of a catchy slogan that we have come across is by an Australian bank, the Commonwealth Bank, which uses the rhetorical question-and-answer tagline: "Which bank? . . . The Commonwealth Bank." After some *repetition* of the *pairing* of the category need and the brand name, subsequent ads only had to say "Which bank?" and most viewers or listeners would automatically fill in, mentally, the Commonwealth Bank brand name. A pause in the tagline is used to allow them to do this, then the brand name is spoken or supered on the TV screen after they've already said it mentally.

Jingle mnemonic devices are trickier. Most effective are originally composed jingles in which the category need and the brand name are associated, in the

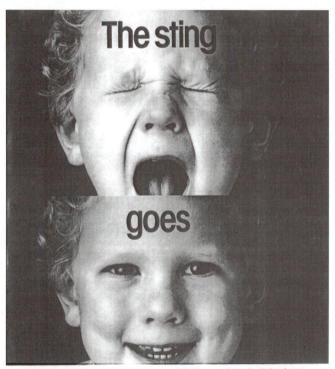

FIGURE 8.4 *Ad for Stingose antiseptic cream in which the category need correctly precedes the brand name for brand recall learning.*

SOURCE: Courtesy of Pfizer Australia Pty Ltd.

correct sequence, in the *lyrics* (e.g., "Beanz Meanz Heinz," a famous tagline which originally was the last words of a jingle). A *risky* practice is the use of *popular songs*; if the song is well-known, listeners are more likely to sing the words of the song to themselves rather than rehearse the category need and brand name.[17] However, popular tunes to which the words are *not* easily recalled are suitable. For example, Decoré, an Australian brand of shampoo, successfully used the tune of the 1962 Gene Chandler song "Duke of Earl"; the singer in the ad, who is in the shower shampooing and thus depicting the category need, sings the lyrics "Dec . . . Dec . . . Dec . . . Decoré, Dec . . . Dec . . . Decoré," (new wording that fits the old tune).

If new, select a recallable brand-item name

Finally, for a *new* product, if the manager has the option to choose the name of the brand-item and knows that the choice process will involve Brand Recall, then the manager should select a brand-item name that is inherently *easy* to recall. Names that refer to the Category Need are about 33% more easy to recall, in response to the category-need cue, than average.[18] Examples are Ultra Slim-Fast, Colgate Whitening toothpaste, and Healthy Choice (a category need applicable across a lot of food product categories and hence a reason why the Healthy Choice brand has been so easily amenable to brand extensions). If the brand name is to be used in Asia, the first orthographic character of the name should refer to the category need.[19] High-imagery brand names – the first two above, perhaps, and also Apple, Mustang, and Dove – exhibit about a 50% recall advantage over low-imagery brand names such as Compaq, Probe, and Neutrogena.[20] Unusual spelling of the brand name also helps recall[21] but we are not keen to endorse this tactic in view of the sufficient problem that children already have with their spelling!

It has to be admitted that, despite a lot of research on memory, we still don't have *sure-fire* tactics, other than the association and repetition tactics, for maximizing Brand Recall. The main problem, even when employing association and repetition in the ad, is that *other* brand names are also trying to attach themselves to the category need in the customer's mind and so interference from competing ads in the category is rampant. This means that, for Brand Recall, *media* repetition of the ad, as far as possible at times when competitors are not advertising – is very important. Brand Recall, being verbal paired-associates learning, is very vulnerable to competitive advertising clutter.[22] Brand Recognition, by contrast, being visual iconic or auditory echoic learning, is not subject to competitive interference, and repetition is not so important. This distinction bears on the Effective Frequency decision in media planning, as we will see in Chapter 12.

Brand-recall-boosted brand recognition

When Brand-Recall-Boosted Brand Recognition is the awareness objective, a combined set of tactics, combining some elements of Brand Recognition and Brand Recall tactics, is advised. These (abbreviated BOTH) are summarized in Table 8.3. As noted in Chapter 6, Brand-Recall-Boosted Brand Recognition is a difficult objective, to be nominated as the brand awareness objective only if the BSM calls for it or if the manager believes recall can be successfully forced on an otherwise brand-recognition choice. Looking ahead to Effective Frequency, the recall component dominates and Brand-Recall-boosted Brand Recognition is treated the same as Brand Recall.

TABLE **8.3** *Advertising tactics for brand-recall-boosted brand recognition.*

BOTH-1	Ensure sufficient exposure of the logo or pack shot – with the brand *name* clearly visible
BOTH-2	Associate the category need and the brand name in the main copy line (or ensure that these two elements are automatically "read" from the visuals) in the sequence: category need → brand name
BOTH-3	Repeat the association (not just the brand name)
BOTH-4	Encourage a personal connection with the brand *or*
BOTH-5	Use a celebrity presenter *or*
BOTH-6	Use a mnemonic device
BOTH-7	(If you have this option) choose a recallable brand name

BRAND PREFERENCE TACTICS

Brand Preference tactics from the grid apply to the in-message *execution* of *the a-b-e benefit claim chain* (or chains if multiple benefits are used, as in a High-Involvement choice) which has been selected for the ad or advertised promotion offer. These tactics are aimed at achieving the a-b-e chain's required brand emotions and brand benefit beliefs and, as their result, Brand Preference.

Tactics for each of the four quadrants of the Brand Preference part of the grid are explained below, beginning with the two Low-Involvement brand preference quadrants and concluding with the two High-Involvement quadrants.

Low-involvement/informational

When brand-item choice for the target customer is **low-involvement/informational**, the most effective persuasion approach could be described as Simple RSP, that is: employ a *simple, rational selling proposition*. The Brand Preference tactics for this quadrant are listed in Table 8.4.

TABLE **8.4** *Advertising tactics for low-involvement/informational brand preference.*

LI/I-1	Emphasize only one benefit or at the very most two benefits
LI/I-2	The key benefit claim should be extreme (curious disbelief)
LI/I-3	Support the key benefit claim with an $e^{--} \rightarrow b \rightarrow e^{+}$ emotion shift (the problem-solution format)

One benefit or, at most, two benefits

First, because the choice is Low Involvement, target customers will not be willing to process (attend to and learn) more than one or two benefits. Usually, only one benefit – the Key Benefit – should be emphasized. The use of two emphasized benefits is necessary only when the brand-item is tapping into the Mixed Approach-Avoidance buying motive, the conflict resolution motive. A good example of conflict resolution is the tagline for Lean Cuisine low-calorie, frozen-prepared meal items: "It's not just Lean. It's Cuisine." In some cases of Low-Involvement choices, an Entry-Ticket Benefit may also have to be clearly mentioned in addition to the key benefit.

Extreme claim

Second, the Key Benefit Claim should be *extreme*. Maloney[23] describes the desired reaction to an extreme claim as **curious disbelief**. The prospective customer should think: "It can't *really* be that good, can it? I'd better try it and see." Consumers have come to expect extreme claims in advertising for Low-Involvement products and services, and a KBC for products and services of this type that is not extreme will not even get considered. An extreme claim induces tentative prospective customers to try. The extreme claim also reinforces the preference of customers who *already* buy the brand or brand-item. In making an extreme claim, the advertiser cannot, of course, state or show an outright lie; in particular, the ad for the product or service cannot state or show that it possesses a particular *attribute* when it does not. However, it is quite legal to make an extreme *benefit* claim. There are four main ways of executing a benefit claim so that it makes an extreme promise. (These extreme claim tactics can be employed in either Low-Involvement/Informational or Low-Involvement/*Transformational* advertising, depending on the purchase motive. To avoid repetition, we list the tactics only in the LI/I section.)

Direct extreme verbal claims are one way of making an extreme benefit claim. Extreme direct verbal claims are less common than extreme implied verbal or implied visual claims (below) because if the claim is direct, the advertiser has to be able to prove it legally. An example is the benefit claim made by Grey Goose vodka: "Rated the No. 1 tasting vodka in the world." This is actually an informational – Intellectual Stimulation and Mastery – appeal because most people cannot taste the differences between vodkas, especially in mixed drinks. As the claim is based on Beverage Testing Institute data from 1998 and in subsequent tests Grey Goose has not been rated number one yet is still running the ads, there is a government case pending against the company at the time of writing.[24] Another example is from Apple Computer in the U.K., who was forced to withdraw TV commercials claiming that the G5 Power Mac is (or was in 2003) "The world's fastest personal computer," based on a test that allegedly favored Apple by running competitor Dell on the Linux O/S rather than Windows, an allegation that Apple Computer disputed but lost.[25] Of course, if you can sustain an extreme direct verbal claim, then you should use it. Examples of extreme direct verbal claims include "Visa – it's everywhere you want it to be," which 65% of consumers rate as believable, and "The wonderful world of Disney," which 78% rate as believable. Interestingly, the well-known extreme claim for BMW autos, "The ultimate driving machine" is rated as believable by only 45% of consumers[26] but that many may be enough!

Implied extreme verbal claims use words with a strong connotative (emotional) meaning to make a claim that seems more extreme than the literal meaning. In school, we learn that the hierarchy of praise is "good, better, best." However, in advertising, it is actually legally easier to claim that an item is "best," meaning *one of the best,* than it is to claim that it is "better" than all other items.[27] An example is the well-known tagline, "Gillette, best a man can get," although it is true that some of the items in Gillette's product lines *are* functionally better than those of competitors.

Implied extreme visual claims, though used more often in Low-Involvement/Transformational advertising, can also be used in Low-Involvement/Informational advertising, most often as a graphic "product demonstration." Advertisers must, in demonstrations, show only what a *typical user* could expect to obtain by way of product or service performance but they can show the *peak* performance obtained by the typical user. An example of peak performance portrayal is the ad for Stingose antiseptic cream, in Figure 8.5, the same ad that was used to illustrate Brand Recall in Figure 8.4.

Paralogic, or what McGuire calls "probabilogic,"[28] is frequently employed to imply an extreme claim as the *conclusion* to an apparently logical argument. Here is an example suggested by D.G. Mick.[29] If an ad states that "All healthy meals are nutritionally balanced" and that "Smith's frozen dinners are healthy," then it is logically correct to conclude that "Smith's frozen dinners are nutritionally balanced." However, the following argument sequence has a logically incorrect conclusion: "All healthy meals are nutritionally balanced" and "Smith's frozen dinners are nutritionally balanced" and therefore "Smith's frozen dinners are healthy." If the first premise is true, healthy meals are a subset of nutritionally balanced meals and it is therefore *logically* possible to have nutritionally balanced meals that are *not* healthy. However, most consumers do not make the effort to check the logic of the argument. Rather, they simply draw the inference that the conclusion is *probably* true (hence probabilogic) if not definitely true.[30] It should be noted that

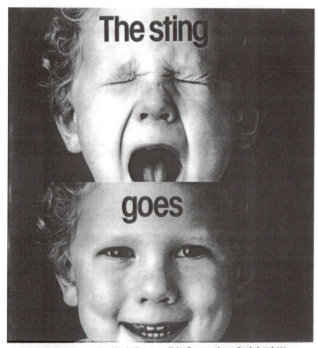

FIGURE 8.5 *Stingose ad showing low-involvement/informational persuasion tactics, particularly the extreme claim tactic.*

SOURCE: Courtesy of Pfizer Australia Pty Ltd.

advertisers employing a paralogical message usually make the first two true claims and leave it up to the consumer to infer, illogically, the third claim (the intended conclusion). This tactic is legal.

Very negative to moderate positive emotion-shift (problem-solution format)

The third and final tactic for Low-Involvement/Informational brand preference concerns how the key benefit claim should be supported *emotionally*. Even though we have referred to the overall persuasion approach for Informationally motivated purchases as a *rational* selling proposition, there should be an emotional component in *all* advertising. In fact, a good case can be made that an ad or promotion offer that does not stimulate at least the basic type 1 emotion of *Arousal* is unlikely to be persuasive.[31] Getting down to the a-b-e level of positioning, the most effective support chain for the key benefit claim for low-involvement/informational products or services will be a chain that can be described as an $e^{--} \rightarrow b \rightarrow e^{+}$ **emotion-shift**. The two different emotions occur before and after the benefit, b, and the shift takes place when the b is introduced. That is, the ad should first press hard on the negative emotion, hence the superscript for e is a double negative, of the consumer problem, then introduce the key benefit which will bring with the benefit belief (via the multiattribute model and specifically the D and I, or desirability, multiplicative term) at least a moderate positive emotion, thus $b \rightarrow e^{+}$. This is the classic *problem-solution* format.

The ad for Stingose in the previous figure nicely illustrates emotion-shift. Typical emotion-shift sequences for the negatively originated, Informational motives are:

- annoyed → relieved (Problem Removal)

- fearful → relaxed (Problem Avoidance)

- disappointed → optimistic (Incomplete Satisfaction)

- conflict or guilt → reassured (Mixed Approach-Avoidance)

- mildly annoyed → contented (Normal Depletion)

The emphasis on a strong negative emotion at the start in the Low-Involvement/Informational quadrant means that the ad is not likely to be likable. Indeed, two of the U.S.A.'s highest-selling TV commercials of all time – Wisk laundry detergent's "Ring around the collar," which ran for 22 years until 1989, and Charmin toilet tissue's "Mr. Whipple, please don't squeeze the Charmin," which ran for about 10 years through the early 90s – were voted first and second, respectively, on the all-time list in the U.S.A. as "most obnoxious" by consumers, according to the TV tracking service Video Storyboard Tests.[32] Disliked they were, but they worked. Their respective creative ideas conveyed an extreme claim about the key benefit, based on a prior negative emotion, that was associated indelibly and uniquely with the brand for a long time.

The target customer's registration of the appropriate emotion sequence – for Informational or Transformational ads – can be easily verified by pre-testing. Recently, the Dutch industrial design researcher, Pieter Desmet[33], has developed pictorial manikin items to represent relevant emotional states. These are shown for some very negative emotions (e^{--}), negative emotions (e^{-}), mild positive (e^{+}) and very positive (e^{++}) emotions in Figure 8.6. Whereas verbal emotion

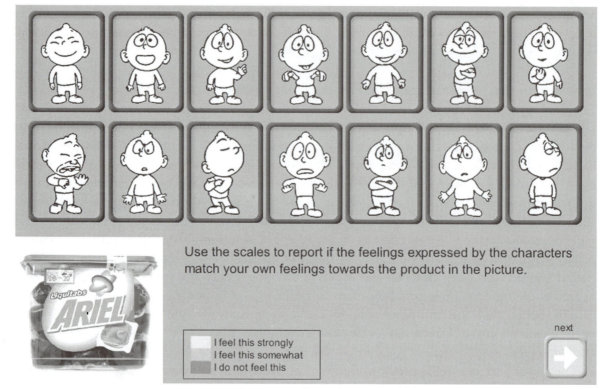

FIGURE 8.6 *Desmet's pictorial manikins for registration of negative and positive type 2 emotional responses.*

SOURCE: Courtesy of P.M.A. Desmet. For more information go to <www.designingemotion.nl>.

scales are usually used in pre-testing, we believe this pictorial method will better capture the target customer's emotional states as induced by the ad.[34] The manikin figures are easily feminized for female respondents.

Low-involvement/transformational

The **low-involvement/transformational** quadrant of brand preference applies to product or service items that represent a *low degree of purchase risk*, with the primary purchase motivation (in the key benefit claim) being *positive-ending*. This is the emotional selling proposition (ESP) quadrant. The main in-ad message tactics for Low-Involvement/Transformational brand preference are listed in Table 8.5.

TABLE 8.5 *Advertising tactics for low-involvement/transformational brand preference.*

LI/T-1	The key benefit claim must be emotionally positively extreme
LI/T-2	The execution of the key benefit claim must be unique to the brand
LI/T-3	The target customers must like the ad

Extreme positive emotion

First, the key benefit claim must be emotionally positively extreme. **Extreme positive emotion-shift** in the Low-Involvement/Transformational case starts with the assumption that the target customer will be in a fairly neutral emotional state when first attending to the message. Thereafter, a strong positive emotion (e^{++}) must be induced via the key benefit claim statement or portrayal. The typical end-emotions for the various positive-ended, or Transformational, purchase motives are:

- desire, delight, or elation (Sensory Gratification)

- mental excitement reflecting inspiration, sometimes edging on smugness (Intellectual Stimulation and Mastery)

- self-assurance, or self-pride (Social Approval)

These very positive emotions are subtly but importantly different. Small-scale quantitative research will often be needed to identify the specific positive emotion, a type 2 emotion, that is most motivating and to develop the most effective $b \to e^{++}$ chain or e^{++} focus. It is vital, at the same time, for the *type 1* emotion of Arousal to exhibit a marked increase to a very positive end-state during processing of the ad or offer. (The pictorial scales of Desmet, earlier, can be used to measure registration of the emotion-shift. Although moment-to-moment "dial" ratings capture the dynamic aspect better[35], the pictorial scales can pick up more-specific *type 2* emotions.) Increased Arousal assists not only Brand Awareness but also Brand Preference, the communication objective that is our concern here.[36]

It should be evident that, in this Low-Involvement/Transformational quadrant, only a *single* benefit claim will realistically be processed by the target customers.

Unique execution

Second, the *execution* of the key benefit claim – which will of necessity be an emotional execution – must be *unique to the brand (or brand-item)*. A common problem in Low-Involvement/Transformational product or service categories is that many brands try to tap into the same buying motive and they end up with look-alike or sound-alike executions. Men's liquor ads and women's cosmetics ads, for example, are two categories where similarity is often a problem. It is very important, therefore, that the emotional execution be "tightly connected" to the brand or brand-item.[37] Examples of brands' ads that are distinctive executionally are: Absolut Vodka ads (which feature the bottle in different cities of the world; see Figure 8.7) and Marlboro cigarette ads (the cowboy, who is still the most-recognized advertising icon worldwide, or, in Marlboro ads in the U.S.A., cowboy-country rural scenes). Summary label for this tactic: **unique execution**.

FIGURE 8.7 *Absolute Vodka "bottle" ads illustrating a unique execution for the brand.*

SOURCE: Under permission by V&S Vin & Sprit AB (publ). Absolut country of Sweden vodka & logo, Absolut, Absolut bottle design and Absolut calligraphy are trademarks owned by V&S Vin & Sprit AB (publ). © 2004 V&S Vin & Sprit AB (publ). Photographer Graham Ford: Absolut Rome, Absolut Milan, Absolut Munich, Absolut Athens, Absolut Berlin. Photographer Vincent Dixon: Absolut Amsterdam, Absolut Naples, Absolut Barcelona.

Ad likability by target audience

Third, the Target Customers, but not necessarily anyone else, must *like* the ad: **ad likability by target audience**. Ad liking is necessary because, in this quadrant, target customers, during the learning phase of ad processing, have to undergo **human evaluative conditioning** by transfer of positive affect (e^{++}, the unconditional stimulus, or US) from the ad to the brand (the brand becomes the conditional stimulus, or CS).[38] A fascinating fact about human evaluative conditioning (HEC) is that it actually works better if the consumer is *aware* of the attempted conditioning. The marketer of Molson, the Canadian beer, has apparently realized this and has employed a humorous, Postmodern spoof (but entirely scientifically serious) execution of HEC, in which an excellent HEC ad aimed at *women,* shown in panel (a) of Figure 8.8, is "explained" in a follow-up ad, shown in panel (b), aimed at *men.* In the first ad, "men who *drink* Molson" is the to-be-conditioned stimulus (the CS) and the "sensitive hunk with puppies" is the positive unconditional stimulus (US$^+$) for the female audience. For the male *target* audience, the necessary process is not HEC but **instrumental, or operant, learning**, which is more cognitive: Molson beer is the to-be-learned positive discriminative stimulus (S^D), the operant response (R) is "to buy and be seen drinking Molson," and the promised positive reinforcer (S^{r+}) is to "attract females." This promise should be regarded as credible because it is very likely that women who see the first ad, which was placed in women's magazines such as *Cosmopolitan*, but not the second ad that reveals the "trick," which was placed in men's magazines only, *will* be favorably conditioned as intended.[39]

Next, we consider the Brand Preference tactics for the two *High-Involvement* brand preference quadrants. Because of the High-Involvement nature of the brand or brand-item choice in these quadrants, entailing *high purchase risk* of either the *functional* (Informational) or *emotional* (Transformational) type, we will see that *believability* becomes paramount in the persuasion tactics. The benefit claims have to be *accepted* in processing for High Involvement, not just learned as in Low-Involvement brand preference.

Panel (a)

Panel (b)

FIGURE 8.8 *Molson beer ads attempting human evaluative conditioning of females, panel (a), and instrumental conditioning of males, panel (b).*

SOURCE: Courtesy of Molson U.S.A., LLC. Agency: Crispin Porter & Bogusky. Photographer: Arnaldo Anaya-Lucca.

High-involvement/informational

The **high-involvement/informational** brand preference quadrant is for ads for a brand-item for which the target audience perceives that the choice is high risk and based on a negatively originated motive. Whereas these brand-items can be advertised in Awareness Ads, it is important to point out that this is the quadrant for most Direct-Response Ads, including most Website ads, direct mail ads, and retailers' ads for durables. Finally, it is also the main quadrant of tactics for another form of marcoms that we cover in Chapter 17 – Personal Selling.

In Low-Involvement persuasion situations, as we saw above, extreme benefit claims should be employed. It does not matter that the extreme claim is blatant because, in low-risk persuasion, the ad's forewarning of its intent to persuade does *not* reduce the persuasion effect.[40] The main reason for this is that in processing a message, comprehension *with* belief comes first, and rejection or disbelief, if it occurs at all, is a second, consciously taken step.[41] Faced with a message about a Low-Involvement choice, the target customer, if he or she bothers to question the claim at all, is likely to suspend disbelief pending trial of the brand-item. The situation is very different for messages concerning High-Involvement choices. Because of the high risk of making an unsatisfactory choice, the target customer is sure to take that extra step of processing effort that is required to estimate the truth of the benefit claim or claims. Benefit claims that are too extreme and therefore not judged as true will "boomerang," meaning that the target customer will mentally retreat and retain his or her pre-exposure brand benefit belief ratings and thus pre-exposure Brand Preference.[42] (There is an important qualification to this conclusion, concerning extreme portrayals of *emotional* benefits in the High-Involvement/*Transformational* quadrant, as explained later.)

The tactics for High-Involvement/Informational (HI/I) brand preference are listed in Table 8.6. For the High-Involvement/Informational quadrant, a complex rational selling proposition (Complex RSP) approach is required and the tactics are very detailed.

TABLE 8.6 *Advertising tactics for high-involvement/informational brand preference.*

HI/I-1	The message must be introduced in a manner that reflects the target customer's initial state of preference toward the brand
HI/I-2	Benefit claims must be pitched at the upper level of the target customer's latitude of acceptance – do not overclaim or inadvertently underclaim
HI/I-3	Order and number of benefit claims: (a) the key benefit claim must be emphasized no matter where it is placed (b) then list (up to) six other benefit claims in the approximate order that the target customer would look for them in the category (c) if a direct-response ad, save a unique, important claim for last
HI/I-4	If the benefit claims have to be more convincing, use an expert, sincere presenter
HI/I-5	For target customer groups who have a negative initial preference – such as Negative NCUs, Unfavorable OBLs, or Unfavorable OBSs – use a very positive opening visual or, on radio, word picture followed by refutational (yes . . . but) benefit claims
HI/I-6	If you are a small brand taking on a large entrenched competitor, use explicit comparison, with a rhetorical "check" question at the end

Acknowledge prior attitude

First, it is essential for the message to be introduced in a manner that acknowledges where the target customer is "coming from" in terms of his or her prior attitude toward the brand-item. The individuals in the target group may have either a *negative* (Negative NCUs, Unfavorable OBLs, or Unfavorable OBSs) or *neutral* (Unaware NCUs, Neutral OBLs, or Neutral OBSs) or just *moderately favourable* (Positive NCUs, primarily) Brand Preference for our brand-item before being exposed to its marcoms message. Because they are making a high-risk choice in considering our brand-item, this prior state of mind must be acknowledged so that the subsequent "selling" part of the message will not be rejected as being "not applicable to me." This fear on the part of advertisers is undoubtedly a reason for the rise of Postmodern Ads but they are not a good solution for anyone other than 18–34 year-olds (see Chapter 7) and, even for that age group, the Postmodern style must not override message content when advertising High-Involvement/Informational purchases (e.g., a laptop computer) because the essential sales points (the benefits) may be missed. The three possible **acknowledge prior attitude** tactics are discussed below.

Negative prior attitude. When the target group's prior attitude is *negative,* the lead-in to the message should acknowledge this head on, and the body of the message should, of course, attempt to convert this to a *positive* attitude. An example is a print ad headline used by Apple for its introduction of the Power Macintosh: "Think of it as the Macintosh for people who thought they could never have a Macintosh." The benefit claims in the body copy of the ad were *sympathetic but firm*, such as ". . . find out about the power that will change the way you think about the Macintosh." When the target group's prior attitude is negative, also use *tactic 5*, which will be explained shortly.

Neutral prior attitude. If the target group's prior attitude is *neutral,* which means that they can be assumed to be *hesitant*, the introduction should be *reassuring* and not extreme or confrontational. An ad for Narhex Cross-Linked Elastin, a wrinkle-reduction product, illustrates exactly the right approach here without overclaiming: "More and more men and women achieve wrinkle reduction in only 28 days, confirming results on a 'world first' scientific study." A sub-headed benefit claim continues: "72% reduction in wrinkles achieved," which is a believable yet still hope-inspiring claim.

Moderately favorable prior attitude. If the target group's prior attitude is just *moderately* favorable, then a tone of *encouragement* should be adopted. For example: "Step up to a GE fully reversible home heating/air-conditioning system. No longer will you have to put up with a home that is too cold in winter and too hot in summer."

Overall, the *prior attitude* tactic helps by reducing the target customer's perception of *intent to persuade*.

Do not overclaim

Second, the message – the benefit claims – must not attempt to persuade by overclaiming. The High-Involvement/Informational benefit claims must be pitched at the **top of the latitude of**

acceptance.[43] If your objective, factual delivery of the benefit is below the top level of what would be accepted, you must not lie by using a direct verbal overclaim; however, you can move the claim up legally with an implied verbal claim or, if applicable, a visual demonstration of the benefit claim (see "how to make an extreme promise," discussed in the section on Low-Involvement/ Informational tactics). You could also try using an expert, sincere presenter – see tactic 4. If, on the other hand, your objective delivery *exceeds* the top of the latitude of acceptance, pull it *back* to the top, because it will otherwise be rejected as an overclaim.

Slipping too far down the latitude will result in an underclaim which is just as ineffective as an overclaim. Some attempted "highbrow" ads, such as on FM radio, tend to underclaim and, we note, underclaiming is likely to be a problem for the Postmodern style of ad in *this* quadrant.

> How can the manager find the Top of the Latitude of Acceptance? The only way to do this is to pre-test benefit claim statements or portrayals that use successive degrees of extremity. See previous discussion of how to make benefit claims extreme. A straightforward method for direct verbal claims is to test a range of increasingly intense adjectival modifiers, in association with the claim, that convey the sense of "quite good," "good," "very good," and then "extremely good" and settle for the level at which a sample of target customers indicate, for the next level, that they don't believe the claim.

Key benefit claim and other benefit claims

Third is a *set* of tactics for *multiple* benefit claims. High-Involvement/Informational messages almost always employ multiple benefit claims – and here we mean claims about distinctly different benefits as identified from the I-D-U analysis for the brand-item. Keller and Staelin[44] show that the first seven *high-importance* benefits are what mainly influence High-Involvement choices; more than this and choice becomes more confusing and may lead the customer to consider another, more concisely described brand. (Benefit chains used to support these benefit claims are usually of the a → b form and there is no similar limit on the total number of *attributes* that can be employed in support; that is, there can be several a's supporting the one b.) One reason for limiting the number of benefits, although seven is already a lot, is that additional benefits are very likely to start delving into benefits of lower importance or desirability and the addition of these can actually *dilute* Brand Preference via a subjective averaging effect (the customer gets the impression that the ad is stretching itself for extra benefits and preference is averaged down as these beliefs are processed).[45] Also, seven is an upper limit – if you can achieve the intended level of brand-item preference with *fewer* benefits than this, then use the lesser number.

Moreover, the message must emphasize the *Key Benefit*. No matter where it is placed in the ad, it should be clearly visible (or clearly audible in a radio ad).

The question then becomes how best to order the other benefit claims. In all cases, place the most important and mostly unique benefit claims first, to take advantage of the "primacy" effect in message processing; then, if it is an Awareness Ad (and hence delayed response), tail off to the relatively less unique (usually Entry-Ticket) benefit claims. However, if the ad or offer is intended to generate an immediate, direct response, save at least one important, unique claim until last because a Direct-Response Ad will, in addition to the primacy effect, produce a "recency" effect in processing.[46] The primacy effect of benefit order is very strong. In an experiment, Kardes and

Herr[47] demonstrated, ethics aside, that they could lead consumers to prefer a slightly inferior model of color TV set when its positive attributes were presented in primary positions in the list describing the TV set, compared with a slightly better model whose positive attributes were spread throughout the list. When the choice was delayed, as it normally would be in seeing an ad first and getting to the store later, the primacy effect was very strong: 80% of consumers in the experiment indicated they would choose the slightly inferior TV set against a chance level of 50%.

With High-Involvement processing, there is also a greater likelihood than with Low-Involvement processing that various benefit claims will *interact*.[48] The Trading-Off option for an inferior benefit that must be mentioned to the customer is an example of a deliberately imposed interaction: the inferior benefit is followed by an offsetting but related superior benefit. Other than this, through Pre-Testing, you must ensure that any related benefit claims interact positively. If two claims are seen as at all redundant, separate them in the list.

An excellent example of the tactics for multiple benefit claims is the ad for Sharper Image's Ionic Breeze Silent Air Purifier in Figure 8.9. It features a capstone claim, does not exceed seven benefit claims, and, as a Direct-Response Ad should, it saves an important, unique claim until last.

FIGURE 8.9 *Sharper Image ad uses multiple benefit claim tactics correctly.*

SOURCE: Courtesy of The Sharper Image.

Consider adding an expert, sincere presenter

Fourth, if your benefit claims have to be more convincing, consider using an **expert, sincere presenter**. As should be evident from the discussion so far, for High-Involvement/Informational persuasion, the benefit claims need to be strong without being too extreme – they have to be convincing but not exaggerate. It is best if the benefit claims can achieve this on their own but quite often in pre-testing it will be found that the claims are not quite strong enough to induce *Acceptance* responses in processing, which are necessary to produce an increase in Brand Preference. In this circumstance, the addition of a presenter (spokesperson) who has an immediately-perceived expertise "hook" and makes a sincere presentation should be investigated (see the CESLIP Model of presenter characteristics later in this chapter). An excellent example of the use of the Expert, Sincere Presenter tactic occurred with the launch of Healthy Choice frozen entrees some years ago. With its high introductory price, its primary target audience of Other-Brand Loyals (Lean Cuisine loyals) and its secondary target audience of New Category Users (who haven't previously bought frozen entrees), Healthy Choice was High Involvement/Informational. The launch TV ad featured the CEO, Charles "Mike" Harper, admitting to having recently suffered a serious heart attack and, in a "change of heart" for one presumed to be solely profit-motivated, deciding that his company, the food company ConAgra, would produce a line of frozen foods that were "Heart-healthy." The new line was to be called Healthy Choice and despite having to enter a crowded market peopled by fussy consumers, it was instantly accepted and became the market leader.

For negative-attitude target audiences, use a very positive opening visual then refutational benefit claims

Fifth – and this is related to the first tactic about prior attitude – for a target customer group who has *objections* to the brand-item (which may also include objections to the category), namely Negative NCUs, Unfavorable OBLs, or Unfavorable OBSs, the ad should use a **very positive opening visual**. The use of a Very Positive Opening Visual – the opening video sequence in a TV commercial, the picture in a print ad, or the opening "word picture" in a radio ad – is a tactic based on a study by Leclerc and Little[49] in which the use of pleasant pictures in FSI coupon ads was shown to strongly attract OBLs, a finding which should generalize to "negative" target audiences. This should be followed by the benefit claims, *refutationally worded*. The **refutational approach** is known in personal selling as the "Yes . . . but" approach, in that you first acknowledge the objection, then counter it. There may be one major objection, or several objections, to be countered. The headline for the presumed negative target group for the Apple Power Macintosh discussed earlier employs the refutational tactic. The refutational approach is especially relevant, too, for social marketing campaigns aimed at habitual offender target groups – technically, brand loyals for the "bad" behaviour – who are likely to object to being told what is good for them (see Chapter 18).

Small brands should use explicit comparison, with a rhetorical "check" end-question

Sixth, for high-involvement/informational persuasion, a small-share brand can make use of the **explicit comparison** message tactic. Explicit Comparison is where the competing brand or brand-item is identifiably shown or openly named, so that the competing brand definitely gets considered alongside your brand. This differs from **implicit comparison**, which does not identify the competing brand in the ad – however, implicit comparison ads become *de facto* explicit comparison ads if consumers reliably fill in the other brand's name when processing the message. The comprehensive empirical evidence on comparison advertising campaigns indicates that, for *market leader* brands, the Implicit Comparison approach – whether or not the competitor becomes explicit in the consumer's mind – is very effective (the change in brand preference is +117%) and the Explicit Comparison approach is extremely effective (+186%). However, there is a view that the use of comparison tactics, implicit or explicit, by the Market Leader brand is predatory market behavior and, indeed, regulators in many countries ban the practice as *unfair*, even if the comparison can be factually verified. The U.S.A. is the only country, to our knowledge, where substantiated comparisons by market leaders are not restricted, either by law or by common agreement among advertisers. Large and small *follower* brands, in most countries, are allowed to use Explicit Comparison. In the U.S.A., the Explicit Comparison approach has been used for many years by Wendy's and Burger King against McDonald's, Pepsi against Coke, Scope against Listerine, Energizer against Duracell, and Avis against Hertz. The evidence shows, surprisingly, that, for *middle-share brands*, Explicit Comparison on average *does little* (persuasion index +8% only), that *Implicit* Comparison actually *hurts* them, on average (–26%) and that a *Non*-Comparative approach is the best option (+28%). These results are difficult to explain but perhaps are due to middle brands not pre-testing comparative messages thoroughly. Most interestingly, though, the *Explicit* Comparison approach is the *only* effective approach, on average, for *small brands* (small brands were defined in the study as those whose market share is half of 1/n or lower, where n is the number of brands – thus 10% or lower share in a five-brand market or 5% or lower in a 10-brand market). Both standard Non-Comparative ads (–109%) and Implicit Comparison ads (–100%) hurt small brands badly. For small brands, only Explicit Comparison ads had an average positive effect on brand preference, small though the effect is (+10%). So, where it is legal, the Explicit Comparison tactic *should* be employed for small brands. Note that there is no ethical issue of predatory behavior in the use of this technique by a small brand because it has "nothing to lose" and is unlikely to damage the fortunes of the big brands.[50]

Recently, an effective type of explicit comparison has been identified by Muthukrishnan, Warlop and Alba, called a **piecemeal comparison**.[51] A piecemeal comparison compares the focal brand (or brand-item) with *several* other brands on a *different* attribute each time, selecting those attributes on which the focal brand is superior to the particular other brand. Consumers are likely to infer that the focal brand is superior *overall* to the other brands.

An effective ending for an explicit comparison ad is a **rhetorical "check" end-question** – the "check" being to encourage the audience to rehearse the right brand! For example, a TV commercial in Australia comparing Herron Blue pain reliever ("Australian") with Nurofen ("Foreign") concludes with the voice-over: "So which do you take – Nurofen or Herron Blue? The choice is in your hands."

High-involvement/transformational

The brand-item of a product or service is classified in the **high-involvement/transformational** brand preference quadrant if the target group perceives the choice as *high risk* and the key benefit claim relies on a *positive-ending* purchase motive, namely, Sensory Gratification, Intellectual Stimulation and Mastery, or Social Approval. "Branding" strategies – using an instinctual selling proposition (ISP), archetypal selling proposition (ASP), or strong emotional selling proposition (ESP) – are *also* classified in this quadrant because for the customer to approach an unknown or little-known brand, in most product and service categories, is *high risk*. The tactics for high-involvement/transformational (HI/T) brand preference are listed in Table 8.7. Again, being high-involvement tactics, they are necessarily quite detailed.

TABLE 8.7 *Tactics for high-involvement/transformational brand preference.*

HI/T-1	Branding – new key benefit positioning of a brand or sub-brand using an ISP, ASP or strong ESP – should be regarded as high-involvement/transformational, and tactics 2, 3 and 5, below, should be applied. (The product or service itself may be in any of the two brand awareness and four brand preference boxes of the grid.)
HI/T-2	The overall ad, and the specific portrayal of the product or service, must be highly emotionally authentic in the reaction of the target audience
HI/T-3	The *transformational* key benefit claim or claims should be extreme (overclaimed)
HI/T-4	There may be secondary *informational* benefits, which should be pitched at the upper level of the target customer's latitude of acceptance (not overclaimed)
HI/T-5	Any person shown or heard in the ad is automatically a presenter and must strongly have the characteristics of expertise (expert *user*) and ideal-similarity (aspirational for the target customer)

First and very important, **branding** is included in this quadrant. *Branding* is new key benefit positioning for the *brand* or *sub-brand,* rather than the brand-item. Why do we regard branding as *High*-Involvement/Transformational? The "brand name" factor can, of course, guide the customer's choice for either low- or high-involvement and either informational or transformational brand-items. However, potential customers regard *new brand names* or *radically repositioned* brand names as somewhat risky, even in otherwise low-risk product categories, and as very risky in high-risk product categories. The conservative classification is therefore High Involvement for branding, with high-involvement tactics required. Moreover, acquisition of brand characteristics or values is just about always Transformational in that the characteristics are based on one of the positive-ending motives of Sensory Gratification, Intellectual Stimulation and Mastery, or Social Approval. For branding, too, HI/T tactics 2 (target audience emotional authenticity), 3 (overclaiming) and 5 (user as presenter) apply.

We said in Chapter 3 that it is worthwhile to investigate a "brain-levels" fundamental positioning approach for brand or sub-brand benefit positioning – an instinctual selling proposition (ISP), archetypal selling proposition (ASP), or strong emotional selling proposition (ESP). Either of these approaches will require executional stimuli *in the message* to create the desired brand preference effect.

Brand delivery on an ISP or ASP "benefit" is quite difficult to measure, as the perceived delivery may be subconscious, or, in the case of sexual stimuli, conscious but "taboo." The most valid measure is likely to be a psychophysiological method such as neuro-imaging (fMRI,

MEG, or SSPT) or, more straightforward, skin conductance response (SCR) coupled with facial electro-myographic response (EMG) such that the SCR measures arousal and the EMG measures positive or, if intended, negative affect.[52]

Alternatively, use the clinical psychoanalytical methods, which are verbal methods but not rating methods, hence we have described them as "non-verbal," of Rapid Word-Association or Projective Interviews (asking the respondent what associations *other people* would have with the brand).

Emotional authenticity (for the target audience)

Second, the main tactic to employ in High-Involvement/Transformational messages is **target audience emotional authenticity**. The entire execution must achieve emotional authenticity for the typical target customer. The desired (subvocal) response when seeing, reading or hearing the ad is: "That could be *me*." This type of cognitive response (which is really an emotional response, too[53]) signals message *acceptance* in processing in the high-involvement/transformational quadrant.

Depending on the *Transformational purchase motive*, there could be various type 2 emotional responses (each an e^{++})[54]:

approachability – the *sublime* feeling of approachability, in which the approach tendency asserts itself over the coincidentally salient avoidance tendency[55]; approachability in the sublime sense is a real insight from the Grey typology of "emotional triggers" as it precisely describes what has to be achieved as a lower-brain reaction for prospective customers facing High-Involvement/Transformational choices, especially NCUs who are "upgrading," or changing their lifestyle (the Diderot unity phenomenon[56]) by buying a branded item in this category. (The motive here is Intellectual Stimulation and Mastery even though the emotion of approachability is felt as a strong *sensory* impulse.)

trust – which is actually the outcome of prior arousal of the Informational Problem-Avoidance motive, but with an emotional end-state tapping into the Transformational motive of Mastery (thus the chain is $e^{--} \rightarrow b \rightarrow e^{++}$). *Trust* is an essential entry-ticket emotional benefit for services brands, and it is worth noting here that different functional benefits support it (thus the b is really $b^f \rightarrow b^e$, where the superscripts denote functional and emotional benefits). For banks, "Customer service" is the main functional benefit that produces trust; for credit cards, "Security;" for airlines, "Safety;" for most other services, "Dependability."[57]

identification – *reinforcement of* one's *ideal* self-image (any presenter of a High-Involvement/Transformational message must have the Ideal-Similarity characteristic – see the CESLIP Presenter Model, shortly – and the motive here in terms of the end-state is, actually, Sensory Gratification, the *thrill* of seeing your *ideal* self in your mind's eye).

empowerment – feeling of confidence and self-assurance, closely followed by a feeling of *freedom* (Intellectual Stimulation and Mastery).

status – feeling of pride in *oneself* as opposed to pride about something external (Social Approval).

Overclaim transformational benefit(s)

Third, there is, practically speaking, *no upper limit* to the Latitude of Acceptance for emotional benefit claims – which means that the *Transformational* key benefit claim or claims should be extreme (overclaimed). (The benefit claim is obviously exaggerated if Parody is used; Parody – one of the Postmodern tactics – is appropriate in the High-Involvement/Transformational quadrant if the target audience age group is 18 to 34 year-olds.) Why is Overclaiming recommended? High-Involvement/Transformational products and services are mostly **credence goods** in that their benefit delivery is difficult for the buyer to judge objectively, even after purchase.[58] For instance, most people buy life insurance based on faith (trust) placed in a close friend or in the agent.[59] Similarly, the envy of your friends when you say you've taken a Club Med vacation or have just bought a new Mercedes SEL sports car is the credence benefit (for you) that the brand-item offers. "Hyperclaimed" advertising for High-Involvement/Transformational products and services is effective in large part because it influences the *public image* of the item among those who may never experience it and thereby not have an opportunity to discount the hyperclaims. This inflated yet accepted public image then raises the buyer's own preference rating of the brand-item to a higher level then it would otherwise have been. Tactic label: **overclaim transformational benefits**.

But don't overclaim on informational benefit(s)

Fourth, because the brand choice is High Involvement and even though the purchase is *primarily* Transformationally motivated, information about functional benefits will usually be needed to "close the sale." If TV is used as the primary advertising medium, the Informational benefits should not be "tacked on to" the primarily Transformational execution but rather should be delivered through linked marketing communications. Interested target prospects – their interest generated by the Transformational TV ad – will search for a print ad or brochure, go to the brand-item's Website or make a personal visit to the retail outlet and encounter a salesperson. These subsequent messages should first *remind* the prospect of the key Transformational benefit or benefits and *then* deliver the Informational benefits, where necessary – using the High-Involvement/Informational tactics described previously. This tactic is summarized as **but credible informational benefits**.

Expert user-presenter with ideal-similarity

Fifth, advertising for HI/I products or services often opts for a **user-as-hero** message where the portrayed user is perceived as an expert *user* and as a person to aspire to. When a User is inserted into the ad (the User may also appear in promotions as well) he or she is automatically perceived as an endorser or spokesperson for the brand-item. The essential characteristics of such presenters are expertise – but *User Expertise* rather than technical expertise, as would be required for the presenter of an informational product or service – and *Ideal-Similarity*, meaning someone whom the typical Target Customer will aspirationally identify with. Identification is achieved by selecting a presenter whose apparent personality is close to the typical target customer's *ideal* self-image rather than the customer's *actual* self-image (only in the very small percentage of "self-actualized" individuals will these two self-images coincide). Any potential presenter to appear in

High-Involvement/Transformational advertising or promotions for the brand-item must be pre-tested for perceived User Expertise and Target Customer Ideal-Similarity (see the CESLIP Presenter Model, shortly). Both characteristics are difficult to evaluate without a pre-test and presenters who have been intuitively selected have a very high rate of failure.[60] Summary label: **expert user, ideal-similar presenter**.

PRESENTERS

Throughout our discussion of the brand awareness and brand preference tactics in the grid, there is frequent reference to the use of a *Presenter*. In standard communication theory, the presenter is the *perceived source* of the message. However, **the presenter approach** is properly described as such in *advertising* only when the source is made *salient* – that is, takes an obvious role – in the message, either by literally delivering the message or by clearly endorsing its content. The presenter is usually a person, but animals, animated characters, or identified organizations can act as presenters.

The **CESLIP presenter model**, summarized in Table 8.8, can be used to select a suitable presenter. CESLIP is an acronym for the six *potential* characteristics of the presenter: Celebrity status, Expertise, Sincerity, Likability, Ideal-Similarity, and Power. One of the characteristics is unconditional in that all presenters must have it: Expertise. The other characteristics depend on the Brand Awareness objective or the Brand Preference grid quadrant of the message and are thus *conditional* characteristics. In the CESLIP Presenter Model, the conditional characteristics are indicated by a question mark.

TABLE 8.8 *The CESLIP presenter model (conditional characteristics are indicated by question marks).*

PRESENTER CHARACTERISTIC	CONDITION
Celebrity?	Use a known-to-target-audience celebrity when a large increase in *brand recall* is the objective (if it's not, a celebrity will not hurt when used for other reasons below)
Expert	(Unconditional) Whether or not the presenter is a celebrity, the presenter must have an immediately evident "expertise hook" to the product or service, either as a *technical* expert or an expert *user*
Sincere?	A so-called *real people* presenter, who is not a celebrity, has to look honest and make a sincere delivery of the message
Likable?	The expert presenter should also be quite *likable* or, in the condition below, ideal-similar
Ideal-similar?	The expert presenter should be *similar* to an *ideal user* if the product or service is *socially conspicuous*
Powerful?	The presenter should be *powerful* (authoritative-looking if a visual ad and an authoritative voice if an audio ad) if the message is a *fear appeal*

Celebrity?

As we saw earlier among the tactics for brand awareness, a Celebrity Presenter is very effective for increasing *Brand Recall*. A celebrity is a person or character who is famous *in the eyes of the target group.* The use of cult-movie actress Gretchen Mol as a presenter in the very successful "Cocktail moments" campaign for SKYY vodka is clever because even if only a few people recognise her – mainly those who are fans of cult movies – she looks rather like the most iconic celebrity of all time, Marilyn Monroe. This SKYY ad is thus a celebrity presenter ad for everybody. (We can't show Gretchen's ad because the talent rights have expired, but you can view it on www.skyy.com. It is a fantastic, theoretically correct ad, and Rossiter's favorite.) A Celebrity brings quick and high visibility for the brand or brand-item which, if the Category Need is also present, will increase Brand Recall. In Japan, the second largest adspend market in the world after the U.S.A., it is reported that 70% of TV commercials use an international or Japanese celebrity perhaps because advertisers there use so many short (5- or 10-second) commercials which have to gain Attention.[61] If, on the other hand, *Brand Recognition* is the objective, a celebrity doesn't help but won't hurt either, as long as the execution of the ad doesn't allow the celebrity to "vampire" the brand. Show the brand name – which is also the brand mark – clearly, to minimize vampiring. You may select a celebrity for strength on another characteristic, also below.

Expert

It is *essential* that the presenter have a quickly perceived **expertise hook** to the advertised product or service. Here are some examples of *celebrities* with an expertise hook to the product, from a study by Rossiter and Smidts[62]: Andre Agassi for a sports deodorant; Julia Roberts for a hair colorant; Michael Dell, CEO of Dell computers, for a new E-news magazine. If the presenter is not a celebrity, then you have to briefly describe his or her expertise in the ad – usually via the presenter's *occupation*. The presenter may be a *technical* expert or an expert *user*. Without this immediately perceived expertise hook to the advertised product or service, the addition of a presenter runs the risk of *reducing* Purchase Intention for the product. Here are some celebrity examples that turned consumers *off* the product in our experiment: Andre Agassi for coffee, where the addition of Agassi as a presenter reduced average purchase intention from 43% for the product alone down to 26%; Ricky Martin for a candy bar, 60% for the product alone down to 30%; Michael Dell for a ski jacket, 32% for the product alone down to 17%. The *negative* effect of a presenter with no hook is revealed by testing a product-only "control" version of the ad.

Sincere?

With a *Celebrity* Presenter, Sincerity does *not* make a difference, probably because celebrities are perceived as just moderately sincere by most consumers. However, when using a normal presenter, a so-called **"real people" presenter** – which you can do if you know your ad is highly attention-getting and you can find a technical expert or user expert who is not perceived as a celebrity by the target audience and who will cost you a great deal less than a celebrity[63] – **sincerity** is necessary. To a large extent, sincerity can be *stage-managed* in a broadcast commercial by doing a number of "takes" of the presenter's delivery until a confident look and sound are achieved.[64] In a print ad, you must choose as the presenter a person who *looks* honest. As examples of sincere-looking presenters, consider the young man and the young woman who are real-person presenters for Lacoste sport shirts, shown in Figure 8.10 (two separate ads).

FIGURE 8.10 *Sincere-looking, ideal-similar presenters for Izod's Lacoste sports shirts.*

SOURCE: Courtesy of La Chemise Lacoste.

Likable?

If and only if the presenter has an expertise product hook, the **likability** of the presenter *additionally* helps for most products and, we presume, most services. Liking seems to work, perversely enough, by enhancing the perceived Expertise of the presenter, either technical expertise or user expertise! In nearly all studies of presenters (including salespersons), their physical attractiveness, the main cue for liking a stranger, increases their perceived expertise.[65]

Ideal-similar?

Again, if and only if the presenter has an expertise product hook, the characteristic of **ideal-similarity**, rather than just likability, is additionally important for presenters of brands or products and services whose usage is *socially conspicuous*.[66] Examples of socially conspicuous *products* are automobiles, clothing, and also personal products whose results you can see, such as shampoo, or smell, such as cologne or perfume; examples of socially conspicuous *services* are department stores and, especially, boutiques and restaurants. Most advertisers of these products or services choose a highly idealized presenter who is extremely attractive (and often a celebrity). This is not quite what is needed. A better choice is a presenter who the target customer can *realistically aspire* to be like – quite highly ideal but not unattainably so in the mind of the typical target customer. The quite good-looking young man and the quite pretty young woman who are the presenter models for Izod's Lacoste sports shirts in the ads in Figure 8.10 not only have the sincerity characteristic, as we noted previously, but also are excellent choices for *ideal-similarity* in the sense that we advocate. It is deliberate that the two models have even been photographed a little "off the ideal" center of the page.

Powerful?

The **power** characteristic – being authoritative-*looking* or, in voice-overs, authoritative-*sounding* – is important when presenting a *fear appeal* message. Fear appeals are common in social marketing campaigns, as we will see in Chapter 18, but, as they tap into the *Problem-Avoidance* motive, some *commercial* products such as life insurance, or services such as home-protection can also use them. The Powerful presenter can be a "real-people" presenter or a celebrity, though a celebrity should be used when Brand Recall is an objective.

Power, the sixth potential characteristic, concludes the CESLIP Presenter Model.

EXECUTIONAL INTEGRATION TACTICS

We noted earlier, in Chapter 4 on benefit positioning, that integration of the ads and the promotions in the marcoms campaign for the brand or brand-item can be achieved in either of two ways: by "cosmetic" integration or by "brand personality." Integration is deliberately focused on the *Brand Identity* element of positioning (again see the key diagram at the beginning of this chapter) because integration is *usually not possible* for the *Category positioning* or the *Key-benefit positioning*. For different target groups, the category need and key benefit *may* differ; the specific key benefit or benefits, and the entry-tickets, will *almost certainly* differ; and the benefit claims themselves will *definitely* differ.

Cosmetic integration

One way to achieve integration is cosmetically – by giving the ads and offers a "look and feel" that is executionally consistent. Cosmetic Integration should be superficial only and *not* extend to the message content. The desired processing responses are: (1) "Look – it's something *new* from [e.g.] Volvo," and (2) "What do they want me to know *now,* or how would they like me to feel *now?*" IBM has been employing the cosmetic integration tactic for the past several years in its campaigns for its sub-brands, "Business Solutions" (blue top and bottom border strips in TV commercials) and "e-Business" (black strips although we note that, in Australia, IBM has not used the black strips in its recent newspaper ads – why, we're not sure, but we think it's a mistake on IBM's part). The Absolut Vodka ads shown earlier in the chapter use cosmetic integration perfectly.

Integration by brand personality

An alternative way to achieve executional integration is by bringing out the brand's or sub-brand's "personality," not only in master-brand or sub-brand ads, but also by "lending" the brand's personality to ads and offers for its *brand-items*. This option for integration assumes that the manager has conducted adequate research and agreed on the Brand Personality Approach by identifying either (a) a concise and communicable set of personality traits as strategically desirable "properties" for the brand or sub-brand to "own" or (b) a personality *Archetype,* as described in Chapters 3 and 4.

A list of brand personality Traits that can be considered is provided by Aaker, although we recommend that the advertiser choose from the *specific* traits listed in her article rather than the *summary* traits which she identified, which are "Sincere", "Exciting", "Confident",

"Sophisticated", and "Ruggedly individualistic."[67] For instance, the new personality trait for the Sprite soft-drink brand is: *"Funky."* In mid-2004 a new presenter character, Miles Thirst, an African-American poet/philosopher with "Hip-Hop sensibility" began in Sprite's TV ads, with "his" own Website, milesthirst.com, to lend the "Funky" trait to the brand.[68] "Funky" is a good example of the need to select a specific trait and not to be limited by Aaker's five summary traits ("Funky" does not fit any of them properly, even the last).

The above is the nomothetic (separate traits) approach to brand personality. In contrast, the Archetype approach is an ideographic (trait cluster, or personality *type*) approach. For instance, "Dickensian," "Mother Theresian" or "Bill Gatesian" are personality *types,* as too are archetypes such as "The Warrior/Hero/Champion," "The Jester," or "The Caregiver." A personality type is based on extreme ratings on just a few traits, as are archetypes.

The brand personality trait list, or the archetypal template, should be employed as "filter" ratings[69] in pre-testing the brand's or sub-brand's ads and promotion offers to ensure that the executions fit.

SUMMARY

The second component of an ad, which takes up most of the ad's time or space, is Brand Awareness tactics and Brand Preference tactics. The tactics differ radically, depending on whether the brand awareness communication objective is Brand Recognition or Brand Recall, and on which one of four types of brand choice process the brand preference emerges from: Low-Involvement/Informational, Low-Involvement/Transformational, High-Involvement/Informational, or High-Involvement/Transformational. These six boxes are formalized in the Rossiter-Percy-Bellman grid.

We will not recite all the tactics here, but will just review the main ones. For Brand Recognition, use a logo or pack shot that inherently has high recognizability. The brand name or logo should be reasonably but not overly prominent in print ads and must receive adequate exposure time (the two-second rule) in broadcast ads. For new brand or brand-item launches, the category need must also be shown. For Brand Recall, the essential realization is that brand names do not simply get recalled on a spontaneous basis. Brand name recall is prompted by the category need arising in the customer's mind. Accordingly, brand-recall ads have to teach customers to associate the category need and our brand name, which is a process of verbal rote learning and repetition. The link of category need to brand name, not just the brand name alone, must be repeated in the ad and should receive further repetition due to advertising frequency in the media. There are also some memory-assisting devices for brand recall that are worth a try, such as mnemonics, personalization, or the use of a celebrity presenter.

All ads have not only the communication objective of brand awareness, but also brand preference. Brand preference tactics for Low-Involvement/Informational choices are to use the most extreme, but legal, key benefit claim possible and to limit the number of claims to one or two. Brand preference tactics for Low-Involvement/Transformational brand choice are to make an extreme emotionally positive key benefit claim and to make sure that the execution of that claim is unique to the brand.

For ads in the two high-involvement quadrants, the tactics become necessarily more numerous. For High-Involvement/Informational brand preference, which is the usual type for durables, for direct-response ads, and for personal selling, the benefit claims have to be tailored not to push too far upwards from the target audience customer's prior attitude but to push just to the top of the prospect's latitude of acceptance. Multiple benefit claims can be employed, up to a maximum of about seven claims, and the key benefit claim must be emphasized. High-Involvement/Informational is also the place to use the two-sided "refutational" approach, preceded by a positive visual, for negative prior-attitude prospects. For small challenger brands, it is the place to employ explicit comparison advertising. For High-Involvement/Transformational brand choice, the tailoring of benefit claims is different – they must focus on emotional authenticity specifically for the target group, and this may require separate executions if the target group includes subgroups of diverse lifestyles. The benefit claims should overclaim on transformational benefits including the key benefit. Many High-Involvement/Transformational products and services, being very expensive, or very risky for one's self-image, secondarily have to provide some informational benefits to close the sale, and these should be just to the top of the latitude of acceptance, not overclaimed. Often, the informational benefit claims are made in follow-up ads, or on the Website, or by personal selling. "Branding" should employ high-involvement/transformational tactics.

A carefully chosen *Presenter* can increase communication effects, particularly Brand Preference. The presenter decision is assisted by the CESLIP Presenter Model. The presenter should be a *celebrity* if Brand Recall has to be increased substantially. The presenter absolutely must be perceived as either a *technical expert* or an *expert user* (providing an immediately evident expertise *hook* to the product or service). If the presenter is a "real people" presenter, not a celebrity, the presenter must be perceived as sincere when delivering the message. The presenter should either be likable, because liking helps to magnify perceived expertise, or be ideal-similar, if the advertised product or service is socially conspicuous. Power is an additional characteristic of the presenter for delivering a "fear appeal" message, as in many social marketing campaigns. Note that the SLIP characteristics work *only if* the presenter is perceived as an Expert.

Also, there are tactics for creative integration *across* ads and promotion offers. Creative integration should be achieved cosmetically rather than in the substantive content of the ads or promotions, which are bound to differ across the marcoms campaigns for the brand. Cosmetic integration proper is achieved by giving the ads and offers the same "look and feel" so that when the prospective customer first sees one of the ads or offers, he or she immediately realizes which brand is being advertised while the content suggests that a new message about the brand is about to be presented. An alternative form of creative integration is integration by brand personality (traits or archetype). If this approach is adopted, all ads and offers for the brand and its brand-items should be pre-screened to ensure that they reflect its personality traits or archetypal character.

DISCUSSION QUESTIONS

8.1 Write the audio script for a Radio commercial designed to increase Brand Recall of the company that fixes your car when it needs servicing or repairs. The script must have some appropriate Brand Preference content as well. Next to the script, point out the tactics that you have used.

8.2 What tactics would you use in an advertising campaign to generate Brand Recognition for a new nationwide online grocery shopping service that will also be advertising on the Web and by direct mail?

8.3 In an ad for a Low-Involvement/Informational product, what specific tactics are available for making the key benefit claim extreme? Illustrate these in a rough ad for Listerine.

8.4 In an ad for a Low-Involvement/Transformational product, what specific tactics are available for making the key benefit claim extreme? Illustrate these in a rough ad for M&Ms.

8.5 Here is a true test of your copywriting ability. On the left-hand side of the page, in double spacing, create a Direct-Response Ad to sell men's or women's custom-made suits. Invent a brand name for the company. On the right-hand side of the page – and you will probably require two or three pages – insert discussion aligned with the tactics that you have used.

8.6 Construct a TV commercial script, with storyboard video scenes, for a ski resort targeting would-be Favorable Brand Switchers in the 18–34 year-old age group.

8.7 Use the CESLIP Presenter Model to evaluate the suitability of the potential pairing of these Presenters with these Products: (a) a "typical customer" testimonial for an investment advisory service, (b) Keanu Reeves, the movie actor, for a new video game, and (c) Kylie Minogue, the singer, for Maybelline lipstick.

NOTES

1. The Rossiter-Percy Grid was first introduced in J.R. Rossiter and L. Percy, *Advertising & Promotion Management*, New York: McGraw-Hill, 1987. Its superiority over the well-known FCB Grid was demonstrated in J.R. Rossiter, L. Percy, and R.J. Donovan, A better advertising planning grid, *Journal of Advertising Research*, 1991, 31(5), pp. 11–21. It was continued, with several updates to the tactics, in J.R. Rossiter and L. Percy, *Advertising Communications & Promotion Management*, New York: McGraw-Hill, 1997. As a planning tool, the Rossiter-Percy Grid has held up well – but here, in the present book, in the Rossiter-Percy-Bellman Grid, we make important modifications to both the brand awareness and brand preference tactics.

2. In their 1997 book.

3. P.W. Henderson and J.A. Cote, Guidelines for selecting or modifying logos, *Journal of Marketing*, 1998, 62(2), pp. 14–30. Henderson and Cote and colleagues repeated their study with Chinese consumers in China and Singapore and found that much the same characteristics of visual brand marks predicted high recognition, with high realism being particularly important; see P.W. Henderson, J.A. Cote, S.M. Leung, and B. Schmitt, Building strong brands in Asia: selecting the visual components of image to maximize brand strength, *International Journal of Research in Marketing*, 2003, 20(4), pp. 297–313.

4. Shapes are likely to be processed only by feature analysis, which is sufficient for recognition, whereas real objects –

especially if shown against a normal background "in context" – are likely to be processed by semantic analysis, for meaning. See S. Shapiro, When an ad's influence is beyond our conscious control: perceptual and conceptual fluency effects caused by incidental ad exposure, *Journal of Consumer Research,* 1999, 26(1), pp. 16–36.

5. R. Thomaselli, Reebok's strategy: play up Vector logo, *Advertising Age,* August 25, 2003, p. 6.

6. Recent neuro-imaging studies prove that a pretty close representation of the icon is indeed imprinted in the brain, in the so-called early visual cortex, whose neurons correspond with the geometric pattern of the retina of the eye. Not only the visual representations of real objects but also self-generated visual images are stored iconically. See S.M. Kosslyn and W.L. Thompson, When is early visual cortex activated during visual mental imagery?, *Psychological Bulletin,* 2003, 129(5), pp. 723–746.

7. See J.R. Rossiter and L. Percy, Visual communication in advertising, in R.J. Harris (Ed.), *Information Processing Research in Advertising,* Hillsdale, NJ: Lawrence Erlbaum Associates, 1983, chapter 4.

8. J.U. McNeal and M.F. Ji, Children's visual memory of packaging, *Journal of Consumer Marketing,* 2003, 20(5), pp. 400–427.

9. Estimate by M. Morrin from Russo and Leclerc's (1994) study. See M. Morrin, The impact of brand extensions on parent brand memory structures and retrieval processes, *Journal of Marketing Research,* 1999, 36(4), pp. 517–525; J.E. Russo and F. Leclerc, An eye-fixation analysis of choice processes for consumer nondurables, *Journal of Consumer Research,* 1994, 21(2), pp. 274–290.

10. R. Pieters and M. Wedel, Attention capture and transfer: brand, pictorial and text size effects in advertisements, *Journal of Marketing,* 2004, in press. Also, Starch ad readership norms show that the brand is noticed 79% of the time in newspaper ads and 86% of the time in magazine ads, among those who notice the ad at all.

11. See the rejection of the "spreading activation" (two-way) model in favor of the "spooky action at a distance" (one-way) model of paired-associates learning, in D.L. Nelson, C.L. McEvoy, and L. Pointer, Spreading activation or spooky action at a distance?, *Journal of Experimental Psychology: Learning, Memory, and Cognition,* 2003, 29(1), pp. 42–52.

12. J.R. Rossiter and L. Percy, 1983, same reference as note 7.

13. R.H. Coulter and M.A. Sewall, A test of prescriptive advice from the Rossiter-Percy advertising planning grid using radio commercials, in C.T. Allen and D. Roedder John, (Eds), *Advances in Consumer Research,* 21, 1994, pp. 276–281. We expect this finding would hold also for TV commercials, as their audio is similar to that of a radio commercial.

14. The P&O and New Zealand examples are from Australian copywriter John Bevins, an expert in personalizing taglines.

15. R.H. Holman and S. Hecker, Advertising impact: creative elements affecting brand recall, in J.H. Leigh and C.R. Martin Jr. (Eds), *Current Issues and Research in Advertising,* Ann Arbor, MI: Graduate School of Business, University of Michigan, 1983, pp. 157–172.

16. K.A. Lutz and R. Lutz, The effects of interactive imagery on learning, *Journal of Applied Psychology,* 1977, 62(4), pp. 493–498; and K. Lutz Alesandri, Strategies that influence memory for advertising communications, in R.J. Harris (Ed.), *Information Processing Research in Advertising,* Hillsdale, NJ: Lawrence Erlbaum Associates, 1983, chapter 3.

17. R.F. Yalch, Memory in a jingle jungle: music as a mnemonic device in communicating advertising slogans, *Journal of Applied Psychology,* 1991, 76(2), pp. 268–275.

18. K. Robertson, Strategically desirable brand name characteristics, *Journal of Consumer Marketing,* 1989, 6(4), pp. 61–71.

19. Y.H. Lee and K.S. Ang, Brand name suggestiveness: a Chinese language perspective, *International Journal of Research in Marketing,* 2003, 20(4), pp. 323–335.

20. K. Robertson, 1989, same reference as note 18.

21. T.M. Lowrey, L.J. Shrum, and T.M. Dubitsky, The relation between brand-name linguistic characteristics and brand-name memory, *Journal of Advertising,* 2003, 32(3), pp. 7–17.

22. R.J. Kent and C.T. Allen, Does competitive clutter in television advertising "interfere" with the recognition and recall of brand names and ad claims?, *Marketing Letters,* 1993, 4(2), pp. 175–184.

23. J.C. Maloney, Curiosity versus disbelief in advertising, *Journal of Advertising Research,* 1962, 2(2), pp. 2–8.

24. K. McArthur, Government to mediate vodka ad dispute, *Advertising Age,* September 8, 2003, p. 92.

25. D. Frith, Fastest claim not provable, *The Australian,* IT Section, November 18, 2003, p. 4.

26. P. Haan and C. Berkey, A study of the believability of the forms of puffery, *Journal of Marketing Communications,* 2002, 8(4), pp. 243–256.

27. Carl P. Wrighter (probably a *nom-de-plume*), *I Can Sell You Anything,* New York: Ballantine, 1984.

28. W.J. McGuire, The nature of attitudes and attitude change, in G. Lindzey and E. Aronson (Eds), *The Handbook of Social Psychology*, Vol. 3, Reading, MA: Addison-Wesley, 1969, chapter 2.

29. D.G. Mick, Consumer research and semiotics: exploring the morphology of signs, symbols, and significance, *Journal of Consumer Research,* 1986, 13(2), pp. 196–214. We have adapted his example.

30. C.S. Areni, The proposition-probability model of argument structure and message acceptance, *Journal of Consumer Research,* 2002, 29(2), pp. 168–187. For earlier use of this approach, see L. Percy and J.R. Rossiter, *Advertising Strategy,* New York: Praeger, 1980, chapter 4.

31. A.J. Kover, S.M. Goldberg, and W.L. James, Creativity vs. effectiveness? An integrating classification for advertising, *Journal of Advertising Research,* 35(6), pp. 29–40.

32. L. Freeman, Wisk rings in a new ad generation, *Advertising Age,* September 18, 1989, pp. 1, 81.

33. P. Desmet, Design and emotion, working paper, Department of Industrial Design, Delft University of Technology, The Netherlands, May 2003.

34. We note, however, that pictorial manikin scales do not have any advantage for recording the *type 1* emotions of arousal and pleasure; the pictorial ratings correlate at least .95 with the verbal ratings. See J.R. Rossiter and L. Percy, 1983, same reference as note 7.

35. H. Baumgartner, M. Sujan, and D. Padgett, Patterns of affective reactions to advertisements: the integration of moment-to-moment responses into overall judgments, *Journal of Marketing Research,* 1997, 34(2), pp. 219–232. The ads tested in this study were for low-involvement/transformational products such as Coca-Cola and Taster's Choice coffee.

36. H. Baumgartner, M. Sujan, and D. Padgett, 1997, same reference as note 35.

37. W.D. Wells, *How Advertising Works,* Mimeo, Chicago, IL: Needham, Harper & Steers Advertising, Inc., 1981.

38. J.R. Rossiter and L. Percy, Attitude change through visual imagery in advertising, *Journal of Advertising,* 1980, 9(2),

pp. 10–16; C. T. Allen and C.A. Janiszewski, Assessing the role of contingency awareness in attitudinal conditioning with implications for advertising research, *Journal of Marketing Research,* 1989, 26(1), pp. 30–43; E.W. Stuart, T.A. Shimp, and R.W. Engle, Classical conditioning of consumer attitudes: four experiments in an advertising context, *Journal of Consumer Research,* 1987, 14(3), pp. 334–349; J.B. Cohen and C.S. Areni, Affect and consumer behavior, in T.S. Robertson and H.H. Kassarjian (Eds), *Handbook of Consumer Behavior,* Englewood Cliffs, NJ: Prentice-Hall, 1991, chapter 6.

39. The Molson case was brought to our attention by P.S. Loroz, an advertising professor at Gonzaga University, Spokane, Washington, U.S.A., in a posting on the e-list, ELMAR, January 3, 2004. She gives Web links to an article on the campaign and to Molson's Website, for the ads.

40. W. Wood and J.M. Quinn, Forewarned and forearmed? Two meta-analytic syntheses of forewarnings of influence appeals, *Psychological Bulletin,* 2003, 129(1), pp. 119–138.

41. D.T. Gilbert, How mental systems believe, *American Psychologist,* 1991, 46(2), pp. 107–119. Also see F.R. Kardes, *Consumer Behavior and Managerial Decision Making,* 2nd edn, Prentice Hall, 2002.

42. The theoretical rationale for this is discussed at length in Wood and Quinn, 2003, same reference as note 40.

43. See C.W. Sherif, M. Sherif, and R.E. Nebergall, *Attitude and Attitude Change,* Philadelphia: Saunders, 1965; also W.J. McGuire, 1969, same reference as in note 28; and L. Percy and J.R. Rossiter, 1980, same reference as in note 30.

44. K.L. Keller and R. Staelin, Effects of quality and quantity of information on decision effectiveness, *Journal of Consumer Research,* 1987, 14(2), pp. 200–213.

45. For recent studies of this, see J. Friedrich, D. Fetherstonaugh, S. Casey, and D. Gallagher, Argument integration and attitude change: suppression effects in the integration of one-sided arguments that vary in persuasiveness, *Personality and Social Psychology Bulletin,* 1996, 22(2), pp. 179–191. Also see T. Meyvis and C. Janiszewski, Consumers' beliefs about product benefits: the effect of obviously irrelevant product information, *Journal of Consumer Research,* 2002, 28(4), pp. 618–635.

46. A.V. Muthukrishnan, M.T. Pham, and A. Mungale, Does greater amount of information always bolster attitudinal resistance?, *Marketing Letters,* 2001, 12(2), pp. 131–144.

47. F.R. Kardes and P.M. Herr, Order effects in consumer judgment, choice, and memory: the role of initial processing goals, in M.E. Goldberg, G. Gorn, and R.W. Pollay (Eds), *Advances in Consumer Research,* 17, 1990, pp. 541–546.

48. S.M.J. van Osselaer and C. Janiszewski, Two ways of learning brand associations, *Journal of Consumer Research,* 2001, 28(2), pp. 167–188.

49. F. Leclerc and J.D.C. Little, Can advertising copy make FSI coupons more effective?, *Journal of Marketing Research,* 1997, 34(4), pp. 473–484.

50. The research evidence on comparison advertising comes from a study of 1,016 TV commercials in which the brand preference measure was a shift to the advertised brand in a pre-exposure then post-exposure choice, by C. Pechmann and D.W. Stewart, How direct comparative ads and market share affect brand choice, *Journal of Advertising Research,* 1991, 31(6), pp. 47–55.

51. A.V. Muthukrishnan, L. Warlop, and J.W. Alba, The piecemeal approach to comparative advertising, *Marketing Letters,* 2001, 12(1), pp. 63–73.

52. For SCR and EMG measures, and validation, see M.K. Greenwald, B.W. Cook, III, and P.J. Lang, Affective judgment and psychophysiological response: dimensional covariation in the evaluation of pictorial stimuli, *Journal of Psychophysiology,* 1989, 3(1), pp. 51–64, and P.J. Lang, M.K. Greenwald, M.M. Bradley, and A.O. Hamm, Looking at pictures: affective, facial, visceral, and behavioral reactions, *Journal of Psychophysiology,* 1993, 30(3), pp. 261–273.

53. Some theorists claim that a very powerful feeling is the primary basis for high-involvement/transformational decisions and that the cognitive rationalization merely follows it. See, for example, A. Dijksterhuis, H. Aarts, and P.K. Smith, The power of the subliminal: on subliminal persuasion and other potential applications, in R. Hassin, J. Uleman and J. Bargh (Eds), *The New Unconscious,* New York: Oxford University Press, in press.

54. Adapted from a presentation by Grey Global Group, Emotional Trigger Points^{TM}, Conference on Branding & Emotion, Rotterdam School of Management, The Netherlands, May 27, 2003.

55. The "sublime" reaction was best analyzed by Immanuel Kant in 1764(!); see J.T. Goldthwait (Translator), *Immanual Kant's "Observations on the Feeling of the Beautiful and Sublime",* Berkeley: University of California Press, 1960, translator's introduction, especially pp. 34–35.

56. T. Davis and G. Gregory, Creating Diderot unities: quest for possible selves?, *Journal of Consumer Marketing,* 2003, 20(1), pp. 44–54; see also G. McCracken, *Culture and Consumption,* Bloomington, IN: Indiana University Press, 1988.

57. *Reader's Digest,* Most Trusted Brands Survey 2002, reported in *B&T Weekly,* November 22, 2002, p. 14.

58. M.R. Darby and E. Karni, Free competition and the optimal amount of fraud, *Journal of Law and Economics,* 1973, 16(1), pp. 67–88.

59. R.A. Formisano, R.W. Olshavsky, and S. Tapp, Choice strategy in a difficult task environment, *Journal of Consumer Research,* 1982, 8(4), pp. 474–479. In this survey, the authors found that 75% of people buying life insurance (median policy amount: U.S.$25,000) sought a quotation from only one insurance company and that 48% bought from the first salesperson who contacted them (thus showing considerable "faith").

60. A. Smidts and J.R. Rossiter, Presenter effects in advertising: the VisCAP model, paper presented at the Marketing Science Conference, Edmonton, Canada, June 27–30, 2002.

61. Channel Nine, Australia, evening news, February 26, 1998.

62. J.R.Rossiter and A. Smidts, A test of the VisCAP and ELM models of presenter effectiveness, paper presented at the Marketing Science Conference, College Park, MD, June 26–29, 2003.

63. Nike's stable of sports-star users, for instance, is costing Nike U.S.$340 million in 2004 alone, including a gamble on tainted star Kobe Bryant, who was recently signed on for U.S.$45 million; see R. Thomaselli, Nike bets big on range of endorsers, *Advertising Age,* January 24, 2004, p. 8.

64. J. Robinson and L.Z. McArthur, Impact of salient vocal qualities on causal attribution for a speaker's behavior, *Journal of Personality and Social Psychology,* 1982, 43(2), pp. 236–247; and P.J. De Paulo and B.M. De Paulo, Can deception by salespersons and customers be detected through non-verbal cues?, *Journal of Applied Social Psychology,* 1989, 19(18), pp. 1552–1577. They cite previous studies showing that professionals – such as detectives, police officers and customs officials – cannot reliably detect lying.

65. G. Patzer, *The Physical Attractiveness Phenomenon,* New York: Plenum, 1985.

66. F. Leclerc and colleagues called these "hybrid" products because they are rated in the middle of a scale of utilitarian

vs. hedonic, which indicates that *both* types of attributes apply. See F. Leclerc, B.H. Schmitt, and L. Dubé, Foreign branding and its effects on product perceptions and attitudes, *Journal of Marketing Research,* 1994, 31(2), pp. 263–270.

67. J.L. Aaker, Dimensions of brand personality, *Journal of Marketing Research,* 1997, 34(3), pp. 347–356. Also see the excellent article by J. Dean, Brand personality: a practitioner's perspective, *Proceedings of the Society for Consumer Psychology,* American Psychological Association, 1994, pp. 57–62. The trait listed last, "rugged individualism," was called "ruggedness" by Aaker but we have labeled it more accurately, we think, by using Hirschman's term for this trait; see E.C. Hirschman, Men, dogs, guns, and cars: the semiotics of rugged individualism, *Journal of Advertising,* 2003, 32(1), pp. 10–22.

68. K. MacArthur and J. Nelt, Sprite shifts gears in quest for street cred, *Advertising Age,* January 26, 2004, pp. 1, 29.

69. The Ted Bates agency, inventors of the famed Unique Selling Proposition, or USP, a single rational selling proposition approach that fits the low-involvement/ informational brand preference quadrant of the Rossiter-Percy-Bellman Grid, apparently adapted a heading in their creative brief form from "tone" to "brand personality" as early as 1980 or thereabouts; see the very good article by A. Azoulay and J.N. Kapferer, Do brand personality scales really measure brand personality?, *Brand Management,* 2003, 11(2), pp. 143–155.

CHAPTER 9

Attention tactics

We said at the outset of creative strategy that an ad is a complex piece of communication. Even the seemingly simplest ads have four components at a deep analysis level. The first three components, as we have seen in the previous two chapters, are the Key Benefit Claim, the Creative Idea, and Brand Awareness and Brand Preference tactics. The fourth component of an ad is Attention Tactics. Attention tactics are structural and executional tactics used to gain attention initially and to hold attention during processing of the message. We also said that Attention is the single biggest barrier facing advertising right now and it will become an even bigger barrier in the future. Pertinent to this chapter, fully half of the variation between ads in their ability to gain and hold attention is caused by the ad's *structural features* – its length or size, and pattern or layout – not by the ad's message content.[1]

Attention tactics, as might be expected, differ according to the advertising *medium* in which the ad or offer is to be placed. Accordingly, Attention tactics are described for each of the major media's ads separately: TV commercials, radio commercials, newspaper ads, magazine ads, directory ads, outdoor ads, and online ads.

TV COMMERCIALS

On average, and this *is* an average, the typical 30-second (alternatively written as ":30") **TV commercial**, on a typical showing, can expect to gain the Attention of 65% of the TV program's viewing audience.[2] This means that the TV viewer has a .65 probability of paying attention to the TV commercial during any particular exposure opportunity. (This and other advertising attention probabilities will be revisited in the section of the book on media strategy because of their obvious importance in media schedules.) Recent research suggests that this probability is about .60 during group viewing and increases to about .70 during TV programs that are viewed by one person in the household, alone (with the increase in available TV channels and the ubiquity of multiple-set households, just over half of all TV viewing in advanced countries is done alone).[3] Therefore, we estimate that for advanced countries the average probability of attention to the average TV commercial is .65. That is now. The probability of attention to TV commercials will become lower for people who adopt digital video recorders (DVRs) such as TiVo or Replay TV. DVRs are expected to be in 20% – or one in five – of U.S. homes by 2007; DVRs are now in 2% of homes and research with DVR owners indicates that they skip (one button-press on the DVR jumps 30 seconds forward) TV ads 70% of the time.[4] Their probability of attention to the full ad, therefore, will drop to $.3 \times .65 = .20$ (they would see the start of the ad to decide whether to skip, but their probability of watching any ad in full would be .20). Although the overall loss of full TV ad "reach" across all U.S. households is estimated to be about 14% in several years time, this is meaningless in practice because it is based on an average of *two very different* viewing groups. The loss of reach applies only to DVR households, with the loss being 70% for them and zero for all other households. DVR ownership will become a factor in describing the Media Target.

The attention *probabilities* by structure for TV commercials are listed in Table 9.1, together with other attention *tactics* discussed below. The structural features and tactics are jointly called "attention factors."

TABLE 9.1 *TV commercial attention factors.*

ATTENTION FACTOR		PROBABILITY OF ATTENTION
30-second commercial (standard):	Overall	.65
	Group viewing	.60
	Viewing alone	.70
90-second commercial or longer		1.00
60-second commercial		.76
15-second commercial		.54
10-second commercial		.45
DVR owner		.3 of the above figures
Fast cuts (15 or more per 30-second commercial)		No difference in attention but lower message recall
Interest pattern:	Informational	Two peaks
	Transformational	Rising to peak plus kick-up at end
Multi-tasking test:	Video	Brand identity and key benefit should
	Audio	be apparent from both
Fast-forwarding test:	Video	Brand identity and gist of message should be apparent when fast-forwarding

Length

The main internal structural factor that affects attention is the commercial's *length*. The standard TV commercial's length worldwide, except for Japan, is 30 seconds. In Japan, the standard length is now just 10 seconds and there are many five-second commercials on Japanese TV!

Considering the worldwide standard of a 30-second commercial, which has an attention probability of .65, a 90-second or longer TV commercial (usually a **TV infomercial**), can be expected to gain 100% attention (1.00 probability). A 60-second commercial, on average, has an attention probability of .76; a 15-second commercial, .54; and a 10-second commercial, .45.

Fast cuts

Cuts are video scene changes that occur on average every half-second or faster, rather than *edits*, which are camera angle changes within a scene. The average number of cuts in a 30-second TV commercial is about 13; more than this is "fast cuts."[5] Fast cutting is suitable for *Transformational* commercials if the creative team wishes to use this format; indeed, fast cuts can increase Arousal during processing, which is desirable.[6] Fast cuts should *not* be used for *Informational* commercials, however, because viewers cannot take in the content of the benefit claim if the ad's structure is changing at the same time.[7] We note here that good Direct-Response TV commercials or Infomercials use fast talking but *not* fast video cuts for the benefit claims. Whereas slow- and fast-paced commercials are equally good at holding *attention* throughout, fast-cut commercials produce lower recall, and therefore less *learning*, of the central message content. With fast cuts, only the peripheral, executional content is likely to be learned; this is usually adequate for Transformational benefit claims, in which the focus is on e^+, or more likely e^{++}.

Interest pattern

For *Informational* commercials, the interest pattern, which can be measured with moment-to-moment ratings by a sample of $n = 30$ from the target group or groups, should be double-peaked: high at the onset as the "problem" is dramatized, a brief pause in the middle as the brand-item's Brand Identity is introduced, followed by a final peak as the "solution" involving the brand-item is shown. This pattern corresponds to the ideal sequence for Operant (Instrumental) Learning, which is how Informational ads work to increase Brand Preference (see Figure 9.1, panel (a)). The "problem" serves as the discriminative stimulus, S^D; the "response," R, is to *use* the brand-item; the "solution" is the reinforcing stimulus that follows, S^{r-}, the minus superscript indicating a "negative" reinforcer, negative in that the reinforcement works by "removing" the problem. The Brand Identity is inserted again at the end to assist brand awareness: to maximize Brand *Recognition*, employ the two-second rule for pack shots or brand marks; to maximize Brand *Recall*, insert the Category Need → Brand Name association just before, and then again after, the high-interest second peak.

For *Transformational* commercials, make sure that the interest pattern of the commercial is one of increasing arousal rising to a high peak with a further short rise or "kick-up" at the end, not a let-down as sometimes occurs by inserting a dealer tag (see Figure 9.1, panel (b)). This pattern will increase both Brand *Recall* (Brand *Recognition* is a matter of holding the pack shot or brand mark for at least two seconds) and Brand Preference.[8] This pattern corresponds to the ideal sequence for Human Evaluative Conditioning[9], which is how Transformational ads work to increase Brand Preference (we mentioned HEC in Chapter 8 for the *women's* Molson beer ad, noting that the men's ad relies on Operant Learning, not HEC). The brand-item, or brand in the case of brand ads, is the to-be-conditioned stimulus, CS, and the instinctual, archetypal, or emotional benefit claim (assuming positive) is the positive unconditional stimulus, US^+, that follows it. The conditioned response, CR, which should now be elicited whenever you think of or see the brand-item, is a more favorable *feeling* about the brand-item, which increases preference for it. The Brand Identity is inserted again at the end, this time not as a visual brand mark or pack shot, because this would undermine the US^+, but *auditorially*, as a voice-over, which would include the ending of a jingle if the audio is a jingle. If the brand awareness objective is *Visual Brand Recognition*, the pack shot or brand mark must be shown early, and clearly, because this produces the most effective conditioning arrangement: forward conditioning, that is, $CS \rightarrow US^+$.

TV ads, both for Informational and Transformational products or services, *do* have to produce *emotional Arousal*. In the Informational case, it is usually a strong *negative* emotion (the "problem") that will produce the arousal. In the words of the advertising agency Clemenger BBDO,

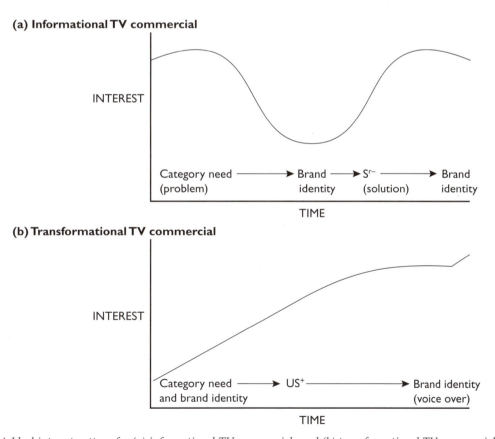

FIGURE 9.1 *Ideal interest pattern for (a) informational TV commercials and (b) transformational TV commercials.*

Melbourne, you want (informational) "ads that kick the door down." The second emotional peak then occurs with the enlightening demonstration of the brand-item as the "solution." On the other hand, in the same agency's words, you want (transformational) "ads that walk straight into your heart." Walking into your heart – with a jump in your heart at the end – nicely characterizes the arousal pattern to aim for with a *positive* emotional execution in Transformational TV ads.[10]

Mystery ads

A **mystery ad** can be either Informational or Transformational. The Mystery Ad format uses the same respective interest pattern but *omits the initial brand identification*, identifying the brand only at the *end*. The "Streaker" commercial for (then) new Nike Shox sports shoes, discussed in Chapter 7 and excerpted in Figure 7.9, is both Postmodern, by pretending to be a live newscast, and a Mystery Ad. The mystery ad format increases Brand *Recall* for a *new* brand or brand-item because it has the right sequence of category need (cue) followed by brand name (response) and it also, apparently, increases brand *name recognition*.[11] However, after seeing the Mystery Ad a *few times*, viewers tend to mentally insert the brand name as soon as the ad begins, so that the Mystery Ad now functions like a Conventional Ad. Thus, eventually it conforms to the respective Informational or Transformational interest pattern.

Mystery Ads should *not* be used for *established* brands or brand-items. The reason is attitudinal: having been led through an intriguing mystery about which brand it could be, viewers are very likely to be disappointed – a negative emotion – when they find out it's a brand they already know of. This places an e^- (actually a US^-) right after the Brand Identity!

So, the mystery ad format is for *new brand or brand-item launches* only.

Independent functioning of video and audio

Whereas the video track and audio track of the TV commercial are meant to work *together*, the advertiser has to allow for the prevalence of multi-tasking, that is, viewers doing something else while watching TV. The manager should arrange a small-scale test of the rough TV commercial to ensure that the Brand Identity and the Key Benefit are apparent (a) when watching the *video* on its own, as when in another part of the room or in a bar or public venue – and that the brand identity and the gist of the message are apparent when *fast-forwarding* by VCR – and (b) when listening to the audio on its own, as when reading or working near the TV. *Silent or partially silent* TV commercials where the verbal message, or part of it, is supered only visually, by written words on the screen, are quite trendy for advertisers at present but they should *not* be used. Silent TV ads may work once, because you think something's wrong with the TV and glance at the screen; but, after that, the ad is likely to be unheard *and* unseen.

RADIO COMMERCIALS

On average, the typical 30-second **radio commercial** engages the Attention[12] of 30% of the audience tuned to the station at the time, meaning that the individual's probability of attention is .30 during any one playing of the ad. This is a bit less than half the attention probability that a 30-second *TV* commercial attracts.

Length

As shown in Table 9.2, the *length* of the radio commercial causes large differences in attention. The standard length, 30-second radio commercial has, on average, an attention probability of .30. Longer radio commercials have a higher probability of gaining attention, .42 for the average 60-second commercial. Shorter commercials score lower: .21 for the average 10-second radio commercial. Length interacts with listener demographics, with adult men being the worst attenders (so use a 60-second ad for them), women above average, and teenagers marginally the best attenders (e.g., .36 for a 30-second ad for teens, versus the all-ages average of .30).

TABLE 9.2 *Radio commercial attention factors.*

ATTENTION FACTOR		PROBABILITY OF ATTENTION	
30-second radio commercial (standard)		.30	
60-second commercial		.42	
25-second commercial		.24	
10-second commercial		.21	
Demographic differences in attention:		30-second commercials	60-second commercials
	Adult men	.27	.36
	Adult women	.33	.45
	Teenagers	.36	.48
Format differences in attention:		30-second commercials	60-second commercials
	Slice-of-life (minidrama)	.42	.51
	Consumer testimonial or interview	.39	.45
	Jingle	.30	.36
	Live announcer-read	.30	.36
Interest-maximizing factors:	Open with absolute-interest words or the preferred music style of listeners		
	Use high-imagery sentences		
	End with rhetorical-doubt question (straight ad); "klitchik" not "klinker" (humorous ad); or upbeat finish (musical or jingle ad)		

Format

Another big factor in attention to radio commercials is the *format* (see Table 9.2). The two formats that attract very high attention, relatively, are *slice-of-life*, also known as the *minidrama*, and *consumer testimonials or interviews*. Two other common formats, live announcer-read commercials and jingles, produce average attention at the 30-second length but they lose attention, relative to the other two types, when extended to 60 seconds.

Within *any* of the above formats for radio commercials, though not mentioned in the table, the same respective *interest pattern* should be aimed for as for TV commercials, the Informational pattern or the Transformational pattern (again see Figure 9.1).

Style

Layered on these format choices for radio commercials are the *style* factors of straight verbal script, humorous verbal script, or musical jingle. *Straight verbal script* commercials, which are usually Informational, should open with an absolute-interest word or words (e.g., "Danger," "Sex," "Money") and employ sentences that generate visual imagery (such sentences use concrete, rather than abstract, words although the whole of the clause must be easily visualized[13], e.g., "Your car's battery *dies*..." not "Your car's battery is *unreliable*...") and an effective ending is a *rhetorical-doubt question*[14] (e.g., "Are you sure *your* battery will last the weekend?" – a question that could be asked as the final words in a commercial that's just recommended that you install a new Exide).

Humorous radio commercials, either Informational or Transformational but especially Informational, must not use the irrelevant-joke ending known as a *klinker* (a common error in humorous *TV* commercials as well) because it will wipe out memory of, and any imagery from, the foregoing selling message. On the other hand, a message-relevant joke ending, known as a *klitchik*, can be very effective because it *reinforces* the message (e.g., the perennial VW Beetle's "Doesn't go in one year and out the other," or a relevant joke that the lads in England will get, "Steinlager. Not just another Australian in Britain").[15] We point out that, contrary to popular belief, humor as a style makes *no difference* to the attention paid to a radio commercial.[16]

Music-dominant radio commercials – including jingles – get high initial attention if the music fits the preference of the radio station's listeners. If the musical commercial is Transformational, the music – again including jingles – must have an upbeat finish.

NEWSPAPER ADS

The average one-page, black and white **newspaper ad** gains the Attention of 43% of the paper's readers, which is an attention probability of .43. This overall attention probability is modified by size, color, and placement[17], as summarized in Table 9.3.

Size and color

A full-color (known technically as *four-color*) one-page newspaper ad has almost the same probability of attention, .64, as a 30-second TV commercial, .65. The addition of one color to black and white (known as *two-color*) also increases attention probability over black and white, to .56. The size chosen for the newspaper ad also affects attention. For new products or services, a two-page ad is worth buying, with an attention value of .52, although the large gain comes from a two-page, four-color ad, which will have an attention probability of .77. *Two* separate *one-page* ads would have an excellent chance, roughly double .43, or .86, of a reader seeing at least one of them. *Four-page or longer* newspaper ads, which technically are inserts (liftouts), achieve very high

TABLE 9.3 *Newspaper ad attention factors.*

ATTENTION FACTOR	PROBABILITY OF ATTENTION		
	BLACK & WHITE	2-COLOR	4-COLOR
1-page newspaper ad (standard)	.43	.56	.64
2-page ad	.52	.68	.77
½-page ad	.30	.39	.45
¼-page ad	.21	.27	.31

Placement factors:

Another ad on opposite page (1-page ad)	.47
Related editorial on opposite pages (1-page ad)	.34
Other ads on same page (½-page or smaller ad)	.17 (.20 if bottom, .22 if outer)
Related editorial on same page (½-page or smaller ad)	.26 (.31 if bottom, .34 if outer)
Sports section (1-page ad)	.22 for women readers

Interest-maximizing factors:

	LOW-INVOLVEMENT BRAND PREFERENCE	HIGH-INVOLVEMENT BRAND PREFERENCE
Picture	Maximize size, with a single dominant focal point	For HI/INFO, write the headline and copy first, but leave at least one-sixth of the full page for the picture; for HI/TRANS, maximize size, with a single dominant focal point
Headline	Complete headline, below picture if visual conveyer	Lead-in headline
Body copy	50 words maximum; lower case	50 to 200 words; lower case; bullet each benefit
Brand name, with brand mark (if any)	Brand-item name in headline, repeat with pack shot or brand mark at bottom right	Brand-item name with brand mark, anywhere below lead-in headline

attention, of course, and would be rated as 1.00 (not shown in the table). They are very expensive but very effective for a *major new product launch*. For instance, in Australia, Toyota launched its Prius petrol-electric hybrid car with a four-color, six-page insert, run twice the same week! Interest in the Prius ran hot immediately, according to dealers.[18] *Small* ads of ¼-page lose only about half of the one-page attention value, so for a short message for an *established product or service*, a series of these in the same issue is worth considering.

At the time of writing, many newspapers in Britain were moving to a compact (half-size) format.[19] The smaller size of the newspaper page will make no difference to the size factor for *ads*.

A one-page black and white ad, for instance, will still have a .43 attention value in the compact newspaper.

Placement

Placement affects attention to newspaper ads. Paradoxically, having *another ad* on the facing page increases attention to our ad somewhat, to .47 from the normal .43. *Related editorial content* on the facing page, however, hurts badly, a drop for our ad to .34 attention (the editorial text apparently distracts readers' attention from the ad – the exception here is when a special section attracts *extra people* to buy and read the paper such that a larger base of readers could outweigh the attention loss). For ads of size ½-*page or smaller*, related editorial on the same page also hurts, with attention falling from .30 to .26, and other ads on the same page really hurt, with attention to our ad falling to .17. There is one *gender* difference that applies, which is that ads placed in the sports section of the newspaper have about 50% lower readership by women, their probability of attention being only .22 for a one-page ad placed there.

Structure

What is the most effective structure for a newspaper ad? As summarized in the table, this depends on whether the ad is for an item whose choice is Low Involvement (low purchase risk) or High Involvement (high purchase risk). In either case, include a *picture* – for a newspaper ad without a picture, attention is about 30% lower, an attention probability of .30 rather than the standard .43!

(We will take this opportunity to recommend the **picture content for all types of print ads**. The picture must have *at least one* of the features[20] listed in Table 9.4. *People or animal pictures* must use at least one of the features in the left column. *Object pictures* must use at least one of the features in the right column.

Also because all types of print ads use a Headline, we define the two most effective types of headline – the **complete headline** and the **lead-in headline** – in Table 9.5. The two types of headline are exemplified in the various print ads in this chapter.)

TABLE 9.4 *Picture content for* all *print ads: 10 attention-getting features, of which the picture must have* at least one.

PERSON OR ANIMAL PICTURE	OBJECT PICTURE
1. Eyes (direct gaze)	5. Beautiful scene or object
2. Baby	6. Danger-suspense scene
3. Erotic	7. Cultural icon
4. Celebrity	8. Bright color
	9. Simple object on white space
	10. Incongruous object (remote conveyer)

TABLE 9.5 *Two main types of headline for* all *print ads.*

COMPLETE HEADLINE

Includes the brand and the benefit. Takes the conversation form of either:

- an announcement
- a command
- a testimonial statement (endorsement)

LEAD-IN HEADLINE

Promises the benefit but doesn't tell you which brand delivers it and thus makes you want to read the body copy. Takes the conversation form of either:

- an instruction (how to . . .)
- an explanation (why . . .)
- a question
- a curious word, phrase, or clause

For a *High-Involvement/Informational* newspaper ad, the verbal text is very important, so the headline and body copy should be written first and the remaining space, though *at least one-sixth* of a full page, left for the picture.[21] For an ad for a product or service in the *other three* brand preference quadrants, *maximize* the picture's size: to at least half the ad's size – the larger the better. To further increase the probability of attention, use a picture that has a *single dominant focal point*.[22] If a visual conveyer is used, which is the normal choice for a low-involvement brand preference ad, the focal point should be the conveyer.

Finish the ad as follows. For a *Low-Involvement* brand preference newspaper ad, use a *Complete* headline, taking as many words and lines as you wish, which mentions the brand-item and its key benefit. If the picture is a Visual Conveyer, place the headline *below it* so that it prompts the conveyer (do not place the headline above or it will interfere with the visual conveyer by pre-labeling the picture). Keep the body copy to no more than 50 words (a lot fewer will do in most cases) and repeat the brand-item name, with its pack shot or brand mark, at the *bottom right* of the ad.

For a *High-Involvement* brand preference newspaper ad, use a *Lead-in* headline (such as VW Beetle's famous ad, shown in Figure 9.2, which uses the curious-word headline: "Lemon") so that prospective customers will read the copy. The copy should be *more than 50 words* and can run to about 200 words with no loss of readership, and each benefit claim should be listed in *bullet points*. The brand-item name and brand mark can be placed anywhere below the headline.

The *headline font* in newspaper ads can be all capitals or in lower case (it makes no difference). The *body copy font* should be lower case, in a serif ("little feet") typeface, and set in dark type on a light background (absence of *any* of these three characteristics will greatly reduce readership of the body copy). Short sentences and short (one- or two-syllable) words do not assist readership but should be favored because they increase attention to the ad overall.[23]

MAGAZINE ADS

Magazine ads produce differences in Attention depending on where they are placed – in broad-audience magazines, a category which includes consumer magazines and general business magazines such as *Fortune* and *Business Week*, or in narrow-audience industry magazines. In general, ads in *industry magazines* have higher attention probabilities because they are read

Lemon.

This Volkswagen missed the boat.

The chrome strip on the glove compartment is blemished and must be replaced. Chances are you wouldn't have noticed it; Inspector Kurt Kroner did.

There are 3,389 men at our Wolfsburg factory with only one job: to inspect Volkswagens at each stage of production. (3000 Volkswagens are produced daily; there are more inspectors than cars.)

Every shock absorber is tested (spot checking won't do), every windshield is scanned. VWs have been rejected for surface scratches barely visible to the eye.

Final inspection is really something! VW inspectors run each car off the line onto the Funktionsprüfstand (car test stand), tote up 189 check points, gun ahead to the automatic brake stand, and say "no" to one VW out of fifty.

This preoccupation with detail means the VW lasts longer and requires less maintenance, by and large, than other cars. (It also means a used VW depreciates less than any other car.)

We pluck the lemons; you get the plums.

FIGURE 9.2 *Probably the most famous lead-in (curiosity) headline of all time: Doyle Dane Bernbach's Sam Levenson's "Lemon" ad for the Volkswagen Beetle.*

SOURCE: Courtesy of Doyle Dane Bernbach.

by more selective, though smaller, audiences. Also, one-page, four-color ads are standard in consumer and general business magazines, whereas one-page, black and white ads are standard in industry magazines. It should be noted that the format of the magazine (page size) does not affect attention to ads within it. Advertisers once had concerns about the small page size of *Reader's Digest* and, in the U.S.A., *TV Guide* but ad attention studies found that ads placed in these small magazines performed no differently than those in regular-sized magazines. The problem with small magazines is not attention, but readability of the body copy; if you take normal-sized copy and shrink it, older readers will have difficulty!

Consumer and general business magazine ads: size and color

Attention factors for *consumer and general business* magazine ads are shown in the first column of Table 9.6. The *size* of the ad and whether it uses *color* are the main determinants of attention. A standard one-page, four-color ad will, on average, be noticed by 49% of the magazine's readers, an attention value of .49. Whereas it might be thought intuitively that a black and white ad would stand out in this all-color advertising environment, the attention figures show that this is not the case. Black and white ads lose attention, at .34, and two-color ads *also* lose, at .39. Therefore, use *four-color* ads. The only factors that substantially increase attention to consumer and general business magazine ads are a very expensive four-or-more-pages, four-color insert, .78; a two-page color spread, .64; or a pop-up insert (the cardboard tag you sometimes see in magazines), at .64; or placing the ad in the very expensive outside back cover position if it's available, which also has a .64 attention value.

TABLE 9.6 *Magazine ad attention factors.*

ATTENTION FACTOR	CONSUMER AND GENERAL BUSINESS MAGAZINE ADS	INDUSTRY MAGAZINE ADS
1-page, 4-color magazine ad (standard for consumer and general business magazines)	.49	.64
With pop-up insert to 1-page, 4-color ad	.64	.83
Multi-page, 4-color insert	.78	n.a.
2-page, 4-color spread	.64	1.00
½-page, 4-color ad	.34	.45
1-page, 2-color ad	.39	.55
1-page black & white ad (standard for industry magazines)	.34	.46
½-page black & white ad	.24	.32
Position in magazine:		
Inside front cover	.59	.83
Inside back cover	.59	.83
Outside back cover	.64	.83
Inside pages	.49	.46

Continues

TABLE 9.6 *Continued*

Interest-maximizing factors:

	LOW-INVOLVEMENT BRAND PREFERENCE	HIGH-INVOLVEMENT BRAND PREFERENCE
Picture	Maximize size; single dominant focal point	At least half of the ad's space should be a picture; single dominant focal point
Headline	Complete headline; up to 8 words; lower case; below picture if picture is a visual conveyer	Lead-in headline; 1 to 5 words; lower case
Body copy	50 words maximum; lower case	50 to 200 words; lower case; bullet each benefit
Brand name, with brand mark (if any)	Brand-item name in headline, then repeat it with pack shot or brand mark at bottom right	Brand-item name with brand mark, anywhere below lead-in headline

Industrial magazine ads: size and color

In *industrial* magazines, *four-color* ads stand out, with an attention value of .64 compared with .46 for a one-page, black and white ad. *Two-color* ads also increase attention over black and white, at .55. Even a $1/2$-page, four-color ad, at .45, gets as much attention as a standard black and white ad. In industry magazines, all *cover* positions have very high attention value at .83 and are worth investigating, despite the high cost, when launching a new product in a large-value industrial market.

Structure

In terms of interest-maximizing factors, magazine ads work the same way no matter which type of magazine they are placed in, consumer or industrial. The main difference is whether the ad is advertising for low-involvement brand preference, or high-involvement brand preference. In the *Low-Involvement* situation, the *picture* is the most important element. The picture should be as *large* as possible[24], occupying at least half the ad's space, and should have a *single dominant focal point*. The picture can include a Visual Conveyer (this would be the dominant focal point) as conveyers are known to increase attention. Always use a picture of a concrete (real) object or presenter, never an abstract or vague picture. The headline in the low-involvement preference ad should be a *Complete headline* of up to eight words, though not more than two lines, naming the brand and its key benefit; this is because with such little risk in trying the product, most people will not bother to read the body copy. The headline should be set in *lower case*, not all capitals. If the picture is a visual conveyer, the headline should be placed below it. What body copy there is should consist of *no more than 50 words* and should be set in readable, *lower-case* type. The brand name should be *in* the headline, as already stated, and repeated with a pack shot or brand mark at the bottom right.

In magazine ads for *High-Involvement* brand preference, the *picture* is still the main attention-drawing element and should occupy *at least half the ad's space – more*, if the ad is half a page or less, because picture size *on the page* is what draws attention. The picture should have *one dominant focal point*. Headline and copy work together for inducing high-involvement brand preference; thus, a *Lead-in headline* of one to five words should be used, designed to make the reader want to read further. The body copy should *exceed* 50 words and can extend to about 200 words without losing readership.[25] Multiple benefits should be *bulleted*. A *lower-case font* should be used for the body copy. The *brand name*, which is not included in the headline if a lead-in headline is used, can be placed with the brand mark, if a brand mark is used to identify the brand, *anywhere below* the lead-in headline. It does not have to be at the bottom right.

Always phrase magazine ad headlines *positively*; a negative-sounding headline will be detected as negative preattentively and will reduce noticing of the ad, pushing the attention probability for the whole ad down from the normal .49 to .37, which of course also means fewer will read the body copy.[26] *Nouns* and *personal words* ("I" or "You") in the headline increase attention to the ad.[27]

Should you apply "KISS," that is, "Keep it simple, stupid!" in the body copy of magazine ads – indeed all print ads? The answer is yes, but not for the usual reasons given for KISSing. Short paragraphs, short sentences, and short words do *not* increase people's understanding of what is being said[28], nor is simplicity more persuasive.[29] Rather, the greater *contrast* between the words and the white space will increase initial attention to the ad.[30]

YELLOW PAGES/DIRECTORY ADS

Yellow Pages and other more specialized **directories** available in various industries – in paper form and increasingly online – are a surprisingly large and important advertising medium. They are often the *only* medium that professionals and tradespeople use. You can buy a regular in-column listing or ads in various sizes (see the categories in Table 9.7). Yellow Pages and other Directory ads, of course, are *Direct-Response* Ads.

Size

Yellow Pages/Directory ads range in *size* from a simple in-column listing of the business name, to in-column ads, to larger ads that go across columns – called Display ads – which occupy approximately a quarter, a half, or three-quarters to a full page. Directory ads are, of course, in place for 12 months, which is 13 four-week "media months," and the cost is added to the firm's monthly phone bill. Whether to go beyond a listing and place a larger ad is a difficult decision for smaller businesses especially – medical or legal professionals, tradespeople, restaurants – because, to provide some U.S. figures[31], a Listing costs about $5,000; the smallest next size up ad, which is a small In-column ad occupying about 5% of the page, costs about $19,000; a half-page Display ad is about $50,000; and a full-page Display ad is about $100,000. The *profit* return on business generated by the ad for the year therefore has to be greater than these costs to justify an ad of that size.

The *usual* measures of Attention, which are Ad Recognition for print ads and Ad Recall for broadcast ads, are not meaningful enough for directory ads because the customer does not have to recognize the ad (apart from "cognizing" it initially) or recall it, but rather has to *act* on it. These

TABLE 9.7 *Yellow Pages/directory ad attention factors.*

DIRECTORY ADS: TYPE AND SIZE	PROBABILITY OF ATTENTION	AVERAGE DIRECT-RESPONSE INQUIRIES (CALLS PER HUNDRED THOUSAND POPULATION PER YEAR)
1-page or at least $^1/_4$-page display ad	1.00	7,255
$^1/_2$-page display ad	.82	5,926
Small display or large in-column ad, .22 to .37 of page size	.72	5,172
Large in-column ad, .10 to .15 of page size	.58	4,165
Small in-column ad, .03 to .09 of page size	.53	3,767
In-column listing, normal or bold	.16	1,148

Interest-maximizing factors:

Picture	Include a photo or line drawing, even if it is a small one, making sure it suits the brand image
Headline	Use a short (1 to 5 words) and prominent lead-in headline
Body copy	Bullet-point the benefit claims and make each very short (1 to 3 words maximum)
Response device	Include details of how to visit (street location, URL), or order (phone, fax) and also payment options (if credit cards are accepted, reproduce *their* logos)
Brand name, with brand mark (if any)	Prominent, at top or bottom

Note: Direct-response data are from A.M. Abernathy and D.N. Laband, 2002, reference in note 31.

are all Direct-Response Ads, not Awareness Ads. The appropriate measure of *attention* for Yellow Pages directory ads is therefore based on the number of *inquiries* (phone calls) generated by ads of different sizes.[32] We have used data provided from a large-scale experiment by Abernethy and Laband[33] to estimate, in Table 9.7, attention probabilities by size of ad based on their relative rates of inquiries. We assume that a very large ad (three-quarters to one-page) has an attention probability of 1.0, in that everyone opening the directory for that category would see it. The successively smaller ads are then indexed down from 1.00, based on the number of calls they attract. It can be seen in the table that an *ad*, as opposed to a Listing, has at least .5 attention probability, which increases with size. A Listing, whether normal or bold, has an attention probability of only .16.

Structure

For Display ads and In-column ads in directories, a *picture always helps*, even if it is small – and it can be a photograph or a line drawing – but make sure it suits the brand image. The headline should be short and take the *Lead-in* form. The copy should also be *short* with benefit claims *bullet-pointed*. The *brand name and logo*, of course, should be *prominent*, though can be placed at either the top or the bottom of the ad. Finally, *response information* is vital (in other words, Purchase Facilitation is necessary): how to visit or how to order, and how to pay.

OUTDOOR ADS

Outdoor ads, called **out-of-home ads** in the U.K., come in many sizes, shapes, and locations. The probability of Attention to an outdoor ad differs somewhat for those who *drive by* it, as their attention is tunneled forward, and for those who *walk by* it. Also, *stand-alone* outdoor ads will get more attention than outdoor ads next to others.

Location

In Table 9.8, we provide estimates of attention probabilities for the main *types* of outdoor ad (which include posters placed *indoors*). There are two sets of estimates, based on a pedestrian audience[34] and a drive-by audience.[35] To arrive at a single estimate for a particular location, take an average weighted by the proportion of prospects who walk or drive by.

TABLE 9.8 *Outdoor ad attention factors.*

	PROBABILITY OF ATTENTION	
LOCATION	PEDESTRIANS	DRIVERS
Overhead pass or line-of-driving outdoor ad	N.A.	.92
Stand-alone outdoor ad, any size	.80	.53
Stand-alone *indoor* poster, moderate to large size	.90	N.A.
With adjacent ad(s)	.40	.38
Bus-site ad, taxi-back ad	.30	.50
Bus shelter	.40	.25

Interest-maximizing factors:

	MOBILE-VIEWED AD	STATIONARY-VIEWED AD
Picture	Large and literal or can use a simple but not complex visual conveyer as long as the product *category* is also shown; single dominant focal point	Write the headline and copy first, leaving remaining space, but at least one-sixth of the ad, for the picture
Headline	Complete headline of 1 to 5 words (this is also the copy) and placed *under* the picture	Lead-in headline, of any length
Body copy	None	50 to 200 words; lower case; serif; dark on light background; bullet each benefit
Brand name, with brand mark (if any)	Brand-item name should precede or start the headline; the brand mark (if any) should precede the headline	Brand-item name and brand mark (if any) prominent, lower right corner

Structure

The interest-maximizing factors for outdoor ads, listed in the table, depend on whether the ad is mobile-viewed or stationary-viewed.

Mobile-viewed outdoor ads have very limited processing time and therefore the picture must signal quickly what the *category* is, even if a (simple) visual conveyer is also shown. Do not use a curiosity picture, as these can be understood in Stationary outdoor ads only. The category in the picture, followed by the brand name in the headline, is the correct sequence (CN → BN) for Brand Recall. Mobile-viewed outdoor ads should use a *Complete headline* of one to five words and *no body copy*. The Complete headline should, contrary to common practice, be placed *under* the picture in Mobile-viewed outdoor ads, for the same reason mentioned earlier: you don't want the headline to pre-label the picture but rather to *prompt* it. A common error is to place the brand-item name and brand mark, if any, after the headline. The brand should be identified *before* the benefit claim, as this is the correct sequence for both Informational operant learning and Transformational evaluative conditioning. For instance, an outdoor ad that we saw for a well-known brand of rain jacket, pictured below a stormy sky, said "Repels all of the above. Columbia." A better sequence would be, "Columbia. Repels all of the above."

Stationary-viewed outdoor ads (meaning indoor as well) are like a *newspaper ad* for High-Involvement preference and they are usually Informational. The interest-maximizing tactics are much the same as for a High-Involvement newspaper ad with a couple of refinements concerning the body copy and the brand mark placement. We stress the admonition against hard-to-read "reverse type" (light type on a dark background) which we are sure deters body copy readership in outdoor ads, especially those placed indoors with poor illumination.

It may be noticed that we have not listed *color* as an attention factor for outdoor ads. This is because, for outdoor ads, there is no evidence of a general advantage of color over black and white. However, the earlier rules for attention-getting pictures apply and *bright color* is one such feature that should work especially well for a *Mobile-viewed* outdoor ad. The launch ads for Apple Computer's iPod sub-brand of consumer electronics employed bright colors behind black silhouettes of young people on posters and bus stands, as shown in Figure 9.3, which we believe have been very effective. The product (the brand-item) is the dominant focal point.

ONLINE ADS

Online ads come in a number of forms, including *permission emails*, *spam emails*, Web *banner ads* (on Internet search engines such as Netscape, Yahoo or Google and in permission emails) and *Websites* themselves. Attention factors for the different forms of online ads are summarized in Table 9.9. It must be emphasized that the attention probabilities apply *within* the online population, which is about two-thirds of children and adults in advanced countries. Also, the reach of any one site (excluding search engines) is not very high, as we'll see later in the media chapters. Levi's (Levi Strauss), for example, abandoned its Web and cinema ad strategy in the U.S.A. several years ago because it did not reach enough of the youth market, and went back to mainstream TV, print and outdoor.[36]

FIGURE 9.3 *Outdoor ads for the launch of Apple Computer's iPod sub-brand consumer electronics. The silhouette is black, the product white, and the background color either pink, yellow, green, or purple. Agency: TWBA/Chiat Day/L.A.*

SOURCE: © Apple Computer, Inc.

TABLE 9.9 *Online ad attention factors.*

ATTENTION FACTOR		PROBABILITY
Permission email (opening)		.68
Spam email (opening)		.34
Banner ad (attention):	Static	.30
	Animated or pop-up	.40
Website (attention for those who go to the site):	Home page	1.00
	Page 2	.24
	Page 3	.21
	Page 4	.15

Interest-maximizing factors:

EMAIL ADS	BANNER ADS	WEBSITES	WEB TV ADS
Use high-involvement *newspaper* ad tactics (Table 9.3)	Use a complete headline or "free offer" headline – and a small picture or logo	Use high-involvement *magazine* ad tactics (Table 9.4) for every page. Link every page to the home page. No long, scrolling pages. No page downloads that take more than 10 seconds	Use *TV* ad tactics (Table 9.1)

Email ads

Survey data indicates that **permission emails** have a .68 probability of being opened.[37] **Spam (unsolicited) emails**, which are banned in the European Union and, at the time of writing, have just been severely limited by opt-out legislation in the U.S.A.[38], have only about half that probability, .34, of being opened, but even this is higher than one might expect given the general negative reaction to Spam. Email ads function in exactly the same way as High-Involvement *newspaper* ads and should employ the same tactics (Table 9.3).

Web banner ads

Web **banner ads** come as "buttons" or as "little billboards" in several sizes up to a half page[39], though most are less than one-tenth of the Web page, and also can be static or dynamic, that is, an animated banner or a pop-up banner or both. The size of the Banner ad does *not* affect attention[40] and we estimate the probability of attention for the average Banner ad to be about .30, based on one-exposure ad recognition.[41] Animated or Pop-Up Banners, annoying as these ads can be, have a higher attention probability, estimated to be .40. Structurally, a Banner ad is exactly like a small Mobile-viewed outdoor ad and should use a *Complete headline* – or "free offer" headline[42] – and a *small picture or logo*. The *sequential frames* of a very good animated Banner ad are shown in Figure 9.4. Dale Computers company doesn't exist, so don't try to go to the site! This Banner ad was designed by some of Rossiter's brilliant students.

Websites

A **Website ad** is a much more complex proposition than the other types of online ad. People completely self-select visits to Websites, so the probability of attention for those who choose to visit the site is 1.00, for the first or "home" page. The probability of attention (clicking onwards) falls by about three-quarters after the home page and falls further for every successive page[43]; for very large sites, such as Dell's at over 200 pages, these falling probabilities would apply within each section or category of the site that is searched. The biggest factor in losing attention to the site as a whole is undoubtedly *navigability*: don't include "orphan" pages not linked to the home page, long scrolling pages, or pages that take more than 10 seconds to download.[44] If a multi-page site has really poor navigability, visitors will rarely make a repeat visit to that site.

What factors maximize interest to Website pages? The answer is that you should use High-Involvement *magazine* ad tactics (Table 9.6) for every page of the site.

Web TV ads

Web buttons or other banner ads can also be clicked on to bring on a full-screen TV commercial – a **Web TV ad** – usually of 15 seconds length.[45] The probability of attention to these is the same as the proportion who click through from the banner. The Web TV ad itself should employ the same attention tactics as for *TV* commercials (Table 9.1).

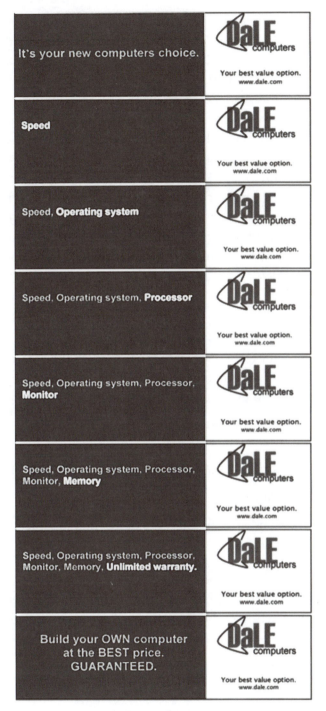

FIGURE 9.4 *An animated banner ad, shown frame by frame from the top down.*

SOURCE: Created and contributed by Ana Luisa Costa, Leonardo Valle Arce, Mohalib Khan, and Suk Yan Cheng, at the University of Wollongong, August 2004.

SUMMARY

If the ad does not gain the attention of prospective customers, it cannot work. Attention is the main barrier to advertising effectiveness in the crowded marcoms environment of today and the attention problem is likely to worsen in the future. Attention tactics must therefore be built into the ad (as the fourth component of creative strategy). Attention tactics differ according to the medium of the ad.

For TV commercials, the probability of attention is mainly a function of the length of the commercial and then attention-holding or "interest" should be managed by its patterning or structure. Informational TV commercials should employ a *two-peaked pattern* with the Category Need in the first peak, the Brand Identity in the lull, and the reinforcing Benefit portrayal in the second peak. Transformational TV commercials should employ a *rising pattern* with a further definite *kick* at the end; the Brand Identity comes first and the positive rise reflects the presentation of the e^{++} which acts as the US^+ in the human evaluative conditioning process.

Radio commercials also have attention probabilities proportional to their length. They should use high-imagery words and, usually if Transformational, music that appeals to listeners' demographics. There are also several other specifically recommended tactics, such as a rhetorical-doubt question at the end for Informational radio commercials and the absolute avoidance of an irrelevant closing joke.

Print ads, which, in their various media, constitute well over half of all ads that prospective customers see, have attention probabilities that differ by size and by the inclusion of color, either two-color (black and white plus one color) or four-color (all color). Both initial attention and attention-holding are strongly and positively influenced by the inclusion of a *large picture* with a *single dominant focal point*. Headlines also affect the readership of print ads and should be a Complete headline for products or services based on Low-Involvement brand preference, or a Lead-in headline for products or services based on High-Involvement brand preference. For Low-Involvement brand preference ads, the body copy should consist of fewer than 50 words and there should be no body copy in mobile-viewed outdoor ads. High-Involvement brand preference ads can employ between 50 and 200 words as longer copy for these types of products or services assists readership. In both, the brand name or logo should be clearly visible but does not have to be grossly prominent. These are the main attention tactics for print ads, although some additional specific tactics are recommended for newspaper ads, magazine ads – and *outdoor* ads and *online* ads. All of these, though the media differ, are *print ads*.

DISCUSSION QUESTIONS

9.1   What Attention tactics would you recommend for a TV commercial to introduce the new Schick Quattro four-blade razor? Justify the length of the commercial and outline an appropriate interest pattern, noting what should go where.

9.2   Design an attention-getting and attention-holding Radio commercial to advertise the services of your local dry-cleaner.

9.3   Design a Newspaper ad for the Chrysler Crossfire automobile (a full ad, not a teaser ad).

9.4   Design a Newspaper ad for Kellogg's Corn Flakes.

9.5   Design an Outdoor ad for Speedo swimwear and specify the types of location in which you would place it.

9.6   Design a Bus Interior ad for the Salvation Army.

9.7   Brainstorm and design two Web Banner ads for The Rotterdam School of Management's MBA program, briefly state why you think each would be effective and suggest where you would place them.

NOTES

1. This is certainly true for print ads (see J.R. Rossiter, Predicting Starch scores, *Journal of Advertising Research*, 1980, 21(5), pp. 63–68) where 45% (R^2) of the variation in initial attention and in readership of the copy is due to mechanical, not message, factors. For broadcast ads, length alone causes a similar degree of variation.

2. The estimates of attention to TV commercials are based on "eyes on screen" studies and the 65% allows for people who leave the room or look away during the whole ad. See M. Ritson, What do people really do during TV commercials?, working paper, London: London Business School, 2003. The estimates of length effects on attention, given in Table 9.1, are derived by applying ad recall indexes to the .65 figure. For ad recall as a function of TV ad length,

see E. Du Plessis, An advertising burst is just a lot of drips, *Admap*, 1996, July–August, pp. 51–55.

3. A. Green, Families no longer watch together, *Television Week*, May 5, 2003 (electronic document).

4. R. Baron, DVR threat real, growing, *Television Week*, October 20, 2003, Website.

5. J. MacLachlan and M. Logan, Camera shot length in TV commercials and their memorability and persuasiveness, *Journal of Advertising Research*, 1993, 33(2), pp. 7–61.

6. P.D. Bowls and D.D. Muehling, The effects of television commercial pacing on viewers' attention and memory, *Journal of Marketing Communications*, 2003, 9(1), pp. 17–28.

7. This was neatly demonstrated in an experiment on learning from video lectures. For learning new material, when content competes with structure for attention, learning of content suffers. See E. Thorson and A. Lang, The effects of television videographics and lecture familiarity on adult cardiac orienting responses and memory, *Communication Research*, 1992, 19(3), pp. 346–369.

8. H. Baumgartner, M. Sujan, and D. Padgett, Patterns of affective reactions to advertisements: the integration of moment-to-moment responses into overall judgments, *Journal of Marketing Research*, 1997, 34(2), pp. 219–232. The ads tested in this study were for low-involvement/transformational products such as Coca-Cola and Taster's Choice coffee.

9. Human evaluative conditioning (HEC) is not the same as classical, or Pavlovian, conditioning (PC). The importance of the differences will become clear when we discuss media frequency for transformational ads, in Chapter 12. See J. De Houwer, S. Thomas, and F. Baeyens, Associative learning of likes and dislikes: a review of 25 years of research on human evaluative conditioning, *Psychological Bulletin*, 2001, 127(6), pp. 853–869.

10. Cited in a book highly recommended for those interested in TV commercial production, by J.Aitchison, *Cutting Edge Commercials*, Singapore: Prentice Hall, 2002, p. 14.

11. See the carefully controlled study of mystery ads by R.H. Fazio, P.M. Herr, and M.C. Powell, On the development and strength of category-brand associations in memory, *Journal of Consumer Psychology*, 1992, 1(1), pp. 1–13. The use of mystery ads for many products and services, for new *and* old brands, seems to have increased over the recent decade, a creative fad no doubt.

12. Obviously there is no radio equivalent to "eyes on screen" – you can't really tell whether someone is "listening" during a radio ad. The only behavioral measure that comes anywhere close to measuring auditory attention was W. Wallace *et al.*'s CONPAAD, but this was only ever used to test attention to TV ads (by willingness to press two foot pedals, otherwise the video would fade on one pedal or the audio on the other). We therefore have to rely on ad recall to measure attention to radio commercials. Our estimates are from over 2,000 radio ad recall tests reported in R. Galen, I saw it on the radio: an overview of radio copy testing approaches, *Copy Research*, New York: Advertising Research Foundation, 1985, pp. 227–286.

13. D.W. Miller and L.J. Marks, The effects of imagery-evoking radio advertising strategies on affective responses, *Psychology & Marketing*, 1997, 14(4), pp. 337–360.

14. D.T. Howard and R.E. Burnkrant, Question effects on information processing in advertising, *Psychology & Marketing*, 1990, 7(1), pp. 27–46.

15. "Klinkers" versus "klitchiks" are terms coined by Sam Levenson, legendary creative director of the original Volkswagen Beetle ads at Doyle Dane Bernbach, U.S.A.

16. M.A. Sewall and D. Savel, Characteristics of radio commercials and their recall effectiveness, *Journal of Marketing*, 1986, 50(1), pp. 52–60. See also J.R. Rossiter and L. Percy, Visual communication in advertising, in R.J. Harris (Ed.), *Information Processing Research in Advertising*, Hillsdale, NJ: Erlbaum, 1983, chapter 4, especially pp. 99–100.

17. The attention measure for newspapers is ad recognition, in which readers of the newspaper are interviewed within 25 hours of receipt of the issue and asked "through the book," for each ad, whether they remember seeing that ad in the issue (the Starch method). The figures are from G. Kelly, How to advertise in print media, proprietary document, Melbourne, Australia, Quadrant Research, 1991.

18. N. McDonald, Green hybrids clean up in local car market, *The Australian*, January 29, 2004, p. 7.

19. Mini-papers boost sales, *The Australian*, Media section, February 19, 2004, p. 17.

20. The attention-getting pictorial features are taken from J.R. Rossiter, T. Langner, and L. Ang, Visual creativity in advertising: a functional typology, *ANZMAC Proceedings*, 2003, electronic document, and the analysis by Starch INRA Hooper, Inc., Creating notable ads: lessons from the winners, *Starch Tested Copy*, 1993, 4(12), p. 8. Note that effective attention features do *not* change over the years.

21. The one-sixth minimum is an educated guess that seems right: divide a page into two columns and three rows, that is, into six parts, and you would think that a picture smaller than a sixth would struggle for attention.

22. Starch Noted score norms show substantially lower attention if the picture has two or more competing focal points or, if multiple, small pictures are used. See *Starch Tested Copy*, vol. 2, no. 17, no year given, whole issue, and *Starch Tested Copy*, 1990, 2(6), pp. 1, 2, 4.

23. R.J. Donovan, A. Oshinsky, and J.R. Rossiter, High involvement print ads and copy readability, unpublished paper, Australian Graduate School of Management, Sydney, 1989.

24. For a recent replication of the importance of picture size in increasing attention to the magazine ad, see G.R. Franke, B.A. Huhmann, and D.L. Mothersbaugh, Information content and consumer readership of print ads: a comparison of search and experience products, *Journal of the Academy of Marketing Science*, 2004, 32(1), pp. 20–31.

25. *Starch Tested Copy*, 1990, 2(11), whole issue.

26. Canadian Starch studies summarized in Reader's Digest Australia's *Research Digest*, 1985, October, pp. 1–2.

27. J.R. Rossiter, 1980, same reference as note 1.

28. J.R. Miller and W. Kintsch, Readability and recall of short prose passages: a theoretical analysis, *Journal of Experimental Psychology: Human Learning and Memory*, 1980, 6(4), pp. 335–355.

29. M.C. Macklin, N.T. Bruvold, and C.L. Sheay, Is it as simple as "keep it simple"?, *Journal of Advertising*, 1985, 14(4), pp. 28–35.

30. R.J. Donovan, A. Oshinsky, and J.R. Rossiter, 1989, same reference as note 23.

31. A.M. Abernethy and D.N. Laband, The customer pulling power of different-sized Yellow Pages advertisements, *Journal of Advertising Research*, 2002, 42(3), pp. 66–72.

32. Eye-tracking has been used to measure attention to Yellow Pages ads and whereas this measure may be helpful to record which content elements are looked at, it tells nothing about whether the ad was processed, unlike ad recognition or ad recall. The study included color ads and found that color greatly increases "look at," but color is still a rarity in directory advertising and also would cancel out competitively if it were to become the norm. See G.L. Lohse, Consumer eye movement patterns on Yellow Pages advertising, *Journal of Advertising*, 1997, 26(1), pp. 61–73. The problem with his sample of ads was pointed out by Abernethy and Laband, see note 31 above.

33. A.M. Abernethy and D.N. Laband, 2002, same reference as note 31.

34. A. Hodges, How poster campaigns perform, *Admap*, 1993, April, pp. 32–33, 35, 36, based on street intercept interviews using the ad recognition method, for 400 campaigns.

35. I. Garland, Measuring the great outdoors, *Admap*, 2003, November, pp. 24–26. To estimate drive-by attention, the study counted the rate of motor vehicles passing by the site, with GPS satellite technology, then adjusted for size, distance, angle, illumination, and typical vehicle speed.

36. Levi's changes for new generation, *Ad News*, April 20, 2000, p. 16.

37. A. Parmar, You have our permission, *Marketing News*, January 3, 2003, p. 3 (based on a survey of over 1,200 online respondents aged 18 and over, conducted by Quris Inc. research company).

38. House votes to put spam back in can, *The Australian*, November 24, 2003, p. 20.

39. NYTimes.com, for instance, sells half-page banner ad units that take up two of the Web page's four columns.

40. Banner ad size does not change click-through probability and, therefore, attention measured as *processing* is unaffected by size; see E. Ahn and S.M. Edwards, Does size really matter? Brand attitude versus click-through in response to banner ads, *Proceedings of the 2002 Conference of The American Academy of Advertising*, 2002, pp. 8–9.

41. Based on five banner ads in an online test, but this is about the same as a quarter-page or smaller newspaper ad and seems right. For the banner ad test, see X. Drèze and F-X. Hussherr, Internet advertising: is anybody watching?, working paper, Wharton School, University of Pennsylvania, July 2003.

42. H.G. Kim and J.D. Leckenby, Creative factors in interactive advertising, *Proceedings of the 2002 Conference of The American Academy of Advertising*, 2002, pp. 58–63. The dependent variable in this study was click-through. They also found that "emotional" (vs. "benefit") headlines predicted well but this label is vague and does not lead to a clear recommendation.

43. The page-by-page site attention probabilities in the table are from a study by R.E. Bucklin and C. Sismeiro, A model of Web site browsing behavior estimated on clickstream data, *Journal of Marketing Research*, 2003, 40(3), pp. 249–267.

44. Recommendations from J. Nielsen, reported in S. Jackson, Dazzle 'em but keep it simple, *The Australian*, September 1, 1999, p. 28.

45. T. Elkin, Unicast rolls out 15-second Web ads, *Advertising Age*, April 28, 2003, p. 66.

CHAPTER 10

Pre-testing rough ads

The manager requires high-quality ads for the campaign and should not sign off on submitted creative until it has passed the first type of pre-test described in this chapter and, in the case of a new campaign, also the second type of pre-test. By "ads" we mean ads in any medium, of course, and also advertised promotions, displays, sales brochures and even sponsors' logos – anything that will function as an ad. All such advertising stimuli should be pre-tested before they are used. We describe two sequential types of pre-tests:

- **Management judgment ad test (MJAT)** in which *managers* systematically evaluate rough ads, including rough versions of promotions and other marcoms materials

- **Customer response ad test (CRAT)** in which good-quality rough ads are pre-tested for response among target *customers*

As we will see, the MJAT should *always* be used even if the ads are just further executions of the brand or brand-item's present creative idea. On the other hand, the CRAT is a further necessary test for ads that employ a *new creative idea* – either a new creative idea for the brand or brand-item's current positioning, or new positioning, which inherently requires a new creative idea.

Also, what is a Rough Ad and why do we recommend that the pre-tests be conducted with *this* form of advertising stimulus? We will explain in this chapter.

MANAGEMENT JUDGMENT AD TEST

As a preliminary step to approving ads or advertised promotion offers for *all* campaigns, a Management Judgment Ad Test (MJAT) should be designed and used. As the name suggests, the

MJAT uses judgments by Managers – usually just marketing department personnel – not target customers. The MJAT is applied at the Rough Ad, or Rough Promotion Offer, stage – to a TV commercial animatic, radio commercial rough recording, print ad sketch-plus-copy, or promotion offer sketch-plus-copy.

The MJAT is fairly easy to design as it is based on the *Creative Brief* that has previously been prepared, although it does require some careful selection and wording of questions. It is easy to conduct and interpret. The MJAT method deserves to be universally known and appreciated but, surprisingly, most marketing managers have never heard of such a pre-test and neglect to put together anything like it. In a recent illustration of this ignorance or neglect, the chief executive of Levi Strauss & Co. was reported in the trade press as lamenting the apparent failure of a very expensive new TV commercial for Levi's Type One Jeans that was run during the U.S. Super Bowl football game in January 2003. The media placement cost for *one insertion* of a 30-second TV commercial in the 2003 Superbowl broadcast was $2.1 million and the production cost of a commercial like that one would be *at least* $1 million, so this is $3 million spent just for a start. The Levi's ad was built around a quite radical creative idea, that of a young couple, wearing Type One jeans, who are wildly improbably caught in a pack of stampeding bison and emerge untouched. "It wasn't a Levi's ad," said the CEO, "[and] it was certainly a poor Super Bowl ad."[1] Well, we say: if it "wasn't a Levi's ad," then why was it approved? This is just one example, albeit a very costly one, but the point is that such hindsight reactions could not happen if an MJAT is conducted first. Contributing to this naïvety, which is not at all uncommon, is the fact that many marketing managers, perhaps most, have blind faith in their agency's ability to come up with a winner. This is like having faith in your GP or doctor – you just *trust* that he or she will give you the right advice and you don't know enough about medicine to question it – nor do you particularly *want* to. In neither case, on the odds, is this blind faith justified. We presented the odds for the success of ads in Chapter 1.[2]

Why the MJAT is necessary

The MJAT makes three very important contributions to the management of the marcoms campaign. First, the MJAT *focuses attention on the Creative Brief* and therefore on the Positioning, Communication Objectives, and Action Objectives that the ad or offer is supposed to achieve. This focus is necessary to prevent the strange amnesia that typically overcomes managers when new rough ads – vaguely called "concepts" – are presented to them by the agency. Typically, the creative brief – the brand or brand-item's positioning, the campaign communication objectives, and the action objective – is forgotten and managers fall back on a "gut reaction" based mainly on whether they, personally, like the ad! If most don't like the ad, the agency then, equally irrelevantly, attempts to justify at length the idea "behind" the ad.[3] Both parties are acting stupidly and it happens frequently. The same problem usually occurs with new promotion offers but we will concentrate on new ads for easier discussion. The discipline of screening rough ads with an MJAT prevents hasty rejection – or approval – by replacing gut reaction with systematic and relevant evaluation.

A second advantage of the MJAT is that it *builds management responsibility for, and commitment to, the creative approach* that is selected. (Recall from the procedure described in Chapter 7 where you have asked the agency for – or you have generated in-house – two Creative Ideas, each represented by two Executions. *One* idea, and at least one execution of it but usually *two*, will need to be selected for the campaign.) The manager, indeed the entire Management Team, must take ownership of the campaign that is selected. Campaign approval must be the manager's call – if the campaign works, as hoped, then both management and the agency take credit; if it does not work after passing the MJAT, the fault is with management, not the agency. A thoroughly pre-tested campaign should work but occasionally it won't. At this stage of advertising development, before in-market results can be known, it is vital that management not only get behind the campaign but take ownership of it. This means communicating the approach to other internal managers, to retailers if they are in the channel, and most importantly to the company's own salespeople. The last thing you want is for your own salesforce and your retailers to be "sprung" by a new campaign about which they have not been informed, because if it's not "theirs" they won't support it and your marketing mix delivery will suffer as a consequence.

A third advantage of the MJAT is that it is *better than no pre-testing*. The MJAT prevents mistakes in ads and thus *reduces the manager's downside risk*. The downside risk is very large; we saw in Chapter 1 that at least 50% of ad campaigns do not break even financially and about 70% are too weak to make much profit.[4] Moreover, the MJAT is the only type of pre-testing that needs to be done for the many campaigns in which the creative idea does not change but *new executions* need to be approved. What the MJAT *cannot* do is predict the *upside* effectiveness of the ads. But eliminating the downside – which the MJAT will nearly always do – is a gain in itself given the substantial observed proportion of ineffective ads. The proportion of ineffective ads is about 30%, and over 50% if we include ads that don't pay back their investment in terms of incremental profit.

Rough ads

Before we start on the MJAT, it will be helpful to provide a couple of examples of what we mean by a **rough ad**. Figure 10.1 shows a magazine Rough Ad for a Birds Eye food product. Figure 10.2 shows the storyboards and script (professionally recorded for the

FIGURE 10.1 *Rough magazine ad (created on a PC) for Birds Eye Create-a-Meal Mexican. For a food product, the rough has to look appealing.*

SOURCE: Courtesy of Simplot Australia Pty Ltd.

| Campaign | "Disgust" Animatics | Length | 30 seconds |
| Execution # | "Maggots" | Format | Video/non-broadcast |

VIDEO SCRIPT 1 : MAGGOTS		AUDIO
Open with close-up of a pack of cigarettes lying on a table		
A hand reaches in and takes a cigarette from the pack		
Pull back to see a young boy put the cigarette to his mouth and light it		
Traverse shot to a girl who looks on. The boy asks her if she'd like a cigarette		BOY: Want one? GIRL: No way
The boy lights the cigarette and inhales. As he does so, the cigarette turns to a cylinder of writhing maggots		BOY: Whatever FX: Inhaling
Cut to girl looking on in disgust	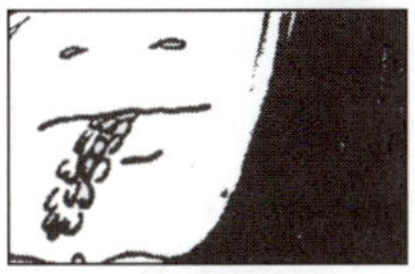	GIRL: Uggh!
Boy (who cannot see maggots, just a cigarette)		BOY: What?
Government department graphic and tagline (to be added)		

FIGURE 10.2 *Rough TV ad for an anti-smoking campaign.*

SOURCE: Courtesy of Dr. Rob Donovan, Curtin University of Technology, Perth, Australia.

pre-test, which is quite low cost) for an anti-smoking TV commercial – working title "Maggots" – for a social marketing campaign.

Line drawings with color – sketches – are easy for an artist to prepare on a PC. A single sketch for a print ad or a sequence of sketches, placed in a booklet or on videotape for a TV ad, with copy or audio added, are completely adequate for pre-testing (both MJAT and CRAT pre-testing). A series of studies over the years – reviewed in, and with a new study contributed by, Morris and Waine[5] – has consistently proven that, at the level of individual ads, not just on average across ads, the storyboard version will produce the same pre-test results as the finished version. This is not only the case for "factual" ads but for "emotional" ads too. A common misconception is that storyboard emotional ads lack the "production values" for a valid pre-test result but the ads in these studies have included rough and finished TV ads for products such as Levi's Jeans, Dr. Pepper soft drink, and Gerber baby formula, all of which would require "emotional" executions. The storyboard version closely predicts the Arousal (type 1 emotional response) and Negative versus Positive Affect (type 1 emotional response) and also the degree of Brand Purchase Intention (a communication objective) generated by the finished version. Not only do the results rarely differ in terms of statistical significance (at the 95% significance level) when rough ads' scores are compared with their counterpart finished ads' scores but, in terms of practical significance, the *same decision* would have been made – to accept, revise, or reject the ad – had only the rough ad version been tested. A rough TV commercial costs *at most* $10,000 to prepare and a rough TV ad storyboard or rough print ad *at most* a couple of thousand dollars' worth of an art person's time and materials. You can afford to pre-test *multiple* rough ad executions at these prices!

MJAT methodology

The MJAT has two sections, which cover evaluation of content and structure. Content consists of ratings of how well the *Target Audience* is addressed in the ad (specifically, the Creative Target, from Chapter 6) and ratings of *Brand Awareness tactics* and *Brand Preference tactics* appropriate to the campaign's communication objectives (from Chapter 8). Structure consists of a checklist of *Attention factors* (from Chapter 9) appropriate to the type of ad – TV, radio, print, etc. The main content ratings and attention factor types are listed in Table 10.1.

Content factors ratings

The **content factors ratings** are made on an *11-point scale*, from 0 to 10, where the lower end-point is 0 = totally unacceptable, the mid-point is 5 = acceptable, and the upper end-point is 10 = excellent.

Six to 10 judges are used to do the ratings (in large companies, you can use as many as 20 judges, remembering that an important purpose of the MJAT is to build the commitment of all members of the management team). If you have only a small management team, recruit others in the office to act as judges and, although this is not always possible, the more similar they are to the target group, the better. In any case, you need a minimum of six judges and it should not be difficult to recruit the safer number of 10 judges. The ratings must be done by each judge *independently*, that is, with no discussion between judges.

TABLE 10.1 *MJAT content factors and attention factors.*

CONTENT FACTORS

1. Target audience decision-maker clearly addressed
2. Category need (if an objective) appropriately reminded or sold
3. Brand awareness tactics appropriate to the objective of brand recognition, brand recall, or both
4. Brand preference tactics appropriate to low-involvement/informational, low-involvement/transformational, high-involvement/informational, or high-involvement transformational
5. Entry-ticket benefits apparent (if required)
6. Purchase facilitation achieved (if required)
7. Clear call to action (if direct-response ad)
8. Mandatory content (if required)

ATTENTION FACTORS (SELECT THE APPROPRIATE MEDIUM)

1. TV commercial (informational or transformational)
2. Radio commercial (informational or transformational)
3. Newspaper ad (low involvement or high involvement)
4. Magazine ad (low involvement or high involvement)
5. Directory ad
6. Outdoor ad (mobile-viewed or stationary-viewed)
7. Web banner ad
8. Website ad (informational or transformational)

Interpreting MJAT content ratings

One member of the rating team collects the ratings obtained by each rough ad on the set of content factors. For each factor, *median* ratings are computed. This is done by arranging the judges' ratings in descending order from highest to lowest and then selecting the *middle* rating value (this will be a .5 number with an even number of judges or a whole number with an uneven number of judges). The median scores are then interpreted as follows:

- If the median score is below 5 on any of the factors: *reject* the ad
- If the median rating on a factor is above 5 but just 6 or 7: the ad goes back to the creative team for *revision* on this factor or these factors
- If the median rating is 8+ on all factors: the ad is *accepted*

This is a *conjunctive* decision rule: any failure, after any necessary revision, means the ad is rejected. Weak ratings on a content factor cannot be offset by strong ratings on other content factors. Rather, *all* criteria must be met.

Attention factors checklist

The **attention factors checklist** is used *only if* the ad was accepted on the Content Factors ratings. Considering that each judge will be evaluating at least four rough ads, it is efficient to withhold this section of the MJAT until the content factors have been rated, then apply it only to the acceptable rough ads. It is common sense that effective attention tactics cannot redeem an incorrectly targeted or inadequately communicated ad. Appropriate attention tactics are "icing on the cake." For an acceptable ad, it is worthwhile and easy to revise and correct attention factors.

> The ratings of attention tactics are a *yes-no checklist*. Interpretation is: the more "yesses" the better but if there are a lot of blank boxes (indicating a high proportion of "no's") then send the rough ad back to the creative team for correction or for a convincing (to management) explanation of why the creative team went this route on the ad's attention tactics. Usually, you will want the revisions.

Examples of MJAT questionnaires

The previous table in which we listed the MJAT content ratings and attention factor types is necessarily quite general. Concrete examples of MJATs will help. We present two examples of MJATs with details slightly disguised to protect confidentiality. The first is for an FMCG product and the second is for a social marketing campaign.

FMCG MJAT

The MJAT questionnaire for the FMCG product is shown in Table 10.2. Here's how the questionnaire was constructed. The brand-item, Birds Eye Create-a-Meal Mexican, is a food product but its Key Benefit is Informational rather than the usual Transformational benefit of Sensory Gratification. The Informational motive in this case is Mixed Approach-Avoidance, specifically an appetizing-looking and great-tasting Mexican meal that requires only 15 minutes to prepare; usually, a meal like this would take more time and effort and this frozen-prepared version resolves the approach-avoidance conflict. The Key Benefit Claim can be stated as "Delicious Mexican meal, quick." However, with food and beverage products, even if the Key Benefit is Informational, there is always a Transformational *Entry-Ticket* Benefit of Sensory Gratification. That is, even if "Preparation convenience," "Low in calories," "High in nutrients," or some other Informational benefit is the unique selling point, the food (or beverage) still has to *look good* or the target decision-maker won't consider it for purchase. This double motivation means that we have to extract Brand Preference tactics from both the Low-Involvement/Informational quadrant *and* the Low-Involvement/Transformational quadrant (these tactics were given in Chapter 8). This is why one of the rating items is "Product shot is appealing" (Sensory Gratification) and also why, for the second-to-last rating item – emotion-shift – there is an implicit, not *explicit*, negative because you do not want negative emotions adjacent to food or beverage depictions in ads! An implicit negative can be achieved by using a "marked" adjective. The headline in this ad uses the word "fast," which is a marked adjective that suggests "slow." Other details, which should be apparent from the rating items selected for the test, are that the brand awareness objective is Brand Recognition (pack recognition) and that the brand preference objective is to Create Strong Preference and is based on presumed Low-Involvement choice. The Attention factors are selected for *consumer magazine ads*, which is the advertising medium for this campaign (see Chapter 9).

TABLE 10.2 *MJAT questionnaire for rough ads for an FMCG food product whose key benefit is informational (mixed approach-avoidance). Brand awareness objective is brand recognition (pack recognition) and brand preference is low-involvement/informational (but with a transformational, sensory gratification, entry ticket).*

AD					JUDGE					
0	1	2	3	4	5	6	7	8	9	10
↑					↑					↑
not at all					just acceptable					excellent

CONTENT (put number in box)

• Meal-planner clearly addressed	☐
• Product category (frozen main meal) quickly apparent	☐
• Brand package clearly visible and name readable	☐
• Product shot is appealing	☐
• Key benefit (delicious Mexican meal, quick) obvious	☐
• Extreme claim for key benefit	☐
• Negative (implicit only) to positive emotion-shift	☐
• Birds Eye logo clearly visible (mandatory)	☐

ATTENTION FACTORS (check box if Yes)

• Large picture	☐	• Headline max. 8 words	☐
• Single dominant focal point	☐	• Headline personal reference	☐
• Product or people	☐	• Copy – max. 50 words	☐
• Celebrity presenter	☐	• Copy – short sentences	☐
• Complete headline	☐	• Copy – short words	☐
• Headline below picture if conveyer picture	☐	• Copy – high-imagery words	☐
• Positive headline	☐		
• Headline upper and lower case	☐		

The rough ad tested (there was only one ad in this case) is the one in Figure 10.1. Without giving the median ratings, which are proprietary, it can be revealed that the MJAT decision was *reject*: Two problem areas, as you might see from the ad, were an unclear Category Need (what is it?) and a weak Brand Recognition stimulus (the small pack shot). Also, among the attention factors, the headline is a Lead-in, whereas a Complete headline should be used for this Low-Involvement ad.

Social marketing MJAT

The second example of an MJAT questionnaire is in Table 10.3. It is for a social marketing campaign to encourage middle-aged (35 to 54 year-old) adults who do not do regular exercise to do so. In this example, to show how easily a comprehensive but straightforward MJAT can be constructed, the questionnaire was constructed by a three-person team of managers attending an executive program. This MJAT covers only the Content factors and it does so efficiently but in a suitably specific way.

The MJAT questionnaire was used (group median ratings are shown) to rate two ad executions that this team created, thus the two boxes for each rating factor. The better of the two executions was "Dog Funeral," an amusing yet pointed TV script in which a dog, Rex, is imagining delivering the eulogy at his own funeral; the eulogy is a lament that his owners didn't do enough exercise to give *him* enough exercise, so he died prematurely (the rough ad is shown in Figure 10.3). This execution, however appealing it may be, was "off strategy" on the benefit claims (see ratings on item no. 4) and was correctly rejected. There was no need to check either ad's Attention factors in this case.

TABLE 10.3 *MJAT questionnaire (constructed by a team in an executive program) for a social marketing campaign to encourage middle-aged adults to do regular exercise.*

0	1	2	3	4	5	6	7	8	9	10
↑					↑					↑
not at all					just acceptable					excellent

	AD 1 = "PARACHUTE"	AD 2 = "DOG FUNERAL"
1. How closely will non-regular exercisers (35–54 year-olds) identify with this ad?	5	8
2. How clearly does the ad convey that activity is part of a healthy life?	6	8
3. How clear is it that this is an ad for regular exercise?	5	8
4. How well does this ad portray the unique benefits from our advertising strategy?		
• it feels good to be alive	7	5
• don't miss those family moments	1	4
5. Do these ads adequately reduce barriers to action?		
• it doesn't need to cost anything	1	8
• it doesn't take much time	4	8
6. How likely are people to take action in response to these ads?	3	7
7. How distinctly does this stand out from other ads for exercise activities?	3	7

FIGURE 10.3 *Rough TV ad "Dog Funeral" created by a three-person management team participating in one of the first author's executive programs. (Thanks, guys, if you see this!)*

CUSTOMER RESPONSE AD TEST

MJAT pre-testing, described above, is conducted with Managers, *not* with Target Customers. To some extent, the managers who act as judges for the MJAT will have attempted to put themselves into the mind-state of a target customer but the validity of the MJAT does not depend on this. This is because any reasonably intelligent person can judge, via the MJAT questionnaire, whether the rough ad is "on strategy" with regard to content and whether it uses or omits appropriate attention tactics. The MJAT is therefore very effective for eliminating mistakes, that is, for reducing *downside* risk.

What the MJAT cannot do, however, is predict the *upside* performance of a rough ad. For this, a rough ad test with a fairly large sample of target customers is required. We recommend the use of a Customer Response Ad Test (CRAT). A CRAT is appropriate if the purpose of the campaign is to launch a new brand or brand-item or to reposition an established one – in other words, whenever a *new creative idea* has to be tested. But before examining the CRAT, let's dismiss two other common options.

No customer pre-test, even for a new creative idea?

Some large advertisers do not do *any* pre-testing with target customers, even for totally new campaigns. It is quite well known that Nike, for instance, does not do any pre-testing – and the highly innovative, often Postmodern, TV, print, and outdoor ads that Nike has run are testimony to the freedom that its agency, Wieden & Kennedy, is given. This approach seems to have worked – mostly – for Nike but they occasionally approve a weak campaign and Reebok and Adidas make inroads on Nike's share when they do.

Only if the creative team's track record exhibits very high performance on average *and* they have produced very few campaigns with lower performance should the manager feel confident, with a campaign based on a new creative idea, to bypass doing a CRAT. In our experience, with TV as well as *print* campaigns, these performance conditions are never met. In our experience, it has always been necessary to do a CRAT on executions when a new creative idea is used.

Not focus groups

The most common form of pre-testing of rough ads with target customers is to show and discuss the ads in **focus groups** (small-group interviews). When advertisers say that their campaign has been "researched," they usually mean that the rough ads have been pre-tested in a few Focus Groups – that is, watched, heard or read in a group setting by about three groups of six to 10 consumers or business customers. Each rough ad is either rejected, fixed up, or approved outright on the basis of those group reactions. This is *not* a valid way to pre-test ads and it is not surprising that many clients are surprised to discover that the campaign does not work after it has been "researched" in this manner. The validity problems with the pre-testing of rough ads in focus groups are that exposure to the ads occurs in an *unnatural setting*, which is social and vocally interactive (whereas nearly all advertising exposures in the real world occur alone or to people acting as if they were alone, and silently, even if they are watching TV or listening to the radio with others); each rough ad is *overexposed*, for much longer than occurs during real-world exposure, which encourages group members to act as critics and overemphasize any positive aspects, overemphasize any negatives and also react to fleeting or small details of the ads that would hardly be noticed during actual exposures; also, the communication objectives of the campaign are usually forgotten so that *any* response from the group, positive or negative, relevant or irrelevant to the objectives, is given *equal weight* in the assessment. Even if pre-test responses from focus groups were valid, which they are not, they would *not be statistically reliable* based on the total sample size of only about 18 to 30 customers.

CRAT method

What is necessary instead is a *large sample of target customers*, per target group, interviewed *individually*. In a CRAT, each rough ad is exposed only for the amount of time it would receive in a real-world exposure. TV and radio commercials are exposed *twice* (if Informational) or *three times* (if Transformational) and on their own, not in a "clutter reel," because the Attention probability (see previous chapter) is allowed for in the media plan. Print ads are exposed *once, ad lib*, but with the instruction to "look at this ad as you would normally." An *unexposed control group* is used for each target group. Only a few *key measures* are taken, as the purpose of this stage of pre-testing is to select which creative idea and which executions to *use in the campaign*, not to re-do the ads. Any revision of ads would happen, if revision is necessary, in the earlier *MJAT* stage of research.

The recommended minimum sample size for a CRAT is *200 target customers per target group* (for instance, the campaign may have favorable brand switchers, FBSs, as the primary target group, and brand loyals, BLs, as the secondary target group, so you would want 200 of each) *per execution*. You also want another 200 of each target group to serve as unexposed *control* groups (they are shown only the pack or logo as the stimulus).

We recommended earlier that the manager should aim to have two creative ideas emerge from the MJAT stage, with two rough ad executions of each idea. (The problem with testing only one execution of each creative idea is that you do not know whether the creative idea will be "campaignable." Also, one execution cannot validly test a creative idea: you may happen to get a good execution of a mediocre creative idea or a poor execution of a very good creative idea. Thus we recommend testing *at least two executions* of each creative idea.)

Each target group sample rates only *one* execution. With two target groups, which is fairly typical, and four executions, this means that the sample size for the exposed groups would be $2 \times 4 \times 200 = 1,600$. Then there is another $2 \times 200 = 400$ for the unexposed control groups. Thus the total sample size is 2,000. These seem like enormous numbers and very expensive: at, say, U.S.$50 an interview the total cost would be $100,000. The large numbers, and the high cost, are necessary as explained below.

Sample size justification

The large sample of 200 target customers per group and per execution is necessary. To obtain statistical precision, you get what you pay for: the larger the sample, providing it is randomly selected, the more accurate the result. In pre-testing, the difference between Creative Ideas, and especially between *Executions* of creative ideas, will often be as small as 10% (see ratings below). To detect a difference as small as 10% and be sure that it is a real difference (here, "sure" means the 95% confidence level) you need sample sizes of at least 200. Table 10.4 shows sample size numbers and degrees of accuracy.

The first panel of the table shows the 95% confidence level around a *single percentage*, such as the percentage of target customers who indicated that they would be willing to try the product; and the lower panel of the table shows the sample sizes needed for a given degree of accuracy when testing between *two percentages*, such as pre-test scores obtained by two Executions. If the manager decides to compromise in an attempt to save money by using target group samples of only 100, the right-hand column of the second panel of the table indicates that the true difference between the ads will need to be at least 14% before it can be confidently detected with sample sizes of 100. This means, for instance, that if you observe a difference between two ads of just 13%, the correct conclusion is that the ads are *equally effective* – you cannot conclude that the higher-scoring ad is better than the other. These are facts of statistics and they cannot be overcome by subjective judgments.

One more example will help to make this clear. Suppose that, using two samples of 200 each, creative idea A, execution 1 achieves a pre-test score of 50%, indicating that 50% of the target group will try the product (again see the intention rating scale and weighting factors in Chapter 8) and that creative idea A, execution 2 obtains a score of 40%. Firstly, using the lower panel of the table, the manager can be sure (95% sure) that execution A1 is truly superior to execution A2. Secondly, by looking at the upper panel of the table, the score of 50% obtained by execution A1 will also contain a degree of inaccuracy due to the sample size; the observed score for A1 could be anywhere between 43% and 57%, which is the degree of error indicated in the last column of the upper table for a sample size of 200. You may notice, and this is pretty sobering for non-statisticians, that even with a sample size as large as 1,000 the absolute error can be as large as plus or minus 3% and the minimum difference detectable by comparing two ads with a sample size of 1,000 each is 5%. Now you can see why such apparently large sample sizes are needed. Even with sample sizes of 200, the results can never be 100% accurate.

Actually, a way of *potentially* saving money with CRAT pre-testing is to run the tests on sample sizes of 100 first. If the differences in results are not large enough to be trusted with 95% confidence, then run the test again with second-sample sizes of 100 and combine the first and second samples' results to achieve the desired sample size of 200 for each execution. Note, however, that if the 100-sample sizes results are significant, you will still lose some absolute predictive accuracy for the winning ad (see table, upper panel).

The cost in perspective

Is U.S. $100,000 or so too much to pay for a CRAT for four ads? To answer this question correctly, you have to consider the chance of *no* profit from running a *weak ad* (about .7 probability if you don't test at all, and still about .5 if the ad has passed the MJAT pre-test). Just one single insertion of a 30-second TV commercial now costs about $475,000 on the U.S. top-rated national TV program, *Friends*[6], and, in a country one-tenth the size, such as Australia, the cost of *one insertion* would be about U.S.$50,000. Is it worth up to $950,000 in the U.S. market or $100,000 in the Australian market, a cost equivalent to two insertions, to be approximately 95% sure, as opposed to 30% (no test) or 50% (MJAT) that you will be running a *successful* ad? In most cases, the rational response is to mentally pull an insertion or two out of the media plan, because a successful ad will need fewer anyway, and commission the CRAT.

TABLE 10.4 *Two useful reference tables for survey or test-result interpretation based on samples of different sizes (95% confidence level).*

A. SINGLE PERCENTAGE

SAMPLE SIZE	PLUS OR MINUS ERROR WHEN THE PERCENTAGE IS CLOSE TO				
	10% OR 90%	20% OR 80%	30% OR 70%	40% OR 60%	50%
1,000	2	3	3	3	3
500	3	4	4	4	4
250	4	5	6	6	6
200	4	6	6	7	7
150	5	6	7	8	8
100	6	8	9	10	10
50	8	11	13	14	14
25	12	16	18	19	20

Example: A reported percentage of 30%, based on a random sample of 200 consumers, has an error rate of plus or minus 6%. That is, we could be "95% confident" that the actual population percentage, had everyone been surveyed, is between 24% and 36%. In other words, it's a safe bet that it is *at least* 24%.

TABLE 10.4 *Continued*

B. DIFFERENCE BETWEEN PERCENTAGES

AVERAGE OF THE TWO SAMPLE SIZES	DIFFERENCE NEEDED WHEN THE AVERAGE OF THE TWO PERCENTAGES IS CLOSE TO				
	10% OR 90%	20% OR 80%	30% OR 70%	40% OR 60%	50%
1,000	4	4	5	5	5
500	4	5	6	6	6
250	5	7	8	9	9
200	6	8	9	10	10
150	7	9	10	11	11
100	8	11	13	14	14
50	12	16	18	19	20
25	17	22	25	27	28

Example: Suppose a TV commercial brand-recall measure, based on a random sample of 200 viewers, indicates a brand recall of 20%. You are disappointed. You decide to repeat the test with a new random sample of 200 viewers, and the commercial now obtains a brand recall of 30%. Are these reliably different scores? The average of the two sample sizes is 150. The average of the two brand-recall scores is 25%. The conservative difference needed is 10% (from the table at the intersection of the 150 row and the 30% column). Yes, you can be 95% confident that the second brand-recall score is higher than the first.

SOURCE: Tables compiled from more detailed tables in Newspaper Advertising Bureau, *The Audience Newspaper Advertising*, New York: NAB, 1978, appendix.

Measures for the CRAT

The two key measures in a Customer Response Ad Test are the ad's ability to generate Brand Awareness and create, increase, or reinforce Brand Preference. If the purpose of the campaign is to remind or sell the Category Need, as for a new brand-item that is pioneering a new product or service category, then you will need a measure of that too. But let's first consider the two essential measures – actually, reconsider them, because they were given in Chapter 8.

Brand awareness

Brand Awareness is difficult to measure in an ad test. This is because if you have just shown a person an ad for the brand (or more specifically, the brand-item) then, unless the ad is unusually obscure about what it is advertising, nearly everyone will be able to recognize the brand – or recall the brand if that is the objective – after such a brief time interval. If the ad happens to be a Direct-Response Ad, in which immediate Brand Recognition is all that is needed, then an immediate measure of Brand Recognition from the pre-test *is* appropriate. However, ads that are not intended to produce a direct response, that is, an Awareness Ad, will in the actual marketplace have a delay between the customer's advertising exposure and the purchase opportunity. Thus, for awareness ads, to obtain a valid measure of brand awareness there should be a *delay* between seeing or hearing the ad and the measurement of whether the target customer can Recognize or, as appropriate, Recall the brand (brand-item). The only way that we know of to solve this problem for awareness ads in an ad test, without an expensive re-interview or telephone callback, is to create an artificial, even if brief, delay during the interview itself. This can be achieved by taking the Brand Preference measure first, then shifting to the collection of demographic information from the respondent, and finally administering the Brand Awareness measure. Note that before all this, there will need to be a quick set of screening questions to classify potential respondents into the Target Group or Groups that you are seeking for the pre-test.

The brand awareness measures are as described in Chapter 8. Brand Recall, if it is an objective of the campaign, should be measured first because it is "unaided." The respondent is presented only with the *Category-Need cue* (e.g., "Financial service advisers") and asked to *call out the brands* that come to mind (e.g., "CitiBank, American Express, ING"). From the Behavioral Sequence Model, the researcher will know how many brands are typically recalled for consideration in this type of purchase decision and should apply an appropriate *cutoff* for that number of brands (e.g., it might be four brands in the consideration of financial services and therefore, to be counted as having generated Brand Recall for that respondent, the advertised brand must be mentioned within that person's first four brands recalled). If it is a brand-*item* that is being advertised, the respondent must get the *item name* correct to count as a brand recaller.

If Brand Recognition is an objective, the respondent is shown a *photo* of brand packages or company logos, as appropriate, and asked to *call out the names* of the brands (if brand-items, they do *not* have to be named by item because the respondent is obviously *looking at* the item, as they would in a store). An example of package photos is shown in Figure 10.4 from ACNielsen's packs@work online pack test procedure. Remember, the brand pack is an ad!

FIGURE 10.4 *Example of competitive pack photos suitable for testing brand recognition. From ACNielsen's packs@work online package testing procedure.*

SOURCE: Courtesy of ACNielsen Australia. packs@work enables marketers to assess new packaging concepts online.

By either type of Brand Awareness measure, the results will be considerably *higher* than they would be with a real-world delay, especially as each respondent has seen the execution very recently and, in the case of broadcast ads, two or three times in succession. There is no good way to correct the Brand Awareness scores downward to reflect real-world scores. Nevertheless, if the respondent cannot Recall the advertised brand, or Recognize it, according to the appropriate brand awareness objective, then the ad has not been effective with that respondent and so the inflated scores are better than making no allowance for brand awareness. The Brand Awareness scores are then used as "qualifiers" for the Brand Preference results (see below). Brand preference scores for those respondents who did not recall or recognize the brand are eliminated from the results count because in the real world, if you do not recall or recognize the brand, it is irrelevant whether or not you prefer it.

Brand preference

The multiple-brand or multiple-logo Brand Recognition *photo* is used to measure Brand Preference. Brand preference is measured for *each* of the half dozen or so brands or companies shown, without the interviewer indicating which was the advertised one so that the subsequent brand awareness measures are not compromised. The appropriate Brand Preference measure differs according to the brand preference *quadrant* in which the brand or brand-item is located.

Recapping these from Chapter 8:

If *Low-Involvement/Informational* or *Low-Involvement/Transformational*, use the *relative* Brand Preference measure: the one brand that I prefer; one of several brands that I prefer; a so-so brand; a brand I don't like. This "softer" brand preference measure, which does not ask for a direct statement of purchase intent, is used because of less emphasis on "buy now" in advertising in this quadrant. The relative brand preference scores are interpreted on a relative "share of requirements" basis, that is, a respondent who says that this is the only brand that they would buy gets a score of 1.00 if that was the advertised brand and zero otherwise; a respondent who nominates the advertised brand along with two others as strongly preferred receives a score of .33.

If *High-Involvement/Informational* or if *High-Involvement/Transformational* the 11-point Juster measure of Purchase (or Action) Intention is used, taken for each of the brand-items or companies. The weighting of the scale starts with .05 and increases in equal increments to reach a maximum of .55 for a respondent who indicates the maximum purchase intention score of 10.

Note that in the two High-Involvement purchase intent situations, the purchase intent measure may need to be qualified by a conditional *Category Need* statement, such as "If you did decide to sign on with a financial service adviser . . ." If *reminding* or *selling* the Category Need was an objective of the campaign, that would be measured separately (before the Brand Preference measure).

Brand emotions and benefit beliefs

After the brand awareness and brand preference measure, it helps for *ad performance diagnosis* to take measures of Brand Emotions and Brand Benefit Beliefs as specified in the campaign positioning statement.

> For Brand Benefit Beliefs, use a *range* measure[7] (exemplified in Figure 10.5). (We note here that a *range* measure of *Brand Preference*, on a scale of –5 = very negative to +5 = very positive, would provide an indicator of the *value-equity elasticity reduction* induced by the advertising.) For Brand Emotions, use Desmet's manikins, as shown in Chapter 8, Figure 8.6, and ask for a "beginning" rating and an "end" rating so that, on an individual respondent basis, you can measure *emotion-shift* of the type intended by the ad.

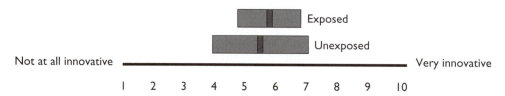

FIGURE 10.5 *Example of the range measure of brand benefit beliefs. The respondent is asked to mark the length of the line in which he or she believes the brand delivers the benefit, that is, with a lower and upper limit, after first marking his or her point-estimate belief. Note: the respondent is not shown the numbers – they are used for coding, later.*

SOURCE: W.T. Moran, 1985, reference in note 7.

Use **ad response modeling** (path analysis) to check whether Brand Preference is or is not influenced by the a-b-e Strategy. Ad Response Modeling is diagnostic – it reveals *how* the ad works on brand preference and where it breaks down if it doesn't work. Ad Response Modeling is not offered voluntarily by most research suppliers, so find out if the supplier has the capability to do ARM (you will pay a bit extra for it) or have a good statistician in your company do it.[8]

> An example of Ad Response Modeling from an article by Mehta is shown in Figure 10.6. This shows the significant paths between elements of the ad, a retail clothing TV commercial that uses a Celebrity (source/model), and the CRAT measures which in this case were Attitude toward the Ad (the TV commercial), Brand Attitude, and Brand Purchase Intention.

Overall scoring in the CRAT

Scoring in the CRAT must be computed on an individual-respondent basis: you have to estimate the *proportion*, the percentage, of each group who meets the *joint* communication objectives.

> As an example, let us consider test results for Awareness Ads that have the communication objectives of (1) Brand Recognition and (2) Low-Involvement/Informational Brand Preference. Suppose that one of the executions achieves Brand Recognition among 120 of the 200 respondents in the target-group sample (among FBSs, for instance). This means, firstly, that the ad can be expected to be successful with approximately, at most, $120 \div 200 \times 100\% = 60\%$ of the FBS target customers. Only these 120 customers' Brand Preference scores are, therefore, counted. Suppose that the Brand Preference scores are distributed as follows:

AD PROCESSING   COMMUNICATION EFFECTS

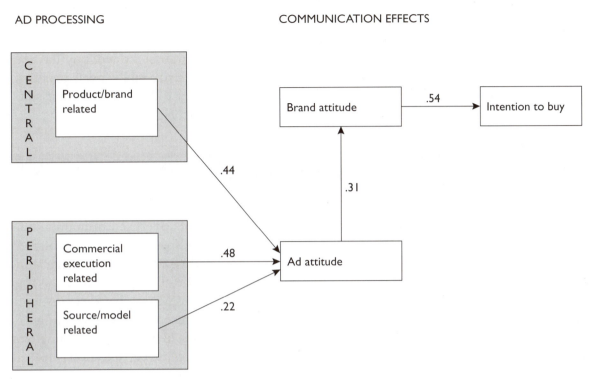

FIGURE 10.6 *Example of an advertising response model based on the results of a path analysis. Standardized regression coefficients are shown.*

SOURCE: From A. Mehta, 1994, reference in note 8, p. 67. Reprinted from the *Journal of Advertising Research* © 1994 by permission of the ARF.

Brand Preference	Sub-sample: respondents who achieved Brand Recognition (n = 120)	Weight	Weighted number
Single preferred	30	1.00	30
One of two preferred	40	.50	20
One of three preferred	30	.33	10
Other	20	.00	0
	120		60

In total, after *weighting* the Brand Preference ratings, the estimated result is that 60 people will buy the product. As a percentage of the original 200 people in the group, this ad's predicted Purchase score is therefore 60/200 = 30%. Because of the sample size, the 95% confidence interval in projecting this predicted Purchase incidence to the target group population is 30 plus or minus 8%, that is, between 22% and 38% (from the sample size table, Table 10.4, upper panel).

The same analysis is conducted for the *control* group, which is not exposed to the ad but *is* exposed to the pack, name, or logo – that is, to *whatever stimulus they would see or hear at the Point of Decision in the real world*. If the score from the ad-unexposed group is 12% or lower, then we conclude that the *ad* has increased the proportion of the target group who will buy the brand. That is, the ad group has to score at least 11% higher (see sample size table, lower panel).

If the ad is for a *High-Involvement* product or service, you use the *Juster 11-point scale* of Brand Purchase (or Action) Intention and *weight* the intention scores as indicated.

SUMMARY

A Management Judgment Ad Test (MJAT) should be constructed by the management team and used to pre-test all Rough Ads and, if applicable, rough versions of advertised promotion offers, prior to approval and final production. The MJAT questionnaire is specific to the campaign. It is constructed by writing rating items that correspond with the Creative Brief (creative target and *all applicable* communication objectives, and the action objective if direct response) and the Brand Awareness and Brand Preference tactics. Added for secondary screening is a checklist of Attention factors (according to the ad or promotion offer's medium). If our recommended procedure from Chapter 7 has been followed, there will be four rough ad executions to be rated, consisting of *two executions* each of the *two creative ideas* that were accepted from the conveyer selection step.

The MJAT provides a systematic and thorough check that the ad execution is "on strategy." The MJAT primarily removes downside risk: it prevents the approval of ads or advertised promotion offers that won't work. This is a very useful achievement. The MJAT is a *sufficient* pre-test for executions that are part of a *continuing campaign*.

For *new campaigns* – that is, when a new creative idea is being introduced, either for a new product or service or for repositioning of an established product or service – the construction and use of a Customer Response Ad Test (CRAT) is recommended because this will predict the upside performance of the ad. The MJAT alone is not sufficient to do this, because it was a test conducted by managers, not with potential customers, and not with a projectable sample size of customers. The CRAT requires a sample size of 200 "test" respondents per target group, per execution, and 200 unexposed "control" respondents per target group. Good-Quality Rough Ads are highly predictive of Finished Ad performance and the CRAT, like the MJAT before it, should be conducted at the rough ad stage, before funds are committed to final production.

The measures for the CRAT must fit the Communication Objectives of the campaign. The CRAT requires a Brand Awareness measure, a Brand Preference measure, and, for diagnostic purposes, measures of Brand Emotions and Brand Benefit Beliefs which are later used to "predict" Brand Preference to determine whether the ad or advertised promotion offer worked as it was intended to. Measures of Category Need, Brand Action Intention, and Purchase Facilitation are added if these are among the campaign's communication objectives.

The results of the CRAT enable a good prediction to be made of the proportion of the target group or groups who are likely to try, buy, or otherwise take the desired Action as a result of the ad or offer.

DISCUSSION QUESTIONS

10.1 Construct and conduct an MJAT for the two Apple Computer's iPod ads, from Chapter 9, Figure 9.3.

10.2 Brainstorm one new Creative Idea for the Birds Eye Create-a-Meal Mexican product and do two Rough Ad executions of it. Then use the MJAT questionnaire in the chapter to pre-test the two executions, and report on your findings.

10.3 Why should managers not use Focus Groups to pre-test ads?

10.4 Why is sample size important in commissioning a CRAT? Is there a way of potentially saving money based on sample size?

10.5 In what circumstances would a CRAT *not* be a rational expenditure from your marketing budget?

10.6 Construct a CRAT for the Coke "Contour bottle" ad from Chapter 7, Figure 7.8.

10.7 Construct a CRAT for the two ads for HSBC bank, from Chapter 7, Figures 7.6 and 7.7.

NOTES

1. As reported in A.Z. Cuneo, Levi's CEO blames slow launch on spots, *Advertising Age*, March 31, 2003, pp. 1, 89. The quotation is from p. 1.

2. Some of the odds for medical treatments will be mentioned in Chapter 18. They are more sobering, even, than marcoms' chances of success.

3. Agencies' verbose rationales for their ad campaigns have been parodied in several movies, most recently to our knowledge by Mel Gibson in *What Women Want*.

4. Based on experience from pre-testing over 3,500 TV ads in diverse countries, Cramphorn also concludes that about 30% of tested ads are "very effective," meaning 70% are not. Given that it is the better advertisers who (quantitatively) pre-test their ads, the success rate in general is surely lower than 30%. See S. Cramphorn, How pre-testing can increase your ROI by 900%, *Admap*, 2003, November, p. 15.

5. J.D. Morris and C. Waine, Managing the creative effort: pre-production and post-production measures of emotional response, in E. Thorson (Ed.), *Proceedings of the 1993 Conference of the American Academy of Advertising*, Columbia, MO: School of Journalism, University of Missouri-Columbia, 1993, pp. 158–176.

6. R. Linnett, "Friends" tops TV price chart, *Advertising Age*, September 15, 2003, p. 1.

7. See W. Moran, The circuit of effects in tracking advertising profitability, *Journal of Advertising Research*, 1985, 25(1), pp. 25–29. The figure is based on his Figure 8, p. 29.

8. Helpful examples of the ARM method are provided in A. Mehta, How advertising response modeling (ARM) can increase ad effectiveness, *Journal of Advertising Research*, 1994, 34(3), pp. 62–74. To clarify the path analysis results, compute cross-tabs. Here is an important insight – and the main reason why we don't use brand emotions and brand benefit beliefs as communication objectives for an overall campaign. For a particular ad, particular emotions or benefit beliefs may be the *intended* way the ad works but the same ad can work in *different* ways for *different* people (e.g., some individuals may be persuaded to try the brand-item because of a startling product demonstration in the ad, "Wow, gotta get one of those!", whereas other individuals may ignore the demo but be glued to the handsome, pretty, or spunky *presenter* who does the demo and think, "I'll have whatever s/he's having, thanks!" The fact that significant correlations are typically observed for *multiple* paths in ARM analysis of an ad supports the "different ways" interpretation. We thank Geoff Eagleson, a stats professor at the Australian Graduate School of Management, for this insight.

PART IV

advertising –

media strategy

CHAPTER ELEVEN

Media-type selection and
the reach pattern 235

CHAPTER TWELVE

Effective frequency and strategic rules for
implementation of the media plan 259

CHAPTER 11

Media-type selection and the reach pattern

There are four main decisions in media strategy. The terminology with which we describe them below will look Martian at first but special terms are necessary and we'll define them carefully. The decisions are:

1. Selection of primary and, usually, secondary media types

2. Formulation of an appropriate reach pattern for the campaign

3. Estimating minimum effective frequency for each advertising and promotion cycle

4. Selection of media vehicles in the media type and insertion of ads in those vehicles so as to efficiently achieve the media plan

The marketing or brand manager should get directly involved in media planning and not delegate these decisions to the media agency or advertising agency! Most of the marcoms budget – about 70% to 90%, depending on the country in which you are advertising – will be spent on media and this warrants a good deal of the manager's thought and time.

Media strategy is covered in two chapters. This chapter, Chapter 11, examines the first two decisions, Media-Type Selection and the Reach Pattern. Chapter 12 examines the third decision, effective frequency estimation, and the final decision, selecting Vehicles and making Insertions for media plan implementation.

PRIMARY AND SECONDARY MEDIA-TYPE SELECTION

Large-audience advertisers, both business-to-business and FMCG, employ two and sometimes three **primary media** to reach the total target audience, and one or two **secondary media** to boost particular communication effects. Smaller-audience advertisers – smaller business-to-business (B-to-B), smaller consumer companies, and retailers – usually employ *one* Primary Medium and *one* Secondary Medium. The terms "primary" and "secondary" with regard to media types are defined below and the media-type selection decision for each of the *main types of advertiser* is explained, that is, large-audience advertisers, small-audience local retailers, small-audience B-to-B advertisers, and direct-response advertisers.

Primary medium

A Primary Medium is the medium capable of delivering *all* of the communication objectives of the campaign. Note that if Purchase Facilitation is an objective, as it might be for a product or service that is not mass-marketed, then the Primary Medium or Primary Media must achieve this too, with a dealer address or URL in the ad. The majority of the media budget is allocated to the primary medium. In this chapter, we will show which primary media options are suitable depending on the brand or brand-item's location in the *Rossiter-Percy-Bellman Grid*, the framework discussed in Chapter 8.

Use of two or three primary media

Most advertisers use only *one* Primary Medium (see Chapter 1, Table 1.2). However, *very large* advertisers cannot reach the whole target audience with one primary medium, or not with enough frequency. An *additional* primary medium is used by very large advertisers to reach target customers who are valuable and worth the extra effort but who have little or no exposure to the first primary medium. The additional medium is primary, even though less is spent on it than on the first primary medium, because it, too, must be capable of delivering *all* the communication effects that are communication objectives for the campaign. Some adults, for instance, watch no television and many, especially 18 to 49 year-olds with annual incomes of U.S.$75,000+ of both genders, are *light* viewers of prime-time TV, when most ads are run, and have recently been viewing even less.[1] Print media are even more skewed and are declining: in most Western countries, a slight majority of adults, just over 50%, do not read any magazines and about 30% do not read newspapers. Young people's exposure to print media is even lower. In Australia, for instance, which is typical of Western countries, just on 50% of "tweenagers" (7 to 14 year-olds) read a magazine and fewer than 30% of this age group read newspapers – and then mainly for the Sunday comics section.[2] In these cases, if a substantial number of your target customers have little or no exposure to the first primary medium that you have selected, another suitable primary medium must be selected. This can be done from Table 11.1, listing primary media options.

For large advertisers who need more than one primary medium, *cross-media optimization* services have emerged recently to help, led, perhaps not surprisingly given its own relatively recent emergence as a medium, by research companies working in conjunction with the Internet Advertising Bureau. The historical alternative for large TV advertisers has been Magazines but with magazine readership falling per capita, Online advertising has become a *third* primary medium for many large advertisers. For new FMCG brand-items, an optimal primary-media mix for maximizing trial includes 10% to 15% spent on Online ads, a remarkable proportion considering that 2% is usual. Most of this comes out of the Magazine spend, with TV, as expected, still dominant with at least 70% of total spend. For example, Colgate-Palmolive Co. found that to reach the target audience of 18 to 49 year-old non-users or occasional users of Colgate Total toothpaste (note: not current regular users), the optimal mix was 75% TV, 14% Magazines, and 11% Online.[3] Two Online ads for Colgate Total are reproduced in Figure 11.1; the left strip is a Banner ad and if you click on that you get to the magazine-like ad shown beside it which is on the brand's Website.

Secondary media

For many campaigns, one or perhaps two Secondary Media are also used. The purpose for employing a Secondary Medium is to boost a *particular* communication effect that is an objective of the campaign.

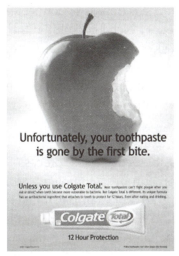

FIGURE 11.1 *Online ads such as this banner ad (left) and Website ad (right) are used as a third primary medium, with TV and magazines, by Colgate Total toothpaste to reach new triers and re-triers.*

SOURCE: Courtesy of Colgate-Palmolive Pty Ltd.

Brand awareness boosting

As we saw in Chapters 5 and 8, Brand Recall, when it is an objective, requires lots of *frequency*; this frequency can be supplemented by a Secondary Medium that reaches the same media target as the Primary Medium. However, media vehicle overlaps in audience are becoming so small that *Impact Scheduling* in the primary medium may be the only solution for achieving high frequency, as explained later. It is worth special emphasis, when Brand Recognition is an objective, to regard *packaging and signage* of all types as an *essential* Secondary Medium. The secondary medium does not have to be capable of carrying all of the campaign communication objectives, only the objective to be boosted, which in the two cases above are Brand Awareness objectives.

Brand preference boosting

For boosting Brand Preference, the Secondary Medium is usually one of the *point-of-decision (P-O-D)* media types discussed later. Apart from P-O-D media, *longer-copy print ads* in Newspapers or Magazines are often used to boost Brand Preference in conjunction with TV ads. The TV ads are still *primary* because they convey all the campaign's communication objectives; it is just that Brand Preference may need some extra, more detailed assistance, which print can provide.

Teaser campaigns: priming

A Teaser Campaign is an effective way for the innovating brand to launch a new product or service category, or for a differentiated new brand to enter an established category. We showed a teaser ad earlier, in Chapter 2, Figure 2.2, for the launch of the Chrysler Crossfire automobile in Australia. A Teaser Campaign employs secondary (incomplete) ads in one medium, to *precede* the primary (complete) ads in the same or a different medium. The incomplete ads give the brand name or logo but don't identify exactly what *category* it is. Later, using primary (complete) ads, Brand Awareness is connected (the category is identified), Brand Preference is established, and Category Need is "sold" if the category is new. A typical Teaser Campaign employs Outdoor, perhaps skywriting or street furniture ads, or short TV or Radio ads (secondary) in the "tease" phase, and then shifts to longer TV, Radio or Print ads (primary) for the "revelation" phase. Teaser Campaigns make use of a processing mechanism known as **Priming**, whereby the incomplete first message motivates the audience, via *curiosity*, to process the second message.[4]

Imagery transfer

Also possible is the *reverse* process – **imagery transfer** – whereby visual or auditory images from the primary medium's "complete" ad are recalled during exposure to the secondary medium's "less complete" ad. For example, Imagery Transfer can be attempted from TV to Radio, where use of the same audio track can prompt recall of the TV ad's video when listening to the Radio ad; or TV to Print, where a Key Visual transferred from the TV commercial to the Print ad can prompt recall of the TV ad's video; or Radio to Print, where music or a jingle from the Radio ad may be recalled if the Print ad uses some of the same wording as the Radio ad. The rationale behind Imagery Transfer is that the two exposures across media count almost as *three* exposures because of the recall of the first during the second. However, there are two requirements for imagery transfer to work: one is a high degree of target audience *overlap* between the cross-media vehicles selected and, second, there must be a *spontaneous* occurrence of imagery during the second ad's exposure. In the 1968 experiment that made Imagery Transfer famous[5], the respondents were *prompted* by the interviewer to recall the first ad. For it to work in reality, imagery transfer has to happen *naturally*.

But not synergy

Apart from when Imagery Transfer is intentionally used, there is no advantage in using multiple media *per se*. So-called "synergy," a multiplicative rather than additive increase in communication effects, is more a hope than a reality.[6] There is, if anything, a *disadvantage* in using multiple media – loss of Effective Frequency because of *reduced Reach overlap* to the target group (this sentence does look Martian but see the next chapter).

PRIMARY MEDIUM SELECTION

The choice of the Primary Medium or sometimes, Primary Media, depends on four factors:

1. Size and type of advertiser (see below)

2. Brand awareness objective (brand recall vs. brand recognition)

3. Brand preference type (low-involvement/informational vs. low-involvement/transformational vs. high-involvement/informational vs. high-involvement/transformational)

4. Then, from the possible primary media remaining, target audience reach

We discuss primary medium selection entirely by *size and type of advertiser*: large-audience advertisers (B-to-B and B-to-C), small-audience local retail advertisers, small-audience B-to-B advertisers, and direct-response advertisers.

Large-audience advertisers (B-to-C and B-to-B)

Large-audience advertisers include large B-to-B companies[7] and large business-to-consumer (B-to-C, mostly FMCG) manufacturers whose distribution covers more than half of the nation. The alternative choices as the Primary Medium for large-audience advertisers are TV, Pay-TV, Newspapers, Magazines, Radio, Stationary- or Mobile-viewed Outdoor, and the Internet (Online). Before considering these, a couple of preliminary points should be made concerning TV advertising, Outdoor, and a medium that is not in the list, Cinema.

TV Advertising is the most effective *mass* medium ever invented[8] and will continue to be for the foreseeable future. Not every advertiser can afford TV, however, and, as we shall see, it is not the best option for advertisers selling High-Involvement/Informational products or services, or for small businesses or small local retailers with relatively small audience numbers.

There is an essential distinction between Stationary-Viewed Outdoor Ads (which function like a Newspaper or Magazine ad) and Mobile-Viewed Outdoor Ads (which function rather like a short, fast-forwarded TV commercial!). *Stationary*-viewed means the outdoor ad is *fixed relative to the customer*, allowing considerable time to process the message. *Mobile*-viewed means either the ad *or* the customer is passing by, so processing time is very brief. Whereas Outdoor is often regarded as a "commuters only" medium, the facts are that most of us *are* commuters. The average American now travels 308 miles (about 500 kilometres) each week including 25 minutes each way to work.[9] In Australia, 94% of 14–54 year-olds make five or more outdoor round-trips a week; the weekly reach of Outdoor is about 60% for the 14–54 age group and 69% for 14–17 year-olds, higher than all print media.[10] Outdoor nowadays is diverse and includes billboards, posters, street furniture, transit and almost any object that can be rented for ad space. In the U.K., these are called *Ambient Media*[11] and are classed with miscellaneous Point-of-Use media (see later in this chapter).

We do not consider **cinema advertising**, which is now available in the U.S.A., as it has been in other countries for years, to be a *primary* medium. Cinema's reach of most groups as well as movie-goers' frequency of attendance are both far too low.

There are, then, really *eight alternatives* as the Primary Medium for large-audience advertisers. Table 11.1 shows their message-carrying capacities for the two universal campaign communication effects of Brand Awareness and Brand Preference. For *brand awareness*, media differ in terms of their capacity to achieve Brand Recognition or to achieve Brand Recall. For *brand preference*, the media differ in terms of their capacity to carry messages suited to the four brand preference strategy Quadrants. The Primary Medium has to carry message content for all of the communication objectives – which means *one* of the two brand awareness types *and one* of the four brand preference strategies for achieving brand preference. For instance, a campaign aimed at achieving Brand Recognition *and* Low-Involvement/Informational brand preference can use, as a primary medium, only those media that can carry both these types of message content. A campaign aimed at generating Brand Recall *and* a High-Involvement/Transformational brand preference must use both those types, and so forth. We explain these message-carrying limitations below.

TABLE 11.1 *Primary media options for large-audience advertisers categorized by brand awareness and brand preference message capacity.*

BRAND *RECOGNITION* AND LI/INFO	LI/TRANS	HI/INFO	HI/TRANS
Television	Television	Pay television	Television (will need secondary medium if information underlay)
Pay television	Pay television	Newspapers (color)	Pay television
Newspapers (color)	Stationary-viewed outdoor	Magazines	Newspapers (color)
Magazines	Mobile-viewed outdoor	Stationary-viewed outdoor	Magazines
Stationary-viewed outdoor	Internet banners	Internet Website	Stationary-viewed outdoor
Mobile-viewed outdoor			Internet Website
Internet banners			

BRAND *RECALL* AND LI/INFO	LI/TRANS	HI/INFO	HI/TRANS
Television	Television	Pay television	Television
Pay television	Pay television	Newspapers	Pay television
Radio	Radio (unless visual required)	Stationary-viewed outdoor	Radio (unless visual required)
Newspapers'	Stationary-viewed outdoor		Newspapers (color)
Stationary-viewed outdoor	Mobile-viewed outdoor		Stationary-viewed outdoor
Mobile-viewed outdoor	Internet banners		Mobile-viewed outdoor
Internet banners			

Brand Recognition requires *visual capacity,* which would normally rule out Radio except in the special case of verbal brand-name recognition. Recognition of the company's name when a salesperson calls would be an example of verbal brand-name recognition. However, in the vast majority of cases, brand recognition refers to recognition of packs and logos – which means it has to be achieved visually. *Transformational* campaigns based on Visual Sensory Gratification, such as for many food products, are also constrained to visual capacity media. Either of these communication objectives rules out radio and also newspapers, the latter because the color reproduction is not good enough.

Brand Recall has a *high-frequency* requirement. So too do Low-Involvement/Transformational brand preference campaigns. If either is an objective, the "slow" medium of magazines is ruled out. Internet *banner* ads, placed on sites that the target audience visits frequently, are suitable.

Lastly, campaigns based on the High-Involvement/Informational attitude strategy for brand preference require *long message* media, the exception being when target customers can be reliably directed to a long-message secondary medium such as a Website, Brochure or an in-bound Telemarketing phone call (in-bound refers to customer-initiated calls, as opposed to out-bound Telemarketing, which is uninvited). Some High-Involvement/Transformational products and services, while transformational on their *key* benefit, also have a heavy informational "underlay" and thus need either a long-message-capacity primary medium or for the target customer to be directed to a long-message-capacity secondary medium. We have listed Internet *Websites* as a suitable primary medium for High-Involvement products but only if the brand awareness objective is Brand Recognition.

The selection of *one* primary medium, or two or three if you are a very large advertiser, for the campaign is made from within the listed types based on **target audience reach**. This means the ability of a set of vehicles in that medium to reach a sufficient number of prospects to deliver the *sales goal*. Cost per prospect *effectively* reached should be the deciding factor thereafter, not the cost per thousand of total reach. We return to the cost factor in the next chapter.

Small-audience local retail advertisers

Local retail advertisers use advertising to attract customers to the store or retail outlet. A retail *chain* can use a mass medium such as television, radio or newspapers to advertise products or services that are common across locations, but an *individual store* in that chain wishing to advertise locally, or a *solely local retailer*, would have too much wasted reach and incur too high an expense to use mass media. Local media are much more appropriate, as listed in Table 11.2.

TABLE 11.2 *Primary media options for local retail advertisers.*

Display ad in local telephone directory (occasionally purchased products or services)
Suburban newspapers
Handbills or flyers (door-to-door mailbox-delivered)
Direct mail (if database marketing is worthwhile)

Small-audience local retailers have Brand Recall and High-Involvement/Informational brand preference to communicate, except for those who sell occasionally purchased products or services that rely on Brand Recognition in the Yellow Pages or local Directories. Suburban Newspapers, delivered once or twice a week to all homes in the suburb, have enough frequency capacity to deliver brand recall for the store. Alternatively, some local retailers invest in weekly door-to-door mailbox pamphlets, also called **handbills** or **flyers**, which have the largest local household reach and command very high levels of Attention (about 74% are looked at, an attention probability of .74) despite their popular description as "junk mail."

Direct Mail is conditionally listed as a local retail medium in the table. This medium should be used if it seems worthwhile for the local retailer to practice Database Marketing. For frequently purchased retail-product stores, such as grocery stores, newsagents, and drug stores, database marketing is neither necessary nor practical. However, for retailers whose products or services are on a *long purchase cycle* (such as dental practices, furnishings, or clothing stores), Database Marketing, either via continued Direct Mail or by Telemarketing, is certainly worthwhile. For a "how to" of Database Marketing, see Chapter 17.

Small-audience B-to-B advertisers

Small-audience B-to-B advertisers usually advertise in **business magazines**, **trade publications** (which are industry-specific) or by Direct Mail, depending on the size of their *small* target audience. Primary medium selection for small-audience B-to-B advertisers is shown in Table 11.3. The print media shown for the larger- and moderate-sized audience B-to-B advertisers are capable of taking two-step, or *double duty*, direct-response ads. A **double-duty ad** is an ad in which a phone number or Website address is *added* to an *Awareness Ad*, to capture inquiries. An Inquiry is the first of two steps to the sale, the second being Purchase itself. Double-Duty B-to-B ads have as their communication objectives Brand Recognition and High-Involvement/Informational brand preference.

TABLE 11.3 *Primary medium selection for small-audience business-to-business advertisers.*

SIZE OF TARGET AUDIENCE (NUMBER OF PROSPECTS)	RECOMMENDED MEDIA
Larger (> 1,000 but distribution less than 50% of the nation, hence small-audience B-to-B advertiser)	Display ad in local telephone directory Business magazines Trade publications Direct mail
Moderate (100–1,000)	Small in-column ad in local telephone directory Trade publications Direct mail
Smaller (<100)	Listing in local telephone directory Personal selling, with brochure or CD sales aids

At the other extreme, less than 100 prospects is too small an audience to advertise to and instead the advertiser would rely on personal selling, with a leave-behind or brochure or CD as a sales aid. All small-audience B-to-B advertisers must use a local directory ad, ranging from a display ad down to a listing according to audience size (see Chapter 9 for the different types of directory ads).

Direct-response advertisers

Direct-Response advertisers are the main cause of the perceived increase in media bombardment. Direct-Response Advertising is more commonly called Direct Marketing because true direct-response ads are *one-step*: they seek the response of Purchase directly.

Direct-Response (DR) media, in approximate magnitude of advertiser expenditure in the U.S.A., are: Telemarketing, Direct Mail, **DR cable (pay) television**, **DR television**, **DR newspaper**, **DR magazine**, **DR radio**, **DR email** (with this new DR medium moving up the list rapidly), and **DR fax**. Telemarketing and the latter two DR media usually have to be permission-based.

Primary medium selection from the DR media alternatives depends largely on the *product or service type*. Table 11.4 shows how the DR media decision is usually made. In the last two categories, one primary medium is selected based on its offering the largest Reach (coverage) of the Target Audience.

TABLE 11.4 *Primary medium selection for direct-response advertisers.*

PRODUCT AND TARGET AUDIENCE	RECOMMENDED MEDIA
Any product or service	Direct mail and email
Product or service category that is well-known and doesn't have to be seen	Telephone (telemarketing)
Product or service with broad target audience but no *mailing list*[a]	Newspaper Television (demonstration products) Pay television (demonstration products)
Product or service whose target audience is well defined by an occupational or other demographic or psychographic readership or listenership group (no mailing list necessary)[a]	Magazine Radio

[a] Select one medium based on the largest reach of the target audience.

SECONDARY POINT-OF-DECISION (P-O-D) MEDIA

Point-of-Decision (P-O-D) media are now so numerous that they are another big cause of perceived media bombardment. **P-O-D media** are *secondary* media – they cannot be used as primary because they cannot generate Brand Awareness *before* the purchase decision. A mass medium is needed for this. However, for those advertisers who rely on P-O-D, the *mass* medium could be regarded as also playing a "secondary" (brand awareness-boosting) role and then the P-O-D medium becomes "primary" in that it communicates all of the intended communication effects: Brand Awareness is reinforced, and Brand Preference and the other communication objectives are established, via the P-O-D ads. **Exterior store signage**, **window displays**, **interior store displays**, and **on-shelf promotions** are some of the many point-of-*purchase* media; **packaging**, **calendars**, home or office **product containers** or **service stickers**, and **recipe or do-it-yourself books** are some of the inventive point-of-*use* media. Point of purchase and point of use are the two main subtypes of P-O-D media.

There is only one appropriate way to select P-O-D media (if the campaign's purpose is to stimulate immediate purchase or usage intentions) and that is by *reach* of *target customers* at the *time* and *location* of the decision. The Behavioral Sequence Model (BSM) of the product or service category decision process (see Chapter 6) helps to identify the best P-O-D media opportunities. Some innovative examples of P-O-D media selection are given in the next chapter in the section on very short-term scheduling.

In summary: selection of the primary medium, and perhaps one or two secondary media, is a rather mechanical process because the selection is *determined* by size and type of advertiser, grid locations for brand awareness and brand preference, and, if more than one primary candidate medium remains, by reach of the target audience. Large-audience B-to-B and B-to-C (including FMCG) advertisers will generally need two or three primary media to achieve total target audience reach at an effective frequency rate. The next two decisions in media planning are more definitely *strategic* – the reach pattern (this chapter) and effective frequency (next chapter).

THE REACH PATTERN

The Reach Pattern controls the degree and timing of *individual continuity* of the messages in the marcoms campaign. Some Reach Patterns require *high* continuity to individuals, whereas others require *little or none*. These *strategic* differences in the way reach is to be distributed cannot be represented by the calendar of insertions that the ad agency or media agency gives you!

To decide upon the appropriate Reach Pattern, the manager first has to conceptualize the entire advertising and promotion schedule from the *individual continuity* perspective. Only then can the manager think about the ad or promotion campaign's reach *across* individuals. A Reach Pattern is essentially a template for the advertising and promotion schedule to which, ideally, the typical target customer should be exposed, graphed to show how *all* target customers should be exposed.

There are eight prototypical Reach Patterns from which the manager can choose: four of these reach patterns are for *new-product* media plans and four are for *established-product* media plans. The manager should seek a good fit for *one* of these reach patterns, or in some cases two reach patterns in an evolving sequence, to the brand-item's advertising situation. Minor adaptations can then be made as necessary (short-term scheduling is discussed at the end of the next chapter). The reach patterns are presented and discussed next.

REACH PATTERNS FOR NEW PRODUCTS

Reach Patterns for *new-product campaigns* are shown in Figures 11.2 to 11.5 and are entitled: the Blitz pattern, the Wedge pattern, the Reverse-Wedge/PI pattern and the Short Fad pattern. Reach of the target audience – the Media Target, or the Actual customer target group or groups if Direct Matching is used – is depicted by the vertical height of the blocks in the bar charts. The *frequency*, per advertising cycle, is depicted – relatively, not yet precisely, because we do not yet know the Effective Frequency number – by the *width* of the bars.

Advertising cycle duration (c)

The duration of an **advertising cycle**, c, in reality, is determined by a practical consideration. The duration is determined by *the time needed to get enough insertions into the media vehicles selected so as to attain the desired amount of reach at the minimum effective frequency (MEF) level. The number of target audience members reached at MEF is the level of Effective Reach.* In the case of media such as magazines and direct mail, the time of the advertising insertion and the time when it is actually seen or read by the target customer may represent a long delay. For broadcast media, in contrast, the insertion and the seeing or hearing are instantaneous. However, from a practical standpoint we need to suggest a duration (for insertions) to aim for. As explained in the next chapter, depending on the size of the frequency requirement, the duration for insertions – the Advertising Cycle, c – will be *one day, one week or two weeks.*

Blitz pattern

It is virtually impossible to over-advertise a new product or service during its introduction, as demonstrated in a well-known review of new product campaigns by Aaker and Carman.[12] The ideal pattern, then, if you can afford it, consists of a "blitz" of continuous advertising – at the minimum effective frequency level *every week* – for the first year or at least for the *introduction period* which applies to many new products. The **blitz pattern** for *introductory promotions*, to gain Trial, would usually occur only for the first six months at most because that is the length of time for which a product or service can legally use the description "new." The blitz pattern is shown in Figure 11.2.

In the Blitz pattern, the advertiser tries to reach 100% of the target audience *every week* and pile on frequency, during each week, at the new category user level (see MEF formula in the next chapter) to the *same individuals*. This Blitz pattern will not only maximize the rate of Trial[13],

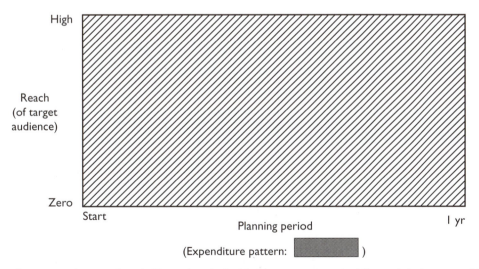

FIGURE 11.2 *Blitz pattern (new products). Shown here is the ideal but very expensive blitz period of one year. More typically, the blitz period is 13 weeks or 26 weeks.*

recognizing that new product trial can take up to two years before maximum penetration is attained[14], but will also tend to suppress the effects of any *competitors'* advertising. That is, an advertiser who uses a blitz pattern is certain to be the "loudest" if not the largest competitor in the category.

For a *really* new product – because of the difficulty of defining a precise target audience as virtually everyone is a potential New Category User – the Blitz pattern can be *very* expensive. Not surprisingly, it has been estimated that, in the U.S.A., the typical advertising cost for a national launch of a new consumer FMCG product with a new brand name is about $35 million, whereas for a not-so-new line extension of a national brand the cost is about $20 million. Consequently, because of the high cost, the highest-budget new FMCG products rarely receive more than a 30-week (usually 26-week) introductory blitz.[15]

With the Blitz pattern, a large "pool" of advertising Executions is needed, built around the same positioning strategy, to prevent Advertising Wearout, which is likely to be rapid with such a heavy schedule aimed at the same people. Three different Executions per quarterly (13-week) period will usually be needed for the blitz, which equates to six executions over 26 weeks and 12 executions over one year.

Wedge pattern

Slightly less effective but also much less expensive than the blitz is the **wedge pattern** for new product launches. The "wedge" actually refers to the pattern of *expenditure*, which begins like a Blitz and then tapers off with each successive advertising cycle. Note carefully, however, that the Wedge pattern for the typical target audience *individual* is *not* wedge-shaped but rather the wedge is received as a succession of advertising cycles – each with the same *Reach* but successively declining *Frequency*. This pattern is shown in Figure 11.3.

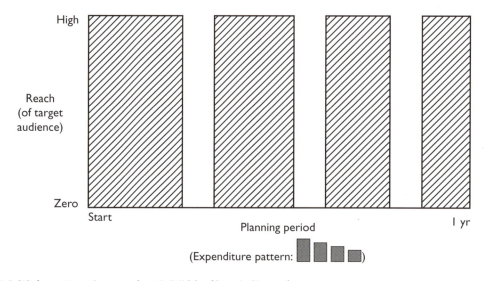

FIGURE 11.3 *Wedge pattern (new products). Width of bars indicates frequency.*

The Wedge is a very good reach pattern for the introduction of new brand-items in *repeat-purchase* product and service categories. High frequency is needed initially to create Brand Awareness for the new product and to enable prospective triers to learn the new product's benefits (Informational advertising) or acquire its intended image (Transformational advertising). Thereafter, most of those who try, if all goes well, will become Favorable Brand Switchers or Brand Loyals who will require less frequency in later cycles to maintain the communication effects (see the Minimum Effective Frequency (MEF) Formula in the next chapter).

In fact, if you can achieve very precise media-vehicle placement of ads, the *really* ideal reach pattern would be to combine a Blitz with a Wedge, such that a Blitz is continued against those who have not yet tried the brand, with trier-rejecters avoided, while a Wedge is offered to those who have tried it and have responded favorably.

Reverse-wedge/PI pattern

As in the wedge pattern, the "reverse-wedge" refers to media *expenditures* over the planning period rather than to exposures as received by the typical target audience individual. The target audience individual receives *increasing* Frequency with each flight, and Reach is held constant at 100% of the target audience. The **reverse-wedge/PI pattern** is shown in Figure 11.4. In the most effective application of this pattern, the target audience consists of consumer *Innovators*[16] or business *Lead Users*[17] initially, and then is broadened to the Mass Market as PI (Personal Influence) from the Innovators takes over. If Direct-Matching media vehicle selection is used, Innovators or Lead Users can be identified in the direct-matching survey with the addition of a few simple questions (see Chapter 14, Table 14.2).

The Reverse-Wedge/PI pattern is most appropriate for the introduction of a new *Social Approval motive* product or service. For the Social Approval motive, the marketer can count on

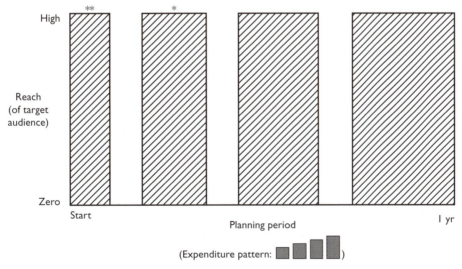

FIGURE 11.4 *Reverse-wedge/PI pattern (new products with social approval motive). Width of bars indicates frequency. Asterisks denote innovator emphasis in target audience.*

personal influence (word of mouth, or visual influence, sometimes called word-of-eye, for products or services that are socially consumed) being generated as a *complement* to the advertising. The idea is that the *low* initial advertising frequency will make the product or service appear to be somewhat "exclusive" both for the innovators or lead users themselves and for any others who happen to see the ads. Many of the Innovators will then act as Opinion Leaders (again see Chapter 14, Table 14.2); the typical estimate is that about 60% will become verbal influencers and almost all innovators who purchase will become visual influencers. Then, as the hoped-for Personal Influence begins to spread, the target audience becomes 100% of Early Adopters, and then later the Late Majority of adopters. Finally, the frequency of ads is gradually stepped up to help persuade the target audience as it becomes more conservative in its adoption behavior. The Reverse-Wedge/PI pattern was first used, as far as we know, by Toohey's Brewery (now Lion Nathan) in Australia for the introduction of its Toohey's Red bitter beer and, later, Toohey's Blue bitter beer. The Reverse-Wedge/PI strategy was very successful and is now imitated, certainly in Australia, by almost all other new beer launches, especially the "boutique" beers whose positioning is almost exclusively based on Social Approval.

The Reverse-Wedge/PI pattern is not limited to FMCG products. There is definitely word-of-mouth pressure in *industry* to "keep up" with new technology, making the Reverse-Wedge/PI pattern applicable for the advertising of new industrial products.[18]

Short fad pattern

Well-discussed in the marketing and consumer behavior literature (for instance, in Robertson's book[19]) is the fact that some products are strictly "fad" products with a *short product life cycle*. Some of these products, such as inexpensive fashion clothes or new toys, may be purchased more than once while the fad lasts.

The **short fad pattern** (Figure 11.5) is like a short Blitz pattern with an important difference: you want to get in early, during the *introduction* stage of the fad life cycle, and this calls for broad Reach (time is too short to try to target innovators first) and high Frequency; the broad reach and high frequency need to be sustained during the *growth stage* of the product life cycle (though this isn't long with most fads) in order to catch the large Middle Majority as they become ready to adopt the fad.

Examples of products that follow the Short Fad pattern include new movies[20], new get-fit or weight-loss programs, and children's toys and games.

REACH PATTERNS FOR ESTABLISHED PRODUCTS

The typical manager is fortunate to spend 10% of his or her time on new product launches. The reality is that about 90% of media plans are for *established* products. Even new products, after their first year or so, become "established" and are no longer introductory unless a new target audience is being sought. However, we note that *re-launching,* or "re-staging," of an established product should be treated as a *new product* launch and one of the above reach patterns used.

There is a choice of four fundamental reach patterns for *established-product campaigns*, and these demand considerable thought if you are serious about saving money in the media plan. The alternative Reach Patterns for established products (and services) are shown in Figures 11.7 to

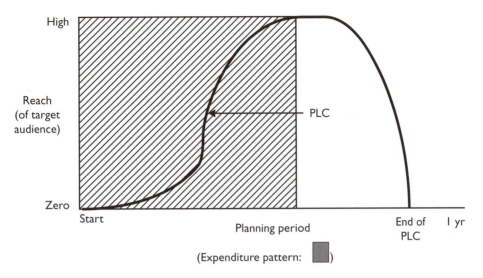

FIGURE 11.5 *Short fad reach pattern (fad products).*

11.10 and are: the Impact Schedule pattern, the Awareness pattern, the Shifting Reach pattern and the Seasonal Priming pattern.

Impact schedule pattern

Our previous recommendation of the Regular Purchase Cycle reach pattern[21] is superseded by an important new analysis of effective frequency – for FMCG products – by Roberts.[22] Roberts' data, shown in Figure 11.6, panels (a) and (b), suggest a pattern of **impact scheduling**, at the individual level, of *one day* approximately every four weeks throughout the year, for an established FMCG brand-item. One day, of course, is a very short advertising duration compared with the typical one-week duration for the other reach patterns. The one-day advertising duration per 28 days advertising cycle applies no matter whether the product category purchase cycle is shorter than 28 days (four weeks), such as about 21 days for coffee; or longer, such as about 90 days for shampoo. As shown in panel (a) of the figure, the Impact Schedule shows an enormous sales effect for three or more opportunities to see (OTSs) received in a concentrated advertising duration of just *one day*. To ensure that an individual receives at least three OTSs, as opposed to three Insertions being made anywhere, this in practice means **triple-spotting** the ad – best is to use *slightly* different poolout versions of the ad to maintain Attention – during one TV program, in a brief time slot on one radio station, in one newspaper issue, or one magazine issue. Again as shown in panel (a) of the figure, Triple-Spotting is much more sales-effective (an average 50% purchase increase) than spending the 3+ OTSs over several days at one OTS per day (an average 20% purchase increase) or over 28 days (four weeks, which yields only 5% purchase increase, on average). Panel (b) is also important: it shows that the spike in purchase caused by Triple-Spotting produces more than *twice* the volume of sales over the *whole 28 days* than is achieved by spreading the OTSs.

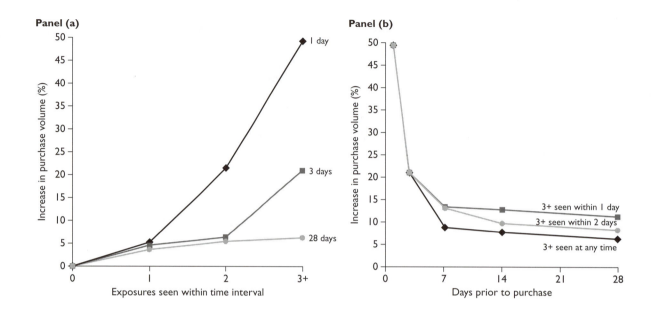

FIGURE 11.6 *Roberts' (1998) data on frequency concentration of ads for FMCG products. The percentage increase in purchase volume (the vertical axis) is over 28 days, even though the exposures are in one day, three days or 28 days, respectively.*

SOURCE: This figure is reproduced with the permission of *Admap*. For more details go to <www.warc.com/admap>.

Although the individual consumer is "dosed with MEF" for one day every 28 days, to take advantage of the fact that individual consumers' FMCG shopping trips tend to be on a regular day of the week, it is best to use *seven* impact schedules, one for each day of the week, which would cover everyone's regular shopping day. One version of this schedule is shown in Figure 11.7, panel (a).

An even better version of the Impact Schedule pattern – usable if you can buy the media time (TV or radio) or space (newspapers) on a *daily* rather than weekly basis – is to spread the seven impact schedule days at *four-day intervals* throughout the four-week period. For example, the placements could be Monday, Friday, Tuesday, Saturday, Wednesday, Sunday and Thursday – that is, *every fourth day* of the month. This "spread" seven-day impact schedule is shown in panel (b). The spread impact schedule has the advantage of distributing the purchase effects evenly over the four-week periods and the year, compared with the first-week "bumps" with the up-front impact schedule. It would also be very difficult for competitors to detect and counter this pattern.

A further refinement to guard against the chance that a large competitor can detect your insertion schedule and try to counter it is to *rotate* the impact schedule placements for each four-week media-*month*; for instance, TV evening news on one channel may be triple-spotted on Monday the first month, Thursday the second month, Saturday the third month, and so forth. On TV, it is actually difficult for a competitor to "sabotage" a schedule, even if it isn't rotated, because

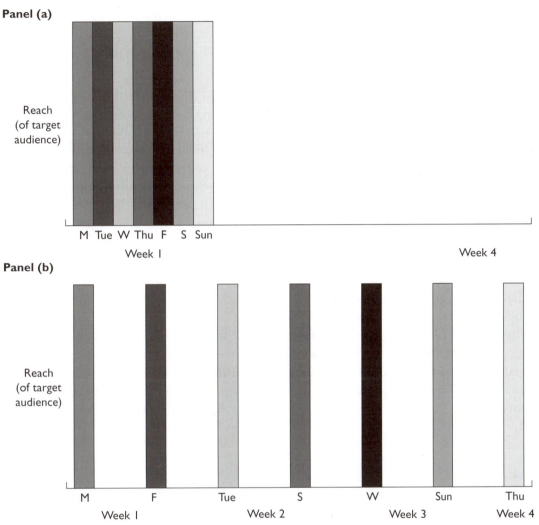

FIGURE 11.7 *Impact schedule pattern for a typical four-week period (established FMCG products or services with a regular purchase cycle throughout the year). In the version in panel (a), seven separate impact schedules are run, one for each day of the week, up front. The pattern is repeated for successive four-week periods throughout the year, thus there are 13 advertising cycles. In the version in panel (b) the seven-day schedule is spread over four weeks, then repeated, which produces 13 contiguous four-week cycles, in effect a 52-week cycle. In both versions, it is preferable to rotate vehicles each month by day of week.*

TV ad buys are made about a year in advance. However, on radio or in daily newspapers, short-term placements are possible, so the rotation is advisable.

In implementing the Impact Schedule pattern, The Reach Rule (see next chapter) should be followed by placing each different impact schedule in a competing vehicle, also on a rotating basis – such as in two or three TV programs that are aired at the same time on different channels, or in the one time slot on several *different* radio stations, or in magazines with *similar* editorial content because each reader is unlikely to read more than one such magazine. Competing vehicles minimize overlap between the impact schedule customer groups.

Awareness pattern

The **awareness pattern** applies to consumer and industrial products and services that have a *long purchase cycle* and a *long decision time*. Long-haul holiday travel, home furnishings and other luxury items would be consumer examples. Installing a new computer system in a company, commissioning major machinery upgrades, or deciding whether to hire a consultant to help set up a customer database would be industrial examples. These products or services are infrequently purchased – perhaps only once every several years – and are typically "pondered" for a long interval before the purchase decision is made. Virtually everyone in the target audience is interested or semi-interested in buying but at any one time only a few of these people actually decide to buy.

This reach pattern, shown in Figure 11.8, is called the "Awareness" pattern[23] because the strategy is to keep all prospects "aware" of the brand, while the timing of the decision to buy is unpredictable for any particular individual prospect. "Aware" has the same meaning as in Awareness Ads, that is, Brand Awareness *and* Brand Preference.

The Awareness pattern consists of very high reach to virtually all prospects but relatively *low* frequency – two or three OTSs per advertising cycle – with the advertising cycles occurring at quite widely spread intervals. If the campaign communication objectives include Brand Recall or Transformational brand preference, then it will be highly sensitive to *competitive* advertising, so if you know that even *one* large competitor will be advertising during your cycles, you will need *five*

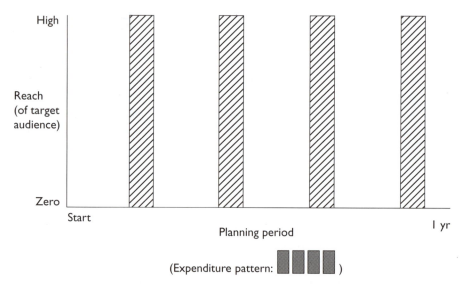

FIGURE 11.8 *Awareness pattern (established products with long purchase cycle, long decision time). Width of bars indicates frequency.*

or six OTSs per cycle. In fact, the *Continuous Tracking* method of survey research[24] is needed to accurately implement this particular reach pattern – in terms of frequency, precisely, rather than reach which always aims to be as high as the budget permits. How long should the *intervals* be? Try about four weeks between cycles and adjust with tracking.

The Awareness pattern is best accomplished by *combining* Awareness Advertising with a Direct-Response Call to Action. Mentioned before, these are Double-Duty Ads, in that they serve an "image" advertising purpose as well as a direct-response purpose.[25] An example is the Paul Hogan (presenter) "Throw another shrimp on the barbie" TV commercials run on cable TV in the U.S.A. by the Australian Tourist Commission. These TV commercials concluded with an 800-number and Website URL "super" on the screen that prospects could contact to obtain further information; after an inquiry is received, the ATC then mails an Aussie travel booklet to inquirers.

The Awareness pattern can be used with double-duty ads for *industrial products* as well. These B-to-B ads usually include a toll-free direct-response number, a mail reply coupon or online reply and ordering details.

Shifting reach pattern

The **shifting reach pattern** applies to products and services with a long purchase cycle and a *short* decision time. The Shifting Reach pattern is a rather unconventional one that regularly *moves its focus*, as shown in Figure 11.9. Individual continuity is thus zero (for about a year) in this pattern.

The logic behind the Shifting Reach pattern is dependent on the realization that although the product or service may have a long purchase cycle, the *decision to buy* is made very rapidly – such as when your present product suddenly dies on you or a service that you use goes out of business.

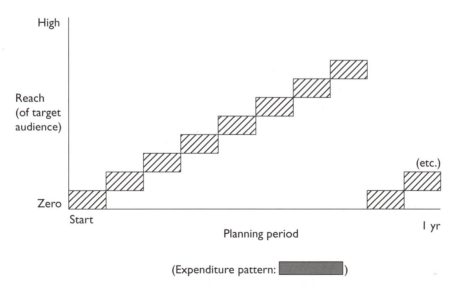

FIGURE 11.9 *Shifting reach pattern (established products with long purchase cycle, short decision time). Width of bars indicates frequency.*

Most of us have had this experience with refrigerators, washing machines, and the other necessities of domestic life. From an advertising perspective, the manager would like the advertising to be "out there" whenever a prospect's Category Need occurs and the prospective customer is thrust into the market. On the other hand, the advertiser cannot afford to be "out there" all the time for everybody, especially as the target consumers are, functionally, New Category Users (NCUs), not having shopped in the category for a long time, and thus they require high frequency to re-learn what the category consists of. Add to this the further realization that once an individual has bought, that individual will once again be out of the market (a non-prospect) for a very long time afterward.

Like a searchlight, the Shifting Reach media plan successively scans a percentage of the prospective population hoping to catch *some* of those who are in the market at that time. The reach *eventually* accumulates to 100% of prospects but on any one advertising cycle it might be only – say – 10% (note that 13 shifts, if this many can be achieved, of about 8% of prospects would cycle through everyone over the year). Why this pattern? The *Blitz* pattern would be most effective but also most wasteful in this situation because once people buy they drop out of the market. The long purchase cycle *long* decision reach pattern, the *Awareness* pattern, is inappropriate because, firstly, it's not a long decision and, secondly, you want to sell the product, not just make people aware; this means heavy frequency in each advertising cycle (with long or large ads – see Attention factors in Chapter 9). The Shifting Reach pattern is the appropriate compromise.

The Shifting Reach pattern is quite an easy media strategy to *implement*. You simply concentrate your advertising on one or two particular media vehicles for one advertising cycle, then change to another non-overlapping small set of vehicles for the next advertising cycle, and so forth. For instance, the first cycle could consist of ads in early morning TV programs, the second cycle in lunchtime TV serials, the third in early evening TV programs, the fourth in prime time, and the fifth in late-night programs. The overlap between these different time slots – even in a relatively "mass" medium like network TV – is so small as to virtually insure that you will achieve a shifting reach of new prospects on each advertising cycle. This reach pattern also has advantages for the Manufacturer and the Retailer because it evens out sales over the year and thus simplifies production and inventory management.

If you can achieve the ideal of 13 shifts in a year, you would have a potential advertising duration of four weeks for each shift-group. However, concentrating the insertions into *one* week of the four-week advertising cycle would work even better to prevent interference from competing ads.

Seasonal priming pattern

The **seasonal priming pattern** is appropriate for products and services whose sales are characterized by one, and sometimes two or three, large *seasonal peaks*. This reach pattern is shown in Figure 11.10, with two seasonal peaks. Low purchase-risk products are often distinctly seasonal, such as cold and flu medicines, sunscreen products, luxury chocolates at Christmas time in the Christian world, and some grocery products such as turkeys at Thanksgiving in the U.S.A. High purchase-risk seasonal purchases would include ski equipment, exterior house paint, and tax consultancy services.

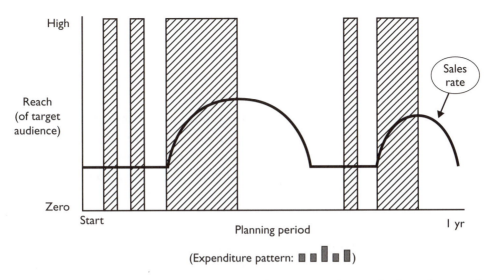

FIGURE 11.10 *Seasonal priming pattern (established products with one or several seasonal sales peaks – two shown here for illustration). Width of bars indicates frequency. The thinner bars represent pre-seasonal primes.*

It is obvious that a seasonal brand's advertising should be timed to reach people near (just prior to or early into) the seasonal peak because it will reach people when their Category Need is strong and thus when they are ready to learn or be reminded about brand differences. However – and this is where the **primes** come in – most other competitors usually will be following the same media strategy, so there will be a lot of competitive advertising around the peak. The Seasonal *Priming* pattern puts in a couple of short flights of advertising a month or two *before* the seasonal peak develops. Simulations conducted by Strong[26] suggest that pre-seasonal advertising does increase the effectiveness of seasonal advertising, by moving consumers toward the effective frequency level that will be needed for the brand *during* the peak. The early priming, of course, reaches people in a low state of Category Need, but can create Brand Awareness without competitive interference. The primes also begin to teach the brand's message, for Brand Preference, although it is expected that customers will not show full interest until the seasonal advertising starts.

COMBINING REACH PATTERNS

One reach pattern may be morphed into a second reach pattern during the media plan. For instance, for a new FMCG item, a *Blitz* pattern may be used for the first three months, to be followed by an *Impact Schedule* pattern thereafter. Or a *Reverse-Wedge/PI* pattern may be followed by an *Awareness* pattern. For established brands, the main variation is likely to be a Seasonal or other promotional "push" *Overlay* on either the *Impact Schedule*, the *Awareness*, or the *Shifting Reach* pattern. These pushes would be, respectively, a reach and frequency increase (to extend the Impact Schedule reach pattern to less-loyal prospects), a frequency increase (to accelerate Purchase), and a reach increase on that shift (such as when the manufacturer or retailer wants to clear excess stock of the product).

The eight reach patterns are *fundamental templates*. With some thought, they can be modified or used in sequence.

The right perspective on the reach pattern decision

Think about what you are trying to do with advertising and promotions at the *individual* level (a good method is to imagine *yourself* in the role of the typical prospective customer). This is the first step toward identifying an appropriate reach pattern. The second thing to think about is that there are a lot of individual prospects to be reached (besides yourself, if you are imagining this through) and you *usually cannot afford to reach all of them, all of the time*. These composite considerations – imagining *within* an individual and *across* individuals – will clearly point to the correct reach pattern.

SUMMARY

There are four major decisions in media strategy: Media-Type selection (primary and secondary); the Reach Pattern; Effective Frequency in the advertising cycles of the reach pattern; and Implementation of the schedule via specific media vehicles. This chapter covers the first two of those decisions.

The Primary Medium or, for a very large advertiser, two or three primary medi*a*, for the campaign must have the capacity to carry all of the communication objectives established for that campaign. A Secondary Medium, or sometimes two secondary media, can be used to boost a particular communication effect or – and this is a widespread use – to place ads that carry further information for prospects who were made aware and interested in the first place by primary-medium advertising.

Selection of the Primary Medium is made on the basis of four factors. The type and size comes first. Then, within type-and-size there is the Brand Awareness objective, the Brand Preference strategy type (the four lower cells of the Rossiter-Percy-Bellman Grid), and, in the case of more than one candidate for the primary medium emerging, by Target Audience Reach. Large-audience advertisers, both B-to-B and B-to-C (including FMCG), will usually require *two or three* primary media if they wish to reach the total target audience with sufficient frequency. Tables for these selection factors are provided in the chapter.

The second decision is choice of the appropriate Reach Pattern for the campaign. For new product launches, either the Blitz pattern, the Wedge pattern, the Reverse-Wedge/PI or the Short Fad pattern is indicated. The Blitz is very effective but very expensive. The Wedge is almost as effective and less expensive. The Reverse-Wedge/PI pattern is suited to the launch of new products or services that are subject to Social Approval (adoption by innovators or business lead-users and followed by opinion leaders' personal influence). The Short Fad pattern is for, as its name suggests, new products that follow a short fad product-category life cycle.

For established products, that is, for ongoing campaigns, the alternative reach patterns are the Impact Schedule pattern, the Awareness pattern, the Shifting Reach pattern, and the Seasonal Priming pattern. The Impact Schedule pattern is best for FMCG products or services that have a short, regular purchase cycle. The Awareness pattern is suited to products or services that have a long purchase cycle and a long decision time. The Shifting Reach pattern is suited to products or services that have a long purchase cycle but a very short decision time. Finally, the Seasonal Priming pattern is, as the name suggests, used for products or services that have a seasonal purchase pattern and the key tactic is to insert one or two high-reach, low-frequency "primes" before seasons and thus the main advertising cycles begin.

DISCUSSION QUESTIONS

11.1 What is meant by the terms Primary Medium and Secondary Medium?

11.2 Which Primary Medium and which Secondary Medium would you select for the advertising of yoghurt, and why?

11.3 Which Primary Medium and which Secondary Medium would you select for the advertising of a luxury cruise liner, and why?

11.4 Which Reach Pattern would you select for the advertising of a luxury cruise liner, and why?

11.5 Which Reach Pattern would you select for the advertising of a local law firm, and why?

11.6 With regard to the reach pattern, why is the calendar of Insertions, as typically provided by the media planner to the manager, uninformative?

11.7 What should "continuity" mean and when is it important?

NOTES

1. In the U.S.A., the three major networks NBC, CBS and ABC recorded a 15% to 20% decline in viewing by the 18–49, $75K+ demographic group in regularly scheduled prime-time programs from October 2002, to October 2003. This age/income group is the most prized by advertisers and its high-rating programs are the most expensive to buy TV ads in. See W. Friedman, Broadcast networks losing upscale viewers, *TelevisionWeek*, December 8, 2003, Website www.tvweek.com.

2. A. Sophocleous, Pestering by kids works, *Ad News*, April 11, 2003, p. 7.

3. T. Elkin, New study: net advantages, *Advertising Age*, February 10, 2003, p. 29.

4. J.A. Edell and K.L. Keller, The information processing of coordinated media campaigns, *Journal of Marketing Research*, 1989, 26(2), pp. 149–163.

5. T. Coffin and S. Tuchman, TV without pix, *Media/Scope*, 1968, 12 (February), pp. 46–53.

6. Studies of multi-media campaigns are reviewed in the PhD thesis – published – by Majorie Dijkstra, who also conducted both forced exposure and voluntary exposure experiments that show no advantage of multiple media over TV ads alone. See M. Dijkstra, *An Experimental Investigation of Synergy Effects in Multiple-Media Advertising Campaigns*, Tilburg University, The Netherlands, 2002 (ISBN: 90-6734-027-8).

7. The 10 largest B-to-B advertisers in the U.S.A. in 2000 were, in descending order: Verizon (U.S.$277 million adspend), Microsoft Corp., IBM Corp., Sprint Corp., SBC Communications, American Express, AT&T Wireless, Compaq Computer (now owned by Hewlett-Packard), Visa, and Bank of America ($123 million adspend). See *Marketing News*, July 8, 2002, p. 18.

8. See W.E. Barlow and E. Papaziou (Eds), *The Media Book*, New York: The Media Book, Inc., 1979, 1980, and Radio Advertising Bureau, Inc., *Radio Facts*, New York: RAB, 1980. These classic field experiments compared sales results from *one exposure* each to TV, radio, and magazine advertising for a

broad range of FMCG brands. For *every* brand, TV advertising generated higher sales – usually 200% to 300% higher, that is, two or three times greater – than either of the other two media. Although one could buy several radio spots or several magazine ads for the price of one TV commercial, the repeated radio or magazine ads could not hope to produce these levels of sales.

9. S. Freitas, Evolutionary changes in the great outdoors, *Advertising Age*, June 9, 2003, p. C4.

10. K. Lyons, Accounting for outdoor, *B&T Weekly*, 2002, October 18, pp. 14, 16.

11. J. Barnes, Creating a difference with ambient media, *Admap*, 1999, February, pp. 46–49.

12. D.A. Aaker and J.C. Carman, Are you overadvertising?, *Journal of Advertising Research*, 1982, 22(4), pp. 57–70.

13. L.M. Lodish and B. Lubetkin, General truths? Nine key findings from IRI test data, *Admap*, 1992, February, pp. 9–15.

14. E.L. Artz, The lifeblood of brands, *Advertising Age*, 1991, November 4, p. 32.

15. R. Baron, How food advertisers use TV, *Television Week*, May 19, 2003, Website www.tvweek.com.

16. D.F. Midgley and G.R. Dowling, Innovativeness: the concept and its measurement, *Journal of Consumer Research*, 1978, 4(4), pp. 229–242; D.F. Midgley and G.R. Dowling, A longitudinal study of product form innovation: the interaction between predispositions and social messages, *Journal of Consumer Research*, 1993, 19(4), pp. 611–625; and S. Im, B.L. Bayus, and C.H. Mason, An empirical study of innovativeness, personal characteristics, and new-product adoption behavior, *Journal of the Academy of Marketing Science*, 2003, 31(1), pp. 61–73.

17. E. von Hippel, Lead users: a source of novel product concepts, *Management Science*, 1986, 32(7), pp. 791–805.

18. D.F. Midgley, P.D. Morrison and J.H. Roberts, The effect of network structure in industrial diffusion processes, *Research Policy*, 1992, 21(6), pp. 533–552.

19. T.S. Robertson, *Innovative Behavior and Communication*, New York: Holt, Rinehart and Winston, 1971.

20. C.B. Weinberg, seminar presented at the Australian Graduate School of Management, Sydney, Australia, 1994; M. s. Sawhney and J. Eliashberg, A parsimonious model for forecasting gross box-office revenues of motion pictures, *Marketing Science*, 1996, 15(2), pp. 113–131.

21. As given in Rossiter and Percy, 1997, chapter 16; and J.R. Rossiter and P.J. Danaher, *Advanced Media Planning*, Boston: Kluwer, 1998, chapter 2.

22. A. Roberts, Recency, frequency and the duration of the sales effects of TV advertising, *Admap*, 1999, February, pp. 40–44.

23. K.A. Longman, *Advertising*, New York: Harcourt Brace Jovanovich, 1971.

24. M. Sutherland and A.K. Sylvester, *Advertising and the Mind of the Consumer*, London: Kogan Page, 2000.

25. A.G. Woodside, Modeling linkage advertising: going beyond better media comparisons, *Journal of Advertising Research*, 1994, 34(4), pp. 22–31.

26. E.C. Strong, The spacing and timing of advertising, *Journal of Advertising Research*, 1977, 17(6), pp. 25–31.

CHAPTER 12

Effective frequency and strategic rules for implementation of the media plan

Following selection of the Reach Pattern, the next decision in media strategy is to choose an *Effective Frequency* level for those people reached during each advertising cycle. As a final step, the media plan must be operationalized – *implemented* via ad placements in specific media vehicles, with these placements constituting the Media Schedule.

Regarding media plan implementation, one term you will *not* see in this chapter or in this book (apart from a passing mention in Chapter 14) is GRPs, an acronym for "Gross Rating Points" (a term that originated in the U.S.A. and is now used worldwide). Nor will you see similar terms such as TVRs, "TV Rating Points" (U.K.); or TARPs, "Target Audience Rating Points" (Australia and New Zealand); or the even more misleading term "Impacts," a synonym for GRPs. However, you will undoubtedly see these terms if you read *other* books or articles about media plans and your advertising agency or media agency will certainly use one of these terms. *GRPs, TVRs, TARPs and Impacts are useless concepts and should be buried, now.* We will now briefly explain the fallacy but not grace these terms by defining them for you. Suppose your agency proposes a media plan that will "deliver 200 GRPs a week." Well so what? This tells you little other than that you will be advertising that week! "Two hundred GRPs" could mean that, in that week, 100% of households will see your ad twice, or 50% will see it four times, or the same 1% of luckless souls will see it 200 times – each of these totally different plans delivering 200 GRPs. "Gross" rating points in the bad sense of "gross" is an apt description. TVRs, TARPs and Impacts are similarly meaningless jargon terms.[1] The proper, alternative, clearly defined replacement term is *Effective Reach*, which is based on *Effective Frequency*.

EFFECTIVE FREQUENCY

The concept of **effective frequency**[2] asserts that an individual prospective customer has to be exposed to a brand's advertising a certain minimum number of times within an advertising cycle in order for the advertising to *influence* the customer's *action* – specifically, to maximize the individual's *disposition* to act. (The action itself might be a Purchase-Related behavior, Purchase, or a Social behavior in the case of social marketing campaigns.) Effective frequency can consist of a *range* of exposures between the Minimum Effective Frequency level and a possible Maximum Effective Frequency level. Exposures within this range raise to a practical maximum the individual's Disposition to Purchase (or Act).

Effective Frequency first requires understanding the input and output concepts of *insertions*, *exposures*, and *disposition to purchase*. Next come the derivative concepts of *minimum* effective frequency and *maximum* effective frequency. We provide a *formula* for estimating minimum effective frequency per advertising cycle (MEF/c). We then show how to adjust MEF/c for the *ad units* used in the media plan.

Insertions and exposures

Insertions of the ad or ads in the media schedule produce Exposures, which should affect individuals' Dispositions to Purchase (or Act).

An **insertion** is simply the placement of an ad in a media vehicle. (A **media schedule** comprises all the Insertions that are placed in all the Media Vehicles used in the plan. The manager, of course, pays for the Insertions.) However – and here is the problem with media schedules shown only as shaded boxes of insertions in a table, which is the standard way they are shown to the manager – there is *hardly ever a one-to-one correspondence* between Insertions in a media schedule and the *Exposures* that result from it:

- *Insertions* are the aggregate input

- *Exposures* are the individual-level result

The difference is easily understood with an example. Suppose an ad is inserted four times in a media schedule. If the four Insertions are in the *same* media vehicle, it is quite likely that everyone reached by that vehicle will get four Exposures to the ad. However, if the four Insertions are in *different* media vehicles, hardly anyone will get four Exposures – most of the individuals reached will get only one Exposure. There have been four Insertions in both cases, but the Exposures to individuals that these insertions produce are very different.

Insertions go in, and a *distribution* of Exposures across individuals comes out. The distribution differs depending on *where* the Insertions are placed. As you may have realized, these different distributions of exposures between individuals and within individuals are the basis of the different *Reach Patterns* postulated in the previous chapter. Now, we turn to the frequency decisions within these reach patterns.

Effective frequency is based on *exposures* to the advertising. **Exposure** means *exposure to the*

Media Vehicle, thereby providing any *opportunity* to pay Attention to the *ad*. The British term for Exposure, **OTS**, or *Opportunity* to See (or hear or read) the advertisement, nicely expresses what is meant. Where we say "Exposure" you could mentally substitute the term "OTS." The plural for multiple exposures is "OTSs."

Whether target audience individuals do in fact see, hear, or read the advertisement – that is, whether they begin to *Process* the advertisement by at least paying initial Attention to it – is jointly a function of: (1) the attention-getting characteristics of the advertising unit (see Chapter 9) for which, it should be noted, the attention-getting characteristics of the different media *types* have already been factored in, and (2) the creative content of the advertisement. The media planner must allow, up front, for (1) and this is achieved by adjusting the *Minimum* Effective Frequency (MEF) estimate for the type of Ad Unit employed in the schedule. If the creative "strength" of the ad or ads is known beforehand, from CRAT pre-test results, then (2) can be allowed for, too, but more typically the strength of the creative is not known until after the campaign has commenced and adjustments to frequency of exposures are made then.

Disposition to purchase (or act)

Whereas any degree of processing that occurs for any of the six communication effects (see Chapter 6) can be said to influence purchase to some extent, the media planner's focus should be on **disposition to purchase (or act)** and the role of Effective Frequency in raising this disposition to the actionable threshold.

Disposition to Purchase (or for the target audience to take *other* targeted Action as specified in the action objective for the campaign – again see Chapter 6) is measured by the individual's "mental state" with regard to *two* communication effects that *jointly* have to be present:

- *Brand Awareness* (a necessary *prerequisite* to Purchase) *plus*

- *Brand Preference* (for a Low-Involvement purchase), *or*

- *Brand Purchase or Action Intention* (for a High-Involvement purchase or action, or a Low-Involvement purchase *with* a promotion offer)

Those familiar with quantitative models of brand choice will see that Disposition to Purchase (or Act) is equivalent to the individual's brand purchase (or action) *probability*. This probability is Brand Preference (preference or intention) *conditional* on Brand *Awareness* at the time of choice.[3] For this conditional probability to be "at threshold," it has to be higher than the conditional probability of purchasing or taking action toward any *other* competing brand-item of which the individual is aware at the time. In a social marketing application, for example drinking and driving, the individual is aware of two brands, "Drink and drive" and "Don't drink and drive," and will choose the one toward which his or her disposition is higher at the time. And notice again that the overall probability of purchase or action – the Disposition – can be raised by increasing either Brand Awareness or Brand Preference (preference or intention) or, of course, by increasing both, which is what advertising and its *frequency* should try to do.

Minimum and maximum effective frequency

Minimum effective frequency (MEF/c)

In estimating the effective frequency for a campaign, the manager or media planner's interest is primarily in the *minimum* effective frequency necessary to raise purchase disposition to action threshold (see Figure 12.1). The Minimum Effective Frequency per advertising cycle, c, is written as **MEF/c**. The minimum is sought because this will produce threshold disposition to purchase (or act) with the fewest insertions – that is, at *lowest cost.*

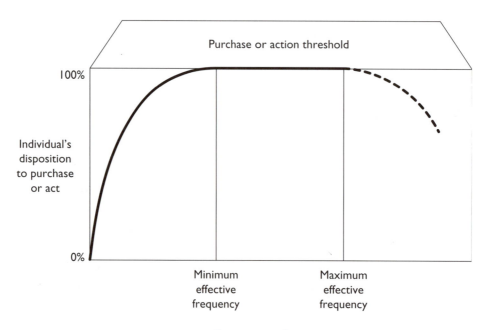

FIGURE 12.1 *Individual threshold of disposition to purchase (or act) as a function of frequency of exposures.*

The lowest Minimum Effective Frequency to cause disposition to purchase would be *one OTS* in the advertising cycle. This may be sufficient for a Direct-Response Ad, such as a direct mail offer – or with a promotion offer – where the target audience only has a chance to go through the buyer response sequence of Exposure-to-Action *once.* Also, as will be seen in the MEF/c formula, an MEF of one may be sufficient in some situations when advertising to our own Brand Loyals.

In most advertising cases, however, the Minimum Effective Frequency per advertising cycle will be *greater than one.* Target audiences *other* than the brand's own loyal customers will increase the required MEF/c by two or three exposures, and more if the target is New Category Users. The nature of the brand's communication objectives or the presence of competing brands' communication effects will also increase the required MEF to a number above one exposure.

The MEF/c Estimation Formula, introduced shortly, incorporates the main factors that determine minimum effective frequency and shows how to estimate minimum effective frequency for any advertising situation. Hereafter, minimum effective frequency will be abbreviated as MEF. Also, to emphasize that MEF must be considered for each advertising cycle, the preferred terminology will be of the form k/c, where k is the required number of exposures, that is, OTSs (the MEF value) and c is the duration of a particular advertising cycle.

What is "c"?

It is best to regard MEF as a *rate* rather than a number or frequency, hence it is written MEF/c, where c is the *duration of the advertising cycle*. As we saw in the previous chapter, the Advertising Cycle is defined as the shortest amount of time that it takes to get the MEF level of exposures delivered to the target audience individuals. The manager should regard the advertising cycle as c = one week for low values of MEF, and c = two weeks if MEF has a high value that cannot practically be delivered via the media vehicles in a one-week timeframe. However, there is one reach pattern, the Impact Schedule pattern, that has an advertising cycle of c = *one day*.

Maximum effective frequency (MaxEF/c)

In Figure 12.1, disposition to purchase becomes a horizontal line when exposure frequency goes beyond the minimum effective frequency needed for purchase and in some cases, discussed shortly, could even turn downwards. Although it may be hard to imagine "too much" effective frequency, this can happen when the individual has been "oversold" after 100% (or probability 1.0) disposition to purchase or act has already been attained. For example, you may be on your way to an IBM computer retailer fully resolved to buy an IBM PC when you hear another advertisement for the IBM PC on your car radio or see a window poster for the IBM PC as you are entering the store. If you were indeed fully resolved to buy, these extra exposures would be "overkill" – unnecessary, because they wouldn't affect your decision. For cost reasons, the manager or media planner may set a *Maximum* Effective Frequency number per advertising cycle, **MaxEF/c**.

The other consideration for MaxEF/c is for ads that can "wear out" if repeated too often or too close together. In broadcast media (TV and radio) there is the risk that purchase disposition can turn *downwards* (see the dotted line in Figure 12.1) especially for Transformational ads excessively exposed to the "captive" audience of a Broadcast program (TV, or news radio). In Print media (newspapers, magazines, outdoor and posters, direct mail) and in the Print-like medium of Internet Websites, the problem is much more likely to be loss of Attention, which won't decrease disposition but won't contribute to it either. The only solution – in both the broadcast case and the print case – is to attempt to find the *individual ad's* MaxEF/c and to introduce a new execution, or executions, at that number. An individual ad's MaxEF/c is highly variable for Broadcast ads and no theoretical guide can be given; direct inspection of tracking survey results has to be used. For Print media, Brown[4] provides evidence that *three OTSs* is the typical MaxEF/c before attention loss becomes substantial, although again of course there are occasional exceptions.

Average frequency is uninformative

Media planners conventionally describe media plans in terms of the *Average* Frequency delivered (among those individuals who are reached) in a particular time period. Average Frequency is uninformative. Indeed, McDonald[5] has called the Average Frequency statistics that appear in conventional media plans "strictly meaningless abstracts." The proof of his point can be illustrated easily with a set of diagrams (Figure 12.2) showing hypothetical **frequency distributions** for alternative media plans. All have an average frequency of exactly two (Total Exposures divided by Reach equals Average Frequency). But in terms of *Effective* Reach, if the MEF is 1, then plans A and B are best; if the MEF equals 2, then Plan A is best; if the MEF equals 3, Plan B is best; if the MEF equals 4, Plan C is best; and if the MEF equals 5, Plan D is best. Obviously, Average Frequency tells us *next to nothing* about a media plan's effectiveness.

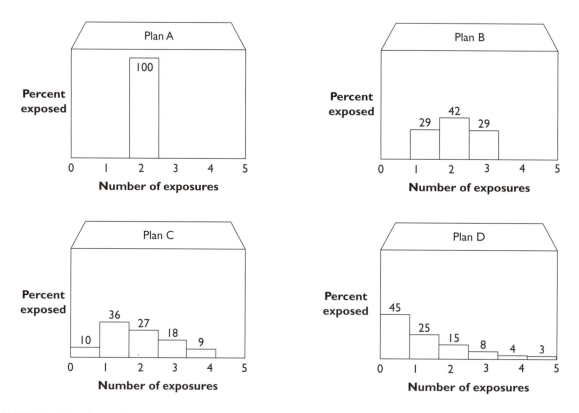

FIGURE 12.2 *Hypothetical frequency distributions of exposures. All have average frequency = 2. Compare them for increasing levels of MEF.*

Indeed, the Average Frequency will almost always *exaggerate* the frequency at which the typical target audience individual is reached. This serious delusion for marketing managers and media planners is due to the fact that most Frequency Distributions (exposure distributions) are right-skewed (peak to the left, or low-frequency end, and tail to the right, or high-frequency end, like

Plan D in the figure). The typical person gets the *mode*, and the mode of a regular right-skewed distribution is always less than the mean. A manager informed that a plan is delivering an Average Frequency of two exposures per week is likely to think that at least half the individuals reached (the "average") are receiving two exposures when in reality it is *far fewer* than half, depending on the degree of skew.

Average Frequency must be replaced by the estimation and reporting of Effective Frequency. Effective Frequency is the only type of frequency that matters, and it is an *individual-level* phenomenon.

MINIMUM EFFECTIVE FREQUENCY (MEF/c) ESTIMATION FORMULA

The Minimum Effective Frequency per advertising cycle (MEF/c) has to be estimated *before* the media schedule of insertions is purchased. Only in the case of an established brand that has been tracked over many years will the manager have a good idea of what the MEF is, and then only if the market hasn't changed. Another expensive and time-consuming option would be to try different frequency levels in different, matched test markets, but few advertisers can afford this. In most cases, therefore, meaning the great majority, the MEF/c will have to be *estimated*.

What can be stated at the outset is that no single number for MEF can possibly be correct for all circumstances, and certainly not without a time period, c, specified. This rules out the use of simplistic, *single-number solutions* such as "three-hit" theory[6], which does not specify a time limit for the three OTSs, and "single-exposure per week," or "1/week recency," theory.[7] Only in very particular circumstances could either of these particular numbers be right, and the time period *must* be specified. For example, 3+ OTSs in *one day* seems, on recent evidence, to be right for the *Impact Schedule reach pattern* but *only* for this pattern. The empirical evidence against there being any one "magic number" for MEF/c for *all* media plans is overwhelming.[8] These in-market studies show that there are wide variations in the number of exposures per time period that will cause the sales of different brand-items to peak. This is as expected, but the knowledge that there *will* be an empirical right number – more precisely a right *rate* – to be found for the campaign in the marketplace does not, as noted, help the manager who must make an estimate before the campaign starts in order to buy the media schedule.

A *rational, up-front approach* is therefore necessary. Our approach to minimum effective frequency estimation is an MEF/c formula. The MEF/c formula assumes that one exposure in the advertising cycle (1/c) is the beginning or "building block" level, then adds – and in one situation subtracts – exposures according to four factors: *target audience* (TA), *brand awareness* (BA), *brand preference* (BPREF) and *personal influence* (PI). Lastly, after its computation, MEF/c is adjusted for *attention* (the ad units employed in the plan).

The formula is MEF/c = 1 + TA + BA + BPREF + PI. The values for these factors are given in Table 12.1. The factors are explained below and then the use of the formula is illustrated.

TABLE 12.1 *Minimum effective frequency (MEF/c) factors and their numerical correction values. The formula is MEF/c = 1 + TA + BA + BPREF + PI. MEF/c is then adjusted for the ad unit attention probability, as explained later.*

FACTOR	−1	CORRECTION (STARTING FROM 1 EXPOSURE IN ADVERTISING CYCLE)			
		0	+1	+2	LC+1[a]
1. Target audience		Brand loyals	Favorable brand switchers	Other-brand switchers, Other-brand loyals	New category users
2. Brand awareness		Brand recognition			Brand recall
3. Brand preference		Informational brand preference			Transformational brand preference
4. Personal influence	High (average contact > .25)	Low (average contact < .25)			

[a] If your brand is the largest competitor (market share leader): use +2 exposures for each of these factors. If your brand is not the leader: set equal to largest competitor's average frequency +1 (called LC+1). LC+1 is additive on the 1 only; for example, a campaign aimed at new category users, with brand recall and transformational brand attitude objectives, would use LC+3 exposures.

Target audience (TA)

The rationale for the Target Audience Correction Factor is that some target audiences have more to learn about the brand than other target audiences. Brand Loyals (BLs) have little or nothing extra to learn, so that no adjustment is needed for advertising to this audience. Favorable Brand Switchers (FBSs) seem to need at least two exposures before switching is induced[9], so one more exposure is added to the building block level of one exposure. Other-Brand Switchers (OBSs) and Other-Brand Loyals (OBLs) – assuming that a message strategy has been found that promises to be effective with these typically more negative target audiences, such as refutational advertising or comparative advertising – have some new learning to undergo, so two more exposures are added (3/c total) when advertising to these groups.

New Category Users (NCUs), on the other hand, are a more variable target audience for whom to estimate effective frequency, as some may be positively disposed toward the category (Positive NCUs) and others may not (Unaware NCUs and Negative NCUs). Most NCU target audience situations will occur with new brands early in the product category life cycle in a growing market, where increased market share, not simply sales, is the objective. Following the argument developed originally by Peckham[10] and later by Schroer[11], the only way to increase market share (assuming equivalent creative effectiveness) is to advertise more than the **largest competitor (LC)**. This means trying to reach more potential New Category Users than competitors are reaching (greater penetration) and reaching each potential user with higher frequency than the *Largest* Competitor. If *your* brand-item is largest, that is, if you are the *Market Leader*, use +2 exposures.

To estimate the Largest Competitor's MEF, run the largest competitor through the MEF/c formula, using +2 instead of LC whenever LC+1 occurs – and remember to nominate the *largest competitor's* target audience. Then advertise to exceed this frequency by at least one exposure (called LC+1) per advertising cycle, therefore producing (LC+1)/c. Exceeding the largest competitor's overall frequency by more than one would be even better, remembering that it is almost impossible to over-advertise a new brand or to over-advertise an established brand to a new-user target. However, a margin of one exposure per cycle, if carefully checked at the individual level by thorough frequency distribution analysis, should be sufficient extra frequency to wage an effective market share battle.

Brand awareness objective (BA)

If Brand Recognition is the objective, the effective frequency needed will be relatively low and no correction is necessary (subject, of course, to the other correction factors). In contrast, if Brand Recall is the objective, then the effective frequency needed will be relatively high. It is virtually impossible to make the frequency for Brand Recall too high.[12] The maximum level for Brand Recall would be everyone in the target audience recalling the brand first, which happens for only a very few heavily advertised brands. Thus, LC+1 is recommended for Brand Recall; that is, set the effective frequency level at least one exposure higher than the estimated effective frequency used by the Largest Competitor, or use +2 if your brand already is the largest competitor, the Market Leader, in the category.

Brand preference strategy (BPREF)

Brand Preference strategy, based on the grid quadrants in Chapter 8, is the other communication factor that changes the required effective frequency in the media plan. The *Involvement* component of brand preference strategy is already allowed for in the Target Audience Correction Factor, whereby purchase risk increases as the audience is changed from Brand Loyals to New Category Users; to correct again would be redundant. However, a correction is applied for the *Brand Purchase Motivation* component. An Informational brand preference strategy should be effective within the first one or two exposures – the brand is perceived immediately as either solving a problem or as irrelevant. Hence no adjustment is recommended for Informational advertising. A Transformational brand preference strategy, by contrast, requires heavy repetition[13] – for build-up *and* for reinforcement of the brand image, and thus LC+1 is used.

The brand awareness and brand preference LC correction factors for effective frequency are *additive on the "+1s" only*. A Brand Recognition/Transformational campaign or a Brand Recall/ Informational attitude campaign would require LC+1 exposures (+2 if you are market leader). A Brand Recall/Transformational campaign would require LC+2 exposures (+4 if you are market leader). Examples of Brand Recall/Transformational campaigns would be the main campaigns for Coca-Cola and McDonald's, who are among the most frequent of every nation's advertisers. If New Category Users are the target for the Brand Recall/Transformational campaign, the requirement is LC+3 exposures (+6 if you are market leader).

Personal influence (PI)

The final correction factor for estimating effective frequency is Personal Influence (PI). This refers to social diffusion of the advertising message, usually via Word of Mouth, including email, but alternatively or additionally by visual influence, or Word of Eye, as when brands are seen by others in a reference group or reference individual context (although see the note on Word of Eye below). PI is *assumed* in the Reverse-Wedge reach pattern, although it can occur, of course, for any reach pattern.

Personal Influence, providing it is favorable[14] (which the advertiser would check during the advertising strategy and ad testing stages of research and then double-check during campaign tracking once the campaign is launched), has a number of advantages over advertising *per se*. First, it is *free*, which means that the advertiser saves on advertising costs. Second, one *word-of-mouth* contact appears to be about *twice* as effective as one *advertising* exposure[15], probably because favorable Brand Preference is nearly always conveyed rather than just Brand Awareness.[16] Third, Personal Influence can operate at *any* stage of the life cycle for *any* type of product, not just new, high-risk products as was commonly believed.[17] In particular, a new *advertising* campaign, even for an old brand, can trigger word of mouth.

Ozga[18] proposed that social diffusion serves as a substitute for part of the total amount of advertising that would otherwise be required. He introduced the notion of a **contact coefficient**, based on the average number of people told about the advertising by the average individual exposed to it (this could be extended to include visual contact, or Word of Eye, for product usage, or service usage, that can be *seen* by others, *if that usage is perceived by others as due to the advertising*). From the available studies of interpersonal influence, it is estimated that a Contact Coefficient of *at least .25* (i.e., $\geqslant$.25) is necessary to justify reducing the effective frequency estimate by one exposure. This means that for every four people reached by the advertising, at least one person contacts at least one other person during the advertising cycle. Because this contact should be doubly effective and because it may spread, it in effect replaces an exposure. Thus, a Contact Coefficient of $\geqslant$.25 seems a reasonable figure to justify a *reduction of one exposure* (i.e., -1) in the minimum effective frequency calculation. For a Contact Coefficient of less than .25 (i.e., <.25), *no adjustment* is made.

With the *one-exposure reduction* in effective frequency under conditions of frequent personal influence, it should be noted that there is *no reduction* in the *Reach* of the media plan. This is because the personal influence phenomenon works best when the "other" person contacted has also seen the campaign (discussing an ad with someone who has not seen it is somewhat frustrating, whereas discussing it with someone who has seen it is usually mutually reinforcing). Thus, the idea is to maintain the Reach while reducing the required number of Exposures because of the bonus exposure created by Personal Influence.

Examples of MEF/c calculations

Several examples will illustrate how the MEF/c formula is applied. The very *lowest* effective frequency would be no advertising (zero exposures) in the advertising cycle. However, this would only occur in *one* circumstance, and not indefinitely but rather *between cycles*. This circumstance would arise for a campaign aimed at Brand Loyals, for a brand purchased via Brand Recognition and sold via an Informational brand preference strategy – which also generated strong Personal Influence. It would be quite rare for a campaign to meet all these criteria simultaneously. In particular, campaigns likely to generate strong Word of Mouth or Word of Eye would be new campaigns rather than campaigns directed with low frequency at Brand Loyals.

Most estimates of minimum effective frequency will be *between one and 11 exposures (or OTSs)* per advertising cycle. Some hypothetical examples of MEFs calculated from the formula include:

- Hellmann's mayonnaise (1), advertising to Favorable Brand Switchers (+1), via a Brand Recognition (0) and a taste-based Transformational brand preference strategy (LC+1). Assume Kraft, the largest competitor, is using +2, giving *its* MEF/c as four exposures per advertising cycle. This gives 2 + 4 + 1 = 7/c for Hellmann's. An Impact Schedule reach pattern should be used for this established brand-item with a favorable target audience, and a 4, 3 OTSs, *two-day* cycle would be recommended.

- Apple computers (1), advertising to Other-Brand Loyals (+2), via a Brand Recognition (0) and Informational brand preference strategy (0) = 3 exposures per advertising cycle, with c = 1 week.

- Hilton hotels (1), advertising to New Category Users, as the Market Leader (+2), via a Brand Recall (+2) and Informational brand preference strategy (0) = 5 exposures per advertising cycle, with c = 2 weeks.

The *highest* MEF, 11/c, would occur with a late-entry brand trying to break into a New Category, with communication objectives that require Brand Recall and a Transformational brand preference, with *no* Personal Influence. This would most likely be in a Blitz or first wave of a Wedge reach pattern.

No adjustment necessary for carryover

MEF/c can remain effective beyond the cycle, c, and in this sense it exhibits **carryover**. However, *loss* of effectiveness, or *decay*, has nothing to do with the elapse of time, as is commonly believed, but rather is due to *interference*[19] from competitors' ads, and specifically when LC+1 is involved. The LC term already *accounts for* competitive interference and there is no necessity to adjust further. Theorists may ask why we bother to specify the duration of an advertising cycle if time doesn't matter. The answer is simple: *too long a duration means it takes too long to get everyone up to MEF.*

Gaps between ad cycles

The phenomenon of carryover does, however, pose the question of how many weeks to leave *between ad cycles* for those reach patterns that rely on *continuity* to the same individuals – the wedge, reverse-wedge, and awareness reach patterns. There is no rational (theory-derived) answer to this question. For the Awareness pattern, we said try four weeks. For the other two reach patterns, *estimate how long* the last ad cycle will take to do its job of *getting the effectively reached prospects to buy or take action* and, if that estimate is too difficult, try a three-week gap after a one-week cycle, or a four-week gap after a two-week cycle. After the campaign has begun, the gaps can be checked, and adjusted if necessary, by using Continuous Tracking research – see Chapter 14.

AD UNIT ADJUSTMENTS TO MEF/c

As the last step in MEF estimation, the MEF number from the formula has to be adjusted to account for ad units' differences in gaining *Attention.* Attention factors for ad units were given in detail in Chapter 9. The main adjustment values for mass-media ad units are *summarized* in Table 12.2. Only if an ad could be guaranteed to get 100% attention from everybody who sees or hears the media vehicle would the ad unit adjustment not be required. However, if you are very sure that the ad's attention value is higher than in the table, then estimate the value upward and divide by (see below) *that* value.

TABLE 12.2 *Ad unit adjustments (contributions to MEF/c) for mass-media ads.*

COMMERCIAL LENGTH	TELEVISION	RADIO	
:60	.76	.42	
:30 (standard)	.65	.30	
:15	.54	.24	
:10	.45	.21	

PRINT AD SIZE	NEWSPAPERS	CONSUMER MAGAZINES	INDUSTRIAL MAGAZINES
2-page spread	.52	.64	.78
1 page (standard)	.43	.49	.46
½ page	.30	.34	.32
¼ page	.21	.20	.18

PRINT AD COLOR	NEWSPAPERS	CONSUMER MAGAZINES	INDUSTRIAL MAGAZINES
4-color	.64	.49 (std)	.64
2-color	.56	.39	.55
Black & white	.43 (std)	.34	.46 (std)

OUTDOOR LOCATION	PEDESTRIANS	DRIVERS	
Competitive (standard)	.40	.38	
Stand-alone	.80	.53	

WEB BANNER AD			
Static (standard)	.49		
Animated or pop-up	1.00		

The adjusted MEF/c estimate is calculated by *dividing* the original estimate by the ad-unit adjustment value.[20] For instance, if the original MEF estimate is 4, and one-page, four-color Newspaper ad units are used (a value of .64 in the table), the adjusted MEF is 4/.64 = 6.25. To be safe, and because MEF must be a whole-number frequency, this number is rounded *up*. Thus MEF = 7. If one-page, black and white Newspaper ads are used, MEF is 4/.43 = 9.30, or 10 rounded up. On the other hand, if half-page black and white ads were used (a value of .30 in the table), the adjusted MEF is 4/.30 = 13.3, or 14 rounded up. In other words, the MEF of 4 could be achieved with either seven full-page color ads, 10 full-page black and white ads, or 14 half-page black and white ads. The ads would have to be placed in the same newspaper, so that these are OTSs for the same individuals, rather than simply insertions.

With all Print ads, when the two ad-unit factors of size and color are used in the one ad, the adjustment values are *multiplied*, and are then compared to the standard black and white ad of that size (for instance, a two-page, four-color Newspaper ad contributes $(.52 \times .64)/.43 = .77$ to the MEF; a quarter-page, two-color Industrial Magazine ad contributes $(.18 \times .55)/.46 = .21$ to the MEF). As before, the resulting value is divided into original MEF value to obtain the ad unit-adjusted MEF/c.

Quite evidently, the ad unit-adjusted MEF numbers are staggering and sobering, because they become so *large*. But this emphasizes the point we have made numerous times in this book – that *Attention is the biggest barrier for advertising*. It pays, in terms of being able to reduce frequency and therefore the cost, to use *high attention-probability units* because the extra cost of these will usually be less than the cost of the extra insertions.

MEF/c and MaxEF/c for direct-response ads and promotions

Common sense suggests that one "good opportunity" to see, read or hear it should be sufficient for a Direct-Response Ad. (The same applies to an Advertised Promotion, which is, essentially, direct response.) This is because DR ads invariably employ an ad unit with an *attention probability of 1.00*. However, MEF depends on the *medium* in which the DR ad or offer appears. With TV Infomercials (90 seconds or longer), two insertions, that is, *two OTSs*, in the *same vehicle* (same program, same day) should be sufficient. Similarly with Direct Mail, two mailings should be sufficient. Shorter DR TV commercials (usually :60s but sometimes :30s are used) and DR print ads in all types of print media – Newspapers, Magazines, Stationary-Viewed Outdoor, and Web Banners – need more insertions because of the vagaries of attention. Survey evidence using sales inquiries or outright purchase as the direct-response measure indicates that almost all prospects, if they are going to respond at all, will have done so after *four OTSs*.[21] Radio DR ads are more difficult to respond to and a safer estimate for radio would be *six OTSs* (or opportunities to hear). These recommendations are summarized in Table 12.3.

TABLE 12.3 *Recommended MEF/c for direct-response ads. Because these MEF/c figures for direct-response ads are adjusted for the number of OTSs to produce the ultimate action response, they do not require adjustment for ad-unit factors.*

DIRECT-RESPONSE AD TYPE	MEF/c
TV infomercial (:90 or longer)	2
Direct mail ad	
TV direct-response commercial	4
Newspaper direct-response ad	
Magazine direct-response ad	
Stationary-viewed outdoor direct-response ad	
Web banner ad	
Radio direct-response commercial	6

Wedge and reverse-wedge changes to MEF/c

Wedge

For the Wedge reach pattern, the MEF/c is steadily *reduced* over cycles. In the Wedge pattern, which is for new products, the target audience requiring the highest MEF/c, which is NCUs, in most campaigns is expected to become BLs, with a dramatic reduction in MEF from LC+1 per advertising cycle to zero (on the target audience correction factor). Similarly, OBLs are expected to convert to BLs for our brand, with a consequent reduction (on the target audience factor) of two exposures per advertising cycle to zero. Other-Brand Switchers, OBSs, should be reduced from two exposures per advertising cycle down to one as they become Routinized FBSs, at least, or possibly BLs. These transitions are likely to occur at different rates across individuals, however. A conservative procedure for the Wedge, therefore, no matter which target group is the initial target, is to use (for the target audience factor) *LC+1* for cycle 1, *LC* for cycle 2, *+2* for cycle 3, and *+1* for cycle 4 and any thereafter. This will give the decelerating frequency required for the wedge.

It is noteworthy that one of the best new-product tracking models for supermarket products, BBDO's NEWS Model,[22] based on case history experience allows only two *purchase* cycles' worth of advertising for trial purchase to occur. The first two *ad* cycles of LC+1 and LC reflect this.

Reverse-wedge/PI

For the Reverse-Wedge/PI pattern, the opposite occurs, that is, MEF/c is *increased* over cycles. For the Reverse-Wedge/PI reach pattern, a reasonable strategy for MEF/c is to reverse the above. Use *zero* for the target audience factor for the first wave (to innovators), then *zero again* for the second wave (reaching innovators once again and also, thinly, the mass market), then *+1*, *+2*, and *LC+1* (stepping up the mass market frequency).

Retailer support

It could make sense to advertise at below MEF in a particular advertising cycle when the Retailer *is also advertising the brand*. In this case, the Manufacturer's extra advertising, even at low frequency, may help to achieve the total MEF. More practically, too, some continued advertising, even in a weak market area, can help to convince Retailers that the brand is being supported in the region and thus is still deserving of shelf space and perhaps special display. Because of the undeniable importance of display to the sales of products sold through retailers[23], this continued advertising can be vital. It is advisable to place it in media or media vehicles to which *the Retailer will be exposed* while occupying his or her out-of-store role as a private consumer. Retail attention to the brand could then maintain sales even though the advertising is not, except by its influence on retailers.

Short-term tactical adjustments in frequency to assist promotions

Short term here is used to mean *less than a year*. The overall reach pattern for the year may need to be adjusted to accommodate *known* events throughout the budgeting year. (Seasonality is excluded here, as it has already been discussed as a reach pattern in terms of balancing low competitive interference before the seasonal peak or peaks – the Primes – against increased Category Need during the Peak or Peaks.) Most often these known events consist of: the *dates* of Promotions to Consumers, or Special Promotions to the Trade.

In the case of Promotion Dates to Consumers, the important tactic is to shift the *timing* of advertising exposures so that they precede the promotion dates and create the Ratchet Effect (see Chapters 1 and 15) by priming the prospective buyer's Brand Preference going into the promotion. This should cause the brand's *Value Equity* to temporarily increase and the promotion to thereby produce more sales. Note that the MEF/c requirement remains the same, so more frequency is not needed, but rather frequency that *precedes* the promotion date.

With Special Promotions to the Trade – that is, to Retailers or other distributors – advertising to *Consumers* is used in many cases to impress distributors that the brand is being given strong consumer support *at the same time* as the Trade drive. Therefore, you should *concentrate some exposures* within the *Consumer* advertising cycle leading up to the *Trade* promotion. Where possible, as noted above, use of media vehicles that the Retailer is also exposed to is desirable because of the dual (trade and consumer) target audience.

Very short-term scheduling

On top of the overall scheduling pattern and the short-term adjustments for known events, the advertiser will want to keep some reserve frequency, and thus part of the budget, for *very short-term* actions and reactions. There are three main types of unpredictable events, discussed next.

LC increases advertising

The most common of these very short-term reactions needed is *response to a leading competitor*. Unanticipated competitive actions, such as the surprise launch date of a new campaign or even a new brand, have the effect of raising our brand's MEF/c under three circumstances: (1) when the target audience is New Category Users (e.g., for personal computers); (2) when Brand Recall is the brand awareness objective (e.g., for airlines); or (3) when the Brand Preference strategy is Transformational (e.g., soft drinks, liquor). All these use the *LC+1* adjustment, so if the "LC" increases advertising, you should too, to maintain your competitive SOV.

Conversely, notice that for target audiences, *other than* NCUs, who are being reached with Brand Recognition/Informational communication objectives, the "LC" term doesn't enter the calculation and *no reaction* would be the appropriate reaction. Many supermarket and drug store (FMCG) products are in this classification and should *not* be concerned about competitive SOV. Rather, they should stay with their present MEF/c rate.

Supply fluctuations

Another very short-term circumstance is caused by *variation in supply*. Just as a factory breakdown or distributor problem could cause advertising to be withdrawn that otherwise would be wasted, a factory overrun or large purchase of stock could require *extra advertising* to stimulate demand. For the brand that is already advertising at MEF/c, this extra advertising would be used to increase the number *reached* at MEF, that is, to increase Effective Reach.

Jumps in category need

A last very short-term action (not a reaction) is opportunistic ad placement to take advantage of *temporary jumps in Category Need*. Some examples:[24]

- Trade show exhibitors using internal hotel TV in the early morning to promote their booths to conventioneers

- FedEx placing ads on late news programs advertising its package-tracking service with the line, "It's 11 p.m. Do you know where your package is?"

- Campbell's Soup's radio ads at 11 a.m. to noon suggesting "Soup for lunch"

- Seasonal product advertisers monitoring weather reports and placing radio or newspaper ads (buyable at short notice), such as Nabisco Cream of Wheat, when cold or snowy weather is forecast, and Windex Outdoor glass spray, when the forecast for the weekend is sunny and above 20°C (70°F)

The increase in Category Need doesn't change the frequency required to direct choice toward a particular brand-item. Rather, it *temporarily shortens the advertising cycle*, thus pushing the frequency *rate* up. Because there is usually a corresponding decrease during opposite weather patterns, the overall effect is to keep total advertising frequency constant while simply varying its timing.

MEDIA DATA, DUPLICATIONS AND STRATEGIC RULES

The manager now has to translate the media strategy into an actual Media Schedule.[25] This requires selection of *Media Vehicles* – specific TV programs, specific radio stations and times, national, local or suburban newspapers and so forth – from within the chosen media type or types, and a decision about *how many ad units* to place in *each* vehicle in *each* advertising cycle.

To select Media Vehicles, the manager has to obtain **media data**, from TV meter panels or media diary surveys that are available to advertisers, in all countries, by subscription. What the manager needs is specific media vehicle *ratings* – the estimated number of people reached by each vehicle, usually also given by gender, age groups, household income, and, for FMCG advertisers, primary grocery shoppers. The media data may also include media vehicle *Duplications*, which are the overlap of people reached by the vehicle over occasions and the overlap of people between the vehicle and other vehicles. If duplication data aren't available, they can be approximated as shown in this chapter.

The *strategic rules* of media vehicle selection have to be understood before going to the computer. As will be shown, these strategic rules greatly help you to correctly implement the media strategy even if you don't use a computer, although a computer model provides valuable precision and optimization to implement the strategy at lowest cost.

For selection of Media Vehicles from the many available, the sole criterion to use is *Reach of the Target Group*, that is, the number of target audience individuals reached by the vehicle. You should not select vehicles on the basis of "media environment" or, the same thing, "quality of the vehicle" because studies of the effects of vehicle quality on the ad's performance have shown these effects to be small.[26] It is better to follow the principle that "A good ad will work anywhere." Any vehicle quality effects are far outweighed by differences between vehicles in the target audience numbers that they reach.

Duplication within and between vehicles

Insertions (of ad units) go into a media plan and *Exposures* or *OTSs* (to the audience) come out. Since not all insertions will be seen or heard by everyone in the target audience, the basic problem in media planning is to concentrate the OTSs for as many individuals as possible (and affordable) so that those individuals will reach the *MEF* in the advertising cycle, c. The complexity in the Insertions → Exposures problem arises because of Duplication of Exposures. Duplication of exposures is necessary if the plan is to produce a frequency of exposure greater than one (unless you use an Impact Schedule pattern, and even this assumes within-program or within-issue duplication). There are two types of duplication:

(1) **Within-vehicle duplication**: For example, how many target audience individuals who saw the TV program *Friends* on one particular weeknight also saw it the following week? And the week after? And how many saw one of these *Friends* programs but not the other two? And how many saw two but not the other one? The extent of audience duplication *within* the vehicle, over successive presentations, has to be known in order to calculate how many exposures various individuals might receive.

(2) **Between-vehicle duplication**: For example, how many target audience individuals who saw *Friends* on a particular weeknight *also* watched *Millionaire* that week (Between-Vehicle Duplication)? Or read *The Wall Street Journal* (*Cross-Media* Between-Vehicle Duplication) that week? If your ad is placed in each of these vehicles, the extent of duplication *between* the vehicles has to be known in order to calculate how many exposures various individuals might receive.

Understanding Within- and Between-Vehicle Duplications helps gain some insight into the broad planning of a media campaign. For instance, if the media strategy is simply to expose your ad to as many people as possible at least once (high Reach), then the media vehicles selected should have very little overlap in audience (low *between*-vehicle duplication). In addition, to minimize *within*-vehicle duplication, each vehicle should have only one insertion of the ad. A perfect set of media vehicles for a high Reach strategy would have *no* overlap in audience, in which case the combined reach is simply the sum of the individual ratings for each vehicle.

Typical vehicle duplications

Typical within-vehicle and between-vehicle duplications for the main media types are shown in Table 12.4. In the first column are typical Reach Percentages (percent of adults aged 18 or older unless indicated more specifically) for that medium's vehicles. For Reach, you in fact want *numbers,* but the percentages shown here facilitate comparison. The remaining three columns show *Repeat-Exposure Proportions* for the different media and, for TV, for various time periods between programs.[27] These are same-medium duplications. Cross-media duplications are discussed later.

TABLE 12.4 *Typical reach and repeat-exposure figures for mass media vehicles. Base = all adults 18+ unless otherwise specified.*

	AVERAGE RATING (% REACH)	PROPORTION REPEATING: DAY-TO-DAY			WEEK TO NEXT WEEK	ANY 2 WEEKS IN 8-WEEK PERIOD
TELEVISION						
Prime-time program	12.0[a]	.53[b]		Households	.40[c]	.28[d]
				Adults	.41	
				Teens	.27	
				Children	.28	
Evening news program	10.7[a]	.54[b]				
Daytime program	5.0[a]	.61[b, e]				
Early morning program	4.4[a]	.44[b]				
Late evening program	4.1[a]	.37[b]				
Any two prime-time programs, *same* channels		.16[e]				
Any two prime-time programs, *different* channels		.13[e]				
Evening news, *different* channels		.12[e]				
Daytime, *different* channel		.05[e]				
RADIO						
Same station	.7[e]	.47[e]				
Different stations		.01[e]				
NEWSPAPERS						
Daily paper	46.2[e]	.82[e]				
Between papers		~.00[f]				
MAGAZINES						
Same magazine	4.3[e]	.50[e]				
Between magazines		.07[e]				
OUTDOOR						
Same site	25.0[e]	.50[e]				
Between sites		~.00[f]				

TABLE 12.4 *Continued*

	AVERAGE RATING (% REACH)	PROPORTION REPEATING DAY-TO-DAY	PROPORTION REPEATING: PAGE-TO-PAGE
INTERNET			
Same site	1.0[g]	.56[g]	.50[h]
Between sites		~.00[f]	

[a] ADWEEK's *Marketer's Guide to Media* (1994)[28]

[b] Headen, Klompmaker, and Rust (1979)[29]

[c] Barwise (1986)[30]

[d] Ehrenberg and Wakshlag (1987)[31]

[e] Stankey (1988)[32]

[f] Judgment

[g] Williamson (1996), updated for Internet access for 30% of households[33]

[h] Industry rule-of-thumb

One type of duplication is Within-Vehicle Duplication. In the table, the TV within-vehicle repeat-exposure proportions indicate, for example, that for evening news programs 54% of the people viewing on one night watch the show again the following night. As the time between exposure lengthens from daily to weekly or longer, within-vehicle repeat-exposure levels are smaller. Day-to-day repeat-exposure levels for radio stations are a little lower than one would expect, at 47%. The highest day-to-day repeat exposure is provided by daily newspapers, at 82%.

The other type of duplication is Between-Vehicle Duplication. Generally, between-vehicle duplications are *smaller* than within-vehicle duplications. In the table, evening news programs illustrate this for the TV medium where duplication between different news programs on different channels is 12% (between vehicle), compared with 54% within the same news program from night-to-night (within vehicle). With TV viewing, there is some degree of program-type loyalty and a slight degree of channel loyalty which push between-vehicle duplications to 13% in prime time, though it's only 5% for daytime TV programs. For magazines, between-vehicle duplication is also low (7%). For radio stations, newspapers, outdoor sites and websites, between-vehicle duplications, on average, are *zero*.

Looking ahead, these figures suggest how a Reach Strategy (low duplication) or a Frequency Strategy (high duplication) can be implemented in the media plan.

Cross-media duplications

One set of duplications not presented in the table is **cross-media duplications** (such as TV plus radio plus magazine). Cross-media data can be obtained by the Direct Matching method, in which survey respondents record their media habits for multiple media and many vehicles (see Chapter 14). However, cross-media calculations turn out to be unnecessary, because *Random Duplication* gives almost exactly the same estimate of multi-media reach, to within plus-or-minus 1%, as the *actual* reach revealed by cross-media, single-source surveys.[34] **Random duplication** means that vehicle duplication *across media types* is equal to the product of the ratings of the two vehicles no matter what these vehicles are. For example, if *Friends* TV show rates 20 with the target group and *Cleo* magazine also rates 20, their overlap will be .20 + .20 = .04 (4%). Random duplication between vehicles across media types produces the conclusion that a Multi-Media Campaign is excellent for *Reach* but very inadequate when there is a *high Frequency* (high MEF/c) requirement.

Strategic rules for selecting the vehicles

Media planning looks very scientific because of the media agency's use of data and computers but the numbers will be misleading unless they are produced by the correct media *strategy*. Media strategy requires considerable judgment, which cannot be delegated to a computer. The Media Strategy is represented in the selection of media vehicles so as to achieve the reach pattern and its effective frequency requirements per advertising cycle. The strategy may call for high reach, or high frequency, or both. The three strategic rules to learn are: *the reach rule*, *the frequency rule*, and *the reach and frequency* rule.

Reach rule

The reach rule is: For high *Reach*, buy *many Competing* vehicles and place *one or only a small number of ads* in each vehicle. Examples of Competing vehicles are TV programs in the same time slot on different channels, radio programs in the same time slot on different stations or magazines that are substitutes, such as *Time*, *Newsweek*, and *U.S. News & World Report*. Competing vehicles provide little or no between-vehicle duplication and thus frequency will be minimized – and reach maximized – by this factor. This buying strategy will tend to scatter the target audience exposures (the OTSs) very widely. The vehicles can be big or small as long as they have good reach of your *target* audience.

One qualification when using *high-rating* vehicles is that they tend also to have high repeat-exposure levels because of the "double jeopardy" effect[35], whereby low-rating vehicles reach a small audience which is also less loyal to the vehicle in terms of repeat exposures. For prime-time weekly TV programs in the U.S.A. for instance, a program with a 9 rating (9% of adults watch it, which is now the average for a prime-time program) will have just 37% of the first-week audience repeat-viewing the next week; a program with a 12 rating will have 51% repeat; and a program with a 16 rating will have 55% repeat.[36] Therefore, if you use a *high-rating* vehicle, place only *one insertion* in it to keep the reach high but also to keep the repeat-exposure low.

Frequency rule

The frequency rule is: For high *Frequency* buy *multiple insertions* in a *few Non-competing, Strip* vehicles (Strip vehicles are those repeated daily or weekly). For example, on TV, buy several big serials or quasi-serials such as *CSI* or *Friends*, which reach 20% to 25% of adults with an average episode; or buy evening news on *one channel* if that has good target audience reach. With daily newspapers, buy ad space frequently in the one paper. With weekly or monthly magazines, concentrate only on a few large-audience magazines, such as *Time* or *National Geographic*. This strategy will reduce Reach but will maximize Frequency (individual continuity of exposures) to the same target group.

Reach and frequency rule

The reach and frequency rule is: For high Reach *and* high Frequency, buy multiple insertions in a moderate number of reasonably big vehicles, especially *Strip* vehicles, that are *Competing*. This strategy is a combination of the previous two strategies. The Competing vehicles will tend to increase Reach, while at the same time multiple insertions in large Strip vehicles (repeat-audience) will increase Frequency. Generally, maximizing both reach and frequency is an *expensive* strategy to implement. It is used most often for new product introductions via the reach patterns of a Blitz or a Wedge, as indicated next.

The rules for each reach pattern

The various reach patterns described in the previous chapter require only a few additions to the three general rules because they are, in effect, specific implementations of those rules.

BLITZ PATTERN The blitz pattern applies the Reach and Frequency Rule . . . to the hilt.

WEDGE PATTERN The Wedge pattern applies the Reach and Frequency Rule initially, then gradually evolves into the Reach Rule, as frequency is gradually reduced on subsequent flights.

REVERSE-WEDGE/PI PATTERN Try to select a set of vehicles that mainly reaches innovators within the target audience initially, and apply the Reach Rule. On subsequent flights, broaden the vehicles beyond innovators to the mass market and gradually evolve into the Reach and Frequency Rule.

FAD PATTERN This is a short blitz; use the Reach and Frequency Rule until the peak of the fad's growth, then stop.

IMPACT SCHEDULE PATTERN Use the Reach Rule on a *weekday* basis, and the Frequency Rule on a within-vehicle basis by triple-spotting (three insertions) in each of the daily vehicles.

AWARENESS PATTERN This is the Reach Rule applied to the hilt, with the *same set* of small, or one-insertion, large competing vehicles bought consistently to produce high individual continuity.

SHIFTING REACH PATTERN This requires the Reach and Frequency Rule but with the Reach part achieved by buying *different sets* of vehicles each time. Frequency is needed as well because you want to "zap" those with the category need who are reached. Longer or larger ads and double- or triple-spotting can assist this.

SEASONAL PRIMING PATTERN Use the Reach Rule for the prime or primes and then the Reach and Frequency Rule for the seasonal growth phases.

The manager or media planner applying one of these rule-governed reach patterns will come pretty close to achieving the right media schedule. However, to *optimize* the schedule – that is, to select the best combination of insertions within the cost of the budget – a media model has to be used.

IMPLEMENTING AND OPTIMIZING THE MEDIA SCHEDULE

The final step of media planning is to actually implement and, ideally, optimize the media schedule. **Optimizing the media schedule** means scheduling Insertions in various vehicles so that they will, in combination, produce the largest Effective Reach per advertising cycle (reach at MEF or higher, that is, MEF/c) of *Exposures* to the target audience, while keeping within the budget.

Media models

Media models input Media Data, consisting of vehicle-audience ratings and duplications, and output an estimate of the entire Exposure Distribution, that is, the proportion of people exposed to none, just one, just two and up to all the insertions in the schedule.

Most of the Media Models used by advertising agencies and media agencies are based on either in-house or syndicated computer software. The single exception is ACNielsen's media service, which uses the media models package we recommend below. A problem with using "black box" media models is that their users, the media managers, rarely know what sort of assumptions underlie the model implemented by the software. The available media models are many and varied. Most of the available models – including the most popular model, the Beta Binomial Model – are not very accurate.[37] If the model is poor, the resulting Reach and Frequency estimates will also be poor. Advertising accountability means that today's *marketing* manager cannot afford to rely on inaccurate media models. This is true for the large advertiser spending millions of dollars as well as for the small advertiser for whom every dollar is precious.

We offer a better solution. This book[38] incorporates (on the Website) a media planning package called *Media Mania,* designed by Peter Danaher of the University of Auckland, a colleague of ours who is widely regarded as the world's leading academic *and* practitioner authority on Media Models. The software package for *Media Mania* offers two new and highly accurate media models *as well as* the popular but not-very-accurate Beta Binomial Model for comparison. *Media Mania* is a Windows-based application that is easy for marketing managers to use. It can, of course, also be used by media professionals and is now used by ACNielsen's media service, as noted. But we strongly advise that you – the *marketing manager* – use it because you will gain a thorough *understanding* of how media models work and, importantly, of how *effectively* your costly media budget is being spent! The mechanics of installing and using *Media Mania* are explained on the Website. In this chapter, outputs from the software are used to demonstrate the implementation and optimization of schedules to fit various media strategies.

Media Mania's models

Media Mania offers three models for performing computations – two very accurate models, Danaher's Approximate Log-Linear Model and Danaher's Canonical Expansion Model, and a standard model for comparison which is Metheringham's Beta Binomial Model, sometimes referred to as the BBD (for beta-binomial distribution) model. Accuracy is determined for media models by comparing the exposure distribution that they *estimate* with the *actual* distribution of exposures. The actual distribution is obtained from a TV-viewing panel or a radio or print survey by the procedure of "giving" each individual respondent an exposure if they had seen, heard or read the particular vehicle when an insertion would have been placed in it, then *physically counting* the number of exposures received by each individual across all vehicles and their insertions. This procedure, necessary for validation of media models, is tedious and time-consuming, which is one reason why many media models are *not* validated. The models in *Media Mania have* been validated using physical-counting checks.

The **approximate log-linear model** is the most accurate overall but is slightly slower computationally for large schedules, that is, when the number of vehicles exceeds six or when there are four or more insertions in a vehicle.

The **canonical expansion model** is almost as accurate and is faster, even for large schedules. The Canonical Expansion Model is therefore the *default model* in the *Media Mania* program should a model not be specified by the program user.

The other model included in *Media Mania,* the **beta binominal model**, is the most popular standard (non-proprietary) model used by media planners. This model is very fast, but is *not reliably accurate*. It is liable to produce two types of error for all media plans and another type of error for media plans that rely heavily on Strip vehicles, that is, vehicles whose audience repeats at a relatively high rate. The Beta Binominal Model usually *overestimates Reach*; predicted reach as a percentage of actual reach is often overstated by 10% or so – for instance, predicting 55% reach when the actual is 50% – which deceives the advertiser into thinking the plan is better than it is. Secondly, it can exhibit the outcome of Reach appearing to be *reduced* when more insertions are added, which is logically impossible. Lastly, because it always produces a "smooth" exposure distribution, it can be *very inaccurate* for media plans that contain *Strip vehicles* (as recommended in the Frequency Rule or the Reach and Frequency Rule). With Strip vehicles, "lumpy" rather than smooth exposure distributions are typical. This is due to, for instance, habitual readership of exactly one issue of a monthly magazine or four issues of a weekly magazine per month, or reading all issues of a daily newspaper, or watching the same TV news program every evening. The problem is more acute in Print media than in Broadcast media but it occurs in both. The Beta Binomial Model is included only as a comparison model, so that the manager can see the sort of errors likely to be observed if he or she does not use an accurate model like the Approximate Log-Linear Model or the Canonical Expansion Model.

In *Media Mania*'s software and instructions, these models are referred to by slightly abbreviated names, rather than their full technical names. The abbreviated model names are: Approximate Log-Linear, Canonical Model, and Beta Binomial.

Model example of reach and frequency strategies

Here is an *example*, using *Media Mania*, of a Reach Strategy and a Frequency Strategy: we show the reach rule, the frequency rule, and the reach and frequency rule in operation.

The product in the example is a BMW car. For simplicity, the primary and sole medium is TV (though *Media Mania* can handle any media type and mix of media types). The *budget* is U.S.$400,000 over a *four-week period*, which would amount to a $5.2 million adspend if BMW were to advertise throughout the entire year (13 media-months) at a constant monthly rate. The media target for this campaign, hereafter called the Target Group, is men aged 35+ who live in urban areas and have above-average income (this is a demographic target group, and a reasonable if broad one although direct matching, as described in Chapter 14, would enable a more precise identification of luxury car prospects and in particular BMW prospects). We use the *Canonical Model*, the default option in *Media Mania* and the faster of the two accurate models.

Eligible vehicle selection

The first task is to identify a list of eligible TV programs. This is best done by examining the *First Insertion Reaches (FIRs)* for the target group from a long list of possible programs. Table 12.5 gives FIRs among the target group, in column 3, for 13 TV programs. The programs are ranked by their FIR percentages (this will be important for implementing the reach rule). Also shown, in column 4, are these programs' *within-vehicle duplications*, night-to-night for daily programs and week-to-week for weekly programs (this will be important for implementing the Frequency Rule). Within-vehicle duplications are given as the percentage of first-episode viewers who repeat by viewing the second (successive) episode of the program. The first two columns, 1 and 2, show the *ratings* of the programs among all people five years of age and older, and the *cost of one advertising insertion* in each program; these data are closely related as costs are mainly determined by total audience ratings. The last column, column 5, shows the *Cost Per Thousand for the Target Group* (**CPMT**) for one insertion.

TABLE 12.5 *Audience and cost information (realistic but not actual) for potential programs in the media schedules.*

PROGRAM	RATING (% OF ALL PEOPLE)	COST PER INSERTION (U.S.$)	FIR (% OF TARGET GROUP)	WITHIN-VEHICLE DUPLICATION (%)	CPMT
Friends	19.2	55,000	18.2	57	3,022.0
Monday Night Football	10.5	41,000	15.8	65	2,594.9
Everybody Loves Raymond	12.0	48,000	15.0	53	3,200.0
60 Minutes	13.7	35,000	14.4	48	2,430.6
ABC News	12.7	50,000	13.5	61	3,703.7
NBC Nightly News	11.5	46,000	12.7	55	3,622.0
20/20	11.3	25,500	12.2	44	2,090.2
CBS Evening News	10.6	40,000	11.6	53	3,448.3
Frasier	8.9	43,000	10.7	45	4,018.7
NYPD Blue	7.5	36,000	9.0	42	4,000.0
Financial Matters	2.8	15,000	4.0	33	3,750.0
Letterman	3.1	18,000	3.6	30	5,000.0
Larry King	2.0	8,000	2.5	25	3,200.0

The most popular vehicle selection statistic used in practice is the (lowest) cost to reach a *target* viewer/listener/reader. This statistic is expressed as cost per *thousand*, where M stands for "thousand," target individuals (CPM Target, or *CPMT*), as in column 5. CPMT is the ratio of cost per insertion to FIR for the target group. A planner who relies strictly on the CPMT selection criterion, in this example, would tend to advertise just in *60 Minutes, 20/20* and *Monday Night Football*, each of which costs under U.S.$3,000 per thousand for the target group, or, perhaps a more easily grasped statistic, U.S.$3.00 per target individual, and would tend to avoid shows like *Letterman* at U.S.$5,000 per thousand, or U.S.$5.00 per target individual. The same number of insertions could cost almost double depending on the vehicles' CPMTs.

However, CPMT leads the planner to focus too much on cost at the early stage of media planning. Remember that an entire budget is available. It is better to consider costs in relation to *estimated Profit*. Consider, for instance, a price-promotion TV campaign for BMW which would follow a *Reach* Strategy – this could be regarded as an *Awareness pattern* with just one, one-week ad cycle. With the discount price, you want to sell a lot of cars to make up total profit. You would therefore have to select *different* high-reach programs (and aim for high Total Reach) regardless of their CPMT differences.

Consider, alternatively, a high *Frequency* Strategy – such as a *Blitz* or *Wedge* – for a new BMW model launch. The relevant statistic would then be cost per thousand *effectively reached* (at MEF/c or higher), not simply reached *once*. With multiple insertions in a program, CPMT does come into consideration because minimizing CPMT at the *effective* reach level will tend to favor the lower CPMT programs. Both the Reach Strategy example and the Frequency Strategy example, as outlined above, indicate that the target group criterion the media planner should be trying to *minimize* (keep as low as possible) is *cost per Effective Reach point*, or CPERP. This is true even for the Reach example, which ignores CPMT, because Effective Reach in this situation is at an MEF/c of only 1 or 2 and you have to use different vehicles to maximize it. CPERP is the cost per percentage point of *effective* reach to the target group, in the advertising cycle. When this cost is divided into the adspend budget, it is equivalent to maximizing the effective reach per dollar of budget.

Implementing a reach strategy

To implement a *Reach Strategy*, as the Reach Rule states, place just one or two insertions in each of many different vehicles that do not overlap much. Three of the vehicles in Table 12.5 earlier are *Friends*, *Raymond*, and *Frasier*, which are comedies and would be expected to have some overlap (this was verified by examining the *between*-vehicle duplications that are available in this dataset), which suggests it would be best not to use all three comedies in the final schedule. A reasonable starting point is to select only two of these three vehicles, namely the two with highest FIR, which are *Friends* and *Raymond*.

Another two *apparently* similar programs are *60 Minutes* and *20/20*, which are scheduled on Sunday and Wednesday nights, respectively, so that viewers can watch both. However, their *actual* between-vehicle duplication is quite low – people tend to view one or the other (if at all). Both are therefore included in the Reach Strategy.

There are three Evening News Shows in the table, all of which *must* have low overlap because they are scheduled at the same time. The news shows are therefore ideal for gaining high reach. The scheduling tactic of placing ads in all three at the same time is called a *roadblock*.

Media Mania (the Canonical Model in the computer program) was then employed, using the Reach Rule, to estimate the reach for various combinations of the TV programs. Working within the budget, which is $400,000, we find that one insertion could be placed in 11 different programs of the original 13, only omitting *Frasier* (omitted earlier) and *Letterman*. The resulting media schedule, given in Table 12.6 (first column), produces a respectable target group MEF/c = 1+/week (one or more OTSs per week) of 75.5%. An option within *Media Mania* is to automatically find the media plan with the highest 1+ reach (using the Optimize feature). Using this feature, it was found that the maximum possible 1+/week obtainable, keeping within the budget, is 75.7%, only fractionally higher than that achieved by using the Reach Rule. The Optimal Schedule (not shown) is very similar to the one selected strategically and uses 10 vehicles, omitting *Frasier* and *Letterman*, along with *NYPD Blue*.

TABLE 12.6 *Media plans using, respectively, the reach rule and the frequency rule.*

PROGRAM	REACH-STRATEGY INSERTIONS	FREQUENCY-STRATEGY INSERTIONS
Friends	1	0
Monday Night Football	1	6
Raymond	1	0
60 Minutes	1	0
ABC News	1	0
NBC Nightly News	1	0
20/20	1	6
CBS Evening News	1	0
Frasier	0	0
NYPD Blue	1	0
Financial Matters	1	0
Letterman	0	0
Larry King	1	0
MEF/c = 1+/1 week	**75.5%**	52.3%
MEF/c = 3+/2 weeks	12.4%	**27.6%**
Total cost	**$399,500**	**$399,000**
CPERP	$5,291	$14,556

Implementing a frequency strategy

Suppose, alternatively, that the media strategy for BMW calls for an MEF/c of three exposures, per two-week advertising cycle (the MEF value of 3 was chosen because *Media Mania* automatically calculates an R3+ percentage; it could be any other value). This is a *Frequency Strategy*. Suppose further that the manager wants to run a short six-week *Blitz* (three consecutive two-week cycles) and has allocated a total budget of $1,200,000 for the campaign (i.e., $400,000 per cycle). The frequency rule's recommendations are almost the opposite of those for getting high reach. As the frequency rule states, it is desirable to have vehicles with high between-vehicle duplication, but especially desirable to have those with high *within-vehicle* duplication. It is almost always the case that within-vehicle duplication for a particular vehicle will exceed the between-vehicle duplication of that vehicle with any other vehicle. Hence, the Frequency Strategy will tend to concentrate the insertions in just a few vehicles, but place many insertions in those vehicles.

Table 12.5 indicates which vehicles these should be. As can be seen from column 4 of that table, *Monday Night Football* has the highest within-vehicle duplication, or repeat-viewing. It also has a high FIR (and a relatively low CPMT for that matter), making it extremely attractive. Indeed, it might seem reasonable to place as many insertions as possible in *Monday Night Football* and have no other vehicles in the media plan. Using *Media Mania*, again the Canonical Model, this strategy would result in nine insertions in *Monday Night Football*, giving an R3+/2 weeks of 20.6%. However, selecting a single vehicle ignores the potential benefits of between-vehicle duplication, so a second vehicle was selected to examine whether the 3+/2 weeks reach of 20.6% could be improved. (Practically, too, there may be a limit of, say, three insertions per week in *Monday Night Football*, which would force the addition of another program.)

Choosing the next vehicle is not as straightforward as the choice of *Monday Night Football* because there are several other programs which have relatively high within-vehicle duplications. *Friends* seems like a good candidate except that it does not have a very high duplication with *Monday Night Football*, probably because *Friends* appeals slightly more to women than men (determined from program ratings by demographic groups). All of the news programs have high within-vehicle duplications and high ratings but they also have high *cost*, meaning that it may be too expensive to place many insertions in these programs. The same can be said of *Raymond*, *Frasier* and *NYPD Blue*. This leaves *60 Minutes* and *20/20*. Using *Media Mania*, insertions were juggled between *Monday Night Football* and either *60 Minutes* or *20/20*. The highest R3+/2 weeks was obtained with six insertions in each of *Monday Night Football* and *20/20*. The results for this plan are given in Table 12.6 (second column). The R3+/2 weeks is 27.6%, being much higher than (relatively, a 34% improvement upon) the earlier value of 20.6% for the campaign having all its insertions in *Monday Night Football*.

Although it is irrelevant in this case, note that the reach (R1+) of the Frequency Strategy is only 52.3%, considerably below that obtained for the Reach Strategy, as expected.

It turns out that *CPMTs* are useful when trying to achieve a Frequency Strategy. This is because the crux of a good Frequency Strategy is multiple insertions. The 12 insertions cost U.S.$399,000 in the above schedule, whereas they would have cost over U.S.$500,000 in *Raymond* or *Letterman*, well beyond the per-cycle budget of U.S.$400,000, and with lower effective (R3+) reach. Certainly you can have more insertions in a lower-cost vehicle but this must be traded off against the vehicle's audience size, hence the value of CPMTs. This is evidenced from Table 12.5, where it can be seen that the lowest CPMTs occur for *20/20*, *60 Minutes* and *Monday Night Football*, in that order. It transpired that these three vehicles were the key ones for developing the Frequency Strategy in this application.

A *Reach-plus-Frequency Strategy* (Reach and Frequency Rule) could easily be implemented with *Media Mania*. For BMW, for instance, the objective of such a media plan might be to

> maximize weekly 2+ reach (reach at a frequency level of 2 or more per week) or, better still, 2-to-3 per week reach (those reached 2 to 3 times *exactly* in one week). Although not shown here, the best schedule employs, as expected, somewhat more media vehicles than the Frequency plan but with more insertions in each than the single insertions in the Reach plan.

We have illustrated some of the capabilities of Danaher's *Media Mania* computer software. To experience the full range of capabilities, the reader should examine the other three examples given on our book's Website. One example is a cross-media, that is, *multi-media* implementation.

Optimization

Media Mania, as currently formulated, offers Optimization of 1+ Reach or 3+ Reach per time period (R1+/c or R3+/c). The selection of 1+ Reach is perhaps obvious because the media planner usually wants to know what the "maximum reach" would be with a set of vehicles and insertions even if this is not the criterion for a particular plan. The selection of 3+ Reach as the other optimization criterion, however, is arbitrary. It would be very time-consuming to run the program if *Media Mania* were programmed to optimize at many different effective reach levels, so the level of R3+ was chosen. But: the "c," the advertising cycle duration, can *vary*. This realization gives the media planner considerable *flexibility* in maximizing effective reach, because effective reach, like MEF, is essentially a *rate* of exposures, a rate of OTSs. By careful consideration of the timing of the vehicles that are candidates for the schedule and the allowable number of insertions per time period (such as per program for a TV show or per issue for a monthly magazine), it is possible to optimize on 1+ Reach or 3+ Reach for a chosen duration of c: per *day*, per *one week*, or per *two weeks*, as desired.

> For example, suppose that MEF/c was estimated to be 6+/2-weekly cycle. The media planner could achieve this *rate* by optimizing R3+/*weekly* and then, using the same vehicles selected by that optimization and following the same pattern of insertions, adding insertions for a further week until the budget amount for that cycle is spent. Because this "variation of c" method is approximate rather than exact, it is very important to adhere to the relevant *strategic rule* when making this type of projection. In fact, if you follow the rule, in this case the Frequency Rule, the 6+/2-week effective reach calculated without optimization will be found to be remarkably close to optimal.

In summary, *Media Mania* allows sufficient optimization flexibility for most media planning applications. It is also easy to use and accurate, with its Canonical Model and Approximate Log-Linear options.

Media budget setting

The **media budget**, also known as the **adspend**, is usually set beforehand for the overall campaign. For instance, a budget of U.S.$400,000 per ad cycle was set in the BMW example. We now provide a task-method check "in reverse" – that is, to see whether the spending rate is *adequate to meet the pre-set sales goal* for the brand. The Task Method is covered in full in the next chapter, but it is appropriate to introduce it here.

We use the high-frequency plan for BMW from Table 12.6. Earlier in the chapter, we said that effective reach is based on maximizing the prospective customer's "disposition," or probability of purchase of the brand. The figures showed that a two-week spend of U.S.$400,000 (actually $399,000) would generate an effective reach of 27.6% of the target group. This means 27.6% of the target group number should be "ready to buy" a BMW – assuming that the creative stimuli (the ads) have been persuasive. Of course, this doesn't mean that 27.6% of them *will* buy. Their favorable disposition has to carry forward into a *showroom visit* and a successful *offer* from the BMW salesperson.

This is where the Task Method comes in. The Task Method (for this particular type of product) requires an estimate of two further probabilities: the probability that an *effectively reached* prospect will visit the showroom and the probability that the average BMW salesperson will convert the visit into a purchase (a sale). Thus, the whole equation is: number in target group × effective reach proportion × p visit × p purchase = sales that month. (For simplification, this assumes that people outside the target group are not influenced by the advertising and that the advertising is the only source of visitors, but these other factors can, if necessary, also be estimated by the Task Method.) Suppose, for illustration purposes, that BMW's market-survey tracking data indicate that one in 20 of those "aware" of the BMW automobile from the advertising (effectively reached) will actually make a visit, thus p visit = .05. Further, suppose that BMW's retail data show a conversion rate of one in three visitors, thus p purchase = .33. The equation now becomes: number in target group × .276 × .05 × .33 = number in target group × .0045; in other words, between four and five individuals (per thousand) of the target group could be expected to buy as a result of each cycle. There are three cycles, so the total number expected to buy is 12 to 15 individuals (per thousand) of the target group – let's say, to be conservative, 12 individuals (per thousand). Suppose further that BMW's profit per vehicle sold, net of all costs except advertising, is U.S.$5,000. The 12 individuals (per thousand) therefore contribute $60,000 in revenue. The adspend was $1,200,000. The break-even number of sales would therefore have to be $1,200,000 ÷ $5,000 = 240 vehicle sales. Since we calculate that 12 vehicles are sold for every 1,000 target audience members effectively reached, the size of the effective reach group required to break even is 240/12 × 1000 = 20,000.

As the effective reach attained was 27.6% of the media target group, this means a media target group size of 20,000 ÷ .276 = 72,464 individuals would be needed to break even. The plan easily covers this media target and the advertising would be very profitable. Exactly *how* profitable depends on the size of the media target – the *number* of effectively reached target audience individuals – that the campaign budget buys.

Another way of looking at this is via **CPERP** (cost per effective-reach point, that is, per 1% of effective reach).

CPERP for the two plans is given in the bottom row of Table 12.6. First we consider the Frequency plan. In the Frequency plan, with CPERP at U.S.$14,556 and profit at $5,000 per vehicle sold, the required net conversion ratio, p visit × p purchase, to break even, is 14,556 ÷ $5,000 = 2.91 individuals per thousand of those effectively reached, a conversion ratio of .00291. If p buy is constant at .33, this implies a p visit of .009, or approximately one in a thousand effectively reached. Above, we estimated the conversion ratio, directly, as being

.05 × .33 = .0165, or 16.5 individuals per thousand. This is 5.7 times higher and may be optimistic. In any event, as one always should, BMW will need to employ high-quality ads to get prospects to visit.

Let's quickly look at the Reach plan, with its CPERP of $5,291. Let's assume that the price discount (e.g., a rebate) on each car is $3,000, so that the Profit per vehicle sold is $2,000. The conversion ratio needed to break even is 5,291 ÷ 2,000 = 2.65 individuals per thousand of those effectively reached, or .00265. With the quite attractive price deal, visitors won't need much convincing by the salesperson, so the key is to ensure that p visit is above .00265, say .003. This is three in a thousand (of the 75.5% effectively reached) and should be quite easily attainable. More than three in a thousand, and the campaign makes a profit, even with the discounted selling price of the car.

Unfortunately, as currently formulated, *Media Mania* cannot go from a Reach or Effective Reach target percentage "back" to the lowest-cost schedule of insertions. Accordingly, you have to use *trial and error* and try increasing the insertions according to the same *strategic rule*, while being careful to watch for insertion limits in vehicles per time period. In practice, this method is not too difficult unless the schedule of vehicles and insertions is *unusually* large to begin with. With the small schedule for BMW, for instance, it is feasible to use this method.

SUMMARY

For the Reach Pattern selected, the manager now has to choose a number representing Effective Frequency for *each* of its advertising cycles.

There is a Minimum Effective Frequency and potentially a Maximum Effective Frequency after which disposition to buy the brand-item, or take other appropriate action, may turn downwards, although this occurs only for ads in Broadcast media that are Transformational, because people are "forced" to watch them or listen to them and they start to dislike them and counter-argue with them.

The most important number to estimate is *Minimum* Effective Frequency (MEF) because you want to bring purchase disposition to a maximum using the fewest necessary number of exposures, that is, at lowest cost. Exposures (or OTSs) beyond the MEF level are wasted but, in trying to maximize MEF for a given budget, it is inevitable that some individuals will receive wasted exposures in mass media campaigns.

It is best to regard MEF as a *rate* rather than a number or frequency, hence it is written MEF/c, where c is the duration of the advertising cycle. As we saw in the previous chapter, the advertising cycle, c, is technically defined as the shortest amount of time that it takes to get the MEF level of exposures delivered to the target audience individuals. The manager should regard the advertising cycle as one week for low values of MEF, and two weeks if MEF has a high value that cannot practically be delivered via the media vehicles in a one-week timeframe.

We provide a formula for estimating MEF/c based on the Target Audience type, the Brand Awareness objective, Informational or Transformational brand preference strategy and Personal Influence. The formula is MEF/c = 1 + TA + BA + BPREF + PI. The resulting MEF/c number (actually a rate) then has to be adjusted upward when the Ad Units used in the campaign have an attention probability of less than 1.00. The ad-unit adjustment greatly increases the required MEF/c and shows a big payoff for using high-attention ad units.

In particular cycles, short-term adjustments to MEF/c may be made. These are to adjust MEF/c downward if there is support advertising by the Retailer; to vary the timing of the cycles if the brand-item is also using promotions so that the advertising *precedes* each promotion event and utilizes the Ratchet Effect. Also, very short-term adjustments may be made for competitive reaction countering; supply fluctuations; and opportunistic advertising to take advantage of jumps in category need. Advertisers who experience these conditions usually keep, say, 10% of the budget aside to move around and reassess the budget quarterly.

To implement the Media Schedule, the manager first has to learn three strategic rules. Appropriate use of these rules, in a good Media Model, will produce an accurate media plan. The respective reach patterns from the previous chapter utilize one or more of these rules. The Reach Rule is to buy many Competing vehicles and place one or only a small number of ads in each vehicle. The Frequency Rule is to buy multiple insertions in a few Non-competing Strip vehicles. The Reach and Frequency rule is to buy multiple insertions in a moderate number of reasonably Large vehicles, especially Strip vehicles, that Compete for the same audience. We provided a media model, *Media Mania*, available on the book's Website, that the manager can use to examine alternative media schedules to select one that achieves high Effective Reach within the assigned advertising Budget. With a little extra effort, an optimal (most cost-effective) schedule can be found using the program's Optimizing feature.

DISCUSSION QUESTIONS

12.1 What is the difference, if any, between the terms "Exposure," "OTS," and "Frequency" as we use these terms here?

12.2 What is the Advertising Cycle Duration, "c," and why is it given a practical duration of one week for low MEF/c plans and two weeks for high MEF/c plans?

12.3 Estimate (calculate) the Minimum Effective Frequency per advertising cycle and the Duration of the advertising cycle, thus MEF/c, for each of the following examples (you will have to select an appropriate advertising unit in each case):

a. Compaq desktop PCs, advertising in Industry Magazines, to Brand Switchers, via a Brand Recall, Informational brand preference strategy.

b. Kraft cheese, advertising on TV, to Brand Loyals, via a Brand Recognition, Transformational brand preference strategy.

c. Jack Daniel's bourbon whiskey, advertising on Billboards, to Other-Brand Loyals, via a Brand Recall, Transformational brand preference strategy, using a campaign that is known to generate favorable Word of Mouth from one in every three people exposed.

d. K-Mart, advertising Sony Walkmans, on Radio, to New Category Users, via a Brand Recall, Informational brand preference strategy.

12.4 How is MEF/c estimated for Direct-Response Ads, Interactive TV or PC Ads, and Promotion Offers?

12.5 (Advanced question that will require looking up media chapters in other advertising texts or a media text.) Below is an example of a media plan for a target audience of 10 people (this could as well be 10 million people, but smaller numbers are easier to work with). It is based on a three-week advertising cycle. An exposure is indicated by an x.

a. According to the definition in the chapter, what is the Reach of this plan?

b. According to the conventional definition of Reach in any advertising textbook, what is the "Cumulative Reach" of this plan for the nine-week period? In a sentence or two, describe why the "Cumulative Reach" figure is misleading.

c. Suppose the Minimum Effective Frequency is estimated or known to be two exposures in an advertising cycle (2/c). Then, as per the conventional textbook definition, calculate the *Average Frequency* for each advertising cycle. Are cycles 1 and 2 equally effective for the advertiser?

d. Suppose that the advertiser is pursuing a *Shifting Reach pattern*, with MEF = 2. What is the Effective Reach of the plan?

e. Finally, suppose instead that the advertiser is pursuing an *Impact Schedule* pattern, with MEF = 2. What is the Effective Reach of the plan?

	Advertising cycle 1 (week no.)			Advertising cycle 2 (week no.)			Advertising cycle 3 (week no.)		
Individual	1	2	3	1	2	3	1	2	3
1			x	x	x		x		x
2									
3	x						x	x	x
4				x	x			x	
5									
6	x	x	x	x					
7					x	x	x	x	x
8			x	x	x	x			
9	x	x							
10		x	x				x		x

12.6 Go to the book's Website and locate *Media Mania*. Do the media schedule exercise for Regaine hair restorer.

12.7 Go to the book's Website and locate *Media Mania*. Do the media schedule exercise for the new call-waiting service for AT&T, the U.S. telephone company.

NOTES

1. Our contempt for GRPs, etc., goes as far back as the first Rossiter and Percy book, in 1987. Media people don't listen – they have a vested interest in keeping clients in the dark about what their media plans are really achieving (the plans achieve much less than the clients believe, usually!). For a recent criticism of "Impacts" in media planning, see R. White, Editorial, *Admap*, 2004, February, p. 3. The knowledgeable reader may note the absence of other similarly mysterious and meaningless media terms in this chapter. If the term isn't here, it is not valid.

2. K.A. Longman, *Advertising*, New York: Harcourt Brace Jovanovich, 1971; A.A. Achenbaum, Effective exposure, a new way of evaluating media, paper presented at the Association of National Advertisers' Media Workshop, Association of National Advertisers, Inc., New York, 1977; M.J. Naples, *Effective Frequency: The Relationship Between Frequency and Advertising Effectiveness*, New York: Association of National Advertisers, Inc., 1979.

3. G.L. Urban and J.R. Hauser, *Design and Marketing of New Products* (2nd edn), chapter 16, Englewood Cliffs, NJ: Prentice Hall, 1993.

4. G. Brown, The awareness problem: attention and memory effects from TV and magazine advertising, *Admap*, 1994, January, pp. 15–20.

5. C. McDonald, *Advertising Reach and Frequency* (2nd edn), Lincolnwood, Illinois: NTC Business Books, 1996.

6. M.J. Naples, 1979, same reference as in note 2.

7. E. Ephron, More weeks, less weight: the self-space model of advertising, *Journal of Advertising Research*, 1995, 35(3), pp. 18–23; J.P. Jones, Single-source research begins to fulfill its promise, *Journal of Advertising Research*, 1995, 35(3), pp. 9–16; J.P. Jones, What does effective frequency mean in 1997?, *Journal of Advertising Research*, 1997, 37(4), pp. 14–20.

8. H. Zielske, Using effective frequency in media planning, *Journal of Media Planning*, 1986, 1(1), pp. 53–56; S. Broadbent,

The gatekeeper takes the lie-detector test, *Admap*, 1996, December, pp. 34–39; C. McDonald, 1996, same reference as note 5; C. McDonald, Advertising sales effects, *Admap*, 1996, April, pp. 39–43; C. McDonald, How frequently should you advertise?, *Admap*, 1996, July–August, pp. 22–25; T. Cowling, New data links for better targeting and planning, *Admap*, 1997, February, pp. 28–31. In an analysis of the sales effectiveness of 113 FMCG brand-item media plans, Starcom media service found that only 14% resembled "recency theory" plans. See V. Evans and C. Wilson, Advertising decay: can it be predicted?, *B&T Weekly*, November 16, 2001, pp. 14, 16.

9. C. McDonald, What is the short-term effect of advertising?, *Special Report No. 71–142*, 1971, Cambridge, MA: Marketing Science Institute; P. Gullen and H. Johnson, Product purchasing and TV viewing: measuring and relating the two, in *New Developments in Media Research*, Amsterdam: ESOMAR, 1986, pp. 345–363.

10. J.O. Peckman, *The Wheel of Marketing*, self-published, Scarsdale, New York, 1981.

11. J.C. Schroer, Ad spending: growing market share, *Harvard Business Review*, 1990, 68(1), pp. 44–48.

12. See studies by S.N. Singh and M.L. Rothschild, Recognition as a measure of learning from television commercials, *Journal of Marketing Research*, 1983, 20(3), pp. 235–248; D.E. Schultz and M.P. Block, Empirical estimation of advertising response functions, *Journal of Media Planning*, 1986, 1(1), pp. 17–24.

13. For recent in-market confirmation of the fact that informational ads do not benefit from repetition (beyond the base MEF/c rate) whereas transformational ads do benefit, a prediction first made in the Rossiter and Percy (1997) book, see D.J. MacInnis, A.G. Rao, and A.M. Weiss, Assessing when increased media weight of real-world advertisements helps sales, *Journal of Marketing Research*, 2002, 39(4), pp. 391–407. As the weight (GRPs) increase was between + 50% and + 100% on TV, this would have mainly increased frequency rather than reach.

14. In a recent study of 12 service categories – including automobile servicing, dry cleaning, and dental care – positive word of mouth was found to be more frequent, often substantially so, than negative word of mouth. See R. East and K. Hammond, The impact and frequency of negative and positive word of mouth, presentation at the INFORMS Marketing Science Conference, 2003.

15. P.M. Herr, F.R. Kardes, and J. Kim, Effects of word-of-mouth and product-attribute information on persuasion: an accessibility-diagnosticity perspective, *Journal of Consumer Research*, 1991, 17(4), pp. 454–462.

16. J.N. Sheth, Word-of-mouth in low risk innovations, *Journal of Advertising Research*, 1971, 11(3), pp. 15–18; G.S. Day, Attitude change, media and word-of-mouth, *Journal of Advertising Research*, 1971, 11(6), pp. 31–40.

17. J.H. Holmes and J.D. Lett, Product sampling and word-of-mouth, *Journal of Advertising Research*, 1977, 17(5), pp. 35–40.

18. S.A. Ozga, Imperfect markets through lack of knowledge, *Quarterly Journal of Economics*, 1960, 74(1), pp. 29–52.

19. Visual memory is virtually permanent or may exhibit a slight, very long-term fade with time, well beyond the duration of advertising effects (see studies reviewed in J.R. Rossiter and L. Percy, Visual communication in advertising, in R.J. Harris, Ed., *Information Processing Research in Advertising*, Mahwah, NJ: Erlbaum, chapter 4, p. 96). Verbal memory is subject totally to competitive interference, not to time-related fading.

20. The simple division adjustment is not strictly accurate but will suffice. A strict adjustment would require dividing by the joint probability of the combined ad units achieving MEF, a very tedious adjustment that would, for high MEF, produce pessimistically large adjusted MEF figures.

21. National Infomercial Marketing Association study reported in *USA Today*, 1994, October 21–23, p. 1A; R.J. Fox, S.K. Reddy, and B. Rao, Modeling response to repetitive promotional stimuli, *Journal of the Academy of Marketing Science*, 1997, 25(3), pp. 242–255; P.J. Danaher and B.J. Green, A comparison of media factors that influence the effectiveness of direct response television advertising, *Journal of Direct Marketing*, 1997, 11(2), pp. 46–58.

22. L.G. Pringle, R.D. Wilson and E.I. Brody, NEWS: a decision-oriented model for new product analysis and forecasting, *Marketing Science*, 1982, 1(1), pp. 1–29.

23. See Chapter 15 and R. East, *The Effect of Advertising and Display*, Boston: Kluwer, 2003.

24. R. Baron, Simple ideas are best creative spice, *Television Week*, August 20, 2003, Website.

25. This section of the chapter is adapted and updated from the specialized book, *Advanced Media Planning*, by J.R. Rossiter and P.J. Danaher, Boston: Kluwer, 1998. We gratefully acknowledge the permission of Peter Danaher and Kluwer publishers to use this material.

26. See J.R. Rossiter and L. Percy, *Advertising Communications & Promotion Management*, New York: McGraw-Hill, 1997.

27. Repeat exposure is one way of showing duplication. It does, though, express a conditional probability: the probability of the next event given that the first has occurred. Computerized media programs usually work with joint probabilities, but this difference need not concern us here.

28. Calculated from 1993 ratings reported in ADWEEK, *Marketer's Guide to Media*, New York: ADWEEK, 1994, 17(1), p. 26.

29. R.S. Headen, J.E. Klompmaker, and R.T. Rust, The duplication of viewing law and television media schedule evaluation, *Journal of Marketing Research*, 1979, 16(4), pp. 333–340.

30. T.P. Barwise, Repeat-viewing of prime-time TV series, *Journal of Advertising Research*, 1986, 26(4), pp. 9–14.

31. A.S.C. Ehrenberg and J. Wakshlag, Repeat-viewing with people meters, *Journal of Advertising Research*, 1987, 27(1), pp. 9–13.

32. M.J. Stankey, Using media more effectively, *Business*, 1988, April–June, pp. 20–27.

33. Study by DoubleClick Network reported in D.A. Williamson, New ammo for click-rate debate, *Advertising Age*, 1996, August 19, p. 24. This study found that the average click-through rate for a Web banner ad seen the first time is 3.6%; the average ad banner is then accessed again by about 2% (that is 56% of the original attenders); and falls to below 1% for any subsequent click-throughs. A "click-through" occurs when a Website visitor clicks on a banner in the advertiser's ad, after first "hitting" the site by downloading the file. The click-through *rate* is the number of click-throughs divided by the number of hits. For a good discussion of measurement issues in online advertising, see I.P. Murphy, On-line ads effective? Who knows for sure?, *Marketing News*, 1996, September 23, pp. 1–38.

34. For instance, see the recent Media in Mind study conducted by media agency Universal McCann, where the assumption of random duplication reproduced the cross-media reach figures to within 1%. Reported in J. Kite, Mixed-media campaigns: can we fix it? Yes we can!, *Admap*, 2001, June, pp. 48–50.

35. G.J. Goodhardt, A.S.C. Ehrenberg, and M.A. Collins, *The Television Audience: Patterns of Viewing* (2nd edn), London: Gower, 1987; N. Donthu, Double jeopardy in program choice, *Journal of the Academy of Marketing Science*, 1994, 22(2), pp. 180–185.

36. T.P. Barwise, 1986, reference in note 30.

37. See M.D. Rice and J.D. Leckenby, An empirical test of a proprietary television media model, *Journal of Advertising Research*, 1986, 26(4), pp. 17–21; R. Rust, *Advertising Media Models: A Practical Guide*, Lexington, MA: Lexington Books, 1986; and P.J. Danaher, Some statistical modeling problems in the advertising industry, *The American Statistician*, 56(5), pp. 255–260.

38. The *Media Mania* media planning package is also available in the specialized book by J.R. Rossiter and P.J. Danaher referenced in note 25.

PART V

budget and tracking

CHAPTER 13

Setting the campaign budget 297

CHAPTER 14

Campaign tracking 312

CHAPTER 13

Setting the campaign budget

The main purpose of this chapter is to demonstrate how to set the budget for a particular marcoms campaign. Before that, however, upper management has to decide the Total Marcoms Allocation for the company or organization for the forthcoming year. We address this decision first. We then move on to Campaign Budget-Setting using the Task Method and, for a multi-regional campaign, Schroer's Method.

THE TOTAL MARCOMS ALLOCATION

The **total marcoms allocation** comprises funds to cover the expected cost of all types of advertising (see Chapter 1) for the year. *Total Adspend* is the largest component and it includes an amount to cover the anticipated cost of *the creative* and *promotional support materials* and an amount to cover anticipated *research projects*. The other component is a sub-budget for sponsorships, event marketing, and PR. Most companies use at least one of these macroms activities and many use all three. Note that the Salesforce Budget is always separate from the Total Macroms allocation and is decided by a different manager.

Total adspend

Deciding how much will be needed for the year's **total adspend**, however, is more difficult, particularly if the manager has never made this decision previously. The theoretically correct way to make the Total Adspend decision is to use the Task Method (see below) to set the adspend for each brand-item and each campaign planned for the year and then *add up the anticipated campaign adspends* to arrive at the total funds that will be needed for the year. Although this is the correct approach theoretically, it is *not really practical*; it overlooks the reality that campaigns are very often initiated at various times during the calendar year and it is not realistic to expect the budgets for these to be worked out in full prior to the year's commencement. Rather, the manager has to make a gross estimate of Total Adspend up front. The most rational way to make this gross estimate is, first, to look up the **advertising-to-sales (A/S) ratio** employed by the company that we most want to *emulate* in the industry and apply that A/S ratio to our own level of sales from the *last* year and, second, *adjust the total adspend upwards* using the average elasticity coefficients from Chapter 1 if a goal of higher sales is desired for the forthcoming year. In the case of a *new* company, where there *is* no last year, the adjustment cannot be made and instead you apply the A/S ratio to your *forecast* amount of sales.

The advertising spending and the sales revenue, and thus the Advertising-to-Sales Ratio, is publicly available information for most companies. The trade newspaper, *Advertising Age*, for instance, annually publishes these figures for U.S. corporations in the U.S. economy. Even if you cannot readily obtain a company's figures for other countries, remember that the *ratio* should stay pretty much the same, at least for other developed economies. Below, we exemplify A/S ratios and show how to interpret them.

Adspend, Sales and Advertising-to-Sales Ratios for selected major companies in various industries are provided in Table 13.1, for the year 2001.[1] As noted, many others are available from the *Advertising Age* source. The figures are *Adspend*, in U.S.$ millions, in measured media, which account for the bulk of most companies' adspend; the total monetary value of *Sales* (profit figures are also often available) in U.S.$ millions; and the *Ratio* of the two expressed as a percentage. There are two aspects to note about these figures: industry differences and company similarities and differences.

Industry differences in value per sales unit

Firstly, companies that sell product or service units each of which has a *high dollar value* – such as automobiles, computers, large household electrical items, clothing, telephone services, and financial services – tend to have *low* A/S ratios, to the order of about 2%; this is because advertising works to sell *units* of a product or service, not their dollar values. In contrast, companies in FMCG categories tend to have *high* A/S ratios because, whereas they sell a lot of units, the dollar value of each is quite small and thus sales revenue in relation to adspend is smaller. Companies that sell household cleaning products, personal care products, or soft drinks are examples of this, with A/S ratios of about 12%. Interestingly, the largest A/S ratios in the table are for the two fast-food restaurants, McDonald's and Wendy's, with each spending about a dollar of advertising to generate five dollars of sales. The A/S ratios for these two restaurant companies were similarly high the previous year but could reflect a market-share battle in an industry that is crowded and rather flat in the U.S.A. at present.

Similarity and deviations within-industry

A second aspect to note is the tendency for closely competing companies in the same industry to exhibit *similar* A/S ratios but for particular companies to *deviate*. We would like to believe that the similarity is due to leading companies having figured out an optimal advertising spending rate rather than being due to blind imitation, but there is no doubt that a good deal of this goes on and indeed we are advocating partially sighted imitation here! On the other hand, there are some notable deviations within industries. As a manager, you should try to think *how these deviations might have arisen*, especially as the reasons for them might affect the setting of your gross adspend budget. For instance, in the telecommunications industry, Deutsche Telekom is a relative newcomer to the U.S. market and is probably spending at a high level relative to its current sales level in order to gain future sales; its A/S ratio is 7.2%, compared with 2.5% for U.S. Telecom giants Verizon and AT&T. In computers, Dell has a very low A/S ratio of only 1.4%, which is possibly due to that company's extensive use of very low-cost, permission-based email and fax ads, which would not be counted in measured media. In electronics, GE's A/S ratio, at 1.7%, is considerably lower than Sony's, at 6.2%; this is harder to explain without looking into both companies' different product lines by sales volume but it is probable that GE sells more larger and higher-priced durables, such as air conditioners and refrigerators, than Sony, which would make GE's A/S *ratio* lower (they each have exactly the same total adspend of $1.3 billion per annum in the U.S.A.). In hotels, the Hilton chain and the Marriott chain each spend almost identical amounts, just under $300 million per year, but the sales base for Hilton is about 70% lower than Marriott's in terms of dollar value; we would have to look into this one to explain why. Among the retailers, Saks' A/S ratio of 4.9% is considerably higher than Target's, at 2.3%, and they both sell clothing; this could represent an aggressive advertising strategy aimed at the upper end of the clothing market by Saks, and also the likelihood that Saks advertises in more expensive upscale TV programs and magazines than does Target. Further, although this would not be reflected in these adspend figures, Target is known for using low production cost ads on television.

Again, whereas the theoretically correct method of estimating Total Adspend is to add up campaign estimates based on the Task Method, a more practical method is to *model the gross budget estimate on the A/S ratio of a company in the industry that your company desires to emulate*.

TABLE 13.1 *Advertising-to-sales ratios for selected major U.S. companies, by industry category alphabetically, in 2001.*

	ADSPEND ($ MILLIONS)	SALES REVENUE ($ MILLIONS)	A/S RATIO (%)
Automotive			
• Ford	2,408	108,296	2.2
• General Motors	3,374	132,339	2.5
Beer			
• Anheuser-Busch	656	12,356	5.3
Cameras, film			
• Eastman Kodak	324	6,419	5.0
Candy			
• Hershey	366	4,557	8.0
Cleaners			
• Clorox	338	3,299	10.2
• S.C. Johnson	479	3,534	13.6
Computers and software			
• IBM	994	35,215	2.8
• Hewlett-Packard	899	31,725	2.8
• Dell	302	21,760	1.4
• Intel	426	9,382	4.5
• Microsoft	920	15,700	5.9
Drugs			
• Johnson & Johnson	1,618	20,204	8.0
• GlaxoSmithKline	881	14,525	6.1
Electronics			
• General Electric[a]	1,310	76,896	1.7
• Sony	1,310	21,127	6.2
Financial services			
• American Express	444	17,552	2.5
• Morgan Stanley Dean Witter	385	16,726	2.3
Food			
• Nestlé	967	15,832	6.1
• Kellogg	422	6,129	6.9
• Campbell Soup	397	5,021	7.9
Hotels			
• Hilton	296	3,050	9.7
• Marriott	288	10,152	2.8
Personal care			
• P&G	2,541	20,334	12.5
• Unilever	1,484	11,315	13.1
• Colgate-Palmolive	355	2,888	12.3

TABLE 13.1 *Continued*

Restaurants			
• McDonald's	1,195	5,396	22.1
• Wendy's	312	1,724	18.1
Retailers			
• Safeway	440	30,866	1.4
• Kmart	597	36,151	1.7
• Target	926	39,888	2.3
• Saks	295	6,071	4.9
Soft drinks			
• Pepsi	2,210	18,215	12.1
• Coca-Cola	903	7,526	12.0
Sportswear			
• Nike	577	4,819	12.0
Telecommunications			
• Verizon	1,462	64,649	2.3
• AT&T	1,372	52,550	2.6
• Deutsche Telekom	289	3,997	7.2
Toys			
• Mattel	449	3,414	13.2

[a] GE's figures are for 2000 because 2001 was an atypical spending year for that company.

SOURCE: Selected from *Advertising Age*'s Leading National Advertisers Report, see note 1.

Purposeful adjustments in total adspend

Adjustments to the gross estimate can then be made by using the **advertising elasticity coefficient** for FMCG products or consumer durables and industrial products, as appropriate, from Chapter 1. Notice that the elasticity figures were computed on sales units, not sales value, but this poses no problem in practice.

> For example, suppose that your company is a financial services provider and that you want to model on the A/S ratio used by American Express company. Suppose further that your sales in dollar value last year were $1 billion. Applying Amex's A/S ratio of 2.5% to this sales amount would produce a gross estimated adspend for your company of $1 billion × .025 = $25 million. Now suppose that your company wishes to increase its adspend to achieve a 10% increase in sales revenue. Even though the elasticities are in sales units, a 10% increase in sales revenue would presumably be equivalent to selling 10% more units, so we do not need to make a conversion. The Advertising Elasticity Coefficient for Durables (in Chapter 1, Table 1.3) indicates that an increase of 10% in adspend for the year would increase sales by 3.6%. Therefore, to increase sales by 10% you would need an adspend increase of 10 ÷ 3.6 = 2.8 × 10% = 28% increase in adspend over the original gross estimate of $25 million, which would be $32 million. Whereas this looks like a much larger amount of adspend, remember that it is on a projected sales revenue base of (now) $1.1 billion, which would represent an A/S ratio of 2.9%.

A further example might help to illustrate this calculation, this time for an FMCG company, let's say a smaller manufacturer of personal care products, also with sales last year of $1 billion. Suppose you model on Procter & Gamble company (P&G); applying P&G's A/S ratio of 12.5% to this sales amount produces a gross adspend estimate of $1 billion × .125 = $125 million. Suppose again you seek a 10% increase in sales. The Advertising Elasticity Coefficient for FMCG products (Chapter 1, Table 1.3) indicates that an increase of 10% in adspend for the year would increase sales by 1.4%, so to increase sales by 10% you would need an adspend increase of 10 ÷ 1.4 = 7.1 × 10% = 71%, which would bring the total adspend to $214 million. This is a massive increase – a new A/S ratio of $214 million ÷ $1.1 billion = 19.5%.

In both examples, the Advertising Elasticity Coefficients assume that the marcoms, mostly advertising, is of *average* quality. If you *know* you are going to have *high*-quality advertising, you would use the coefficients from Chapter 1, Table 1.4, and the required adspend would be lower. However, if you guess optimistically and are wrong, your budget will fall short of being able to deliver the 10% sales increase.

Whereas it is not usual for large, market-leading companies such as most of those named in the table to change their adspend from year to year by more than plus-or-minus 10%, it is *quite usual for companies with medium or small market shares to do so*. For instance, in the U.S.A. for the year 2000 compared with the year 2001, Nextel Communications increased its adspend by 27%, Mazda Motor Corporation reduced its adspend by 14% while Hyundai Motor Corporation increased its adspend by 18%, Bank of America increased its adspend by 37%, Levi Strauss & Co. reduced its adspend by 16% and Philips Electronics reduced its adspend by 22%.[2] Changes of these magnitudes would be expected if a company is aggressively chasing market share or has been doing so for a year, or anticipates a downturn in sales for the coming year for whatever reason.

Adspend policy in an industry recession

Since we are talking about gross spending plans, a related issue is the question of whether the company should reduce its total adspend during an industry recession. Buying-intention surveys can help forecast the size and duration of an anticipated recession in an industry.[3] A reduced adspend is usual but there is another school of thought that sees an opportunity to gain market share while competitors' budgets are reduced by *increasing* adspend during a recession. A couple of well-publicized studies published, incidentally, by media organizations who would stand to gain from increased spending, claimed to demonstrate that companies that increased adspend during a recession in the industry (defined as when one-year sales growth falls below the previous four years' sales growth by 5% or more) were able to increase their market share.[4] These studies were flawed in that they were *cross-sectional* rather than examining results within companies over time. As Broadbent has pointed out, there are many other differences between brands and their marketing programs during recessions, not just differences in adspend.[5] Not only that but what was not given emphasis in the reports were two important qualifications: the fact that the adspend increases were massive (20% to 50%) for relatively small market share gains (0.9% to 1.5%) and the fact that the market share gains were not *profitable*. Regarding profit, big spenders lost as much as everyone else in the 1982 industrial market study and in the 1990 consumer market study big spenders experienced –27% ROI, compared with only –1.6% for those companies that reduced their advertising.

A recent *longitudinal* study (which is the appropriate methodology) covering 2,622 U.S. companies over almost 30 years (1972 to 2000) and using, as the dependent variable, earnings in the current year and several years into the future, produced much more definitive findings. The study found that there *is* a *small* beneficial effect on earnings for *consumer product (FMCG and durables) companies* that increase their adspend during recessionary periods. However, no advantage was shown for *industrial companies* and *services companies* that did so.[6] An important additional finding is that companies' increased earnings due to increased advertising during recessions was of exactly the same magnitude as increased earnings due to increased advertising during *normal* periods (in short, advertising works, regardless of when the money is spent and there is no unusual extra profit to be made in recessions). Most reassuring, finally, is the finding that if a company *does* reduce its adspend for one or two years while the recession lasts, it can bounce back quickly to its normal sales level by increasing its adspend to the normal level afterwards.[7]

Adspend set and a competitor attacks

Once a company has set its Total Adspend for the year, should it worry that the amount might be inadequate in the event of a large adspend attack by a competing company? Surprisingly, the evidence suggests that it should *not* worry. In a study of typical consumer product brands (and there have been several studies with similar results for industrial products), when attacked brands did nothing, only 10% of them lost any sales over the next year as a result.[8] These odds can be generalized to total adspend for the year: should a competitor attack after the budget is set, the odds are 90% in favor of doing nothing. Of course, if you are one of the unlucky 10%, you could always increase your total adspend slightly after the start of the year if it becomes apparent that your sales are suffering.

CAMPAIGN BUDGET-SETTING

The brand manager has to set and justify the budget for a specific Brand-Item Campaign (and for a Brand Campaign if a "branding" exercise is the objective). The most important consideration for the campaign budget is that it be *adequate to meet the Sales Goal*. The Sales Goal is typically handed down by upper management and if the budget that the brand manager sets is too small, then that goal cannot be met. This is logical, but managers at both levels seem to neglect this logic, with disappointment all round. The main reason for this is that proper budget-setting is difficult: it requires the Task Method, which involves a lot of thinking and judgment. We illustrate the Task Method next.

The task method

At the campaign level, the Task Method of budget-setting should be used. The Task Method is used by the majority of leading companies. The Task Method is based on the fact that the marcoms campaign has to accomplish three main tasks, in this sequence: Exposed → Aware → Action. "Exposed" is a media task and it means *exposed at MEF*. "Aware" is shorthand for the individual prospective customer's attainment of *all* the communication objectives of the campaign. It is a task that depends both on media plan effectiveness and creative effectiveness. "Action", the final task, can be pre-purchase, purchase, or post-purchase or some other behavioral action and it might be separated as trial and repeat if multiple purchases or behaviors are required from each prospective customer. The main judgment to be made in the Task Method is the *Conversion Ratio from Aware to Action*.

In the case of multiple media for a campaign, the Task Method becomes the Task Matrix Method. In the **task matrix method**, the manager has to estimate the Aware-to-Action conversion ratio for *each* media type and, to complicate this further, the various *overlaps* of the target audience from one media type to another. For instance, the Awareness (more precisely, Brand Awareness plus Brand Preference) generated by advertising is much less likely to convert a prospect to purchase than is Awareness generated by a free sample or product demonstration. If the respective conversion ratios for the media types are not known from historical data or from test marketing of the present product or service, they must be estimated. Usually, there are some closely applicable norms available to assist with these estimates. Ah, but then you must also estimate the c.r. for those who received both!

In the Task Method (and the Task Matrix Method) the three marcoms tasks are nested between three other steps. These are steps in the sequence of setting the budget rather than tasks to be achieved. The whole sequence is as follows:

Adspend → Insertions → Exposed → Aware → Action → Sales Goal

In applying the Task Method to estimate the required Adspend, the manager works *backwards* through the sequence, thus:

Sales Goal → Action → Aware → Exposed → Insertions → Adspend

By starting with the Sales Goal and working logically back along the sequence to the Adspend, the manager ensures that the adspend *will be big enough* to deliver the necessary sales (to the best of the manager's ability to estimate accurately). If upper management has pre-decided the adspend and the manager's estimate is that the adspend *won't* be big enough to do the job, then the manager should request (a) a budget increase to the necessary level or (b) a commensurate downward revision of the sales goal. If (a) or (b) is not granted, the manager should preserve his or her integrity by finding another job that has more intelligent upper management rather than doing what many managers do, which is to fire the ad agency at the end of the year for not meeting the sales goal, a sales goal that is an impossibility with the adspend granted unless by chance or skill the creative turns out to be spectacularly successful! Be warned, and you can cite this book in support.

The managers must understand what to do when the forecast level of sales includes a mix of *Trial* purchasers, many of whom will not repeat, and *Repeat* purchasers. The answer depends on the primary customer target, as follows.

New-trier target

If a new product is being launched *or* if the target market includes new triers of the brand, then the Task Method should be estimated entirely on *trial purchase* numbers: Aware → Trial. The advertising (or other marcoms) aimed at triers will also be seen by repeat purchasers, so that the advertising frequency rate required to generate trial will be sufficient, indeed more than sufficient, to maintain repeat purchase among those who have previously tried the brand. What needs to be estimated is the number of Triers to be added each media-month to meet the Unit *Trial* Goal for the year. A media-month is a four-week period and there are 13 of them in a year (52 weeks is 13 media-months).

Also, for products or services with a purchase cycle longer than one year, trial *is* purchase and thus the Task Method is estimated on the number of *Purchasers*, and the Aware → Trial conversion ratio becomes an Aware → Purchase conversion ratio.

Repeat-purchaser target

On the other hand, for most established brands, the target market is *repeat purchasers* (BLs and FBSs) and so the Task Method in these cases should go straight from awareness to repeat purchase: Aware → Repeat. There are, after all, no new triers being actively sought although some customers will try the brand for the first time almost incidentally. The advertising *frequency rate* in the media plan, per media-month, then becomes sufficient to maintain Repeat Purchase at the targeted rate of sales. What needs to be estimated is the number of Repeat Purchasers required, at the *incremental* repeat-purchase rate, to meet the Unit Sales Goal for the year.

Steps in the task method

The Task Method proceeds *backwards* through the sequence of steps, as follows:

1. Begin by selecting the Sales Goal (in units) for media-month one.

2. Break down (estimate) the sales goal into the number of Purchasers required for a long-purchase-cycle product or, for a shorter-purchase-cycle product, into the number of Triers required. Then, if some of those triers are likely to repeat during the month, estimate the number of Repeaters (from the Trial → Repeat ratio) and how often, on average, they will repeat that month, because repeat purchases will also contribute to the sales goal. For an established product with a short purchase cycle and a target audience of current buyers of the brand-item so that sales are due totally to Repeat Purchasers, estimate the number of them required based on their average repeat rate within the month (this will be a rate of less than one if the category purchase cycle is longer than four weeks).

3. Continue the breakdown into purchasers or triers and repeaters for each of the 12 remaining media-months of the year. Allow for possible lag of sales several months beyond the campaign's actual ad cycles, which can be due to the persistence of the communication effects or to delayed reading of magazine ads if magazines are in the plan.

4. Focusing on the monthly numbers of purchasers or triers (for a trial-purchaser primary target) or just on the monthly number of repeaters (for a repeat-purchaser primary target), estimate the number of target customers who need to be made *Aware* of the brand-item during each media-month. Aware individuals have a purchase disposition of 100% (communication objectives

fully topped up) but this doesn't mean that all of them can or will purchase. You will need to estimate another conversion ratio: either Aware → Purchase; Aware → Trial; or Aware → Repeat, as appropriate. If your company does not know these ratios, some help from normative figures is given shortly.

5. Estimate the number of people in the media target who will need to be Effectively Reached (reached at the MEF/c) in each ad cycle to deliver the required number of Aware target customers during each of the 13 media-months.

6. Using a media model, preferably *Media Mania's* Canonical Model or, for a schedule with six or fewer vehicles, the Log-Linear Model, calculate the number of ad Insertions (in the media vehicles) in each ad cycle that will generate each ad cycle's Effective Reach number.

7. Cost out the ad Insertions for all ad cycles. Add the cost of the Creative and any additional cost for Research. The total is your campaign budget.

Several different worked examples of the Task Method are provided below. We have deliberately included one example in which the campaign budget *won't* be adequate to meet the Sales Goal, so as to illustrate the point made earlier about management's neglect of proper budget-setting. Also, we short-handed the descriptions considerably to save space. See if you can follow our reasoning.

Example of task method budget: shifting reach pattern

Product: LG refrigerators with PC screen and modem to be sold in the U.S. regional market of Westchester County, New York. Sales goal = 50 units every 4 weeks for 1 year = 650 units. This means that you will require 50 purchasers per media-month, assuming people come into the market at random times throughout the year so that the sales rate is constant each month. Estimate the Aware → Purchase conversion ratio to be .08 if you have no better data (see Chapter 1, average elasticity for durables advertising). Therefore you need $50 \div .08$ = 625 awares every 4 weeks. These should be *different* awares each month (the Shifting Reach pattern). Using one-page black and white newspaper ads, with MEF/c = 3 per 4 weeks, divided by .43 for ad attention = 7 exposures per 4 weeks (to minimize competition interference of brand recall it would be best to concentrate the insertions, which will be more than 7 if 7+ exposures, or OTSs, are required, over a *2-week cycle* each media-month). Place the insertions in local newspapers. Shift reach by using different-area newspapers for each of the ad cycles (Greenwich, Hartford, Mamaroneck, Great Neck, White Plains, Rye and other upmarket population centers). Say that the media model optimization solution requires 15 insertions to result in enough prospects reached at 7+ (ER7+) to generate 625 awares, and that the average cost per ad placement is $500. This is $15 \times \$500 = \$7,500$ per 4 weeks (or per 2 weeks of every 4 weeks if the placements are concentrated as recommended), or $97,500 for the 13-month year. Add research and creative at, say, $20,000. Total budget = $117,500. The expected cost per sale is $\$117,500 \div 650 = \$181$, so LG's profit per unit sold to the *retailer* has to exceed this for it to be profitable for LG to advertise. A profit margin of 25% on a $2,000 unit, that is, $500, would be fairly usual, and the advertising would thereby return $500 − $181 = $319 profit per unit to LG after the advertising is paid for.

Example of task method budget: wedge pattern

Product: Birds Eye Omega-3 Fish Fillets (new product) in the Australian market of 6 million households. Sales goal = 40% penetration × 6 purchases per year = 14.4 million units per year. Estimate the Trial → Repeat ratio to be .40 (the company would have more precise norms in fact). So you need 4.8 million triers. Then 1.92 million of them will buy 5 more times in the year. This totals 14.4 million units. Assume a trial curve with decelerating growth for this new FMCG product. Allocate the adspend over bi-months. This gives trial goals of 1.7, 1.1, .8, .5, .4, and .3 million triers per bi-month. Estimate the Aware → Trial conversion ratio to be .20 (again the company would have norms in fact) which means generating 1.7 million ÷ .20 = 8.5 million awares in the first bi-month, 1.1 million ÷ .20 = 5.5 million awares in the second bi-month, and so forth, noting that these are the *same people* each time (the Wedge pattern has individual continuity). The 8.5 million awares exceeds the number of households in Australia (about 6 million), and thus grocery buyers, so the sales goal on this basis *cannot* be achieved. Re-think each step and try again, or get the sales goal revised drastically down.

Example of task method budget: impact schedule pattern

Product: Shell petrol (gasoline) purchased at service stations in The Netherlands market of 12 million drivers. Purchase cycle = 2 weeks. Sales goal = 25% market share = 3 million drivers, all repeaters. Estimate the Aware → Repeat ratio to be .60. This means a target of 5 million awares who are FBSs for Shell.

MEF/c = 3 exposures per day (impact schedule). Use 30-second TV ads so ad-unit adjusted MEF/c is 3 ÷ .65 = 5 per day. Reach target individuals 1 day per media-month, that is, every second purchase cycle on average, though remembering that the Impact Schedule's MEF should last for about 28 days. Using the media model, estimate an effective reach, ER, of 80% of FBSs per media-month, requiring 30 insertions of the TV ad per media-month. Cost per insertion on prime-time TV = €10,000 per insertion = €300,000 per media-month for 13 media-months = €3.9 million. No research. Creative cost €0.8 million for three TV commercials. Total budget = €4.7 million for the year. At least 80% of the target 3 million drivers would be effectively reached each media-month = 2.4 million FBSs per media-month. Calculate (before approving the budget!) the expected incremental profit from their switch-in purchases of petrol (say 1.2 million × €20.00 per media-month) = €24 million, so the campaign is expected to produce €24 million minus €4.7 million = €19.3 million profit.

Schroer's method

The manager of an *established brand-item* distributed in *multiple regions* – that is, most managers most of the time – should consider the budgeting procedure proposed by Schroer, a strategist with the consulting firm of Booz, Allen & Hamilton.[9] **Schroer's method** has a good deal of logic behind it and is also consistent with empirical evidence on the difficulty of achieving large sales or market share gains in established, mature product categories. If your brand-item's market share is identical across regions and you want to keep it that way, you should use the Task Method nationally. However, most companies know or can easily find out that equal market shares of a brand-item across regions is hardly ever the case. A recent survey by Bronnenberg, Dhar, and Dubé found that market shares for nationally distributed brand-items in fact varied more across regional markets than they did *within* regional markets over time! Two explanations for this are regional differences in advertising concentration for brand-items (TV and radio ads are often bought on a "spot," or local market, basis; virtually all newspapers are local to particular cities; and magazines also produce many local editions) and the now-usual practice of retailers setting the brand-item's *price* locally.[10] Bronnenberg *et al.*'s study confirms, as did Schroer's study earlier, that it is more profitable for companies to lead in selected markets and accept lower market share in the others than it is to attempt to compete to attain parity shares in all markets.[11] In what averages out to the economist's notion of equilibrium, most companies will tolerate a competitor's dominance in one market if they are allowed to be dominant in another market. Also, pertinent to Schroer's Method, retaliation following an attack is surprisingly infrequent.[12]

Procedure

Schroer's Method assumes that the product category has reached maturity in the product category life cycle – that is, primary demand cannot be increased and therefore *a market share increase* (presuming this increases profit) is the objective. His procedure is as follows:

1. Budgets should not be set nationally but rather locally, *market by market*. ("Locally" normally means geographically; for instance, Campbell Soup Company reportedly divides the U.S. market into 22 "strategic" geographic regions. However, the market-by-market divisions could be applied to different *end-use* markets or *demographic* market segments – *if* the media plan can reach them separately.

2. The two aspects to examine in each local market are: (a) the *largest competitor's* share of total advertising spending in the category (SOV) in relation to the largest competitor's, LC's, market share (SOM); and (b) *our brand-item's* market share (SOM) in that local market and, specifically, whether we are *the leader* or a *follower* in the market.

3. If the largest competitor's SOV is *below* its SOM, this signals an opportunity for our brand to *attack*. (Of course, we may *be* the largest-share brand and would therefore wish to maintain our market share; see Table 13.2.) If our brand is going to successfully attack the largest competitor (LC), then we must be prepared to make a *large increase* in spending (large in that local market) and be prepared to sustain the expenditure increase over the year (13 media-months). The required expenditure increase is estimated to be equal to 20 to 30 *percentage points* of share of voice *above* the LC's spending, which usually means approximately double the LC's adspend in that market.

4. In other markets where the LC's SOV is *equal* to its SOM, for our brand-item we adopt a *defensive* strategy, which requires *matching* the LC's expenditure; if the LC's SOV is *greater* than its SOM, we retreat, that is, we *reduce* our expenditure to *zero* in that market.

TABLE 13.2 *Schroer's method of regional (local market) budget-setting.*

	LARGEST COMPETITOR (LC) IN LOCAL MARKET	
OUR BRAND'S SOM IN LOCAL MARKET	LOW SOV/SOM (BELOW 1.0)	HIGH SOV/SOM (1.0 OR HIGHER)
Follower	*Attack* – with a large SOV premium, approximately twice that of the LC, and sustain it for a year or more	*Retreat* – reduce spending to zero
Leader	*Maintain* – set our SOV/SOM at 1.0	*Defend* – increase spending to match that of the LC

Local market adspends

The spending strategies for each local market are summarized in the table. The *local market focus* is the key to the success of this budgeting approach. As Schroer points out, few market leaders would be willing to allow another brand to outspend them by double on a *national* basis. However, when expenditures and market shares are analyzed on a *local* basis, plenty of opportunities for attack exist. And, even if the largest competitor is astute enough and quick enough to pick up the pattern, the chances of retaliation are surprisingly low. Schroer gives a number of case histories of this budgeting approach being used with great success. We believe this procedure deserves close examination by the manager of an established, multi-regional brand. (However, because of the likely crucial consequence if a large competitor retaliates, it is *not* appropriate for a *single-region local advertiser*. Such an advertiser should use the Task Method for budget-setting.)

SUMMARY

The manager first has to set a gross budget for total marcoms for the year – the Total Marcoms Allocation. We recommend doing this by forecasting total sales revenue expected for the forthcoming year and then applying an advertising-to-sales ratio modeled on that of a company in the industry that the manager wishes to emulate (for market leaders, this could be their own company). More precisely, if a change, either up or down, from last year's sales is expected, the relevant advertising elasticity coefficient from Chapter 1 can be applied to adjust the A/S ratio-derived amount based on last year's sales to derive the anticipated amount needed to produce the *forthcoming* year's sales. Whereas the ideal method of setting Total Adspend would be to add up the estimated budgets from the respective campaigns that are planned, this is unrealistic because the details of those plans are rarely known at the beginning of the year.

A budget for each separate marcoms campaign then has to be estimated and justified. The Task Method is best for this (for multi-media campaigns, there is also the Task Matrix Method, which we did not attempt to illustrate in the chapter but rather assumed that the advertiser would be using one primary medium and can roughly add the cost of any secondary media to this). The Task Method is very demanding because it requires the estimation of a conversion ratio from Aware to Action, which may be Aware-to-Purchase, Aware-to-Trial, or Aware-to-Repeat, as well as in the latter case a breakdown of total sales into trial-only sales and repeat purchases by previous triers. The Task Method must be used for every new budget-setting requirement. This is to prevent the common problem of setting a campaign's budget by some other means with the result that the manager has no idea whether it is inadequate (the usual problem) or wastefully overadequate (an occasional problem) to meet the Sales Goal. An A/S ratio applied at the campaign level is much too blunt to produce an accurate estimate because the advertising funds can be spent in many different ways. The expenditure has to be followed through in a sequence of steps culminating in expected sales.

For Established, Multi-Regional brand-items, which constitute a large majority of what marketing managers manage, Schroer's Method of local budget allocation is recommended. Instead of setting a single budget nationwide, the adspend is varied in each local market depending on the brand-item's relative market share against the leading competitor in that market. Attacking, maintaining, defending, and retreating policies are followed on a local market basis.

DISCUSSION QUESTIONS

13.1 Imagine you are a new entrant in the soft drinks industry. You need to set a Total Marcoms Allocation for Germany. Do so, explaining your reasoning.

13.2 Imagine you are a new entrant in the consumer electronics industry. You need to set a Total Adspend for Japan. Do so, explaining your reasoning.

13.3 Set and justify an Advertising Campaign Budget for a brand of air conditioners for residential apartments in Hong Kong. Use a Web search or the library to find some realistic population and sales figures.

13.4 Set and justify a Multi-Media Advertising Campaign Budget for Schweppes Lemonade in England (although unrealistic, assume that there are no regional variations in the brand-item's market share, so you can use the Task Matrix Method). Use a Web search or the library to find some realistic population and sales figures.

13.5 Set and justify an Advertising Campaign Budget for a law firm specializing in domestic disputes, Jones Family Lawyers, in your home town. Use a Web search or the library to find some realistic population and sales figures.

13.6 You are the manager of Canon copiers and your largest competitor is Xerox copiers. Set out below are Xerox's SOV in four key regions as well as Xerox's SOM and Canon's SOM. Set your (Canon's) SOV in each region using Schroer's Method, explaining your reasoning.

	Region A	Region B	Region C	Region D
Xerox SOV	20	10	25	15
Xerox SOM	20	30	10	15
Canon SOM	15	20	20	20

13.7 Which campaign budgeting method should you use if you are a small, local copier manufacturer distributing only in Region A above? You won't be able to give exact figures but outline the procedure you would use to set the budget.

NOTES

1. Ad Age Leading National Advertisers Report, *Advertising Age*, Website, accessed June 26, 2003. At the time of access, 2001 was the most recent complete year for which these data were available and we could make the point with *any* year's A/S ratio data.

2. Advertisers ranked 101 to 200, *Advertising Age*, Website, accessed June 27, 2003.

3. J.S. Armstrong, V.G. Morwitz, and V. Kumar, Sales forecasts for existing products and services: do purchase intentions contribute to accuracy?, *International Journal of Forecasting*, 2000, 16(3), pp. 383–397.

4. The studies are by Cahners/SPI, *Media Advertising When Our Market is in a Recession*, Cambridge, MA: Cahners Publishing Co., January 1982, in which the PIMS database of industrial products and services was examined, and A. Biel and S. King, *Options and Opportunities for Consumer Business: Advertising During a Recession*, New York: The WPP Center for Research and Development, October 1990, which also examined the PIMS database, but this time for consumer products.

5. S. Broadbent, Tough times, *Admap*, 1999, April.

6. K.D. Frankenberger and R.C. Graham, Should firms increase, decrease or maintain advertising expenditures during recessions?, working paper, Cambridge, MA: Marketing Science Institute, April 2003.

7. K.D. Frankenberger and R.C. Graham, same reference as note 6.

8. J-B.E.M. Steenkamp, V.R. Nijs, D.M. Hanssens, and M.G. Dekimpe, Competitive reactions to advertising and promotion attacks, working paper, Cambridge, MA: Marketing Science Institute, May 2003. At the recent (June 2004) Marketing Metrics Conference at London Business School, D.M. Hanssens also provided large-scale evidence that any sales decrease due to one brand's aggressive marketing mix change is usually distributed over several competitors such that none is particularly damaged. The industrial product studies include W.T. Robinson, Marketing mix reactions to entry, *Marketing Science*, 1988, 7(4), pp. 368–385, and H. Gatignon, E. Anderson, and K. Helson, Competitive reactions to market entry: explaining interfirm differences, *Journal of Marketing Research*, 1989, 26(1), pp. 44–55.

9. J.C. Schroer, Ad spending: growing market share, *Harvard Business Review*, 1990, 68(1), pp. 44–48.

10. B.J. Bronnenberg, S. Dhar, and J-P. Dubé, Spatial asymmetries in market shares of brands of packaged goods, paper presented at the Marketing Science Conference, 2003.

11. D. Soberman, Questioning conventional wisdom about competition in differentiated markets, paper presented at the Marketing Science Conference, 2003.

12. B.J. Bronnenberg, Multi-market competition in packaged goods: sustaining large local market advantages with little product differentiation, paper presented at the Marketing Science Conference, 2003.

CHAPTER 14

Campaign tracking

To make sure that the marcoms campaign is working and also to manage the campaign, the campaign must be tracked – that is, monitored by research. The least expensive but least accurate method of tracking is Aggregate Tracking, which uses secondary data on marcoms expenditure over time and sales over time. However, to find out *how* the campaign is working and to manage the campaign while it is working requires a Customer Tracking Survey, using either the *Panel* method, the *Wave* method, or the best method, which is *Continuous Tracking*. These tracking methods are described in this chapter, together with how to *manage* tracking research, of the customer survey type, and to detect and prevent Advertising Wearout.

The majority of campaigns are *not* tracked formally; instead, the manager observes the brand's sales trend before and during the campaign and then *infers* that the marcoms have produced the sales result – up or down.[1] As we saw in Chapter 1, about 20% to 30% of marcoms campaigns produce a large sales increase, but, at the other end of the scale, about 30% of marcoms campaigns are so weak that the brand-item loses sales! Advertisers who do not track their campaigns may have a nasty shock awaiting them – too late to take corrective action.

CUSTOMER TRACKING SURVEY

Large-budget advertisers conduct a **customer tracking survey** even when all signs in the market-place imply that the marcoms program *is* meeting its Sales Goal. The manager wants to be sure that the advertising, and promotions, if used, are *causally contributing to sales*. Remember, sales changes could be caused by changes in distribution, price, or personal selling in the marketing mix, or in competitors' marketing mixes, by competitors' actions rather than our own, or by changes in economic demand industry-wide.

A Customer Tracking Survey, or CTS, is expensive. First of all, the manager will need to conduct a *pre-campaign survey* to obtain a "benchmark" reading of advertising, other marcoms, and brand effects (covering our brand and competing brands). Then one or more "waves" of surveys will be needed *during the campaign* to compare evolving effects against the benchmark and thus "track" the campaign's progress. Each survey wave could cost $20,000 or more, depending on sample size, the length of the survey questionnaire, and the incidence of eligible survey respondents.

MEASURES USED IN TRACKING

The Customer Tracking Survey (CTS) uses measures of all six steps of the marcoms effects sequence: (1) Exposure, (2) Ad Processing, (3) Brand Communication Effects, (4) Target Audience Action, (5) Sales or Market Share, and (6) Brand Equity. This effects sequence cuts across levels from Exposure (which the advertiser does), to the Ad Processing polyarchy and Brand Communication Effects, to Customer Decision Stages (all of which the customer does). See Chapter 1.

Aggregate tracking (AT) omits the intermediate steps: it employs only measures of step (1) Exposure and step (5) Sales or Market Share, although if relative prices are tracked it can measure step (6) Brand Equity as well.

Exposure measures

Exposure is a *media measure* – specifically, a *rate of media input* which can then be related to the brand's Sales rate, or, in the Customer Tracking Survey, to the intermediate steps of the effects sequence. The rate of media input can be measured in various ways, ranging from gross measures such as advertising dollars ($) or gross rating points (GRPs), to measures that more closely approximate exposure itself, such as reach at minimum effective frequency (Effective Reach). Note that Effective Reach (per advertising cycle) was the input measure in the campaign examples in the previous chapter.

The media input measure is expressed as a rate for a particular time period. The time period can be weekly or monthly – depending on the corresponding rate at which the manager wants to measure (or has available) changes in sales or any other intermediate effect. Usually, the time period is four-weekly, and the media input measure is converted to a four-weekly rate.

Advertising dollars
The *rate of expenditure on advertising* – Adspend – is what most concerns senior management. The *expenditure* rate (in dollars or the relevant currency) in relation to the rate of *sales* growth or decline (in units *and* in monetary value) provides the overall input-output evaluation in *Aggregate Tracking*.

Gross rating points (GRPs)
The rate of **GRPs** *per time period* also provides a measure of Exposure. Total GRPs per week or month can be found by adding the *audience* figures (percentages reached) for all vehicles in which the ad was placed in the time period. GRPs take no account of how many exposures an

individual receives and are simply a count of the (often repeated) exposures that are "out there" to be attended to, and for this reason of its "grossness" we do not recommend using GRPs (see the beginning of Chapter 11). Nevertheless GRP rate can be related to dollar-expenditure rate to see whether the advertising money is being spent *efficiently* (GRPs per dollar, over time periods). A high ratio means an efficient media buy; a low ratio means that you're paying more than usual for each exposure. Efficiency, however, indicates nothing about the *effectiveness* of media spending and is a further reason for not using GRPs.

Reach at minimum effective frequency (effective reach)

The incidence of *target audience* reach at minimum effective frequency calculated over *sales* time periods (usually four weeks), called Effective Reach, or ER, is the most precise measure of Exposure. ER can be obtained from the (achieved) media schedule and correlated to the sales rate.

If the *number* of target audience individuals effectively reached in the period doesn't relate to the sales rate in that period, then there's likely to be something wrong – not with the media plan but with either the positioning strategy or with its creative execution (either of which signals a major problem). The Customer Tracking Survey, since it traces the effects sequence, can usually isolate the location of the problem, as we will see with the remaining measures. Aggregate Tracking cannot identify the problem but merely can signal that there *is* a problem.

Ad processing measures

Ad Processing, as we explained in Chapter 2, consists of the individual's *immediate* responses to the ad (Attention, Learning, Emotional responses and, if it is a High-Involvement product choice, Acceptance). The "ad" could equally well be a promotion or a sponsorship or some other marcoms event, but we will focus on ads here. Ad Processing cannot be measured directly in a tracking survey because interviewers obviously can't be present when every *exposure* occurs. Instead, Processing is measured *indirectly* by a delayed self-report of *Attention* to the ad. Attention assumes at least partial *processing* of the ad, because the respondent has to have *learned* in order to remember the ad when the interviewer calls. The most frequently employed attention measures are Ad Recognition (AR and MAR), Brand-Prompted Ad Recall (BPAR), and Category-Prompted Ad Recall (CPAR). We will now define each of these measures and explain its purpose.

Ad recognition

There are two ways to measure ad recognition: *branded* ad recognition (called Ad Recognition) and ad recognition with brand identifiers *removed* from the ad (called Masked Ad Recognition). Usable with either of these is an additional measure, Ad Recognition Frequency.

> **Ad recognition (AR)** Tracking study respondents are shown – or for radio, played – the ads from the campaign and asked whether they have seen or heard them before. Answer categories are "Yes," "Not sure," and "No." Only the "Yes" answers count as signifying Ad Recognition.

The memory cue or stimulus (the "prompt") is the *ad* itself and the response required is ad (*not* brand) recognition.

Masked ad recognition (MAR) In the "masked" recognition measure, the ad is shown or played with the pack, logo or brand name blanked out and then respondents are asked to name the brand (the brand-item). Technically, Masked Ad Recognition requires the respondent to *recall* the brand, so it is somewhat of a misnomer. Masked Ad Recognition offers an additional diagnostic advantage over Ad Recognition in that it measures the extent to which respondents can remember the ad but not which brand it was advertising (an all-too-common occurrence). If there is a problem with *actual* Brand Recognition or Brand Recall (see later measures), Masked Ad Recognition may show the problem to reside in the execution of the ad.

Ad recognition frequency (ARF) Those respondents who recognize the ad are then asked about Ad Recognition Frequency: how many times they have seen, read, or heard the ad, usually asked with reference to a given time period, usually the last four weeks if the tracking results are being analyzed on that basis. This *claimed* exposure frequency provides a check on the achieved Effective Reach level in the media plan. The claimed reach, R1+, per time period is called Mental Reach.[2] If you know that the media *vehicle* reached the percentage of people specified in the *media* plan, yet the percentage who recognize the ad on the *survey* is lower than this, then the problem is most likely with the creative execution – specifically, with its *ability to gain attention in actual media environments*. If your campaign has a Mental Reach problem and you are confident that it's had sufficient frequency of exposure, the first corrective action should be to compare the ad with the recommended Attention Tactics in Chapter 9 and fix it!

Brand-prompted ad recall (BPAR)

Brand-prompted ad recall (BPAR) demonstrates that an ad has been linked to the brand correctly during in-media processing. The memory cue or stimulus (the prompt) is the *brand* and the response is the ad. Recall of the ad's *content* is necessary to prove that it was indeed the right ad. However, managers should note that the widely used Millward Brown measure of Advertising Awareness, which is the basis for the ad's Awareness Index in Millward Brown's tracking service, uses only *claimed* recall – stage 1 below. That is, if people *think* they've seen or heard an ad for the brand, this, in Millward Brown's experience, is just as effective as having actually been exposed.

The BPAR measure is a two-stage measure:[3]

1.   Show a list of brands (if Brand Recall is the objective) or pictures of brands (if Brand Recognition is the objective). Then ask: "Which of these brands have you seen or heard advertised recently?"

2.   For each brand named, say: "Please describe the advertisement or advertisements for this brand in as much detail as you can remember and, in particular, what the advertisement showed or said about the brand." Probe thoroughly. Say: "Tell me more about the advertisement. What else did it show or say?"

Scoring (coding) for this measure is as follows: For *Claimed BPAR*, nomination of the brand as having advertised (stage 1 answer only) is all that counts. For *Proven BPAR*, the respondent (in the stage 2 answer) has to describe the advertisement, recalled for the brand, in sufficient detail to satisfy the coder that the advertisement was indeed seen or heard or read, and that the respondent is not guessing or describing some other brand's advertisement – hence the need for thorough probing during the second-stage answer. Classify the recalled content of the advertisement or advertisements into categories corresponding to the brand's emotions and benefits to infer what emotions and beliefs the advertising caused.

Category-prompted ad recall (CPAR)

Whereas Ad Recognition is proof that people attended to the ad (ad-prompted) and *Proven* Brand-Prompted Ad Recall is proof that people processed the ad in relation to the brand (brand-prompted), the third measure, **category-prompted ad recall (CPAR)**, is the toughest test of the ad's ability to gain attention in media (to "cut through the clutter" of other ads) and be processed by the target audience. MarketMind, a tracking service offered by Taylor Nelson Sofres, specializes in the CPAR measure of advertising awareness (but, of course, anyone can use it, just as they can use BPAR).

The Category-Prompted Ad Recall (CPAR) measure doesn't ask people what advertising they remember in general because that question would be too vague. Instead, the recall task is directed by giving them the *product category* as the cue or prompt (e.g., "fast-food restaurants"), and asking them what ads they remember for *that category* of product or service. Then they are asked what *brand* was being advertised, if the brand was not mentioned spontaneously in their description of the recalled ad.

CPAR should be measured for *each medium separately* (e.g., first for TV advertising, then for magazine advertising). This is to further direct the recall task and to curb the tendency for people to think that the question refers only to TV, as may happen if the question were to use the general term "advertising." Separate questions are needed for each advertising medium of interest.

The responses are then coded for adequate description of the advertisement's content and scored for correct or incorrect association of the brand with the advertisement. Branded CPAR is what is wanted; a high incidence of recall of the ad but not the brand (Unbranded CPAR minus Branded CPAR) indicates Processing failure.

The relationships between the various measures of Ad Processing are shown in Figure 14.1. They have different diagnostic strengths and are *not* substitutes.[4] Also shown are the links necessary for *Brand* Communication Effects. Brand Communication Effects must not be confused with Ad Processing; rather, these effects should be the *results* of processing of the ad or ads (given effective frequency).

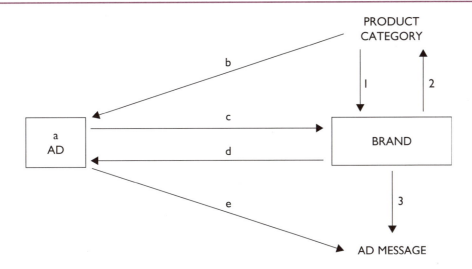

FIGURE 14.1 *Linkages between the ad, product category, brand, and ad message. This diagram shows the locations and directionality of ad processing measures (letters) and brand communication effects (numbers).*

KEY

a   Ad recognition
b   Category-prompted ad recall (unbranded)
c   Category-prompted ad recall (branded) following b
d   Brand-prompted ad recall (claimed)
e   Brand-prompted ad recall (proven) following d

1   Brand recall
2   Brand recognition
3   Brand emotions and benefit beliefs induced by the ad (for brand preference)

Brand communication effects measures

The Brand Communication Effects measures in the CTS research should be *exactly* the same as those measures used in the *Ad Pre-Testing* research. These measures were presented in detail in Chapter 6, referred to in Chapter 10 in conjunction with the CRAT method of pre-testing, and are recapped later in the present chapter, in the IBM PC tracking example.

However, there is an important change in the *order* of the measures. Brand awareness – Brand Recall or Brand Recognition, and in this order if both – in the customer tracking survey is measured *first*, though *preceded* by *category* communication effects if Category Need is an objective. Unlike in pre-testing, there is no need for a delayed measure of brand awareness due to recent exposure to the ad. The ad or ads have had plenty of time to operate and so Brand Recognition or Brand Recall must emerge first (before Brand Preference) if purchase is to occur.

Target audience action measures

Target Audience Action, at the individual customer level, is the next measure in the CTS. It measures the final step in the customer response sequence of Exposure → Ad Processing → Brand Communication Effects → Target Audience Action.

The Target Audience Action measure is a self-report of brand-items bought in the survey period, or of pre-purchase or post-purchase behavior, or of another Action that is the behavioral objective in a social marketing campaign. In place of self-reports, FMCG marketers sometimes use scanner-recorded purchases from households, captured in-store at checkout or after arriving home, via a barcode "wand" and a modem.

The customer tracking survey sample

Think about what should happen during the campaign. If the campaign is successful, the *current buyer* individuals in the target audiences of Brand Loyals (BLs) and Favorable Brand Switchers (particularly Routinized FBSs) should stay as the "inner" audience. However, individuals who were in the "outer" target audiences of NCUs, OBLs, OBSs (and perhaps Experimental FBSs) prior to the campaign should *move out of those audiences* and into the "inner" audience. For example, new category users, if a target, should *become category users*, not stay as NCUs. In fact, we want NCUs to become FBSs, or better still, BLs, for our brand.

This means that one index of the campaign's performance is *the changing incidence of prospect group membership itself*.[5] For example, in a campaign aimed at new category users, the percentage of consumers who are NCUs should get *smaller*. At the other end of the target audience spectrum, the percentage of consumers who are BLs should *not* get smaller. An analysis of tracking data by target audience subgroups – see Table 5.1 in Chapter 5 – *could* show changes in size for all 13 subgroups. To measure changes in group size, we need a *random sample of the total potential audience* (e.g., all adults for an adult-purchased consumer product, or all firms in the industry for an industrial product).

The Target Audience Action measures – trial, or repeat, percent switching in versus switching out – then must be taken on the *total base*. For example, if we mistakenly sampled *only* NCUs throughout the tracking study, trial would always be zero! Yet the campaign might be very successful because the base of NCUs is itself getting smaller relative to the total base.

A further good reason for tracking changes in target audience status is that the campaign's *MEF/c requirement* in individual continuity reach patterns – the Blitz, Wedge, and Reverse-Wedge/ PI *new product* patterns in particular – (see Chapter 11) depends on it. The manager can gradually reduce MEF/c during the campaign *only if* the tracking proves that individuals are becoming more loyal.

Sales and market share measures

Sales can be estimated by aggregating customer self-reports of purchases or measured directly from retail sales records. Sales – the unit rate of sales over four-weekly time periods – is *always* a vital measure to focus on in tracking.

Market share is percentage relative sales, that is, our brand-item's sales (in units) divided by total sales of the category (in units). Market Share is important mainly during a *new product category introduction*: your brand's sales should be rising faster than those of competitors and this can only be indexed by a *Unit Market Share* increase. Market Share can also be expressed in dollars (or whatever currency applies). Comparison of *dollar* share with *unit* share reflects the relative price of the brand-item in the category. However, relative price should be tracked precisely – it is needed for the Brand Equity measures, next.

Brand equity and profit measures

Brand Equity (here referring to the brand's upside and downside price elasticity) measures were described in Chapter 1. Value Equity is measured by the rate of sales *increase* when the item's price falls below the category average. Uniqueness Equity, which you also want, is measured by the rate of sales *decrease* when the item's price rises *above* the category average – you want the rate of decrease to be low or, ideally, zero.

Profit can be tracked directly by substituting dollar *contribution* for dollar sales revenue, per period, and then subtracting the advertising expenditure per period. However, we emphasize that Brand Equity (both VE and UE) *has primacy* for *campaign management*. The reason is that Brand Equity (high VE and high UE, which are both influenced by advertising) produces *sustained* profit.

The Customer Tracking Survey, it should be remembered, measures inputs and outputs for our brand-item and *also those* of *all major competitors*. You can, of course, monitor *competitors' Brand Equity*. Also, the CTS input measures should include not only advertising but *Sales Promotions*, *Personal Selling* drives, *Sponsorships*, and *PR* – and fluctuations in *Distribution*.[6]

METHODOLOGIES FOR TRACKING SURVEYS

Customer tracking survey methodology

CTS can employ one of three survey methodologies: Panel, Wave, or Continuous. Each has advantages and disadvantages but, as we explain shortly, the *Continuous* survey method – called Continuous Tracking – is the best overall.

Panel method

To diagnose the causality of advertising through every step, the most valid method – in theory – is a *panel* survey. In a **panel survey**, the *same* consumers are interviewed in the benchmark (pre-campaign) wave and in each successive (during-campaign) wave. This allows *causality* to be established at the individual consumer or customer level. Although panels survive in most countries, they are *expensive*. There is also recent evidence that successive interviews can *sensitize* respondents and make them more likely to buy in the product category. Finally, panels typically provide *slow data* and therefore slow management response.

Wave method

Interviewing *separate samples* of consumers or customers each time – a **wave survey** – allows the customer response steps to be related only on an *aggregated* basis. You can relate Exposure (e.g., advertising dollars) to percent Processing, or percent Processing to percent acquiring the Communication Effects, or percent acquiring the Communication Effects to percent taking Action and, finally, Action to Sales. But you can't *causally* conclude that the processing led to communication effects and then to action because you have not tracked the same individual respondents over time. Also, if the survey waves are far apart – say, three months or six months as is typical – the data are *slow* and, again, so is management response.

Continuous method

In the Continuous survey method, called **continuous tracking**, small random samples of consumers or customers are selected for an interview from the potential target audience population on a *daily or weekly* basis.[7] Instead of interviewing, say, 600 respondents nationwide every quarter in a wave survey, the Continuous survey method would interview, say, 50 respondents a week – a new sample of 50 respondents every week – for 12 weeks. These weekly samples of 50 cumulate to 600 a quarter (or actually 650, since there are 13 weeks in a quarter). Thus, instead of four waves of 600 respondents measured at quarterly intervals, you have the same number of interviews spread evenly throughout the year. In Continuous tracking, the small sample size in any one week – which produces imprecise results due to small-sample error – is overcome by plotting the results as a *moving average*. This is called "rolling the data" and is an *unweighted* moving average, that is, each week's data in the window of the roll receive equal value. For instance, a four-week roll would plot the first data point as weeks 1–4, the second point as weeks 2–5, the third point as weeks 3–6 and so forth, yielding data points based on 200 observations each. These observations are not independent, as they overlap many of the same respondents with each roll. Classical statistical analysis therefore cannot be applied to the rolled results but only to the raw data. The raw data can of course be aggregated – not rolled – for analysis over longer periods, such as four weeks or a quarter, but cannot be interpreted for the significance of short-term changes because the week-to-week sample is too small. What you do is *eyeball* the rolled data week by week.

Continuous Tracking has emerged as the method of choice. There is no sensitization of respondents as the continuous method is not a panel. Although Continuous Tracking is essentially a wave survey (a very short-cycle wave survey) rather than a panel, and therefore does *not* allow causality to be inferred at the individual level, it does have the considerable advantage of allowing the manager to "read" causal factors in the market *as they occur*. The causes and effects are *inferred* from *aggregate trends* in the results. Specifically, for instance, if an upward trend in the aggregate level of branded Category-Prompted Ad Recall (CPAR) is followed shortly afterward by an upward trend in the aggregate level Brand Recall (for instance), the manager can infer that the former caused the latter. Although it is possible that the same individuals did not produce the two trends – which is to say, there is no causality – this is presumed unlikely. The causality can be reasonably checked, after the fact, by *cross-tabulating* the current-period state of Ad Processing (yes-no) with the current-period state of Brand Communication Effects (yes-no for *each* of them) and the Action effect (yes-no) for successive steps in the customer response steps (these sequential cross-tabs are called **CHAID analysis**). A large proportion of respondents demonstrating CPAR at time *t and* Brand Recall (for instance) at time *t* would tend to rule out the "different respondents" danger though would not be proof of *sequential* causality as all were interviewed at time *t* (see the turnover Table 14.3 later in this chapter).

Let's briefly look at an example of continuous tracking results (Figure 14.2). The data are from a campaign by Tourism Australia, the government organization that promotes tourism to that country. For privacy reasons, we have not named the country in which the survey was taken and the data are *not* current. The graphs show the rolled results of CPAR, BPAR, and Ad Recognition with percentage results for these measures indexed on the left vertical axis. The bar graphs rising from the bottom axis and indexed on the right vertical axis show the weekly advertising GRPs. You can see (by eyeball analysis) these tracking measures responding to the cycles of ads.

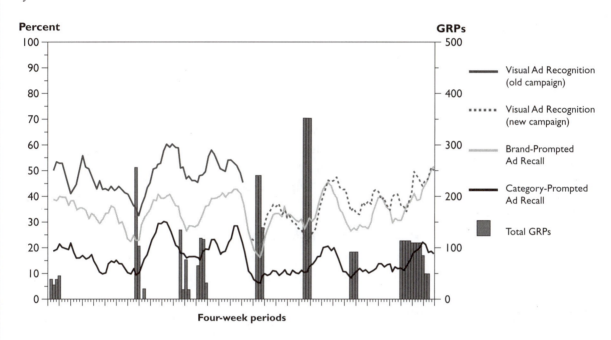

FIGURE 14.2 *Continuous tracking results from a campaign by Tourism Australia. Country of survey and year of survey not identified to protect confidentiality.*

SOURCE: Courtesy of Tourism Australia and MarketMind research company, Australia.

Customer tracking survey interview methods

Tracking studies *should* use **face-to-face interviews** because the interviewers have to show *ads* to respondents to measure ad processing (attention by the Ad Recognition measure). Further, if Brand Recognition is the brand awareness objective, which it is for most FMCG products, the interviewers have to show *pictures of the brand-items* to respondents.

However, Face-to-Face Interviews simply cannot compete with **telephone interviews** for cost in countries such as the U.S.A. and Australia (in contrast with the U.K., most of Europe, and Asia). The sacrifice when using Telephone Interviews is that measures of Ad Recognition (unless it's a *radio ad* campaign) and Brand Recognition, if that's the brand awareness objective, have to be verbally (orally) administered (without visual aids). Bruzzone Research Company in the U.S.A.

gets around this problem by mailing out Storyboard versions of TV ads, but they use a Panel, with guaranteed cooperation. Mailouts would be impractical with Wave or Continuous surveys.

If using Telephone Tracking, the manager should insist that the research company conduct, beforehand, a *small-scale face-to-face pilot study* in which a sample of 30 or so target audience respondents are shown the ads and brands to be surveyed and asked to describe them in their own words. These descriptions are then *summarized* and used in the telephone interviews. It is very important to know that *unpiloted* Verbal Ad Recognition produces much lower scores (37%, on average) than the much more valid Visual Ad Recognition (61%, on average), and the major reason for the lower scores is not doing the pilot study. Worse is that the verbal scores are not *systematically* lower, so you cannot simply transform a verbal score upward to get a visual score! If you don't do the pilot study, you will underestimate Mental Reach, that is, telephone tracking will suggest that the ad is faring a lot worse in attracting attention than it actually is. Do not let your research service tell you otherwise. You must insist on the *piloted* Verbal Ad Recognition measure when using telephone interviewing.

If the target population for the survey overlaps highly – say at least 80% – with the *online* population, then **Web-based interviews** are feasible.[8] On the Web, you *can* show ads, packages and logos. Only some products and services have such a target population but the number of suitable products and services is growing with increased penetration of in-home Internet connections.

Order of measures in the customer tracking survey

The recommended order of measures in the CTS is shown in Table 14.1. Note that the measures of Ad Processing (2, 4 and 10) and Exposure (11) and Action (5) are interspersed with the measures of Brand Communication Effects. This is to prevent *order bias* – that is, answers to early questions affecting or "giving away" answers to later questions.

TABLE 14.1 *Order of measures on the tracking survey.*

1.	Screening questions (to screen in potential and actual category users)
2.	Category need
3.	CPAR
4.	Brand recall
5.	Brand recognition
6.	BPAR
7.	Action
8.	Brand action intention
9.	Brand preference
10.	Brand emotions and brand benefit beliefs
11.	Ad recognition
12.	Target audience classification questions
13.	Direct-matching questions (or separate survey)

The order-of-measures rationale can best be explained with the aid of a *simplified* set of questions for the IBM laptop computer, as follows.

Category Need ("Do you intend to buy a personal computer?") comes first, before any brands are asked about. For the same reason, *Category-Prompted Ad Recall, CPAR* ("What TV ads have you seen recently for laptop computers?" "What magazine ads . . .?"), must be placed early in the sequence, because it stems from a category cue. Respondents are, however, asked to name the brand in the CPAR questions, so it is now appropriate to move to brand questions. There may be some bias, but measuring *Brand Recall and Brand Recognition* before CPAR would totally bias the CPAR results.

Brand Awareness may require Brand Recognition measurement, Brand Recall measurement, or both (if both are objectives of the campaign). If both, then *Brand Recall* ("What brands of laptop computer first come to mind?") should precede *Brand Recognition* ("Which of these brands have you seen before?") as the first is "unaided" whereas the second is "aided" in that the brands are shown to (or named for) the respondent.

Brand-Prompted Ad Recall ("What TV commercials have you seen recently for IBM Laptop Computers?") is measured next. Even if we've measured Brand Recognition and thus "given" the respondent the brands, this causes no bias, because the BPAR measure is based on the brand-as-cue and gives the brands anyway.

Action measures are then taken. Depending on the action objectives, these may be *purchase action* ("Which brand of laptop computer have you bought recently?"), *pre-purchase action* ("Which computer stores or retail outlets that sell computers have you visited recently?"), or *post-purchase action* ("Which brand or brands of laptop computers, if any, have you recommended to a friend or colleague recently?"). Quite logically, *Brand Action Intention*, which is intended action, is the next measure ("If you were going to buy a laptop computer for your own use, how likely would you be to buy an IBM Laptop Computer?").

Brand Preference ("Overall, how would you rank the IBM Laptop Computer for personal use – the single best, one of several best, etc.?") and then brand *Emotions* and *Benefit Beliefs* ("How does the name IBM make you feel?" "How does the IBM Laptop Computer rate on low price, good performance, adequate service support, and so on?") are then measured, with their later order based on the avoidance of having the respondent "compute" a new overall attitude (preference) from considering the questionnaire-provided emotions and benefit beliefs.

Ad Recognition and *Ad Recognition Frequency* ("Have you seen this commercial on TV before?" and if so, "How many times in total?") are placed as the *last* processing measures – of in-media competitive attention – because now we're showing the respondent the ads. To have shown the ads earlier would have biased every following measure.

Target Audience classification questions come next. These include the 13 subgroups classification to identify NNCUs, UNCUs, PNCus, etc., and demographics or corpographics if you want to profile target audiences by these characteristics.

Direct Matching (media) questions are placed last or may be placed in a separate survey with a large (N = 500) potential and actual category user survey together with the Target Audience classification questions taken every six months or at least yearly. An efficient example of a Direct Matching questionnaire used for a study with university students in Australia is given in Table 14.2. In the *Panel survey method*, media exposure can be measured very precisely by having each panelist maintain a *diary* of TV viewing habits, radio listening, readership of newspapers and magazines, Internet use, and so forth; and such questions would not appear on the questionnaire. Without a diary – that is, using Direct Matching questions – only *approximate* frequency of exposure to regularly scheduled TV programs can be measured but exposure to vehicles in the other media is reported from memory quite accurately. The Direct Matching survey generates what is called "single source" data because media exposure and brand purchases are sourced from the same respondents. At the time of writing, there remained only one commercial single-source service, Taylor Nelson Sofres' (TNS') MediaSpan, and it is expensive. Do-it-yourself is a good, low-cost alternative.

TABLE 14.2 *Example of a direct matching questionnaire. Survey population: university students in Australia.*

1. Following is a list of magazines. Please tick the ones that you read:

	Sometimes read it	Always read it
Australian Personal Computer	☐	☐
Australian Penthouse	☐	☐
Australian Women's Weekly	☐	☐
B	☐	☐
Bulletin	☐	☐
Business Review Weekly	☐	☐
Cleo	☐	☐
Cosmopolitan	☐	☐
Dolly	☐	☐
FHM	☐	☐
Girlfriend	☐	☐
Good Medicine	☐	☐
Inside Sport	☐	☐
Instyle	☐	☐
Marie Claire	☐	☐
Men's Health	☐	☐
Motor	☐	☐
New Woman	☐	☐
New Idea	☐	☐
NW	☐	☐

TABLE 14.2 *Continued*

	Sometimes read it	Always read it
PC User	☐	☐
People	☐	☐
Picture	☐	☐
Ralph	☐	☐
Reader's Digest	☐	☐
Street Machine	☐	☐
Take 5	☐	☐
That's Life	☐	☐
TV Week	☐	☐
Wheels	☐	☐
Woman's Day	☐	☐

2. Following is a list of weekend newspapers. Please tick the ones that you read:

	Sometimes read it	Always read it
Daily Telegraph (Sat)	☐	☐
The Weekend Australian (Sat)	☐	☐
Sydney Morning Herald (Sat)	☐	☐
Sun-Herald (Sun)	☐	☐
Sunday Telegraph (Sun)	☐	☐
Illawarra Mercury (Sat)	☐	☐

3. Following is a list of radio stations. Please tick the ones that you listen to:

	Sometimes listen	Always listen
I-98 FM	☐	☐
Power FM (94.9)	☐	☐
Radio ABC Illawarra (97.3)	☐	☐
Wave FM (96.5)	☐	☐
Triple J	☐	☐
ABC Classic FM	☐	☐
TRIPLE M (104.9)	☐	☐
WFS FM (101.7)	☐	☐
One-FM (96.1)	☐	☐
2-Day FM (104.1)	☐	☐
Other FM station	☐	☐
AM station	☐	☐

Continues

TABLE 14.2 *Continued*

4.   During a typical week, how often do you watch TV during the following time periods?

	Every day	Most days	Some days	Never
Before 9.00am	☐	☐	☐	☐
9.00am–12.00 noon	☐	☐	☐	☐
12.00 noon–2.00pm	☐	☐	☐	☐
2.00pm–4.00pm	☐	☐	☐	☐
4.00pm–6.00pm	☐	☐	☐	☐
6.00pm–7.30pm	☐	☐	☐	☐
7.30pm–8.30pm	☐	☐	☐	☐
8.30pm–10.30pm	☐	☐	☐	☐
After 10.30pm	☐	☐	☐	☐

5.   During a typical week, which of these evening programs do you usually watch (*please circle no more than one program for each time slot on each evening*)?

		MONDAY		
7.30	The 7.30 Report	The Great	Friends	Big Brother	Soccer
	Australian Story	Outdoors	Malcolm in the Middle		
8.30	Four Corners	24	Who Wants to be	Secret Life	South Park
	Media Watch		a Millionaire	of Us	Pizza
9.30	Enough Rope	The Practice	Who Wants to be	White Collar Blue	World News
			a Millionaire (cont.)		Tonight
					Queer as Folk

		TUESDAY		
7.30	The 7.30 Report	Better Homes	Gilmore Girls	Big Brother	The Sea Kingdom
	Reality Bites	& Gardens		Everybody Loves	Mum's The Word
		Surprise Chef		Raymond	
8.30	The Bill	All Saints	CSI: Crime Scene	Law & Order:	The Cutting Edge
			Investigation	Criminal Intent	
9.30	Foreign	Cold Feet	Stingers	Rove Live	World News
	Correspondent				Tonight
	The Office				

TABLE 14.2 *Continued*

	WEDNESDAY				
7.30	The 7.30 Report The New Inventors	Surprise Wedding	McLeod's Daughters	Big Brother Skithouse	Australia by Numbers The Movie Show
8.30	The Big Picture	Blue Heelers	Comedy Inc.	The Guardian	Dateline
9.30	Grass Roots	The Jury	Survivor VI: Amazon	The Panel	World News Tonight
	THURSDAY				
7.30	The 7.30 Report Catalyst	Surprise Wedding	Getaway	Big Brother Charmed	Inspector Rex
8.30	Kumars at No. 42 Manchild	Greeks on the Roof	ER	Law & Order: SVU	Insight
9.30	Linda Green True Stories	Will & Grace	The Footy Show	Law & Order: SVU (cont.)	World News Soccer
	FRIDAY				
7.30	Stateline	House Calls to the Rescue	Burke's Backyard	Big Brother The Simpsons	Business Show Living Black
8.30	The Fat	Movie	Rugby League	Movie	About Us
9.30	Taggart – New Life	Movie (cont.)	Rugby League (cont.)	Movie (cont.)	World News Tonight

6. Let's change topics now. Think about consumer electronics products – mobile phones, portable CD players, DVD players, and other new electronics products.

   a. Are you regarded by your friends as knowledgeable about consumer electronics products such that they often ask you for your advice before they buy?
       Yes ☐   No ☐

   b. Are you always among the first to try new electronics products and new models of these products?
       Yes ☐   No ☐

(*Note*: "tick" means "check" in the U.S.A.)

ANALYSIS OF CAMPAIGN TRACKING RESULTS

There are two methods of analysis of tracking study data: causal or quasi-causal analysis of Customer Tracking Survey (CTS) data, and exposure-to-sales analysis of Aggregate Tracking (AT) data.

Causal analysis

For a **causal analysis**, the survey results have to come from a CTS *Panel survey*. Strictly speaking, individual-level causal analysis (over time) is possible only with the *same respondents* interviewed at time *t*, time *t* + 1, time *t* + 2, and so on, through to the end of the tracking. (Shortly, we will comment on what can be inferred if you used Wave surveys or Continuous surveys.) At minimum, two interviews with the same respondents (most often the benchmark interview and one follow-up interview at the peak of or immediately after the campaign) would be required.

With a *Panel* sample, the results are arrayed into a series of "turnover" tables, which link *successive pairs* of measures that represent the buyer response steps, or the more specific hierarchy of effects hypothesized for the campaign, for successive time periods. **Turnover tables** track what happened to respondents from time *t* to time *t* + 1 and to successive time periods if surveyed – for example, whether Exposure did or did not result in Brand Recognition or whether Brand Preference (given Brand Recognition) did or did not produce Brand Action Intention – until all the steps of Exposure → Ad Processing → Brand Communication Effects → Target Audience Action are linked. An example of a Turnover Table for *one* pair of hypothesized successive measures is shown in Table 14.3. The turnover incidence for each cell indicates which diagnosis of causality is appropriate. If the campaign is working (here, by increasing Brand Recognition), most (Exposed) respondents should be in the top right-hand cell, indicating that (recent) Exposure caused Brand Recognition. The lower right-hand cell shows the incidence of Brand Recognition due to *other* causes – such as advertising exposure *prior* to time *t*, or *in-store exposure* to the brand.

TABLE 14.3 *Turnover analysis for inferring causality in panel survey results (example).*

	DID NOT RECOGNIZE BRAND AT TIME t + 1	RECOGNIZED BRAND AT TIME t + 1
Exposed at time t	Campaign not working	Most of the *exposed* respondents should *end up in this cell*
Not exposed at time t	Most of the *unexposed* respondents should be here	Campaign not the cause of brand recognition

Quasi-causal analysis

Quasi-causal analysis, only, is allowable if the CTS has not tracked the same individuals over time. With the *Wave* survey method, causal inference is a major problem – and more so the further apart the waves are, as the chain of causes and effects are badly dislocated in time. With the recommended *Continuous* survey method, however, the observations of inferred causes and effects are virtually continuous, and although different individuals are observed, causality is a *reasonable* conclusion. Quasi-causal analysis is achieved with Continuous Tracking data by **eyeball analysis**, which is statistically crude but *diagnostically sufficient* for management of the campaign. Continuous Tracking, it will be remembered, allows management of the campaign *during* the campaign because this tracking method provides fast data.

Little known but very valuable is *same time-period* CHAID Analysis of Continuous Tracking data. For this, you need a large sample size, so you take at least 12 and preferably 26 weeks of respondents' data and do the CHAID on this large sample. Each respondent's data are, of course, from one time period (the day of the interview) and so you cannot examine "turnover" from one period to the next. But you can learn a lot about causality by, for instance, cross-tabulating Exposed vs Unexposed respondents by Brand Communication Effects, or Ad Recognition Frequency by Brand Communication Effects. Within the BCEs, you can cross-tabulate Brand Recognition (or Brand Recall if that's the brand awareness objective) by degrees of Brand Preference.

Exposure-to-sales analysis

So far, we have assumed that the manager is interested in knowing *how* the advertising campaign is working. This requires Customer Survey Tracking (CTS) so as to document the chain of customer response steps.

However, the manager, once convinced that a good understanding of the likely causal process has been gained, may then choose to track at a more general level *without* doing a survey. This we call Aggregate Tracking because it jumps from Exposure in aggregate to Sales in aggregate. Most often, it consists of relating one of the *gross exposure* measures (Advertising Expenditure rate or GRP attainment rate) to an *aggregated* marketing objective measure (Sales or Market Share; you could also track Brand Equity).

Aggregate Tracking requires some form of direct input-output analysis. This is usually just an Eyeball Analysis of advertising input trends with sales output trends. However, large companies with long time-series of aggregate tracking data sometimes use **econometric modeling**, also called **sales modeling**, to infer future input-output relationships from past ones. Based on honest reports in the literature[9] on Sales Modeling as to the subjectivity that this modeling involves underneath its objective-looking results, we do not recommend it over Eyeball Analysis. To track Brand Equity (Value Equity and Uniqueness Equity) with aggregate data, you simply plot Unit Sales over time against the Relative Price of the brand-item – as shown in Chapter 1, Figure 1.3 – and *eyeball* the trends. Beyond eyeballing, you can compute upside and downside elasticities quite easily as percentage sales changes divided by percentage price changes per four-weekly periods.

TRACKING AND CAMPAIGN MANAGEMENT

Campaign Tracking is used to *manage* the campaign. The Customer Tracking Survey methodology is best for this, and indeed only two and three below could be done with Aggregate Tracking. Five managerial actions can result from tracking:

1. Determining why the marcoms campaign is or is not working

2. Adjusting the budget

3. Adjusting the media plan

4. Adjusting the exposure ratio of individual ads in the pool

5. Making minor improvements in ads

Determining why the campaign is or is not working

The most important managerial result of tracking, at least initially, is *to determine why the marcoms campaign is or is not working (meeting its Sales Goal)*. Until the campaign is actually launched, the manager has been operating only with the marcoms *plan* – which, all things considered, is no more than a *hypothesis* about how the advertising, or other marcoms, is *expected* to work. A smart manager will always want to test this hypothesis and a Customer Tracking Survey is the only way to test it. The exception is Direct-Response advertisers, who have a relatively easy tracking job because *sales are immediate* and inevitably *caused* by the ad or ads, which the advertiser can experimentally vary to find out what works.

Adjusting the budget

Media budget adjustments – increases or decreases in the rate of Adspend – can be made *without* conducting a CTS. Aggregate Tracking, that is, input-output tracking – such as Advertising Expenditure rate related to Sales rate – is sufficient for this.

Adjusting the media plan

Gross adjustments of the media plan, such as increasing or decreasing Adspend in various *geographic* markets, as in Schroer's Method of budgeting (see previous chapter), requires only Aggregate Tracking as above. However, *fine-tuning* of the media plan in terms of adjusting the reach and frequency obtained by ad placements to increase *Effective Reach* requires a Customer Tracking Survey, either Continuous tracking or Panel tracking. The Ad Recognition incidence (Mental Reach) and Ad Recognition Frequency data can only come from a survey.

Adjusting the exposure ratio of individual ads in the pool

Ad Processing measures can be used to adjust the **exposure ratio** of ads in the campaign's pool of ads. The "winner" in pre-testing, for example, may turn out not to be significantly more attention-getting in campaign conditions than the number two ad. Their exposures could therefore be equalized. Or a new winner may be found, or losers discovered, that should be upweighted or downweighted, respectively. For example, American Express, we know from a tracking study, adjusted the ratio of its "Do you know me" TV commercials (Robert Ludlum, Mel Blanc, Benny Goodman and others) to reflect their apparent effectiveness within the campaign. IBM is another company that usually runs a pool of three or four executions (such as, at the time of writing, it's "Little guy" small-business series) which can be individually tracked by Ad Recognition and the ratio of the executions' TV spots adjusted to emphasize the better ones in the schedule.

With Continuous Tracking, ratio adjustments can be made frequently. This can help to forestall Advertising Wearout, as explained later in this chapter.

Making minor improvements in ads

The final and more emergency-initiated management action from survey tracking is, if necessary, to make *small improvements in the executional content of particular ads* while they are *in* the campaign. For example, a TV video "super" (written text superimposed over the video images) can be added to reinforce a Benefit Claim. Or the audio can be re-recorded to mention the Brand Name more often – in association with the Category Need. Magazine ads and outdoor ads have quite a long insertion commitment to the media, meaning that revised ads cannot appear immediately. Changes to newspapers and radio ads can be made at short notice.

HOW OFTEN TO TRACK

How often, or for how long, should you track the campaign? Even "continuous" tracking is rarely continued for 52 weeks of the year. Only by understanding the purpose and methods of tracking can this decision be made correctly. Initiation, Change, and Maintenance are the three campaign considerations that determine the frequency and the *type* of tracking research that should be conducted (see Table 14.4).

TABLE 14.4 *What type of tracking to conduct and how often to track.*

STATUS OF CAMPAIGN	TYPE OF TRACKING	FREQUENCY OF TRACKING
Initiation	Complete causal: Customer Survey Tracking with panel or continuous methodology	Several purchase cycles minimum for FMCG; or six months minimum for durables
Major change by competitor or in market	Aggregate Tracking at first, then complete causal if serious problem	One purchase cycle (two waves) initially for FMCG; then several more if needed; or three months for durables
Maintenance	Aggregate Tracking	Four-weekly, with major review at mid-year and end-of-year planning period

Campaign initiation

When a new campaign is Initiated – either a new brand's first campaign or a new campaign for an existing brand – the causality of the campaign's plan should be tested. This will require a survey, using the Panel or Continuous survey method, for a minimum of six months. All measures are needed. (It is wise to include Brand Recall as well as Brand Recognition in case the new brand or new strategy causes a change in the way the product is purchased. It is not expensive to include both measures.) Use of lead-indicator measures only, or less than complete measurement, will leave gaps in causal inference of effects.

PR tracking

For a new product launch especially but also for a major new campaign, it is additionally worthwhile to track *PR coverage*, which is publicity – positive and sometimes negative – in the media. PR in print media is easy and low cost to track *online* on the Web using a topic search. Hampton[10] of Millward Brown Precis conducted PR tracking of the launch of Coke's ill-fated Dasani mineral water (it was basically bottled tap water) in the U.K., the results of which are reproduced in Figure 14.3. PR, like advertising, can of course influence Brand Communication Effects and, as was the case with Dasani, Target Audience Action.

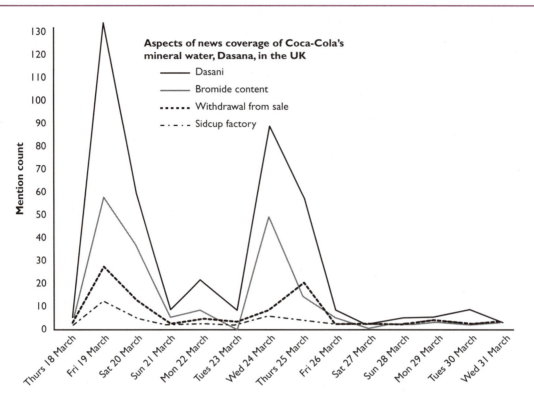

FIGURE 14.3 *Example of PR tracking using a topic search in online versions of newspapers during the launch of Coca-Cola's Dasani mineral water in the U.K.*

SOURCE: F. Hampton, 2004, reference in note 10. This figure is reproduced with the kind permission of *Admap*. For more details go to <www.warc.com/admap>.

To establish reliable causal inferences, a sufficient time period of tracking must be allowed for campaign Initiation. For *short*-purchase-cycle products and services, the period should be *at least three to four purchase cycles*, which for most of these means about six months. For *long*-purchase-cycle products and services, the period should be *at least six months*. Six months should mean that enough purchases have occurred to build up a causal picture of the campaign's effects.

Major change

Major Change does not refer to a major change by the advertised brand, which would be classified as Initiation in our table. Rather, it refers to (1) a major change in a competitor's strategy or (2) a major change in the market itself, such as a new government regulation, or consumer boycotting of a product because of a health scare, or perhaps fortuitously *positive* publicity. Any change likely to affect *our* brand's marcoms performance should be tracked as soon as it occurs.

First, a quick and inexpensive *Aggregate* Tracking assessment of the market should be made. Aggregate measures, notably Sales and Market Share, taken over one purchase cycle (two waves) for FMCG products, or one month apart for three months (four waves) for Durables, should be enough to decide whether the change is serious and likely to continue (hence the multiple waves, to measure the trend). If a substantial effect on our brand's Sales is forecast, then complete *causal* tracking should be resumed, again for several purchase cycles or several months as applicable. This second phase is to determine whether our brand will need to react with a new advertising strategy or even with a new marketing strategy – which would take the campaign back to *Initiation*.

Maintenance tracking

Aggregate Tracking should be undertaken during the remaining periods of market "equilibrium" and this can be regarded as *Maintenance Tracking*. Aggregate data are easy to compile – the company usually has the necessary figures. The usual aggregation period is four-weekly, for the year.

Graphic (not just numeric) reports online directly accessible by the manager are the most useful. They regularly signal whether the market is indeed steady and whether the company's advertising is proceeding as planned. The more sophisticated of these graphic reporting procedures incorporate Expert System software to statistically detect deviations from the normal effects pattern. Information Resources Inc. (IRI) offers an aggregate tracking model that is notable for providing expert system-generated periodic reports to the manager that prompt corrective actions when needed.

It is good management practice to schedule major reviews in which the client and agency are required to read and submit written comments on all available input and output trends, then meet to discuss the trends face-to-face. Quarterly reviews are best and, if not, six-monthly reviews should be the minimum basis of planning during Maintenance periods. These regular reviews will help managers to decide when the current advertising campaign has run its course. This leads to our final topic in campaign management: Wearout.

CAMPAIGN WEAROUT

Everyone thinks they know what *wearout* is. They think wearout "is when the ad or ads aren't working any more." However, the situation is far more complicated than this. We will see that there are three possible conclusions to be drawn when the advertising campaign does not seem to be working any more. Any of the three can cause **campaign wearout:**

1. Positioning strategy out of date

2. Media plan slippage

3. Creative idea or execution wearout

To detect where the problem lies, and thus to draw the right conclusion and apply the right corrective actions, you need *three* audits, conducted in this order: (1) *the marketing plan* – to check for the positioning strategy not being current; (2) *the media plan* – to check for media plan slippage; and (3) *the ads themselves* – to check for **advertising wearout** in its proper sense, that is, wearout of the *creative idea or the creative executions*. The audits or checks should be conducted in the stated order because if the problem is found in an earlier audit, you won't need the next one, but you will have a lot of new planning to do!

First audit: the marketing plan

Before the manager can conclude that a sales decline is caused by advertising wearout, alternative causes must be considered. A **marketing audit** has to be conducted because the problem may be with the brand's marketing plan. A marketing audit should be conducted *first* because, if undetected, this problem will cause the most damage, and very quickly. There are actually three possible problems: changes in the marketing mix, changes in a large competitor's marketing mix, and changes in consumer or customer values.

Changes in the brand's marketing mix

A first set of reasons for a decline in sales, not due to advertising, is changes in (other) components of the Brand's Marketing Mix. A change in product formulation or service design, distribution, price, or promotion other than advertising could be the cause of the sales decline.

- Even a small change can act as a purchase inhibitor. If a small change, the advertising strategy should be *adapted* to counter the inhibition. (See the discussion of Purchase Facilitation as a communication objective in Chapter 6.) This is a minor correction within the same advertising strategy.

- A major change in the brand's marketing mix would, of course, call for a *new* advertising strategy. However, a revised advertising strategy will not save the brand if the marketing mix change has been too severe.

  For instance, Burger King in the U.S.A. has suffered a 22% drop in patronage over the past six years, mainly due to the inconsistent quality of its burgers and fries.[11] Over the six years, four agencies have tried to turn the brand around, without success, and a fifth agency has been brave enough to try, signing on at the beginning of 2004. Despite a generous advertising budget of $335 million, no *advertising* strategy is likely to succeed until Burger King fixes its *product* problem.

  New FMCG brands represent a special case. After the launch of a new FMCG brand-item, a Sales decline often occurs due to the brand achieving its true repeat-purchase incidence and rate; that is, high initial sales in most cases represent the inflationary effect of introductory promotions, so that a drop-off occurs when less than 100% of the triers repeat, or when individual repeaters' rate of purchase *without* price promotions deals stabilizes to the brand's "true" repeat rate.

- The true repeat effect for a new brand would not normally call for a change in Advertising strategy, although it may signal an assessment of the Promotion strategy if the repeat rate is too low (see Chapter 15's discussion of Repeat-Purchase Promotions).

Changes in a large competitor's marketing mix

A second set of reasons for a sales decline is changes in a Large Competitor's Marketing Mix.

  A major new brand introduction, such as Apple's iPod range of personal electronics products, can redefine the market and cause sales and market share declines for other brands, such as Sony's venerable Walkman.

Under the heading of changes in a Large Competitor's Marketing Mix we include changes in a large competing brand's *advertising strategy* (the target audience or the key benefit) but *not* changes in the competitor's *media* strategy *unless* the latter changes follow from a changed advertising strategy. Changes in a large competitor's media strategy alone are discussed later.

- Changes in a large competitor's *marketing mix other than advertising or promotion* that cause our brand's sales to decline will call for a revised *Marketing* Plan and, along with it, a completely revised Advertising Strategy.

- Changes in a large competitor's *advertising (or promotion) strategy* that cause our brand's sales to decline can, more narrowly, often be countered by a change in our brand's *positioning strategy*.

Some years ago, Miller Beer changed its positioning strategy (specifically, it positioned the brand into a new Category Need). The "It's Miller time" theme brought the Miller High-Life brand out of the doldrums in the beer market. Rival Budweiser attempted to counter by simply revising *its positioning* strategy to reflect even broader situational use than Miller's with the "When do *you* say Budweiser?" theme but indications were that it didn't hurt Miller, which creatively had found one of those sayings that become part of popular culture while the campaign runs. In the soft-drink market, more recently, "Always Coca-Cola" was the epitome of this strategy of "all situations" category positioning, which attempts to nullify other brands' *specific* situational positioning (the slogan also meant "Always choose it [Coke]," an extension of "Coca-Cola is it," and was an example of *central positioning* by the *market leader* – see Chapter 3). We say "was" because Coke has since walked away from this position.

Changes in consumer or customer values

A third set of reasons for a sales decline is changes in consumers' or business customers' **Values**. Changes in Values are manifest in altered importance or evaluation weights (I_i's in our multi-attribute formula for the I-D-U model – see Chapter 4) placed on the *attributes* (more accurately, the *benefits*) sought in the product or service category.

The toothpaste market in all Western countries, for instance, historically underwent changes in consumers' Benefit Importance with the emergence of "Decay prevention" as a major consideration, and later, "Plaque reduction", and still later, "Whitening." Likewise, health-initiated sociocultural changes, also just in Western countries, saw "Low tar" emerge as a consumer benefit in the cigarette market (offset, unfortunately, by smokers smoking more and inhaling harder[12]); "Low carb(ohydrates)" emerge as a consumer benefit in the food and beverage markets in the U.S.A.; and "Lite" emerge as a consumer benefit in the U.S.A. for just about anything!

Changes in consumer or customer Values resulting in altered Benefit Importance weights (including the emergence of a new benefit, such as "Whitening" in toothpaste, which previously had little importance except for a small segment of adults) can be addressed in two ways:

- If the altered or new benefit threatens to *substantially re-partition* the category need (see Chapter 3), then the usual response will be to quickly seek a product reformulation or new formulation, resulting in a change in the *Marketing Plan* that will enable our brand to compete successfully in the new submarket (e.g., Crest toothpaste brought out its own whitening toothpaste to match the pioneer brand Colgate Whitening).

- Alternatively, an adequate response may be to revise the advertising strategy: the Target Audience, the Category Need, or the Key Benefit that is emphasized in the ads. Our brand could focus on a more sharply defined target audience, such as *sub-category* users, and try to boost the importance of a previous benefit to reinforce their Brand Preference (e.g., Ultra-Brite and Close-Up continued to go for the "cosmetic" Category-Need segment of the market after the fluoridated toothpastes entered, leaving the latter to the "therapeutic" segment, even though both these brands contain the *attribute* of fluoride).

Second audit: the media plan

If the Market Audit shows no problem, the problem must be occurring in Exposure (step 1) or Ad Processing (step 2) in the customer response steps. This is because, if the advertising strategy is still appropriate, something must be breaking down in the steps *leading to* Brand Communication Effects (step 3) and Target Audience Action (step 4). You should begin with the Exposure step, by conducting a **media plan audit**.

Changes in media vehicle audiences

The pattern of exposures to the advertising could have changed because of *changes in media vehicle audiences*. Changes in media vehicle audiences are missed if you use Aggregate Tracking indicators such as the dollar amount spent on advertising or total GRPs. It is quite possible to be spending the same amount, say, each quarter or to be achieving the same level of GRPs, yet to have a substantial change occur in the rate of Effective Reach – the number of target audience individuals reached at the minimum effective frequency level per advertising cycle. TV programs, in particular, wax and wane in popularity, and seasonal differences in the ratings of established programs are remarkably large; it is not unusual for prime-time TV program ratings, for instance, to vary by 25% to 30% over the four quarters of the year, and this is not just during summer re-runs. Magazine circulations, especially those of magazines that experience a large proportion of their sales from news-stands, fluctuate markedly. As we have emphasized, the advertiser needs to know each vehicle's reach of the *target audience* and this knowledge is not obtainable from GRPs.

The most common mistake in tracking, in fact, is failure to demand an estimate from the media agency of the *achieved* four-weekly effective reach of the campaign, because without this the performance of the ads in terms of Mental Reach (of which Ad Recognition is the best measure) is *not interpretable*. A monthly Ad Recognition incidence of 40%, for instance, would be an excellent result if the Effective Reach of the media schedule that month is about 40% but a terrible result if it was, say, 60%. *Achieved* ER can fluctuate a lot and that might be the problem – a media plan problem, not a problem with the creative.

So, first check Vehicle Audience Figures (Ratings) from the media owners or, if you're using one, your media agency. You should also *update the Direct Matching survey* of the *target audience's* media vehicle exposure. For a brand using Corpographic, Demographic, or Psychographic matching rather than Direct Matching, the ability to detect media plan "slippage" is considerably lessened by the indirect fix on the target audience. Nevertheless, a media plan check is still required and this would be a good time to institute a Direct Matching survey.

Effective frequency check

As we stated in Chapter 12, the calculation of the Minimum Effective Frequency per advertising cycle, MEF/c, is necessarily an *estimate*. The MEF/c estimate is usually made prior to testing the ads that the creative team produces; that is, it assumes *average quality ads*. However, the ads could be so weak or so strong that they require more (if weak) or less (if strong) frequency to achieve the brand's communication objectives. If so, the MEF/c will need to be adjusted upward or downward, as appropriate. A problem that results in *pseudo-wearout* is to run the ad at too low a frequency, so that it never "wears *in*." **Wearin** refers to the tendency of an ad to require fewer exposures on successive cycles (as in the Wedge pattern) to achieve its communication objectives. In any event, it is worth the time to investigate *achieved* frequency during tracking.

MEF/c can be checked in tracking, as we noted before, by asking respondents, in conjunction with the *Ad Recognition* question, the *Ad Recognition Frequency* question: how many times they think they've seen or heard the ad in the last four weeks. Self-reported frequency is remarkably accurate up to about 10 exposures.[13] The reported frequency of the ad (or all ads in the campaign) can be checked against the media plan's intended frequency for each advertising cycle. If too few people report receiving the MEF level, then chances are you're losing Effective Reach. This is likely to be due to the *achieved* media schedule rather than to the ad or ads losing Attention, as very little attention is needed to report simply *seeing* (or hearing) an ad. It is also true that *very* attention-getting ads will tend to have their frequency *over*reported, but that is a nice bonus – you can then reduce the MEF by at least one OTS per advertising cycle.

Maintenance plans

For a new brand campaign or for a new campaign for an existing brand, the advertising is often cut back to a Maintenance level after the heavy initial burst. But usually *too little thought is given to what the Maintenance plan actually delivers*. Again, gross statistics, such as "half the GRPs" (an especially common statistic) or "half the Reach" or "half the Average Frequency" tell us nothing about what the plan is actually delivering. A so-called Maintenance plan may look like it's achieving half the "impact" of the original plan but in fact it may be delivering far less than this, particularly if it drops nearly everyone in the target audience below the Minimum Effective Frequency level required in the advertising cycle.

There is also the question of *who* is being maintained – by way of the target audience. It is one thing, for example, to maintain a target audience of Brand Loyals with relatively low-frequency advertising but quite another to attempt to maintain a target audience of Favorable Brand Switchers with the same maintenance plan. Yet such distinctions rarely enter into the evaluation of reduced media plans. Instead, all detailed consideration is buried in meaningless figures like GRPs, as though the target audience responds to advertising expenditure dispensed in any shape or form.

Make sure you know what "Maintenance" means before you approve such a plan.

Final audit: the ads themselves

Finally, we arrive at Advertising Wearout in the proper sense of the term: that the *creative idea* itself or the *creative executions* are no longer meeting the sales goal even though the advertising strategy is correct and the media schedule is unchanged. The problems could be in the processing responses of Attention, Learning, or Acceptance, or with Emotional responses in Brand Preference learning or Benefit Claim acceptance. We will see that the solutions may require changes in the creative executions *or* changes in the media plan.

Attention wearout

The first response in the processing of all advertisements is Attention. Initial attention to ads was examined extensively in Chapter 9. *Diminished* attention to an advertisement at the individual audience member level after it has been processed several times is a common cause of wearout. Diminished attention is particularly likely to affect campaigns in *Print media* where the easy response for the prospective customer is to turn the page. It is less of a problem in *Broadcast media*, particularly TV, where the easy response is to watch or listen, although increasing clutter is making it a problem.

To alleviate the problem of diminished attention to a campaign, *slightly different advertising executions of the same advertising strategy* (the same Benefit Positioning and Creative Idea) are the lowest-cost solution.

> Miller Lite in the U.S.A. was perhaps the first to do this on a comprehensive scale on TV, with its "ex-jock" pool of commercials, and Blue Nun wine was an early example on U.S. radio. But in *Print media*, where the problem of holding the reader's attention can be severe, advertisers have been somewhat slower to use variations on a theme. Continuous tracking data from Millward Brown suggests that Print ads (magazine and probably newspaper ads) experience a major drop in processing, as measured by Brand-Prompted Ad Recall (BPAR), which measures the proportion of people who link the ad to the *brand,* after three OTSs.[14] *Note* that this may be considerably more than three *insertions*, depending on the reach pattern of the media schedule, as explained in Chapter 12; and it may be more *or* less than three insertions in a particular publication if multiple publications are used in the plan. Print advertisers who use multiple executions include food brands such as Kraft Singles and liquor brands such as Johnny Walker. Figure 8.7, in Chapter 8 showed variations on a theme for Absolut Vodka's international campaign; these ads are shown in *global* media vehicles, such as the world airline magazines, to communicate the positioning benefit (U in the I-D-U model) that Absolut is "The most preferred vodka internationally."

If executional variations don't seem to be sufficient to restore Attention to the campaign (easily measurable in continuous tracking), then it is time to start looking for a *new Creative Idea*. As emphasized in Chapter 7, prospective new Creative Ideas must be thoroughly pre-tested to ensure that the idea selected does not depart from the brand's current Key Benefit (a positioning change is not the correction intended here).

Learning (interference) wearout

Wearout can also occur in the second response in processing: Learning. As explained in Chapter 8, Learning is necessary for two communication effects – *Brand Awareness*, in which the customer must learn the connection between the Category Need and the Brand Identifying Name, Pack or Logo, and *Low-Involvement Brand Preference*, in which the customer must learn the connection between the Brand Identity and its Key Benefit.

Learning failure is very often due to *prior Attention failure*, in which case it would be diagnosed in the foregoing Attention analysis. If so, the solution would be, as before, *variations on a theme* – using new stimuli to regain attention. However, Learning failure can also occur in its own right due to *interference* from learning produced by competing brands. Interference can readily occur when one or more major competitors change their media schedule to attain greater frequency against target audience individuals than previously (called Dominance); or change the ratio of ads in their pool, or change their advertising message execution slightly to achieve stronger associative learning of (their brand-item's) Brand Awareness or Brand Preference.

Changes in scheduling or changes in executional emphasis by a Large Competitor can produce very large interference effects.[15] An increase in *achieved* Effective Frequency by an astute competitor along the lines suggested in Chapter 12 (which would also be the result of using Schroer's Method of local budget-setting, as outlined in the previous chapter) could find the competitive brand dominating in terms of the customer's opportunities to learn the Brand Name as a top-of-mind response to the Category Need (Brand Recall) and simultaneously strengthening the connection between the Brand Identity and its Benefit or Benefits (Brand Preference). Similarly, a competitor whose brand is chosen at the *point of purchase* may increase its executional emphasis on pack shots (better Brand Recognition) or improve its portrayal of benefits (Brand Preference) and make large inroads on your brand – without the competitor altering its media expenditure or its advertising strategy at all!

Also, your brand's *previous* campaign can interfere for weeks or months when you introduce a new campaign – see Sutherland's book for examples.[16] In this case, the interfering "competitor" is you! The solutions to this problem, however, are just the same as when an actual competitor is doing the interfering.

Interference is the major problem that affects *Recall* Learning, which underlies Brand Recall awareness and Low-Involvement Brand Preference. Interference is *not,* however, a significant factor in *Recognition* Learning.

- If *Brand Recall* is the appropriate type of brand awareness communication objective for the brand, then *Dominance* in the advertising cycle (increasing MEF/c above that of the largest competitor – see Chapter 14) is the best corrective tactic. This will require an increase in Adspend – the media budget.

- If *Brand Recognition* is the objective, then the problem is almost certainly due to insufficient Brand Identity exposure (size in print, size and duration in TV ads) *in the ad itself*. This problem can be *fixed* inexpensively in Print ads and, though more expensive, it must be fixed in TV ads.

Acceptance (overexposure) wearout

Negative reactions due to Overexposure are *most unlikely with Print ads*, because the consumer or customer can simply turn the page (for a magazine or newspaper ad or figuratively for a Website ad), or look away (from an outdoor ad), or throw out the ad (direct mail). The wearout problem with print ads is almost certain to be *Attentional wearout*, or possibly *Learning wearout* caused by Interference, but not wearout due to Overexposure. A customer is most unlikely to counterargue with a print ad! Outdoor ads in public view *might* be an exception.

On the other hand, *Broadcast ads are very susceptible to Overexposure wearout* because most people sit passively and attend to the ad. This is particularly true of TV commercials, though less true of Radio commercials because of radio's frequent use as a background medium. In fact, *Attitudinal wearout* (negative shifts in Brand Preference upon repeated exposure) has been demonstrated *only* with TV commercials and not with advertising in any other medium.[17]

What corrective actions should be tried for advertising that has worn out due to Overexposure to, and counterarguing and rejection by, too many members of the target audience?

- If the advertising is *Low-Involvement/Informational*, *ignore* the rejection responses, as they are not relevant to this brand preference quadrant.

- If the advertising is *Low-Involvement/Transformational*, however, *drop the ad immediately*, as negative reactions are fatal in this quadrant.

- For *High-Involvement* brand preference advertising, be it Informational or Transformational, the best solution is to implement *variations on a theme*. The advertiser has to remove offending elements or not present them as often, so as to delay wearout, and replace them with interesting elements. This means different advertisements must be used. A related and less expensive but less satisfactory solution which may work in the short run is to *rotate* the individual ads more often.

- A particular solution applies to target audiences who have fully learned (Low Involvement) or accepted (High Involvement) a strong Brand Preference – these would be *BLs* or *Routinized FBSs* – and this is to use *shorter ads*. Brief TV or Radio commercials (10-second or 15-second spots) and smaller or reduced-copy Print ads should serve to maintain Brand Awareness. Brand Recognition or Brand Recall should, in turn, "carry" the favorable Brand Preference (by reminder) without the ad having to provide much benefit content. Indeed, further exposure of the already-loyal audience (BLs *and* Routinized FBSs) to the full benefit content could paradoxically stimulate counterarguing and wearout! Shorter ads should be used *only* for favorable target audiences. They are *not* suitable for other audiences whose communication effects are not at full strength.

Before assuming Overexposure is the cause, we again emphasize that the advertiser has to be alert for the other internal campaign causes of wearout, including Exposure Slippage (which is *not* wearout but rather constitutes a problem with the media plan), Attention, and Learning. Also, it should be evident that the advertiser *must not lose sight of the Brand Preference strategy*.

The classic American Express Travelers Checks' "Mr Wong" campaign provides a telling example: high-involvement measures of processing, notably cognitive response acceptance, would almost surely have suggested that the irritating "Mr. Wong" TV commercial had worn out early; however, acceptance was irrelevant to the low-involvement/informational way in which this commercial worked.

A summary of *Advertising* Wearout causes and solutions is given in Table 14.5.

TABLE 14.5 *Advertising wearout: causes and solutions.*

CAUSE OF WEAROUT	CORRECTIVE ACTION
Attention – diminished attention (especially to print ads)	*Variations* – different executions of the same advertising message strategy, to hold attention
Learning – unlearning due to competitive interference (Brand Recall and *low-involvement* Brand Preference) or to too brief or small exposure of the pack or brand mark (Brand Recognition)	*Dominance* in the Brand Recall case – extra frequency per cycle to offset competitive interference *Fix the ads* in the Brand Recognition case – longer or larger pack shot or brand mark
Acceptance – rejection responses (especially to broadcast ads) emerging with prolonged repetition; affects Category Need, *high-involvement* Brand Preference, *low-involvement /transformational* Brand Preference, induced Brand Action Intention, and Purchase Facilitation (when these are objectives)	*Variations* – different executions of the same advertising message strategy, to delay rejection of elements: *faster rotation* of existing ads, although this is only a short-term solution; also *shorter ads* for favorable target audience

SUMMARY

When you launch an expensive marcoms campaign, you need to find out as soon as possible whether it is working as planned and you need immediate feedback to manage the campaign if there are problems by adjusting the media schedule and changing or rotating ads. For a Branding campaign (an Awareness campaign), the best way to do this is to conduct Continuous Tracking research using a Customer Tracking Survey, which consists of benchmark interviews before the campaign commences and weekly interviews during the campaign with different random samples of respondents, the results of which are graphed on a rolling (usually four-weekly) basis. Direct-Response campaigns are different: these produce immediate target audience action such as store visits, inquiries, or direct purchases, and continuous interviewing of prospects is not necessary (although periodic interviews can be helpful to find out what's going wrong if the direct-response ads aren't working).

The Customer Tracking Survey is complicated to design and conduct properly. We recommend that you design and commission your own tracking research rather than use a syndicated service because this allows you to select an appropriate survey method (Continuous is best), interview method (Face-to-Face is the most valid because you can show ads and packages, although Online interviews, where you can do likewise, are emerging as an equally good alternative with the rapid increase in in-home Internet usage in advanced countries), and, most important, you can base your survey on the most valid measures. These measures cover media plan delivery (Effective Reach), exposure (Ad Recognition and Ad Recognition Frequency and also exposure to *other* forms of marcoms, if used, including PR), attainment of communication objectives (Brand Communication Effects), and the behavioral effects of the campaign (Target Audience Action representing the relevant behavior or behaviors). Eyeball Analysis, supplemented by turnover table analysis of monthly data, is sufficient to dictate changes and corrections to the campaign.

It is important to conduct a Customer Tracking Survey for campaign Initiation and whenever an evident Change occurs in the market. At other times, called Maintenance periods, it is sufficient to conduct only Aggregate Tracking, which consists of relating the main advertising input (usually Advertising Expenditure but preferably Effective Reach per four-week period) to the main output (usually Sales and also, preferably, Brand Equity).

A major purpose of the Customer Tracking Survey is to detect Advertising Wearout – the tendency of individual ads to lose their selling effectiveness during the campaign. Advertising Wearout is difficult to diagnose correctly – although the solutions are straightforward, once the right cause has been detected. For the manager who is spending millions of dollars on the company or brand's campaign, however, Campaign Tracking is a vital and necessary ongoing and concluding stage of marketing communications management.

DISCUSSION QUESTIONS

14.1 Measures of so-called "advertising awareness" are not created equal. What are the main alternative measures of advertising awareness and what diagnostic information does each provide for the manager?

14.2 The Customer Tracking Survey is meant to establish causality from advertising inputs to brand communication effects to target audience action. Three Survey Methods were examined in the chapter. Discuss how each of the methods fares with regard to establishing causality.

14.3 In Western countries, Telephone Interviewing is by far the most widely used interview method because of its low cost. Measuring Ad Recognition by telephone, however, is a major problem unless we are talking about a campaign consisting only of Radio ads. How can the research company minimize this problem? If Brand Recognition is a campaign communication objective, the telephone interview method will also be problematic. Try to suggest a way round this problem using telephone interviewing.

14.4 What is same time-period CHAID Analysis and when should it be used? Construct a 2 × 2 cross-tabulation table with synthetic results to show how Quasi-Causality can be inferred.

14.5 Several years ago Dannon Yogurt lost its market leadership in the U.S.A. to a then-new brand, Yoplait Yogurt. The coup was attributed to Yoplait's TV ads. However, what audits should the manager of Dannon have done, and why, before accepting this conclusion?

14.6 You are the marketing manager for Lacoste tennis shirts and you want to run a Magazine ad campaign using ads like those in Chapter 8, Figure 8.10, in a Seasonal Priming reach pattern commencing before next summer and going 12 weeks into the summer period. What *two* tactics would you employ to prevent the magazine ads from suffering Attention Wearout?

14.7 Tracking studies results indicate that your campaign's TV commercials are wearing out more quickly than you expected due to heavy competitive Interference. What corrective step or steps should you take?

NOTES

1. The fact that most advertising campaigns are not formally evaluated is reinforced in an interesting article by P.R. Klein and M. Tainiter, Copy research validation: the advertiser's perspective, *Journal of Advertising Research*, 1983, 23(5), pp. 9–17. These investigators followed up on 1,165 TV commercials from 412 campaigns tested by the McCollum Spielman testing service. Although many were very large budget campaigns, few were formally tracked. A likely reason for this, apart from money, is that managers almost inevitably fall prey to "hindsight bias" – that is, they believe they know (after the fact, of course) why a campaign did or did not work. Pressure for accountability in all areas of business, including advertising, is rapidly removing this excuse for not tracking campaigns. See T.B.C. Poietz and H.S.J. Robben, Individual reactions to advertising: theoretical and methodological developments, *International Journal of Advertising*, 1994, 13(1), pp. 25–53, for the observation on hindsight bias; and M. Sutherland and A. Sylvester, *Advertising and the Mind of the Consumer*, Sydney: Allen & Unwin, 2000, for the diminishing excuse and sound business reasons for campaign tracking. Advertising agencies, too, should support the use of a customer tracking survey. Why? If the client loses market share for two quarters in a row, the agency is likely to get fired! The agency may not be at fault but you can't know without tracking. See M.S. Kulkarni, P.P. Vora, and T.A. Brown, Firing advertising agencies, *Journal of Advertising*, 2003, 32(3), pp. 77–86.

2. A.M. Sutherland and A. Sylvester, 2000, same reference as above.

3. S. Colman and G. Brown, Advertising tracking studies and sales effects, *Journal of Advertising Research*, 1983, 25(2), pp. 165–183.

4. Dramatic evidence that alternative proprietary measures with the same label of "ad awareness" are not measuring the same thing can be found in a study in which 60 TV commercials were put through three different pre-testing systems (they use some of the same measures that are used in tracking). See J. Kastenholz, C. Young, and G. Kerr, Does day-after recall testing produce vanilla advertising?, *Admap*, 2004, June, pp. 34–36.

5. C. McDonald, Point of view: the key is to understand consumer response, *Journal of Advertising Research*, 1993, 33(5), pp. 63–69.

6. For an interesting analysis of the effects of different marcoms tools for leader and follower brands, see

R.J. Schuring and D. Veerman, High brand equity: a mixed blessing, *Admap*, 1998, November, pp. 40–42.

7. S. Colman and G. Brown, 1983, same reference as note 3; M. Sutherland and A. Sylvester, 2000, same reference as in note 1.

8. A. Wilson and N. Laskey, Internet based marketing research: a serious alternative to traditional research methods?, *Marketing Intelligence & Planning*, 2003, 21(2), pp. 79–84.

9. For instance, an experienced modeler, L. Cook, recently reviewed the difficulties of correctly interpreting the econometric results of campaigns that have multiple inputs such as advertising, promotions, various brands' prices and achieved distribution, which are typical. Multicollinearity is a big problem. And you usually need several years of data – too backward-looking! See L. Cook, Econometrics and integrated campaigns, *Admap*, 2004, June, pp. 37–40.

10. F. Hampton, How to manage online corporate reputations, *Admap*, 2004, June, pp. 27–29.

11. K. MacArthur, What's eating Burger King, *Advertising Age*, January 26, 2004, pp. 1, 30.

12. J. Wilkenfeld, J. Henningfield, J. Slade, D. Burns, and J. Pinney, It's time for a change: cigarette smokers deserve meaningful information about their cigarettes, *Journal of the National Cancer Institute*, 2000, 92(2), pp. 90–92.

13. L. Hasher and R.T. Zacks, Automatic processing of fundamental information: the case of frequency of occurrence, *American Psychologist*, 1984, 39(12), pp. 1372–1388.

14. BPAR indexes for magazine ads are 1st OTS = 1.0, 2nd = 1.0, 3rd = 0.75, 4th = 0.25, and 5th and later = 0.1 each. G. Brown, The awareness problem: attention and memory effects from TV and magazine advertising, *Admap*, 1994, January, pp. 15–20.

15. Dramatic interference effects were demonstrated in a neatly designed experiment that varied the relative frequency (or "share of voice") of competitive advertising and also the creative effectiveness (or "reward value") of competing ads. Although this was a laboratory experiment, the conditions were quite similar to brand recall learning and low-involvement brand attitude learning in the real world, where competitive interference and not time between exposures is postulated to be the "unlearning" process. See L.A. Lo Sciuto, L.H. Strassmann, and W.D. Wells, Advertising weight and the reward value of the brand, *Journal of Advertising Research*, 1967, 7(2), pp. 34–38.

16. M. Sutherland and A. Sylvester, 2000, same reference as in note 1.

17. Some studies misleadingly suggest that counterarguing is rarely a problem with broadcast commercials because their presentation lasts such a short time and then is supplanted immediately by another commercial or by the program. The evidence for minimal counterarguing with broadcast commercials, however, has been based on *single-exposure* studies. With multiple exposures, as in the vast majority of actual campaigns, counterarguing and consequent rejection clearly can occur. For the two viewpoints and evidence, see P.L. Wright, Cognitive responses to mass media advocacy, in R.E. Petty, T.M. Ostrom, and T.C. Brock (Eds), *Cognitive Responses in Persuasion*, Hillsdale, NJ: Lawrence Erlbaum Associates, 1981, pp. 263–282; and B.J. Calder and B. Sternthal, Television commercial wearout: an information processing view, *Journal of Marketing Research*, 1980, 17(2), pp. 173–186.

PART VI

other marcoms

CHAPTER FIFTEEN
Sales promotions 347

CHAPTER SIXTEEN
Corporate image advertising, sponsorships, and PR 375

CHAPTER SEVENTEEN
Personal selling: direct selling and telemarketing 401

CHAPTER EIGHTEEN
Social marketing campaigns 430

CHAPTER 15

Sales promotions

Sales promotions – often just called Promotions – are incentives to "act now." Promotions in most cases operate *temporarily* on the Brand Action Intention communication effect – just long enough to buy the product. However, when implemented with correct tactics, called consumer or customer franchise-building tactics (CFB), promotions can increase Brand Awareness and Brand Preference over the longer term and thereby increase the brand-item's Value Equity. When used by retailers, promotions can also increase Category Need, which raises the sales of all brand-items in the category.

In this chapter, we will consider Manufacturer's Promotions first. These are the manufacturer's trial promotions to retailers, trial promotions to end-customers, and repeat-purchase promotions to end-customers. In the second part of the chapter, we consider promotions originated by the Retailer, of which there are eight main types: store layout, retail atmosphere, retail feature ads, point-of-purchase displays, price-off promotions, store brands, card-based loyalty schemes, and home shopping.

MANUFACTURER'S TRIAL PROMOTIONS TO RETAILERS

If a manufacturer's brand-item is sold through retailers, rather than sold direct, **trial promotions to retailers** are almost invariably used *to try to gain distribution*. The objective is to make the item available in as many stores as possible. This is not easy, because any new item must displace an existing item stocked by the retailer. For mass-marketed products and some types of services that are mass-marketed, such as franchised services, broad retail distribution is crucial for gaining consumer Trial of the brand-item and, thereafter, for retaining its Repeat-Purchase rate.

The widely observed **double jeopardy phenomenon**[1], whereby the fewer the number of people who buy the brand, the less frequently they buy it, is mainly caused by insufficient distribution.[2] Smaller brands are less available in big stores and small stores tend to avoid smaller brands, stocking only several of the largest-selling brands. An analysis by Farris and colleagues reveals the typical relationship, for FMCG products, between the extent of retail Distribution achieved and Market Share, which is shown in Figure 15.1. Most brand-items cannot get beyond about 10% market share until they have achieved approximately 50% of total potential distribution. Thereafter, with increasing distribution, market share *accelerates* (double jeopardy in reverse, that is, the "double benefit" effect of the brand-item reaching more triers and being more available to them for repeat purchase). However, although the curve in the graph goes up to 100% distribution, even the biggest brand-items rarely achieve more than 80% distribution. Although we are talking about mass-marketed products and services, the same relationship between Distribution and Market Share would be expected to apply for *specialized* brand-items where distribution, for them, is defined as the proportion of *specialized retailers* who carry the item.

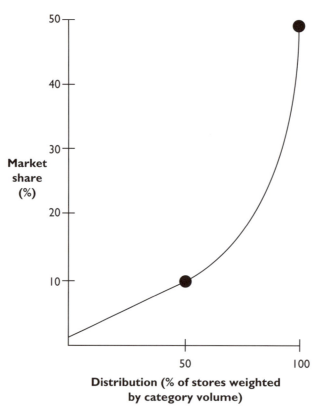

FIGURE 15.1 *As the brand-item's distribution increases, so does its market share. Market share accelerates once 50% distribution is exceeded (the "double benefit" result of being available to more triers and more available when they want to repeat).*

SOURCE: Based on P. Farris *et al.*, 1989, reference in note 2.

Manufacturers employ several types of Trial Promotions to Retailers, which are usually preceded by a personal-selling trade presentation and always by a written commitment by the manufacturer to advertise the new item to *consumers*. These trial promotions are:

- Introductory price allowance
- Returns
- New line fee

Introductory price allowance

Most common of the three – almost universal – is an **introductory price allowanc**e, which is a straight reduction in the selling price to the retailer. When offered an established brand-item, the price discount is called an **off-invoice** promotion. The time window on both types of deal is two to four weeks, during which retailers tend to stock up their warehouses at the lower price.

Returns

Less common is the type of promotion known as **returns**, by which the manufacturer agrees to buy back the retailer's unsold quantities of the product.

The extreme form of returns is distributing **on consignment**, which means that the retailer pays nothing to the manufacturer until the product is sold.

New line fee

A third type of retailer trial promotion is a **new line fee**, also called a **slotting allowance**, which is most often a straight cash payment to the retailer or sometimes a proportion of the stock donated free, so that the retailer will stock the product – at least for a short trial period of several months. New Line Fees have become normal for new FMCG products sold through major chains, both grocery and pharmacy, and the FMCG volume sold through major chains is increasing in all Western countries. Small stores, on the other hand, are powerless to demand a New Line Fee. The fee varies from (U.S.)$5,000 to $10,000 per item per chain, and can amount to as much as a third of the marcoms budget for the new item. With the general trend toward concentration of retailers into large chains, New Line Fees are expected to spread to other products besides FMCG.[3]

> The relative effectiveness of the three types of retailer-trial promotions is not known but the following general principle holds: the stronger the manufacturer relative to the retailer, the lower the percentage price-off or the smaller the New Line Fee.

MANUFACTURER'S TRIAL PROMOTIONS TO END-CUSTOMERS

There are seven types of trial promotion that can be offered by Manufacturers to their Business Customers (direct), or by Consumer Products Manufacturers to Consumers (direct or through retail):

- Product or service sampling
- Rebates

- Bonus packs

- Direct price-offs

- Warranties

- Premiums

- Coupons (for FMCG products and services)

These seven types of trial promotion have several variants, as discussed in the next sections.

Product or service sampling

Sampling can be used as a promotion technique by all types of marketer.[4] **Sampling** is essentially a low-cost or free trial of the product or service and it takes different forms for different types of marketer:

- Industrial marketers – trade shows, feasibility studies, demonstrations

- Consumer durables marketers – demonstrations, home-trial offers

- Consumer FMCG marketers – a "unit" of the product or service given free or at a large discount

Sampling is expensive but it is the strongest trial-generating technique. For *High-Involvement* products and services, sampling is effective because it builds a feeling of reciprocal obligation if the customer agrees to try.[5] For instance, once a prospective customer organization has allowed a supplier company to perform a Feasibility Study, the organization develops a felt commitment to continue. Once you have agreed to Test-Drive a new car, you usually feel more commitment toward that particular model, and toward the salesperson, than if you had not agreed to take the trial. After a salesperson has helped you to select an item of clothing at a clothing store, you feel more obliged to buy it. The feeling of *reciprocal obligation* from sampling builds a strong likelihood of purchase at the full price.

The two most widely used forms of sampling – Trade Shows for industrial marketers and Product Sampling for FMCG marketers – are discussed in more detail below.

Trade shows

Trade shows are the most widely used sampling method by industrial marketers. On average, Trade Shows account for about 20% to 25% of industrial marketer's marcoms budget, second only to expenditure on ads in business publications[6], as indicated in the media expenditures table, Table 1.1 in Chapter 1. The average industrial firm exhibits at six Trade Shows a year.

The reach of Trade Shows (of the population of customers in that industry) is the main consideration. On average, according to one large and representative survey, 63% of visitors to the firm's booth will be talked to, at a cost per contact of about U.S.$200. An average conversion ratio figure is not that meaningful as conversion varies enormously by product type, though 5% conversion (a .05 conversion ratio) to a follow-up sales contact for a major purchase would be a very good result. Usually at least one follow-up sales call is required to close the sale, bringing the total cost of converting a customer to approximately U.S.$450.[7] The quality of the booth personnel and their rate of contact, which ranges from about 12 to 20 prospective contacts per salesperson per hour, are the most important factors in Trade Show effectiveness.

FMCG sampling

With Sampling of *Low-Involvement* products and services, the trier is not likely to feel commitment to reciprocate by buying. Rather, the product or service has to work immediately – that is, be favorably evaluated from the sample of it. Normative data from Trial-Sample Promotions of FMCG Products are that about 75% of consumers who receive a sample will try it and about 15% to 20% will then proceed to make a subsequent full-priced purchase.[8] In other words, the conversion ratio for Trial-Sampling of FMCG products is in the range of .15 to .20.

Consumer Product or Service Sampling is best used in the following situations: (1) new product category introduction, to gain a "first mover" advantage for the brand-item; (2) when introducing a demonstrably superior brand-item into an established category; (3) when advertising is not really adequate to demonstrate the brand-item's benefits; and (4) to force retail distribution, because sampling generates fast action at the retail level at little or no cost to the retailer.

Samples, since they *are* the product or service, are automatically customer franchise-building (CFB) by their nature.

Rebates

A **rebate** is a *partial* money-back offer. "Rebate" is the correct term but the term "Refund" is sometimes used, even though it does not mean a full refund or a Money-Back Guarantee. (A Money-Back Guarantee is a type of Warranty, as discussed later.)

Rebates can be used as a trial offer for *any* product or service. They are common in the automobile industry, as well as for consumer durables in general and, sometimes in the form of "bounce back" coupons for a further purchase rather than cash back, for FMCG products.

Whereas the redemption rate of Rebates is only about 1% to 2%, the conversion rate to purchase is actually higher, about 3% to 4%, a conversion ratio of .03 to .04, which indicates that a properly presented Rebate offer can function similarly to an *advertisement*, in that half the customers buy *without* redeeming the offer.

The Rebate offer should be presented CFB executional tactics. If the purchase will occur by Brand Recognition, reproduce a *picture* of the *package* or of the service's *logo* on the rebate offer or, if by Brand Recall, include the *brand name and category* prominently. To assist Brand Preference, the *key benefit claim* should be featured on the rebate certificate.

Bonus packs

A **bonus pack** offers more of the product, or longer use of the service, at the normal unit price or sometimes at a reduced price – thus, bonus packs are a *price-off* promotion. (Bonus Packs, obviously, can only be used for products or services that are sold in *divisible units*. Consumer durables, such as refrigerators or computers, are *not* divisible and any "add-ons" would be Premiums, not Bonus Packs.) Bonus Packs are most suitable for *Low-Involvement* products and services because you get more of the product than you would normally use; they are not suitable for *High-Involvement* products or services, because you would want to try a *smaller* rather than a larger sample. When Bonus Packs are used as a promotion, *retail sell-in* by the manufacturer is vital because bonus packs usually require more shelf space or, for services, more personnel time.

> A big problem with using Bonus Packs as a *trial* promotion is that they are easily purchased instead by Brand Loyals and Favorable Brand-Switchers – who would have bought the brand-item anyway. The best a manager can do is to *label* the bonus pack with wording such as "Try this!" and then *monitor* the take-up by new triers versus others. No normative figures are available for Bonus Packs as a trial promotion, that is, for conversion from the bonus pack to a regular purchase, mainly because the manager rarely bothers to measure who is buying the bonus packs.

Direct price-offs

A **direct price-off** is a reduction in the brand-item's usual retail selling price, initiated by the *manufacturer.* However, Direct Price-Offs offered by the manufacturer cannot be relied on in today's retailing channels because *retailers* like to set the actual selling price and mostly they have the power to do so. Direct Price-Offs can, on the other hand, be relied on for products and services sold *direct* to the End-Customer.

Direct Price-Offs are *not* a good way to introduce a new product category or a *really* new brand-item because no "reference price" has yet been established in the prospects' minds to evaluate the worth of the discount.[9]

> Michelob Ultra, for instance, which is a new, very low carbohydrate beer from Anheuser-Busch, was positioned to sell at a price about 20% higher than regular beers. Such a high reference price to consumers could not have been established with introductory price discounts to consumers.

Direct Price-Offs *can* be used to attract new users to a *familiar* brand-item in an established product category (for which these prospects would have a reference price). As we will see, however, direct price-offs usually have only a small success rate for attracting triers: only about 5% of price-off purchases are made by new triers of a familiar brand-item in the typical FMCG category (see Table 15.2).

> Purchase by genuine triers should be monitored to make sure sales are not just going to regular buyers of the brand-item.

Warranties

A **warranty**, also known as a **guarantee**, is a contract offered by the manufacturer to a customer to provide *restitution* in some form – such as money back, replacement of the item, or free repairs or servicing – should the product prove deficient within a stated time period. The presence of a Warranty acts as an immediate incentive to buy; is seen by the customer as something that prevents wasting money and therefore a type of price-off.

Warranties function by *reducing perceived risk* and are therefore best suited to generate trial of *High-Involvement* products. Warranties can also be used for High-Involvement *services*, such as car servicing, but only for those in which there is a *tangible product* delivered, as it is the product that carries the warranty, not the service.

Some retailers, such as Sears in the U.S.A. and Kmart, worldwide, have made a 100% Money-Back Guarantee, in the form of credit toward another item or items purchased in the store, an incentive to purchase more products than you would if you were shopping in a "normal" store.

The warranty *offer* should be *pre-tested* to make sure that it is sufficiently attractive to potential buyers. Assuming that it is, a warranty will work regardless of the introductory price or the manufacturer's reputation.[10]

Warranties are CFB in that they increase Brand Preference – you like the item more if it offers a good warranty.

Premiums

A **premium** is an article of merchandise offered free, or at a price less than its retail value, as an incentive to buy one unit or several units of the brand. A **free premium** is just this – a giveaway – and it is always inexpensive merchandise. A **self-liquidating premium**, by contrast, offers an expensive additional product or service (e.g., a vacation trip) for which the customer sends money with the proof of purchase of the original brand-item, enough money to cover the marketer's costs of the premium's purchase and delivery (hence self-liquidating) while still presenting to the customer a price (for the premium) that is well below its normal retail price.

Because the product or service offered as a Premium tends to have *selective appeal* to consumers, premiums have a limited conversion rate, usually about 1%, a conversion ratio of .01. To stimulate trial purchase, a *single-purchase requirement* should be made (multiple-purchase requirements for premiums are a repeat-purchase promotion and are discussed in that section of the chapter).

It is essential to *pre-test* potential premiums, especially if it is a Self-Liquidating Premium offer. Simonson and colleagues demonstrated in a consumer experiment that an ill-considered premium can make the original brand-item less attractive to purchase![11] Remember, you pay *more* than the normal retail price if you buy a product with a Self-Liquidating Premium and, if you don't like the premium, the extra price is not worth it.

In order to encourage trial of the original item at its full price, the Premium should be chosen to be CFB, in that it should reinforce the brand-item's *key benefit*. For instance, Vaseline Intensive Care lotion, positioned during the summertime as an after-sun remedy, offered the Premium of beach T-shirts (discreetly endorsed with the brand logo). Hoover vacuum cleaners at one time used a lightweight indoor stepladder (which also fits the brand's slogan: "Hoover – one step ahead of the rest").

Coupons (for FMCG products and services)

A **coupon** is a voucher or certificate that entitles the buyer to a price reduction on the brand-item. Coupon trading, as the transaction is called, is prohibited by law in some countries, such as Australia, but is widely prevalent in the U.S.A. and European countries for FMCG products. There are two types of coupon. **Manufacturer's coupons** are distributed by the manufacturer – in the U.S.A. the vast majority, 86%, of coupons appear in free-standing inserts (FSIs) in newspapers, 6% as handouts, 2% in direct mail, 3% in magazine and newspaper ads, 0.2% in Web ads, and 2.4% in or on the pack[12] – and can be redeemed direct to the manufacturer or at any retail store that carries the item. **Trade coupons** are designed and distributed by the retailer although partly paid for by the manufacturer (an arrangement called co-op funding) and are redeemable only at the outlet or outlets of the particular retailer who offers them.

Coupon usage tends to be skewed toward Favorable Brand Switchers. In U.S. supermarkets, about a quarter of consumers carry coupons with them and about 19% of consumers are able to use them in the store that day because the promoted item is in stock.[13]

> For a particular brand-item, the conversion rate for Coupons is normally between 3% and 5%, a conversion ratio of .03 to .05. As with all price-off promotions for FMCG products, there is a real problem in directing coupons usage to triers of the brand-item, as opposed to its regular buyers (BLs and FBSs). A partial solution is to employ *in-ad* distribution of coupons in publications read by relatively more users of other brands. This requires a Direct Matching media survey (see Chapter 14).

Coupons can be designed in a CFB manner by showing a *picture* of the product or of the service's logo on the certificate as well as mentioning its *key benefit*. This way, the coupon can function like an ad, even if the coupon is not redeemed.

MANUFACTURER'S REPEAT-PURCHASE PROMOTIONS TO END-CUSTOMERS

The proper purpose of a **repeat-purchase promotion** is to increase the *long-run* rate of repeat purchase of the brand-item at its full price. That is, Repeat-Purchase Promotions should be occasional and provide intermittent reinforcement of purchase.

The manufacturer has four main options for Repeat-Purchase Promotions but, as we shall see, only the last three are good CFB options:

- Direct price-offs
- Multi-purchase sweepstakes or contests
- Multi-purchase "loyalty" premiums
- Packaging

Direct price-offs

Direct Price-Off promotions, which are by far the most common option of the four above, are a failure as a manufacturer's repeat-purchase tool. Several major studies, including a broad-based recent study by Dekimpe and colleagues, have shown conclusively that Price-Off promotions for repeat-purchase products (mainly FMCG) do not increase the rate of full-price purchasing, and that during the promotion the manufacturer always loses profit even though unit sales go up. (We note, at the time of writing, that the emergence of *Scan-Back* trade deals, whereby the price-off to the retailer is given only for units *sold*, not units bought, may change this no-profit conclusion in the future.[14]) It is not unusual to see a brand-item's unit market share jump in the short run from, say, 15% up to 40% with a price-off promotion.[15] This is one reason why managers are so tempted to use them (the other is defensive, because competitors use them, but this threat is totally exaggerated by managers). After these jumps in sales, there is *always* a corresponding *dip*. Interestingly, too, about one-third of price promotions do *not* increase unit sales, so it's not *guaranteed* that you'll get a short-run jump in sales. Direct price-off promotions leave the *long-run* sales rate of the brand completely unaffected! No long-run effect on repeat purchase is observed for 96% of price-off promotion campaigns and you would have to be an extreme optimist to believe that your price-offs will be among the 4% that do have a positive long-run effect.[16] For consumer durables, if new car sales are a typical example, Pauwels and colleagues have recently shown that Rebates, another form of price-off, have no effect on repeat-purchase "loyalty" to the brand or make of car bought next time.[17]

> If you use Direct Price-Off promotions, always "ratchet" them on a cycle of *advertising* first (see Chapter 1 and Chapter 14) so as to remind consumers of the brand's Value Equity. This will make even a small price-off more attractive. If you don't pre-advertise your price-off promotions, you'll experience what happened in the battery market to both Duracell and Energizer – they are now both commodity brands with no Uniqueness Equity, due to long, aimless price cutting.[18]

Sweepstakes or contests

A **multi-purchase sweepstakes** or a **multi-purchase contest** is another possible repeat-purchase promotion. A Sweepstakes is based purely on chance and requires no skill to enter. A Contest, on the other hand, must require of participants some degree of skill in order to win the prize. Note that to stimulate *Repeat Purchase*, there must be a *purchase requirement to enter* and *multiple entries* are encouraged.

> Sweepstakes and contests, however, are difficult to execute, produce very low conversion rates – on average about 1%, for a conversion ratio of .01 – and do not inspire greater liking (CFB) for the original brand-item associated with them. The manager should pre-test the idea of the sweepstakes or contest with the target group to gauge the appeal of this type of promotion.

Multi-purchase premiums

Multi-purchase premiums have had many successes for children's products and are under-used for adult products and services.

> Parents of young children will know the irresistible appeal to children of the Fad Premiums utilized by McDonald's restaurants, for instance, and children's cereals are another product category where Multi-Purchase Premiums seem to be mostly successful. However, although these multi-purchase premiums increase repeat purchase, they do not seem to increase "loyalty," – that is, Brand Preference – which would be evidenced by increased repeat purchase when the premium is *not* offered.[19] As long as the premiums are Self-Liquidating, however, they will make a profit on sales.

Multi-Purchase Premiums for *High-Involvement* (mainly adult) products and services do appear to have *some* positive effect on Brand Preference[20] (as well as the direct effect of increasing repeat purchase) perhaps due to the *reciprocal obligation* phenomenon noted earlier. For adult products and services, the most widely used multi-purchase premium is not really a premium (a tangible reward) at all but rather a price-off promotion, namely, a *Heavy-User Discount*. (A more considerate term in the current Western climate would be heavy *usage* discount, but you know what we mean.)

However, to execute a Heavy-User Discount in a CFB manner, the discount, contingent on a target rate or volume of purchase, should be described – positioned – as a *reward*. The correct positioning, for instance, is seen in offers such as "Buy three and get a fourth one free" or "Sign up for six visits for the price of five," that is, a free *extra* product or service is emphasized rather than the discount.

Framing as a *reward* cannot be accomplished by simple naming. The frequent-flyer programs of most airlines, for instance, refer to "reward points," though the fact is that more than 90% of the points are used to claim free flights[21], not upgrades or other positive reinforcements (the true meaning of "reward"). Most people do *not* mentally thank the airline when taking a free flight but rather feel that they are entitled to it. Some quite dramatic proof that frequent flyer "reward" points do not increase loyalty comes from an experiment, not by an airline company but by a credit card company. The credit card company conducted a split-run test in which new card prospects were direct mailed either an incentive of 5,000 frequent flyer miles for signing up for the card or, in the randomly selected other half of the mailout, were sent a straightforward direct mail ad that emphasized the value of the card to the customer. The frequent-flyer incentive offer pulled in 34% more new cardholders than the ad did. However, careful analysis of what happened after that revealed that just one year later, the *ad-recruited* new customers generated 2.5 times the revenue that was received from the average incentive-attracted customer. Despite the smaller number of ad-attracted customers, they were far and away more profitable in total, and this was just for the first year![22]

It is alternatively possible to select *Attractive Gifts*, chosen by a survey of the preferences of your heavy-user customers, that could also be made contingent on multiple purchases. Choice of prestige products of the type seen in airline duty-free catalogues, for instance, would be an attractive free premium for repeat visitors to expensive hotels, a reward for favored patronage. Loyal patrons of particular retailers, such as department stores or supermarkets, would also be likely to respond to suitable premiums. *Databasing* is the best way of executing such premium offers, so that they come as a surprise rather than requiring patrons to submit proof of purchase.

Packaging

The manager has to think: What happens to my product or service after the buyer has bought it? Are there opportunities to increase the chance of repeat purchase through take-away or leave-behind communication vehicles? **Shopping bags** and **product containers** of all types are opportunities for post-purchase advertising of products. **Service stickers** provide this opportunity for services.

Packaging, of course, should be executed in a CFB manner: the *brand name or logo* should be prominent and also the *key benefit* illustrated or stated. For brands whose purchase is motivated by Social Approval, the package *itself* can be a benefit claim.

RETAILER'S PROMOTIONS

Retailers employ **retailer's promotions** for three main purposes: (1) to increase the number of visitors to the store; (2) to increase the profit return from the total product or service category, including profit from the retailer's own brand or brands; and (3) to clear stock to make space for new items, especially those that attract from the manufacturer a new line fee or sizeable trade deal.

Retailers have eight main promotion tactics available to them:

- Store layout
- Retail atmosphere
- Retail feature ads
- Point-of-purchase displays
- Price-off promotions
- Store brands
- Card-based loyalty schemes
- Home shopping

To provide background for the Retailer's Promotion techniques, it is useful to first describe *customer behavior* for the retail store category that we patronize most often – *grocery stores* (supermarkets and small stores). The U.S. term "grocery stores" sounds a little narrow to those of us who live in other countries, as these stores sell much more than "groceries," but we will stay with this label for want of a better one.

The grocery retailer's sales come from two main types of customer: *Store Loyals*, who will buy at that store anyway and are not price-sensitive (about 35% of customers, on average), and *Favorable Store Switchers* (about 65% of the store's customers) who are distinctly price-sensitive.[23] Unless the store or store chain is new, very few sales come from Other-Store Switchers, Other-Store Loyals or New Users of that category of store.

To illustrate the grocery store shopping pattern, we first go back to ground coffee – a product category that we examined in Chapter 5 in conjunction with target audience purchase behavior and brand loyalty – and consider now the same category with regard to retail shopping behavior. Take a typical supermarket chain such as Safeway, the U.S. chain. Safeway's *average* ground coffee purchaser makes only about one-third of his or her ground coffee purchases at Safeway – and two-thirds at other stores. However, there is a heavy skew toward the small group of *relatively* store-loyal Safeway customers. For instance, and this depends on where we make the cutoff for "store loyalty," the 12% of shoppers who buy more than half their ground coffee at Safeway, its Store Loyals, will account for 49% of all ground coffee volume sales at Safeway; if we loosen the cutoff for store loyalty to include those who are Favorable Store

Switchers, the 54% of Safeway shoppers who buy their ground coffee at Safeway two or more times a year will account for 86% of Safeway's ground coffee sales.[24]

Moreover, remarkably, each of the supermarket *chains* has approximately the same *proportion* of store-loyal and store-switching shoppers (although again there is a "double jeopardy" effect for smaller stores, namely mini-market chains and independents). Big chains with a lot of retail outlets not only have a higher penetration in terms of people who shop there but also a higher repeat-shopping rate than smaller stores.

Store loyalty, as we would expect, diminishes as the analyzed time period lengthens: the longer the time period, the more likely it is that shoppers will have visited other stores.

This is shown clearly in a study of 10,000 households' grocery (chain supermarket *and* small stores) shopping behavior by the research firm of Information Resources Inc.[25] To allow for the occasional "emergency" or "side trip," Store Loyals were defined by IRI as those who made 85% or more of their shopping trips to the one store. As shown in Table 15.1, the proportion of Store Loyals, by the quite strict 85%+ criterion, is quite high over the short period of one week (58%) but declines to only about one in three shoppers over a six-month period (34%). Also shown in the table is the distribution of stores shopped over a middle-length time interval, three months (12 weeks): the average shopper visits three to four grocery stores over a three-month period and only 8% of consumers shop exclusively at a single store over a three-month period. Most important, and consistent with the importance to retailers of store switchers who take advantage of price deals (price specials outside the U.S.A.): the more stores visited, the more the shopper is likely to be purchasing on deal.[26]

TABLE 15.1 *Shopper loyalty to retail grocery stores (supermarkets and small stores) declines with time.*

	TIME PERIOD			
STORE LOYALTY	1 WEEK	4 WEEKS	12 WEEKS	24 WEEKS
Percentage doing 85% or more of their grocery shopping at *one* store	58	44	36	34

ACTUAL NUMBER OF STORES SHOPPED (BY *ALL* SHOPPERS) IN A 12-WEEK PERIOD		
	PERCENT	INDEX OF ON-DEAL PURCHASES
1 store only	8	100
2 stores	18	
3–4 stores	48	116
5 or more stores	26	133
	100	

Sample = 10,000 households in 1984.

SOURCE: IRI data reported in J.C. Totten and M.P. Block, 1987; see note 25.

An average of 40% of all FMCG retail sales in the U.S.A. are on deal – in other words, the *typical* brand-item is sold at a discount price 40% of the time![27]

The average grocery shopping trip lasts just 22 minutes (in the store).[28] However, this represents an average of major trips every two weeks (about 44 minutes) and quick trips every two to four days (about 10 minutes each).[29] Approximately half of the shoppers at a supermarket will buy 10 or fewer items on a quick trip – those shoppers use the express checkout lanes. The other half will buy perhaps 50 to 60 items in the 40–50 minutes they are in the store. Whereas this seems like an item chosen every 50 seconds or so, the rate is actually much faster than this when you subtract the walking time and the checkout time.[30] Observational studies of supermarket shopping behavior indicate that sighting the display to putting the item in the shopping cart is only 9.4 seconds, with 48% of purchases requiring less than five seconds![31] This highlights the importance of packaging – for Brand Recognition – for FMCG products, as we emphasized in Chapter 8.

STORE LAYOUT

The physical Layout of the store can have a large effect on what is purchased. Customers do not go to every area of the store. A typical supermarket, for instance, has 30 zones of broad product categories but the average customer on the average shopping trip passes only 25% of them (manufacturers should consider how this affects *actual* distribution!).

In-store traffic flow and volume can be measured by direct observation, by infrared sensors, or by using electronic tags on shopping carts in stores that have these.[32] Interestingly, a right-side front entrance encourages an anti-clockwise traffic flow and, in supermarkets, shoppers who go that way spend about $2 more per trip. Store image-forming items should be placed at the front of the store. "Must buy" items, such as milk and other staples in the case of grocery retailers, or replacement parts in the case of automotive or electronic retailers, should be placed at the back of the store in order to draw customers through the aisles past other product displays.

At the micro level, the retailer should experiment with shelf "layout," using a computer program such as ACNielsen's SPACEMAN to allocate products to shelf space in a way that maximizes profit.

For instance, one retailer's application of SPACEMAN turned around a 10% below-industry average in shampoo sales to 10% above the industry average within six months and all brands showed a profit increase, across all stores.[33]

Quite surprisingly, the organization of brand-items *within* product categories can produce increases in sales for the store.[34]

For instance, arranging cereals by brand produces more sales than arranging them by cereal type; arranging soft drinks by manufacturer produces more sales than arranging them by bottle size; and sales of toothbrushes increase when they are placed in the middle of the toothpaste section rather than next to it. The retailer should experiment with within-category layouts.

Up to this point we have been talking about retail layout for Supermarkets – a type of store that does and should use a *grid layout*. The **grid layout** facilitates *routine* shopping behavior.[35] Store types that can benefit from customers *browsing* before purchase – fashion clothing stores, bookstores, for instance – should use a **freeform layout**, which is just what it sounds like, namely asymmetric and with varied displays and plenty of room to move between displays. Store types that have difficulty encouraging customers to *visit multiple departments* – such as, indeed, department stores – should use what is called the **racetrack-boutique layout**, a complex design consisting of *semi*-separate display areas connected by almost a *maze* of paths so that shoppers frequently uexpectedly come across a department they did not plan to visit. This interesting layout, first identified apparently in the retailing management textbook by Lewison[36], has been adopted in recent years by many department stores.

RETAIL ATMOSPHERE

Quite independent of the physical layout of the store is its psychological atmosphere. The internal **retail atmosphere** of the retail outlet – a store, reception area, or office – is encoded immediately by customers in terms of two (type 1) emotional dimensions – Pleasantness (or Affect) and Arousal. Basic as these emotional responses may be, they have a large effect on customers' willingness to spend time in the store and also to *purchase more*.[37]

> The two dimensions interact in an important manner. In *pleasant* (Positive Affect) retail environments, such as department stores or boutiques, the retailer should keep the *arousal level high*, via stimuli such as bright colors or fast music. In contrast, in *unpleasant* (Negative Affect) retail environments, such as doctors' or dentists' offices, *and* supermarkets, the retailer should tone *down* the arousal level, via softer colors or slow music.

Color, music, and olfactory cues are the main stimuli that affect Pleasantness *and* Arousal. There is also the stimulus of credit card stickers. The four stimuli are examined below.

Color

Color in a retail environment is low cost to implement and has large effects on store atmosphere (arousal, pleasantness) *and* beliefs about the retailer. To *increase* arousal, use colors toward the red end of the color spectrum and make them intense. Conversely, to *decrease* arousal, use colors toward the violet end of the color spectrum and make them more pastel.[38] To increase *pleasantness*, on the other hand, there is *no general rule about color* because pleasantness is judged *jointly* with the object (the product or service category).

> For example, blue is not a good color for food retailing environments whereas it may be pleasant for electronics retailing. The retailer must further be alert to learned *cultural* reactions to colors – type 2 emotional responses in our terminology – which are pronounced and often contrary to the extent that cultural color beliefs may override the color × object evaluation. To give just a couple of examples, the "color" white means "Purity" in most Western cultures but is the color of "Death" in Asia; green means "Healthy" and "Go" in the West, whereas it means "Danger" in Malaysia and "Sincerity" in China.[39] Multinational retailers, or retailers who have clientele from different cultures, must be sensitive to cultural color associations.

Music

Music – as installed by providers such as MUZAK – is a promotional stimulus that can be used in most selling environments. Music is inexpensive to manipulate. In the several experiments that have been conducted to date, music has shown remarkable effects on sales. The effects are so large and the process is so clearly subconscious that it is a wonder music in retail environments has not been legislated against on ethical grounds (the teleological objection would be to overspending and the deontological objection to the means). Anyway, it's legal, so if a retailer with an unpleasant or somewhat stressful environment – supermarkets – wants people to spend more, they should use *slow* music, which is 60 bpm, or "heartbeat" rate.

In Milliman's famous experiment in supermarkets – well, famous among consumer behavior academics anyway – in which he varied only the music tempo, as no vocals were played, gross sales per store per day averaged $16,740 on days when 60 bpm music was played and $12,113 when 120 bpm (rock 'n roll tempo) music was played, a 38% sales increase for slow music![40] In restaurants and bars, people will drink faster if the background music is slow, to bring their mental stimulation level up to optimal. In bars that play country & western music, this could also be partly due to vocal content – the songs are mostly so sad that you need to *get* stimulated!

Actually, music *content*, not just its tempo, also makes a difference.

In one experiment conducted in the section of a U.K. supermarket where alcoholic beverages are sold, the researchers arranged for distinctly French music to be played on alternate week days over a two-week period and distinctly German music to be played on the other days. There was a baseline preference for French wine but, on days when the French music was played, French wine outsold German wine by 40 bottles to eight; whereas on days on which German music was played, German wine outsold the French wine by 22 bottles to 12. Fewer than 10% of the shoppers who were interviewed and asked extensive probe questions afterwards had any idea that the music had influenced their choice.[41]

Olfactory cues

Olfactory cues – the everyday term is **odor** – can be employed in any retail environment. Like color and music, Odors in the air elicit type 1 and usually type 2 emotions. The type 1 reaction is phylogenetically primitive (lower brain) and seems to be mainly an Approach-Avoidance reaction, although there is reasonable evidence also for an erotic Arousal response from the smell of pheromone chemicals present in certain scents[42], the principal effect of which would be to reinforce approach behavior and make people linger longer. This may make them spend more.[43]

When Olfactory Cues are injected in a retail environment without customers being able to detect their presence, our opinion is that this is unethical seller behavior. Even the *attempt* to persuade people subconsciously is deontologically unethical, whether the attempt is successful or not. However, we would regard the use of *detectable and reportable* scents – even if artificial – as being fair.

Of course, grocery retailers also – quite ethically – use *actual* scent, such as the real smell of baked goods near that department, which they have found to increase sales quite dramatically.

Credit card stickers

Finally, we should mention the remarkably strong – though ethically questionable – effect of the presence of **credit card stickers**. The prominent display of pictorial logos of credit cards, to signify that these cards are accepted by the retailer, has been shown, in both simulated store settings and in retailers' catalogs, to make consumers *more willing to buy* the item as well as to pay a *higher price* for it.[44] For willing customers, credit card payment is a convenience but an expensive one, because they are more likely to buy than otherwise and less likely to shop around for a lower price. Some shoppers know this (the first author is a willing credit card shopper) but, for many, the phenomenon is totally unwitting.

> The ethical solution would be to allow credit card purchase but not *advertise* the fact. Visa and MasterCard would support this suggestion, no doubt, as they have the widest retail distribution!

RETAIL FEATURE ADS

Retail feature ads are retailers' major marcoms expense. Retail Feature Ads are placed in city and suburban newspapers, on local television, in local editions of magazines or in door-to-door brochures or flyers. These ads showcase – hence "feature" – a *number* of products which are usually (but not always) offered at a discount price.

In Feature Ads, decisions have to be made *every time* about (a) which items to include and (b) at what amount of discount. The typical supermarket retailer, for instance, has to decide which items to include from among 1,000 to 3,000 items (mainly those on trade promotion deals from the manufacturer) per *week!* A typical weekly or twice-weekly retail feature ad, either in a cluttered one-page format or in a less-cluttered three-page format, includes about 15 items.

> An *Expert System* developed by McCann and colleagues shows how this could be achieved for a supermarket retailer.[45] The longer three-page format should be used because it is less cluttered and will gain – and for retail shoppers, hold – attention. Feature four "hot items" on the first page – leading brands deeply discounted due to manufacturers' case allowances; then five "good deals" on the second page – leading brands with medium turnover offered at not quite as deep a discount (but still those permitting a discount from the case allowance). Finally, feature six items with good margins for the retailer on the final page – which could be any brands from low turnover categories which are actually offered at *no discount* but represent a profit to the retailer because they were bought on deal from the manufacturer. Supplementary rules are to spread the "hot items" across a range of product categories and not to repeat any item in the product category during its purchase cycle.
>
> In **retail catalogs**, profit for the retailer will be maximized by adjusting the ad space devoted to each product such that the profit per square inch (or square centimeter) is equal across products.[46] For instance, an item generating $2,000 profit per week should get twice as much ad space as an item generating $1,000 profit per week. This rule would also apply to **online catalogs**, which are a common form of Website ad.

Many retailers use "bait and switch" advertising, despite it being illegal. Bait and switch (b & s) is the practice whereby retailers advertise an item at a low price that they know will be attractive to consumers (to get them into the store) but then deliberately stock only a limited number of the discounted item so that they can try to persuade interested customers to switch to a higher-priced or higher-margin substitute once they are in the store. *Although bait and switch is illegal, it continues to be practiced by many retailers because it is very difficult to police.*

Gerstner and Hess take the ethical view that the "end" justifies the illegal "means" by showing in a survey that consumers are usually *more satisfied* with the substitute item than with comparable items bought without being b & s'd.[47] We note, however, that the reported satisfaction could stem from *dissonance reduction*. In any case, bait and switch is a deliberate attempt to deceive and should not be condoned.

POINT-OF-PURCHASE DISPLAYS

A **display** at the point of purchase, sometimes called a **POP display**, is a widely used retailing device for drawing customers' attention to a *promotion* – well, to an *apparent* promotion, as there is no legal requirement that the items on display have to have their shelf price reduced!

Because a Display is a contrasting stimulus, one important way in which a display works is by eliciting *reflexive* attention to the promotional message and thus to the brand. However, displays also work through the process of *selective* attention. Because consumers in the past have been rewarded (more correctly, negatively reinforced by saving money) for purchasing promoted brands from displays, the mere *presence* of a display causes them to believe that the brand on display is also "on special" when in reality it may not be, or when in reality the "deal" might be very minor. An illusory price cut, of course, is an ethically questionable retail promotion technique.

The "On Special" Effect was hypothesized long ago for special displays by Engel and Blackwell[48] and the sales effect of displays *without* a price cut has been confirmed in at least two studies[49] and also by Information Resource Inc.'s (IRI) research.

Displays are very effective for *retailers* in their quest to move products. An analysis of the three main forms of retailer's promotions – Retail Feature Ads, Displays and Price-Offs – demonstrates that displays are relatively the most effective.

Figure 15.2 shows an analysis conducted by IRI[50] based on 780 brands in 116 product categories over the course of a year. The simplest type of promotion, a 10% Price-Off, increases sales by 20%. When this Price-Off is featured in a prior Retail Ad, sales increase a further 78%. Alternatively, if the price-off is part of an in-store Display, sales increase 105%. The effect of all three promotional devices used *together* is a massive (short-term) 203% increase in sales – with the Display being the single largest factor, coupled with the considerably boosted effect of the display following feature advertising (which is a Ratchet Effect).

The problem of cluttering aisles, however, places a physical limit on the number of displays that can be accommodated by the retailer on any shopping day.[51]

Price-off promotions

A **price-off promotion** is a *temporary* reduction, made by the *retailer*, of the "normal" price of the brand-item. (Retailers can implement price-offs in a number of ways: through *feature ads* in newspapers or other media, including *store flyers*, which announce the price-off available at the point of purchase; through *price-off coupons* included in these ads or available at the shelf or at the cash register; by using a *display* with a price reduction; by a *shelf-price reduction*, clearly designated

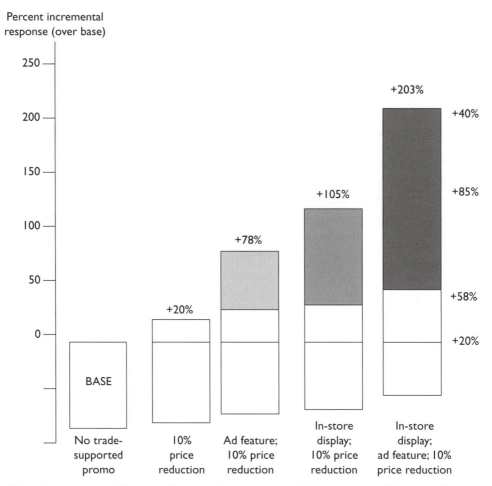

FIGURE 15.2 *Sales results for 10% price-offs, retail feature ads and POP displays (and their combinations). Unit sales increases, indexed to no-promotion base sales, are here averaged over 780 brands in 116 retail grocery product categories.*

SOURCE: IRI results reported by G.M. Fulgoni, 1987; see note 50 at end of chapter. This figure is reproduced with the kind permission of *Admap*. For more details go to <www.warc.com/admap>.

as such; or by reducing the price with *no mention* of the reduction. Henderson[52] has found some evidence that these various "media" of price-offs tend to attract different consumers and it is probably in the retailer's interest to use a variety of means of implementation in order to attract a larger number of different individuals to the store.)

The retailer's Price-Offs may well attract *store* switchers, as they certainly attract *brand* switchers. For FMCG products, over 80% of the extra sales due to a price-off come from Favorable Brand Switchers (probably Routinized FBSs) as shown in Table 15.2.

Price-Off promotions are very rarely profitable for the FMCG *manufacturer*; as we stated previously, 96% of them produce no long-run sales increase after the initial blip and dip. However, price promotions juggled over many manufacturers' items are obviously profitable for the *retailer*, otherwise these hard-nosed experimentalists would not use them so much. It should be noted, by the way, that FMCG retailers typically operate on profit margins as low as 1% of dollar sales.

TABLE 15.2 *Target audience responses to a typical brand of supermarket product at its normal price and when offered on a price-off deal, measured in sales units (with rounding, the total is 99%).*

TYPE OF BUYER	PERCENT OF SALES AT NORMAL PRICE	PERCENT OF PURCHASES DURING DEAL	INCREASE	PERCENT OF BRAND'S BUYERS RESPONSIBLE FOR THE *ADDITIONAL* SALES
Brand loyals (80–100% loyal)	52	68	+16	11
Brand switchers (less than 80% loyal to any brand)	43	156	+113	83
Other-brand loyals (80–98% loyal to *another* brand)	2	6	+4	3
New category users (first purchase in category)	3	6	+3	2
	100	236	+136	99

SOURCE: Adapted from IRI data reported in J.C. Totten and M.P. Block, 1987; see note 25 at end of chapter.

It is worthwhile to examine retailer's price-off *tactics*, if only for our education as consumers! There are four main variables: the wording of the price-off offer; whether the savings are stated in monetary or percentage terms; the effects of price-endings; and a stated time limit or limited purchase amount.

Price-off wording

The retailer's *wording* of the price-off offer in feature ads or in point-of-purchase signage seems to exert quite a strong effect. *Explicit comparative* wording, either "Total value/Sale price" or "Regular price/Sale price," is perceived as better value for the money than the implicitly comparative wordings, "Now only" or "Our price."[53] Both types of wording are implicated in the controversial issue of **high-low pricing** whereby retailers set the original price at an artificially high level for a brief period and then discount the item for a *long* period against the original price.[54] (This term should not be confused with the identically worded misnomer that has emerged as a contrast to the supermarket practice of **everyday low price**, EDLP. The true contrast to EDLP is simply **variable pricing**.) In the U.S.A. some 60% to 75% of the volume of consumer durables is sold via low prices offered against an artificially high "usual" price. Some U.S. states have introduced legislation to limit this practice. For instance, Massachusetts law requires that 30% or more of the item's sales must occur at the normal (original) price, *or* that this price must be in use for at least

15 continuous days prior to the sale and that the sale price can then be offered for no more than 45% of the next 180 days.[55]

Price wording may also imply an unfair *competitive* claim. In a famous example in the U.S.A., Wal-Mart stores was forced in 1994 by the National Advertising Review Board to stop using its slogan "Always the low price. Always." Wal-Mart has since amended its slogan to "Always low prices. Always. Wal-Mart."[56] Wal-Mart can no longer imply *the* low price, that is, the low*est* price available.

Monetary or percentage savings

Price-off *savings* can be shown in terms of *monetary* savings, in dollars or cents, or in *percentage* terms.[57] For a single item, indicating the monetary savings would appear to be more effective than indicating the percentage savings. In practice, the fact that retailers more often use the monetary savings format suggests it is the more effective. However, for a retailer who is trying to attract customers to the store by offering savings on *many* items, the retailer has to state some sort of *average* percentage savings. The retailer could bluntly use what is strangely known as an "objective" claim, if the *average* savings is 25%, of "Save 25%." However, the savings on some items would be less than this unless all items were priced at exactly 25% off, and the objective claim would then be misleading. The same effectiveness would probably be achieved for the case of buying many items by stating the truthful claim "Average savings: 25%." Alternatively, the retailer can use what is known as a "tensile" price claim, in which a *vague reference* is made to the amount of savings. The most common forms of tensile claims are *maximum,* such as "Save up to 40%"; *range,* "Save 10 to 40%"; and *minimum,* "Save 10% or more." The *maximum* claim seems to be most effective, because when asked to state what they thought the *maximum* discount would be for a claim of "Save up to 40%," most interestingly 80% of consumers thought that the maximum would be 40% to 49%, being optimistic about the maximum possible deal.[58] The Maximum claim is technically true and thus ethical, and more effective than an Average savings claim.

Price-endings

The third implementation tactic for retailer's price-offs (which also applies to pricing in general) is the use of particular *price-endings.* It has long been known that various price-endings have subjective or "psychological" connotations. Schindler, the leading researcher of price-ending effects, points out that (a) a price-ending of 95 or 99 cents, such as $49.99, suggests a *discount*; (b) an unusual ending such as 63 cents, as in $7.63, suggests a *carefully determined price* where the retailer has perhaps offered the maximum savings down to some fixed margin; and (c) a 00 or rounded ending, such as $400, suggests a *high-quality* product (or store).[59] Moreover, customers certainly notice, and respond to, price-endings and not just the general price.[60]

Limited time or purchase amount

As consumers, we are all susceptible to The Scarcity Effect.[61] An announced limit on a price-off promotion, such as "This week only" or "Limit two per customer," works very well for retailers.[62]

The practice is legal for retailers to adopt and the offer, once decided by the retailer, is truthfully stated. However, if the limit is imposed just to sell more product and if most consumers believe that there must have been some necessary reason for the limit, then the practice is deceptive and should be prosecuted.

STORE BRANDS

Store brands are products made by major manufacturers but packaged under the retailer's "own" label (known as a **private label** in the U.S.A.). The label can be the name of the store or a "house brand" name invented by the retailer. The practice of store branding has largely *replaced* the earlier practice of **generic branding**, which is somewhat different in that Generic "no name" brands were typically made and put on the market by groups of smaller manufacturers who could not afford to advertise and therefore banded together to offer a clearly *un*advertised low-priced "brand." Store Brands, and Generic Brands where they still exist, are typically sold at a price that is *at least 20% lower* than the average price for **national brands** (also called **name brands**) and sometimes up to 50% lower. Their perennially lower price makes Store Brands a *promotion* tactic.

The success of Store Brands varies widely by category and retailer. In the U.S.A., in the *average* supermarket product category, one in five of that category's sales are the store brand.[63] For supermarkets in the U.K., the market share of store brands is considerably higher.

Among leading supermarket retailers, ASDA sells about 32% of its total turnover under its own label; and the highest incidence of own-label sales is observed at Sainsbury's, where 54% of its products are sold under the Sainsbury label. The general share for European supermarkets is that 40% of sales are store brands.[64] Upmarket clothing retailers in the U.S.A., such as Brooks Brothers, and in the U.K., such as Marks & Spencer, probably have an even higher percentage of store brand sales. In effect, the more upmarket store brands have become *Name Brands* and are advertised similarly.

Interestingly, the Store Brand's share of sales in a given product category is *not* proportional to the degree of price differential in comparison with the National Brands. Rather, the store brand's share of sales mainly increases with the extent to which the product *category* is perceived to be commodity-like with brands differing little in perceived quality, such as milk in supermarkets or aspirin in chain drugstores.

In the U.K.[65] and, we suspect, in other countries, there *tends* to be a segment of shoppers who prefer Store Brands in every store in which they shop. In most countries this segment appears to be of substantial size and this would explain why most retailers now offer a store brand.

CARD-BASED LOYALTY PROGRAMS

Many big retailers have introduced a **card-based loyalty program** (based on their own charge cards). However, like airline frequent-flyer programs before them, these have mainly had the *null* effect of keeping retailers' market shares constant in the category. Card usage is rarely exclusive to one retailer.

For instance, in England, 35% of Sainsbury's Reward Card holders also have a Tesco Clubcard, and 30% of Tesco Clubcard holders have a Sainsbury's Reward Card.[66] It has been widely reported in the British trade press that Tesco is the only food retailer that has made a profit from introducing a card-based loyalty club – not because their customers have become more frequent or larger-volume shoppers at that store, but because Tesco's management invested wisely in establishing a proper database of customer characteristics and they *work* the database very effectively with reminders and cross-promotions.[67]

The retailer should not rush into offering a loyalty scheme without first conducting a small-scale but thorough *pre-test*.

The experience of Delvita, a high-quality supermarket chain in Czechoslovakia, is instructive here. In 1996, Delvita launched a card-based loyalty program to try to counter the U.K. chain Tesco and also the French chain Carrefour, both of which had recently entered the Czech market. The card scheme cost Delvita more money than it brought in in extra revenue. A subsequent survey of customers found that 88% said they would shop at Delvita anyway, card or no card. In response to a related question, 83% said they would continue to shop there if the card were withdrawn (a negligible 1% said they would leave if the card were withdrawn, and the other 16% were non-committal). Delvita killed the card scheme late in 2001. The previous card budget was used to reduce prices on a long-term basis on 1,000 product lines; Delvita gave each previous cardholder a small cash bonus and also remodeled some of its stores and improved its service throughout the chain. The result in the year after the card was dropped was a 5% increase in sales, which is a massive increase for an established supermarket retailer.[68]

HOME SHOPPING

Home shopping is a retailer's promotion that appeals by *time saving* rather than monetary saving, as delivery costs make it more expensive to shop from home in most cases. There are two forms of home shopping: via *Direct-Response* ads, and *Online* ads.

Home shopping from Direct-Response ads has been around a long time. This includes TV shopping channels, catalogs, direct mail, and direct-response ads in mass media. The purchase order is made by mail, fax, or phone. It is paid for by credit card, check, money order, or cash on delivery – in fact the last three methods far outweigh credit card payments in Europe. It used to be that some manufacturers distributed only by home shopping, such as L.L. Bean and Talbots, but now nearly all also have retail stores or distribute to retailers.

Online home shopping has been made possible by *interactive* TV and PC ads (on Websites). Offered mainly by retailers, TV or PC Online Home Shopping can, like Direct-Response Ad Home Shopping, be offered by manufacturers as a bypass-the-retailer form of Direct Marketing. The necessary component for the consumer or customer is access to the Internet. The purchase may or may not be made online. It can be made by telephone (a call or an SMS), by fax or mail – or in person, as many prefer to search and evaluate online and then go to the store to buy the item. For some retailers, shoppers can access an interactive digital version of the store at a trade or consumer show, at a kiosk in a shopping mall, or even in the store itself.

In Asian countries especially – together the largest consumer base in the world – people love to shop and Online shopping has very little appeal.[69]

It is clear that Home Shopping is attractive only for certain types of products and services. Direct-response ad home shopping and Online ad home shopping suits some customers but will not replace retail stores. In fact, as new shopping channel options are introduced, the traditional retail channels usually attract *more* business, not less. For instance, with the introduction of ATMs and, later, online banking, the number of bank branches in the U.S.A. has *grown* by about 30%.[70] The exception, you would think, would be airline travel agents, but no loss of business in that industry has been reported since Online bookings have been available. As Nunes and Cespedes observe, these new intermediary retailers face a survival problem if *payment* is not made through them.[71]

SUMMARY

Promotions are incentives to "act now." And most have the temporary effect of doing just that. To make them work beyond the immediate action or purchase event, managers should design promotion offers so that they also function to increase Brand Awareness and Brand Preference. Promotions that incorporate tactics for these two universal communication objectives are called customer franchise-building (CFB) promotions.

The action objective for promotions is either Trial or Repeat Purchase for FMCG products and services, or Purchase for durables (or other action equivalents of purchase behaviors).

Manufacturers use promotions, first of all, to get Retailers to try – that is, stock and distribute – their products or services. An Introductory Price Allowance, a policy of Returns, or, for FMCG retail especially, a New Line Fee are the retail trial promotions most typically used by manufacturers. Retail distribution, it should be emphasized, is the most important success factor for new products and also for established products. Advertising to consumers and promotions to retailers, the two other success factors, leverage themselves on prior distribution.

Manufacturers also offer Trial promotions to End-Customers. These trial promotions are offered directly or through retailers. Product or Service Sampling is an end-customer trial promotion technique that can be employed by business marketers or consumer marketers and is the strongest trial-generating technique. The other six possibilities, though not possible for all types of marketers, are Rebates, Bonus Packs, Direct Price-Offs, Warranties, Premiums, and Coupons (FMCG) in countries where coupons are allowed.

Manufacturers have four main techniques available for Repeat-Purchase promotions. The most widely used technique is Direct Price-Offs, usually just called Price Promotions. Price Promotions (price-offs) stimulate a sharp rise in sales followed by a corresponding dip when the promotion is stopped. Extensive evidence indicates that price promotions are not profitable for the manufacturer and they should be avoided if possible. However, this evidence does not isolate "ratcheted" price promotions, which use a burst of advertising before the promotion and are more likely to be profitable. Other techniques for repeat-purchase promotions are Multi-Purchase Sweepstakes or Contests, Multi-Purchase Loyalty Premiums (most of which are in fact multi-purchase *price-offs*), and Packaging. These should be executed in a CFB manner.

Retailers can employ eight main promotion techniques: Store Layout, Retail Atmosphere, Retail Feature Ads, Point-of-Purchase Displays, Price-Off promotions, Store Brands, Card-Based Loyalty Programs, and Home Shopping.

Store Layout and variables affecting Atmosphere can have a remarkably strong effect on the propensity to purchase the product or service. However, the manipulation of such environmental variables as store layout, color, music, and also lighting (a variable which we have not discussed because of the absence of systematic research), to the extent that they are not consciously perceived by customers, could be regarded as unfair trading although we know of no consumer complaints about these techniques, unlike the frequent complaints about advertising and about occasionally deceptive retailer's promotions!

Retail Feature Ads are the largest marcoms expense for most retailers. The two decisions for the retailer are which items to feature in each ad and how much discount to offer on them, if any, because many of these advertised items are the result of trade deals from the manufacturer so that the retailer makes a good profit without lowering the price to the consumer. A retail ad from a large multi-line retailer, such as a supermarket chain, will usually feature about 15 items spread over two or three pages or in a flyer. A format of "hot items" first, followed by "good deals" and ending with trade dealt non-discount items, seems to be effective. Limited line retailers, such as furniture stores, often advertise on TV and therefore can feature far fewer items, usually just the "hot items." Bait and Switch Advertising is an illegal but widespread practice, widespread because it is difficult for regulators to police every instance of this and industry bodies do not seem to see it as an ethical concern.

Point-of-Purchase (POP) Displays are a highly effective means of increasing sales of the brand-item, so much so that their use is limited only by the need to prevent intolerable in-store clutter. POP Displays work doubly well if the item is featured beforehand in a retail ad. Most POP displays include a price-off offer on the item although legally they do not have to. Consumers have learned to expect that displayed items have a discounted price but they do not usually check this.

Price-Off promotions by the *Retailer*, in which the retailer reduces the manufacturer's recommended retail price, are the *most widely used* retail promotion technique. As we noted at the beginning of the chapter, where we summarized retail shopping behavior, about 40% of all FMCG sales are made with some form of price discount. Usually called just Price Promotions, they are essential to the FMCG retailer's profit, which is typically only about 1% of sales anyway. Price-Off offers are marketing communications and the explicit comparative price-off wording works best, although there is another ethical issue here with the widespread practice of High-Low Pricing, whereby retailers use an artificially high "usual" price and offer the discount against that. So-called tensile price claims, such as "Save up to 40%," are likely to be optimistically interpreted by customers. Price-ending effects are surprisingly influential, whereby 5 and 9 endings suggest a discount, other ending numbers suggest a carefully worked out price, and "00" endings suggest quality.

Store Brands are used as a promotion technique by most retailers. There is genuine value here as most of these products are made by the major manufacturers and they can be purchased at 20% or more lower price. The store brands of upmarket retailers have become well-valued brands and often are just 10% or so lower priced than name brands. There appears to be a segment of shoppers who prefer store brands no matter which type of retail store they are shopping in.

Card-Based Loyalty Programs do not engender true loyalty and when all retailers in a category offer them, market shares stay the same. The only way to make incremental profit from a loyalty-card program is to *database* the cardholders in terms of what they buy and then run *reminder* promotions and cross-promotions.

Home Shopping, via traditional Direct-Response ads or, increasingly, Online ads, represents an alternative retail channel. With *online* shopping, perhaps as many as half of customers use TV or PC interactive ads to search for information to make their choice but then go to the physical retail outlet to make the purchase. Home shopping seems to assist, rather than replace, bricks-and-mortar retailing. The catch for the intermediary retail agent, however, is to try to capture payment direct to them.

DISCUSSION QUESTIONS

15.1 Outline several examples of how Sampling might be used to encourage *retailers of durables* to try a line of new products. Then outline several examples of how Sampling can be used with their *end-customers*. Finally, outline several examples of how Sampling could be used for end-customers for *services*.

15.2 Collect two Warranties for any product or service you can find. How do they match up with the characteristics for an effective warranty as described in the chapter?

15.3 What are the limitations of Direct Price-Offs as a trial-generating technique for end-customers? Think up some CFB implementation tactics to lessen these limitations.

15.4 Choose and evaluate, for Heineken beer, a Free Premium and a Self-Liquidating Premium.

15.5 As a repeat-purchase promotion technique aimed at end-customers, Direct Price-Offs are not recommended for general use because they are not profitable. How might you implement a *series* of Direct Price-Off promotions so that their CFB effects are maximized and their chances increased of being profitable?

15.6 Choose and evaluate a suitable Loyalty Premium for customers of a luxury hotel chain.

15.7 We said that Packaging can act as a repeat-purchase promotion technique. How?

15.8 Team project. Select the local outlet of a multi-line retailer and do an observational traffic count, being careful to sample across opening hours. Then make recommendations for improving the store's Layout so as to increase sales. If you can, also recommend improvements in within-category layouts.

15.9 How can the retailer ethically improve Retail Atmosphere in a retail outlet that is (a) neutral or negative in pleasantness and (b) already pleasant?

15.10 Interview the manager of a small supermarket, such as a 7-Eleven or a gas station mini-market and design a Retail Feature Ad for that week.

15.11 In the same store, if you wish, first observe shoppers and then interview the manager about the use and effectiveness of POP Displays, then write a brief report.

15.12 Discuss the ethics of Retail Price-Off promotions.

15.13 Across several types of retail stores, compare the price differences between Name Brands and Store Brands. What factors might account for the *percentage* difference?

15.14 Write a brief report of your experiences with Online Home Shopping. If you've never done it, interview a friend who has.

NOTES

1. A.S.C. Ehrenberg, G.J. Goodhardt, and T.P. Barwise, Double jeopardy revisited, *Journal of Marketing*, 1990, 54(3), pp. 82–91.

2. P. Farris, J. Olver, and G. de Kluyver, The relationship between distribution and market share, *Marketing Science*, 1989, 8(2), pp. 107–127.

3. A.R. Rao and H. Mahi, The price of launching a new product: empirical evidence of factors affecting the relative magnitude of slotting allowances, *Marketing Science*, 2003, 22(2), pp. 246–268.

4. F.R. Kardes, *Consumer Behavior and Managerial Decision-Making*, Englewood Cliffs, NJ: Prentice Hall, 2002.

5. R.B. Cialdini, *Influence: The Psychology of Persuasion*, New York, NY: Quill, 1998.

6. S. Gopalakrishna and J.D. Williams, Planning and performance assessment of industrial trade shows: an exploratory study, *International Journal of Research in Marketing*, 1992, 9(19), pp. 207–224. The U.S. expenditure is closer to 20% and the European expenditure closer to 25% according to sources cited in S. Gopalakrishna and G.L. Lilien, A three-stage model of industrial trade show performance, *Marketing Science*, 1995, 14(1) pp. 22–42.

7. Estimates from Cahners Advertising Research Report #542.1F, 1992, as interpreted by S. Gopalakrishna and G.L. Lilien, 1995, same reference as in the previous note.

8. Based on estimates by H. Aniero, an expert promotion consultant, in a privately circulated document.

9. For an excellent discussion of the importance of reference price and a summary of recent findings, see G. Kalyanaram and R. Winer, Empirical generalizations from reference price research, *Marketing Science*, 1995, 14(3, part 2), pp. G161–G169.

10. T.A. Shimp and W.O. Bearden, Warranties and other extrinsic cue effects on consumers' risk perceptions, *Journal of Consumer Research*, 1982, 9(1), pp. 38–46. Shimp and Bearden examined the effect of warranties on the trial purchase of three high-risk, innovative products: a multiscreen TV set, a plastic auto tire, and a computerized indoor jogging device.

11. I. Simonson, Choice based on reasons: the case of attraction and compromise effects, *Journal of Consumer Research*, 1989, 16(2), pp. 158–174.

12. NCH Marketing Services Inc. figures for the U.S.A. in 2002, reported in *Marketing News*, May 26, 2003, p. 3.

13. These figures come from a POPAI/DuPont study summarized in L.J. Haugh, Buying-habits study update, *Advertising Age*, June 27, 1977, pp. 56–58.

14. X. Dreze and D.R. Bell, Creating win-win trade promotions: theory and empirical analysis of scan-back trade deals, *Marketing Science*, 2003, 23(1), pp. 16–39.

15. E. Garner, Do sales promotions really work?, *Admap*, 2002, July–August, pp. 30–32.

16. M. Dekimpe, EMAC Conference presentation, Glasgow, May 2003; also see S. Srinivasan, K. Pauwels, D.M. Hanssens, and M. Dekimpe, Do promotions benefit manufacturers, retailers, or both?, *Management Science*, forthcoming. Also see K. Pauwels, D.M. Hanssens, and S. Siddarth, The long-term effects of price promotions on category incidence, brand choice, and purchase quantity, *Journal of Marketing Research*, 2002, 39(4), pp. 421–439.

17. K. Pauwels, J. Silva-Risso, S. Srinivasan, and D.M. Hanssens, The long-term impact of new product introductions and promotions, presentation at INFORMS Marketing Science Conference, College Park, MD, June 2003.

18. J. Neff, Duracell market share sags in spite of turnaround effort, *Advertising Age*, January 5, 2004, pp. 3, 21.

19. Y. Yi and H. Jeon, Effects of loyalty programs on value perception, program loyalty, and brand loyalty, *Journal of the Academy of Marketing Science*, 2003, 31(3), pp. 229–240; see also E. Garner, Do sales promotions really work?, *Admap*, 2002, July–August, 30–32.

20. Yi and Jeon, same reference as in previous note.

21. D. Parker, Upgrade the best option, *The Australian*, Business Travel section, February 27, 2004, pp. 1–2.

22. R. Briggs, Does bribery build brand loyalty? Reported in G. Stephenson, Garbage in, garbage out, *Viewpoint*, 1999, July (reproduced on the ARF Website).

23. Estimates compiled from the following sources: R.E. Bucklin and J.M. Lattin, A two-stage model of purchase incidence and brand choice, *Marketing Science*, 1991, 10(1), pp. 24–39; R.C. Blattberg, G.D. Eppen, and J. Lieberman, A theoretical and empirical evaluation of price deals for consumer nondurables, *Journal of Marketing*, 1981, 45(1) pp. 116–129; K. Helsen and D.C. Schmittlein, How does a product market's typical price-promotion pattern affect the timing of households' purchases? An empirical study using UPC scanner data, *Journal of Retailing*, 1992, 68(3), pp. 316–338.

24. M.D. Uncles and A.S.C. Ehrenberg, The buying of packaged goods at U.S. retail chains, *Journal of Retailing*, 1990, 66(3), pp. 278–296.

25. 1984 IRI study of 10,000 households' shopping behavior, reported in J.C. Totten and M.P. Block, *Analyzing Sales Promotion: Texts and Cases*, Chicago, Il: Commerce Communications, Inc., 1987.

26. IRI study, same reference as previous note.

27. M. Dekimpe *et al.*, same reference as in note 16.

28. K. Deveny, Displays pay off for grocery marketers, *The Wall Street Journal*, October 15, 1992, pp. B1, B5.

29. B.E. Kahn and D.C. Schmittlein, Shopping trip behavior: an empirical investigation, *Marketing Letters*, 1989, 1(1), pp. 55–69; L. Rickard, Shopping lists tell just half the real story, *Advertising Age*, January 9, 1995, p. 20.

30. K. Deveny, same reference as note 28.

31. See J.R. Rossiter and L. Percy, Visual communication in advertising, in R.J. Harris (Ed.), *Information Processing Research in Advertising*, Hillsdale, NJ: Erlbaum, 1983, chapter 3; and also Chapters 8 and 9 in this book for more on the two learning processes.

32. See H. Sorensen, The science of shopping, *Marketing Research*, 2003, 15(3), pp. 30–35, for the findings cited here.

33. See A. Mitchell, Category captains, *Marketing* (UK), April 8, 1993, p. 24; and C. Buckingham, Onset of the category management phenomenon, *Admap*, 1993, pp. 12–16.

34. R. Gibson, The fine art of stocking a supermarket's shelves, *The Wall Street Journal*, October 15, 1992, pp. B1, B10.

35. A.P. Vrechopoulos, R.M. O'Keefe, G.I. Doukidis, and G.J. Siomkos, Virtual store layout: an experimental comparison in the context of grocery retail, *Journal of Retailing*, 2004, 80(1), pp. 13–22.

36. D.M. Lewison, *Retailing*, 5th edn, New York: Macmillan, 1994.

37. R.J. Donovan and J.R. Rossiter, Store atmosphere: an environmental psychology approach, *Journal of Retailing*, 1982, 58(1), pp. 34–57; R.J. Donovan, J.R. Rossiter, G. Marcoolyn and A. Nesdale, Store atmosphere and purchasing behavior, *Journal of Retailing*, 1994, 70(3), pp. 283–294.

38. Studies reported in the classic C.E. Osgood, G.J. Suci, and P.H. Tannenbaum, *The Measurement of Meaning*, Urbane, IL: University of Illinois Press, 1957.

39. Cultural associations to color – some from controlled studies, others anecdotal – are reviewed in M.M. Aslam, A cross-cultural investigation into color as a marketing cue, working paper, University of Wollongong, December 2003.

40. R.E. Milliman, Using background music to affect the behavior of supermarket shoppers, *Journal of Marketing*, 1982, 46(3), pp. 86–91.

41. A.C. North, D.J. Hargreaves, and J. McKendrick, The influence of in-store music on wine selections, *Journal of Applied Psychology*, 1999, 88(2), pp. 271–276.

42. D. Butler, H. Gibson, K. Noble, and P. Salz-Trautman, Attention all shoppers, *Time*, August 2, 1999, pp. 44–49.

43. Observational study conducted in a large London department store, reported in the *Time* magazine article in the previous note.

44. R.A. Feinberg, Credit cards as spending facilitating stimuli: a conditioning interpretation, *Journal of Consumer Research*, 1986, 13(3), pp. 348–356. Feinberg also found that donations to charity (United Way) were higher in the presence of credit card stimuli – student donations averaged $4.01 in the credit card condition and only $1.66 in the absence of credit card cues. Does the end (social good) justify the means (possible unfair persuasion technique)?

45. J. McCann, A. Tadlaoui, and J. Gallagher, Knowledge systems in merchandising: advertising design, *Journal of Retailing*, 1990, 66(3), pp. 257–277.

46. V. Rao and J.L. Simon, Optimal allocation of space in retail advertisements and mail-order catalogs: theory and a first approximation decision rule, *International Journal of Advertising*, 1983, 2(2), pp. 123–129.

47. E. Gerstner and J.D. Hess, Can bait and switch benefit consumers?, *Marketing Science*, 1990, 9(2), pp. 114–124. B & s is current and prevalent. One of Australia's largest electronics retailers recently lost a court battle for advertising a computer software package worth $900 (AUD) for just $199 (AUD) and then not ordering enough stock to meet the expected demand; see Retailer's "bait" ads, *The Australian*, August 11, 2004, p. 3.

48. J.F. Engel and R.D. Blackwell, *Consumer Behavior*, 4th edn, Hinsdale, IL: Dryden, 1982, pp. 554–556.

49. P.M. Guadagni and J.D.C. Little, A logit model of brand choice calibrated on scanner data, *Marketing Science*, 1983, 2(3), pp. 203–238; J.J. Inman and L. McAlister, A retailer promotion policy model considering promotion signal sensitivity, *Marketing Science*, 1993, 12(4), pp. 339–356.

50. G.M. Fulgoni, The role of advertising – is there one?, *Admap*, 1987, 23(4), pp. 54–57.

51. *The Wall Street Journal*, October 15, 1992, pp. B1–B6.

52. C.M. Henderson, Promotion heterogeneity and consumer learning: refining the dual-proneness construct, in C.T. Allen and D. Roedder John (Eds), *Advances in Consumer Research*, 21, 1994, Provo, UT: Association for Consumer Research, pp. 86–94.

53. A study by Friedmann and Hains confirms the attraction of the word "sale" in retail newspaper ads and also the word "wholesale." They note that the word "sale" can be used in compliance with FTC guidelines only if the reduced price is indeed for a "limited" selling period. As we shall see shortly in conjunction with "high-low" pricing, the FTC's vague prescription allows wide latitude. See R. Friedmann and P. Hains, An investigation of comparative price advertising and newspapers, *Journal of Current Issues and Research in Advertising*, 1991, 13(1), pp. 155–173.

54. P.J. Kaufmann, G. Ortmeyer and N.C. Smith, Deception in retail sale pricing, in G. Bamossy and W.F. van Raaij (Eds), *European Advances in Consumer Research*, 1993, 1, pp. 345–351.

55. P.J. Kaufmann *et al.*, same reference as in previous note.

56. Always a slogan, *Marketing News*, June 20, 1994, p. 1.

57. In a content analysis of retail newspaper ads, Friedmann and Hains found that about two-thirds of retailers stated price-offs in monetary terms whereas one-third used percentage statements. See R. Friedmann and P. Hains, same reference as in note 53.

58. A. Biswas and S. Burton, An experimental assessment of effects associated with alternative tensile price claims, *Journal of Business Research*, 1994, 29(1), pp. 65–73. Biswas and Burton were careful not to over-generalize the results of their study, and in an earlier study provided some evidence, and a very good discussion, of situations in which using a range of savings or even the minimum level of savings may be more effective for the retailer. They found that a range of savings could be perceived as more honest if in fact very few items are offered at the maximum savings, and a minimum savings might be effective if the retailer were offering a very narrow range of savings with a low maximum. See A. Biswas and S. Burton, Consumer perceptions of tensile price claims in advertisements: an assessment of claim types across different discount levels, *Journal of the Academy of Marketing Science*, 1993, 21(3), pp. 217–229.

59. R.M. Schindler, Symbolic meanings of a price ending, in R.H. Holman and M.R. Solomon (Eds), *Advances in Consumer Research*, 18, 1991, Provo, UT: Association for Consumer Research, pp. 794–801.

60. M. Stiving and R.S. Winer, An empirical analysis of price endings with scanner data, *Journal of Consumer Research*, 1997, 24(1), pp. 57–67.

61. R.B. Cialdini, *Influence of Science and Practice*, Glenview, IL: Scott Foresman, 1985.

62. J.J. Inman, A.C. Peter, and P. Raghubir, Framing the deal: the role of restrictions in accentuating deal value, *Journal of Consumer Research*, 1997, 24(1), pp. 68–79.

63. M. Boyle, Brand killers, *Fortune*, August 3, 2003, pp. 62–68.

64. M. Boyle, 2003, same reference as in previous note.

65. S. Buck, Own label and branded goods in fmcg markets: an assessment of the facts, the trends and the future, *Journal of Brand Management*, 1993, 1(1), pp. 1–8.

66. S. Hastings and M. Price, Money can't buy me loyalty, *Admap*, 2004, February, pp. 28–31.

67. Marketing consultant P. Hunby presented impressive examples of databased promotions by Tesco at the June 2004 Marketing Metrics conference in London organized by the Marketing Science Institute. Hunby reported that his company has been engaged by the giant U.S. retail food chain, Kroger.

68. S. Hastings and M. Price, 2004, same reference as in note 66.

69. M Hollands, Online trolleys on right track, *The Australian*, July 24, 2001, p. 43.

70. P.F. Nunes and F.V. Cespedes, The customer has escaped, *Harvard Business Review*, 2003, November, pp. 96–105.

71. P.F. Nunes and F.V. Cespedes, 2003, same reference as in previous note.

CHAPTER 16

Corporate image advertising, sponsorships, and PR

Corporate Image Advertising, Sponsorships, and Public Relations, or PR – which is the general term now for all forms of manufactured publicity – are *conceptually identical* types of marcoms. From the manager's standpoint, Corporate Image ads, Sponsorships, and PR are direct means of generating awareness and preference for the **corporate brand** (e.g., Canon, Gillette) or **master brand** (e.g., Foster's, Pepsi) rather than for the specific brand-item.

In the most significant change in marcoms policy for many years, the previous "hidden giants" among consumer product manufacturers – Unilever, Procter & Gamble, Johnson & Johnson, SC Johnson, and Kao – which is the name of the Japanese company that previously branded its products in the U.S.A. under the name Andrew Jergens Co. – are each now featuring their respective corporate names prominently on product packages. SC Johnson began a corporate ad campaign several years ago using patriarch Samuel Johnson as the presenter (use of the CEO or company founder as a presenter is a well-known corporate image advertising and also PR tactic) and Kao, at the time of writing, was about to launch a global corporate brand campaign.[1]

Corporate Image Advertising, we estimate, is engaged in by about 50% of U.S. companies and a recent survey indicates that about 70% of *large* companies use it.[2] Among user companies however, Corporate Image advertising typically receives only a small percentage of the total marcoms allocation.

For instance, in 2004, Toyota U.S.A. spent $50 million on a seven-month brand image campaign for one of its Master Brands, Lexus cars (key benefit claim: "Pursuit of perfection").[3] This seems like a big spend but in fact it is just 0.3%, less than 1%, of Toyota Motor Corp.'s annual U.S. adspend of $1,550 million.[4]

With so much corporate branding spilling over into sponsorships and PR these days, it is fairly difficult to isolate the expenditure on corporate image advertising but counts of corporate image ads placed in measured media typically put the expenditure on corporate image advertising in the U.S. at about 1% of total advertising expenditure. This figure has probably doubled in the last year or so, however, with the emergence of **company-branded generic-need advertising**. Generic-Need (GN) Ads dramatize a need rather than promote a product but the company's name in the ad suggests, to many consumers, that this company's product is best for meeting the need.

Manufacturers of prescription-only pharmaceuticals have led this increase with so-called "disease awareness" ads aimed directly at consumers. An example is an ad aimed at men with erectile problems, urging them to see their doctor for a consultation; this wise advice is brought to you, via the corporate I.D. at the end of the ad, by Pfizer, the company that makes the potency drug, Viagra. A legal loophole, too, in the U.S.A., is that a company can transport creative elements – such as a spokesperson – from its over-the-counter (OTC) product ads for the brand into the generic ads, that is, when the brand covers both OTC and prescription drugs, which would suggest the specific *brand* rather than just the corporate name.[5]

Many other corporate image ads, of course, are GN ads, advertising the need to clean up our environment or reduce pollution, while implying that the company is contributing toward these worthy ends, without mentioning any of the company's products.

Sponsorships are a *bigger* category of marcoms than Corporate Image advertising. The total U.S. expenditure on Sponsorships is estimated to be approximately $9 billion to $10 billion per year; to put this in perspective, this is only about 3% of total marcoms expenditure (see Chapter 1) but it is larger than each of the advertising expenditures on the Internet (at present), Outdoor, Business Publications, and Trade Shows.

Three countries spend double this percentage on sponsorships, mainly of sports – Italy, South Africa, and Australia.[6] The typical sponsorship expenditure per brand in the U.S.A. among those companies that use sponsorship, though, is actually quite low at $1.2 million only, per annum.[7] In the U.S.A., and probably worldwide, more than two-thirds of all sponsorships, about 70%, are of sports teams or sports events. The other 30% of sponsorships are fairly evenly distributed across the categories of entertainment (a big subcategory is rock bands and their concerts), festivals and fairs, causes and charities, and the arts.[8]

Sponsorships – which include ongoing sponsorships as well as short-term sponsorships of special events, called *Event Marketing* – have an alarming rate of failure. Most sponsorships do not show any demonstrable effect on company stock prices or on sales. Curiously enough, the corporate naming of sports arenas (in our view an obnoxious practice that began in the U.S.A. with the naming of Busch Stadium, owned by leading U.S. brewer Anheuser-Busch, and has spread almost worldwide), does apparently have a positive effect on the sponsor's stock price.[9] However, sponsorship of the biggest event of them all, the Olympic Games – although some may contend that the football World Cup is bigger – typically produces no noticeable effect on stock prices and only a very short-term effect on sales.[10]

A major reason for this failure is that Sponsorships are usually conceptualized poorly and their effects are measured wrongly (if they are measured at all).[11] For example, in a study by the NBC television network, which carried the U.S. telecast of the 1992 Olympic Games, the sponsors did not bother to track Sales, deeming sales results outside the scope of the research. Instead they concluded that because there was a positive correlation, in a one-shot survey, of .27 between Liking of the Ads the sponsor ran during the games and the sponsor's corporate Image Ratings, the sponsorship was therefore a success.[12] Might it not be that those respondents who were already favorable toward the company tended also to evaluate the company's *ads* more favorably, regardless of the Olympics? This is typical of the naïve sort of measurement that goes on with Sponsorships. We will explain later what *should* be measured.

Public relations and **publicity** – lumped together nowadays as **PR**, is impossible to put an exact figure on because much of it appears as "free" publicity, even though it can cost the company, in the case of positive publicity, quite a lot of money to get it widely publicized and, in the case of negative publicity, a lot of money to counter it! One guesstimate for the *worldwide* expenditure on PR is about U.S. $10 billion per year and the U.S. figure would be about half that.[13] These guesstimates are rubbery because almost all *Sponsorships* use *Corporate Image TV advertising* that quite often features the *PR spokesperson*.

For example, in one of the most successful PR and advertising tie-ins ever, Coca-Cola company in 1984 paid the then-enormous sum of $8.5 million for singer Julio Iglesias (no, not Enrique, but his then-famous Dad) to promote Coke and Diet Coke during his 36-city U.S. summer tour, which was subsequently extended to tours in Europe, South America, Africa and Australia in the next year – and to appear in TV commercials aired in 155 countries. Of this amount, $3 million went straight into Julio's bank account and $5.5 million went to pay for the PR and advertising. Julio Iglesias in that era was the darling of 18–49 year-old women – the main *grocery buyer* demographic – worldwide. During the tour, sales of Coke and Diet Coke, combined, reportedly doubled (+100%) in almost every market, which astounded even the company's managers.[14]

Viewers' attention to TV advertising has declined, as we documented in Chapter 9, on Attention, and applied in Chapter 12, on Effective Frequency. Perhaps as a result, **product placement**, in regular TV programs and in movies, is on the increase. (Despite ethical concerns – for example, consumer activist Ralph Nader has petitioned both the U.S. Federal Trade Commission and Federal Communications Commission to have Product Placements properly labeled in TV programs and movies.[15] We hope he is successful; it is scandalous that regular ads have to be clearly identified as such whereas deliberate product placements don't.)

On TV we are witnessing a return to the era of the "soap operas," with program characters carrying through into the ad breaks to deliver testimonials for the sponsor's product.[16] One of the first of these instances in recent times was Jerry Seinfeld for the American Express credit card. An extreme example of program and product plugs blurring will occur if Miller Brewing Co. in the U.S.A. goes ahead with a plan to turn its popular five-year-old ad campaign for Miller High Life into an Archie Bunker style, blue-collar comedy TV series – guess what brand most of the characters will drink.[17]

Nielsen Media Research, the leading supplier of TV program and advertising audience ratings, recently introduced ratings of audience numbers exposed to branded products and brand names – depicted or mentioned – in TV programs.[18]

In this chapter, we examine the *conceptualization* and *planning* of Corporate Image campaigns, Sponsorships, and PR activities. Because Sponsorships and PR are typically so poorly conceived and badly planned, we are going to examine these two types of marcoms first. Corporate Image advertising is usually better planned, so we'll cover that last.

SPONSORSHIPS, PR, AND PRODUCT PLACEMENTS

Proposals for Sponsorships, Event Marketing, Product Placements, and other PR opportunities are usually presented *to* the marketing manager by the events' owners or organizers. The decision for the marketing manager is therefore which, if any, to accept. There are two major, and complex, criteria on which this decision should be made, and in this order:

1. Will it work – creatively?

2. If yes, does it offer good media value – what amount of target audience reach will be obtained, in what reach *pattern*, and for what cost?

A third implicit question is: how will we be able to measure whether it has worked? The next sections examine these questions.

Will it work – creatively?

A Sponsorship, a PR event, or a Product Placement must achieve at least the basic C-B links of positioning from the T-C-B model and generate the right communication effects. Specifically, each of these types of marcoms has to work via the basic positioning model that we said to keep in mind when considering creative tactics for advertising (see Chapter 8). The basic positioning model is reproduced in Figure 16.1.

For a Sponsorship, PR event, or Product Placement to work, it must, just like Advertising: (1) connect the Brand Identity to the Category Need – in both directions to cover Brand Recognition (upward) and Brand Recall (downward); and (2) connect the Brand Identity to the Key Benefit – in this one direction (see Figure 16.1) to cover Brand Preference. These two creative links are explained below.

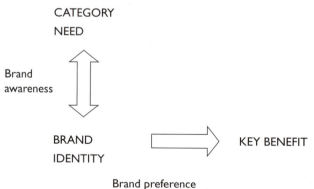

FIGURE 16.1 *The basic positioning model. This model assumes aim at the target customer (T) and focuses explicitly on the C and B links of positioning (C = category need and B = key benefit) with the brand identity. By these two links the two universal communication effects, brand awareness (brand recognition and brand recall) and brand preference, are achieved.*

The brand awareness link

The first link, the Category Need to Brand Identity two-way connection, sets up the *brand awareness* responses of Brand Recognition and Brand Recall. This link will only be established if the *event* clearly signals the Category Need (e.g., Löwenbräu beer sponsoring a beer festival) or if the target audience is likely to mentally fill in the Category Need when they see or hear the brand name or see its visual identifier because of *previous* exposure to ads for the brand or previous exposure to its products or services (e.g., the Lacoste logo – "Oh yes, they make sports clothing"). If the Category Need that the brand represents is *not* spontaneously evident to most of the target audience, then the logo should be extended to include it by adding a *slogan*, or *another graphic*, that tells you its *category*. The word "logo" comes originally from the Greek *logos*, "word," but in marketing it has come to mean either the brand name in a stylized font (e.g., Dell uses all caps and tilts back the E), a graphic symbol owned by the brand (e.g., Nike's "Swoosh"), or the two together (e.g., the Shell logo with a shell graphic and the name). The further graphic (sometimes used, especially in Yellow Pages and other directory ads) or slogan (short slogans are called word marks and a better name for both is *tagline*) is *additional* to the logo. An addition like this is necessary for all marcoms involving the logo, not only Sponsorships or PR, although the problem is most severe with these because they usually permit *only* the logo – the brand name or brand graphic – to be displayed at events.

> Here's the test you should conduct. Show a sample of target audience customers (N = 200 would be enough) the brand identity that you are planning to use, and ask each person to think aloud. If most (let's say 85% or more) spontaneously mention the category (correctly), then fine. If fewer do, then you must *add a few words or a picture* to teach people its category.

The brand preference link

The second link, the Brand Identity to Key Benefit connection, which sets up *Brand Preference*, has to be made *indirectly* by the *nature of the event* that the sponsorship is for or the PR is about. Figure 16.2 shows two examples, for Qantas and Volvo. Qantas, the Australian "flag carrier" airline, uses the tag line "The spirit of Australia" and sponsors mainly Australian events or Australian sports teams, reinforcing its "Quintessentially Australian experience" Key Benefit. Volvo, the Swedish car and truck manufacturer, typically uses in its logo the tagline or word mark "Volvo for life" (a double meaning referring to the brand's reputation for "Safety" and its reputation for "Longevity"). It then uses an emotional, evaluative conditioning approach (*HEC*) to link one of its *other* intended Key Benefits – "Classy" – by sponsoring only prestigious, that is, classy, sports tournaments such as major tennis, golf, and sailing events.

> Events and even specific product placement situations have to be chosen for their capacity to communicate the brand's Key Benefit – or at least one of its Key Benefits if there is more than one (as in the case of Volvo). Note that the Key Benefit may be an *emotional benefit* rather than a functional benefit, and specifically a type 2 emotion (see Chapters 3 and 4 for the distinction of benefits and for examples of type 2 emotions).

VOLVO

for life

FIGURE 16.2 *The Qantas logo has the word mark (or slogan) added to communicate the brand's key benefit. The Volvo logo adds a word mark to communicate one of its key benefits (it sponsors "classy" events to communicate another).*

SOURCE: Logos courtesy of Qantas Airways and Volvo Car Australia.

How can the manager check on the suitability of a proposed Sponsorship or PR opportunity for communicating the brand's Key Benefit?

Commission a survey of, say, N = 200 randomly selected members of the target audience, including 100 of each stakeholder group if there is more than one stakeholder group that you are targeting. Ask them to state the first two or three *thoughts* that come to mind and, as the second question, the first two or three *feelings* that they have in relation to the proposed *event* – for example, the World Cup, the Superbowl, the Chicago Symphony Orchestra, a James Bond movie, a Quentin Tarantino movie (like most movies, Tarantino's movies are probably open to product placements, though we're not sure of this). If the key benefit or key emotion, depending on your positioning goal, is *not* among the top three associations listed by – let's pick a reasonable number – 80% of target respondents, reject the Sponsorship or PR proposal. Do not use rating scales, an *aided* measure, for this test (e.g., asking people to rate the Wimbledon tennis championship on "prestige," which Volvo might want, or to rate a Russell Crowe movie on "Australianness," which is what Qantas might want) because the association has to emerge on a *spontaneous* basis during the sponsorship or placement.

For a *new, unknown* company brand, the logo will require pictorial content or words added to achieve (1) the Brand Identity link to the Category Need and (2) the Brand Identity link to the Key Benefit. A hypothetical example for a new company, Smith's, is shown in Figure 16.3. In panel (a) we see the company name – the word mark – alone, which tells the audience nothing about Smith's. In panel (b) the Category Need has now been added pictorially – Smith's is a road transport company. In panel (c) a tagline has been added to denote Smith's transport company's Key Benefit – "Reliable delivery Australia-wide." Now the logo is conceptually complete.

In some sponsorship or event marketing situations, *no logo can be shown* – in radio broadcasts, for instance, or in live TV coverage when a sponsor's logo can't be shown on screen. In such cases, a *Tagline* has to do the two-link communication job. Because Taglines come under creative tactics, we discuss the conceptual considerations for them at the *end of the chapter*. This is somewhat arbitrary as Logos, too, are creative tactics. After reading the present discussion of logos, you could look immediately at the end-of-chapter discussion of taglines.

Panel (a)

Panel (b)

Panel (c)

FIGURE 16.3 *The logo for a new, unknown company shown in panel (a) requires an addition to identify its category need, as in panel (b), and a further addition to identify the company's key benefit, as in panel (c).*

The Manager of the *Event*, on the other hand, would want to know to which *Companies* to offer a sponsorship or PR opportunity. This reverse process – for an event, find sponsors that would have a suitable fit – was used in a recent U.S. study by Gwinner and Eaton.[19] First, they looked at functional-benefit relationships, reasoning that the participants in the event should be expert users of the potential sponsoring brand's product. For the Indianapolis 500 auto race, the brands Goodyear tires, Pennzoil motor oil, and Shell gasoline were thought to have a good functional fit; for the annual NCAA basketball tournament, the brands Champion uniforms, Reebok shoes, and Powerade sports drink were thought to have a good functional fit. Second, as an alternative selection criterion, they looked at emotional-benefit fit, which they referred to as image fit. For the U.S. Open Golf championship, the brands Acura automobiles, Sony, and Michelob beer were regarded as having a good image fit; for the Kentucky Derby horse race, the brands American Express, Oldsmobile cars, and John Hancock Insurance were regarded as having a good image fit. The researchers also identified some no-fit or bad-fit examples. For the World Cup soccer tournament, the brands Dell computers and Clorox bleach were rated as having no fit, and Camel cigarettes, interestingly, though in hindsight, obviously, was rated as having a negative fit with this sporting event; for the Rose Bowl football game, the brands Irish Spring soap, Renuzit air fresheners, and Levi's jeans were rated as having no fit. These examples show the nature of the evaluation that has to be made when the Event Manager is considering a sponsorship proposal.

For the *test* phase of their study, the researchers employed an appropriate measure of fit between the event and the brand in that the association had to be made spontaneously. The measure is adapted from a previous measure of self-image congruence developed by Sirgy, Grewal, Mangleburg, Park, Chon, Claiborne, Johar, and Berkman[20] and is reproduced here:

> Take a moment to think about the [event name]. Think about the various images and experiences one would encounter when they attended or watched this event on TV. Imagine this event in your mind . . . Now think of the company or brand [insert brand] . . . To what extent is your image of [event] and [brand] consistent – are they: very inconsistent ☐, not consistent ☐, moderately consistent ☐, or highly consistent ☐?

Product placements

As we made plain at the beginning of the chapter, we believe Product Placements – *Brand* Placements usually, though sometimes an industry places a generic Category – to be an ethically contemptible form of marcoms. For years, magazines such as *Reader's Digest* have been prohibited from slipping product endorsements into their news stories and articles – so-called **advertorials** – unless the magazine clearly marks any story that carries a branded product or service endorsement with the words "The following is an advertisement." Similarly, in European TV programs a well-recognized on-screen signal and an audio sound-chime must appear at the beginning *and* end of the commercial break. Product Placements are unethical – deontologically unethical, that is, morally wrong – in our opinion, because they represent an attempt at persuasion without the recipient's guaranteed understanding that such an attempt is being made. It does not matter whether many of the audience in fact recognizes these placements for what they are – advertisements – but rather it is the *intention* to deceive that is unethical regardless of what proportion of people are in fact deceived.

Having said this, Product Placements are, to our amazement, quite legal. Therefore they must, under present law, be regarded as a marcoms option. Conceptually, like a sponsorship or PR event, the product placement must create the brand awareness link between the Brand Identity and the Category Need (usually obvious by the timing of the placement) and the brand preference link between the Brand Identity and the brand's Key Benefit (most often achieved by a Celebrity Presenter effect – see Chapter 8). The brand might be generic (e.g., smoking by actors).

Ethical or not, whether product placements are *effective* is another matter. There are some impressive anecdotal cases, but controlled experiments, two of which we will summarize shortly, are not so encouraging. The earliest known product placement in a movie was the appearance of a bottle of Jack Daniel's bourbon whiskey in use by the star, Joan Crawford, in the film *Mildred Pierce* in 1945.[21] For many years after that, the brands of liquor, beer and cigarettes used in films had their labels covered or appear indistinctly to prevent brand identification; this was apparently by motion picture industry agreement rather than legal restriction. How times have changed. This tacit agreement was ditched in the early 1990s and product placements in movies are now commonplace, with up to 10 products being featured, for example, in each of the recent *James Bond* films. There have been several *anecdotal reports* of spectacular increases in brand sales following product placements in movies.

Reportedly, the placement of Reece's Pieces candy in the movie *E.T.* produced a 65% increase in sales (for how long we don't know and we also do not know whether the profit from the extra sales exceeded the cost of the placement, although this is very likely). Another anecdotal report is that actor Tom Cruise's use of Ray-Ban sunglasses in the movie *Top Gun* increased the sales of this brand which, prior to the movie's release, was losing market share (again we don't know the financial details).[22] Product placement costs are not insubstantial; for instance, Mars reportedly spent £2 million (U.S. $3,660,000) for product placements within a recent *Mr. Bean* film, which means that a good deal of profit would need to be generated from increased sales to cover the large cost.[23]

However, the few *experimental* studies that have been conducted examining product placements in movies have indicated very patchy results to the extent that it is far from a guarantee that a product placement will increase sales.

For instance, in one experiment, Johnstone and Dodd asked college students to watch a 33-minute, self-contained, actual segment from a film, *Spice Girls – The Movie,* in which no less than six types of product were visible including, for two of the product categories, more than one competing brand. Of the four single brands, only *one* exhibited a statistically significant increase in top-of-mind recall from the pre-exposure measure to the post-exposure measure. In the two competing-brand categories, the brand that received the longest on-screen exposure exhibited a significant increase in top-of-mind brand recall while the lesser-exposed competing brands did not. Another experiment on product placements in movies, by Karrh[24], also studied actual placements in a 33-minute segment of a real movie – the 1987 comedy *Raising Arizona.* Karrh used an experimental group (exposed to the film, then measures taken) and a control group (not exposed, but measures taken).[25] In the film segment there were single placements for five branded products – Huggies diapers (36 seconds, shown and mentioned), Coca-Cola Classic (27 seconds, shown and mentioned), Budweiser beer (26 seconds, shown in use), Kellogg's Corn Flakes (three seconds only, shown in use) and the fast-food chain Dunkin' Donuts (one second, mentioned in dialogue). The first measure taken was Category-Cued Brand Recall, relevant mainly to Coke, Budweiser and Dunkin' Donuts; unfortunately, Brand Pack Recognition, relevant to these *and* to the other two products, Huggies and Corn Flakes, was not measured. Anyway, only *one* brand, Huggies, showed a significant increase in Brand Recall as a result of the placement. However, Coke and Budweiser were pretty much at maximum recall in the unexposed control group (a "ceiling effect") and Corn Flakes and Dunkin' Donuts were only briefly exposed, so perhaps the Huggies result (a brand which had "room to move up") is encouraging. The second measure taken, Brand Preference, revealed no effects of placement but we note here, as we did in Chapter 6, that an increase in Brand Recognition or Brand Recall, depending on the choice process – would increase choice *even if* Brand Preference remained constant.

In general, whether Sales will be increased by a product placement to an extent that offsets the *cost* of the placement, however, is impossible to predict. *The only method of determining this would be for the advertiser to conduct a product placement test in a preview version of the TV show or movie, using an experimental group and a control group as Karrh did.*

Target audience effective reach and reach pattern

Once the manager has determined that there is a good creative fit of the Corporate Brand or Master Brand with the proposed sponsorship, PR event, or product placement vehicle, there are two further assessments to be made prior to accepting or rejecting the proposal. Both relate to the *media value* of the proposal: Target Audience Effective Reach, and the proposal's achievable Reach *Pattern*.

Target audience effective reach

The Effective Reach of the Target Audience or Audiences Poses the question of what *number* of stakeholders will be reached with sufficient frequency to generate Action? *Simple* Reach is itself easy to estimate; the numbers attending or – even bigger and more important because you can run TV ads as well – watching TV coverage of sports events, concerts, gala functions, and so forth, have a long historical record from which good predictions for forthcoming events can readily be made. The tricky factor to estimate is achievement of the *MEF/c*. You have to estimate the number and Attention values of the OTSs in terms of their contribution towards MEF – which is difficult because of the *varying length and quality of brand exposures* during a Sponsorship, PR event, or Product Placement. As we saw in Chapter 12, the attention probability greatly affects contribution to MEF. Believe it or not, there are research firms who systematically pore through the videotapes of every race and measure the amount of time that each sponsor's logo is reasonably visible. This duration measure is strictly an OTS – there is no measure of the incidence of race viewers who *actually* see the sponsor's logo or for how long. Management judgment has to be used here to estimate attention probability and attention duration.

> In theory, eye-tracking research could be used whereby respondents watch a videotape of the event. In practice, eye-tracking isn't used because it is prohibitively expensive to record and analyze this much data. (Perhaps a sample of the race coverage could be taken. It's an important issue for other events, too, such as TV coverage of football, baseball, tennis, and golf.)

Achievable reach pattern

Also to be considered is whether the desired Reach Pattern will be reasonably *achieved* by the sponsorship or other type of proposal. For example, sponsorship of Formula 1 motor racing, which receives its largest coverage from TV broadcasts of the races, looks very impressive as a sponsorship opportunity because, over the lengthy racing season, approximately 50% of all adults in the U.S.A. (which is about 70 million people in that country), Japan, Britain, Germany, Hungary, Belgium, and Italy are reached.[26] However, the adult Reach in these countries for any *one* broadcast of a Formula 1 race – across its 26-race, one per fortnight, season – is only 10% (which, incidentally, is a lot more than the 1% who watch at least one day's coverage of a typical major golf tournament, although that 1% tends to be affluent viewers, attractive to advertisers of luxury products). Considered from a Frequency criterion, only about 20% of adults watch Formula 1 broadcasts "loyally," in that they watch (some or all) of 10 or more races in the 26-race season. Only among this number of viewers could you therefore achieve a repeat-audience (high-continuity) reach pattern. About 50% of adults watch (some or all) of only *one* race during the whole year. Of course, sponsors' logos are typically visible many times during one race, but this would be very concentrated frequency, an ad cycle of once a year! If you think about it, this would be good for the Shifting Reach pattern – but for that you'd have to use TV ads, as logos would not be sufficient communication devices in this pattern, because the Shifting Reach pattern is for long-copy, direct-response types of ads.

Marketing guru Al Ries advises companies to use PR *in place of* advertising.[27] Like his earlier pronouncements on positioning[28], this is sensational but simplistic. The reason why PR will not take over from corporate image advertising or sponsorships is the lack of predictability and control of the *reach pattern* achievable by a PR campaign. For example, an average company among the top 100 (Fortune 100) companies in the U.S.A. achieves almost 80% of its PR coverage from newspaper stories.[29] Only by hindsight (historical content analysis) could you pick a reach pattern from that (which is worth doing, by the way).

The main reason that PR – and here we mean *positive publicity* – survives at all is that it is very *persuasive* among those who *are* reached. This is because publicity, in comparison with advertising or sponsorship, is seen as "objective," that is, as "news." It's like personal influence via word of mouth and, indeed, the four-to-one PI contact coefficient ratio (see Chapter 12) could be applied to positive publicity exposures (divide the required MEF by four).

Measuring the effects of sponsorship, PR, or product placement

Just like all other marcoms, a sponsorship, PR event, or product placement must – for the corporate brand or master brand – increase Brand Awareness and increase or reinforce Brand Preference.

Brand awareness

As we mentioned at the outset of the chapter, researchers – both academics[30] and practitioners[31] – almost without exception focus on an irrelevant measure. The irrelevant measure is whether people can recall or recognize the companies that *sponsored* the event. As a corollary mistake, users of this measure also regard *false* sponsorship recall or *false* sponsorship recognition as evidence of successful **ambush marketing** – where a company that is *not* a sponsor deviously pretends to be, often by running ads at the same time as the event. The results produced by the "which company was a sponsor?" measure are meaningless because they do not validly represent the way in which consumers or customers have to recall or recognize the corporate or flagship brand in the real world. When choosing an airline, for example, travelers will not first think of major events and then the airlines that sponsored them, yet that is what would have to happen if the "which company was a sponsor?" measure were to have any relevance. It doesn't; it is completely independent of the way that prospects remember and choose a company. In a Brand Recall situation, the recall process is triggered by the normal Category Need cue (air travel, to a particular destination) and then brands are recalled – without any reference whatsoever to events or sponsorships that may be associated with those brands.

The correct measure of the brand awareness effect of sponsorship or PR activities is simply the measure that you would normally use in tracking: *Category-Cued Brand Recall*.

Only one published study that we have come across has used this correct measure. In a study of sponsors and non-sponsors of the 1992 Barcelona Olympic Games[32], the results of a Customer Tracking Survey (Wave method) showed that there was a brand recall boost for sponsor brands but that the increase occurred *only* during the four weeks of the games and was unlikely to be worth the cost of the sponsorship (which was about $35 million in 1992).

> Similarly, if choice of the corporate or master brand is by Brand Recognition – such as would be the case for consumer choice of brands such as Esso, Adidas, or Kellogg's, or for business customers receiving personal sales visits from a potential vendor company – then the normal tracking measure of *Brand Recognition* should be used, not "Recognition as a sponsor."

Brand preference

To measure the effect of a sponsorship, PR event, or placement on Brand Preference for the corporate or master brand, the question that was wrong above has to be asked in *reverse*. Give respondents the name of the company and ask them to recall what *events* it sponsors. This question must be asked *after* the brand awareness measure(s).

> Provide respondents with the company or flagship brand name if the prior communication objective is Brand Recall, or with the brand mark or logo if the prior communication objective is Brand Recognition, and then ask respondents, totally unaided, who or what, if anyone or anything, the company is a sponsor of.

However, it should be noted that a sponsorship, PR activity, or product placement *could* have a positive effect on Brand Preference *without* recall of the event. For example, few people, even those who are regular attenders of ballet in Australia, can recall – even when asked the proper question of what the telephone company, Telstra, sponsors – that Telstra sponsors the Australian Ballet. However, we would be very surprised if the favorability of overall attitude toward Telstra has not risen among the ballet audience and among other audiences who have seen this sponsorship advertised, despite lack of recall of it. If they *like* ballet, and not everyone who goes does, then positive evaluative conditioning (*HEC*) should occur, especially if the theatre goers see the to-be-conditioned stimulus, Telstra, first, as they would in the foyer or when skimming the ballet program booklet before the performance starts. If they *do* recall this sponsorship, that is, they are "aware" of the attempted conditioning, the effect will be even stronger.[33]

Action effects

In addition to communication effects, the two most essential being Brand Awareness and Brand Preference, the behavioral Action effects of the sponsorship, PR campaign, or placement should also be measured. If Action effects can't be demonstrated, then who cares whether Brand Awareness and Brand Preference were increased? You shouldn't.

> You should track Target Audience Action before, during, and after the event or events – such as job applications, customer referrals to the company and, of course, Sales – over time, as a function of the sponsorship, PR, or placement input (these in terms of Effective Reach per media-month). It is also vital that *other* marcoms inputs during the same period be simultaneously tracked because target audience action could be caused by one form of marcoms but not the other, but hopefully both.

There are some success stories. In an early application of econometric analysis to tracking-study data, Volvo's management estimated that its five-year sponsorship of tennis tournaments, its first venture into sports sponsorships, returned $8 extra revenue for every $1 spent for the sponsorship, a $2 million net profit return. Cornhill Insurance company's sponsorship of test cricket in England put this company on the map at much lower cost than the company would have had to pay for equivalent coverage via media advertising.[34] QBE Insurance company in Australia reportedly grew from a market share rank in the teens to the top four with a football team sponsorship – the Sydney Swans in the Australian Football League – although it must be acknowledged that the company complemented the sponsorship with TV, radio and print *media* advertising.

CORPORATE IMAGE ADVERTISING

Before outlining the conceptual aspects of Corporate Image Advertising, it is worthwhile to distinguish certain other, *related concepts* that are useful to know first – Vision, Mission, and Corporate Identity. The best definitions that we have come across of these three terms are as follows:

- **Company vision** – an inspirational statement of what you expect to do with the company brand.[35] For instance, the company vision of Disney Corporation is "To make people happy"; Microsoft's is "To empower and enrich people in the workplace, at school, and at home"; the corporate brand Pepsi's is "To beat Coke"; and Leo Burnett Advertising Agency's is "To create superior advertising."

- **Company mission** – the operational prescription for what you need to do to *accomplish* the vision.[36] Examples of these are less often reported in the public domain, although Leo Burnett's rather elaborate mission to achieve its vision of creating superior advertising is, reportedly, "By making ads that are interrupting, daring, fresh, engaging, human, believable, and well focused as to themes and ideas."

- **Corporate identity** – the visual, verbal, and auditory symbols that the company uses to identify itself to people; most often-used symbols are Brand Name, Brand Mark, Slogan or Tagline, and Livery (corporate colors, stationery, motor vehicle signage, and so forth).[37]

Okay, now we can define the main term, Corporate Image, and the resulting term, Corporate Reputation, that are our focus here. **Corporate image** is the set of functional and emotional benefit beliefs and type 1 and type 2 emotional associations connected to – and spontaneously elicited by – the corporate brand. **Corporate reputation**[38] is corporate brand *preference*; it is the *overall* evaluation of the company and is composed by the stakeholder from the subjective evaluative weighting and summing of the benefit beliefs and emotional associations (as in the I-D-U benefit positioning model in Chapter 4). Corporate Reputation is the summary evaluation deriving from the components of the company's Corporate Image.

A reasonable measure of Corporate Reputation, used by *Fortune* magazine in the U.K. originally and now in the U.S.A. as well, is nomination as a *"most admired"* company.

In Asia, collectively the world's largest consumer market, the corporate brand reputation of global (mainly Western) brands counts for more than patriotic allegiance to Asian (or specific

Asian country) brands, among young adults especially. In a recent survey of young adults aged 15 to 28, admittedly in one of the more affluent regions of Asia, the Pearl River Delta region of China, 100% of "moderately patriotic" young people said they prefer to drink Coke but so, too, do 94% of the "most patriotic" young people; Nike footwear rules over the leading Chinese brand, Li Ning; and Disney theme parks are preferred over local ones such as the Happy Valley Amusement Park. A likely cause of this trend is that the ads in Western-originated magazines (articles in Chinese) distributed in Asia, such as *Esquire, Elle*, and *Cosmopolitan*, which are read mainly by Generation-X 18-to-35-year-olds, educated and affluent, now reflect modernity rather than tradition and also tend to be more individualistic than ads on mainstream Chinese TV (which is government controlled).[39] An end-result is that just 19% of these young Asian adults consider that country of origin should be a factor in brand choice, which is pretty close to the observed low weight of country of origin in choice experiments in Western countries.[40] On the other hand, astute global brands such as Coke and Wrigley select sponsorships and PR events in Asia that are distinctly Asian, to try to build the local appeal of the brand. See, for instance, Coke's extreme use of the "happiness and joy" color, red, extreme even for Coca-Cola which owns red as a corporate color, in the poster ad in Figure 16.4 (the ad's background is red, which you'll have to imagine in this non-color reproduction, the same red as on the Coke bottle's label, and the Chinese words top left are the Word Mark "Coca-Cola"). In the same vein, Anheuser-Busch, the U.S. company that makes Budweiser beer, never runs U.S. commercials in Asian countries without pre-testing them for local appeal and sensitivity to local culture; in fact, Bud runs many *old* U.S. campaigns in overseas markets, such as the "Ants" TV commercial, famous in the U.S.A. several years ago, which is at the time of writing being shown in China.[41]

FIGURE 16.4 *Poster ad for Coca-Cola in China emphasizing the "happiness and joy" color, red.*

SOURCE: Courtesy of Coca-Cola (China) Beverages Ltd. Special thanks to Mr. Oscar Wang. Coca-Cola, Sprite, Fanta, and Smart (the products shown in the ad) are trademarks of The Coca-Cola Company.

Dowling identifies the *circumstances* in which Corporate Image Advertising – as distinct from regular advertising for specific products or services – should be used.[42] These conditions are so important and useful that they are worth highlighting in a table (see Table 16.1). The company or organization should use Corporate Image Advertising to advertise to other stakeholders – should their number or influence be substantial – who are not often exposed to the company's product or service (brand-item) advertising; or if the *company* brand name contributes value equity to its brand-items; or if the purchase cycle is longer than a year; or if the need for issue management is expected; or to thank its own employees periodically. Corporate Image Advertising should be placed in media vehicles that reach the *stakeholder* target audience or audiences that the company wishes to influence; it does not have to reach everybody.

TABLE 16.1 *When to use corporate image advertising.*

1.	If there are *other stakeholders* who don't see much of your *product* advertising.
2.	When the customer "buys the company" as well as the product or service. If customers "don't care who made it," then use only product advertising.
3.	If the *purchase cycle is long*, that is, 12 months or longer, because when customers are out of the market, they tend not to notice your product advertising.
4.	When the company needs to manage an *issue*, be it a crisis or an ongoing issue.
5.	When the company needs to *thank employees* to boost morale – it is a good idea to thank your employees in this public manner in any case, at least once a year, and twice a year is better.

SOURCE: G. Dowling, 2001, reference in note 37.

Communication objectives of corporate image advertising

Corporate Image Advertising aims to increase Corporate Reputation, but before that it has to increase Corporate-Brand Awareness because awareness is the *carrier* of the reputation. From a creative tactics perspective, these two communication objectives, as in any marcoms, have to be addressed as two independent objectives to be achieved. *They are also measured as separate effects although, as you should understand by now, you must measure Brand Preference – here, Corporate Reputation – conditional on prior Company Brand Recall or Company Brand Recognition, whichever of these awareness objectives applies.*

How do corporate image ads create or increase the Brand Reputation of the company or organization? They do so by creating or increasing Brand Benefit Beliefs. This process is usefully conceptualized by using the CESLIP Presenter Model.

The CESLIP presenter model and corporate brand benefits

We foreshadowed in Chapter 8 that the CESLIP Presenter Model is applicable to Corporate Image Advertising because *the company is the presenter* in a corporate image ad, even if a special presenter, such as a CEO or celebrity, is additionally used. The Presenter characteristics of CESLIP can be aligned with specific *Benefit Beliefs* that the company or organization wishes to communicate in order to increase Corporate Reputation (Corporate Brand Preference). The functions of the CESLIP presenter characteristics applied to corporate image ads are summarized in Table 16.2. The first characteristic, *Celebrity Status*, functions to increase Corporate Brand Awareness *and* the corporate brand Benefit Belief of "Esteem, respect." Also to increase its perceived "Esteem, respect," the company must present itself in ads as an *Expert*. If it wants to increase "Trust" (which necessarily must result in an approach tendency), it must achieve *Sincerity* in its ads. If the company wishes to be seen as a "Good citizen," it must ensure that it is portrayed as *Liked* in its ads. More complex is getting stakeholders to "Identify with" the company as this requires really a corporate *Brand Personality* approach, portraying the company as similar to the stakeholder's Ideal Self (the Corporate Brand Personality approach is discussed below). To increase "Obedience, compliance," the company – more likely a government regulatory organization – should use *Power* symbols in its ads.

TABLE 16.2 *The CESLIP presenter model and corporate brand benefits.*

PRESENTER CHARACTERISTICS (OF THE COMPANY)	AWARENESS AND BENEFIT BELIEFS (OF THE STAKEHOLDERS)
1. Celebrity (typically the founder, the CEO, or a paid celebrity presenter)	Corporate brand awareness and Esteem, respect
2. Expert	Esteem, respect
3. Sincere	Trust, meaning that the customer is confident to approach and do business with the company
4. Liked	Good citizen
5. Ideal similar	Identify with
6. Powerful	Obey, comply with

All the Benefit Beliefs are potentially important (in the sense of the I-D-U multiattribute Brand Preference model) for all the Action objectives. (The Action objectives are deliberately placed at the end of the chapter.) Empirically it may be found that the importance of a particular Benefit Belief varies with the particular Action objective but we expect that each of them would make enough of a contribution to be worth targeting them all in corporate image advertising.

More practically, you should *track* them all and then set as communication *objectives* any that appear to need to be strengthened. In other words, special attention should be given in the creative to any presenter attributes on which the company is perceived to rate low. For many companies these days an important creative focus is *sincerity*, because it builds *trust*.

Corporate brand emotions

Brand Emotions connected to the corporate brand can also influence Brand Reputation. An emotional benefit that is relevant to the image of many brands is "Cool" (most probably, this emotion, a type 2 emotion, affects the Benefit Belief of *"Esteem, respect"* in the CESLIP conceptualization just discussed). An academic from the University of Utrecht in The Netherlands has designed an international survey which he calls the Global Cool Hunt (subsequently purchased by the big PR company Hill & Knowlton).[43] Unilever, for instance, is one global FMCG company that subscribes to the Global Cool Hunt study.

> At the time of writing, the coolest brands as rated by young adults worldwide include Puma, Diesel, Zara, H&M, Apple's iPod, Starbucks (although Starbucks is trending downward in the "Cool" stakes) and Nudie, a cool, catchy name that is a brand of natural fruit drinks in some countries (e.g., Australia) and a brand of apparel in others (e.g., European Union countries). As young people know, coolness is fickle! Puma, the overall number-one-ranked cool brand globally, was a very uncool, unpopular brand in the early 1980s and has made a spectacular comeback. Converse All Stars, on the other hand, has always been a cool brand for as long as we can remember, and Dunlop Volley is a perennially cool retro brand of sports shoes in Australia.

Dowling points out that companies in *controversial or distasteful industries*, sometimes called "demonized" industries, such as munitions manufacturers, nuclear power companies, tobacco companies, sex workers, and legal pornographers, will deliberately opt for *low* brand awareness – among the *general public*.[44] Philip Morris, ironically the one tobacco company that does not manufacture *only* tobacco products, recently gave up; it now calls itself the Altria Group. Most demonized companies could not afford a name change, nor is there really a need to change. Among their respective *Target Audiences*, high brand awareness and *positive* benefit beliefs, both functional and emotional, are still essential communication objectives to aim for.

The brand personality approach to corporate image advertising

In Chapter 3, on positioning, we said that it is worth trying to position the brand – in this case the Corporate Brand – via a lower brain level, if this can be achieved. The more functional approach just described is the more conventional corporate image advertising approach and it operates at a high (cortical) brain level. At a lower level are the possibilities of positioning the Corporate Brand – or even just a Master Brand – by giving it the personality of an Archetypal character (the holistic or idiographic approach) or giving it a set, a small set, of Personality Traits (the trait or nomothetic approach).

For the Archetype Approach, Pearson (Carol Pearson, not our publisher!) has proposed a very interesting theoretical framework in which well-known archetypes can be used to emphasize the "evolution" of the company – basically what stage it has reached in its own life cycle – on the one hand, and one major corporate attribute or "value," on the other.[45] Pearson's framework is summarized in Table 16.3.

TABLE 16.3 *Pearson's theory of archetypes that communicate the stage of the company's evolution (going down the columns) and the one major corporate value (going across).*

EVOLUTIONARY STAGE	STABILITY AND STRUCTURE (ADMINISTRATOR-TYPE COMPANY)	PEOPLE AND BELONGING (FACILITATOR-TYPE COMPANY)	RESULTS AND MASTERY (MANAGER-TYPE COMPANY)	IDENTITY AND LEARNING (MENTOR-TYPE COMPANY)
1. **Preparation** (new company)	Caregiver (altruist)	Orphan (regular guy or gal)	Warrior (hero)	The Innocent (a simple good person)
2. **Journey** (growing company)	Creator (artist)	Lover (the leading lady or the leading man)	Destroyer (outlaw)	Seeker (explorer)
3. **Return** (established company)	Ruler (the boss)	Jester (fun-maker)	Magician (miracle worker)	Sage (expert or guru)

The Trait Approach to corporate brand personality can be illustrated by **internal corporate image communications**. As many of us have suspected, it turns out that the personality of the chief executive officer (CEO) rubs off quite strongly on the company's top management teams (TMTs), the elite groups that operate the company, and affects their management style.[46] The top management teams' management style factors that correlate most highly with income growth, as a company performance indicator, are *optimism* ($r = .53$), *flexibility* ($r = .48$), *cohesiveness* ($r = .45$) and *risk taking* ($r = .44$). CEOs (real company CEOs) were rated on the "big five" personality traits – agreeableness, conscientiousness, emotional stability, openness to experience, and extraversion – and their trait ratings were compared to their company's TMT management style, rated in terms of the four factors. The *optimism* trait of the company's TMTs was not related to any of the CEO's personality traits. However, three of the five traits of CEOs were strongly related to the rated *flexibility* of TMTs, namely, conscientiousness, emotional stability (the opposite of neuroticism), and openness to experience. Three of the five traits were also strongly related to the *cohesiveness* of the TMTs, namely the agreeableness, conscientiousness, and emotional stability of the CEO. And one of the five traits was strongly related to the rating of the TMTs for *risk taking*, namely the CEO's openness to experience. Extraversion, the only one of the "big five" traits that has not been mentioned, was not significantly related to any of the four income-growth management styles. What are the personality traits of several well-known CEOs? Lee Iacocca, the previous CEO of the Chrysler Corporation who led it out of the red, was, at the time when he headed it, very emotionally stable, very extraverted, moderately conscientious, but not so open or agreeable. Roberto Goizueta, recent CEO of Coca-Cola, was also very emotionally stable, very extraverted, quite conscientious, not very agreeable, but more open to new experiences than was Iacocca. Worst rated – in the study – was Ron Miller, previous CEO of Disney, who was classified as quite highly neurotic, slightly extraverted, and low on conscientiousness, agreeableness, and openness to experience.

It would not be too difficult for your marketing group to gather internal employees' ratings of your company's CEO. Perhaps he or she might possess the personality traits – agreeableness, conscientiousness, emotionally stability, and openness to new ideas – that appear to stimulate a useful management style in the company's top management team or teams. If not, the findings are strong enough, we believe, to recommend that your company hire a suitable presenter for internal corporate communications – a mouthpiece for the boss. If this makes the CEO seem too remote from his or her top people, the company could kick the CEO upstairs to Chairman of the Board and install the presenter type as the CEO.

Company founders long departed or dead are certainly too remote to have a brand personality effect on TMTs despite the popular belief that founders with strong personalities leave their residual effects. Living founder-CEOs, of course, do have a ruboff effect on management – Richard Branson and Bill Gates come readily to mind.

Taglines (slogans)

As we have seen with Sponsorships, PR, and Product Placements, and now similarly applicable to Corporate Image Ads, *a company logo alone* is usually insufficient to achieve the two basic positioning objectives of linking the Corporate or Master Brand to the appropriate Category Need and communicating its Key Benefit (see the basic positioning model in Figure 16.1). To achieve both objectives, it is often necessary to add a *slogan*, also called a *tagline*. (Both these terms are still in wide use. "Slogan," the original term, comes from the Gaelic word for "war cry" and also has acquired somewhat distasteful political party overtones over the years. "Tagline" is the more contemporary term – though, in theory, the tagline has to put *two* tags on the brand and could thus more correctly be called a "tagsline.")

Theoretically-correct taglines indicate both the Category Need and the company brand's (or master brand's) Key Benefit. Some well-known taglines that are *theoretically correct* include:

- BMW – "The ultimate driving machine."
- Saturn – "A different kind of car company."
- United Airlines – "Fly the friendly skies of United."
- Lufthansa – "There's no better way to fly."
- Apple Computer – "Think different." (Note that the *category need* is in the *brand name* and does not need to be in the words of the slogan part.)
- EBay – "The world's online marketplace."

Many other taglines fail by *omitting the category need* into which the brand is positioned. Examples:

- Kinko's – "Express yourself."
- Nissan – "Enjoy the ride."
- Toshiba – "Don't copy. Lead." (Unlike in the Apple example, above, the category need is *not* in

the name; also, "Don't copy" may remind people of the well-known stereotype that Japanese companies often *do* copy and, also, in colloquial U.S. English "Don't copy" means "I don't understand"!)

- Tyson – "It's what your family deserves."

As we commented earlier, the only saving argument for category-less taglines is if the marketer is sure that the target customers will automatically mentally plug in the category need when they see or hear the brand name. Nissan would probably get by on this argument. Kinko's would be pushing to demonstrate that everyone automatically plugs in the category need (copying services). But, as Ries asked in his regular critic's column recently, "What's a Tyson?" Tyson, which happens to be quite a large food company in the U.S.A., in 2003 spent $40 million on a branding (corporate image) campaign using the above tagline.[47] In this case, we agree with Ries: the campaign was a waste of money. Ries also criticizes the famous Nike tagline, "Just do it" because, he claims, it required over $500 million of advertising each year to put across. Here, we *disagree* with his assessment. Nike is one brand for which, we believe, people automatically think of sports footwear or sportswear clothing, for the category-need element. Also, "Just do it" was (and is) a benefit claim, reflecting the imperially aggressive personality of the brand (and the company itself), that entered the culture as an idiom very quickly and would *not* have taken a lot of money to establish.

Other taglines employ hopelessly vague statements of the *key benefit*. Examples:

- Sears – "Where else?" (This ill-chosen invitation to think about the competition has since been replaced by a new tagline for Sears, "Good life. Great price.")

- Delta – "On top of the world."

- Aventis – "Our challenge is life."

- Hitachi – "Inspire the next."

- Ernst & Young – "From thought to finish."

The Aventis, Delta, and Hitachi taglines are among those criticized by Ries as being insipid[48]; we think the problem is that they are much too vague as to what the *key benefit* might be, rather than too weak.

Finally, we do *not* recommend the use of *puns* (ambiguous taglines) for communicating the brand's key benefit. There is simply too great a likelihood that readers or listeners will fail to focus on the *beneficial* interpretation of the pun. Examples:

- Volkswagen – "Drivers wanted."

- Kinko's – "Express yourself."

- Viagra – "Let the dance begin." (A really obscure reference to "horizontal folk dancing," we presume.)

- UPS – "Moving at the speed of business." (An unfortunate pun on, and comparison with, "Moving at the speed of light.")

> The company or organization is going to have to live with its Tagline for a long time. Theoretically-incorrect taglines are just as easy to imprint on the public as theoretically-correct ones, so you should do some thinking beforehand, and also some pre-testing, to choose one that is theoretically correct.

Action objectives of corporate image advertising

Corporate Image Advertising is useless unless it influences behavior (Action). The Action objective of Corporate Image Advertising for *end-customers*, as for Sponsorships and PR activities, is increased Purchase of the company's products or services. However, the Action objectives for *other stakeholders* are not purchase behaviors but rather are other important behaviors that ensure the future healthy life of the company. The most typical Action objectives for Corporate Image Advertising are:

- **Purchase** – an action objective for end-customers, who may be the company's business customers or consumer customers.

- **Invest in** – an action objective for traders on the stock market if the company is publicly listed and for providers of finance such as banks.

- **Supply to** – an action objective for suppliers of raw materials and input services.

- **Work for** – an action objective for graduates of universities and trade schools.

- **Don't attack** – an action objective (where the objective is *inaction*) for government regulatory and industry self-regulatory bodies and lobby groups, and sometimes for intimidation of competitors.

SUMMARY

Corporate Image Advertising, Sponsorships, and PR are all related in that they are specialized means of generating awareness and preference for the Corporate Brand or Master Brands. When considering Sponsorship offers or PR opportunities, the manager should make sure that two questions can be answered affirmatively: Will it work creatively? Will it provide good media value in terms of target audience reach and the desired reach pattern? It's easier to plan Corporate Image Advertising to achieve both these objectives than it is to plan Sponsorships and PR to do so.

From the creative perspective, a Sponsorship or PR activity must enable generation or reinforcement of a brand awareness link and a brand preference link. The *brand awareness link* is between the Brand Identity and the Category Need into which the brand is positioned. This link may have to operate both ways: from Category Need to Brand Identity for *brand recall*, and from Brand Identity to Category Need for *brand recognition*. The *brand preference link* has only to operate in one direction: from Brand Identity to its Key Benefit. Sponsorships and PR events typically allow only a display of the company brand or master brand logo (the stylized brand name, its distinctive visual graphic or, in rare cases, its distinctive audio signal, such as Intel's "chimes"). Unless the brand's category is spontaneously plugged in whenever the target audience sees the logo, the category should be added as a brief word mark or in an additional graphic. The *key benefit claim*, on the other hand, cannot be spelled out by adding a lengthy slogan or tagline but rather has to be communicated *indirectly* by association with the type of event that the brand is sponsoring or in which it has PR participation. Make sure you test prospective offers of sponsorship or PR for their spontaneous associations; if none of the top-of-mind associations fits your key benefit, then your brand should not sponsor or appear in that event. By using the same testing procedure, the manager of an event who is seeking sponsors or companies to invite for a PR appearance can easily produce a list of companies to approach that would have a good functional fit or a good image fit with these spontaneously emerging characteristics of the event.

Product Placements, which are usually *brand* placements, in movies, TV programs or in print media for that matter, are a pernicious form of sponsoring or PR, in our opinion. They are an unfair business practice because they attempt to persuade people without warning them, which in our view is sufficient to have product placements legislatively prohibited. On the practical side, despite isolated anecdotal reports of success, the few experimental studies of product (actually brand) placements have revealed a discouragingly low rate of success in increasing either brand awareness or brand preference.

The second consideration when evaluating potential Sponsorships and PR opportunities – their media value – is more difficult to assess but this assessment must be made. Simple reach of the target audience is quite easy to estimate from the event's audience figures but the Reach *Pattern* that can be achieved requires individual-level survey data and then some hard analysis by the manager. Estimating Effective Reach, which depends on minimum effective frequency, MEF, requires a further difficult judgment, which is the *attention probability* of the brand's exposure or exposures during the event. Failure to consider the creative adequacy of Sponsorship and PR opportunities is one reason for their very low success rate, and optimistic guesswork about their media value is the other.

Corporate Image Advertising, the other alternative for corporate brands and master brands, is on the increase with the trend, both globally and nationally, toward corporate branding and reputation building. Even previously "hidden" brands such as P&G, Unilever and Kao are now coming out of the closet with corporate image campaigns and prominent corporate branding on packaging. Demonized-industry brands are either staying hidden, except to their immediate stakeholder audiences, or changing, at great expense, to a new, neutral-sounding company name that does not carry historical negative connotations.

Corporate Image Advertising, like sponsorships and PR, is not just about "image." Corporate Image Advertising has to generate corporate brand or master brand *awareness* (Brand Recognition is usually the more relevant, but Brand Recall may also be the objective), *brand preference* (Corporate Reputation), and, further, it has to cause appropriate *action* (Behavior) or else it is not worth the expenditure. Action outcomes which should be tracked are: Purchase, Investment, Supply, Employment, and the inhibitory response of "Don't attack" (an inaction objective).

To plan the *content* of corporate image advertising, we suggest the CESLIP Presenter Model from Chapter 8, because the company is automatically a presenter even if, additionally, a special spokesperson is used in the ads. When applying CESLIP, Celebrity Status will increase corporate brand awareness and esteem and respect; Expertise will increase esteem and respect; Sincerity will increase trust; Likability will increase the "good citizen" perception; Ideal Similarity will increase identifying with (on the part of stakeholders); and Power, which is sometimes relevant, will increase compliance with the company's or organization's (such as a government office's) policies. The CESLIP Presenter Model aims to instill emotional benefits rather than emotions or instincts. As with brands in general, it is worth an attempt to position the Corporate Brand, or a Master Brand, at a "lower brain" level by considering an archetypal positioning or taking advantage of the CEO's personality traits that can inspire its top management teams.

We also identified, from a thoughtful analysis by Dowling, five alternative conditions in which companies should engage in Corporate Image Advertising and *not rely on product advertising alone*.

In Corporate Image Advertising, a Tagline (the contemporary term for a Slogan) represents a critical conceptual choice that the company has to live with. An effective tagline refers to the Category Need, unless this is patently obvious and automatically inserted whenever people see or hear the Brand Identity, and explicitly points to the Key Benefit that the corporate brand or master brand wants to be known for.

DISCUSSION QUESTIONS

16.1 Identify two product categories and one service category for which "Cool" is an important emotional benefit. Survey about 20 young adults and identify the two coolest brands, currently, in each of these categories. Why are these brands "Cool"? What benefit beliefs or emotional associations give them their "Cool" status? In this answer, use the a-b-e model of benefit claims. Then select *one* brand and outline how you would use PR to maintain the brand's "Cool" image.

16.2 Let's assume that a Sponsorship allows the Brand Mark, the Brand Name and a *short* Tagline to be shown. The current corporate tagline of MasterCard is "Priceless." Suggest two Sponsorships – which could be ongoing or particular events – that would fit the key benefit claim of "Priceless."

16.3 Suppose that the marcoms campaign for the Corporate Brand – a new "creative boutique" ad agency – would be most effectively implemented with a Reverse-Wedge/PI reach pattern (review this pattern in Chapter 11). Plan a PR campaign for the year of the launch of the new agency.

16.4 Find two Corporate Image Ads from magazines and analyze and discuss their content using the CESLIP Presenter Model.

16.5 See Carol Pearson's Archetypal approach to corporate brand personality, summarized in Table 16.4. What stage of corporate "evolution" would you judge your company or organization to be in: Preparation, Journey, or Return? Also, which would you say is the company's or organization's major "value" type: Administrator, Facilitator, Manager, or Mentor? Now locate the Archetype that best fits the intersection of these two dimensions. Which archetypal character is it? Read some more about the traits that this archetypal character represents and then discuss how you would implement an archetype-based

Corporate Image campaign for your company or organization. You can use PR as well as advertising.

16.6 Recruit a sample of 10 colleagues from your company or organization (which may be a university if you are a student) and have them rate the CEO (or president or dean) on the "big five" personality traits of: emotionally stable/neurotic; introverted/extraverted; ultraconservative/open to new experiences; agreeable/disagreeable; and not a detail person/conscientious. Have the respondents rate each trait on a 1 to 9 scale, and then score the Neuroticism end, the Extraversion end, the Openness end, the Agreeableness end and the Conscientiousness end as 9. Now look at the chapter – or the Peterson *et al.* article in note 46 – and see whether any of the distinctive traits of your CEO are correlated with income-growth management styles. Do you see an opportunity for a brand-personality-based Internal Corporate Image campaign? Explain why or why not.

16.7 Evaluate the following corporate taglines: (a) Philips – let's make things better; (b) GE – we bring good things to life; and (c) LG – life's good.

NOTES

1. J. Neff, Unilever stamps corporate name on all packages, *Advertising Age*, March 1, 2004, pp. 3, 37.

2. Association of National Advertisers, New study reveals corporate advertising budgets at all-time high, News Release (see ANA's Website), New York, April 1, 1998. The survey was conducted among member firms of the (American) Association of National Advertisers, which would be large companies. We've projected the trend to 2004/2005.

3. J. Halliday, Lexus readies launch of a $50m brand effort, *Advertising Age*, December 8, 2003, p. 6.

4. Toyota's U.S. adspend for 2002, *Advertising Age*, Fact Pack, 2004.

5. R. Thomaselli, Marketers seize DTC ad loophole, *Advertising Age*, February 16, 2004, p. 10.

6. T. Meenaghan, Current developments and future directions in sports sponsorship, *International Journal of Advertising*, 1998, 17(1), pp. 3–28.

7. T. Meenaghan, 1998, same reference as in previous note.

8. The U.S. figures are from the article, Event/sponsorships, *Marketing News*, July 8, 2002, p. 23. In the U.K., too, about 70% of sponsorships are of sports; see T. Meenaghan, The role of sponsorship in the marketing communications mix, *International Journal of Advertising*, 1991, 10(1), pp. 35–47. In a follow-up analysis, Meenaghan incorrectly included broadcast coverage in the corresponding table; see

T. Meenaghan, 1998, same reference as in note 6. In most countries, sports sponsorship dominates.

9. J.M. Clark, T.B. Cornwell, and S.W. Pruitt, Corporate stadium sponsorships, signaling theory, agency conflicts, and shareholder wealth, *Journal of Advertising Research*, 2002, 42(6), pp. 16–32. We note with glee that Candlestick Park in San Francisco got its name back after a public outcry over using a sponsor's name.

10. A.D. Miyazaki and A.G. Morgan, Assessing market value of event sponsoring: corporate Olympic sponsorships, *Journal of Advertising Research*, 2001, 41(1), pp. 9–15; see also a related study of the effects of sponsorship during the 1992 Barcelona Olympic Games, in J. Crimmins and M. Horn, Sponsorship: from management ego trip to marketing success, *Journal of Advertising Research*, 1996, 36(4), pp. 11–21.

11. Gregory, Public relations and evaluation: does the reality match the rhetoric?, *Journal of Marketing Communications*, 2001, 7(3), pp. 171–189.

12. H. Stipp and N.P. Schiavone, Modeling the impact of Olympic sponsorship on corporate image, *Journal of Advertising Research*, 1996, 36(4), pp. 22–27. Another study that drew the unwarranted conclusion that Olympic sponsorship is effective is by S. Wally and A.E. Hurley, The torch stops here: Olympic sponsorship and corporate reputation, *Corporate Reputation Review*, 1998, 1(4), pp. 343–355; in their study, look at the results for 1994, a year and a half *before* the 1996 Atlanta games.

13. For instance, Gregory, 2001, same reference as in note 11, analyzed the case reports of 25 recent award-winning PR programs in the U.K. and found that reach was measured in less than 5% of cases, and communication effects and action – generously considered as either – were measured in only about 10% of cases, and yet it was claimed that all 25 campaigns were successful!

14. J. Rovin, *Julio!*, Toronto: Bantam, 1985, chapters 24, 25.

15. C. Atkinson, Nader on advertising, *Advertising Age*, March 1, 2004, p. 35.

16. B. Harvey, Measuring the effects of sponsorships, *Journal of Advertising Research*, 2001, 41(1), pp. 59–64. The two largest "soap companies," Unilever and P&G, as well as Coca-Cola and PepsiCo, already produce programs featuring their products and attempt to sell these programs to TV stations, and pharmaceutical companies have been producing "doctors' TV" programs, for use in waiting rooms, for years; see T. Meenaghan, 1998, same reference as in note 2.

17. R. Linnett, High Life spots to spawn sitcom, *Advertising Age*, January 12, 2004, pp. 1, 41.

18. J. Mandese, Nielsen unveils new service, *Television Week*, December 8, 2003, Website. The service is called Nielsen Product Placement Measurement Service and is available at present only in the U.S.A.

19. K.P. Gwinner and J. Eaton, Building brand image through event sponsorship: the role of image transfer, *Journal of Advertising*, 1999, 28(4), pp. 47–57.

20. J.M. Sirgy, D. Grewal, T.F. Mangleburg, J. Park, K.-S. Chon, C.B. Claiborne, J.S. Johar, and H. Berkman, Assessing the predictive validity of two methods of measuring self-image congruence, *Journal of the Academy of Marketing Science*, 1997, 25(3), pp. 229–241. We have further adapted their measure.

21. Reported in I.D. Nebenzahl and E. Secunda, Consumers attitudes toward product placement in movies, *International Journal of Advertising*, 2000, 12(1), pp. 1–11.

22. Both the previous examples are reported in the article by E. Johnstone and C.A. Dodd, Placements as mediators of brand salience within a U.K. cinema audience, *Journal of Marketing Communications*, 2000, 6(3), pp. 141–158, although the original reports come from other articles cited in that publication.

23. R. Baird, Patent place, *Marketing Week*, 1997, 19(49), pp. 46–49; we were referred to this citation by the Johnstone and Dodd, 2000, article, same reference as in previous note.

24. J.A. Karrh, Effects of brand placements in movies, in K.W. King (Ed.), *Proceedings of the American Academy of Advertising*, Athens, GA: University of Georgia, Department of Advertising and Public Relations, 1994, pp. 90–96.

25. In fact, the "control" group underwent the sequence: pre (the control measure), exposure, post. In the control group's pre-to-post scores, Karrh found a lot of evidence of increases due to sensitization – which means that the Johnstone and Dodd study should have revealed more effects than it did (it found a positive effect for only one brand out of six).

26. S. Vickers and I. Thompson, Sponsorship: the real deal, *Admap*, 2002, October, pp. 19–22.

27. A. Ries and L. Ries, *The Fall of Advertising and the Rise of PR*, New York: HarperBusiness, 2004; and A. Ries, The disintegration of integrated marketing, *Advertising Age*, February 16, 2004, electronic AAP37R on AdAge.com.

28. A. Ries and J. Trout, *Positioning, The Battle for Your Mind*, New York: McGraw-Hill, 1971.

29. Analysis of PR expenditures by Fortune 100 companies in the Delahaye Media Reputation Index database, for Q2 of 2003, reported in J. Mandese, Quantifying PR by medium, *Television Week*, September 1, 2003, Website.

30. For example, see G.V. Johar and M.T. Pham, Relatedness, prominence and constructive sponsor identification, *Journal of Marketing Research*, 1999, 36(3), pp. 299–312.

31. For example, see J.A. Tripodi, M. Hirons, D. Bednal, and M. Sutherland, Cognitive evaluation: prompts used to measure sponsorship awareness, *International Journal of Market Research*, 2003, 45(4), pp. 435–455.

32. J. Crimmins and M. Horn, 1996, same reference as in note 10.

33. Human evaluative conditioning (HEC) was discussed in Chapters 8 and 9, as well as the contribution of respondent awareness – which helps!

34. Case reported in T. Meenaghan, The role of sponsorship in the marketing communications mix, *International Journal of Advertising*, 1991, 10(1), pp. 35–47.

35. K.J. Clancy and P.C. Krieg, *Counterintuitive Marketing*, New York: The Free Press, 2000, p. 109.

36. K.J. Clancy and P.C. Krieg, same reference as in previous note, p. 110.

37. G. Dowling, *Creating Corporate Reputations*, Oxford, U.K.: Oxford University Press, 2001, p. 19.

38. The term "corporate reputation" was apparently coined by Charles Fombrun in 1990 – see C. Fombrun and M. Shanley, What's in a name? Reputation building and corporate strategy, *Academy of Management Journal*, 1990, 33(2), pp. 233–258 – and has better connotations than "attitude" toward the company. However, in 1983, *Fortune* magazine in the U.S.A. began publishing a rating of "most admired", companies, which was subsequently imitated by British and Asian publications and we think that "most admire" is the best single-item representation of what "reputation" means. Note that individuals can nominate several, even many companies as those they "most admire" and are not confined to naming just one. See C. Fombrun, Indices of corporate reputation: an analysis of media rankings and social monitors' rankings, *Corporate Reputation Review* (a journal started in 1997 by Fombrun and Cees van Riel), 1998, 1(4), pp. 327–340.

39. J. Zhang and S. Shavitt, Cultural values in advertisements to the Chinese X-generation, *Journal of Advertising*, 2003, 32(1), pp. 23–33.

40. N. Madden, Study: Chinese youth aren't patriotic purchasers, *Advertising Age*, January 5, 2004, p. 6.

41. The Associated Press, Anheuser dusts off popular U.S. ads for foreign markets, *Marketing News*, March 1, 2004, p. 4.

42. G. Dowling, same reference as in note 37.

43. P. McIntyre, Quest for cool as necessary as detergent, *The Australian*, Media Section, December 11–17, 2003, p. 10.

44. G. Dowling, Corporate reputations: should you compete on yours?, Working paper, Sydney, Australia: Australian Graduate School of Management, University of New South Wales, June 2003.

45. C. Pearson, Archetypes 101, www.herowithin.com/arch101, accessed January 23, 2004. Carol Pearson's Website includes a questionnaire for locating your company's best-fitting archetype.

46. R.S. Peterson, D.B. Smith, P.V. Martorana, and P.D. Owens, The impact of chief executive officer personality on top management team dynamics: one mechanism by which leadership affects organizational performance, *Journal of Applied Psychology*, 2003, 88(5), pp. 795–808.

47. A. Ries, Wasting money on bad advertising slogans, *Advertising Age*, January 12, 2004, AAP27J on AdAge.com.

48. A. Ries, 2004, same reference as in previous note.

CHAPTER 17

CHAPTER 17

Personal selling: direct selling and telemarketing

Personal Selling is by far the largest form of marcoms. Round-figure estimates for the U.S.A. are that companies spend $500 billion annually on **direct selling**[1], which is face-to-face selling, and a further $45 billion on **telemarketing**, which is solicitation-by-telephone personal selling.[2] The combined total is more than double the estimated expenditure in the U.S.A. on media advertising, including sponsorship and events (see Chapter 1, Table 1.1).

In most large companies and organizations a *Sales Manager*, rather than the Marketing Manager, is responsible for Direct Selling and for Telemarketing, if this is used. The functional separation of sales and marketing is widest in FMCG companies because, for the salesforce, *retailers* are the brands, whereas for marketing managers or brand managers the specific *products* are the brands.[3] In most companies, too, the Salesforce Budget is regarded as separate from the Marcoms Budget (i.e., selling is regarded as an activity distinct from advertising, sales promotions, and PR). However, personal selling activities must be regarded as marcoms – and integrated and coordinated with the company's *other* marcoms *conceptually* if not always practically. This is realized by the fact that Direct Selling and Telemarketing proceed from the *same brand positioning* analysis and have the *same communication objectives* that the brand or brand-item has in general, no matter which type of marcoms is employed in the campaign. We need not, therefore, repeat these steps here.

The recommendations for the management of Personal Selling depend on the *type of selling*. In this chapter, we distinguish six main types of selling (one of which is Telemarketing). Two of the types are relatively passive, order-taking and order-filling types of selling, where the sales exchange is initiated and largely controlled by the customer. The other four types are active, salesperson-initiated and involve an exchange process that is reciprocally controlled by the salesperson and the customer. It is only to these *active* types of selling that the well-known Stages of Selling apply, which we will label as Approach, Benefit Presentation, De-Resistance, Closing and Follow-Up.

The sales manager has two broad variables to work with – the salesperson and the message. The *salesperson variable* is important in all six types of selling; decision factors within the salesperson variable include hiring, payment policy, and, to the extent that this is feasible, assignment to customers. Decision factors for the *message variable* focus on the best tactics for the stages of (active) personal selling. The tactics can be taught to salespeople via sales training, although it is the individual salesperson who is responsible for actual selection of tactics and their implementation.

In this chapter, we will consider the salesperson factors for each type of selling separately, because they differ so sharply. We will then consider message strategy, which is jointly applicable to the four *active* types of selling.

SALESPERSON FACTORS BY TYPE OF SELLING

We distinguish *six main types of selling*. These are summarized in Table 17.1, together with the *sales management recommendations* that will be discussed under each type. The first three types of selling pertain to the selling of *low-tech* products and services: Regular Retail Selling, Small Business Selling, and Trade Selling. The second three types involve the selling of *high-tech* products and services: Telemarketing, High-End Retail Selling, and Technical Selling.

TABLE 17.1 *Types of selling, hiring factors, pay policy, and assignment to customers.*

TYPE OF SELLING	CUSTOMER	SALES ENCOUNTERS	SALES-PERSON'S ROLE	HIRING FACTORS	PAY POLICY (SALARY: COMMISSION)	ASSIGNMENT TO CUSTOMERS
LOW-TECH PRODUCTS AND SERVICES						
Regular retail selling	Consumers	Transactions	Passive	• Mathematical ability • Social skill	90 : 10	Fixed
Small business selling	Business customers, trade customers, or consumers	Relational	Passive	• Fixed	Fixed	Fixed
Trade selling	Trade customers (wholesalers or retailers)	Relational	Active (stages)	• Experience • Conscientious-ness *given* social skill	60 : 40	AIO matching

TABLE 17.1 *Continued*

HIGH-TECH PRODUCTS AND SERVICES						
Tele-marketing	Consumers	Transactions	Active (stages)	• Voice and speech quality • ASQ	80 : 20	Ethnic matching by telephone exchange area
High-end retail selling	Consumers	Transactions	Active (stages)	• Attractive appearance • Voice and speech quality • Social skill	80 : 20	Fixed
Technical selling	Businesses, professionals or consumers	Relational	Active (stages)	• ASQ	80 : 20	AIO matching

Regular retail selling

We designate this category as **regular retail selling** to distinguish it from High-End Retail Selling, which is clearly more complex and interactive and is discussed later. Regular Retail Selling is *over-the-counter* selling to *consumers* as customers. It is mainly customer initiated and consists of one-off transactions. These conditions characterize the selling process in most department stores, drugstores, and supermarkets. They also characterize the selling process for many consumer services such as banks, for their basic services such as check accounts, savings, and cash withdrawal, as well as the consumer services provided by hotels, rental car agencies, and travel agents.

Hiring

Regular retail salespeople are basically responsible for taking customers' orders and filling them correctly (although, in some industries, there is certainly some scope for add-on sales; see pay, below). It follows that the most important hiring factor, a factor that can be evaluated in an initial employment interview, is **mathematical ability**. It so happens that the single best predictor of success in *any* type of job, from low-skilled jobs through to high-skilled jobs, is General Mental Ability, GMA[4], which is the current more politically correct name for what used to be called I.Q. Most impressive, the prediction holds *within the range* of the GMAs of the types of people that would apply for these jobs. For retail clerical work, it is particularly the *mathematical* component of I.Q. that is important. This can be assessed reasonably briefly and reasonably accurately during an applicant interview with a straightforward test such as the one given in Table 17.2, devised some years ago by Lumsden.[5] *Managers will need to develop norms on the typical range of scores obtained by applicants and should hire at the top end of that range.*

A second desirable hiring factor, which should be predictive of add-on sales – and customer satisfaction – is **social skill**. In a recent study of non-technical retail selling, social skill was shown to be a good predictor of supervisor-rated salesperson performance.[6] People rate themselves quite honestly, and the scale items are shown in Table 17.3. The retail salespeople in the study scored an average of 3.7 out of 5, *so it is advisable to hire applicants who score higher than average, say 4.0 or higher.*

TABLE 17.2 *Number series test for assessing mathematical ability.*

EXAMPLES:

2	4	6	8	10	12	…	…
9	8	7	6	5	4	…	…

DO AS MANY AS YOU CAN IN 3 MINUTES:

2	2	3	3	4	4	…	…
1	7	2	7	3	7	…	…
3	4	5	6	7	8	…	…
10	15	20	25	30	35	…	…
8	7	6	5	4	3	…	…
3	6	9	12	15	18	…	…
5	9	13	17	21	25	…	…
8	1	6	1	4	1	…	…
27	27	23	23	19	19	…	…
1	2	4	8	16	32	…	…
9	9	7	7	5	5	…	…
8	9	12	13	16	17	…	…
11	13	12	14	13	15	…	…
19	16	14	11	9	6	…	…
2	3	5	8	12	17	…	…
18	14	17	13	16	12	…	…
29	28	26	23	19	14	…	…
20	17	15	14	11	9	…	…
81	27	9	3	1	$\frac{1}{3}$	…	…
1	4	9	16	25	36	…	…
16	17	15	18	14	19	…	…
3	6	8	16	18	36	…	…

SOURCE: J. Lumsden, see note 5.

TABLE 17.3 *Social skill questionnaire (self-rated).*

	STRONGLY DISAGREE				STRONGLY AGREE
I find it easy to put myself in the position of others	I	2	3	4	5
I am keenly aware of how I am perceived by others	I	2	3	4	5
In social situations, it is always clear to me exactly what to say and do	I	2	3	4	5
I am particularly good at sensing the motivations and hidden agendas of others	I	2	3	4	5
I am good at making myself visible with influential people in my organization	I	2	3	4	5
I am good at reading others' body language	I	2	3	4	5
I am able to adjust my behavior and become the type of person dictated by any situation	I	2	3	4	5

SOURCE: L.A. Witt and G.R. Ferris, see note 6.

Pay policy

Despite the description of Regular Retail Selling as "passive," the fact is that retail salespeople show remarkably high variation in the amount of retail sales associated with them (the obvious exceptions here are those retail sales jobs where the salespeople are *strictly* order-fillers, such as supermarket checkout personnel and bank tellers as contrasted with, say, bank desk personnel). In chain department stores, hotels, and rental car agencies, for example, some salespeople are "naturals" who have the knack of encouraging upgraded or add-on sales. Individuals' performance should be *objectively tracked*, not subjectively judged by the management supervisor, as subjective judgments are not very accurate.[7] This knack should not be overly encouraged, of course, or the salesperson might become too aggressive and turn customers off, especially when customers expect to be in control of the exchange, but it does seem to be worth some acknowledgment and reward. We recommend, in this situation, a policy of *paying 90% fixed salary and 10% commission.*

Assignment to customers

In the examples of Regular Retail Selling that we have been discussing, the manager's capacity to assign salespeople to customers is essentially *fixed*, meaning that the manager cannot make assignments. If anything, the opposite occurs – customers assign themselves *to salespeople*, within the limits of who is available at the retail counter. Nevertheless, the sales manager may find, through accidental experimentation or observation, that particular salespeople seem to do better with particular types of customers, perhaps distinguished by age, gender, or ethnicity. Provided the salesperson is willing, we see no harm in *reassignment* to different branches or offices based on compatibility with customer types. Such transfers would be profitable for both the store and the salesperson.

Small business selling

We distinguish **small business selling** as a category because there are so many small businesses in every country and they are economically and personally very important. Primarily, small businesses are owner-managed and the sales staff usually consists of the owner himself or herself and members of the owner's family. These small businesses may sell to Business Customers, as do most secretarial services, drafting services, and small equipment suppliers; to Trade Customers, as do local hardware stores or smallgoods stores; or to Consumers, as do local grocery shops, drycleaners, or hairdressers. For each of these types of customer, the exchange process is *relational* rather than simply transactional, because most customers are repeat customers. On the other hand, the salesperson's role is usually passive, as an order-taker and order-filler. It is true that in some small business industries, the seller has considerable scope to vary the price. Auto mechanics, plumbers, and indeed most tradespersons seem to do this. Excessive variation, however, we believe to be unethical (price discrimination) and we would not wish to encourage this with recommendations of incentive payments or incentive self-payments in any way, shape or form.

Basically, in the case of small business selling, the *hiring* factors are *fixed* – limited to self and close family; the *pay policy* is *fixed* – 100% salary; and self-assignment to different types of customer is not possible because the small business is captive to its location.

Trade selling

Trade Selling is where many young marketing trainees begin their careers and it is also a full-time career for many salespeople. **Trade selling** is selling within the channel of distribution: Manufacturers selling to Wholesalers or Retailers, and Wholesalers selling to Retailers. Typical trade selling industries are FMCG food and beverages, health and beauty products, over-the-counter drugs, textiles, and clothing. Trade Selling is *relational* (success definitely depends on relationship marketing) and it is an active form of selling in which the salesperson employs the standard Stages of Selling (see below).

Hiring

The best predictor of success in Trade Selling is *Experience*. Although trade selling is often used as a temporary training ground for marketing trainees and provides essential frontline exposure to wholesalers and especially retailers' decision processes, the salespeople who sell the most are generally those over 35 years of age who have made trade selling a career.[8] There is therefore a fair amount of hiring away from other companies with the promise of larger commissions as the main incentive.[9] Other than Experience, which discriminates against hiring younger salespeople, there is one personality factor that predicts performance quite well in trade selling and that is *Conscientiousness* – being a planner, organized, hard-working, responsible, and persistent – but this only works if the salesperson is above average on *Social Skill*.[10] Self-ratings of the Conscientiousness trait characteristics are quite valid and could be easily employed in the job application questionnaire following the Social Skill self-ratings. The items measuring Conscientiousness should be mixed with items measuring other "Big Five" personality trait characteristics such as Extraversion and Neuroticism (even though these don't predict) to disguise the otherwise obvious purpose of the test.

Pay policy

Of all the types of selling, Trade Selling has the highest proportion of pay in the form of *commission*, typically *a 60:40 ratio of fixed salary to variable commission*. It is much too easy for trade selling to lapse into becoming a series of routine calls on regular customers, so a high incentive should be built into the pay policy to ensure that extra sales become the purpose of these visits. At the same time, there is a good deal of necessary routine activity in the form of shelf-stocking and order-taking. This activity must be broken up with genuine opportunities to sell and Newton (that's Derek, not Sir Isaac) recommends that three to five such opportunities per day is a reasonable goal that will keep the trade salesperson interested and motivated (and well rewarded).[11]

Assignment to customers

As mentioned, Trade Selling is *relational selling* and success in this depends mainly on the similarity of **attitudes, interests, and opinions (AIO)** between the salesperson and the customer.[12] As far as possible, therefore, trade salespeople should be allowed to *choose the customers* they wish to sell to because, after some trial and error, they will naturally gravitate toward those with whom they get along well. The implication for the sales manager, accordingly, is to hire salespeople with a *diversity of AIO characteristics* because customers will surely exhibit similar diversity.

Telemarketing

As predicted in Chapter 1, Telemarketing looks likely to continue to be a giant form of marcoms everywhere in the developed world except for the European Union, where unsolicited, "outbound" telemarketing is prohibited by law. This is despite the advent of the U.S. National "Do Not Call" Registry in October 2003, with a similar registry soon to be introduced in Australia. As far as we know, Asian countries, comprising the largest consumer market in the world, do not have a "do not call" restriction prohibiting unsolicited telemarketing. (In the U.S.A., long-prohibited telemarketing practices are *automated dialing*, whereby a computer program tries random digits within exchanges until someone answers, and the use of an *artificial or pre-recorded voice* to open the sales call and even, in some cases, make the sales pitch, unless the called party has given express consent for such calls, which is rare[13]; these practices are prohibited by the Telephone Consumer Protection Act of 1991. Live telephone solicitations to private residences are allowed, *unless* the telephone number is registered as "do not call," and even then *exemptions* have been obtained by financial institutions, non-profit organizations and charities, and, somewhat unfairly it would seem, government offices.[14])

Telemarketing is targeted primarily at *consumers*, B-to-C, although there is a small amount of B-to-B telemarketing. Most telemarketing campaigns are *transactional*. Most sales calls are one-off attempts, such as for insurance, credit cards, phone plans, and home improvement services. Even in the categories of products or services that rely on regular re-ordering, such as stationery supplies as a product example and medical and dental visits as service examples, each repeated call is more like a transaction than a relationship. The salesperson's role is definitely active, employing the traditional Stages of Selling.

Hiring

The first and foremost characteristic on which to hire telephone salespeople is **voice and speech quality**. The opening 30 seconds of the telemarketing sales call is crucial because that is the typical interval during which the prospective customer decides whether to allow the call to be continued or to terminate.[15] Listeners automatically make judgments of the status and likability of the caller *from the voice* in just 10 to 15 seconds[16] and if the caller seems to be of lower status than the prospective customer, or is simply dislikable, the customer will terminate the call as quickly as possible. In fact, in a study of the causes of refusal in phone calls made by telephone survey interviewers, a job which has obvious relevance to telemarketing, it was found that the *content* of the introduction (the Approach) had very little effect on whether the call would be successful whereas the interviewer's voice and speech had a big effect.[17] Everyone experiences refusals, but callers with the lowest refusal rates, and therefore the highest success rates in completing the call, exhibited the following voice and speech characteristics:

- Relatively rapid speech (approximately 200 words per minute) which can be easily determined by recording, say, 30 seconds of a candidate's normal speech and then counting the number of words.

- A somewhat higher than average voice pitch, but also variation in pitch.

- Distinct articulation of words and clear pronunciation.

- An accent that is equal in status or higher than that of the person called; a lower-status accent is an immediate turnoff (this applies within ethnic accents when ethnic salespeople are used in telemarketing).

Hiring on the basis of Voice and Speech Quality can be defended as functionally related to the job. A telemarketing job applicant who feels discriminated against on the basis of voice quality would have a difficult, if not impossible, task of proving discrimination in this functional capacity.

There is a second criterion that should be employed for hiring telemarketers, which is **attributional style**. All types of active selling are accompanied by frequent refusals or rejections during the selling process, and Telemarketing would have to be highest on this count (even higher than door-to-door selling, which was disappearing in the U.S.A. but may make a comeback with the recent restrictions on telemarketing[18] and is still prevalent in other parts of the world) because it is easier for the customer to terminate on the phone than in person, that is, face-to-face. The average person, if placed in the role of a telemarketing salesperson, would soon feel confidence dropping and self-esteem being dented[19] from the repeated refusals and rejections. The Attributional Style Questionnaire (ASQ), developed by Seligman and colleagues, originally for use in clinical psychology, measures the extent to which an individual tends to blame negative events on external causes and at the same time tends to take personal credit for positive events.[20] The combination, within the same individual, of strong Optimism and almost a complete lack of Pessimism turns out to be a very strong predictor of personal selling performance. The ASQ, scored as the composite score for positive events minus the composite score for negative events, an index called CPCN, predicts two aspects of personal selling performance, both of them extremely valuable in hiring. First of all, individuals with high CPCN scores (see Table 17.4) are much less likely to quit following sales training. Second, CPCN also predicts upside sales performance and in a linear manner; for instance, in Seligman and Schulman's prospective study of life insurance salespeople, individuals scoring above the median on the CPCN sold a 35% greater value of life insurance policies in the second six months following the initial six months of training than did individuals scoring below the median. Further indicating a linear relationship, those in the top quartile sold 73% more than those in the bottom quartile.[21] The ASQ is reproduced in Table 17.4 from published sources.[22] Note that, for actual use, the questionnaire has to be prepared from the information in the table (the classification of events, of course, does *not* appear on the questionnaire, and the rating items have to be adapted to fit the 12 events).

> You might find it revealing to take this test and see how you would fare as a salesperson. It cannot give perfect prediction at the individual level, of course, but it is highly likely that if you tend to be a pessimist, or tend to be fatalistic about *both* good and bad events, then you are not cut out to be a hard-core salesperson.

TABLE 17.4 *Attributional Style Questionnaire (ASQ).*

Instructions

Please try to vividly imagine yourself in the situations that follow. If such a situation happened to you, what would you feel would have caused it? While events may have many causes, we want you to pick only one – the *major* cause if this event happened to *you*. Please write this cause in the blank provided after each event. Next, we want you to answer some questions about the *cause*. To summarize, we want you to:

1. Read each situation and vividly imagine it happening to you.

2. Decide what you feel would be the *major* cause of the situation if it happened to you.

3. Write one cause in the blank provided.

4. Answer three questions about the *cause*.

5. Go on to the next situation.

The 12 events (on the questionnaire, place them in the order shown in the parentheses and delete "event type" and "domain"):

EVENT TYPE	DOMAIN	EVENT
Positive	Achievement	(3) You become very rich.
		(10) You apply for a position that you want very badly (e.g., important job, graduate school admission) and you get it.
		(12) You get a raise.
	Affiliation	(1) You meet a friend who compliments you on your appearance.
		(6) You do a project that is highly praised.
		(9) Your spouse (boyfriend/girlfriend) has been treating you more lovingly.
Negative	Achievement	(2) You have been looking for a job unsuccessfully for some time.
		(5) You give an important talk in front of a group and the audience reacts negatively.
		(8) You can't get all the work done that others expect of you.
	Affiliation	(4) A friend comes to you with a problem and you don't try to help.
		(7) You meet a friend who acts hostilely toward you.
		(11) You go out on a date and it goes badly.

Continues

TABLE 17.4 *Continued*

<u>The four questions – including ratings of internality (question 2), permanence (question 3) and generality (question 4) for each event – illustrated here for event no. 2. Adapt wording of questions 2, 3 and 4 to fit the event.</u>

You have been looking for a job unsuccessfully for some time.
1. Write down the one major cause_____

_____

_____

2. Is the cause of your unsuccessful job search due to something about you or to something about other people or circumstances? (circle one number)
   Totally due to other people or circumstances   1   2   3   4   5   6   7   Totally due to me
3. In the future when looking for a job, will this cause again be present? (circle one number)
   Will never again be present   1   2   3   4   5   6   7   Will always be present
4. Is the cause something that just influences looking for a job or does it also influence other areas of your life? (circle one number)
   Influences just this particular situation   1   2   3   4   5   6   7   Influences all situations in my life

<u>Scoring</u>
<u>Add ratings on items 2, 3 and 4 for all positive events and divide by 6 (called CoPos). Add ratings on items 2, 3 and 4 for all negative events and divide by 6 (called CoNeg). Then total score CPCN = CoPos – CoNeg. The maximum possible CPCN score is 18, the minimum is –18, and the midpoint is 0. Norm for sales applicants, male or female: median = 6.2. Norm for undergraduate students: median = 1.1. Sales applicants are more optimistic than students in general.</u>

SOURCES: C. Peterson *et al.*, 1982, 1984, see note 20; and Seligman and Schulman, 1986, see note 21.

Pay policy

Because Telemarketing typically involves the selling of relatively high-tech products or services, it appears prudent to follow the payment policy for this type of selling, which, in the U.S.A., is usually an *80:20 ratio of fixed salary to commission*.[23] The incentive of earning just 25% more than your base salary (which produces an 80:20 ratio) seems to be quite low, but the fairly stressful nature of telemarketing, even for personality types suited to it via the ASQ, suggests that paying 80% fixed salary will result in a greater sense of job security. Of course, telemarketing sales managers, in our experience, are quite ruthless about firing salespeople who are not attaining the company's historical minimum number of successful calls per day and so job security is something that only *successful* telemarketing salespeople can rely upon!

Assignment to customers

If the company's telemarketing sales area and target customers include ethnic segments, it may make sense to assign telemarketing salespeople with a certain *ethnic* background to a telephone exchange area that has a high proportion of households with the same ethnicity as the salesperson. Ethnic differences are a fact of life in most large cities and metropolitan areas now throughout the world and it would be poor business practice to ignore this trait. At the same time, the sales manager should realize that the equal or higher *status* effect – which in telemarketing is exhibited solely by voice and speech quality – operates *within* ethnic groups. This means that telemarketing companies should hire not only salespeople of suitable ethnic backgrounds but also well-educated, and therefore apparently higher status, salespeople.

High-end retail selling

High-end retail selling, as distinct from Regular Retail Selling discussed above, requires *specialized knowledge* of the product category or service category. This is acquired, of course, by *sales training*, with six months of training at a cost to the company of about $30,000 per trainee being fairly typical. Because it is retail, the great majority of the sales exchanges are *transactional*, that is, one-off purchases by the customer. Industries that employ High-End Retail Selling, mainly of the transactional type, include automobile sales, consumer electronics and expensive household goods, insurance of all types, real estate, and legal services.

Hiring

With High-End Retail Selling – and here it will be useful to keep typical examples in mind, such as for car sales, home furnishings, major home electronics items, or expensive apparel – the customer comes to the salesperson and thus the salesperson does not face the problem of having to make a "cold call" approach and also faces much less chance of encountering an outright rejection. Rather, the salesperson's task is to *help the already interested customer make a good choice* and, quite frankly, to *try to upgrade* that choice and encourage the customer to buy peripherals and add-ons that will increase the value of the total sale. Add-on sales are obvious for new cars but you might also keep in mind home furnishing accessories such as drapes and cushions, even paintings, electronics accessories such as room-to-room headphones, and apparel accessories such as ties, scarves, belts, bags, and perhaps footwear. Salesperson factors that help to do this are: Attractive Appearance, Voice and Speech Quality, and Social Skill.

It has long been known that *reasonably attractive, well-groomed* salespeople tend to sell more in high-end retail settings. They are also more likely to be hired in the first place.[24] With highly Transformational products, such as furnishings and apparel, there is a functional reason for this; customers would not feel comfortable asking a sloppily dressed or clearly lower-social-class salesperson for fashion advice. But even for non-transformational, more Functional products, physical attractiveness and good grooming appear to be effective high-end retail selling. For instance, pharmaceutical company salespeople, calling on physicians as customers, achieve a remarkably higher level of prescriptions written for their brand the more "good-looking" the salesperson is! The effect of physical attractiveness on sales is larger when making new calls on physicians but is still evident during a longer association between the particular salesperson and the particular physician.[25] What are the effective appearance cues for salespeople? Despite changing fashions and fashion cycles, the *clothing cues* that give the impression of knowledge-ability and credibility have not changed in decades.

> For men, the cues are a conservative suit or blazer, worn with a tie. For women, it is a dress or blouse with a tailored look; a jacket or blazer can help but if it looks too casual, as in the semi-crumpled and looser European style now in vogue, it probably detracts from the authoritative impression. For women, it is important, on the one hand, not to dress in an overly feminine and informal manner, but on the other hand, not to go so far as to appear "butch" or masculine,

with such things as pin-stripe jackets or suits or pseudo-ties as neckwear.[26] The main stimulus dimensions in the masculinity versus femininity of clothing are summarized in Table 17.5. Listed are the extreme endpoints of each dimension – remember, the advice is that women avoid the obviously feminine side and opt for *moderately* masculine clothing cues rather than extreme masculine. John T. Molloy's well-known books on "dress for success," which cover recommendations for men and women, remain an observationally astute guide to creating an effective impression. These books also recommend some subtle distinctions between dressing for sales situations in contrast with, for example, dressing for aspirations to the boardroom.[27] Although it is logical that job applicants for sales positions could be taught to dress appropriately, the reality is that appropriate clothes selection is more a matter of well-established habit. Clean, polished footwear, for both men and women when footwear is visible to the customer, is also a further superficial but meaningful cue to competence. Not only clothing but *personal grooming* is important. For men, hair trimmed, nails clean and cut; for women, hair looking clean, not too much makeup or heavy perfume. Although it seems fake to suggest that men or women salespersons should wear glasses if they do not need them, an early and classic study of judgments of photographs of the same people with and without glasses (rimless, plain clear glass, not tinted) found that glasses added to the impressions of intelligence, industriousness and honesty.[28] A later study replicated the intelligence and dependability effect of regular glasses for both sexes, and replicated the honesty effect but for women only. Also, in case you are concerned, it found no difference in rated attractiveness in the glasses-wearing conditions compared to the same people without glasses (note that physical attractiveness helps in selling situations and had there been a negative effect of wearing glasses, we would recommend against them).[29]

TABLE 17.5 *Extreme femininity versus extreme masculinity cues in clothing.*

FEMININE	MASCULINE
Rounded silhouette	Straight silhouette
Horizontal lines	Vertical lines
Soft texture	Hard texture
Small-scale details	Large-scale details
Light colors	Dark colors

Vocal cues – *voice and speech quality* – are also influential in the transactional situation that is characteristic of High-End Retail Selling. Effective voice and speech cues are the same as for Tele-marketing: namely, relatively rapid speech (approximately 200 words per minute); a somewhat higher than average voice pitch, but also variation in pitch; distinct articulation of words and clear pronunciation; and the accent should be at least equal in status or higher than that of the customer.[30] The final hiring factor for High-End Retail salespeople is *social skill*, the same factor that is important for successful low-end retail selling. The social skill of the salesperson is influential despite the more careful, considered choice that the customer is making.

Pay policy

As we said, *technical expertise* is a requirement for High-End Retail Selling and Newton[31] recommends that the company's technical salespeople, on *average* be paid on an *80:20 ratio of base salary to commission*. In other words, the typical high-end retail salesperson should be expected to be able to earn an amount, percentaged on his or her total sales, that is 25% extra on top of his or her base salary. The manager does not want to *over*-reward pushiness for add-on sales and at the same time an attractive base salary makes the salesperson feel more like a valued, non-transient employee.

Assignment to customers

This type of selling is *retail*, where customers come to you, so that assignment of salespeople to customer types is not really an option. Between retail locations, however, geographic reassignment (for demographic matching) should be used when possible.

Technical selling

Technical selling, as the name suggests, involves the personal selling of *complex products and services* to business customers or consumer customers. Although Technical Selling initially requires a new-business solicitation, or "cold call," in most cases thereafter it becomes *relational* with continuing product ordering or service renewals and, in many cases, annual contract renewal. Technical Selling is the major form of marcoms in a wide range of industries, such as: chemicals, machinery, transport and logistics, insurance, corporate financial services, and company health programs, all with business customers; and personal financial advisory services, as well as specialist medical, dental, health, and beautification services, for private consumers. You may wonder why we include physicians and dentists as examples of technical *salespeople*, but in the realm of private as contrasted with government health care, these professionals have the scope to recommend special services and – little restricted by professional associations' guidelines – to set their own prices. While we may not like to think of this as selling, it is. In all areas of technical selling, the salesperson is presumed to be offering expert advice in line with each individual customer's needs, but the sale still has to be made.

Hiring

Technical salespeople are highly paid and Technical Selling is, for many, a sought-after career that is competitive to get hired into and easy to fail at. For instance, in the life insurance industry, companies typically hire only about 8% of applicants for sales positions and almost four out of five of those 8% hired will quit the industry, not just the company, within the first three years.[32] In Technical Selling, training costs are very high because of the technical nature of the products or services, and frequent updating training sessions are required because most of these industries are subject to relatively rapid technological advances. A recent estimate is that it costs $60,000 to replace a salesperson who quits.[33] A hiring method that can predict not only who will succeed but also who will stay with the company is therefore of enormous value to the sales manager. *Attributional Style*, the same test we recommended for hiring telemarketers, appears to be able to predict both low turnover and high value of sales among Technical Salespeople. Prediction is achieved by using the CPCN score (see Table 17.4 earlier).

The idea in Technical Selling is to convert successful initial calls into *relationships* with customers. This means a relationship on a personal basis between the customer and the individual salesperson, *not a pseudo-relationship* whereby the customer deals with the same company but is attended to by whichever salesperson happens to be available; pseudo-relationships are no more profitable than mere transactions.[34]

Pay policy

The normative recommendation is to pay Technical Salespeople a relatively high *fixed salary component of 80%*, to emphasize that they are highly respected employees of the company, but with a commission rate set on their cold calls and total sales for the year such that the average salesperson in a typical year should be able to earn an extra 25% above the fixed salary, which makes the typical ratio of fixed to variable salary about 80:20. Because cold calls are so important in most technical selling jobs, approximately half of the *commission* should be paid on the basis of meeting cold-call quotas, with the other half paid on the dollar volume of completed sales.[35] The obvious exception here is health professionals, who are prevented by law or industry self-regulation from soliciting business; they are paid 100% by fixed salary but the salary should be increased annually if they sell more successfully.

Assignment to customers

The salespeople within the company's salesforce are likely to be similarly knowledgeable about the technical aspects of the products or services that the company sells. The best predictor of whether a successful *relationship* will be developed between the individual salesperson and the individual customer is *similarity of Attitudes, Interests, and Opinions (AIO)*. Actually, the effective variable in AIO similarity is the proportion of *topics* on which the two agree rather than the absolute number of agreements, as these could be outweighed by numerous specific disagreements on one or two topics. The usual topics that come up in the course of an extended relationship are politics and religion, and non-political social issues such as the acceptability of alternative contemporary lifestyles, or even sports teams! A high *proportion* of topics agreed on is what counts.[36] We are not suggesting, by any means, that salespeople should hide their personal views from customers known to disagree with many of them, but rather that the senior sales manager should do his or her homework on prospective new account customers and try to assign individual salespersons to them who are most likely to achieve interpersonal compatibility.

STAGES OF SELLING AND MESSAGE TACTICS

The action objectives and communication objectives for Direct Selling or Telemarketing campaigns are straightforward. The ultimate Action Objective is always Purchase, although a finer-grained analysis of the purchase decision via the Behavioral Sequence Model, the BSM, may suggest that Pre-purchase action should be attempted first, such as a dealer or showroom visit, if the prospective customer is not already at the retail location, or that the initial action objective should be a Trial purchase rather than a fully committing complete purchase. Appropriate action objectives are easily identified for a particular direct selling or telemarketing campaign.

The Communication Objectives that need to be achieved to ensure Action also directly parallel those that are set for an advertising campaign and are in fact exactly the *same* as those that would be set for a *Direct-Response advertising campaign*. Just as a direct-response ad has to achieve the communication objectives in one or two exposures, Direct Selling or Telemarketing has to achieve the communication objectives *in one or two salesperson-customer exchanges*. First, Category Need may have to be sold using a category-level purchase motive, unless the customer comes to the sales exchange with the need to buy in the category already established. Second, in a salesperson-initiated exchange, the brand awareness objective is Brand *Recognition:* where the brand may be the company or organization that the salesperson represents, or particular brands of products or services that the salesperson sells. The BSM will indicate whether this will be *Visual* Brand Recognition, when the customer is making a choice at the retail location (e.g., rental car company logos or brands of consumer electronics products in a retail store) or *Verbal* Brand Recognition, which is the only type of recognition possible in *telemarketing* or when the initial customer contact is made by *telephone* in personal selling and is the type necessary in *face-to-face* personal selling when the initial contact is made by the *salesperson*. Indeed, a major communication objection of Corporate Image advertising (see previous chapter) for companies that rely on *personal selling* is to generate *Verbal* Brand Recognition so that the company name will be known by the customer when the salesperson initiates the *Approach* (see Stages of Selling, below). With an *unknown* company or brand name, where prior advertising or publicity has not been engaged in or is not affordable, the salesperson has to quickly establish his or her company's credibility during the approach, which takes up valuable time and may not be very convincing. Third, brand benefits and emotions are critically important in direct selling and telemarketing to achieve the communication objective of Brand Preference (these are covered in the Benefit Presentation stage, below). Fourth, Brand Action Intention must be *generated* (as the purchase decision is High Involvement). Fifth, Purchase Facilitation is always an objective (usually incorporated in Closing the Sale, which is the penultimate stage of the selling process, below).

Direct Selling and Telemarketing differ from Advertising, however, even from infomercials and interactive Website ads, in that their marcoms messages proceed through a *definite sequence of stages* – this is really the major difference between personal versus media-delivered marcoms. Each stage is *two-way and reciprocal* between salesperson and customer, unlike the one-way communication that characterizes all other forms of marcoms (with the exception of interactive TV or PC advertising, though this operates at a considerably lower level of interactivity and reciprocity than direct selling and telemarketing).

The **stages of selling** in personal selling and telemarketing are somewhat like the customer decision stages that we described in Chapter 1, except that because the stages are *initiated* by the salesperson they are described from the *seller's* perspective. Textbooks and sales training manuals differ somewhat in their labeling of the stages and also in their number, but a useful generic stage model, with the optional first stage of prospecting, is listed in Figure 17.1. We describe the stages as *Prospecting* (optional), *Approach*, *Benefit Presentation*, *De-Resistance*, *Closing*, and *Follow-Up*. In the next sections of the chapter, we discuss **effective selling tactics** for each of these stages. The tactics are drawn, in part, from the book by Schell[37], whose study of selling tactics is uniquely valuable in that the tactics were researched with prospective buyers to determine which ones *they* regard as effective – a nice application of customer orientation!

PROSPECTING
(OPTIONAL)

APPROACH

BENEFIT PRESENTATION

DE-RESISTANCE

CLOSING

FOLLOW-UP

FIGURE 17.1 *Stages of selling.*

Prospecting (optional)

Prospecting – identifying prospective customers to be approached – is listed as an optional stage because it is applicable in only two of the types of selling: Telemarketing and Technical Selling. These are the two types of selling where *cold calls* on prospective new customers are a large part of the business. Whereas cold calls on smaller or new distributors are sometimes part of Trade Selling, the majority of trade sales calls are made on established buyers to whom the salesperson has sold previously.

Prospecting is very much like target audience selection for advertising except that it is on a one-on-one basis rather than a group basis. The salesperson looks for prospects who will be most interested in the category and tries to find out with whom their current loyalty, if any, is placed. The most common methods of prospecting are:[38]

- Personal research (the Internet holds an incredible amount of information about companies and government organizations as prospects and sometimes includes personal profiles of the individuals to whom you want to sell)

- Referrals

- Networking in the industry, including attendance at trade shows and conferences

- Community contacts

Individuals are the targets. In particular, the salesperson needs to identify the individual (even though the sales presentation may be made to a group or buying center) who is the *key decider* and who has the *authority to approve the purchase.* Finding this person is not as easy as it sounds, because decision authority is not always well indicated by job titles, in large companies particularly. Key decider identification is an essential part of successful prospecting.

Approach

The **approach** is the first stage of the actual sales exchange and takes place in the *first few minutes of the sales call* or, as noted earlier, in the *first 30 seconds of the telemarketing call.* The literal content of the approach is fairly standard and, as we will see shortly, is less important than *how* the content is presented. The Approach is usually opened with:[39]

- a statement about *yourself*, the name of your *company* accompanied by a brief ISPS, and, if the prospect is a referral, the name of the person who *referred* you. An ISPS[40] is an **industry-specific positioning statement**, which, in marcoms planning, you should have previously prepared anyway. Examples: "We specialize in lower inventory management costs for electronics companies"; (to a university) "We are a growing company that makes consumer household products and we want to recruit top undergraduates in marketing"

and followed with:

- a *compliment* if you know that the prospect is already interested in what you have to offer or, if you are not sure, a *question* as to the prospect's interest.[41] Keep the compliment on the topic; do not try to elicit "feel-good" answers with a clichéd opening such as "How are you today?", a good reason being that it *is* a cliché and another being that people in a *negative* mood are more likely to buy.[42]

More important than the literal content of the approach is the necessity of quickly building **rapport** with the prospect. Rapport is largely determined by paraverbal stimuli rather than literal verbal stimuli. Two tactics can be employed by the salesperson to assist in establishing Rapport: *gradual convergence of speech rate*, and *NLP matching*.

Gradual convergence of speech rate

In discussing salesperson selection, we have already emphasized the importance of voice cues in generating a first impression; voice cues are absolutely determinant in telemarketing and equally determinant, with appearance cues, in face-to-face personal selling. The tactic of **speech rate convergence** goes beyond the initial impression and begins to build rapport. Speech Rate Convergence means adjusting your speech rate to that of the listener but slightly faster, and doing so gradually rather than obviously and abruptly.[43] Judgments of the speaker's Expertise and Trustworthiness generally increase with a fast rate of speech, towards 200 words per minute, and most people actually prefer to listen to fast speech, in the range of 175 to 200 words per minute. However, converging towards the *listener's* speech rate increases the listener's "Identify-With" judgment of the speaker.[44] The *prospective customer's* speech rate should be evident in the *first 10 seconds or so* of the conversation. If the prospect speaks *slowly*, the salesperson should gradually reduce his or her speech rate to just a little faster than that of the prospect. Conversely, for a *fast-speaking* prospect, the salesperson should gradually increase his or her speech rate, even going as high as 250 words per minute. It is at the slow and fast extremes that convergence is likely to go off the rails as being either condescending or ingratiating and the salesperson has to be very careful to not let this happen – it can be a fine balance, but an effective one.

NLP matching

Neuro-linguistic programming (NLP) sounds like it refers to manipulation of the mind but really it is quite the opposite, namely reading of and sensitivity to the other's mind. NLP, developed by Bandler and Grinder[45] is well-established in psychotherapy[46] and reportedly is used by some major companies as part of sales training.[47] NLP theory postulates that individuals tend to prefer and habitually employ one of three modes of information processing: Visual, Auditory, or

Kinesthetic.[48] Whether these individual differences are inborn or learned early in childhood is not known but the fact is that they are real and quite pronounced differences. NLP theory further postulates that communication will be most effective if the communicator *matches* the preferred mode of the recipient. This applies to *one-way* communication, as in advertising, as well as to *two-way* communication, as in the dyadic exchange that characterizes direct selling and telemarketing. Confirmatory evidence of the effectiveness of NLP matching in one-way communication is provided in a fascinating study by Orr and Murphy in which three versions of a radio commercial for a BMW automobile that emphasized either the look of the car (Visual), the sound of the car (Auditory), or the feel of the car (Kinesthetic) generated higher purchase intention among the respective groups of Visual processors, Auditory processors, and Kinesthetic processors, as predicted by NLP theory.[49] Confirmatory evidence of the effectiveness of NLP theory in two-way communication comes mainly from anecdotal clinical reports.[50] It should be emphasized before we go any further that individuals *do switch* between all three modes of processing, as we will exemplify shortly, but here we are concerned with identifying their preferred or *habitual* mode of processing. The person's habitual mode of processing can be detected quite easily, in either face-to-face selling or telemarketing, by **speech sampling**.[51] Classification is achieved most objectively by recording and analyzing several minutes of the person's speech. However, because it is illegal to record conversations without the participant's prior consent, the salesperson will have to become skilled at detecting the customer's preferred mode "on the run," without the aid of the voice recording. Table 17.6 provides typical *clues* to assist classification. The salesperson will then communicate more effectively – build Rapport – by:

- *slightly exceeding* the speech rate of the customer (as noted under convergence, previously)
- employing verb types and colloquial expressions, called *predicates*, that correspond to the customer's preferred modality.[52]

On average, according to Bandler and Grinder's early report, about 70% of the population are Visual processors, 15% are Auditory Processors and 15% are Kinesthetic processors. If the salesperson cannot pick up the preferred mode of the customer, or in the rare event that the customer prefers *mixed* modes, the best tactic in the benefit presentation stage of the sales exchange (see next) is to employ *all three* modes; although the single best bet would be to employ only the Visual mode, chances are that 30% of prospects will not relate to that mode but will prefer one of the other two modes, hence the recommendation to mix them. *Most effective, of course, is to detect the customer's preferred mode and use that.* Obviously, as well, the preferred NLP mode should be continued through the remaining stages of selling.

Benefit presentation

The types of product or service sold through face-to-face selling or telemarketing will generally be High-Involvement/Informational or High-Involvement/Transformational and it therefore follows that the Brand Preference tactics for **benefit presentation** which were given in Chapter 8 for media advertising should be employed – *with some modifications to fit selling*. The modified tactics are listed in Table 17.7 and explained next. But:

- First, *write out* the **two key benefit statements** that you want to communicate (these should be deliverable in a total of 15 seconds).[53] Example: "We mainly work with Fortune 500 companies like yours." "We don't have the lowest prices in the industry but we *do* have the best product – you want the best, don't you?"

- Second, keep **supplementary benefit claims** handy – also written out.

TABLE 17.6 *Speech clues for classifying customers as either visual, auditory or kinesthetic processors.*

	VISUAL PROCESSORS	AUDITORY PROCESSORS	KINESTHETIC PROCESSORS
Speech rate	Rapid rate, higher pitch	Medium rate, melodious	Slow rate, lower pitch, and with more pauses
Verb type	Seeing, e.g.,	Hearing, e.g.,	Feeling, e.g.,
(understand)	I see what you mean; I get the picture	That rings a bell	That feels right; I get your drift
(don't understand)	I'm in the dark	That's all Greek to me	I can't make head or tail of it
(don't know)	It's not clear	I can't tell if that's right	I don't have a handle on that
(think)	My view is . . .	Something tells me . . .	I hold these views . . .
(confused)	It's too obscure	It doesn't sound like a good idea	This doesn't fit what I want

SOURCE: The verb-type examples are from J. O'Connor, 2001, p. 61, see note 46.

TABLE 17.7 *High-involvement benefit presentation tactics for personal selling (face-to-face or telemarketing).*

PS-1	Write out the two key benefit statements that you want to communicate (make sure they can be delivered in a total of 15 seconds). Keep handy the supplementary benefit claims – also written.
PS-2	The message must be introduced in a manner that reflects the target customer's initial state of preference toward the brand.
PS-3	Try to detect the target customer's preferred NLP mode, if not already known, and describe the benefits in this mode. If the preferred mode is not detectable, describe the key benefit in visual (see), auditory (hear) and kinesthetic (feel) wording, even though this will take a little longer.
PS-4	Also try to gauge the target customer's upper-limit latitude of acceptance for the important benefits: if *transformational*, overclaim; if *informational*, claim at estimated upper limit, provided this is within the range of truth.
PS-5	Be prepared to answer comparison questions, truthfully, if the customer brings up a comparison with another brand.
PS-6	Use refutational (yes . . . but) answers to any hesitations with acceptance of benefit claims but admit if the claim can't be truthfully refuted.

Adjust the message introduction to suit the customer's initial state of preference

The message must be introduced in a manner that reflects the target customer's *initial state of preference* toward the brand (or the company as brand). This tactic corresponds with the opening tactic for High-Involvement/Informational Advertising and is equally important in Personal Selling. A prospective customer who seeks you out as a salesperson – for instance, in High-End Retail Selling – can be presumed to have a quite favorable attitude toward the product already and you should reinforce this. On the other hand, in "cold call" selling – in Trade Selling (occasionally), Telemarketing, or Technical Selling – the prospective customer may hold any of a range of predispositions toward your brand of product or service, including never having heard of it.

- If the target customer's prior state of preference has not been determined from thorough prior prospecting, you must determine it quickly by asking an opening question before the benefit presentation: a *direct question*[54] is best, such as: "What do you think of our product?"

Prospects will usually give a pretty straight answer, which will enable you to lock in on the likely initial attitude and proceed from there. If the target customer's initial attitude is very negative, rather than risk a termination jump straight to tactic 4, Comparison, or tactic 5, Refutational. Normally, however, prospects will have either a neutral or moderately positive preference and so you can proceed immediately to the Benefit Presentation phase.

NLP matching

Now comes the actual Benefit Presentation phase. The tactics center on **NLP matching**, as follows:

- If it is not already known, the salesperson should try to quickly detect the target customer's preferred NLP mode and describe the benefits of the product or service in this mode predominantly.

The Visual mode can be addressed effectively in face-to-face selling with *illustrations* (e.g., a video presentation or a brochure) of the product or service in use; however, in Telemarketing, you have to use *words* – nouns that conjure favorable visual imagery and also visual verbs and predicates (see earlier). The Auditory mode, applicable in both face-to-face selling and telemarketing, is just *straight verbal descriptions of the benefits*. The Kinesthetic mode is most effectively implemented in Face-to-Face selling, where the prospect can touch product samples or be given a live demonstration of the service; in Telemarketing, the only way to tap this mode is to use *tactile verbs and predicates* ("will help you stay ahead of the game," "leading edge," "state-of-the-art," and so forth).

- If the prospect's preferred mode is not detectable, describe the key benefit in wording that reflects *all three modes*, even though this will take a little longer.

An example of all three modes, quickly used, is: "You can see the quality (or, if telemarketing, will see . . .)"; You've probably heard how good . . ."; and "I think this will fit your requirements very well . . ."

If the key benefit is transformational, overclaim; if informational, state the key benefit claim at the estimated upper limit of the customer's latitude of acceptance subject to the truthful limit of benefit delivery that your product or service offers

With this Benefit Presentation tactic, there is a dichotomy depending on whether the major purchase motivation (and thus the key benefit claim) is Transformational or Informational. New cars, luxury vacations or fashion clothing would be examples of products or services where the primary purchase motivation is likely to be Transformational and, accordingly, the subjective key benefit in these cases should be *overclaimed* – not unbelievably exaggerated but described in the most glowing terms. "Glowing" is the Visual mode, so we should add "best-sounding" for the Auditory mode and something like "a great experience" for the Kinesthetic mode. At this point, it may be worth looking back at Chapter 8 to see why we do not regard the overclaiming of subjective claims as being unethical and, indeed, argue that the hedonic welfare of the customer is increased by doing so. The situation is entirely different, however, when the major purchase motive (and thus the key benefit claim) is Informational, that is, when the choice is based on the verifiable extent to which the brand-item solves the problem, prevents it, resolves it, or meets an ideal (the main Informational motives). Much of Trade Selling, Telemarketing and Technical Selling is informationally based. The salesperson's ethical obligation is to make a benefit claim that does not go beyond the objectively determinable – that is, truthful – *limit* of product or service delivery. An interesting and important sub-tactic arises here. If the prospective customer's upper limit of latitude of acceptance (upper limit of believability) is *below* the objective delivery limit, then the salesperson should moderate the benefit claim *down* to that level. This is because the prospect would not believe the stronger claim anyway, even when it is truthful, and, when the product or service does turn out to deliver better than expected, in actual use, the buyer's satisfaction will be *increased*, which is very important for future purchases and for referrals.[55] In the converse case, when the prospective customer's believability limit is *higher* than the objective delivery limit, then that's too bad – the salesperson must not be tempted to exaggerate (lie) about the objective quality or performance of the product or service! Should the salesperson lie, he or she risks the subsequent loss of the customer to the company, possible legal redress, possible loss of his or her own job, and damage to the reputation of the company that he or she is representing.[56]

Truthful comparison, if prompted

Comparisons with competitors' products or services are not an effective tactic when initiated by the salesperson.[57] However, if the *customer* brings up a Comparison *as a question to the salesperson*, then you are best advised to give a direct and truthful answer. Of course, with High-Involvement products and services, a multiattribute comparison is always possible and we see nothing wrong with you emphasizing the advantages of your product or service after having truthfully answered the prospect's comparative question, which may show your product or service to be inferior or just equal on one or more of these attributes.

Use refutational answers to any hesitations

This last tactic can also be part of the next stage of selling, De-Resistance, but it is quite likely to come up during the Benefit Presentation stage, namely, when the prospect exhibits a clear hesitation (a long pause, indicating doubt) or sometimes a direct verbal disputation of the claim that you have just presented. Assuming you have just told the truth, then tell it again as the refutation; if you sense that this hasn't worked, go for compensating benefits. (A Transformational overclaim, however, is different, and you should probably back off just a bit.)

- To refute a hesitational objection, a skilled salesperson will use the *refutational* "yes . . . but" or "offset" method[58]: acknowledge the objection (or the presumed objection in the case of a clear hesitation) but offset it either with the truth again, or by drawing attention to compensating benefits

De-resistance

De-resistance, which is our summary label for the standard selling stage of "Handling objections and overcoming resistance," is always identified as a stage of the selling process.[59] Customer resistance is not an inevitable occurrence, of course, but is quite likely to occur in *cold-call* selling, whether this be face-to-face or telemarketing.

- The most ethical tactic to try to achieve *de-resistance* is to adopt the *refutational* method, as described above.

Among the tactics that must *not* be employed in an attempt to overcome resistance are the high-pressure tactics known as "Standing room only" and another known as "Door-in-the-face." The tactic known as "Standing room only" is an outright lie to the effect that the salesperson's offer is limited by either number or time, so that if the prospect does not agree to buy now, he or she will miss out. The legal ground here is tricky because it is not illegal to make an offer on a limited number of items or for a restricted time period, but when this offer is made artificially, and thus in effect is offered to everyone with the limitations never honored, it is clearly unethical. Similarly, the tactic known as "Door-in-the-face" whereby an overly expensive offer is made first, with every expectation that the customer will reject it, and then a switch is made to a more reasonable offer, is also unethical.[60] The DIF tactic works, all too well, because of the psychological phenomenon of *reciprocity*: the salesperson has apparently just done you a favor by making a concession and you will often feel obliged to comply. The concession offer, however, was always the intended real offer and thus presenting it in the context of a sham offer is outright deception. Here, we should clearly distinguish one form of concession that is *legal and ethically proper*, and that is the salesperson's discretion to offer a price concession from a *realistically quoted* initial price. This is discussed further in the penultimate stage of the selling process, Closing the Sale.

Closing the sale

The next to last stage of selling is **closing the sale**.

- Unless the prospective customer spontaneously says "I'll take it," the salesperson must close the sale – that is, ask directly for the order.

The best and most ethical method of Closing the Sale is known as the **summary close**, in which the salesperson summarizes the benefits and asks directly for the order. (*Preceding* this, however, if you believe that the prospect *is* ready to buy, the most effective close is actually **silence** – to say nothing and let the prospect volunteer the decision.[61]) If the prospect remains hesitant, even after you have taken care of other hesitations and objections, then you should interrupt with the Summary Close. It may be met with a "no, thanks" but is the least wasteful of both the salesperson's and the customer's time. It is also less offensive than another popular closing tactic, which we have to admit is effective, dammit, known as the "Presumptive close," easily recognizable from salespersons' catchphrases such as "How did you want to pay for that?" or, in a retail setting, "Can I wrap that for you?" The "Presumptive close" would seem bizarre in Technical Selling, so prospects for this type of selling escape it!

Follow-up

The final stage in the standard selling process is **follow-up** after the sale has been made – or even if it has not.

- Follow up with a fax or email even if you didn't get, or haven't yet got, the sale[62] (this is especially important for Telemarketing sales – to prove your company is legitimate and that you are sincere).

- Make a list of what you promised to deliver and do it ASAP[63] (response time is the factor that is most irksome to customers).

The salesperson is obliged to Follow Up on *customer-initiated* contact when the customer calls back or revisits with a question or seeks further advice. However, contrary to the standard text-book recommendation for personal selling, we do *not* believe it to be necessary for the salesperson to contact – by phone or face-to-face or sending a note – the customer after the sale. In the case of *one-off* purchases, the customer is unlikely to see the salesperson again, so post-sale contact would seem rather unusual beside being economically pointless. Salesperson-initiated follow-up in *relational* selling, we believe, poses a different problem, though perhaps less so in the U.S. culture where overservicing seems to be normal; it is almost always perceived by the customer as just an attempt to make a future sale, rather than as genuine concern for the customer's satisfaction. Think back to the last friendly phone call or "Thank-you" note that you received from a salesperson. We would guess that if you did not know the salesperson well, you would have found the call somewhat awkward, and would have suspected the salesperson of being manipulative. We also suspect that a small segment of the population, and you many be one of these people, would treat the thank-you as incurring an obligation and would feel pressured to place a further order with that salesperson even if they really did not need or want to. This kind of felt reciprocity is not uncommon and, in our view, it is insidious.[64]

In clear contrast to the ulterior-motivated Follow-Up that we have been talking about, there can be a legitimate and useful reason for a follow-up contact *if* the salesperson has a new product or a new, better-value service that would really benefit the customer. This, however, would be better labeled the *follow-on* stage of personal selling.

SUMMARY

Personal selling is a major form of marcoms for many companies – the largest companies down to the smallest one-person business. In the large companies, personal selling is usually accompanied by (preferably preceded by) Advertising and perhaps PR, although the reality is that these other marcoms are managed by the Marketing Manager, whereas personal selling is managed by a separate Sales Manager. It is actually in *small* companies where advertising and personal selling are most likely to be integrated because there is one manager, and the advertising is quite likely to be limited to display ads or brochures or flyers.

There are two principal variables that the sales manager has to manage: the Salesperson and the Message. Tactical recommendations for managing the salesperson variable and the message variable differ according to the *type* of selling. We identify six main types of selling: Regular Retail Selling, Small Business Selling, Trade Selling, Telemarketing, High-End Retail Selling, and Technical Selling. The first three of these types of selling involve the sale of low-tech products or services and the last three pertain to high-tech products or services.

The Salesperson is really part *of* the message – the highly salient *presenter* of it. The salesperson is important even in the relatively passive forms of selling (Regular Retail Selling and Small Business Selling) and is crucial in the active forms (Trade Selling, Telemarketing, High-End Retail Selling, and Technical Selling). Because of the importance of the salesperson, the hiring policy for each of these types of selling is vital. We have carefully identified from the literature the hiring criteria that we believe will best predict success in each of these types of selling. These range from the quite superficial criteria of *voice cues* (essential in Telemarketing) and *appearance cues* (important in all forms of Face-to-Face selling) to a somewhat deeper criterion called *social skill*, and a very entrenched criterion, which cannot be changed, called *attributional style*.

The recommended monetary compensation policy also varies between the types of selling, from straight salary in Small Business Selling, to as much as a 40% of the salesperson's pay earnable as a commission on sales in Trade Selling. The norm for the other types of selling is more like 80% salary and 20% commission and in the types of selling where cold-calling is required, half of the commission should be paid on calls attempted rather than sales made. In Trade Selling and Technical Selling, the sales manager also has the ability to assign salespeople to particular customers. This is most effective when the assignment is made on the basis of similarity between the salesperson's and the customer's *attitudes, interests, and opinions (AIO)* as this similarity has been found to be a good predictor of sales results in relational, as contrasted with transactional, selling.

The Message is the other principal variable in selling. In Regular Retail Selling and in Small Business Selling, there may be very little message, as such, because the salesperson is mainly an order-taker and order-filler. However, in these passive or customer-controlled selling situations, the astute salesperson will politely suggest Upgrades or Add-Ons and, again based mainly on voice cues and appearance cues, individual salespeople can be remarkably effective at persuading customers to make further purchases. How the salesperson conveys the message is possibly more important than what the salesperson actually says.

In the other four forms of selling, a distinct series of *seller-initiated* Stages typically occurs and the stages have to be planned for. The stages are Prospecting (in telemarketing and technical selling only), Approach, Benefit Presentation, De-Resistance, Closing, and Follow-Up.

Prospecting – identifying prospective customers to be approached – is best accomplished through personal research, nowadays usually on the Internet, through referrals, and by "networking" in the industry, and through community contacts.

The Approach stage refers to the first few minutes of the sales call or the first 30 seconds of a telemarketing call. How the approach is made, rather than literally what is said, is crucial. However, as you should have done already, prepare an industry-specific positioning statement (ISPS) for opening the contact. We identify two interesting variables that assist the "how" of the approach. One is the *gradual convergence of speech rate* to a rate that is just slightly faster than that of the customer. The other is an advanced technique called *NLP matching*, in which the salesperson tries to detect the preferred sensory processing mode of the customer – which could be Visual (how things look), Auditory (how things sound), or Kinesthetic (how things feel) – and then introduces into the approach words that match the customer's mode. We do not think there is an ethical issue with NLP matching and, to the contrary, it could be justified as producing more effective and more satisfying communication.

The Benefit Presentation stage is the "crunch" stage of the active selling process; although we say "active," remember that the sales exchange is always a two-way process. First, write out your Two Key Benefit Statements; these should be deliverable in 15 seconds. Second, keep handy a Written List of Supplementary Benefits. For the benefit presentation itself, we recommend a set of tactics modified from the *High-Involvement* Informational and, where applicable, Transformational quadrants of the Rossiter-Percy-Bellman Grid. Briefly summarized here, these are to (1) take into account the target customer's initial state of preference toward the brand; (2) try to detect the target customer's preferred NLP mode and state the benefits in that mode but, if not known, employ a mixed-mode presentation of the key benefit claim; (3) if the target customer's major purchase motivation is transformational, overclaim the key benefit and any other transformational benefits but, if informational, state the key benefit claim only at the upper limit of the target customer's estimated latitude of acceptance, even if you could objectively make a stronger truthful claim; (4) be prepared to answer comparison questions truthfully, though only if the customer brings up a comparison; and (5) use refutational answers to any hesitations or outright objections, either a direct refutation, if truthful, or a compensatory refutation, if indeed your brand is inferior on the benefit in question.

The De-Resistance stage may not arise but it often does in personal selling. De-Resistance is best accomplished with either of the two refutational rebuttals, as just described, or, where the salesperson has discretion over pricing, by improving the deal.

Closing the Sale, if the customer does not do this for you by saying "I'll take it," is best achieved by *asking for the order directly*. Even if the potential sale seems as though it is being lost, the salesperson should go for a direct close, as this will save everyone's time and also the apparently reluctant customer might surprise and say "Yes." Not going for the close means a probably wasted additional sales call. When the prospective customer is obviously interested but is hesitating, an effective strategy is simply to wait it out, that is, employ silence. Make a list of what you promised to deliver, and deliver promptly.

The final stage of the selling process – Follow-Up – should be done by fax or email. Follow up with a personal call only if the customer seeks post-purchase assistance or if you genuinely have something new and beneficial to suggest to the customer.

DISCUSSION QUESTIONS

17.1 Why is the Salesperson such a crucial variable in personal selling and what are the three areas of sales management policy that may possibly be employed to make the salesperson variable more effective?

17.2 Look at our classification of the six main Types of Selling and find two industry examples of each (other than the examples given in the chapter).

17.3 Construct a Hiring Interview Protocol (written and oral) for hiring salespeople for Technical Selling.

17.4 Imagine you have been hired as a Telemarketing salesperson for the worldwide charity, World Vision. Go to World Vision's Website and find out what this organization does. Then copywrite three alternative Benefit Presentation scripts – one Visual, another Auditory and the other Kinesthetic. Explain not only the differences between the scripts but also how you have pitched the key benefit claim, and why.

17.5 Suppose that your company's service in terms of objectively measurable attributes such as customization, responsiveness and delivery time is actually better than the prospective customer expects. Should you point out these superiorities?

17.6 What should you do when a prospective customer disputes a benefit claim that you have presented, as apparent from his or her prolonged hesitation or verbal disagreement?

17.7 What tactics are appropriate for Closing the Sale? When, if at all, should you Follow Up?

NOTES

1. A.A. Zoltners and S.E. Lorimer, Sales territory alignment: an overlooked productivity tool, *Journal of Personal Selling & Sales Management*, 2000, 20(3), pp. 139–150.

2. Telemarketing was listed in Chapter 1 as the largest form of media marcoms in the U.S.A., with an expenditure of $67 billion in 2001, but we noted that legal restrictions on unsolicited telemarketing calls have reduced this to an estimated $45 billion by now.

3. B. Dewsnap and D. Jobber, The sales-marketing interface in consumer packaged-goods companies: a conceptual framework, *Journal of Personal Selling & Sales Management*, 2000, 20(2), pp. 109–119.

4. M.J. Ree, J.A. Earles, and M.S. Teachout, Predicting job performance: not much more than g, *Journal of Applied Psychology*, 1994, 79(4), pp. 518–524. Also see N.R. Kuncel, S.A. Hezlett, and D.S. Ones, Academic performance, career potential, creativity, and job performance: can one construct predict them all?, *Journal of Personality and Social Psychology*, 2004, 86(1), pp. 148–161.

5. J. Lumsden, A factorial approach to unidimensionality, *Australian Journal of Psychology*, 1957, 9(2), pp. 105–111.

6. L.A. Witt and G.R. Ferris, Social skill as moderator of the conscientiousness-performance relationship: convergent results across four studies, *Journal of Applied Psychology*, 2003, 88(5), pp. 809–820. Their study 4 was on low-tech retail selling. Supervisor-rated sales performance correlated $r = .19$ ($p < .05$) with the salesperson's self-rated social skill and an amazing $r = .68$ ($p < .01$) with supervisor-rated social skill of the salesperson, but this second correlation is probably biased upward because the supervisor made both

ratings. To rate the social skill (seven aspects) of someone else, you would have to know them well and therefore, in a job interview, the sales manager has to rely on the applicant's self-ratings.

7. M. Levy and A. Sharma, Relationships among measures of retail salesperson performance, *Journal of the Academy of Marketing Science*, 1993, 21(3), pp. 231–238.

8. D.A. Newton, Get the most out of your salesforce, *Harvard Business Review*, 1969, 47(5), pp. 130–143. This early article on pay policy and management has not been bettered since.

9. D. Godes, In the eye of the beholder: an analysis of the relative value of a top sales rep across firms and products, *Marketing Science*, 2003, 22(2), pp. 167–187.

10. M.R. Barrick, M.K. Mount, and J.P. Strauss, Conscientiousness and performance of sales representatives: test of the mediating effects of goal setting, *Journal of Applied Psychology*, 1993, 78(5), pp. 715–722.

11. D.A. Newton, 1969, same reference as in note 8.

12. J.D. Lichtenthal and T. Tellefsen, Toward a theory of business buyer-seller similarity, *Journal of Personal Selling & Sales Management*, 2001, 21(1), pp. 1–14.

13. P.J. Batista, Telemarketing and the TCPA: let the seller beware, *Journal of the Academy of Marketing Science*, 2003, 31(1), pp. 97–100.

14. D.L. Vence, Less ringing in the ear, *Marketing News*, December 8, 2003, p. 14.

15. D. Sanchez, When your company speaks, do people listen?, *Telemarketing*, 1985, July, pp. 70–72.

16. L.S. Harms, Listeners' judgments of status cues in speech, *Quarterly Journal of Speech*, 1961, 47(2), pp. 164–168.

17. L. Oksenberg, L. Coleman, and C.F. Cannell, Interviewers' voices and refusal rates in telephone surveys, *Public Opinion Quarterly*, 1986, 50(1), pp. 97–111.

18. S. Reeves, "Do not call" revives door-to-door sales, *Marketing News*, December 8, 2003, p. 13. The retail value of door-to-door sales in 2002 was $28.7 billion.

19. However, contrary to popular belief, high self-esteem is not a predictor of success in selling and neither are two other "obvious" traits, extraversion and machiavellianism (the tendency to exploit other people and interpersonal situations for self-gain). The everyday observation that successful salespeople are confident and extraverted is more likely due to reverse causality – those who experience success show an

increase in their self-esteem and become more extraverted (social extraversion is reinforced by successful "cold calling," in particular) whereas those who continue to work for the company but without the same success show no significant change (though no loss) on these two traits. See A.A. Turnbull, Selling and the salesman's prediction of success and personality changes, *Psychological Reports*, 1976, 38, pp. 1175–1180. The ASQ has been shown in prospective (predictive longitudinal rather than cross-sectional) studies to be useful for hiring salespeople who will succeed.

20. C. Peterson, A. Semmel, C. von Baeyer, L.Y. Abrahamson, G.I. Metalsky, and M.E.P. Seligman, The Attributional Style Questionnaire, *Cognitive Therapy and Research*, 1982, 6(3), pp. 287–300; C. Peterson and M.E.P. Seligman, Causal explanations as a risk factor for depression: theory and evidence, *Psychological Review*, 1984, 91(3), pp. 347–374. Martin Seligman, currently President of the American Psychological Association, emphasizes optimism and teaches a course on "positive psychology," suggesting ways to live a pleasant, good, and meaningful life; see www.psych.upenn.edu/seligman.

21. M.E.P. Seligman and P. Schulman, Explanatory style as a predictor of productivity and quitting among life insurance sales agents, *Journal of Personality & Social Psychology*, 1986, 50(4), pp. 832–838.

22. The main questionnaire is taken from the article by Peterson *et al.*, 1982, same reference as in note 20, but includes some amendments made later by Seligman and Schulman, 1986, reference in previous note.

23. D.A. Newton, 1969, same reference as in note 8.

24. S. Forsythe, M.F. Drake, and C.E. Cox, Influence of applicant's dress on interviewers' selection decisions, *Journal of Applied Psychology*, 1985, 70(2), pp. 374–378; E.W. Stuart and B.K. Fuller, Clothing as communication in two business-to-business sales settings, *Journal of Business Research*, 1991, 23(3), pp. 269–290; T.W. Leigh and J.O. Summers, Initial evaluation of industrial buyers' impressions of salespersons' nonverbal cues, *Journal of Personal Selling & Sales Management*, 2002, 22(1), pp. 41–53.

25. M. Ahearne, T.W. Gruen, and C.B. Jarvis, If looks could sell: moderation and mediation of the attractiveness effect on salesperson performance, *International Journal of Research in Marketing*, 1999, 16(4), pp. 269–284. In keeping with the well-established physical attractiveness halo effect, attractive salespeople were also perceived as more expert, trustworthy, likable, and as having better communication ability. Each of

these factors, except perceived expertise, which was possibly at a ceiling level, had significant positive relationships with market share of prescriptions obtained via the salesperson.

26. S. Forsythe, M.F. Drake, and C.E. Cox, 1985, same reference as in note 24.

27. J.T. Molloy, *New Dress for Success*, New York: Warner Books, 1988; see also J.T. Molloy, *New Woman's Dress for Success*, New York: Warner Books, 1996.

28. G.R. Thornton, The effect of wearing glasses upon judgments of personality traits of persons seen briefly, *Journal of Applied Psychology*, 1944, 28(3), pp. 203–207.

29. T. Bartolini, J. Kresge, M. McLennan, B. Windham, T.A. Buhr, and B. Pryor, Perceptions of personal characteristics of men and women under three conditions of eyewear, *Perceptual and Motor Skills*, 1988, 67(2), pp. 779–782. The third condition in this experiment was sunglasses, which produced exactly the opposite of the effects that a salesperson would want to convey.

30. T.W. Leigh and J.O. Summers, 2002, same reference as in note 24.

31. D.A. Newton, 1969, same reference as in note 8.

32. Life Insurance Marketing Research Association survey figures, cited in M.E.P. Seligman and P. Schulman, 1986, same reference as in note 21.

33. Survey of companies with large salesforces by Hewitt Associates, press release (on Website), June 19, 2001.

34. B.A. Gutek, A.D. Bhappu, M.A. Liao-Troth, and B. Cherry, Distinguishing between service relationships and encounters, *Journal of Applied Psychology*, 1999, 84(2), pp. 218–233.

35. D.A. Newton, 1969, same reference as in note 8.

36. J.D. Lichtenthal and T. Tellefsen, 2001, same reference as in note 12.

37. M. Schell, *Buyer-Approved Selling: Sales Strategies from the Buyer's Side of the Desk*, Vancouver, BC: Marketshare Publications, 2003.

38. S. Dwyer, J. Hill, and W. Martin, An empirical investigation of critical success factors in the personal selling process for homogenous goods, *Journal of Personal Selling & Sales Management*, 2000, 20(3), pp. 151–159.

39. S. Dwyer, J. Hill and W. Martin, 2000, same reference as in previous note.

40. M. Schell, 2003, same reference as in note 37.

41. This second opening is our adaptation of the "prospect-focused approach" defined by S. Dwyer *et al.*, 2000, same reference as in note 38.

42. S. Maxwell and A. Kover, Negative affect: the dark side of retailing, *Journal of Business Research*, 2003, 56(7), pp. 553–559.

43. S.M. Ketrow, Attributes of a telemarketer's voice and persuasiveness, *Journal of Direct Marketing*, 1990, 4(3), pp. 7–21. In an excellent analysis of telemarketing success factors for fundraising, it was found that the "How are you?" approach produced 10% lower incidence of pledges; see L.L. Simmel and P.D. Berzer, The art of the *ask*: maximizing verbal compliance in telefundraising, *Journal of Interactive Marketing*, 2000, 14(3), pp. 12–40.

44. Again, see S.M. Ketrow, 1990, same reference as in previous note, for a summary of this research and, for a recent confirming study, see D.M. Eveleth and L. Morris, Adaptive selling in a call center environment, *Journal of Interactive Marketing*, 2002, 16(1), pp. 25–39.

45. R. Bandler and J. Grinder, *The Structure of Magic 1* and *The Structure of Magic 2*, Palo Alto, CA: Science and Behavior Books, 1975 and 1976.

46. NLP, like most other forms of psychotherapy, is well-established despite mixed evidence in controlled studies. NLP has been particularly difficult to "prove" but the retort by NLP advocates is that the tests have not involved experts. The severest critic of NLP has been an Australian, C.F. Sharpley, but he concedes that "the process of predicate matching to enhance support is worthwhile" (1987, p. 105) and that is the NLP process that we focus on here. See C.F. Sharpley, Research findings on Neurolinguistic Programming: nonsupportive data or untestable theory?, *Journal of Counseling Psychology*, 1987, 14(1), pp. 103–107.

47. H. Alder, *Mind to Mind Marketing*, London: Kogan Page, 2001. A 1997 survey of direct marketing companies in the U.K. found that in their salesperson training program 58% used "mirroring" of customer's pace of speech, including 22% who used NLP specifically; see C. Nancarrow and S. Penn, Rapport in telemarketing – mirror, mirror on the call?, *Marketing Intelligence & Planning*, 1998, 16(1), pp. 12–21.

48. There are also small incidences of individuals with either an olfactory (smell dominant) or gustatory (taste dominant, which actually depends on smell) preference but they are usually grouped with kinesthetic (feel, touch) preferrers.

See J. O'Connor, *NLP Workbook*, London: Thorsons, 2001.

49. B.H. Orr and J.H. Murphy, Neuro-linguistic programming: implications for advertising copy strategy?, in P.A. Stout (Ed.), *Proceedings of the 1990 Conference of the American Academy of Advertising*, Austin, TX: Department of Advertising, The University of Texas at Austin, 1990, pp. RC-111 to RC-116.

50. See, for example, Bandler and Grinder's books, in note 45, Alder's book, in note 47, and O'Connor's book, in note 48.

51. In a face-to-face situation, very skilled observers can also detect visual and auditory patterns, though not kinesthetic, from eye movements. Visual processing is upward eye movements or fixed staring into space; auditory is lateral movements and also down to the participant's left, while kinesthetic (which may be a mixed factor consisting of bodily awareness versus tactile) is supposedly down to the right; see M. Buckner, N.M. Meara, E.J. Reese, and M. Reese, Eye movement as an indicator of sensory components in thought, *Journal of Counseling Psychology*, 1987, 34(3), pp. 283–287. R. Dilts <nlpu.com/research.htm> also claims to have identified reliable differences in EEG patterns between modes of sensory processing. Verbal predicates are much easier to reliably detect.

52. The verb-type predicates in the table are from J.O'Connor, 2001, same reference as in note 48, p. 61. For more examples of these, see H. Alder, 2001, same reference as in note 47, pp. 241–243.

53. M. Schell, 2003, same reference as in note 37.

54. S. Dwyer *et al.*, 2000, same reference as in note 38.

55. P.K. Kopalle and J.L. Assunção, When (not) to indulge in "puffery": the role of consumer expectations and brand goodwill in determining advertised and actual product quality, *Managerial and Decision Economics*, 2000, 21(6), pp. 223–241; and P.K. Kopalle and D.R. Lehmann, Strategic management of expectations: the role of disconfirmation sensitivity and perfectionism, *Journal of Marketing Research*, 2001, 38(3), pp. 386–394.

56. See especially P.K. Kopalle and J.L. Assunção, 2000, same reference as in previous note.

57. S. Dwyer *et al.*, 2000, same reference as in note 38.

58. S. Dwyer *et al.*, in 2000, same reference as note 38.

59. The classic reference for the stages of selling is A.J. Dubinsky, A factor analytic study of the personal selling process, *Journal of Personal Selling & Sales Management*, 1980, 1(1), pp. 26–33.

60. See R.B. Cialdini, *Influence: The Psychology of Persuasion*, New York, NY: Quill, 1998; and R.B. Gialdini and N.J. Goldstein, Social influence: compliance and conformity, *Annual Review of Psychology*, 2004, 55, pp. 591–621.

61. S. Dwyer, *et al.*, 2000, same reference as in note 38.

62. M. Schell, 2003, same reference as in note 37.

63. M. Schell, 2003, same reference as in note 37.

64. For instance, in one study that demonstrates the pressure of felt reciprocity, half of the shoppers entering a bookstore were approached with a catalog handout and the greeter touched them lightly on the upper arm, while the other half of the shoppers were offered the catalog but not touched, with these two conditions being randomly determined. Touched shoppers spent longer in the store, an average of 22 minutes versus 13 minutes if not touched, and spent almost one-fifth more: average purchase $14.90 versus $12.20 for those not touched. See J. Hornik, Shopping time and purchasing behavior as a result of in-store tactile stimulation, *Perceptual and Motor Skills*, 1991, 73(2), pp. 969–970. There is a similarly dramatic finding in a study of the effect of waitresses' extent of smiling when delivering the bill – a broad but natural smile almost triples the gratuity left by male customers and almost doubles the gratuity left by female customers. See K.L. Tidd and J.S. Lockard, Monetary significance of the affiliative smile: a case for reciprocal altruism, *Bulletin of the Psychonomic Society*, 1978, 11(6), pp. 344–346.

CHAPTER 18

Social marketing campaigns

Social marketing covers two activities: the *de-marketing*, to use Kotler and Zaltman's term, of "bad" products, services and behaviors judged by our elected government officials to be harmful to individual and social well-being, and the *promotion* of "good" products, services and behaviors judged to be beneficial to individual and social well-being.[1] Note that even non-government social marketing organizations are bound by the elected government's decisions about what is "bad" and what is "good." These decisions are highly subjective and they vary not only with who's in power but in many cases also between government departments.[2] In this chapter, we will try to accept current Western governments' classifications but we will also question some governmental and corporate social marcoms strategies on ethical grounds (see end of chapter).

A **social marcoms campaign** is a mass-media or direct-response media campaign that has the de-marketing of the "bad" or the promotion of the "good" as its primary purpose. Social Marcoms Campaigns are launched by government departments, quasi-government organizations that depend on government funding, private charitable organizations, and special-interest groups among the public. It is important to recognize that Social Marcoms Campaigns are also launched by commercial industry groups or companies with a vested interest in either the "bad" (to minimize legislation that would restrict it) or the "good" (if their products or services profit from it).

Social marcoms campaigns, overall, have a much lower success rate than *commercial* marcoms campaigns because the behaviors that they target are usually much harder to change. Commercial marcoms campaigns change people's behavior – increase their purchase and use of the brand of product or service – in about 50% of campaigns and profitably so in about 30% of campaigns, as we reported in Chapter 1. Social marcoms campaigns, by and large, do not do as well: a rough estimate is that only about 10% of them produce any measurable changes – meaning reduction of "bad" behavior or production of "good" behavior – and then in only some people's behavior.[3] As Rothschild has observed in an excellent analysis of social marketing approaches, most of the changes in social behaviors that have been achieved have been the result, not of social marcoms campaigns, but of *legislation* making "bad" behaviors illegal, or of the introduction of *economic disincentives* (read higher prices due to taxes or else heavy fines for offenders) that discourage them and, less widely, of *economic incentives* to encourage "good" behaviors (such as lower-than-regular prices for low-alcohol beer, reduced insurance premiums for non-smokers and, more recently, for non-obese individuals).[4] We will avoid the difficult and controversial judgment of whether social marcoms campaigns – successful campaigns – are the more efficient use of funds, compared with law enforcement and economic subsidies and, for addictive behaviors, direct clinical treatment programs.[5]

There are examples, if not a high percentage of the total, of social marcoms campaigns that have been successes, and in this chapter we attempt to identify and recommend the steps toward getting your campaign into that category.

In this chapter, we regard social behaviors as *brands*. We conceptualize the *target audiences* for social marcoms campaigns, as for all marcoms campaigns, as New Category Users, Other-Brand Loyals, Other-Brand Switchers, Favorable Brand Switchers, and Brand Loyals (demographics cut across these brand-loyalty-defined target audiences). However, we define *Brand Loyals* in social marketing as referring to the "bad" behavior. The de-marketing of the "bad" behavior is almost always the primary purpose of a social marcoms campaign, so we give bad-behavior loyals top billing from a targeting perspective. For *habitual* "bad" behaviors, which are the focus of the large majority of social marcoms campaigns and of most of our examples, we also use more descriptive terminology and label BLs as Offenders, FBSs as Vacillators, and OBLs as Conformers.

Turning to *creative strategy*, we start with *brand positioning* for the social marketing brand, then consider the *communication objectives* for its campaign and the *grid tactics* that might be employed for its marcoms messages. The grid tactics for social marcoms messages focus on *punishment* appeals and *reinforcement* appeals. We will see that Threatened Punishment works best with Anxious individuals as a deterrent to the "bad" behavior. On the other hand, Promised Reinforcement for the "good" behavior offers the best hope for Impulsive individuals. In social marcoms, unlike in commercial marcoms, it is worthwhile to segment the target audiences in terms of these two *personality* traits.

Next, we look at *media strategy* for social marcoms campaigns and discuss situations where a Reach emphasis is required and other situations that depend on Frequency (and individual continuity).

Then, we propose how *ad testing* and *campaign tracking* research should be used in social marcoms campaigns.

Last, we discuss *ethics* in marcoms messages. Our proposed two-part principle of ethics covers all marcoms messages but we emphasize its applications to social marcoms messages.

A preview summary of the steps we recommend for planning a social marcoms campaign is provided in Table 18.1. Special terms are capitalized and may be checked in the Glossary if you don't recall them from previous chapters.

TABLE 18.1 *Summary of planning steps for a social marcoms campaign.*

1. Conduct a situation audit on the topic via secondary research and then commission primary qualitative research (Individual Depth Interviews: at least n = 20 with individuals who habitually do the "bad" behavior and n = 20 with individuals who mostly do the "good"). Specify in precise operational terms the "bad" behavior (which may be a set of behaviors) and the counterpart "good" behavior (which again may be a set of behaviors). Conceptualize these behaviors as brands. Construct three separate BSMs for Conformers, Vacillators, and Offenders.

2. Do a quantitative survey of each group (n = 200 per group) measuring individuals' gender, ethnicity, and literacy. Decide whether divisions of gender, ethnicity, and literacy are substantial enough to be further segmentation variables (further in that segmentation within the Conformer, Vacillator, and Offender groups by the personality traits of Anxiety and Impulsiveness is *assumed* in employing a dual benefit-positioning strategy).

3. For each of the three groups, Conformers, Vacillators and Offenders, construct (from the qualitative research) an I-D-U matrix of the facilitators and deterrents of the "bad" brand vs the "good" brand. From this, again for each group, identify a dual benefit-positioning strategy that punishes the "bad" behavior and reinforces the "good" behavior. If some of these six strategies are almost the same, you can economize by selecting the stronger of the overlapping pair. For the punisher strategy and the reinforcer strategy, generate and select a Key Benefit Claim and then generate and select a Conveyer. Construct rough ads including Grid tactics and Attention tactics. Pre-test with the MJAT method only.

4. Select an appropriate Reach Pattern. Estimate the MEF/c per ad cycle. Review the BSM and also commission a Direct Matching survey to select media types and media vehicles. Finalize the media schedule using *Media Mania* software.

5. Commission a Continuous Tracking Survey to monitor the campaign. Adjust media and creative as indicated, paying special attention to potential media-caused or creative wearout.

TARGET AUDIENCES IN SOCIAL MARKETING

For social marcoms campaigns, in contrast with commercial marcoms campaigns, we recommend two stages of segmentation to identify the target audience. As you might expect, the first is *brand loyalty segmentation*, as employed in commercial marcoms campaigns (see Chapter 5). The second stage, exclusive to *social* marcoms campaigns, is segmentation by *personality traits*. In this second stage, there should be an additional check on possible differences by *gender* and in many countries by *ethnicity* and, if print media are to be used in the campaign, by *literacy level*.

Stage 1: Segmentation by brand loyalty

Target audiences in social marketing should be approached from the Brand Loyalty perspective (not from the widely used Stages-of-Change perspective, because this has not proven helpful for social marcoms *message* planning[6]). The most difficult target audience for social marketing campaigns are those citizens who are loyal to what society deems to be "bad" behaviors, especially bad behaviors that, for individuals, have become habitual. These Brand Loyals we call **offenders**. From this perspective, citizens already doing the "good" behavior are *Other-Brand* Loyals, or, in the case of habitual behaviors, **conformers**. The rest, aside from those too young to possibly enter the category, are Favorable Brand Switchers – whom we call **vacillators**. Vacillators are those who are contemplating *taking up* the "bad" behavior or else they engage in it but only *occasionally*. For example, the 32% of young adults aged 18 to 24 in Minnesota who are *regular* smokers of cigarettes, which is well above the national average of 21% of all U.S. adults who are current smokers, would be regarded as Offenders, but at least a further 7% would be regarded as Vacillators in that they smoke *occasionally* and do not *see* themselves as smokers (when asked).[7] We should add here that, contrary to popular belief, occasional smoking carries no less health risk than regular smoking.[8] Vacillator smokers are a large and growing group in the U.S.A.; from 1996 to 2001, the most recent year for which The Centers for Disease Control and Prevention's (formerly The Centers for Disease Control and note the ambitious new name) survey results are available, a constant 23% of U.S. *adults* were "daily" smokers but in 38 of the 50 states the number of "some days" smokers has increased, with most being new, *occasional* smokers rather than regular smokers who have cut down (an almost impossible feat for the addicted smoker, who is more likely to be able to quit than to adjust to a lower nicotine dosage[9]). Approximately 25% of all *smokers* in the U.S.A. now are non-addicted, occasional smokers – Vacillators.[10]

A second example of a target audience well described as Vacillators would be the 25% of men and 40% of women in the U.S.A. who, at any one time, report they are dieting to control their weight. (Excess weight is, at the time of writing, deemed to be the *distal* cause of approximately 17% of deaths in the U.S.A. and is about to overtake smoking, at 18%, as the alleged[11] leading distal cause of deaths; these two causes are way ahead of the third distal cause, alcohol, at 3.5%.[12] A distal cause refers to the risky *behavior*, whereas the proximal cause is the resulting *disease*, such as heart disease or cancer.) Although 95% of people fail on their initial attempt to diet[13], they try again and again, so the constant struggle of willpower and temptation is indeed a state of vacillation. Offenders would be overweight people who *don't* try to lose weight. Given that 66% of U.S. adult men and 46% of U.S. adult women are overweight (as evaluated by the Body-Mass Index statistic, which seems to produce slightly higher estimates than the simpler Waistline measure statistic that seems to be recently favored by health researchers[14]) and 25% of men and 40% of women are dieting, then about 41% of men, though just 6% of women, must be Offenders. Of course, some of them could be trying to lose weight by taking up regular *vigorous* exercise – a behavior that is far more likely to work than dieting and provide a cardiovascular benefit too – but, as we will see later, they are very few![15]

A third example of brand loyalty segments is indeed the social-marketing-targeted product category of physical exercise, though among *children*. In the demographic group of children aged 5 to 14, a group which consists primarily of "tweenagers," ages 7 to 14, a recent survey in Australia indicates that just 62% of this age group participate in sport beyond the school system's two hours total of compulsory physical education a week – a scandalously low incidence, in our opinion. Although it is possible that *some* children get sufficient exercise from informal sports activities such as skateboarding, a conservative estimate is that the size of the Offender group – the sedentary behavior group – in this age bracket is 38%. There is a gender difference here, too, in that 31% of tweenage boys do not participate in organized sport and 44% of tweenage girls do not.[16]

Brand awareness, brand attitude, and action

The *brand loyalty* perspective on target audiences requires that we know the status not only of the individual's behavior (Action) but also his or her Brand Awareness and Brand Attitude with regard to both the "bad" behavior and its "good" alternative behavior. The concept of Attitude rather than Preference is more appropriate in social marcoms because the individual may not *prefer* the behavior he or she is engaging in – "bad" or "good"! Indeed, as we stated at the outset, it is government policy makers who decide the goodness and badness of our behaviors.

Attitude, in particular, is *necessary* to know because there is a world of difference from a marcoms standpoint between New Category Users (non-users up to now) who are aware of and have a *negative* attitude toward the "bad" behavior and those who are aware of it and are *favorably curious* ("favorably curious" describes, e.g., most incipient underage drinkers of alcohol and many incipient triers of cannabis or of ecstasy, known simply as E) who would be *Positive* NCUs or, to adopt a stricter perspective, *Favorable Brand Switchers*. With ecstasy, a drug that produces a relaxed but euphoric state and is known as the "rave party" drug or "clubbing" (i.e., night-clubbing) drug, the number of regular users is increasing rapidly. A recent survey in Australia of 20 to 29 year-olds, the prime age group of "clubbers," found that 20% had tried E, and 33% of the triers, that is, 6% to 7% of *all* 20-somethings, now take it weekly and show signs of *psychological* addiction in that they have come to believe that they "Can't have a good time at dance clubs without it." These young people (and some younger and some older) would be the Offender segment for taking the drug, ecstasy. Those who don't believe that E is *necessary* for having a good time, even though they take E, would be – attitudinally – Vacillators. The long-term effects of regular use of ecstasy aren't yet known but dangerous short-term side effects *may* include nausea, panic attacks, and paranoia.[17]

Target audiences include all at-risk groups

Notice that while we distinguish *target audiences* – because they will require different messages – we *do not* use *Leverage* to choose between them. In social marcoms, there is, we believe, a *deontological* ethical obligation, based on social justice, *to try to help everyone who is at risk* (see the section on Ethics at the end of the chapter). It is morally wrong to exclude from the target audience the most endangered group, the Offenders, even though, for addictive behaviors, they have *very low* Leverage – this means little hope of more than *some* of them changing *completely* for the good, not most of them changing a little for the good, which never happens. Offenders must be explicitly included among the target audiences for the campaign unless, and only unless, the social marketer can demonstrate that the Offender group is being adequately reached by *personal* social marketing. This means government-sponsored community outreach programs and one-on-one counseling and, if necessary, referral for medical treatment.

Stage 2: Segmentation by personality and perhaps by gender, ethnicity, or literacy

Social marcoms can utilize punishment of the "bad" behavior and rewarding of the "good" behavior. Depending on two different and uncorrelated personality traits – called Anxiety and Impulsiveness – individuals react very differently to punishment stimuli and reward stimuli. Actually, the distinction is a little more complicated than implied by the everyday terms "punishment" and "reward," as we will see in the section following shortly on persuasion, but these two terms will suffice to start with. There may also be gender differences that either affect the relationship between personality and persuasion for particular types of social behavior, or gender differences that directly affect persuasion and behavior independently of personality. Furthermore, *language ability* segments may be present in the form of different Ethnic groups, or in terms of Literacy within any ethnic group.

> We provide measures of the relevant personality traits, Anxiety and Impulsiveness, in the section after next. Gender differences are straightforward to measure, as is Ethnic group membership. Literacy is trickier to measure and is usually based on *spoken* language proficiency rather than a reading test. Individuals who report that they are unable or only a little able to converse in English (or whichever is the dominant language in the region) with one's doctor, with one's bank manager re financial matters, with co-workers, and with retail clerks when shopping will require a low-literacy (mostly pictorial) message.[18]

BRAND POSITIONING IN SOCIAL MARKETING

The first research step in planning a social marcoms campaign (see Table 18.1) is to find out how the Target Audience Groups *themselves* Position – from their perspective, *perceive* – the brand. Only after an understanding of the Category Need met by the brand and the Key Benefit (or Key Benefits if the behavior has a complex motivational basis, as health behaviors often have[19]) that it provides for the Target Audience can the *third* step proceed, which is for the social marcoms manager to explore possible ways to *reposition* the brand. By "positioning" here, we mean the T-C-B Model which requires selecting the Category Need and the Key Benefit for the *Target Customer*.

In practice, as we have suggested, there will be at least two brands to potentially be repositioned – the "bad" behavior and the "good" behavior – and more if either comprises a *set* of relevant behaviors. Also, there will be at least three target audiences (three types of target customer) to position *both* brands to – Conformers, Vacillators, and Offenders.

Failure to understand how the typical *Vacillator* customer positions the brand is probably the main reason for the failure of so many social marcoms campaigns. Following are three examples of this.

Milk Funded by the U.S. milk-producer industry[20], the "Got milk?" campaign could be regarded as social marketing because it attempts to change the nutritional intake of the American public. Anyway, *we* are going to consider "Got milk?" as social marcoms and the brand as "Drinking milk." This very likable advertising campaign, which features celebrities such as ex-President Bill Clinton, supermodels Naomi Campbell and Christie Brinkley, *Friends* and movie star Jennifer Aniston, as well as senior celebrities such as Tony Bennett and Lauren Bacall – each photographed in ads with a "milk mustache" – has failed to stem the steady decline in per capita consumption of milk in the U.S.A. If we segment by gender, we find that most teenage girls and young adult women do not drink milk – because they believe it is fattening.[21] The fact that these celebrities drink milk – though the implication that they drink it *regularly* stretches credibility – is of no consequence to teenage girls and young women because milk just *seems* to be fattening. The fact that milk has fewer calories than a lot of things they *eat* will not wash. Had the campaign and brand been "Got *lite* milk?", it may have had a chance of working with these important demographic target customers. How *should* the brand "Drinking milk," that is, *regular* milk, be positioned? Only in Australia has a campaign (actually two campaigns) ever been able to reverse the decline of the last 20 years or so in per capita milk consumption (mainly regular milk) and turn the brand "Drinking milk" around. The two campaigns, by the Victorian Milk Board, and both masterminded creatively by the John Bevins Agency in Australia, were diligent in their research efforts – solely *qualitative research* – to locate a respective persuasive Key Benefit. One campaign, which targeted young children as Users and their mothers as Influencers and Deciders, was code-named "Molecular Reconstructor"; the TV commercial for this campaign showed the kitchen of the future in which all the breakfast items were constructed in a futuristic-looking microwave-type machine – except one item, milk. The tagline was to the effect that milk is "perfect already," with the implication that it is also all-natural, and that no substitute beverage could possibly be constructed to improve upon it. The second campaign was equally insightful. It repositioned "Drinking milk" to meet what, for milk, was a new Category Need. The campaign targeted young men, the demographic group in which, in Australia, the most severe decline in regular milk consumption had been observed for the previous decade, and repositioned it as a competitor to heavy *beer* drinking for the Category Need of *casual sex*! To dramatize the Key Benefit, the Creative Idea of sexual innuendo was used by implying if you drink milk "You can keep going all night." This Key Benefit Claim was depicted metaphorically in the TV commercial by the setting of a country dance in which all the young men, who were dancing with all the young ladies, gradually fall into drunken stupors – except two of them, who chose to drink milk at the bar instead of beer and who get to dance with all of the ladies as the evening wears on and the beer drinkers wear out. Both campaigns worked in terms of changing *behavior*, among mothers of children, and among young men, and the decline in per capita milk consumption in the *total* population reversed and showed a steady increase during the course of, and for a considerable time after, the campaigns.[22]

Overweight "Being thin" has undoubtedly emerged as a desirable social brand in its own right, at least for Western women and not just young women. It is no coincidence, for instance, that the prevalence of overweightness is much lower for Western women than for Western men (although the prevalences are nevertheless at epidemic levels for both genders, 46% for adult women in the U.S.A. and 66% for men, and worsening). Women's role models such as Callista Flockhart, who plays the character Ally McBeal in the TV series of the same name, and Jennifer Aniston, who was reported to weigh 60 kg (about 133 pounds) before signing on for the hit TV series, *Friends,* and has shed a further 15 kg (about 33 pounds) during it[23], and teenage girls' role models such as Sarah Michelle Gellar have epitomized the social brand of "Being thin" for women. Coincidentally, the average hip measurement for women's shop dummies (mannequins is a nicer word) is reported to have shrunk from 86.5 cm (34 inches) in 1950 to 79 cm (31 inches) in the 1990s.[24] The Key Benefit for the brand "Being thin" is essentially the motive of Social Approval. With increasing concern about women's weight problems, it will be interesting to see whether Western health authorities can successfully attach the Key Benefit of *better long-run health*, which follows the *different* motive, Problem Avoidance, to the brand "Being thin." We are skeptical because overweight women (and men) seem to be most motivated by immediate Sensory

Gratification. To try to introduce the delayed benefit of better long-run health via the motive of Problem Avoidance seems doomed to fail. Also, the facts are that dieting produces long-term weight loss for only 2% to 5% of dieters worldwide (although they spend an estimated $33 billion a year on weight-loss programs and diet products) and about 90% of dieters, in the long run, will put on more weight than they lost![25] The only remedy likely to work on a large scale for weight loss will not be behavior change but, rather, a pharmaceutical drug breakthrough, which is likely soon.[26]

Body organ donation An interesting challenge is the brand positioning of an Altruistic behavior – the *counterpart* of which is *not* a "bad" behavior in that it is not directly harming any person, self or other. Consider, for example, "Body organ donation after my death" as the brand. This is obviously not a habitual or addictive behavior and it would not be fair to characterize those people who won't donate as Offenders or those who will as Conformers, but most people *could* be labeled Vacillators in that most are hesitant and undecided. An excellent qualitative study by Sanner[27] makes it clear that the only positioning that will work is to invoke the metaphor (a Conveyer, actually) that "The human body is like a machine and as such it needs replacement parts." This positioning conflicts, however, with two other prevalent perspectives, that the body is a "temple" not to be desecrated even after death and the "magical contagious" belief that the personal characteristics of the donor will come with the body part! Because most adults have firmly made up their minds about which perspective is correct, the marketing of "Body organ donation after my death" is not just a matter of positioning but of *attitudinal target audience identification* – to identify and appeal to Positive NCUs, in our terminology.

> It is essential for determining brand positioning in social marketing to conduct thorough *qualitative research* – using Individual Depth Interviews. The IDIs should be conducted and analyzed by an experienced *clinical* psychologist who *also* knows a fair bit about marketing and persuasion. The analyst should convert his or her inferences into an *I-D-U matrix*. As indicated in Table 18.2, at least three I-D-U matrices (tables) are required: one for Conformers (mainly to verify what deters them from adopting the "bad" behavior), one for Vacillators (usually the most difficult to get right because of the individual's attractions to *both* behaviors) and one for Offenders (which, in the case of addictive "bad" behaviors, may include physiological attributes). If there are gender differences, as there certainly are for Dietary behavior, for instance, then six I-D-U models are required. There are at least two brands: the "bad" behavior and the "good" behavior. Also, the benefits are separated into *facilitators* and *deterrents*, as will be explained.

TABLE 18.2 *To develop the positioning for a social marketing brand, you will need at least three I-D-U analyses.*

(a) Offenders

	BRAND BELIEFS		
BENEFITS(i)	"Bad" behavior	"Good" behavior	E_i
• Facilitators			
■	—	—	+ve
■	—	—	+ve
■	—	—	+ve
• Deterrents			
■	—	—	−ve
■	—	—	−ve
■	—	—	−ve

(b) Vacillators

	BRAND BELIEFS		
BENEFITS(i)	"Bad" behavior	"Good" behavior	E_i
• Facilitators			
■	—	—	+ve
■	—	—	+ve
■	—	—	+ve
• Deterrents			
■	—	—	−ve
■	—	—	−ve
■	—	—	−ve

(c) Conformers

	BRAND BELIEFS		
BENEFITS(i)	"Bad" behavior	"Good" behavior	E_i
• Facilitators			
■	—	—	+ve
■	—	—	+ve
■	—	—	+ve
• Deterrents			
■	—	—	−ve
■	—	—	−ve
■	—	—	−ve

PERSUASION IN SOCIAL MARCOMS

The most valid theoretical model of persuasion in social marcoms is the **Fishbein extended model**.[28] With slight variations, this model has also been called the Theory of Planned Behavior and the Theory of Reasoned Action, but these names understate the contribution of *emotions* to persuasion. The basic equation for the Fishbein Extended Model is:

$$\text{Action Intention}_{act} = \text{Attitude}_{act} + \text{Social Norm}_{act}$$

The first term or component on the right-hand side, Attitude toward the act, or $Attitude_{act}$ as it is symbolized in the equation, is very similar to the I-D-U Multiattribute Model of persuasion in commercial marcoms (see Chapter 4). We will expand on this component shortly. The new component is the second term on the right-hand side, Social Norm regarding the act, symbolized as $Social\ Norm_{act}$ in the equation. Fishbein and colleagues actually call this the *subjective* norm component but it is really the individual's perception of the *social* norm and so we have labeled it as such. The $Social\ Norm_{act}$ concept is especially relevant in social marcoms. (It can also be applied in commercial marcoms in product and service categories where there is substantial social influence but usually "what other people think of the product or service brand" is simply folded back in as another Benefit Belief in the summation of benefit beliefs rather than broken out as a separate component.) It has been argued by R. Hornik, we believe correctly, that social marcoms campaigns often do not have much effect on the Attitude component but can, with repetition over time, have a substantial effect on the Social Norm component.[29] Two obvious examples of this point are smoking and gay sex. In both these cases, people's perceptions of the *risks* of the act (encapsulated in $Attitude_{act}$) have changed very little whereas *social tolerance* of the two acts has certainly changed (encapsulated in the $Social\ Norm_{act}$ component). In the U.S.A. and Australia, social tolerance of smoking has declined markedly (smoking has virtually become "immoral"). On the other hand, in the case of gay sex, social tolerance in those two countries and in most of Western Europe has increased considerably so that it is now tolerated (though *not* actively advocated) by a majority of the public. What this means is that a person's Action Intention (and the Behavior itself) can change *without* any change in one's *personal attitude* toward the act ($Attitude_{act}$). That is, the change could be entirely *socially induced* (via $Social\ Norm_{act}$).

Following is the expansion of the $Attitude_{act}$ component:

$$Attitude_{act} = \text{(Sum over every) Belief that the act will lead to a particular consequence}$$
$$\times \text{ Evaluation of that consequence} + \text{(net positivity or negativity of) } Emotions_{act}$$

The first two (multiplicative) terms on the right-hand side are essentially the I-D-U model. (In the social science applications that you will want to read, and influenced originally by Rogers' Protection Motivation Model, Belief is also called *susceptibility*, a word that correctly implies that it is the *individual's* believed probability of experiencing the consequence, and the Evaluation of the consequence is called its *severity*, which is not a good word because the evaluation can be negative, as implied by the word "severity", which makes the consequence a Deterrent, or it can be *positive* in that there are some things that people *like* about "bad" behaviors and these attributes are evaluated positively, which makes the consequence a Facilitator.) We added the $Emotions_{act}$ component, the last term on the right-hand side; it is not in the original Fishbein Extended Model but it should be. Back in Chapter 3, we talked about a deeper level of positioning using an instinct, archetype, or strong emotion of the type 1 ("gut") or type 2 (cognitively labeled) variety. These are *not* "believed" consequences but are simply "attached" emotions – automatically felt when the individual thinks of or encounters the act or object. It is the net positivity or negativity of these emotions that counts because in quite a few cases there will be "mixed," that is, mixed *valence*, emotions attached to the social brand of behavior.

The Social Norm$_{act}$ component is also expanded into its constituent components and is similar in structure to the Attitude$_{act}$ component, but with different labels:

Social Norm$_{act}$ = (Sum over every) Belief that a reference group or reference individual endorses (or proscribes) the act × Degree of compliance with referent

This time, instead of different attributes or consequences, there are different reference groups (e.g., family, friends, the general public) and reference individuals (e.g., God or another deity, or the King, Queen or President of your country). The first term on the right-hand side captures what *you* perceive that others believe and it is *bipolar* (endorse, a Facilitator, vs proscribe, a Deterrent). The second term in effect is an evaluative weighting factor, as it measures the extent to which you feel compelled to comply or go along with the particular reference group or reference individual.

The Fishbein Extended Model applied to social marcoms is a powerful model and is the model of persuasion that is *implicitly* followed by most social marketers even if they do not recognize it in the formal terms described above. However, there are *two major problems* with the model. One problem is practical. This is that use of the model has not been shown to make much headway against *addictive* behaviors.[30] Hard-core addicts don't care too much about social norms or, if they do secretly care, this is drowned out by the addiction. The second problem is ethical (see also the final section of the chapter). Both for negatively evaluated and positively evaluated consequences, social marcoms campaigns based on this model rely on *exaggerations* to achieve persuasion. To put it plainly, they rely on lying. The typical social marcoms campaign, on the negative side, tries to scare the you-know-what out of people by exaggerating the severity of negative consequences or, if it doesn't do that, it certainly exaggerates the probability that the actor will suffer those negative consequences (susceptibility). One of the emotions typically employed in the Emotions$_{act}$ component, too, has an inherent ethical problem, namely fear, where exaggeration results in arousal of *excessive* fear.[31]

An ethical alternative

Now the crucial question: is there an ethical way to persuade people in social marcoms? We think there is. The ethical way is to match types of message appeals with types of people – through personality traits. This does not require exaggeration or lying in any form. Rather, it is entirely a matter of effective targeting, that is, aligning the most effective message type with the type of individual most likely to respond to that message. Moreover, effective targeting is easy because, as we'll explain, all message types are sent to everyone and individuals by type can be counted on to "self-select."

The message types are based on an expansion of the nature of Consequences. Earlier, we drew the distinction between Facilitators and Deterrents. A more technical term for Facilitators is *reinforcers*, and it is important to understand that reinforcers themselves come as two subtypes: Positive Reinforcers and Negative Reinforcers. Despite the word "negative," both types of reinforcement *increase* behavior. **Positive reinforcement** is where the behavior is increased because it turns *on* an appetitive or rewarding consequence. **Negative reinforcement** is where the behavior is increased because it turns *off* an *aversive* consequence. The positive and negative refer to turning on and turning off, not to the nature of the *consequence*.[32] Deterrents are punishers, which *decrease* behavior, and punishers also have two subtypes: **positive punishment**, where the behavior turns on an aversive consequence, and **negative punishment**, where the behavior now *fails* to turn on a previously received *positive reinforcer* (Negative Punishment only works when the behavior has been positively reinforced; the punishment is *not to get* the expected positive reinforcement). These distinctions set up the analysis of persuasion based on personality traits – actually, personality *types* – as explained next.

Personality traits and perhaps gender – and persuasion

By "personality" here we mean *internal* personality traits, not personality traits in the sense of dimensions of external descriptions of people (as in the "Big Five" personality traits) or of brands (as in "brand personality").[33] Our approach here uses *biological* personality traits.

Personality traits, biological *or* descriptive, do not correlate much with category purchase and brand choice for FMCG products or for Durables – but they do show impressive correlations with a wide range of Health and Safety Behaviors. Personality differences are mainly genetic and are pretty much fixed by the time a child is three years of age.[34] Biological personality traits – which are reliably classifiable by clinical psychologists observing three-year-olds, and which hold up consistently on personality questionnaire self-ratings at age 18 – are remarkably predictive of risky health and safety behaviors at age 21.[35]

Gray's theory of anxiety and impulsiveness

The best-established biological-trait theory of personality is **Gray's theory**[36], which is a modification of Eysenck's earlier theory.[37] Eysenck's theory of personality is a three-trait theory consisting of the traits of Psychoticism, Neuroticism, and Extraversion-Introversion. Gray focused on Eysenck's second and third traits – Neuroticism and Extraversion-Introversion. These two traits are independent, thus forming axes at 90 degrees when plotted together. Based on a thorough review of the research on human *classical* conditioning as a function of these two traits, Gray suggested a 45-degree rotation of the two dimensions such that the dimensions are located on two of Eysenck's sub-factor traits: *Anxiety* and *Impulsiveness*.[38] In our conceptualization of Gray's theory, these two traits are actually *unipolar*, that is, they both start at "zero." Being unipolar and independent, Anxiety and Impulsiveness can be plotted as a right-angle diagram (Figure 18.1). The area near the bottom-left (zero, zero) coordinate represents the small proportion of very calm, very conscientious individuals in the population. Also shown are the theorized gradients of responsiveness to punishers (P) and reinforcers (R) that go with these two traits. Anxious individuals' responsiveness to punishment is stronger than Impulsive individuals' responsiveness to reinforcement, so the punisher gradient goes to PPP strength whereas the reinforcer gradient goes only to RR. Although first developed to explain individual differences in classical conditioning, Gray's theory has since been applied to the more important – for health and safety behaviors – *instrumental discrimination learning*.

Questionnaire measures of Anxiety and Impulsiveness are given in Table 18.3 because we recommend that researchers use these measures to segment the target audience for any social marcoms campaign.[39] The two new traits are also independent, that is, uncorrelated, in that your score on one has nothing to do with your score on the other. This means, by definition, that

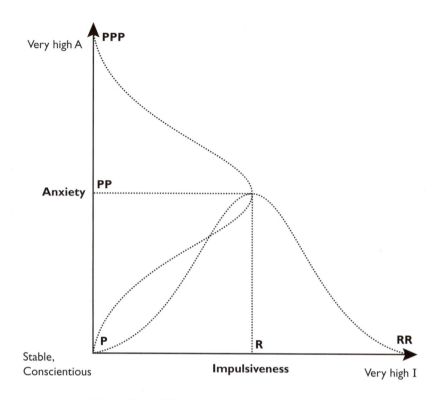

FIGURE 18.1 *Our representation of Gray's theory. The diagram shows the two independent traits of Anxiety and Impulsiveness as the independent (uncorrelated) axes and the Ps and Rs indicate degrees of responsiveness to punishers (P) and reinforcers (R). The dotted normal curves show the distribution of each trait in the general population.*

approximately half the population is medium to very high on the respective traits, one or the other, with few high on both and few people low on both traits.

Gray's theory makes the prediction that Anxious individuals will respond best to signals of *punishment*, and that Impulsive individuals will respond best to signals of *reinforcement*. Note, and note carefully, that "reinforcement" here means both reward in the everyday sense, that is, Positive Reinforcement, and *also* escape from punishment, that is, Negative Reinforcement, which is negative only in the sense that an aversive consequence is *removed* contingent on performing the behavior. Similarly, "punishment" here means both punishment in the everyday sense, that is, Positive Punishment in that an aversive consequence (including *excessive novelty*) is *presented* if you perform the behavior and Negative Punishment, also known as omission training, or frustrative non-reward, whereby a previously occurring reinforcer is now *withheld* if you perform the behavior.

TABLE 18.3 *Self-rating questionnaires for the traits of Anxiety and Impulsiveness. For Anxiety, items 2, 3, 10, 13, 14, 18, and 23 are reverse-scored (No = Yes). For Impulsiveness, items 1, 4, 6, 10, 11, 20, 24, 25, and 27 are reverse-scored (No = Yes). For each scale, the score is the total number of Yes answers, ignoring undecided (?) and No. The theoretical range for each is 0 to 30.*

ANXIETY

1.	Do you blush more often than most people?	Yes	?	No
2.	Would you say that you seldom ever lose sleep over your worries?	Yes	?	No
3.	Are you usually calm and not easily upset?	Yes	?	No
4.	Do you sometimes feel that you have so many difficulties that you cannot possibly overcome them?	Yes	?	No
5.	Is life often a strain for you?	Yes	?	No
6.	As a child were you afraid of the dark?	Yes	?	No
7.	Do you often feel restless as though you want something but do not really know what?	Yes	?	No
8.	Are you inclined to tremble and perspire if you are faced with a difficult task ahead?	Yes	?	No
9.	Are you often afraid of things and people that you know would not really hurt you?	Yes	?	No
10.	Are you less prone to anxiety than most of your friends?	Yes	?	No
11.	Do you often worry unreasonably over things that do not really matter?	Yes	?	No
12.	Are you anxious about something or somebody most of the time?	Yes	?	No
13.	If you have made an awkward social error, can you forget it quite easily?	Yes	?	No
14.	Can you relax quite easily when sitting or lying down?	Yes	?	No
15.	Are you easily startled by someone appearing unexpectedly?	Yes	?	No
16.	Do you find it difficult to sit still without fidgeting?	Yes	?	No
17.	Do you worry a great deal over money matters?	Yes	?	No
18.	Can you drop off to sleep quite easily at night?	Yes	?	No
19.	Are you easily embarrassed in a social situation?	Yes	?	No
20.	Are you easily "rattled" if things don't go according to plan?	Yes	?	No
21.	Do you often wake up sweating after having a bad dream?	Yes	?	No
22.	Does your voice get shaky if you are talking to someone you particularly want to impress?	Yes	?	No
23.	Would you stay calm and collected in the face of an emergency?	Yes	?	No
24.	Do you sometimes get into a state of tension and turmoil when thinking over your difficulties?	Yes	?	No
25.	Do you worry too long over humiliating experiences?	Yes	?	No
26.	Would you describe yourself as self-conscious?	Yes	?	No
27.	Do you worry unnecessarily over things that might happen?	Yes	?	No
28.	Are you inclined to get yourself all worked up over nothing?	Yes	?	No
29.	Have you ever felt you needed to take tranquillizers?	Yes	?	No
30.	Are you a nervous person?	Yes	?	No

Continues

TABLE 18.3 *Continued*

IMPULSIVENESS

1.	Do you like planning things well ahead of time?	Yes	?	No
2.	Do you usually make up your mind quickly?	Yes	?	No
3.	Do you often change your interests?	Yes	?	No
4.	Before making up your mind, do you carefully consider all the advantages and disadvantages?	Yes	?	No
5.	Do you often buy things on impulse?	Yes	?	No
6.	Do you know what you will be doing on your next holiday?	Yes	?	No
7.	Can you make decisions quickly?	Yes	?	No
8.	Do you often get into a jam because you do things without thinking?	Yes	?	No
9.	Do you generally do and say things without stopping to think?	Yes	?	No
10.	Do you usually think carefully before doing anything?	Yes	?	No
11.	Would you rather plan things than do things?	Yes	?	No
12.	Are you an impulsive person?	Yes	?	No
13.	Do you prefer activities that just happen to those planned in advance?	Yes	?	No
14.	When you meet new people, do you very quickly decide whether you like them or not?	Yes	?	No
15.	Do you often do things on the spur of the moment?	Yes	?	No
16.	If it were practically possible, would you like to live each day as it comes along?	Yes	?	No
17.	Do you like doing things in which you have to act quickly?	Yes	?	No
18.	Do you often get involved in things you later prefer to opt out of?	Yes	?	No
19.	Are you an easy-going person, not generally bothered about having everything "just so"?	Yes	?	No
20.	When you go on a trip, do you like to plan routes and timetables carefully?	Yes	?	No
21.	Do you mostly speak before thinking things out?	Yes	?	No
22.	Do you think an evening out is more successful if it is arranged at the last moment?	Yes	?	No
23.	Do you get so "carried away" by new and exciting ideas that you never think of the possible snags?	Yes	?	No
24.	Do you prefer to "sleep on it" before making decisions?	Yes	?	No
25.	Do you prefer work that needs close attention most of the time?	Yes	?	No
26.	Do you need to use a lot of self-control to keep out of trouble?	Yes	?	No
27.	When you want to buy something expensive, can you save up for some time patiently?	Yes	?	No
28.	Would you agree that planning things ahead takes the fun out of life?	Yes	?	No
29.	Do you hate standing in a long queue for anything?	Yes	?	No
30.	Do you get bored more easily than most people doing the same old things?	Yes	?	No

SOURCE: H.J. Eysenck and G. Wilson, 1976, reference in note 39, chapters 2 and 3.

The *action implications* of Gray's theory are based on the fact that individuals who rate high on the Anxiousness trait are sensitive to "no-go" signals, whereas individuals high on the Impulsiveness trait are sensitive to "go" signals. Social marcoms message appeals directed to Anxious individuals should aim to make them *inhibit* the *"bad"* behavior by threatening punishment *or* non-reward; whereas message appeals directed to Impulsive individuals should encourage them to *perform* the *"good"* behavior by pointing out rewarding *or* escaping consequences.

Gray's theory, as we mentioned earlier, applies well to *instrumental discrimination learning*. Instrumental discrimination learning refers to voluntary, operant responses or behaviors that compete (in the individual's mind) in the stimulus situation or setting. The extent to which addictive behaviors are "voluntary" is a debatable point but "voluntary" here is used in contrast with "involuntary," that is, elicited reflex responses that the individual cannot decide against. Even with severe addictions, we have to assume that voluntary decision-making is possible or all is lost for social marcoms, although medical treatment offers hope. The individual has to learn to discriminate between two, at least, competing responses or behaviors, that is, to learn when it is appropriate to perform the one or perform the other. The instrumental discrimination learning paradigm fits most health and safety behaviors. For example, young people, and older people too, have to learn to discriminate between consuming a safe, moderate amount of alcohol per occasion versus consuming immoderately to the extent that their alcohol consumption puts them at high risk of personal accidents, fighting, or dangerous operation of motor vehicles. Moderate drinking and Excessive drinking are, in this case, two competing responses; another competing response, of course, but less attractive to the regular drinker, is to Not drink on that occasion. Indeed, alternatively, the response competition could be between the performance of the response and the complete suppression or inhibition of it. The performance versus suppression distinction would fit the cases of most drug-taking: the response competition is between Doing the drug and Not doing it at all.

Individuals above the midpoint on Impulsiveness, and increasingly so, are most responsive to "go" signals, that is, to *Doing* behaviors that promise either positive reinforcement (reward) or negative reinforcement (escape); this means in social marcoms that you should emphasize doing the *"good"* behavior (and demonstrate its efficacy) when targeting Impulsives. In contrast, individuals who are above the midpoint on Anxiety, and increasingly so, are most responsive to "no-go" signals, that is, to *Not doing*, or inhibiting, behaviors that promise either positive punishment (punishment) or negative punishment (omission of reinforcement)[40]; this means in social marcoms that you should emphasize *not* doing the *"bad"* behavior when addressing Anxious individuals. Take the behavior of smoking cigarettes as an example. The Anxiety trait operates as a cause of adolescents avoiding smoking and the Impulsivity trait is a cause of them taking up smoking. Perversely, however, illustrating the complexity of motivation, if the adolescent does take up smoking, then the Anxiety *state*, that is, temporary anxiety, plays a *reversed* role by helping to maintain the smoking through anxiety reduction and negative reinforcement. Anxiety – chronic anxiety, the *trait* – as well as its frequent accompanying state, depression, is actually protective against drug-taking.[41] Impulsivity, in contrast, is strongly related to drug-taking onset and the acquisition of a long-term habit.[42]

The fundamental personality difference also widens the gap between Conformers, who "just can't understand" why some people do all these bad and often self-endangering things (drugs, alcohol, speeding, etc.), and Offenders, who *know* the others don't understand and see the others as unsympathetic. Anxiety is likely to make anxious people pay more attention to "punishment" messages *and* to increase their perceptions of their personal risk (their perceived susceptibility);

Anxious people, most of them Conformers, are therefore more likely to believe exaggerated claims by government.[43] Impulsives – often disproportionately Offenders – do not respond to these messages. Why and how will the gap widen? The prevalence of very high Impulsives is likely to remain fairly constant because the trait is mainly genetic and not caused by parental permissiveness as many believe. On the other hand, the prevalence of Anxiety and also the closely related trait of Neuroticism, or emotional instability, in the U.S. population has increased almost a full standard deviation – in plain terms, an absolute increase of about 16% in the proportion of highly anxious individuals in the population – since the "calm" 1950s.[44] The large increase has occurred among children and teenagers (nine to 17 years of age) as well, with the average American tweenager now reporting higher chronic anxiety than tweenage psychiatric patients of the 1950s. The causes of the increase in Anxiety and Neuroticism appear to be the steady breakdown in social connectedness (particularly the divorce rate and the incidence of people living alone) and increased environmental threats (terrorism, crime, and fear of plague-like diseases such as AIDS and SARS). From the increase in Anxiety, and in its closely related trait Neuroticism, it is possible to predict a corresponding increase in the prevalence of individuals with clinical depression, psychosomatic health problems, and lessened coping ability when disease strikes in later life. The trend constitutes a major and rising barrier for public health campaigns to attempt to surmount. They may not be able to: the most likely remedy is, sadly, wider intake of (legal) drugs.

Another barrier that will foreseeably be very difficult, and perhaps impossible, to get over with health education programs is the very big differences, found in every society, in the health status of *social classes*, with *all* types of health, physical and mental, increasing linearly with social class.[45] Social class differences are ultimately and almost entirely due to differences in Intelligence, or General Mental Ability, which is not something that education programs – the "environment" – can do much about.[46]

Further tactics for "no-go" and "go" appeals

Note that distinction between "no-go" and "go" appeals is not the same as the distinction between Informational and Transformational appeals in commercial marketing. Informational and Transformational appeals, respectively, are escape (negative reinforcement) and reward (positive reinforcement) appeals that *both* reinforce "go" behaviors, that is, *Doing* behaviors, such as Purchase behavior. The two new types of appeals – positive punishment and negative punishment, or omission – both apply to *Not* doing, that is, to "no-go" behaviors, as in not drinking and driving, restraining from engaging in unsafe sex, limiting your intake of harmful fats in food, and so forth. "No-go" versus "go" is the main difference in effective message appeals for Anxious people and Impulsive people, but there are some further tactical differences that are summarized in Table 18.4 regarding Humor, the presence of Other People in the message, and the use of Presenters.[47]

The campaign has to use *both* "no go" and "go" message appeals at the same time. There is no conflict in using both together. This is because the personality traits of Impulsiveness and Anxiety are, as we said, independent, or uncorrelated, which means that one type of appeal will not turn off the other segment but rather will simply be ineffective among those individuals, and the same for the other type of appeal.

In Figure 18.3, examples of the two types of "no-go" ads are shown in panel (a) and the two

TABLE 18.4 *Differences in persuasion tactics for chronically anxious individuals and impulsive individuals.*

ANXIOUS INDIVIDUALS	IMPULSIVE INDIVIDUALS
• Target "no-go" behavior (response inhibition) under threat of *positive punishment* (aversive consequence would follow if you were to respond) or *negative punishment* (appetitive consequence would be withheld if you were to respond)	• Target "go" behavior (performance of the response) with the promise of *positive reinforcement* (appetitive consequence follows if you *do* respond) or *negative reinforcement* (aversive consequence is avoided or terminated if you *do* respond)
• Show familiar surroundings and objects (highly novel stimuli are aversive)	• Show novel surroundings and objects (highly novel stimuli are exciting)
• Show single individuals (wants to be alone when stressed)	• Show a group (seeks company of others when stressed)
• Use cognitive humor, i.e., an intellectual joke, or humor incorporating incongruity or surprise	• Use sexual humor and aggressive humor
• Presenter can be male or female (males and females respond equally well to a presenter of either gender)	• Presenter should be crossed in media vehicles skewed toward one gender (males and females respond better to a presenter of the opposite gender)

types of "go" ads are shown in panel (b) of the figure. The targeted behavior, in all four ads, is physical exercise and specifically the Australian government's recommendation to exercise regularly. The first two ads are "no-go" appeals, explaining in a threatening sense what will happen if you *don't* do regular exercise, positive punishment in the first ad and negative punishment in the second ad. The second two ads are "go" appeals, explaining what will happen if you *do* regular exercise, positive reinforcement in the first ad and negative reinforcement in the second ad. In all cases, the consequences are quite likely and attainable and are supported by a considerable amount of previous research on the health problems of prolonged physical *in*activity, on the one hand, and benefits of regular exercise on the other. However, we must be careful, as always, in marcoms campaigns not to exaggerate or promise untrue consequences. We recognize that these are not great ads in other respects (a single, explicit Key Benefit Claim for each would be more effective than the present implied ones of "Lots of bad things" and "Lots of good things"). However, the ads do clearly exemplify the conceptual mechanisms of positive punishment, negative punishment, positive reinforcement, and negative reinforcement.

MEDIA STRATEGY IN SOCIAL MARCOMS CAMPAIGNS

The media strategy *decisions* for a social marcoms campaign are exactly the same as for a commercial marcoms campaign. It is useful to look back through Chapters 11 and 12, because the same concepts apply here. In the following sections, we will point out the main applications of media strategy in social marcoms campaigns.

Media type selection

The manager has to select a Primary Medium (see Chapter 11) capable of carrying all of the campaign's communication objectives, and, usually, one or two Secondary Media for a hard-to-reach

Panel (a)

Panel (b)

Why Exercise?...........

Because...if you DON'T exercise regularly, you could:

- Be tired and lacking in energy
- Feel bad about yourself and your body
- Become or remain fat
- Become or remain unfit
- Become or remain overweight
- Have weak muscles and poor body strength
- Experience pain and discomfort associated with occasional exercise

For more information on the benefits of regular exercise, talk to your family doctor, or contact the Department of Human Movement & Exercise Science at the University of Western Australia

S-ON

Why Exercise?...........

Because...if you DO exercise regularly, you could:

- Get even more energy
- Feel good about yourself and your body
- Get or stay slim
- Get or stay fit
- Achieve or maintain your correct weight
- Have firm muscles and good body strength
- Get to enjoy the experience of regular physical activity

For more information on the benefits of regular exercise, talk to your family doctor, or contact the Department of Human Movement & Exercise Science at the University of Western Australia

S-ON

Why Exercise?...........

Because...if you DON'T exercise regularly, you won't:

- Get even more energy
- Feel good about yourself and your body
- Get or stay slim
- Get or stay fit
- Achieve or maintain your correct weight
- Have firm muscles and good body strength
- Get to enjoy the experience of regular physical activity

For more information on the benefits of regular exercise, talk to your family doctor, or contact the Department of Human Movement & Exercise Science at the University of Western Australia

S-OFF

Why Exercise?...........

Because...if you DO exercise regularly, you won't:

- Be tired and lacking in energy
- Feel bad about yourself and your body
- Become or remain fat
- Become or remain unfit
- Become or remain overweight
- Have weak muscles and poor body strength
- Experience pain and discomfort associated with occasional exercise

For more information on the benefits of regular exercise, talk to your family doctor, or contact the Department of Human Movement & Exercise Science at the University of Western Australia

S-OFF

FIGURE 18.3 *The two types of "no-go" appeals, in panel (a), and the two types of "go" appeals, in panel (b), illustrated here for the health behavior of regular physical exercise.*

SOURCE: S.C. Jones, Message presentation effects in health behaviour communications, Ph.D. dissertation, University of Western Australia, 2003.

group or groups or to boost a single communication objective, the most likely of these being Brand Recall – that is, recall of the brand of "no-go" behavior or "go" behavior that is being targeted, with the *situation or opportunity to choose between the behaviors* serving as the Category-Need cue.

For the *primary* medium, radio is a good choice for targeting these behaviors because radio can handle Brand Recall and High-Involvement/Informational messages. Late-night TV is also often a good high-reach primary medium choice. Print media readership – newspapers and magazines *and* the Internet – is negatively related to Intelligence and most vehicles in print do not have very good reach for targeting "problem" behavers, who tend to be below average intelligence.

So-called "street" media are likely to emerge as a very good *secondary* medium to reach addicted illegal drug users as they also provide timely Brand *Recognition*. *Mobile-viewed* (quick exposure) outdoor is good as a "reminder" secondary medium for dangerous driving, speeding, drink-driving, and, a growing problem, driving under the influence of illicit drugs.

Reach pattern selection

Some social marcoms campaigns should be conceptualized as selling a new product and so the *Fad* reach pattern, or a *short Blitz*, which is essentially the same thing, should be employed. (Reach Patterns were explained in Chapter 11.) An example would be the safe-driving campaigns, targeting the driver behaviors mentioned above, leading in to holiday periods such as, depending on the country and its people's predominant religious preference, Christmas and Easter or other public holidays. A substantially new *positioning* for an established social behavior brand would also require the use of a reach pattern as for a new product. The *Wedge* reach pattern would be the most typical selection, although thoughtful consideration could be given to a *Reverse-Wedge* reach pattern for social behaviors subject to opinion leadership among peers, of which the taking of "party" drugs, such as ecstasy, would be an example.

Duration (continuity)

Most social marcoms campaigns should require a total advertising duration of *no more than three media-months* (12 weeks) because, if they are going to work at all, they should have demonstrated most of their effects on behavior by this time. However, there are some exceptions. Planners of anti-speeding road safety campaigns, for instance, have argued that continuous bursts of advertising, much like an *Awareness* reach pattern, is necessary, as driving a car and deciding to speed (or not) is something that most drivers do every day.[48] However, the decision to speed, or alternatively to drive within the appropriate speed limit, is an ongoing series of short-cycle decisions rather than one long, contemplative decision and this would suggest the use of the *Shifting Reach* pattern, with short shift durations so that all drivers are effectively reached several times a year.

Minimum effective frequency per advertising cycle

The MEF/c formula (see Chapter 12) for estimating Minimum Effective Frequency per advertising cycle is again applicable to the social marcoms campaign. The frequency (OTSs) requirement will undoubtedly be high because nearly all social marcoms campaigns have to include New Category Users in the target, a frequency factor that requires the use of LC+1, where "LC" is usually the competing *"good"* behavior. On the other hand, if the campaign is focused on promoting the "good" behavior, then LC becomes the competing "bad" behavior. In both cases the MEF/c is calculated for the competing behavior and plugged back in to the formula. In terms of the second and third factors that affect MEF, the campaign may emphasize Brand Recognition or it may emphasize Brand Recall, and it may be based on either Punishment (handled like an Informational campaign – an aversive consequence will require only low frequency) or Reward (handled like a Transformational campaign – high frequency will be required). Personal Influence may also be a factor required in the formula, especially if a Reverse-Wedge reach pattern is employed; the PI factor is calculated in the usual manner. When the Awareness reach pattern is employed, the Minimum Effective Frequency requirement should be taken to be the same as for a *direct-response* ad (the MEF recommendations for Direct-Response ads, depending on the media type, were given in Chapter 12, Table 12.3).

Media vehicle selection and use of the media model

As with commercial marcoms campaigns, media vehicle selection – from within the media types – is made on the basis of Target Audience Reach, subject to the overall cost constraint imposed by the media budget. And remember, if the campaign will have limited Effective Reach, then you must cut back the Action goals – using the Task Method of budget-setting (Chapter 13). The media model provided in Chapter 12, *Media Mania*, is well suited to selecting the most cost-effective vehicles and for determining the number of ad insertions in each.

Media vehicle selection does not escape *ethical* judgments (our perspective on ethics is given at the end of the chapter). Incredibly, Simmons Market Research Bureau recently began providing, to TV advertisers in the U.S.A., indexes of which TV programs are most watched by, respectively, underweight, normal, overweight, and obese people.[49] Without wishing to endorse this, we should give a "for example"; well, obese individuals differentially favor crime shows, while underweight individuals, surprise, surprise, are very keen on *American Idol*. Simmons provided these data ostensibly to help fight the overweightness epidemic in the U.S.A. but the data must be tempting for food advertisers for whom overweight people literally are heavy users![50]

RESEARCH IN SOCIAL MARKETING

The most important research required for a social marcoms campaign is up-front *qualitative research* to develop the Behavioral Sequence Models (BSMs) and the subsequent brand positioning strategy models (the I-D-U models).

The BSMs Development of the BSMs necessitates qualitative research: Individual Depth Interviews and possibly Group Depth Interviews in the case of peer-influenced or family-influenced social behaviors. The research needs to be carefully handled by a qualified clinical psychologist as moderator. It is usual to conduct this research with separate samples of Conformers, Vacillators, and Offenders. However, requiring great care but capable of yielding extremely valuable insights is to deliberately run "conflict" focus groups which mix participants from the different target groups. In conflict groups, individuals get to defend their chosen behavior – "good" or "bad" – and these defense statements can illuminate Facilitators and Deterrents for behavior-change attempts.

Separate BSMs will be needed for each of the target audience groups. Remember also that the social marketer has an ethical obligation to include everyone who is either currently or potentially at risk from the "bad" behavior.

The I-D-U models Research for the I-D-U models, one for each target group (see Table 18.1), in which the *true* Facilitators and Deterrents to both the "bad" behavior and the competing "good" behavior must be identified, can be greatly enhanced by *secondary research*: a literature search of clinical experimental and survey studies on the focal social behavior topic. Throughout this chapter, we have given numerous examples of relevant studies that are available on all of the major social marcoms topics. We chastise advertising agencies or, more directly, their government agency clients, for not delving into this specialized literature. Whereas it is true that many social marcoms campaigns are done *pro bono*, that is, free or for the cost of materials only, this is no excuse for not doing proper homework on the focal topic, assuming that the sponsor really wants the campaign to work. Note that you should additionally and afterwards commission primary qualitative research (the research outlined above) in which the facilitators and deterrents identified from the secondary research are investigated directly.

Deterrent beliefs in the I-D-U formula The benefits used in the I-D-U model for *commercial* products and services are generally Facilitators, that is, positive or negative *reinforcers*, and, for these, the usual *multiplicative* relationship between brand delivery and importance or desirability, $D_{bi} \times E_i$, is correct (see I-D-U formula in Chapter 4). However, social marcoms messages often use Deterrents, positive or negative *punishers*, to discourage the target audience from performing a "bad" behavior, and Shah and Higgins[51] have suggested, with some experimental support, that deterrent beliefs and their evaluations are processed by people *additively*. In the terms of Rogers' Protection-Motivation theory[52], this means that intention to *avoid* the behavior (reflecting negative Brand Preference, in our terms) will be increased by perceived personal susceptibility to the consequence (e.g., your estimate of the chance of your having an accident due to speeding) *plus* perceived severity (e.g., how fearful the thought of such an accident makes you). The "plus" means that a message that increases *either* the individual's perceived susceptibility *or* the perceived severity of the event will be effective; in other words the message does not have to increase both. The additive function for deterrent beliefs explains why threat appeals can make us scared even if we are not that susceptible to the threat, or if we are *very* susceptible to just a mild threat.

Once the I-D-U analysis has been carefully assessed and the benefit strategy worked out, there is then the creative development to be done, which includes the identification of a Key Benefit Claim and generation and testing (by an MJAT) of potential Creative Ideas (Conveyers). The creative development and screening procedure, followed by the insertion of Grid tactics and Attention tactics for the ad, proceed exactly as they would for a commercial marcoms campaign (see Chapters 8 and 9).

Customer response ad testing The pre-testing of social marcoms ads with "consumers" – a customer response ad test, or CRAT – is not always advisable. For non-clinically caused behaviors, such as littering, environmental good citizenship, and energy-conserving activities, we would advise yes, put the ads through a CRAT with Brand Recall and Action Intention as the criterion measures. However, for ads targeting clinically caused behaviors (addictions) or strongly habitual behaviors (quasi-addictions), some pretty deep conditioning mechanisms might be employed and people may not be able to report whether the mechanisms have had an influence.[53] The only valid test of the results of these – quite unlike asking a consumer whether the ad makes them prefer a product – is a *behavioral test*. Self-reports of responses to fear appeals, for instance, are notoriously poor predictors of actual behavior, not just under-predicting it but often predicting the contrary behavior! For example, the first author's research with "shock" ads (positive punishment) aimed at deterring speeders showed that whereas viewers *said* the ads would make them slow down, a *behavioral* test of their driving-speed choices immediately after revealed that on average they *sped up*, most likely due to residual unrelieved arousal.[54] We suspect that social marcoms ads that employ rewards (positive reinforcement), which require *multiple* learning trials, would also be invalidly self-reported in a typical one-exposure CRAT.

However, in most cases it will not be feasible to set up a behavioral test. This means you have to rely on the MJAT. Design the MJAT questionnaire carefully (see Chapter 10) and use a minimum of 10 conscientious judges.

THE ETHICS OF MARKETING COMMUNICATIONS: OUR VIEW

A discussion of – and a clear recommendation for – ethical considerations in marcoms messages is appropriately placed in this chapter on social marcoms because, paradoxically, as we will see, it is in social marcoms, which ostensibly try to do good, that ethical problems most often arise. The same ethical problems can be found in commercial marcoms but, we believe, to a much less serious extent.

There are two great schools of thought, or theories, of ethics: *deontological* (from the Greek *deon,* meaning "that which is binding and proper"), which emphasizes doing the right thing regardless of the consequences, and *teleological* (from the Greek *tele,* meaning "afar"), or consequentialist, which considers only the net good consequences from doing *anything*. In teleological ethical theory, "the end justifies the means" and so, in the most notable case, not telling the truth – lying – is justifiable if it leads to a good outcome.

Neither theory is sufficient, alone, to guide every ethical decision. The two limitations of deontological theory are, firstly, that the "categorical imperative" of Kant, the principal deontological theorist, is that one should do only those acts which one would be willing to advocate as *universally* right, such as, in Kant's view, never killing someone. However, this fails to cover circumstances in which it seems justified to kill another person, such as if you were being attacked and in mortal danger, or in a legally declared war.[55] Secondly, that the categorical imperative of doing the right thing cannot handle *conflicts* of duty, that is, a choice between right acts, which can be illustrated by the well-known story of Anne Frank, whereby the Dutch family hiding the Franks, who were Jews, had a duty to help the refugee Frank family but also a duty to tell the truth, no matter that this truth is being told to the Nazis, the pursuers. A consideration of *consequences* seems to be necessary to resolve the universalism objection and the conflict problem.[56] Teleological theory, or consequentialism, on the other hand, has the major limitation that it cannot handle considerations of *justice*, which means treating every individual as being of equal worth. The classic illustration of this is known as the "scapegoat" problem, in which, to relate a typical version, a town is shocked by a brutal murder which continues unsolved, respect for the police falls, youth crime in the town increases, and everyone is scared. The chief of police decides that the police have to act and so he orders the arrest of a derelict at random found sleeping on a through train, conducts a sham trial, and has the unfortunate innocent condemned to death. No further murders occur in the town, the police are praised, youth crime diminishes, and fear abates. Despite the widespread utilitarian good that has resulted, this case is an obvious miscarriage of justice.[57]

We have to therefore get around the problem of universal duties or obligations by introducing the possibility of a *prima facie* (Latin: "first impression") duty that overrides others in a given situation by virtue of its more beneficial *consequences* (a teleological addition to an otherwise deontological rule).[58] The conflict-of-duties dilemma can *also* be resolved by applying the same teleological addition: that of choosing the action alternative that has the greatest-good outcome (explained further below). On the other hand, the failure of teleological theory to cope with considerations of justice can only be overcome by preceding the goodness-of-outcome consideration with the purely moral *proviso* that individuals be treated equally as far as possible. This *proviso* of justice does not assume that people *are* equal, on characteristics such as intelligence, attractiveness, athletic ability, or even criminal ability, but rather that they be *treated* equally, that is, equally without prejudice.

> Our own version of this necessary concatenation of deontological and teleological ethical theories is a two-part principle: (1) that *truth* is the primary standard but that (2) truth can be overridden in a particular circumstance by an assessment that there are substantial harmful consequences of telling the truth.

In marcoms situations, our principle of ethics leads to the following judgments about common questionable practices:

- **Subliminal presentation of stimuli** – unethical because it is untruthful by omission (you have not informed the audience that a persuasion attempt is being made). As we have seen in Chapters 8 and 9, and contrary to the outdated account in most advertising textbooks, subliminal persuasion works, provided it is administered via the correct human evaluative conditioning (HEC) procedure.[59] A difficult ethical decision arises in that subliminal HEC can be used to improve self-esteem, a "good" health outcome.[60] However, we regard subliminal HEC as deontologically wrong and, further, there is no good teleological override defence, because there are alternative *supraliminal* procedures that raise self-esteem (such as focusing on one's successes, or simply getting some vigorous exercise, including, interestingly, "power" weight-lifting[61]). We note that subliminal HEC could be used in personal selling, telemarketing and advertising to *lower* the consumer's self-esteem and likely make the consumer more easily persuaded – which is *also* deontologically bad.

- **Supraliminal stimuli but subliminal process**[62] – unethical because it is untruthful by omission (you *have* told the audience that a persuasion attempt is being made by the fact that the stimuli are perceivable but you have *not* informed them that the *process* by which these stimuli persuade is hidden). Examples are personal selling techniques such as foot-in-the-door, door-in-the-face and the low-ball tactic; companies' distribution of free, branded gifts to students, including medical students[63]; and *also* the deliberate use of Freudian symbolism in ads, which consists of including an everyday object or objects that subconsciously trigger sexual arousal. Potentially the use of a Jungian archetype would fall into this category – *if* people can't see it for what it is. But if that's a lot of people, then you haven't executed the archetype clearly enough.

- **Omission of material facts** – where "material" means that the audience, not aware of the fact, could suffer harm, whether or not harm actually occurs. The most common examples of unethical omissions are health side effects with medications, foods and beverages; and safety hazards with machinery, appliances, and toys. Under "omission" we include warnings, conditions of offer, and price disclosures in print which is so small that it is almost impossible for consumers, especially older consumers, to read them.[64] Another form of omission consists of statements that do not present the facts accurately. Major contributors to this form of omission are "the media" when reporting on health and safety issues. Worst of all are those reporters who pass themselves off, with their bylines, as health or biological science authorities. With few exceptions – *The Wall Street Journal* and *The Australian Financial Review,* although they are business newspapers, have some of the more responsible reporters – self-styled health and science reporters continually reveal an alarming, and dangerous, level of ignorance. Most of them merely summarize without evaluation abstracts or news releases from medical or health journal studies obviously without having read those studies or understood them. These reporters also tend to highlight the worst from story to story, in the interest of "news," a practice that contributes greatly to the level of fear in the general public about most health and safety issues.[65]

- **Lying, which is exaggeration of attribute or benefit claims** – unethical with two *exceptions:* (a) subjective metaphors (a product or service can be *likened to anything,* as in the Conveyer ad examples in Chapter 7, such as HSBC's "footballs," without claiming that the product or service *is* that thing, which would be a simile, a literal claim, and a pointless lie) and (b) obvious puffery (obvious, that is, not just to the "reasonable consumer" but to the least intelligent and least educated sectors of society, though excluding imbeciles; an example is the claim by Greenseas Tuna in a TV ad in Australia that "Greenseas Tuna stay 98% fat-free by running from sharks!" In the U.S.A. now, under the self-regulatory Uniform Commercial Code that covers TV ads, the aggrieved *buyer* has to prove that puffery was actually an affirmation of fact and that it became part of the agreement with the seller[66]). We further discuss, below, the widespread practice and complex ethical issue of lying.

Lying can be justified if and only if the truth would cause harm

The widespread practice of lying in social marcoms practice is the one in which we can see a possible teleological override (the second part of our principle) in the form of harm being done by telling the *truth;* lying by omission also counts here if telling the *whole* truth produces harm. There are five main types of harm and we discuss these together with some cases in which it may be ethically defensible to depart from the truth. We note that there are no absolute truths other than tautologies; by "the truth" we mean the prevailing expert opinion on the topic.[67] Five types of harm can be distinguished: injury harm, health harm, economic harm, psychological harm, and moral harm. These are approximately in ascending order of difficulty of objective measurement.

Injury Harm is the most objective in that it is relatively easy to quantify the incidence and extent of bodily injury caused by defective products, risky products such as extreme vehicles or extreme sports, and speeding and dangerous driving of motor vehicles. The main difficulty with injury harm is with products for which testing on humans is too dangerous, in which case an expert assessment of the risk of injury to humans must be substituted. For injury harm, neither minimization nor exaggeration of the warning message is ethical (the best expert estimate of the truth must be used).

Health Harm, by which we mean damage to *physical* health, should be relatively easy to quantify according to medical experts, but we disagree. The situation of the advertising of alcoholic beverages in the U.S.A. supports our claim that it is *not* easy, and this case of health harm is quite typical.[68] At present, there is no consequentialist evidence to support any sort of prohibition on alcohol advertising in the U.S.A. and there is certainly no deontological reason to do so before that (alcohol ads do not have to lie to get their messages across).

Cigarettes, alcohol, foods high in bad fats, and practices or products that cause air or water pollution are the main issues with regard to causing harmful health consequences. However, it must be commented that health harm assessors seem never to take into account the beneficial effects of some of these products such as alcohol (in *moderation*, alcohol reduces stress[69], improves overall health, and thus one's work productivity and income[70]), cigarettes (smoking is protective for Alzheimer's disease[71] and Parkinson's disease[72] and depression[73]), high-fat foods (for temporary relief of depression) and perhaps even air and water pollution (if economic savings are factored in with health harm, although economic savings cannot justify air pollution caused by driving gasoline-powered or diesel-powered vehicles in congested areas or the similar pollution of indoor air where we spend 90% of our time[74]).

Health harm has one application where exaggeration – lying – seems justified, and that is in *medicine*. If the truth were widely known about the extent of misdiagnosis preceding doctors' recommendations and about the average cure rates of common medicines and treatments, most people would lose faith – faith, as in religious faith, is an apt description – in medicine and not seek *any* help.[75] Similarly, if people knew the true extent of the placebo effect in medical treatments that *do* work, then about 75% of the time they would *not* work![76]

Economic Harm is a more contentious type of harm because it is difficult to quantify the amount of monetary loss attributable to the "bad" behavior. The main two issues here are robberies initiated by drug addicts and economic hardships imposed on families by gambling addicts. Gambling is a particularly difficult case because there is plenty of evidence that, as with alcohol, *moderate* gambling has considerable psychological benefits for its adherents.[77]

Excessive gambling can only be treated by counseling, and that is voluntary. Note that economic harm in the forms of taxes and fines is a prevalent way of encouraging "good" behavior. The average U.S. citizen uses twice as much energy (gasoline and electricity mainly) as does the average Western European or Japanese citizen, in large part because the taxes in the latter societies make excessive consumption of energy unaffordable for nearly everyone.[78]

Psychological Harm gets into a very gray area as many judges and courts have found. Mental or psychological health is accorded, in modern society, as much weight in making judiciary awards as physical health. There are not many *legal* products that we can think of that are alleged to cause psychological harm, although guns, violent video games, and various gender or character dolls are candidates that are thought by many (including some governments) to send the "wrong message." In most cases this turns out to be alleged *moral harm* rather than demonstrated psychological harm. In terms of actual messages, *fear appeals* – because they almost always greatly exaggerate the actual risk probability, that is, susceptibility – can cause psychological harm in the form of prolonged anxiety and may cause *health harm* in the form of non-compliance with medical advice. For instance, a team of medical researchers recently advocated a policy of making women worry even more than they do now about getting breast cancer by raising further their already exaggerated perceived risk of contracting the disease (the predominantly white, better-educated sample estimated their average chance of getting breast cancer in their lifetime to be 34.4%; the actual probability for this sample was calculated to be 8.1%) because worry has been shown to motivate screening visits – despite acknowledging that other studies have shown that *too much* worry can deter women from seeking screening, especially those with a family history of breast cancer.[79] There is both a deontological ethical problem (lying) and a utilitarian ethical problem (avoidance of screening) here!

As any advertising creative employee knows, you can lie with pictures more effectively and less detectably than with words. A case of pictorial lying which has caused unwarranted fear is the approach used now in almost all anti-smoking ad campaigns worldwide. As we have said, the package is a medium of advertising. The respective governments have mandated the addition of gruesome visuals on cigarette packs in Canada since 2001, and in Brazil since 2002. The identical proposal is being considered, at the time of writing, by the national governments of England and Australia. An example of these visuals, shown on a generic pack, appears in Figure 18.4. At present in Canada, cigarette-

FIGURE 18.4 *Example of the graphic warnings on cigarette packs proposed for England and Australia and already mandated in Canada and Brazil.*

SOURCE: <www.quitnow.info.au>. © Commonwealth of Australia.

makers are required to rotate 16 different visuals presumably to prevent "wearout," due to diminishing attention, of any one picture's effect. The visuals include the brain of a stroke patient, part of lungs blackened with cancer, a man in a hospital bed breathing through a ventilator, a "blinded" eye as in the figure, and some less drastic possible consequences such as nicotine-stained teeth. These visuals lie by exaggerating the probability of the consequence, which, from a deontological perspective, should be sufficient to stop the use of these packs.[80] Their use would not be retrievable with a teleological override because an empirical test would doubtless show that they create more fear than health-enhancing quitting.

Moral Harm is the most contentious and subjective form of harm: it means *an offense to community standards of decency.* Community standards of decency are usually set by a large minority (say one-third of the adult population) rather than the majority. The standards are highly variable across cultures as anyone who has seen or heard ads in various countries of the world can attest. In advertising, moral harm stipulations apply to portrayals of nudity and sex, aggression, and disgusting objects or acts[81], as well as speech – even jokingly – that makes a religious slur or a racial slur. In some countries – you would be surprised at how few – gender slurs, ageism slurs, and slurs on homosexual lifestyles are regarded as indecent and are not allowed in ads. Countries that are relatively liberal on some things, such as sex, can be conservative on others, such as disgusting objects or acts. For instance, a British ad for Barnardo's, a charity for homeless children, showed a cockroach in a baby's mouth (faked of course); the ad caused a huge outcry of disgust and had to be withdrawn. Standards of decency can be specific to a single country. For instance, Australians were outraged by a TV ad for Dorf Taps (faucets) in which a jilted lover left all the taps in the house running; Australia was in the grip of a drought at the time and complaints about this indecent (or should we say inconsiderate) portrayal led to banning of the ad.[82]

> *The apparent decision rule for moral harm prohibitions:* The rule of thumb appears to be approximately that as long as one-third of sentient adults claim that they or their children are harmed morally by a practice, a prohibition will go into effect. In all cases of alleged moral harm, even with hard-core pornography, benefits, and not just economic benefits or profit, can be demonstrated for *some* people. In all cases of alleged moral harm, there are difficult assessments to be made of the prevalence and (negative) value of the harm compared with the prevalence and (positive) value of the benefits. But, usually, the rule of one-third claiming moral harm prevails.

SUMMARY

Social marketing campaigns are extremely difficult to plan effectively and, because they are usually performed *pro bono* by advertising agencies, they are usually poorly planned, if at all (many are dreamed up on the spot, by one copywriter, working for nothing). Social marcoms campaigns also have a low success rate compared with commercial marcoms campaigns because the types of behaviors that they target are often *habitual* or even *addictive*, unlike Purchase behaviors – although "shop 'til you drop" addicts may dispute that point!

Moreover, despite the undoubted good intentions of social marketers, the persuasive tactics that they employ and the side-effect outcome that often occurs – fear – are ethically contentious. Nevertheless, it is possible to design a social marcoms campaign that will work and will work in an ethically acceptable manner.

For every social marketing issue, there are always two brands: the "bad" behavior and the "good" behavior. Of course, finer distinctions of the two behaviors are sometimes worth making. Target audiences should be classified, just as in commercial marketing, in terms of brand-loyalty groups. The most relevant classification for most social marketing issues is in terms of Brand Loyals for the "bad" behavior (Offenders); Favorable Brand Switchers between the "bad" behavior and the "good" behavior, including those contemplating taking up the bad behavior (Vacillators); and those who are loyal to the "other" brand, the good behavior (Conformers). We believe that social marketers are deontologically ethically obliged to try to help all at-risk groups, unlike in commercial marketing where the manager would target the group or groups with the highest leverage. A further stage of segmentation is recommended using the personality traits of Anxiety and Impulsiveness (Gray's personality model), noting that there is a strong tendency for Anxious individuals to be Conformers and Impulsive individuals to be Offenders. For dietary behaviors and perhaps exercise behaviors, which are highly relevant in Western society at present given the increasing epidemic of life-threatening overweightness, further segmentation by gender is also necessary, and perhaps further by ethnicity or literacy.

The reason for the further segmentation by personality traits is that social marcoms message appeals differ sharply in their persuasiveness as a function of individuals' Anxiety and Impulsiveness. Individuals above the median on Anxiety respond best to (threatened) punishment appeals, which use either Positive Punishment (presentation of an aversive consequence) or Negative Punishment (loss of a previously received reward) of the "*bad*" behavior; in other words, Anxious individuals are sensitive to "no-go" signals. In contrast, individuals above the median on Impulsiveness respond best to (promised) rewards for performing the "*good*" behavior, where, and this gets tricky, the reward may be a Positive Reinforcer (presentation of an appetitive, or pleasant, consequence) *or a Negative Reinforcer (removal of a threat)*. As the total at-risk population is made up of both types of individuals and includes a somewhat smaller group who are both highly Anxious and highly Impulsive, it is necessary to use the two types of appeal – punishment for the "bad" and reward for the "good" behaviors – in the campaign. Splitting the two types of appeal further by gender may also be appropriate, as it certainly is for the problem of overeating of foods of the health-threatening variety. At the very least, the social marcoms campaign will require a "no-go" appeal simultaneous with a "go" appeal. There are other differences in persuasive tactics for Anxious individuals and for Impulsive individuals: familiarity versus novelty, solitude versus socializing, cognitive versus sexual or aggressive humor, and the use of a same-sex versus opposite-sex presenter.

The media strategy decisions for a social marcoms campaign are made in the same way – and employ the same concepts of media types, reach and frequency – as for a commercial marcoms campaign. For media type selection, there will be a primary medium and very often a secondary medium. TV and print media, which are the two most often chosen for advertising commercial products and services, are not that good for advertising for many social issues in view of the demographic skew of the offender group. Most social marcoms campaigns sell either a new (social) product or substantially reposition an established product, and so the reach pattern will be either a short Blitz like the Fad reach pattern, a Wedge, or a Reverse-Wedge for social behavior subject to opinion leadership among peers. Three media-months (minimal 12 weeks) is the usual duration of a social marcoms campaign – if it is going to work at all, it should work within that time period given, of course, a sufficiently high Effective Reach. Effective Reach means calculating Minimum Effective Frequency for each advertising cycle. The MEF/c formula is used. If the ads are targeting "no-go" on the "bad" behavior, then "LC" is the competing "good" behavior. If the ads are targeting "go" for the good behavior, the subject of LC is the bad behavior. Note, however, that because many social marcoms ads are Direct-Response in nature, the MEF recommendations for those should be used, which depend on the media type.

Intensive research is crucial for designing a successful social marcoms campaign. You will need thorough qualitative research – with a very good, and probably clinically trained, analyst – to develop the BSMs (one for each group: Offenders, Vacillators, and Conformers) and especially to construct the relevant I-D-U models. The benefits – those that Facilitate and those that Deter – must be very carefully identified rather than merely guessed at, which is what typically happens in the planning of social marcoms campaigns.

Pre-testing of social marcoms ads should always involve a Management Judgment Ad Test (MJAT). Whether to then proceed with a Customer Response Ad Test (CRAT) is not so clearcut. For ads that target non-clinically caused behaviors, yes. But for ads that target behaviors that have a strong clinical cause (addictions) or habitual character (quasi-addictions), a CRAT is not usually indicative of the likely behavioral effect of the ads because conditioning and repetition are necessary for counter-addictive processes to have their effect.

At the end of the chapter, we provided a perspective on the ethics of marketing communications, with emphasis on social marketing communications. Our two-part principle of ethics is (1) that *truth* is the primary standard but that (2) truth can be overridden in a particular circumstance by an assessment that there are substantial harmful consequences of telling the truth. We are against the subliminal presentation of stimuli; the use of supraliminal stimuli with a subliminal process; omission of material facts; and, usually, lying – except when the telling of the truth, or the whole truth, would cause harm. Some commercial marcoms campaigns and many social marcoms campaigns by these standards are unethical and should be stopped.

DISCUSSION QUESTIONS

18.1 Why do social marcoms campaigns typically produce a much lower behavioral success rate than commercial marcoms campaigns? Answer in detail using a range of social marcoms topics to exemplify your answer.

18.2 Who do the terms Offenders, Vacillators, and Conformers describe from a brand-loyalty segmentation perspective? Answer using the applications of (a) driving a vehicle beyond the posted speed limit; (b) the use of a legal substance, alcohol; and (c) the use of "recreational" illicit drugs, such as ecstasy.

18.3 Explain the difference between Eysenck's theory of personality and the subsequent modification of that theory by Gray. Rate yourself on the traits of Anxiety and Impulsiveness using the questionnaire provided in the chapter and then discuss what types of social marcoms advertising appeal you believe have been effective in inhibiting or changing the relevant behaviors in your case.

18.4 We recommended not using the almost-standard model of segmentation in social marketing, the Stages-of-Change, or Transtheoretical Model (see note 6). Why is it not useful? Can you suggest a way in which this popular model might be saved? If so, how?

18.5 Conduct some thorough research – secondary and primary – and outline an advertising campaign that you expect will be effective in encouraging people who are definitely overweight, or obese, to moderate the quantity and raise the quality of their daily food intake.

18.6 Outline a campaign to encourage all individuals, overweight or not, to regularly do physical exercise. From your secondary research (of the clinical literature) and from some primary research interviews with at-risk individuals, make clear recommendations about frequent mild exercise and less-frequent but vigorous exercise.

18.7 A recent Canadian study replicated an earlier finding suggesting that driving a car when listening to music with a tempo faster than 60 beats per minute increases heart rate and blood pressure and lowers reaction time by about 20% – a potentially fatal delay in most driving conditions – and the louder the fast music, the worse the effect.[83] Should the government mount a marcoms campaign to discourage such listening while driving? Answer in terms of ethical implications.

NOTES

1. P. Kotler and G. Zaltman, Social marketing: an approach to planned social change, *Journal of Marketing*, 1971, 35(3), pp. 3–12.

2. Here's some evidence to back up this allegation. We will focus on U.S. examples because they are no less subjective than elsewhere in the Western world. First, what is the monetary value of one life saved (by a medical, safety, or social marketing intervention)? If you are going to evaluate whether an intervention is worthwhile, absolutely, or better than an alternative use of public funds, relatively, then you *have* to put a money value on human life. The most commonly used measure is based on "willingness to pay," which in simple terms is the amount that the government (via taxpayers) would be willing to pay to save *one* human life. Human life is valued very highly although it is not priceless. One estimate is that the U.S. government in total spends $21.4 billion a year on life-saving interventions (medical, safety, and social marcoms) to save approximately 56,700 lives; see T.O. Tengs and J.D. Graham, The opportunity costs of haphazard social investments in life-saving, in R.W. Hahn (Ed.), *Risks, Costs, and Lives Saved: Getting Better Results from Regulation,* New York: Oxford University Press, and Washington, DC: The AEI Press, 1996, pp. 167–182. This works out to a *cost* of $377,425 to save each life, that is, one life. Presumably, if such interventions are going to be "cost effective," then one human life must be assigned a *value* of more than this amount. According to one U.S. government department, the Environmental Protection Agency, the value of one human life (in the U.S.A.) is $4.8 million. The EPA estimate was based on a review of many different studies and so they published this figure as an average with a 95% confidence interval of plus-or-minus $3.2 million, that is, a range from a low of $1.6 million to $8.0 million. The $4.8 million average estimate by the EPA happens to be the same as this department's estimate of the value of saving the life of a person at 50 years of age. However, the U.S. Food and Drug Administration values the saving of a 50-year-old's life at only $1.2 million. And the

U.S. Department of Agriculture values it at only $0.72 million (which is still approximately double the $0.37 million cost to save a life estimated by Tengs and Graham). But there is also a value to be placed on *prolonged* life under debilitating illness or injury. This judgment is statistically important because illnesses and injuries per year far outweigh deaths per year. An increasingly popular measure is to adjust the value downwards of a life saved by making an estimate of the "quality" of life that the person will have during whatever years are left (the so-called quality-adjusted life year, or QALY, approach); for example, the survivor of an initial heart attack might have an estimated 30% "quality" a year chopped off. The QALY approach has the economically rational but morally perverse implication that *saving* the life of a healthy person is preferable to saving the life of an ill or injured person! Not only this but if the *general public* is asked to estimate their willingness to pay to prevent various causes of death, which is hardly ever done except by academic health economists, it seems that *how* you die affects the value of saving your life! For example, cancer scares everyone and is valued at three times the value of accidental death by motor vehicle, and heart disease, another scary diagnosis, is valued at twice the amount of a death by motor vehicle. Presumably, government officials are also influenced by these entirely illogical subjective considerations. These examples are cited in D. Kenkel, Using estimates of the value of a statistical life in evaluating consumer policy regulations, *Journal of Consumer Policy,* 2003, 26(1), pp. 1–21. The second major difficulty is that we need to estimate not only the value of saving or prolonging an individual life but also the *probability* that the individual – the *average* individual, it should be emphasized – will die, or contract the illness, or experience injury, given the so-called "risk factor." For example, if you are going to try to estimate the worthwhileness of getting people to quit smoking, then you have to estimate the extent to which smoking is a "risk factor" for the most prevalent life-shortening diseases, namely, lung cancer, coronary heart disease, and, for smoking in particular, emphysema. A risk health factor does not have to be a *cause* of the outcome but rather has only to be correlated significantly (i.e., significantly more than zero) with the outcome. This lack of insistence on reasonable causal proof leads to all sorts of spurious factors which nevertheless qualify under the literal definition of a risk factor. A spurious but nevertheless definitionally correct risk factor for lung cancer, for instance, is drinking one or two glasses of whole milk per day (a relative risk estimated at 1.62 which is larger than the 1.19 relative risk for exposure to second-hand smoke; see C. Mettlin, Milk drinking, other

beverage habits, and lung cancer risk, *International Journal of Cancer,* 1989, 43(4), pp. 608–612). A further problem with risk factors is the widespread failure to acknowledge that various risk factors might not only be interactive but *depend* for their effect on one or more of the *other* risk factors. See especially L.R. Novick and P.W. Cheng, Assessing interactive causal influence, *Psychological Review,* 2004, 111(2), pp. 455–485. Yet what we see in the health literature is very precise-looking estimates for each risk factor separately. Another problem is that there are different ways of computing the *degree* of risk which differ between in the fields of medicine, epidemiology, and social science – and they produce estimates that are different enough to the extent that the same factor might be regarded as a significant risk by one field and not by another. See H.C. Kraemer, A.E. Kazdin, D.R. Offord, R.C. Kessler, P.S. Jensen, and D.J. Kupfer, Measuring the potency of risk factors for clinical or policy significance, *Psychological Methods,* 1999, 4(3), pp. 257–271. We do not mean to undermine these necessary efforts but rather to point out how subjective they are.

3. For instance, despite mass-media appeals to the adult public in Australia to donate blood – appeals which are conducted at least twice yearly nationwide – and with about 10% who are unable to donate, only 3% of adult Australians have *ever* donated blood. See radio news report, 2WS FM, March 18, 2004. As another instance, in 1990 the National Heart Foundation of Australia ran a heavy campaign (2,000 GRPs, and while we don't advocate using this term or concept, it would be roughly equivalent to 100% of households seeing or hearing the message an average of 20 times) to encourage people aged 14 and older to exercise by regular walks. An unbelievably high proportion of people, over 70%, reported "walking for exercise in the previous two weeks." Everyone, except perhaps professional athletes, exaggerates the amount and intensity of exercise they do. (On almost any desirable trait, at least 70% of individuals judge themselves to be better than the average individual when, of course, no more than 50% could be. For instance, about 80% of automobile drivers believe they are better drivers than the average driver and this is believed to result in most drivers ignoring road safety campaigns as applying only to "bad drivers"; see D. Walton and P.C. McKeown, Drivers' biased perceptions of speed and safety campaign messages, *Accident Analysis and Prevention,* 2001, 33(5), pp. 629–640.) Also, even if 70% *do* walk for exercise, only 40%, at most, get *enough* exercise (30 minutes of moderate exercise at least five days a week or three days of 30 minutes' vigorous exercise) to achieve any health

benefits; see, for example, The University of Adelaide's Male Ageing Study, 2004. The 70% prevalence was *before* the campaign started; immediately after it, there was no significant increase. So the campaign was repeated the following year with 2,200 GRPs behind it. Once more, the campaign had no effect on the reported prevalence of walking or on exercise in general. See N. Owen, A. Bauman, M. Booth, B. Oldenburg, and P. Magnus, Serial mass-media campaigns to promote physical activity: reinforcing or redundant?, *American Journal of Public Health*, 1995, 85(2), pp. 244–248. In what must be the biggest social marcoms campaign of all time, the U.S. White House's Office of National Drug Control Policy spends $145 million *per year* which, to put this in perspective, is equivalent to about one-quarter of McDonald's restaurants' annual U.S. adspend, to attempt to prevent the uptake and use of illicit drugs by children in that country; *another* U.S. government office, the National Institute on Drug Abuse, recently completed a four-year evaluation and concluded that the anti-drug marcoms had "little impact" (essentially no effect, if you read the report, as those exposed most to the campaigns exhibited beliefs afterwards that were no different from those little or not exposed). See I. Teinowitz, Study faults White House anti drug ads, *Advertising Age*, January 19, 2004, online. An earlier assessment wrongly concluded that the campaign was working in that recalled exposure to the ads was correlated with less drug usage, but this could be due to "conformers" paying more attention to the ads, with the ads less attended to by "offenders." See L.G. Block, V.G. Morwitz, W.P. Putsis Jr., and S.K. Sen, Assessing the impact of antidrug advertising on adolescent drug consumption: results from a behavioral economic model, *American Journal of Public Health*, 2002, 92(8), pp. 1346–1351.

4. M.L. Rothschild, Carrots, sticks, and promises: a conceptual framework for the management of public health and social issue behaviors, *Journal of Marketing*, 1999, 63(4), pp. 24–37. A radical "let's change our institutions" approach to social marketing has been advocated by M.E. Goldberg following a review of the weak effects of most social marcoms campaigns; see M.E. Goldberg, Social marketing: are we fiddling while Rome burns?, *Journal of Consumer Psychology*, 1995, 4(4), pp. 347–370.

5. See, for example, M. Dekimpe, L.M. Van de Gucht, D.M. Hanssens, and K.I. Powers, Long-run abstinence after narcotics abuse: what are the odds?, *Management Science*, 1998, 44(11, part 1), pp. 1478–1492.

6. A popular model for segmenting audiences for social marcoms campaigns is Prochaska and DiClemente's

Stages-of-Change Model, or Transtheoretical Model. See J.O. Prochaska and C.C. DiClemente, Stages and processes of self-change in smoking: toward an integrative model of change, *Journal of Consulting and Clinical Psychology*, 1983, 51(3), pp. 390–395; also see J.O. Prochaska, C.C. DiClemente, and J.C. Norcross, In search of how people change: applications to addictive behaviors, *American Psychologist*, 1992, 47(9), pp. 1102–1114. The stages of change – which are Precontemplation, Contemplation, Preparation, Action (the change from the "bad" behavior to the "good" behavior) and Maintenance – are recommended in most health promotion textbooks as *the* way to segment the total "bad" behavior, category-user group into subgroups. This segmentation is recommended not only for addictive behaviors, such as smoking, chronic excess consumption of alcohol, and possible addiction to high-fat and high-sugar foods and beverages, but also for most other bad behaviors that pose a health risk but are clearly *not* addictive, such as inadequate sun protection and poor oral hygiene. The face validity of the stages-of-change is high in that it seems obvious, for addictive behaviors at least, that individuals can be classified into relatively discrete states or stages which *should* follow a progression if the individual is giving up the addictive behavior. For instance, in a recent large-scale *prospective* (over time) study conducted with smokers, 47% of the smokers at the time of the baseline measure were Precontemplators (not seriously thinking about quitting smoking in the next six months), 37% were Contemplators (seriously thinking about quitting in the next six months, though not within the next month and not having attempted to quit in the past year), and 16% were Preparers (seriously thinking about quitting within the next 30 days and had made at least one attempt to do so in the past year). On the whole, most did progress over the subsequent two years but *not* as a result of the stages-of-change model's message interventions. The smokers were randomly assigned to either an intervention condition, which involved anti-smoking education classes, group activities, and brochures, conducted over a two-year period, and a control condition in which smokers received only written information on smoking cessation. As with so many social marcoms campaigns, the two-year follow-up comparison between the intervention and control worksites revealed no differences in smoking cessation. The dispute is not about the stages, which are evidently valid, for addictive behaviors at least, but rather about the behavior-cessation procedures and attitudes that are hypothesized in the model to *move* people to progress from one stage to the next (the three above), culminating in the Action stage (in the case of quitting smoking, Action is defined as abstinence for six months and Maintenance is defined as abstinence beyond six months). See T.A. Herzog, D.B. Abrams, K.M. Emmons, L.A. Linnan, and W.G. Shadel, Do processes of change predict smoking stage movements? A prospective analysis of the transtheoretical model, *Health Psychology*, 1999, 18(4), pp. 369–375.

Support for the movement influences in the stages-of-change model has been based only on *cross-sectional* surveys. Longitudinal *prospective* studies fail to show a causal influence of these factors, as in the smoking study discussed above. A second prospective study of stages-of-change was a study of an intervention among U.S. Blacks to encourage them to eat more fruit and vegetables. In this study, none of the psychosocial variables predicted transitions and, most damaging for the stages model, Precontemplators, who said at the beginning that they were *not* thinking about changing, showed in fact a large increase in their intake of fruit and vegetables by one year later. Indeed, one year later, the earlier-designated Precontemplators were eating as much fruit and vegetables as the earlier intending changers, the Contemplators! See K. Resnicow, F. McCarty, and T. Baranowski, Are precontemplators less likely to change their dietary behavior? A prospective analysis, *Health Education Research Theory & Practice*, 2003, 18(6), pp. 693–705.

7. J. Stieger, A. Mowery, and K. Oestreich, Survey finds young adults smoking at twice the rate of older Minnesotans, Academic Health Center, University of Minnesota, news release on Website, January 22, 2004.

8. The remarkable finding about smoking and lung cancer is the lack of a dose-response relationship. That is, it is the number of years that you smoke for, rather than the number you smoke per day or per year, that affects your chance of getting lung cancer; see H.J. Eysenck, *The Causes and Effects of Smoking*, London: Sage, 1981. Also see S.S. Hecht, S.E. Murphy, S.G. Carmella, C.L. Zimmerman, L. Losey, I. Kramarczuk, *et al.*, Effects of reduced cigarette smoking on the uptake of a tobacco-specific lung carcinogen, *Journal of the National Cancer Institute*, 2004, 96, pp. 107–115.

9. Blood-test studies of nicotine content, the only valid method of determining whether a smoker has truly quit, suggest a quit rate of about 2% of the 100% of smokers a year, and the true quitters are mainly older smokers diagnosed with a severe health problem.

10. Centers for Disease Control and Prevention, *Annual Smoking Report 2001*, Atlanta, GA: CDCP, 2002.

11. The main health risk from smoking is, of course, lung cancer and ever since the U.S. Surgeon General's report in 1964, lung cancer has been overdiagnosed as the cause of death if the deceased was a smoker – see the studies reviewed in H.J. Eysenck, same reference as in note 5, 1981, pp. 37–40. Overdiagnosis of lung cancer as the *cause* of death is estimated to be 45% to 50%. For a reporter's view of how the health risks of smoking have been greatly exaggerated in the media, see D. Oakley, *Slow Burn*, Roswell, GA: Eyrie Press, 1999.

12. A.H. Mokdad, J.S. Marks, D.F. Stroup, and J.L. Gerberding, Actual causes of death in the United States, 2000, *Journal of the American Medical Association*, 2004, 291(10), pp. 1238–1245. As is unfortunately typical with medical writers, academics and journalists, it would be much more informative to report the data for *premature* deaths, because everyone dies of something and for diseases it's more a matter of how soon and to some extent how painfully.

13. Figures cited in A. Ward and T. Mann, Don't mind if I do: disinhibited eating under cognitive loads, *Journal of Personality and Social Psychology*, 2000, 78(4), pp. 753–763.

14. As the authors are Australians, they note with shame that Australia is the world's second fattest nation with a total overweightness prevalence of about 60% among adults compared with 65% in the U.S.A. and in both countries about 30% (as measured by a BMI of greater than 30) are obese, a condition in which the risk of heart disease, stroke, and Type 2 ("adult") diabetes is greatly accelerated, and in both countries, about 15% of grade school children and 16% of high school adolescents are obese. For white men, a combination of two-thirds BMI and one-third Waistline (waist circumference) best predicts the likelihood of developing cardiovascular disease; for white women, Waistline alone is the best predictor – see S. Zhu, S. Heshka, Z. Wang, W. Shen, D.B. Allison, R. Ross, and S.B. Heymsfield, Combination of BMI and waist circumference for identifying cardiovascular risk factors in whites, *Obesity Research*, 2004, 12(4), pp. 633–645. Obesity prevalence is just under 5% in China, Japan, and most of Africa – but this is a lot of people! See World Health Organization Website, Obesity and overweight, 2003. Practical hint: to discourage overweight people from buying and, in restaurants or at home, eating full-fat foods, social marketers and perhaps you as a self-marketer should install a mirror in the situation. See S.M. Sentyrz and B.J. Bushman, Mirror, mirror on the wall, who's the thinnest one of all? Effects of self-awareness on consumption of full-fat, reduced-fat, and no-fat products, *Journal of Applied Psychology*, 1998, 83(6), pp. 944–949.

15. B.H. Marcus, P.M. Dubbert, L.H. Forsyth, T.L. McKenzie, E.J. Stone, A.L. Dunn, and S.N. Blair, Physical activity behavior change: issues in adoption and maintenance, *Health Psychology*, 2000, 19(1, supplement), pp. 32–41. By the way, we believe the evidence favors three times a week vigorous exercise (heart rate elevated at least 20%) over most days 30 minutes' moderate exercise; see Letters to the Editor, *Journal of the American Medical Association*, October 27, 1999, pp. 1515 ff.

16. B. Tasker, TV rules but kids leap at sporting life, *Illawarra Mercury*, January 31, 2004, p. 13. As you may see by the header on this news item, the news reporter was lauding an increase in participation in organized sport in this age group. The 62% appeared to be an absolute 2% increase on the 60% figure reported in a survey four years previously, although the difference could be within the range of sampling error. In any event, the absolute level of participation is hardly praiseworthy. TV watching is also a likely contributor to children's weight problems. Overweight and especially obese children tend to spend more time than normal-weight children watching TV and one study has shown, consistent with the theory that TV is a conditioned relaxant, that all children have a lower than *resting* metabolic rate (less energy expended) while watching TV! Kids often snack while watching, which increases calorie intake and further lowers energy expenditure. See R.C. Klesges, M.L. Shelton, and L.M. Klesges, Effects of television on metabolic rate: potential implications for childhood obesity, *Pediatrics*, 1993, 91(2), pp. 281–286.

17. G. Kaszubska, Users struggle to break ecstasy's grip, *The Australian*, April 20, 2004, p. 5.

18. The four scenarios were suggested from a good study (but with erroneous analysis of the scale items) by S. Limidis, P. Reddy, I.H. Minas, and J. Lewis, Brief functional English proficiency measure for health survey research, *Australian Psychologist*, 2004, 39(2), pp. 154–165.

19. Addictive health behaviors are the most complex in terms of their motivational bases. See R.L. Solomon, The opponent-process theory of acquired motivation, *American Psychologist*, 1980, 35(8), pp. 691–712; and T.B. Baker, M.E. Piper, D.E. McCarthy, M.R. Majeskie, and M.C. Fiore, Addiction motivation reformulated: an affective processing model of negative reinforcement, *Psychological Review*, 2004, 111(1), pp. 33–51.

20. The client is the National Fluid Milk Processor Promotion Board.

21. This observation was made by advertising researcher Lee Weinblatt, and reported in a critical analysis of the "Got milk?" campaign in A. Ries and L. Ries, *The Fall of Advertising and the Rise of PR*, New York: HarperCollins, 2002, pp. 34–35.

22. See M. Sutherland and A. Sylvester, *Advertising and the Mind of the Consumer*, Chicago, IL: Independent Publishers Group, 2000.

23. R. Neill, Incredible shrinking fashion victims, *The Australian*, August 31, 2001, p. 13.

24. R. Neill, 2001, same reference as in previous note.

25. E. Tom, Faith can move mountains but it's not going to remove your flab, *The Australian*, May 8, 2002, p. 11.

26. At the time of writing, Australian pharmacological researchers at Melbourne's St. Vincent's Institute of Medical Research and CSIRO had identified the structure of the enzyme that controls the body's reaction to food and exercise; the enzyme synthesizes, among other things, fat and cholesterol but is not "switched on" all the time. Development of a drug that switches the enzyme on or mimics its functions could see in the era of easy weight loss. Of course, it would probably not improve cardiovascular fitness, which is another major health risk factor here. See C. Pirani, Exercise in a pill? No sweat, *The Australian*, July 16, 2004, pp. 1, 6.

27. M.A. Sanner, Exchanging spare parts or becoming a new person? People's attitudes toward receiving and donating organs, *Social Science & Medicine*, 2001, 52(10), pp. 1491–1499.

28. See I. Ajzen and M. Fishbein, Attitudinal and normative variables as factors influencing behavioral intentions, *Journal of Personality and Social Psychology*, 1972, 27, pp. 41–57; M. Fishbein and I. Ajzen, *Belief, Attitude, Intention, and Behavior*, Reading, MA: Addison-Wesley, 1975; and M. Fishbein, Extending the extended model: some comments. In B.B. Anderson (Ed.), *Advances in Consumer Research*, Vol. 3, Ann Arbor, MI: Association for Consumer Research, 1976, pp. 491-497; I. Ajzen and M. Fishbein, *Understanding Attitudes and Predicting Social Behavior*, Englewood Cliffs, NJ: Prentice Hall, 1980.

29. R.C. Hornik (Ed.), *Public Health Communication: Evidence for Behavior Change*, Mahwah, NJ: Lawrence Earlbaum Associates, 2002. See especially Hornik's introductory chapter, pp. 1–19.

30. A meta-analysis of studies using the Fishbein Extended Model (there called the Theory of Reasoned Action) which

included most major health behaviors found impressive predictive results; see B.H. Sheppard, J. Hartwick, and P.R. Warshaw, The theory of reasoned action: a meta-analysis of past research with recommendations for modifications and future research, *Journal of Consumer Research*, 1988, 15(2), pp. 325–341. However, the studies were predominantly about prediction of current behavior not behavior *change* as in reducing or curing an addiction.

31. S.L. Brown, Emotive health advertising and message resistance, *Australian Psychologist*, 2001, 36(3), pp. 193–199.

32. Most consumer behavior books confuse negative reinforcement with punishment, wrongly stating that negative reinforcement decreases the behavior when it does just the opposite. B.F. Skinner, who invented the fourfold classification, should not have used "positive" and "negative" in this way. "Reward learning" and "Escape learning," others' terms, are clearer. See B.F. Skinner, *Science and Human Behavior*, New York: Macmillan, 1953.

33. This distinction in uses of the term "personality" was made by H.J. Eysenck in many of his early publications and is also well discussed in R.T. Hogan, Personality and personality measurement, in M.D. Dunette and L.M. Hough (Eds), *Handbook of Industrial and Organizational Psychology*, Vol. 2, Palo Alto, CA: Consulting Psychologists Press, 1991, pp. 873–919.

34. A. Caspi, D. Begg, N. Dickson, H. Harrington, J. Langley, T. Moffitt, and P. Silva, Personality differences predict health-risk behaviors in young adulthood: evidence from a longitudinal study, *Journal of Personality and Social Psychology*, 1997, 73(5), pp. 1052–1063. Also see L. Wasylkiw and G.C. Fekken, Personality and self-reported health: matching predictors and criteria, *Personality and Individual Differences*, 2002, 33(4), pp. 607–620.

35. Some of the risky health behaviors that have been tracked as a function of personality are sexual intercourse with casual partners without using condoms, and dependence on alcohol; and some of the risky safety behaviors are various dangerous driving practices, and violence committed against others. Habitual offenders, for each of these behaviors, tend to be much higher on the personality trait of Impulsivity, which is lack of self-restraint, and considerably lower on chronic negative emotionality, or Anxiety. See M. Rutter and J. Silberg, Gene-environment interplay in relation to emotional and behavioral disturbance, *Annual Review of Psychology*, 2002, 53, pp. 463–490. Further confirmation of the relationship between basic personality traits and risky health behaviors

comes from a study among young Swiss adult university postgraduate students, average age 25, which employed a personality *type* approach – combining trait ratings in an idiographic manner, reflecting the same distinction we made earlier between the archetype and the trait approach to personality. The study found large differences between the types in terms of smoking (regular smokers are higher on Neuroticism, probably giving them hypersensitivity to withdrawal symptoms – see T.B. Baker, *et al.*, 2004, same reference as in note 19 – and they are higher on Impulsiveness); regularity of getting drunk (where Impulsiveness as a single trait was by far the most predictive); and frequent use of cannabis (Impulsiveness again). See M. Vollrath and S. Torgersen, Who takes health risks? A probe into eight personality types, *Personality and Individual Differences*, 2002, 32, pp. 1185–1197.

Pertinent to the current major health issue in Western countries – overweight children and adults – which is still likely to be the major focal issue for social marcoms in Western countries when this book is published, is an important study conducted at the University of Adelaide, Australia. The study found that four basic personality traits – Psychoticism, Extraversion, Neuroticism, and External Locus of Control – predicted people's intake of the main nutrient types in foods, but that they predicted somewhat differently between males and females. The relationships between personality traits and nutrient intake were as strong as the well-known relationships between demographic factors, notably occupational status, which is the main indicator of social class, and nutrient intake. Rather disturbingly from a marcoms perspective, the only type of nutrient intake that was *not* predictable by *either* demographics or personality was fat intake; unfortunately, though, the researchers did not distinguish between "good" fats (that is, mono-unsaturated or polyunsaturated fats, which lower the rate of heart disease) and "bad" fats, (that is, saturated fats and trans fats – re-cooked fats, as in making potato chips and cookies), which increase it. See, for instance, Cutting through the fat, *Choice*, March 2004, pp. 16–19. Cholesterol intake (but among men only, not women), refined sugar intake, and sodium intake were predicted quite strongly by personality traits, though with differences in the significant predictors between males and females. The Australian study is reported in H. Falconer, K.I. Baghurst, and E.E. Rump, Nutrient intakes in relation to health-related aspects of personality, *Journal of Nutrition Education and Behavior*, 1992, 25(6), p. 307. Because the personality traits also influence the persuasiveness of different message types, this means that personality and gender are important segmentation variables for marcoms designed to encourage healthy eating. Campaigns that do not acknowledge these differences will not work, or will work only on that part of the population which happens to be attuned to the message by personality and gender.

Personality traits are established early in childhood and the relationships with risky behaviors in young adulthood are quite strong but they are certainly not 100% predictive, so we would not recommend, as some have – such as in the case of psychoticism and future violent crime (see H.J. Eysenck, *Crime and Personality*, 2nd edn, London: Routledge & Paul, 1977) – a program of early screening and monitoring. Rather, we suggest that *message appeals* may be effectively designed to take advantage of personality differences because, as we have suggested and will explain shortly, responsiveness to different types of message *also* relates to basic personality traits.

36. See J.A. Gray, A critique of Eysenck's theory of personality, in H.J. Eysenck (Ed.), *A Model for Personality*, Berlin, West Germany: Springer-Verlag, 1981, pp. 246–276. Also see J.A. Gray, *The Neuropsychology of Anxiety*, Oxford, England: Clarendon Press, 1982; J.A. Gray, Perspectives on anxiety and impulsivity: a commentary, *Journal of Research in Personality*, 1987, 21, pp. 493–510; P.J. Corr, A.D. Pickering, and J.A. Gray, Personality and reinforcement in associative and instrumental learning, *Personality and Individual Differences*, 1995, 19(1), pp. 47–71; A. Gomez and R. Gomez, Personality traits of the behavioural approach and inhibition systems: associations with processing of emotional stimuli, *Personality and Individual Differences*, 2002, 32(8), pp. 1299–1316; R. Poy, M. del C. Eixarch, and C. Ávila, On the relationship between attention and personality: covert visual orienting of attention in anxiety and impulsivity, *Personality and Individual Differences*, 2004, 36(6), pp. 1471–1481. Lastly, see a very important study by S.L. Gable, H.T. Reis, and A.J. Elliot, Behavioral activation and inhibition in everyday life, *Journal of Personality and Social Psychology*, 2000, 78(6), pp. 1135–1149.

37. H.J. Eysenck, The place of anxiety and impulsivity in a dimensional framework, *Journal of Research in Personality*, 1987, 21, pp. 489–493; and H.J. Eysenck and M.W. Eysenck, *Personality and Individual Differences: A Natural Science Approach*, New York: Plenum Press, 1985.

38. Gray's Impulsiveness trait is *related* to Eysenck's original other trait, Psychoticism. The difference appears to be that Impulsiveness produces sensitivity to conditioned (learned) rewards, such as verbal praise or money, whereas Psychoticism more strongly produces sensitivity to

unconditioned (innate) rewards, hence the selfish hedonistic, that is, sadistic, behavior of psychotics; see J.A. Gray, 1981, first reference in note 36. Gray's theory also has a more plausible neurobiological basis than Eysenck's. Recent evidence suggests that the behavioral inhibition system (BIS, related to chronic anxiety) is marked by higher chronic cortical activity in the right prefrontal cortex, whereas the behavioral activation system (BAS, related to chronic impulsivity) is marked by chronic cortical *and* autonomic *underarousal*; see G.G. Knyazev, H.R. Slobodskaya, and G.D. Wilson, Psychophysiological correlates of behavioural inhibition and activation, *Personality and Individual Differences*, 2002, 33(4), pp. 647–660.

39. H. Eysenck and G. Wilson, *Know Your Own Personality*, Harmondsworth, England: Penguin Books, 1976.

40. R. Zinbarg and W. Revelle, Personality and conditioning: a test of four models, *Journal of Personality and Social Psychology*, 1989, 57(2), pp. 301–314.

41. R.A. Wise and M.A. Bozarth, A psychomotor stimulant theory of addiction, *Psychological Review*, 1987, 94(4), pp. 469–492. For instance, studies in which drug-addicted laboratory animals are subject to uncontrollable stress (which would probably not be approved by university ethics committees now) show that they avoid freely available drugs. If you've unfortunately ever suffered depression, you don't feel like having a drink or getting high on drugs, and if you're a smoker you will smoke less frequently even though smoking helps alleviate depression (see references in note 74).

42. Both these findings, from various research reports, are summarized in T.B. Baker, T.H. Brandon, and L. Chassin, Motivational influences on cigarette smoking, *Annual Review of Psychology*, 2004, 55, pp. 463–491.

43. D. DeSteno, R.E. Petty, D.T. Wegener, and D.D. Rucker, Beyond valence in the perception of likelihood: the role of emotional specificity, *Journal of Personality and Social Psychology*, 2000, 78(3), pp. 397–416; D. DeSteno, R.E. Petty, D.D. Rucker, D.T. Wegener, and J. Braverman, Discrete emotions and persuasion: the role of emotion-induced expectancies, *Journal of Personality and Social Psychology*, 2004, 86(1), pp. 41–56.

44. J.M. Twenge, The age of anxiety? Birth cohort change in anxiety and neuroticism, 1952–1993, *Journal of Personality and Social Psychology*, 2000, 79(6), pp. 1007–1021.

45. See, for instance, the data on physical and mental health by social class stratum reported and discussed in M. Argyle,

The Social Psychology of Everyday Life, London: Routledge, 1992.

46. For the most recent meta-analysis of general mental ability and occupational attainment, which is the main determinant of social class, see F.L. Schmidt and J. Hunter, General mental ability in the world of work: occupational attainment and job performance, *Journal of Personality & Social Psychology,* 2004, 86(1), pp. 162–173; and for evidence on the argument that intelligence is the main direct cause of social class inequalities in health, see L.S. Gottfredson, Intelligence: is it the epidemiologists' elusive "fundamental cause" of social class inequalities in health?, *Journal of Personality and Social Psychology,* 2004 (86(1), pp. 174–199.

47. J.R. Rossiter, Based on an unpublished review of studies of personality, conditioning, and persuasion.

48. Transport Accident Commission of Victoria, Marketing road safety, in Advertising Federation of Australia (Eds.), *Effective Advertising: Casebook 1992,* Sydney: Advertising Federation of Australia, 1993, pp. 193–212.

49. J. Mandese, Sizing up audiences by body type, *Television Week,* September 8, 2003, online.

50. A really dumb study published in a prestigious journal found that normal-weight people's brains light up when the people are deprived of food and then exposed to actual food stimuli. From this wholly unremarkable finding, the team of numerous authors, which seems to be the norm in medically oriented journals these days, drew the sweeping policy conclusion that *advertising* for food products should be prohibited as it is "likely to contribute to the epidemic of obesity" (p. 1790). See G.-J. Wang, N.D. Volkow, F. Teland, M. Jayne, J. Ma, M. Rao, W. Zhu, C.T. Wong, N.R. Pappas, A. Geliebter, and J.S. Fowler, Exposure to appetitive food stimuli markedly activates the human brain, *NeuroImage,* 2004, 21(4), pp. 1790–1797. Much more relevant is an earlier study by Steinberg and Yalch which found that normal-weight individuals are most likely to impulsively purchase extra food items in the supermarket the longer it has been since they last ate, whereas obese individuals are more likely to make impulse food purchases the more *recently* they have eaten, suggesting that eating disinhibits eating in obese individuals. See S.A. Steinberg and R.F. Yalch, When eating begets buying: the effects of food samples on obese and nonobese shoppers, *Journal of Consumer Research,* 1978, 4(4), pp. 243–246.

51. J. Shah and E.T. Higgins, Expectancy × value effects: regulatory focus as determinant of magnitude *and* direction,

Journal of Personality and Social Psychology, 1997, 73(3), pp. 447–458.

52. R.W. Rogers, Cognitive and physiological processes in fear appeals and attitude change: a revised theory of protection motivation, in J. Cacioppo and R. Petty (Eds), *Social Psychophysiology,* New York: Guilford Press.

53. See especially C.K. Turner, Don't blame memory for people's faulty reports on what influences their judgments, *Personality and Social Psychology Bulletin,* 1988, 14(3), pp. 622–629.

54. J.R. Rossiter and J. Thornton, Fear-pattern analysis supports the fear-drive model for anti-speeding road safety ads, *Psychology & Marketing,* 2004, 21(11), in press.

55. At the time of writing, the Israeli army had assassinated the leader, and one month later the new leader, of the militant Palestinian organization, Hamas, in what is *not* an internationally (e.g., the United Nations) sanctioned war. Such acts are deontologically wrong unless we accept the Israelis' argument that they were in mortal danger (the second leader, Dr. Rantissi, was on record as vowing that "we will not leave one Jew in Palestine"). See *The Australian,* April 19, 2004, p. 1.

56. For further explanation of Kant's theory and of its merits and limitations, see J.W. Cornman and K. Lehrer, *Philosophical Problems and Arguments: An Introduction,* New York: Macmillan, 1968.

57. Again, see J.W. Cornman and K. Lehrer, same reference as in previous note, for further discussion of the failings of a strict consequentialist theory as regards the principle of equal justice for all.

58. The *prima facie* and override approach was suggested by D. Ross, *The Right and the Good,* Oxford, England: Oxford University Press, 1955.

59. A. Dijksterhuis, H. Aarts, and P.K. Smith, The power of the subliminal: subliminal perception and possible applications, in R. Hasin, J. Uleman, and J.A. Bargh (Eds), *The New Unconscious,* New York: Oxford University Press.

60. A. Dijksterhuis, I like myself but I don't know why: enhancing implicit self-esteem by subliminal evaluative conditioning, *Journal of Personality and Social Psychology,* 2004, 86(2), pp. 345–355.

61. Power weight-lifting ("lifting to the max") helps to bring relief to most older (age 60+) people who suffer depression: 60% of older male and female participants, chronic depressives, showed a 50% reduction in their levels of

depression; low-intensity lifting had the same effect as standard medical care, averaging a 30% reduction. Research by N. Singh at Royal Prince Alfred Hospital, Sydney, Australia, reported in L. Deighton, Ironing out the wrinkles of elderly depression, *The Australian,* 16 April 2004, p. 5.

62. See especially J.A. Bargh, Losing consciousness: automatic influences on consumer judgment, behavior and motivation, *Journal of Consumer Research,* 2002, 29(2), pp. 280–285.

63. W.A. Rogers, P.R. Mansfield, A.J. Braunack-Mayer, and J.N. Jureidini, The ethics of pharmaceutical industry relationships with medical students, *Medical Journal of Australia,* 2004, 180(8), pp. 411–414. Rogers *et al.* claim that pharmaceutical companies' gifts to medical companies create a conscious reciprocal obligation or a subconscious one.

64. Advertisers still try to pull the "fine print" stunt. A recent instance is an ad for broadband connection by a leading Australian telephone company which placed a 400-word disclosure in print that could not be read by people with normal 20/20 vision; see S. Canning, *The Australian,* April 22, 2004, p. 21.

65. The reporters apparently have never heard of statistical confidence intervals and favor the more alarming upper end of almost every statistic. Another common error is to report various diseases or lifestyle practices as "causes of death," when what is really meant is the more controversial and difficult-to-estimate "causes of *premature* death." Another dangerous error is to hype the announcement of every new wonder drug that comes on the market, indicating that the reporters, or most of them, uncritically swallow pharmaceutical companies' PR. Viagra (generic name sildenafil) is a case in point. The hype about Viagra as a cure for male impotence, in general and after prostate treatment, has led to a tragic state of affairs whereby affected men try it once and, if it doesn't work the first time, they become severely distressed and feel even more impotent and emasculated than they did before they tried it. See J.M. Tomlinson and D. Wright, Impact of erectile dysfunction and its subsequent treatment with sildenafil: qualitative study, *British Medical Journal,* March 29, 2004, online at bmj.com/bmj.38044.662176.EE. Viagra is a highly effective drug, with a success rate much higher than almost any other drug, but what is not known by most men – because it has not been adequately reported – is that it may have to be taken up to six times before it starts working and that anxiety about it not working, due to expectations raised by the hype, can, by "mind over matter," prevent it from

working due to insufficient relaxation. See Dr. D. Lording, Cabrini Health, Melbourne, Australia, reported in H. Tobler, Viagra has a downside, *The Australian,* March 31, 2004, p. 10. A careful follow-up of cancer treatment "wonder drug" reports in the media reveals that they nearly all prove less effective than originally claimed – but reporters rarely do follow-ups. E.S. Ooi and S. Chapman, An analysis of newspaper reports of cancer breakthroughs: hope or hype?, *Medical Journal of Australia,* 2003, 179 (1/15 December), pp. 639–643. A strong case could be made for editing for moderation in health and safety reporting – both on the "disease" side and on the "cure" side. This is not an exercise of "freedom of speech;" it is irresponsible, dangerous, and deceptive speech, and it should be legislated against.

66. C. Ross, Marketers fend off shift in rules for ad puffery, *Advertising Age,* February 19, 1996, p. 41.

67. See J.R. Rossiter, The five forms of transmissible, usable marketing knowledge, *Marketing Theory,* 2002, 2(4), pp. 369–380; and J.R. Rossiter, What is marketing knowledge? Stage II: evidence to establish marketing knowledge, Working paper, Wollongong, Australia: University of Wollongong, 2002.

68. A.G. Woodside, Advertising and consumption of alcoholic beverages, *Journal of Consumer Psychology,* 1999, 8(2), pp. 167–186. Until 1996, advertising of hard liquor (distilled spirits) was banned on U.S. television and radio; both wine and beer advertising have always been permitted. Liquor, of course, is a legally purchasable product in the U.S.A. and thus there is no deontological reason why it should not be advertised in any TV and radio program, since minors, that is, those under 21 years of age, are not allowed to buy any form of alcohol in the U.S.A. Woodside conducted an econometric analysis of the effect of distilled spirits advertising, wine advertising, and beer advertising (computed as shares of total alcohol advertising) on total alcohol consumption per adult. In his careful analysis, Woodside found some statistically significant but practically very small effects. A 10% increase in the *share* of alcohol advertising devoted to hard liquor would increase per capita alcohol consumption by .01% (that's one-hundredth of 1%) and an increase in the *share* of alcohol advertising devoted to wine advertising would increase total per capita alcohol consumption by .02% (that's two-hundredths of 1%); the share of alcohol advertising devoted to *beer* advertising had a very small *negative* effect on total per capita alcohol consumption, of – .01% (again, this is a decrease of one-hundredth of 1%). Avid consequentialist policy makers could

interpret these findings as calling for a ban on hard liquor advertising and wine advertising and an *increase* in beer advertising, because it appears to be mildly preventative for total per capita alcohol consumption; this is also the policy interpretation suggested in Woodside's article. There is also a not-too-subtle implication in Woodside's interpretation that the consumption of hard liquor is somehow more dangerous than the consumption of wine or beer as far as problem drinking is concerned, which is quite naïve as there are plenty of alcoholics who drink only beer, and, as most teenagers know, binge drinking can be accomplished quite effectively with just beer. However, the increase in the per capita consumption of alcohol could well be a *beneficial* social outcome if it represented more U.S. adults consuming *moderate* amounts of alcohol, as the health benefit of moderate consumption of alcohol, and, interestingly, the work benefit and economic benefit, are well established in Western populations (approximately one-third of U.S. adults never drink alcohol; 57% are light to moderate drinkers; and just 10% are heavy drinkers, although they drink 61% of total alcohol by volume; see M. Chase, Health journal: Americans seem to drink a lot or hardly at all, *Wall Street Journal,* December 30, 1996, p. B2). In fact, to have any relevance for policy from a consequentialist standpoint, the analysis would have to show that an increase in alcohol advertising of any type increases not the per capita amount of alcohol drunk, which may possibly be a good thing, but specifically contributes to the prevalence of alcoholism or, even more specifically, to the prevalence of premature deaths and drink-driver accidents and injuries. This was not examined and therefore not demonstrated.

69. C.M. Steele, L. Southwick, and R. Pagano, Drinking your troubles away: the role of activity in mediating alcohol's reduction of psychological stress, *Journal of Abnormal Psychology*, 1986, 95(2), pp. 173–180. And see C.M. Steele and R.A Josephs, Drinking your troubles away II: an attention-allocation model of alcohol's effect on psychological stress, *Journal of Abnormal Psychology*, 1988, 97(2), pp. 196–205.

70. Interesting example of a reverse risk factor (but a cause?) and significant for men only. For U.S. males, any drinking is beneficial: see G.A. Zarkin, M.T. French, T. Mroz, and J.W. Bray, Alcohol use and wages: new results from the national household survey on drug abuse, *Journal of Health Economics*, 1998, 17(1), pp. 53–68. But in Canada it's definitely only moderate drinking that helps (1.5 to 2.5 drinks a day): see V. Hamilton and B. Hamilton, Alcohol and earnings: does drinking yield a wage premium?, *Canadian Journal of Economics*, 1997, 30(1), pp. 153–151. The "moderate for men"

finding was replicated in Australia but we can't find the working paper!

71. H.J. Eysenck, 1981, same reference as in note 8; and Memory goes up with a puff, *The Australian*, November 10, 1999, p. 11.

72. I.I. Kessler, Epidemiologic studies of Parkinson's disease. III: a community based survey, *American Journal of Epidemiology*, 1972, 96(4), pp. 242–254.

73. B. Hickman, Smokers prone to the blues, *The Australian*, January 18, 1999, p. 3; and J.D. Kassel, L.R. Stroud and C.A. Paronis, Smoking, stress, and negative affect: correlation, causation, and context across stages of smoking, *Psychological Bulletin*, 2003, 129(2), pp. 270–304.

74. J. Margo, Sick-building syndrome leads to unwell staff, *The Australian Financial Review*, May 6, 2004, p. 19.

75. R. McGreevy, Prescription medicine is hit or miss for most, *The Australian*, December 9, 2003, p. 10.

76. I. Kirsch and S.J. Lynn, Automaticity in clinical psychology, *American Psychologist*, 1999, 54(7), pp. 504–515.

77. P.S. Loroz, Golden-age gambling: psychological benefits and self-concept dynamics in aging consumers' consumption experiences, *Psychology & Marketing*, 2004, 21(5), pp. 323–349.

78. T.P. O'Brien and S.J. Zoumbaris, Consumption behaviors hinge on financial self-interest, *American Psychologist,* 1993, October, pp. 1091–1092.

79. The medical researchers are I.M. Lipkus, M. Kuchibhatia, C.M. McBride, H.B. Bosworth, K.I. Pollack, I.C. Siegler, and B.K. Rimer, and the advocacy was made in their article, Relationships among breast cancer perceived absolute risk, comparative risk, and worries, *Cancer Epidemiology, Biomarkers & Prevention*, 2000, 9, pp. 973–975.

80. The deontological (right means) issue is that the visual warnings are exaggerated. For example, the probability that a lifelong smoker in the U.K. – and presumably in Australia, which has much the same racial stock, race (or genetics) being a causal factor for all cancers – will contract lung cancer is about 16% (see R. Peto, S. Darby, H. Deo, P. Silcocks, E. Whitley, and R. Doll, Smoking, smoking cessation, and lung cancer in the UK since 1950: Combination of national statistics with two case-control studies, *British Medical Journal*, 2000, 321, pp. 323–329), but the picture of the cancerous lungs, as well as the earlier verbal warning "Cigarettes cause lung cancer," implies a much higher probability. Already, the public, including otherwise knowledgeable people, typically estimate the

probability of a lifelong smoker getting lung cancer to be about 60% (J. R. Rossiter, Unpublished survey results, N = 120, University of Wollongong, March 2004), which is a gross exaggeration. Not to minimize the horror of various diseases associated with smoking, but the other diseases that are claimed to be caused by smoking have even lower probabilities. The irony is that the main justification for these fear appeals according to their supporters is "better informed smokers." See R. Borland and D. Hill, Initial impact of the new Australian tobacco health warnings on knowledge and beliefs, *Tobacco Control*, 1997, 6(4), pp. 317–325. Their conclusion was even more ironic: that "the new health warnings are resulting in better informed smokers" as if the warnings are *producing* more and smarter smokers! Hardly; smokers, and non-smokers, are being *misinformed.* The teleological (good consequences) issue is that there is no valid behavioral evidence that the graphic cigarette pack warnings are working. Instead, the questionable claim of success comes from a survey of 1,398 (self-reported) non-smokers and 633 smokers 18 months after the packs' introduction, conducted by the Canadian Cancer Society, who might have a vested interest in proving the campaign to be a success. In the society's survey, many smokers said the warnings had increased their motivation to quit, but the fact is that 42.5% of smokers said that they "seriously intend to quit within the next six months" *before* the packaging change, and about the same proportion, 41.2%, said this after the change. Actual quitting, for three months after the packaging change in Canada, was reported by 11% of smokers, but since intentions did not change, *we* conclude that the quitting *cannot* be attributed to the packaging change. See D. Hammond, G.T. Fong, P.W. McDonald, R. Cameron, and K.S. Brown, Impact of the graphic Canadian warning labels on adult smoking behaviour, *Tobacco Control*, 2003, 12(4), pp. 391–395. An insidious consequentialist outcome is that the new packs will be paid for by addicted consumers, many of them ill-able to afford the outrageous price of cigarettes in Canada – as is the case in the U.K. and Australia – and guess who pockets most of the extra revenue? We have to wonder whether governments want these campaigns to work; again, the government is lauded, by the scientifically naïve public, as "doing something" about the problem!

81. T.A. Shimp and E.W. Stuart, The role of disgust as an emotional mediator of advertising effects, *Journal of Advertising*, 2004, 33(1), pp. 45–53.

82. S. Canning, Selling offensive, *The Australian*, Media and Marketing section, April 15, 2004, pp. 17, 20.

83. M.A. Recarte and L.M. Nunes, Mental workload while driving: effects on visual search, discrimination, and decision making, *Journal of Experimental Psychology: Applied*, 2003, 9(2), pp. 119–137.

glossary

NOTE: Terms in the definitions that are written with initial capitals are themselves defined in the glossary.

Acceptance: A response in the Processing of an ad or promotion offer in which the customer mentally agrees with a Brand Benefit Claim made in the ad or offer (that is, the claim is regarded as credible). Necessary only in processing of messages for High-Involvement brand-item choice. Acceptance is a combination of Learning and a *positive* Emotion.

Acknowledge prior attitude: Essential tactic for the High-Involvement Brand Preference strategy. There are three possible prior attitude states – Negative prior attitude, Neutral prior attitude, and Moderately favorable prior attitude – and the advertiser has to figure out which one applies to the target audience and acknowledge it in the message.

Action objective: What we expect the Target Audience to *do* as a result of seeing or hearing our marcoms. Action is *observable, measurable behavior.* The most common action objectives are *pre-purchase* behaviors, such as Visits and Inquiries; *purchase* behaviors, such as Trial and Repeat Purchase (and Purchase, itself, for durables); and, occasionally, *post-purchase* behaviors, such as Display or a particular type of Usage.

Ad likability by target audience: If the purchase decision for the brand-item is Low-Involvement/ Transformational, the Target Customers, but not necessarily anyone else, must like the ad.

Ad recognition (AR): Customer Tracking Survey respondents are shown – or, for radio, played – the ads from the campaign and are asked whether they have seen or heard them before. Answer categories are "Yes," "Not sure," and "No," and only the "Yes" answers signify Ad Recognition.

Ad recognition frequency (ARF): Follows the Ad Recognition measure in a Customer Tracking Survey. Those respondents who recognize the ad are asked how many times they have seen, read, or heard the ad, with reference to a given time period.

Ad response modeling (path analysis): Used to check whether Brand Preference is, or is not, influenced by the a-b-e Benefit Claim Chain. It is diagnostic and reveals how the ad works on brand preference and where it breaks down if it doesn't work.

Adspend: See Media Budget.

Advertising: Comes from the Latin verb *advertere* which means "to turn toward," indicating that the purpose of advertising is to "turn the mind" of the prospective customer toward the brand (which means making the customer aware of the brand and preferring it).

Advertising cycle: The duration of an Advertising Cycle is determined by the time needed to get enough insertions into the media vehicles selected so as to attain the desired amount of reach at the minimum effective frequency (MEF). Depending on the size of the frequency requirement, the duration for insertions – the Advertising Cycle – will be one day, one week, or two weeks.

Advertising elasticity coefficient: Multiplier on unit Sales reflecting the effectiveness of the advertising.

Advertising strategy: Decisions encompassing the target audience (whom you want to talk to) and the message (what you want to show and say). But not *how* you show or say it, which is Creative Strategy.

Advertising-to-sales ratio (A/S ratio): Total Adspend (monetary) as a percentage of total Sales (monetary) for the year. Imitating a leading competitor's A/S ratio is one way of setting your total adspend if you're new.

Advertising wearout: The *Creative Idea* or the *Creative Executions* are no longer meeting the sales goal even though the benefit positioning strategy is correct and the media schedule is unchanged. The problem could be Attention wearout, Learning (interference) wearout, or, if a High-Involvement brand choice, Acceptance wearout.

Corrective actions include Variations, Faster rotation, Shorter ads, and, if Brand Recall learning is suffering, achieving greater Dominance in your ads' media schedule.

Advertorials: Publisher allows manufacturer to slip brand endorsements into news stories and articles (paid for).

Aggregate tracking (AT): Omits the Customer Survey and employs only measures of Adspend or Exposure, as input, and measures of Sales or Market Share, and if you are smart, Brand Equity, as output.

Ambush marketing: A company that is *not* a sponsor pretends to be, often by running ads before and during the event.

Approach: First stage of the actual sales exchange and takes place in the *first few minutes of the face-to-face sales call*, or in the *first 30 seconds of the telemarketing call*.

Approachability: The *sublime* feeling of approachability, in which the approach tendency asserts itself over the coincidentally salient avoidance tendency. "Sublime" is E. Kant's term and is used to describe the reaction to classic "explorer beholds new vista" paintings.

Approximate log-linear model: The most accurate Media Model overall, but slightly slower computationally for large schedules, that is, when the number of vehicles exceeds six or when there are four or more insertions in a vehicle.

Archetype: An emotionally-laden, universally recognized, character (an idiographic personality type). Examples: The Hero, The Outlaw, The Earth Mother, The Magician. Jung invented the concept in the early 20th century and others such as Carol Pearson have popularized and applied archetypes to marcoms content.

Associate and repeat: A tactic to increase Brand Recall whereby the Category Need and Brand Identity (usually the Brand Name) are repeated as a *pairing* in the ad.

Attention: First and necessary response in Processing (level 1 of how marcoms work). Initial and then successive attention responses are necessary for the prospective customer to learn from and respond emotionally to an ad or offer. Attention should be measured by self-report post-test of recognition of elements of the ad's or offer's content. Psychophysiological measures such as eye-tracking or brain or skin reactivity are insufficient as they include "sensory register" responses that don't reliably prove (too many false alarms) that the consumer mentally focuses on the stimulus element that he or she is exposed to.

Attention factors checklist (in the MJAT): Second part of the management judgment ad test (MJAT). A checklist of Attention tactics and used only if the ad was accepted on the first part, the Content Factors Ratings. The Attention tactics differ according to the ad's medium (see Chapter 9 for these in detail).

Attention tactics: Tactics that will be most likely to attract and maintain the Target Customer's mental focus on the message in the ad or offer. These are mainly *structural* factors such as ad duration or size, picture size, form of headline, brand-identity placement; and for TV and radio ads, which take form over *time*, the "interest pattern" that the commercial stimulates dynamically. Attention can be reflexive (elicited by contrasting stimuli in the ad or offer) or selective (when the viewer, reader, or listener has a Motive in mind and is searching for content relevant to it).

Attitudes, interests, and opinions (AIO): Person's outlook on life as expressed in conversations with others. In Trade Selling and Technical Selling, try to fairly well match salesperson and customer on their AIOs.

Attributional style: Excellent hiring factor for Technical Selling and Telemarketing (predicting both success in selling and retention of the salesperson). Look for salespeople who are optimists – attributing successes entirely to themselves and rationalizing rejections to external factors (such as the customer).

Awareness advertising, also called Brand advertising: Advertising that is placed in mass media such as TV, radio, cinemas, newspapers, magazines, and outdoor, and that is "mind-turning," not direct-response, in its purpose.

Awareness pattern: Reach pattern suited to consumer and industrial products and services that have a *long purchase cycle* and a *long decision time*. High target-audience reach, low frequency per cycle (often using Double-Duty ads).

Behavioral sequence model (BSM): One-page diagram constructed to illuminate the buyer behavior basis of marcoms strategy – "who we should talk to," "where," "when," and to some extent "what" we'll need to say (see stage 5 of the BSM). The BSM identifies (1) the main stages of the decision; (2) who the role-players are at each stage; (3) where the decision stages take place; (4) over what time intervals and at what times each decision stage takes place; and (5) how the decision at each stage is achieved by the main role-player at that stage.

Benefit claim chain: Sequence of attribute(s), the benefit, and emotion(s) used to achieve a Benefit Claim. (See the a-b-e Model in Chapter 4.)

Benefit claims: Brands and brand-items are benefit-positioned by a benefit *claim* rather than the benefit itself. Benefit Claims are what customers see or hear (and are thus reality). Just to prove this, remember that competing brands can offer the same benefit but be strongly differentiated in customers' minds by the claim each makes about that benefit. The actual benefit promised is in the claim; it is not in the abstract benefit. The claim may be made pictorially or verbally and sometimes by sound effects or other-sense stimuli such as touch (POP) or scratch and sniff, in-ad sampling.

Benefit presentation: Next Stage of Selling in Personal Selling after the Approach stage.

Beta binominal model: The most popular standard (nonproprietary) Media Model used by media planners. This model is very fast, but is *not reliably accurate*, tending to overestimate Reach in all media and not modeling magazine ad exposures well.

Between-vehicle duplication: In Media Data: the extent of pairwise duplication *between* the vehicles on a typical co-occurrence of the vehicles.

Blitz pattern: The advertiser tries to reach 100% of the target audience *every week* and piles on frequency, during each week, "at the NCU level" to the *same individuals*.

Brand action intention: Fourth of the Communication Effects (level 2 of how marcoms work) and necessary only for high-risk product or service choices. The intention must occur in the prospect's mind consciously as a self-instruction to act.

Brand advertising: See Awareness advertising.

Brand architecture: The process of ensuring that the positioning of the Master Brand or Sub-Brand comes across in the positioning of those brands' specific brand-items while still distinguishing those brand-items from each other.

Brand attitude: Means the same as absolute Brand Preference although Brand Attitude is a more appropriate term in social marcoms because it is possible to have a favorable attitude (overall evaluation) of a bad or good behavior without personally preferring to do it.

Brand awareness: Second of the Communication Effects (level 2 of how marcoms work). Necessary in order that the brand-item can be considered for purchase; the brand-item either has to be recognized as an item that belongs in that category (Brand Recognition) or recalled as an item *when* the Category Need arises in the decision process (Brand Recall). In some purchase situations, both of the brand awareness responses need to be made, recalling the item and then recognizing it in the store or in a catalog (Brand-Recall-Boosted Brand Recognition).

Brand awareness tactics: These tactics execute and structure the brand awareness message content to achieve Brand Recognition, Brand Recall, or both. The tactics are taken from the Rossiter-Percy-Bellman Grid.

Brand communication effects: See Communication Effects – we don't use this term any other way than to refer to mental responses attached to the *brand* (or *brand-item*). Not responses to the ad (or offer).

Brand equity: Principal measure of marketing communications' long-run success. At the Corporate Brand level, brand equity is measured by the brand's monetary valuation (e.g., Interbrand). At the Brand-Item level, brand equity should be measured by Value Equity and Uniqueness Equity (W. Moran's method).

Brand-item: The specific purchasable unit of a branded product or service.

Brand loyals (BLs): Those loyal to *our* brand or brand-item. In some product or service categories, BLs can be divided into Single-Brand Loyals and Multi-Brand Loyals.

Brand loyalty segmentation: Used to define the potential target audience groups. "Loyalty" is defined as the propensity to choose the brand-item *caused by* awareness of it and preference for it. There are five broad brand loyalty segments: Brand Loyals, Favorable Brand Switchers, Other-Brand Switchers, Other-Brand Loyals, and New Category Users. For a big brand, the manager can further segment these into 13 brand loyalty subgroups (see brand loyalty group definitions).

Brand personality approach: One way of achieving integrated marcoms (Cosmetic Integration is the other). Consists of identifying either (a) a concise and communicable set of personality traits as strategically desirable "properties" or (b) a personality *Archetype*, and attaching it (via marcoms) to the Master Brand or Sub-Brand. The trait set or archetype is then reflected in *all* marcoms right down to the brand-item level.

Brand positioning: An attempt to create and maintain a unique representation of the brand in customers' minds, a representation that is expected to stimulate choice of that brand. The representation (or "schema") is the Brand Identity positioned to a Target Customer type (T); into a Category Need (C); and onto a Key Benefit (B). This is the T-C-B Model of Positioning. Compare Key Schema.

Brand preference: Third of the Communication Effects (level 2 of how marcoms work). Brand preference can be measured as absolute, in which case it is equivalent to Brand Attitude, or relatively, which indicates preference for the brand over other brands.

Brand preference score: Output of numerical calculations from the I-D-U Matrix of ratings that, for each of the competing brands or brand-items (and an "ideal" one), measures Brand Preference. Because the score is "scale-less," it should be expressed as *percent of ideal*.

Brand preference tactics: These tactics execute and structure the Brand Emotions and Brand Benefit Claims needed to achieve the Brand Preference communication objective. The tactics are taken from the Rossiter-Percy-Bellman Grid.

Brand-prompted ad recall (BPAR): Demonstrates that an ad has been linked to the brand correctly during in-media processing. Can be Claimed or Proven recall. Leading tracking supplier Millward Brown uses the former in the well-known Awareness Index.

Brand recall: To teach the target customer to think of the brand or brand-item's Brand Identity (its name, or what it looks like sufficient to buy it) whenever the Category Need arises.

Brand-recall-boosted brand recognition: To teach the target customer to recall the brand *prior* to the point of purchase and then later to recognize it so as to find it *at* the point of purchase.

Brand recognition: To teach the target customer the Brand Identity – what the brand's *logo* or the brand-item's *package* looks like, or in the occasional case of auditory brand recognition, what the brand or brand-item's name sounds like – and what *category* it belongs to, that is, the Category Need.

Branding: Key benefit positioning for the *Master Brand* or *Sub-Brand*, rather than the brand-item. The branding benefit should be emotional: an Instinct, an Archetype, or an Emotional Selling Proposition.

Business magazines: Magazines whose editorial content covers business in general, not a particular industry.

But credible info: The creative tactic for the *second message* – which may be placed in separate marcoms – in a High-Involvement/Transformational ad. The subsequent message should first *remind* the prospect of the key Transformational benefit or benefits and then deliver the Informational benefits, where necessary, using High-Involvement/Informational tactics.

Campaign wearout: Positioning strategy is out of date, Media plan has slipped, or the Ads themselves are wearing out. See Advertising Wearout.

Canonical Expansion Model: Media Model that is almost as accurate as the Approximate Log-Linear Model, and is faster, even for large schedules.

Card-based loyalty program: Manufacturer's or retailer's promotion tactic recorded from either a third-party's or the retailer's charge card transactions designed to reward frequency or volume of purchase, or both.

Rewards are usually some type of discount on future visits or purchases or (the increasingly unusable) frequent-flyer points.

Carryover: MEF/c can remain effective beyond the cycle, c, and in this sense the ad or ads exhibit "carryover."

Category need: First of the Communication Effects (level 2 of how marcoms work) and is the target customer's acceptance that the *category* (the product or service in general) is necessary to remove or satisfy a perceived discrepancy between the customer's current motivational state and his or her desired motivational state. May arise as an effect in the customer's mind by naturally-occurring business or consumer circumstances or may be sold or reminded by marcoms.

Category need explicit: A tactic to increase Brand Recognition whereby the Category Need should be *mentioned* or *portrayed* in the ad *unless* it is immediately obvious (that is, unless it spontaneously comes to mind when the Target Customer sees or hears the Brand Identity).

Category-prompted ad recall (CPAR): In a Customer Tracking Survey. The recall task is directed by giving people the *product category* as the cue or prompt and asking them what ads they remember for *that category* of product or service. Then they are asked what *brand* was being advertised, if the brand was not mentioned spontaneously in their description of the recalled ad.

Celebrity: Person, human character, or animal character who is famous in the eyes of the *target audience*.

Celebrity presenter: A tactic to increase Brand Recall; the celebrity presenter increases attention to the ad which, if the presenter's role is executed so that the presenter interacts with the brand rather than swamping it, should increase recall of the brand.

Central me-too positioning: Benefit positioning strategy in which the brand-item claims to offer the same benefits as the Central brand-item and with a substantial price saving.

Central positioning: Benefit positioning usually adopted by the Market Leader, claiming that its brand-item delivers best on the *set* of benefits that meet the Category Need, including the short-cut assertion that it's the best overall in the category.

CESLIP presenter model (The): This model can be used to select a suitable presenter. CESLIP is an acronym for the six *potential* characteristics of the presenter: Celebrity status, Expertise, Sincerity, Likability, Ideal-Similarity, and Power. One of the characteristics is unconditional in that all presenters *must* have it: Expertise.

(The expertise must be Technical expertise for an Informational product or service and User expertise for a Transformational product or service.) The other characteristics depend on the Brand Awareness objective or the Brand Preference grid quadrant of the message and are thus *conditional* characteristics.

CHAID analysis: Cross-tabulating the current-period state of Ad Processing (yes-no) with the current-period state of Brand Communication effects (yes-no for *each* of them) and Action effects (yes-no) for successive steps in the customer response steps so as to examine the apparent causality of the campaign.

Change the choice rule: The I-D-U benefit positioning strategy of persuading customers to change their choice rule for the category so that the new rule favors our brand. Numerically, the new choice rule means a change in the importance (or desirability) weights, with some going to zero.

Cinema ad: Nowadays, a cinema or movie ad is a TV commercial shown before the movie starts – with the big screen and surround sound, they are blow-you-away ads and agency creatives and producers often put their best work into these commercials (many of which run only in cinemas, not on TV).

Closing the sale: The next to last stage of selling – asking directly for the order.

Color: A retail promotional stimulus that has large effects on store atmosphere (arousal, pleasantness) *and* beliefs about the retailer.

Communication: Comes from the Latin word *communicus* which means "common," and refers in the marcoms context to the establishment of a commonality – ideally, an identity – between the marketer's intended communication message and the customer's interpreted communication message (more particularly, between the marketer's *intended* Positioning of the brand and the customer's *perceived* Positioning of the brand).

Communication effects: Brand-based responses that the marcoms campaign is expected to create, increase, or reinforce in the prospective customer's mind. The five communication effects are Category Need, Brand Awareness, Brand Preference, Brand Action Intention, and Purchase Facilitation.

Communication objectives: Those Communication Effects that are *targeted* by the campaign. Communication objectives are selected from a set of *options* for each communication effect where, in the cases of Category Need, Brand Action Intention, and Purchase Facilitation, one option is to *omit* that communication effect as an objective.

Company-branded generic-need advertising: Generic-Need Ads dramatize a need rather than promote a product but the company's name in the ad suggests, to many consumers, that this company's product is best for meeting the need.

Company mission: The operational prescription for what you need to do to *accomplish* the Company Vision.

Company vision: An inspirational statement of what you expect to do with the company brand (the Corporate Brand).

Conformers: Those already doing the "good" behavior.

Consideration set: The set of brand-items seriously – that is, favorably – considered as alternatives for purchase. The prospective customer must (1) be aware of the brand and (2) have a positive, if tentative, preference for it, for it to be in his or her consideration set.

Contact coefficient: Fractional multiplier of Personal Influence. If it is greater than or equal to .25, you can drop 1 OTS from the MEF (reduce the required MEF by 1).

Content factors ratings (in the MJAT): Target audience decision-maker clearly addressed; category need (if an objective) appropriately reminded or sold; brand awareness tactics appropriate to the objective of brand recognition, brand recall, or both; brand preference tactics appropriate to low-involvement/informational, low-involvement/transformational, high-involvement/informational, or high-involvement/transformational; entry-ticket benefits apparent; purchase facilitation achieved; clear call to action (if direct-response ad); mandatory content.

Continuous tracking: A Customer Tracking Survey method in which small random samples of consumers or customers are selected for an interview from the potential target audience population on a *daily* or *weekly* basis, that is, near enough to "continuously," then the results are cumulated as moving averages (usually rolling 4-weekly) for reporting.

Conveyer (U.S. spelling; Conveyor is the usual British spelling): Remote (apparently incongruous) visual or wording that increases the effectiveness of the ad by starting in motion a sequence of four steps – Attention, Curiosity, Search, and Resolution.

Corpographic proxies: "Proxy" is a contraction of "an approximation" and in B-to-B marcoms it means using company or organizational descriptive measures (most often used are industry type and small, medium, and large firms) to try to identify the target audience that you really want, which should be a brand loyalty group or subgroup. Not recommended.

Corporate brand: Brand name of the company or organization (e.g., Canon, Gillette, The U.N.).

Corporate identity: The visual, verbal, and auditory signals that the company uses to identify itself to people.

Corporate image: The set of functional and emotional Benefit Beliefs and Type 1 and Type 2 Emotional associations connected to – and spontaneously elicited by – the Corporate Brand or Master Brand.

Corporate image advertising: Advertises the Corporate Brand or one of its Master Brands, rather than specific Brand-Items.

Corporate reputation: Corporate brand *preference*; it is the *overall* evaluation of the company and is composed by the Stakeholder from the subjective evaluative weighting and summing of the benefit beliefs and emotional associations (i.e., of the Corporate Image responses).

Cosmetic integration: One of the two strategies for integrated marketing communications (the other is integration by Brand Personality). Cosmetic Integration means that the ads and promotion offers across the entire line should share the "same look and feel." The desired effect is that the consumer notices immediately that it is an ad or offer from that brand but also that it is a new message for the brand-item.

Coupon: A voucher or certificate that entitles the buyer to a price reduction on the brand-item.

CPERP: A media schedule's cost, per percentage point of Effective Reach.

CPMT: A media schedule's cost, per thousand of the target audience.

Creative (The): The marcoms term for advertisements and also for the materials used to support promotion offers. (The creatives, plural, refers to the people in the agency who think up and produce the creative.)

Creative idea: Way of dramatizing the Key Benefit Claim. The ad is *built around* this component: the ad basically *is* the Creative Idea.

Creative strategy: Decisions made encompassing the Key Benefit Claim, the Creative Idea, Grid tactics, and Attention tactics.

Creative tactics (or Grid tactics): In-ad tactics designed to achieve the two universal campaign communication objectives of Brand Awareness and Brand Preference. In this book, the tactics are based on the Rossiter-Percy-Bellman Grid.

Creative target: The individual in a particular *decision role* to whom the advertising message or promotion offer is "addressed." That individual will be an Initiator, Influencer, Decider, Purchaser, or User – depending on where your brand-item's main problem is located in the decision stages of the BSM.

Credence goods: Products or services whose benefit delivery is difficult for the buyer to judge objectively, even after purchase.

Credit card stickers: The prominent display of pictorial logos of credit cards in retail stores, direct-response ads, catalogs, or Website ads makes customers *more willing to buy* the item as well as to *pay a higher price* for it.

Cross-media duplications: In Media Data: the extent of pairwise duplication between vehicles that come from different media *types*.

Curious disbelief: Precisely the reaction you want to the benefit claim(s) for a low-involvement/informational brand-item. Concept invented by J. C. Moloney. The prospective customer should think: "It can't *really* be that good, can it? I'd better try it and see."

Customer franchise-building (CFB): Description given to Promotions designed to contribute to long-run Brand Awareness and Brand Preference as well as induce immediate Action.

Customer response ad test (CRAT): Use in high-risk advertising situations (new product or new creative idea). In the CRAT, good-quality rough ads are pre-tested for response among *target customers* – a large sample of them (200 per ad) because you need reasonably statistically accurate results to decide whether to accept or reject the ad or have it revised and retested.

Customer response steps (The): Exposure → Ad or Promotion Processing → Brand Communication Effects → Target Audience Action. These are the four essential "gates" that the campaign must get through if the marcoms campaign is going to produce Sales. The four customer response steps also indicate the types of measures to be taken in Ad Testing (the last three) and Campaign Tracking (all four).

Customer tracking survey (CTS): Type of survey necessary when the manager wants to be sure that the advertising, and promotions, if used, are *causally contributing to sales.* Based on interviews with the total potential audience to measure Processing, Brand Communication Effects, and Action.

Database marketing: Capturing prospective customers' and current customers' contact details and purchase history in an electronic database and then "working" (analyzing and acting on) the database to target individuals for Trial, Repeat, or Purchase of the brand-item and of related brand-items.

Decrease a competitor's delivery: The I-D-U benefit positioning strategy of decreasing a competitor's perceived delivery on an important benefit (this means Explicit Comparison advertising).

Demographic proxies: "Proxy" is a contraction of "an approximation" and in B-to-C marcoms it means using a demographically described Media Target (most often used are gender and age demographics) to try to identify the target audience that you really want, which should be a brand loyalty group or subgroup. Not recommended.

De-resistance: The Personal Selling stage of "Handling objections and overcoming resistance." Not inevitable but very likely to arise in a "cold call" (first contact with prospect).

Differentiated positioning: Benefit positioning that should be adopted for each Follower brand-item (unless the manager chooses Central Me-Too Positioning). Differentiated Positioning refers to the attempt to establish relatively uniquely superior perceived delivery on at least one, and usually just one, *important* benefit.

Direct extreme verbal claim: One way of making an extreme benefit claim. Less common than extreme *implied verbal* or implied *visual* claims because if the claim is direct, the advertiser has to be able to prove it legally.

Direct mail: Type of Direct-Response Advertising that uses the country's postal system or, sometimes, private contractors, as letter distributors.

Direct-marketing promotion: A Promotion offer in a Direct-Response Ad.

Direct matching: Recommended method of selecting media vehicles for the media schedule by directly surveying a random sample of approximately 500 people from the target audience and asking them which TV programs they most often watch, which radio stations they listen to and when, which newspapers they read and how often, and the same for magazines, as well as cinema attendance, commuting pattern (for outdoor media vehicles), and Web usage.

Direct price-off: The most common Repeat-Purchase Promotion.

Direct-response advertising, also called Response advertising: Ads placed in mass media or in narrower, direct-to-customer media which attempt to be immediately mind turning so as to produce immediate action (a sales inquiry, retail visit, or purchase).

Direct selling: Face-to-face personal selling.

Direct-to-customer trial promotions: Product or Service Sampling, Bonus Packs, Direct Price-Offs, Coupons, Premiums, Warranties, or Rebates – offered by the manufacturer, not the retailer – to encourage Trial purchase or full Purchase.

Display: See Point-of-Purchase Display.

Disposition to purchase (or act): Indicated by the individual's "mental state" with regard to *two* communication effects – the individual has to have Brand Awareness *and* Brand Preference or Brand Action Intention.

Don't attack: An action objective (where the objective is *inaction*) for government regulatory and industry self-regulatory bodies and lobby groups, and sometimes for intimidation of competitors.

Double-duty ad: An ad in which a phone number or Website address (URL) is *added* to an *Awareness* Ad, to capture inquiries, thus making it an Awareness ad *and* a Direct-Response Ad.

Double jeopardy phenomenon: Brands (brand-items) with limited distribution have fewer people who buy them and because the brands are harder to find, they buy them less often, thus there is a double penalty due to limited distribution. Conversely, widely distributed brands have more buyers who buy those brands more often (a double benefit) because they are available in more stores both for trial and easy repeat. Of course, there's a reciprocal-causality cycle here: retailers stock brands because the brands are popular in the first place.

DR cable (pay) television: Direct-response ad next to or during a Pay-TV program.

DR email: Direct-response ad sent via email

DR fax: Direct-response ad sent to your facsimile machine (by the vendor's fax or by email).

DR newspaper: Direct-response ad in a newspaper.

DR radio: Direct-response ad on a radio station.

DR television: Direct-response ad next to or during a Free-to-Air TV program.

Econometric modeling, also called Sales modeling: Time-series regression analysis used to infer future input-output advertising-to-sales relationships from past ones.

Effective selling tactics: These fit the Stages of Selling and are too detailed to list here (see pp. 416–423 and then check the Glossary definitions of those bolded).

Emotion: Short-term "feeling" response generated during Processing of an ad or promotion offer that should be attached (by Learning) to the brand or brand-item such that when the brand or brand-item is encountered later on its own, the same feeling response emerges automatically. There are two types of emotions (emotional responses): Type 1 (Arousal, Positive Affect, and Negative Affect) which do *not* require the person to mentally label them; and Type 2, the more complex human emotions that *do* have to be labeled consciously by the person (e.g., Ecstasy, Delight, Nostalgia, Pity, Empathy).

Emotion-shift: Essential mechanism for portraying motives in ads (and it's in the a-b-e benefit claim chain). The emotion-shift is Negative-to-Mild-Positive (Informational motives) or Neutral-to-Extreme Positive (Transformational motives).

Empowerment: Feeling of confidence and self-assurance, closely followed by a feeling of freedom.

Entry-ticket benefits: Benefits that the target customer expects the brand-item to have as "par for the course" in that category, but needs to be explicitly shown or told that it *does* have.

Event marketing, also called Event sponsorship: Sponsorship of a one-off event such as a concert, or a celebrity's visit, that the advertiser hopes will attract a large number of target customer prospects. See also Sponsorship.

Event sponsorship: See Event Marketing.

Everyday low price (EDLP): Retail pricing strategy of setting the brand-item's price at a constant, attractively low price for relatively long periods that is still profitable for the retailer.

Experimental favorable brand switchers (Experimental FBSs): Favorable Brand Switchers early in the product category life cycle, who are still "trying out" brands (or brand-items), including ours. Really "their" life cycle with regard to the product category (they may be new to an established category).

Expert, sincere presenter: Effective creative tactic for High-Involvement/Informational Brand Preference – a spokesperson who has an immediately-perceived expertise "hook" and makes a sincere presentation.

Expert user, ideal-similar presenter: Any potential presenter to appear in High-Involvement/*Transformational* advertising or promotions for the brand-item must be pre-tested to be perceived as an Expert *User* and have Target Customer Ideal-Similarity. Both characteristics are difficult to evaluate without a pre-test and presenters who have been intuitively selected have a very high rate of failure.

Expertise hook: If the presenter is not a celebrity, then you have to briefly describe his or her expertise in the ad – usually via the presenter's *occupation*. The presenter must be a technical *expert* (Informational) or an expert *user* (Transformational). The addition of a presenter without this immediately perceived expertise hook to the advertised product or service runs the risk of *reducing* Purchase Intention for the product.

Explicit comparison: Where the competing brand or brand-item is identifiably shown or openly named in the ad, so that the competing brand definitely gets considered alongside your brand. Definitely use if yours is a small brand-item taking on a large competitor.

Exposure: The individual prospective customer's single exposure to the Media Vehicle, thereby providing an *opportunity* to pay Attention to the ad (an OTS).

Exposure ratio: The proportion of times each ad in a pool of ads for the campaign is inserted (better still, seen or heard by the average individual) in the Media Schedule.

Exterior store signage, Window displays, Interior store displays, On-shelf promotions: Point-of-*purchase* media.

Extreme positive emotion-shift: The Transformational emotion-shift mechanism. Starts with the assumption that the target customer will be in a fairly neutral emotional state when first attending to the message. Thereafter a strong positive emotion must be induced via the key benefit claim statement or portrayal. The target customer must feel the emotion shift and the end-emotion.

Eyeball analysis: For Customer Survey Tracking or Aggregate Tracking data, a statistically crude but diagnostically sufficient method of analysis for management of the campaign.

Face-to-face interviews: In a CTS, the interviewers have to show *ads* to respondents to measure Ad Processing, and show packs or logos to measure Brand Recognition, so face-to-face interviewing is best. Internet surveys (Web-based) may be used instead if the total potential audience is well represented by the at-home online population.

Favorable brand switchers (FBSs): Current customers for whom our brand is one of several acceptable brands. Can be divided into Experimental and Routine switchers depending on how experienced they are with the category as a whole.

Favorable other-brand loyals (Favorable OBLs): Not our customers; are strongly loyal to another brand, but would consider trying our brand.

Favorable other-brand switchers (Favorable OBSs): Not our customers at present; they do switch between brands, don't include ours, but would consider including it.

Fishbein extended model: Social psychological model that explains behavior (actions) as caused by the individual's attitude toward the act and his or her perceptions of whether relevant others endorse the act. Main persuasion model (even if implicit) in social marcoms.

Focus groups: These are small-group interviews in which semi-structured questions are asked by a moderator and open-ended answers are given, by target audience customers. Most widely used – and dangerously misleading – method of pre-testing ads. However, used for strategy development, focus groups can be extremely valid – depending on the ability of the analyst (who should do the moderating).

Follower: Any brand-item other than the market leader brand-item.

Follow-up: Final stage in Personal Selling. After the sale has been made or even if it has not, you should follow up by fax or email – but not with a personal call unless the customer calls you or you have something genuinely new to offer.

Free premium: A giveaway – always inexpensive merchandise.

Freeform layout: Store layout that is asymmetric, with varied displays and plenty of room to move between displays.

Frequency rule (The): For high *Frequency*, buy *multiple insertions* in a *few Non-competing, Strip* vehicles (those repeated daily or weekly).

Generic branding: Generic "no name" brands were typically made and put on the market by groups of smaller manufacturers who could not afford to advertise and therefore banded together to offer a clearly unadvertised low-price brand.

Goal: Objective made specific as to the magnitude to be achieved and the time period in which it is to be achieved.

Gray's theory: Biological-trait theory of personality highly applicable to social marcoms. Postulates that anxious individuals are most responsive to "no-go" signals (threatened punishment of the "bad" behavior) whereas impulsive individuals are most responsive to "go" signals (promised reinforcement of the "good" behavior).

Grid layout: Conventional row layout of store as in most supermarkets. Facilitates *routine* shopping behavior.

GRPs: Gross Rating Points. One GRP is achieved by a media vehicle that reaches 1% of the audience but at higher percentages GRPs confound Reach and Average Frequency. Definitely not recommended – for media planners or for managers.

Guarantee: See Warranty.

Handbills or flyers: Some local retailers invest in weekly door-to-door mailbox pamphlets which have the largest local household reach and command very high levels of Attention. The old name is "handbills" and the more recent name is "flyers."

Headline: There are two main types of headline for print ads – a Complete Headline, which includes the Brand Identity and the Key Benefit; or a Lead-in Headline, which promises the key benefit but doesn't tell you which brand delivers it and thus makes you want to read the body copy.

High-end retail selling: Requires specialized knowledge of the product category or service category acquired through sales training. But preselect trainees on attractive appearance, voice and speech quality, and social skill, because failed training is expensive!

High involvement: For those people who have not bought our brand or brand-item before or not bought in the category for a long time, and especially those who have previously been loyal to another brand or brand-item, the decision is classified as High Involvement, meaning that there is a personally substantial economic or psychosocial loss at stake should the customer make a poor choice.

High-involvement/informational: Brand Preference strategy for ads for a brand-item for which the target audience perceives that the choice is high risk and based on a negatively originated purchase motive.

High-involvement/transformational: Brand Preference strategy for ads for a brand-item *or brand* for which the target audience perceives the choice as *high risk* and the key benefit claim relies on a *positive-ending* purchase motive.

High-low pricing: Illegal but widely practiced pricing strategy whereby the retailer sets the original price at an artificially high level for a brief period and then discounts the item for a *long* period against the original price.

Home shopping: A promotion that appeals by *time saving* rather than monetary saving, as delivery costs make it more expensive to shop from home in most cases.

Human evaluative conditioning (HEC): How Transformational ads work to increase Brand Preference. The learning process (called "conditioning" because the consumer is passive – it happens automatically) involves a to-be-conditioned stimulus (the brand-item, or CS), immediately followed by another stimulus known to reliably elicit (unconditional stimulus, US) the Emotional response of Positive Affect (the unconditional response, UR) such that after repeated pairings of the first and second stimuli, the first stimulus (the brand-item) now elicits a Positive Affect response (the conditioned response, or CR). Human counterpart of Pavlovian or "classical" conditioning in lower animals but actually works better if the consumer realizes what's going on, and it is resistant to extinction after conditioning (unlearnable only by counterconditioning, that is from *interference*).

Ideal-similarity: For presenters of brands of products and services whose usage is *socially conspicuous*, assuming that the presenter has an expert-user hook, it helps for persuasiveness if the presenter is similar in appearance (and inferred personality) to the typical target customer's ideal self-image.

Identification: Feeling of reinforcement of one's ideal self-image with a Sensory Gratification end-state.

Imagery transfer: The *reverse* process to Priming. In Imagery Transfer, the visual or auditory images from the primary medium's "complete" ad are recalled during exposure to the secondary medium's "less complete" ad. Because imagery transfer is cross-media, make sure the media vehicles used have high target-audience overlap so that many of the same individuals see or hear both ads.

Impact scheduling: Reach pattern that provides at least three OTSs in one day, approximately every four weeks throughout the year, for an established FMCG brand-item.

Implicit comparison: Where the competing brand is not identified in the ad – the usual reference is to the "other brand" or "other brands" – but implicit comparison ads become *de facto* explicit comparison ads if consumers reliably mentally fill in the other brand's name when processing the message.

Implied extreme verbal claim: Uses a word or words with a strong connotative (emotional) meaning to make a claim that seems more extreme than the literal meaning.

Implied extreme visual claim: Visual claims can be metaphorical or literal. A visual conveyer can easily suggest an extreme level of a benefit or emotion metaphorically. Literal visuals can only make an extreme claim in broadcast ads (not print ads) via a demonstration. Advertisers must, in demonstrations, show only what a *typical user* could expect to obtain by way of product or service performance but they can show the *peak* performance obtained by the typical user.

Impulse purchase: A purchase triggered entirely by the package and its display at the point of purchase. If you have never seen this item before, the Communication Effects for it (the whole five) get acquired in the first exposure, or, if you have seen the item before, then communication effects 1, 4, and 5 get acquired in one exposure, and 2 and 3 get reinforced. Either way, you make the Purchase immediately.

Increase delivery: The I-D-U benefit-positioning strategy of increasing our brand's perceived delivery on an important benefit – a benefit which is, or could be made, unique to our brand.

Increase importance: The I-D-U benefit-positioning strategy of increasing the perceived importance of a benefit on which our brand already delivers uniquely.

Individual-group-individual (I-G-I Method): A method of brainstorming in which individuals individually generate Creative Ideas; then meet as a group to develop the ideas; then split as individuals again to rate the developed ideas independently.

Industry-specific positioning statement (ISPS): Personal Selling tactic used in the Approach stage. The salesperson tailors the Short Positioning Statement to the prospect's industry and writes it down beforehand.

Inferior benefit: The brand-item may be perceived as having *inferior delivery* on a particular, important benefit. The inferior benefit – assuming it is important – is traded off (compensated) or omitted (risky if important, and in some cases illegal) in the brand-item's marcoms.

Informational: Label given to ads in which the buying motive for the advertised brand or brand-item is *negatively originated*. The negatively originated motives are Problem Removal, Problem Avoidance, Incomplete Satisfaction, Mixed Approach-Avoidance, and Normal Depletion.

Insertion: The placement of an ad in a media vehicle.

Instinct: Defined by psychologist William McDougall (in 1908) as "an . . . innate . . . disposition which determines its possessor to perceive, and to pay attention to, objects of a certain class, to experience an emotional excitement of a particular quality upon perceiving such an object, and to act in regard to it in a particular manner, or, at least, to experience an impulse to such action." Wordy old-day definition but still valid, in our opinion, for contemporary marcoms.

Internal corporate image communications: Corporate image advertising and personal selling inside the organization.

Internet ads: See Online ads.

Introductory price allowance: Straight reduction in the selling price of a new brand-item to the retailer.

Invest in: An action objective for traders on the stock market if the company is publicly listed.

Key benefit: The emotional (possibly Instinctual or Archetypal) or functional benefit that the brand or brand-item will emphasize in its marcoms. Answers the hypothetical question asked by a prospective customer, "What does *this* brand (or brand-item) offer?"

Key benefit claim (KBC): Defined as an accurate, persuasively sufficient, succinct statement of the Key Benefit. May be explicitly stated as the campaign's headline or tagline or stated for internal use *only*, for the purpose of generating the Creative Idea, and then *implied* in the campaign. The KBC is the first thing that needs to be "created" for the ad. *One* KBC has to be selected.

Key benefit prompt: In the headline, body copy, or tagline of an ad, it reveals to the prospective customer what the brand or brand-item's key benefit is.

Key schema: Uses the C and B of the T-C-B Positioning model – assumes you are addressing the Target Customer and shows the key directional associations between the Brand Identity and the Category Need (for Brand Awareness) and the Brand Identity and the Key Benefit (for Brand Preference). The Key Schema is reproduced on the book's back cover because it is of paramount importance for marcoms planning.

Largest competitor (LC): See Market Leader.

Learning: A response in Processing necessary for the formation and strengthening of Brand Awareness (Brand Recognition, Brand Recall) and for the consumer to attach Brand Benefit Beliefs and Brand Emotions (which may be an Instinct or Archetype) to the brand or brand-item. Also see Visual Iconic Learning; Verbal Echoic Learning; Verbal Paired-Associates Learning; Human Evaluative Conditioning; and Operant (or Instrumental) Learning.

Leverage calculations: Method of assessing Target Audience groups' or subgroups' potential based on the expected increase in the monetary profit from sales to that group or subgroup (if the marcoms campaign successfully persuades them) divided by the monetary cost of the campaign. Leverage is a ratio and should be greater than 1.0. If 1.0 or less, don't target that group or subgroup. In social marcoms, the cold judgment of the monetary value of life and health has to be made and the experts put these values very high (see Chapter 18) which makes the leverage of social marcoms campaigns look good when they're not (it's the *incremental* value *caused* by the campaign that should count).

Likability: If and only if the presenter has an expertise hook, it helps for persuasiveness if the presenter is also likable.

Local retail advertiser: As distinct from a national or regional retail advertiser (though *they* can run local ads too, we mean a retailer who sells in one area only).

Long-form positioning statement: Detailed written statement of the positioning strategy for the brand or brand-item that incorporates the T-C-B, I-D-U, and a-b-e models.

Low involvement: The decision by the target audience customer to purchase *our* brand or brand-item on the *next* purchase occasion is classified as Low Involvement if only a small economic or psychosocial loss is at stake should the customer make a poor choice.

Low-involvement/informational: Applies to a brand-item whose purchase, for the customer, represents a *low degree of risk*, with the primary purchase motivation (in the key benefit claim) being *negatively originated*.

Low-involvement/transformational: Applies to a brand-item whose purchase, for the customer, represents a *low degree of risk*, with the primary purchase motivation (in the key benefit claim) being *positive-ending*.

Management judgment ad test (MJAT): Fully structured pre-test (questionnaire based on the Creative Brief) in which 6 to 10 *managers* systematically evaluate rough ads for the campaign, including rough versions of promotions and other marcoms material. An MJAT pre-test should be used prior to *every* campaign.

Manufacturer's coupon: Coupon certificate distributed by the manufacturer and can be redeemed direct to the manufacturer or at any retail store that carries the item.

Market leader, also called Largest competitor (LC): Brand-item that has the largest unit market share in the market (in the Category-Need category).

Market share: Your brand-item's current rate of sales as a percentage of everyone else's brand-items' sales in that product or service market – actually, in the *Category Need* category (managers can fool themselves by arbitrarily specifying the "market" to make their brand-item look good). Also, check that it's *unit* market share because units are what you sell and dollar market share obscures sales performance due to price differences.

Marketing audit: The first research step to determine the cause of a sales decline during the marcoms campaign. Check for changes in your brand's marketing mix or in a large competitor's marketing mix and check for changes in consumer or customer values.

Marketing communications (marcoms): Marketer-originated messages, placed in various media, their purpose being to sell the brand by showing it, saying things about it, or both, in a manner that establishes the marketer's desired Positioning for the brand in the minds of Target Customers.

Masked ad recognition (MAR): In Customer Tracking Survey: the ad is shown or played with the pack, logo or brand name blanked out (masked) and then respondents are asked to name, that is, to recall the brand (the brand-item).

Master archetypes: Carol Pearson's typology that classifies the 12 main archetypes (Jung identified more) loosely but reasonably in terms of whether the brand's best option for benefit positioning is to make it be seen as an "order keeper" versus a "change agent" (the vertical dimension) and, cutting across this dimension, as "self-oriented" versus "group-connected" (the horizontal dimension). See Chapter 4, p. 66, Figure 4.1.

Master brand: One of the main brands in the company's or organization's portfolio. May be the Corporate Brand if only one.

Mathematical ability: The single best test for hiring Regular Retail Selling employees (correlates highly with I.Q. and the score should be at least 50% correct on the test we provide on p. 404). Necessary even with the advent of electronic scanner cash registers.

Media budget: The contemporary term is Adspend and is the amount spent to place (insert) the ads and offers in the Media Vehicles. The term Total Adspend we use to mean Adspend *plus* the cost of the creative and the cost of any research that is done to design and evaluate the campaign.

Media data: Specific media vehicle ratings – the estimated number of people reached by each vehicle. Usually broken out by gender and age groups, sometimes by household income, and, for FMCG advertisers, by primary grocery shoppers. In Direct Matching, the breakout is by Target Audience groups or subgroups. The media data may also include media *Duplications*, which are the overlap of people reached by the vehicle over occasions and the overlap of people between the vehicle and the other vehicles that are being considered for the schedule.

Media models: Media Models input media data (consisting of vehicle-audience ratings and duplications) and output an estimate of the entire distribution of Exposures (or OTSs), that is, the proportion of people exposed to none, just one, just two, and up to all the insertions in the schedule. *Media Mania*, the software on the book's Website, developed by P. Danaher, includes three media models: Beta Binominal, Approximate Log-Linear, and Canonical Expansion.

Media plan audit: Second research step to determine the cause of a sales decline during the marcoms campaign. The ads may be working but media vehicle audiences may have changed (a reach problem) or the real MEF/c is greater than what you estimated when you bought the media schedule (a frequency problem).

Media schedule: Spells out the *number* and *timing* of the Insertions in the Media Vehicles used in the media plan. But it is just the inputted Insertions, not the outputted Exposures (or OTSs).

Media strategy: Decisions encompassing Primary and Secondary Media Types, the Reach Pattern, Minimum Effective Frequency per advertising cycle, and the Media Schedule.

Media target: Description (almost always demographic or corpographic) that hopefully covers the target audience groups or subgroups and preferably does so without much wastage on non-target customers. Described demographically or corpographically because that's the traditional way of describing the audiences of Media Vehicles.

Media type selection: Choice of a Primary Medium (one, usually, but sometimes, for a widely-selling brand-item, two or three Primary Media), and one or two Secondary Media, if needed, for the campaign. Media Types are broad categories (Free-to-air TV, Pay TV, Radio, etc.), rather than specific programs, timeslots, locations, or publications, which are Media Vehicles.

Media vehicles: Specific publications, programs, timeslots, locations, etc., in which an ad or ads (or a promotion offer) can be placed in a Media Schedule.

Minimum effective frequency (MEF/c): Asserts that an individual prospective customer has to be exposed to a brand's advertising a certain minimum number of times within an Advertising Cycle, c, in order for the advertising to influence the customer's action – specifically to maximize the individual's *disposition* to act.

Mnemonic device: A prompt to rehearse the Category Need → Brand Name association to increase Brand Recall. Can be visual or verbal or musical such as a jingle (only verbal or musical in a radio ad).

Mobile-viewed outdoor ads: The ad is moving or the viewer is moving – thus "mobile viewed." These have very limited processing time and therefore the illustration in the ad must signal quickly what the *category* is, and the copy must identify the brand and the key benefit briefly (often by employing a Complete headline with no other copy).

Moderately favorable prior attitude: A tone of *encouragement* should be adopted in the ad.

Multiattribute model (I-D-U Model): A model for use by the *manager* to find an effective "way in" to creating, increasing, or maintaining Brand Preference by the target customer.

Multi-brand loyals (Multi-BLs): Current customers who buy and *prefer* two or three brands, including ours, in the category.

Multi-purchase contest: A contest requires of participants some degree of skill in order to win the prize, but you have to buy multiple units of the brand-item to enter.

Multi-purchase premium: Usually a self-liquidating premium received at the end of a string of purchases or a series of them received one per purchase or visit.

Multi-purchase sweepstake: A sweepstake is based purely on chance and requires no skill to enter, but you have to buy multiple units of the brand-item to enter.

Multiple benefit claims: High Involvement/Informational messages almost always employ multiple benefit claims. Use only as many as necessary to convince the prospect to buy (never more than seven and don't "pad" with weak claims or you'll dilute the message effect). One claim, usually the first, should be a capstone or summary benefit claim, then order claims from most to less unique. If direct-response, save one important claim till last.

Music: A retail promotional stimulus that has large effects on store atmosphere (arousal, pleasantness) *and* beliefs about the retailer.

Mystery ad: Can be either Informational or Transformational. The Mystery Ad format uses the same respective interest pattern as an Informational or Transformational ad but *omits the initial brand identification*, identifying the brand only at the *end*. Works well for new products but not for established ones. Be sure to apply the Two-Second Exposure Rule for the brand identification at the end (too brief an exposure of the brand name or logo is a common error made in Mystery Ads).

National brands, also called Name brands: Brand-items that carry the brand name of a national or international manufacturer.

Need arousal: Second of the Customer Decision Stages (level 3 of how marcoms work). The prospective customer acknowledges that the general product or service type (category) could solve his or her problem or increase his or her positive emotional state.

Negative new category users (Negative NCUs): Have heard about the category and are uninterested, unimpressed, or actively dislike the category. Whatever the reason, they will be a tough if not impossible sell. In social marcoms, if the new category is a beneficial health or safety program, you are ethically obliged to try to persuade them, that is, to include them in the target audience.

Negative prior attitude: The lead-in to the message should acknowledge this head on, and the body of the message should, of course, attempt to convert this to a *positive* attitude.

Negative punishment: Decreases the behavior because the behavior now *fails* to turn on a previously received *positive reinforcer*.

Negative reinforcer: Increases the behavior because the behavior turns *off* an aversive consequence.

Negative-to-mild-positive emotion-shift: The Informational emotion-shift mechanism. Starts with a negative emotion (the problem) and ends with a mild positive emotion (the solution). The target customer only has to recognize, not actually feel, the emotions for this shift.

Neuro-linguistic programming (NLP): NLP is the ability to "read" and be sensitive to the other's mind and is based on the theory that individuals use either a visual person, an auditory person, or a kinesthetic person in their habitual mode of information processing.

Neutral other-brand loyals (Neutral OBLs): Currently loyal to another brand. Not our customers; have not heard of our brand (or brand-item) or know nothing about it.

Neutral other-brand switchers (Neutral OBSs): Currently switch between other brands. Not our customers; have not heard of our brand (or brand-item) or know nothing about it.

Neutral prior attitude: The introduction in the ad should be reassuring and not extreme or confrontational.

New benefit: The I-D-U benefit positioning strategy of adding a new benefit – if technically feasible to do – on which our brand delivers uniquely.

New category users (NCUs): Not our customers – in fact at present they are not even customers of the category. Their potential must be assessed as *new* users, by classifying them as Positive NCUs, Unaware NCUs, or Negative NCUs.

New line fee, also called a Slotting allowance: A straight cash payment to the retailer, or sometimes a proportion of the stock donated free, so that the retailer will stock the product – at least for a short trial period of several months.

Newspaper ad: On-page or insert ad in a newspaper.

NLP matching: Tactic used in the Benefit Presentation stage of Personal Selling, requiring detection of the target customer's preferred NLP mode and then describing the benefits of the product or service in this mode predominantly.

Not in the market: First of the Customer Decision Stages (level 3 of how marcoms work). The prospective customer as yet, or at present, has no need for the product or service category.

Objective: Broad directional aim. In contrast with a Goal, no magnitude is specified and the time period may or may not be specified.

Off-invoice promotion: When the manufacturer offers the retailer a price reduction on an established brand-item, the price discount is called an Off-Invoice Promotion.

Olfactory cue (odor): A retail promotional stimulus that can elicit type 1 and sometimes type 2 emotions.

On consignment: The retailer pays the manufacturer only if, and after, the product is sold; if it's not sold within an agreed time period, the manufacturer takes the product back or instructs the retailer to dispose of it.

Online ads: These ads come in a number of forms, including Permission emails, Spam emails, Web banner ads, and Websites.

Online catalogs: A common form of Website ad.

Online home shopping: Made possible by interactive TV and PC ads (on Websites).

Operant or instrumental learning: How Informational ads work to increase Brand Preference. The learning process involves a discriminative stimulus or "signal" (the brand-item), a mental action response (brand action intention), and a reinforcer promised if you take that action (a "negative" reinforcer in that it solves the "problem").

Optimizing the media schedule: Scheduling Insertions in various media vehicles so that they will, in combination, produce the largest Effective Reach per Advertising Cycle, while keeping within the Media Budget.

Order of measures on a customer tracking survey: Screening questions (potential and actual category users), category need, CPAR, brand recall, brand recognition, BPAR, action, brand action intention, brand preference, brand emotions, brand benefit beliefs, ad recognition, ad recognition frequency, target audience classification questions, direct-matching questions.

Other-brand loyals (OBLs): Not our customers; are strongly loyal to another brand. With regard to our brand, however, they may be Favorable, Neutral, or Unfavorable.

Other-brand switchers: Not our customers; they switch between other brands but not ours. However, can be divided into Favorable, Neutral, and Unfavorable with regard to our brand.

OTS: Opportunity to See (or hear or read) the ad. Plural: OTSs.

Out-of-home advertising: See Outdoor advertising.

Outdoor advertising, also called Out-of-Home Advertising: Ads on outdoor, indoor, or in-vehicle sites.

Overclaim transformational benefits: "Hyperclaimed" _transformational_ benefits in an ad for High-Involvement/ Transformational products and services. Effective in large part because the hyperclaims influence the _public image_ of the item among those who may never experience it and thereby not have an opportunity to discount the hyperclaims. This inflated yet accepted public image then raises the buyer's own preference rating of the brand-item to a higher level than it would otherwise have been.

Overclaiming: What the advertiser should do with _Transformational_ benefits, in both Low-Involvement and High-Involvement ads.

Own brand(s): See Store Brand(s).

Packaging, Calendars, Product containers, Service stickers, Recipe or do-it-yourself books or pamphlets: Point-of-_use_ media.

Panel survey: A Customer Tracking Survey method in which the _same_ consumers are interviewed in the benchmark (pre-campaign) wave and in each successive (during campaign) wave. This allows _causality_ to be established at the individual consumer or customer level.

Paralogic: Frequently employed to imply an extreme claim, explicit or inferred, as the _conclusion_ to an apparently logical argument. Usually set up by separate sentences or clauses but can also be set up by a sequence of visuals.

Permission emails: Recipient has given prior permission (usually by registering on the Website) for the vendor to send these. About two-thirds are actually opened by the recipient.

Personal influence: Word of mouth – or visual influence, sometimes called word-of-eye – for products or services that are socially consumed.

Personal selling: Umbrella term that covers Direct Selling (face-to-face) and Telemarketing (on the phone).

Personalization: A tactic to increase Brand Recall whereby a personal connection with the brand is encouraged by using personal words (especially first-person "I" or "We" but also second-person "You") in the tagline.

Picture content: We identify 10 types of pictorial content that will increase attention to the ad: incongruous (remote conveyor); danger-suspense; eyes (direct gaze); baby; erotic; celebrity; beautiful scene or object; cultural icon; bright color; simple object on white space.

Piecemeal comparison: Compares the focal brand (or brand-item) with _several_ other brands on a _different_ attribute each time, selecting those attributes on which the focal brand is superior to the particular other brand. Tactic identified by L. Warlop.

Point-of-decision (P-O-D) media: These are _secondary_ media – they cannot be used as primary because they cannot generate Brand Awareness _before_ the purchase decision.

Point-of-purchase (POP) display, also known as a Point-of-sale (POS) display or simply a Display: Retailer's promotion, though usually provided by and largely or wholly paid for by the manufacturer, that gives physical (and thus visual) prominence to a brand-item and increases the probability of the consumer's Attention. The Display should include a Price-Off but is not legally required to.

Point-of-sale (POS) display: See Point-of-Purchase Display.

Positive new category users (Positive NCUs): Have heard about the category and are favorably disposed toward it but have not yet made a trial purchase of any brand-item in the category.

Positive punishment: Decreases the behavior because the behavior turns *on* an aversive consequence.

Positive reinforcement: Increases the behavior because the behavior turns *on* an appetitive or rewarding consequence.

Power: Effective characteristic for the presenter of a fear appeal message. Authoritative-*looking* or, in voice-overs, authoritative-*sounding*. The Powerful presenter can be a Real People Presenter or a Celebrity, though a celebrity should be used when Brand Recall is an objective.

PR: Literally the abbreviation for Public Relations activities but includes (positive) Publicity issued by the company or organization – all called "PR."

Presenter approach (The): The presenter is the *perceived source* of the message. The Presenter Approach is properly described as such in *advertising* only when the presenter dominates in the message – either as the person showing or speaking the message or undeniably endorsing its content.

Price-off promotions: Retailer's promotion tactic of offering a temporary reduction in the customary price of a brand-item. Can be implemented in Feature Ads, Flyers, Coupons, Shelf Tags – or Direct (unannounced).

Primary medium or media: A Primary Medium is the medium capable of delivering *all* of the communication objectives of the campaign. Up to three may be employed for a big brand or brand-item.

Primes: The high reach, low frequency cycle or cycles before a seasonal peak in the Seasonal Priming reach pattern.

Priming: Teaser campaigns make use of a processing mechanism known as Priming, whereby the incomplete first message motivates the audience, via *curiosity*, to process the second message. This is completely overt priming, not Subliminal Affective Priming. The Chrysler Crossfire ad in Chapter 1 was an example. The second-message (full ad) has just appeared in Australia but too late to include in the book. U.S. readers probably saw it a while ago – especially those "in the market" for a new car.

Print advertising: Ads distributed by direct mail, or in newspapers, magazines, directories, outdoor, business publications, flyers, calendars, or on the Web.

Processing: Collective term for the responses at level 1

of how marcoms work. Processing responses occur during exposure to each ad or promotion offer and again if the same ad or promotion offer is seen or heard again. The responses in Processing are Attention responses, Learning responses, Emotion responses, and, if the ad or offer poses a high-risk (High-Involvement) brand choice, Acceptance responses.

Product or service representation: Visual or verbal identification of the brand or brand-item in an ad.

Product placement: Really a brand or brand-item placement since the placed product has to be branded to be of any PR value to the company (though an exception is industry generic placement, such as smoking depicted in movies and magazines, and sometimes on TV, or visible use of condoms in movies or sometimes on TV). Represents an attempt at persuasion without the recipient's guaranteed understanding that such an attempt is being made.

Profit: Can be tracked directly by substituting dollar *contribution* for dollar sales revenue, per period, and then subtracting the marcoms expenditure per period.

Promotion strategy: Decisions encompassing the target audience for the promotion (whom you want to receive the offer) and the type of promotion (the mechanism of incentive to act now).

Promotions: Comes from the Latin verb *promovere* which means to "move forward or advance," indicating that the aim of promotions is to produce immediate purchase of the brand. Promotions offer an incentive to *act now*.

Prospecting: Identifying prospective customers to be approached.

Public relations: See PR.

Publicity: These days, subsumed under the term "PR" even if it originated outside the company or organization.

Purchase: Fourth of the Customer Decision Stages (level 3 of how marcoms work). The physical acts of acquiring and paying for the brand-item.

Purchase facilitation: Fifth of the Communication Effects (level 2 of how marcoms work). Necessary for some high-risk product or service choices so that the customer can act on the Brand Action Intention and complete the Purchase (or other targeted behavior).

Quasi-causal analysis: In a Customer Tracking Survey: achieved with Continuous Tracking data by Eyeball Analysis.

Racetrack boutique layout: Store layout that is a complex design consisting of *semi*-separate display areas connected by almost a *maze* of paths so that shoppers frequently unexpectedly come across a department they did not plan to visit.

Radio commercial: Radio ad. Pre-recorded or announcer-read live.

Random duplication: The assumption (a very accurate one) that vehicle duplication *across media types* is equal to the product of the ratings of the two vehicles no matter what these vehicles are.

Rapport: Personal Selling tactic largely determined by paraverbal stimuli rather than literal verbal stimuli and achieved by graduate convergence of speech rate and, if you are skilled, by NLP matching.

Ratcheting strategy (The): The strategy, invented by W. Moran, of scheduling a cycle of advertising to precede each promotion period – that is, to run promotions only after advertising cycles. The ad reminds customers of the brand-item's benefit(s), increasing its Value Equity, and makes the promotion work better because it is then seen as a better-value deal.

Rational approach (The): Method of persuasion in which Key Benefit is a functional performance benefit and the Key Benefit Claim is a Rational Selling Proposition (RSP). Correct approach for an Informationally-motivated brand or brand-item (bought to satisfy one of the negatively originated motives).

Reach and frequency rule (The): For high Reach *and* high Frequency, buy multiple insertions in a moderate number of reasonably big vehicles, especially *Strip* vehicles, that are *Competing*.

Reach pattern: Controls the degree and timing of *individual continuity* of the messages in the marcoms campaign. Some Reach Patterns require *high* continuity to individuals, whereas others require *little* or *none*. These *strategic* differences in the way reach is to be distributed cannot be represented by the calendar of ad insertions (which may include promotion insertions) that the ad agency or media agency gives you.

Reach rule (The): For high *Reach*, buy *many Competing* vehicles and place *one or only a small number of ads* in each vehicle.

"Real people" presenter: Use a presenter who is a "real person" (not an "artificial" person, i.e., a Celebrity) if you know your ad is highly attention-getting and you can find a technical expert or user expert who is not perceived as a celebrity by the target audience. This will cost you a great deal less than a celebrity.

Realism curved: A tactic for increasing Brand Recognition – the logo or pack photo should be realistic, have some natural curvature, be highly but not perfectly symmetrical and balanced, and have some internal repetition. If color is possible, which it usually is, choose a distinctive color.

Refutational approach (The): Known in personal selling as the "Yes . . . but" approach – you first acknowledge the objection, and then counter it. Use in a High-Involvement/Informational ad if you know the target audience has a well-known objection to the product or service category or brand-item.

Regular retail selling: This is *over-the-counter* selling to *consumers* as customers and called "regular" because the salespeople are selling low-tech products or services.

Remote conveyer model (RC model): A very effective model for generating Creative Ideas for ads. The RC Model has three elements – the Conveyer, the Product or Service Representation, and the Key Benefit Prompt.

Repeat-purchase promotion: Any promotion offer intended to increase the rate of repeat purchase of the brand-item (e.g., Next-Purchase Coupon, Multiple-Purchase Premium or Contest or Sweepstakes) or more units *this* time (quantity Price-Off or Bonus Pack).

Response advertising: See Direct-response advertising.

Retail atmosphere: Internal sensory environment of a store or reception area or office. Encoded immediately by customers in terms of two (type 1) emotional dimensions – Pleasantness (or Affect – Positive or Negative) and Arousal.

Retail catalogs: Books of the retailer's products or services, hard copy or electronic.

Retail feature ads: Retailer's promotion tactic of selecting half a dozen or so brand-items from the entire stock and putting them in an ad with Price-Offs on each, thus these items are "featured" in the ad.

Retailer's promotions: Promotions initiated by the retailer to increase the number of visitors to the store; increase the profit return from the total product or service category, including profit from the retailer's own brand or brands; or to clear stock to make space for new items.

Returns: The manufacturer agrees to buy back the retailer's unsold quantities of the product.

Reverse-wedge/PI pattern: Most appropriate for the introduction of a new *Social Approval* motive product or service, this reach pattern targets innovators on the first cycle or two then broadens to the mass market in which many of the innovators become opinion leaders and publicize the product via Personal Influence – Word of Mouth or "Word of Eye."

Rhetorical "check" end-question: Encourages the audience to accept the key benefit claim by mentally answering the question affirmatively (e.g., "Aren't you glad you use Dial?"). Can be used in ads in any medium but especially effective in a radio ad. Pre-test to make sure most do answer affirmatively!

Rossiter-Percy-Bellman grid: The Rossiter-Percy-Bellman Grid is a 6-cell grid, consisting of the Creative Tactics for *two* types of Brand Awareness (Brand Recognition and Brand Recall), and *four* types of Brand Preference (Low-Involvement/Informational, Low-Involvement/Transformational, High-Involvement/Informational, and High-Involvement/Transformational).

Rough ad: An ad (or a promotion offer) produced at low cost in pre-final form: a TV animatic (sequence of frames, videotaped, with the actual audio track); a finished radio ad (low cost in any case); a print ad mocked up on a PC with a realistic sketch or borrowed visual and the final headline, main copy, and brand identification). If it's Transformational, use good production (easy these days), especially for Sensory Gratification products.

Routinized favorable brand switchers (Routinized FBSs): Favorable Brand Switchers late in their product category life cycle; their switching behavior can be expected to persist.

Sales: Purchases per time period (thus rate) of units of the product or service. Sometimes given as dollar sales, as distinct from unit sales. Unit sales allow a clearer evaluation of performance.

Sales modeling: See Econometric Modeling.

Sales promotions: See Promotions.

Salesforce promotions: Sales commissions, bonus payments, or non-cash rewards such as frequent-flyer points (air miles) designed to encourage the salesperson to sell more or faster.

Schroer's method: Very good way to decide Adspend by region for a multi-regional brand-item. Budget in each region is varied to attack, defend, maintain, or retreat, depending on what the largest competitor in each region is doing with its share of voice in relation to its share of market.

Search and evaluation: Third of the Customer Decision Stages (level 3 of how marcoms work). The prospective customer looks for alternatives at the brand-item level and evaluates them.

Seasonal priming pattern: Reach pattern suited to products and services whose sales are characterized by one, and sometimes two or three, large *seasonal peaks*. Sort of "pre-announced Fad" pattern with one fad per season.

Secondary media: The purpose of employing a Secondary Medium or two (rarely more) Secondary Media is to boost a *particular* communication effect that is an objective of the campaign.

Self-liquidating premium: An expensive additional product or service for which the customer sends money with the proof of purchase of the original brand-item, enough money to cover the marketer's costs of the premium's purchase and delivery, while the price the customer pays is well below the premium's normal retail price.

Service stickers: Opportunities for post-purchase advertising of services.

Shifting-reach pattern: Reach pattern suited to products and services with a long purchase cycle and a *short* decision time. On each ad cycle, the reach is shifted to a new subset of the target audience and starts again after all subsets have been zapped with MEF.

Shopping bags and product containers: Opportunities for post-purchase advertising of products.

Short fad pattern: A new product reach pattern in which you need to get your brand-item's ads in early, during the *introduction* stage of the fad life cycle, and this calls for broad Reach of the target audience and high Frequency.

Short positioning statement: Very brief statement (sufficient, and better than no explicit statement, for developing the Creative) of the positioning strategy for the brand or brand-item, and based on the T-C-B model – "To target customers (T), brand X is the brand of category need (C), that provides key benefit (B)."

Silence: A closing-the-sale tactic in Personal Selling, used if you sense that the prospect is ready to buy: say nothing and let the prospect volunteer the decision.

Sincerity: Necessary in presentation when using a "real people" presenter. Can be stage-managed in the ad.

Single-brand loyals (Single-BLs): Current customers who buy our brand or brand-item on *most* purchase occasions. The incidence of single-brand loyals depends on the exact cutoff used to operationalize "most occasions."

Six-step marcoms planning approach: The sequence of planning steps followed in this book. The steps are Brand Positioning, Campaign Objectives, Creative Strategy, Promotion Strategy, Media Strategy, and Campaign Management.

Slotting allowance: See New Line Fee.

Small audience B-to-B: Business-to-Business advertiser with distribution covering less than 50% of the nation. Usually advertise in Business Magazines, Trade Publications (which are industry specific) or by Direct Mail, depending on *how small* a target audience the advertiser has.

Small business selling: Owner-managed business, usually, and the salesperson may be the owner or, often, a family member.

Social marcoms campaign: A mass-media or direct-response media campaign that has the de-marketing of the "bad" or the promotion of the "good" as its primary purpose.

Social marketing: De-marketing of government-judged "bad" products, services and behaviors and the promotion of government-judged "good" products, services and behaviors. The de-marketing or the promotion may be attempted by the government, industry bodies, public interest organizations, or commercial companies!

Social skill: A desirable hiring factor in personal selling, which should be predictive of add-on sales and customer satisfaction, for Regular Retail salespeople, Trade salespeople, and High-End Retail salespeople.

Spam (unsolicited) emails: Banned in the European Union and have been severely limited by opt-out legislation in the U.S.A. A Spam email has only about half the probability of being opened that a Permission email has (recipients open about a third of Spams).

Speech rate convergence: Personal selling tactic of adjusting your speech rate to that of the listener but slightly faster, and doing so gradually rather than obviously and abruptly.

Speech sampling: Recording and analyzing several minutes of the prospective customer's speech to detect the prospect's NLP mode. Not legal without the other's consent, so the salesperson has to speech sample "on the run."

Sponsorship: Marcoms arrangement in which the advertiser donates cash or privileges to a person, team, or series in return for Publicity. The advertiser can also advertise the sponsorship.

Stages of selling: Prospecting (optional), Approach, Benefit Presentation, De-Resistance, Closing, Follow-Up.

Stakeholders: Different types of customer. The main types are Suppliers, Distributors, Investors, Regulators, prospective *and* current Employees, and End-Customers.

Stationary-viewed outdoor ads: The ad and the viewer are stationary with respect to each other (the ad could be inside a moving public transport vehicle). These have virtually unlimited processing time and are like a *newspaper ad* for High-Involvement brand preference and are usually Informational.

Status: The emotion portrayed in an ad of feeling pride in *oneself* as opposed to pride about something external.

Store atmosphere: See Retail Atmosphere.

Store brands: The store's private label brands (a confusing American technical term) or own-named brands (U.K. and clear, as is the term Store Brands itself).

Store layout: Retailer's promotion tactic of arranging the "furniture" and its spacing to facilitate the flow of customer traffic to all areas of the store.

Sub-brand: Brand name coupled with the Master Brand name.

Subliminal affective priming: A variety of Human Evaluative Conditioning (HEC) in which positive or negative affective stimuli too subtle to be consciously noticed nevertheless get attached in the customer's mind to the primed object (e.g., a brand) so that the brand as a conditioned stimulus (CS) elicits the corresponding Type 1 Emotion as the conditional response (CR). (You can't subliminally prime a *Type 2* Emotion because it requires cognitive labeling, which is of course a *conscious* response to the stimulus.)

Summary close (The): The salesperson summarizes the benefits and then asks directly for the order.

Supplementary benefit claims: Personal Selling tactic used in the Benefit Presentation stage. Written list of supplementary benefit claims follows the tactic of Two Key Benefit Statements.

Supply to: An action objective for suppliers of raw materials and input services.

Tagline (Slogan): Written or spoken words added to an ad or written words added to a logo that, if either is not evident, should identify the brand-item's Category Need and its Key Benefit.

Target audience: The target customer *groups* or *subgroups* to whom the marcoms *campaign* is directed. There are five potential groups at the broad level and 13 potential subgroups for fine targeting. The Primary target audience is the group or subgroup from whom most of the incremental sales are expected to come and Secondary target audience is the group or subgroup who produce most of the current sales and just need to have their brand communication effects reinforced. See Brand Loyalty Segmentation.

Target audience action: The final step in the customer response sequence of Exposure → Ad Processing → Brand Communication Effect → Target Audience Action.

Target audience emotional authenticity: The key creative tactic for Brand Preference in the *High-Involvement/Transformational* grid quadrant. The desired response when seeing, reading, or hearing the ad is: "That could be *me*."

Target audience reach: The ability of the combined *set* of media vehicles to reach a sufficient number of prospects to deliver the *sales goal*. Really, to reach them *effectively*, that is, at MEF/c for all the ad cycles.

Target customer: Who the brand (corporate brand, master brand, sub-brand, or brand-item) is *for*.

Task matrix method: In the matrix extension of the Task

Method for setting the Media Budget, the manager has to estimate the Aware-to-action conversion ratio for *each* media type and the various Exposure *overlaps* of the target audience from one media type to another.

Task method: Best (most accurate) way of setting the Media Budget. Based on the fact that the marcoms campaign has to accomplish three main tasks, Exposed → Aware → Action, which are embedded in the full sequence: Budget → Insertions → Exposed → Aware → Action → Sales Goal. The manager starts from the Sales Goal and works back through the tasks to arrive at the estimated Media Budget.

T-C-B positioning model: See Brand Positioning.

Technical selling: The personal selling of *complex products and services* to business customers or consumer customers (the type of selling that most marketing students think of as a sales career).

Telemarketing: Personal selling via the telephone.

Telephone interviews: Cheapest form of interviewing for a Customer Tracking Survey in large Western countries. Measures of Ad Recognition and Brand Recognition, if that's the brand awareness objective, have to be verbally (orally) administered (without visual aids), so make sure you develop the interviewers' description of these from a pre-sample of consumers.

Top of the latitude of acceptance: If your objective, factual delivery of the benefit is below the top level of what would be accepted, you must not lie by using a direct verbal overclaim; however, you can move the claim up legally with an implied verbal claim or a visual demonstration of the benefit claim.

Total marcoms allocation: Funds to cover the expected cost of all types of marcoms that the company or organization expects to use for the year.

Trade coupons: Coupon certificate designed and distributed by the retailer although partly paid for by the manufacturer (co-op funding) and redeemable only at the outlet or outlets of the particular retailer who offers them.

Trade promotions: Monetary incentives offered to wholesalers and retailers to encourage them to stock and promote the product.

Trade publications: Industry-specific magazines or newspapers.

Trade selling: Selling within the channel of distribution – Manufacturers selling to Wholesalers or Retailers, and Wholesalers selling to Retailers.

Trade show: An exhibition of products and services by manufacturers in an industry or in many related industries – and an opportunity for Direct (face-to-face) Selling.

Transformational: Label given to ads in which the buying motive for the advertised brand or brand-item is *positive-ending*. The positive-ending motives are Sensory Gratification, Intellectual Stimulation or Mastery, and Social Approval.

Trial promotions to retailers: Used by the manufacturer to try to gain distribution. The objective is to make the item available in as many stores as possible. Most often used are an Introductory Price Allowance, Returns, or payment of a New Line Fee.

Triple-Spotting: The media scheduling tactic of placing three ad insertions in the one vehicle on the one occasion; this will usually produce three OTSs in one day for the Impact Schedule reach pattern.

Trust: A feeling (that accompanies a conscious belief and doesn't occur on its own) which is the outcome of prior arousal of the Informational Problem-Avoidance motive, but with an emotional end-state tapping into the Transformational motive of Mastery. Trust is an essential entry-ticket emotional benefit for services brands.

Turnover tables: In a Customer Tracking Survey using the Panel method, you can link successive pairs of measures that represent the Customer Response Steps, or the more specific hierarchy of effects hypothesized for the campaign, for successive time periods.

TV advertising: Ads that appear during or between Free-to-air TV and Pay TV programs.

TV commercial: Also called a TV ad ("commercial" is the U.S. term for broadcast ads, both TV and radio).

TV infomercial: A 90-second or longer TV commercial.

TV or PC interactive shopping: An ad on TV (with modem) or via your PC (with modem) that prompts you and allows you to hunt through the ad (as through a catalog) when searching for and possibly purchasing a brand-item.

Two key benefit statements: Personal Selling tactic used in the Benefit Presentation stage. Salesperson should write out statements for *two* key benefits, deliverable orally in 15 seconds.

Two-second exposure rule: A tactic for increasing Brand Recognition whereby the pack shot or brand name or logo (depending on how the brand must be identified during recognition for choice) is shown on screen for at least two seconds in the TV ad and the brand name repeated for a total of at least two seconds in the radio ad.

Unaware new category users (Unaware NCUs): Have not heard about the category.

Unfavorable other-brand loyals (Unfavorable OBLs): Not our customers and not likely to be if they have previously tried our brand and disliked it. If they *haven't tried* it, there's hope, and the advertising (and perhaps an attractive promotion) should be designed to get them to try it.

Unfavorable other-brand switchers (Unfavorable OBSs): Not our customers; they switch between brands, don't include ours, and are not presently disposed toward including it. May have tried our brand in the past and disliked it, or may dislike it on the basis of its advertising or its packaging.

Unique execution: In a Transformational ad, the execution of the key benefit claim must be unique to the brand or brand-item. Why? Because in most Transformational product or service categories, the brands and brand-items are differentiated mainly – even solely – by their advertising! This truth was first pointed out by W. Wells.

Uniqueness equity: Rate at which our brand-item's sales go down if we raise its price or if a close competitor cuts its price ("downside" price elasticity). Indicates a range from complete substitutability of to extreme insistence on our brand-item.

Usage: Last of the Customer Decision Stages (level 3 of how marcoms work). The phase of post-purchase use of the brand-item, or "consumption" broadly speaking, which may extend to re-use and disposal.

User-as-hero: Creative tactic in which the ad revolves around a Presenter – an expert *user* and a person to aspire to.

Vacillators: Those who are *contemplating* taking up the "bad" behavior or else they engage in it but only *occasionally*.

Value equity: Rate at which our brand-item's sales go up in response when we cut its price ("upside" price elasticity). Indicates benefit(s) perceived per unit price – that is, value – delivered by the brand-item.

Variable pricing: The normal retail pricing strategy: the retailer chooses when to deeply discount the brand-item.

Verbal conveyer: Headline or tagline that includes a simile (literally comparing by saying "same as" or "is like") or a metaphor (implying the similarity) in which the product or service representation is compared to another entity – the conveyer. Famous example of a verbal metaphorical conveyer: "Esso. Put a tiger in your tank." In general, not as effective or widely usable as a Visual Conveyer.

Visual conveyer: The other entity to which the product or service representation is compared in a pictorially communicated metaphor (an implied comparison). A visual conveyer ensures that visual imagery about the Key Benefit is accurate; is generally more effective than a non-conveyer picture or a Verbal Conveyer; and can be used internationally and globally.

Voice and speech quality: First and foremost characteristic on which to hire Telemarketing salespeople and the second most important characteristic on which to hire High-End Retail salespeople: comprises relatively rapid speech, slightly higher than average voice pitch but with pitch variation, distinct articulation, and an accent of equal or higher status to the typical customer.

Warranty, also called a Guarantee: A contract offered by the manufacturer to a customer to provide restitution in some form should the product or servicing of the product prove deficient within a nominated time period.

Wave survey: A Customer Tracking Survey method in which *different* consumers are interviewed in each survey period (waves). The waves are usually spaced quarterly. Allows the customer response steps to be related only on an *aggregated* basis.

Wearin: The tendency of an ad to require fewer exposures on successive cycles to achieve its communication objectives. The required MEF/c should decline as more of the target audience individuals become FBSs or BLs.

Web banner ads: These come as "buttons" or "little billboards" in several sizes.

Web-based interviews: In a Customer Tracking Survey with Web-based interviews, you can show ads, packages and logos, just like in face-to-face interviews. Check sample coverage before using this method.

Web TV ad: The probability of attention to these is the same as the proportion who click through from the banner onto the Website. Web TV ads are usually just 10 to 15 seconds long.

Website ads: People self-select visits to Websites, so for *them* the attention probability to the first or home page is 1.0. Website ads function exactly like a long brochure or catalog.

Wedge pattern: Used for new product launches (most common pattern for these). The "wedge" actually refers to the pattern of *expenditure*, which begins like a Blitz and then tapers off the frequency (only) with each successive advertising cycle.

Within-vehicle duplication: In Media Data: the extent of audience duplication *within* the media vehicle over successive presentations of it.

Work for: An action objective in Corporate Image advertising (and sometimes in PR) for graduates of universities and trade schools.

index

a-b-e benefit claim model 42, 71–2
Absolut Vodka 166, 180
acceptance response 28, 29
acknowledge prior attitude 169
ACNielsen 226
acquisition 26–8
action objectives 33, 81, 90–3
Adidas 386
adspend 11, 286, 297–303, 313, 330
advertisers
    direct-response 242–3
    large-audience 239–41
    media use by individual 10–11
    small-audience 242–3
advertising 6, 7, 9, 21
    awareness 6, 27, 170
    cinema 239
    company-branded generic-need 376
    competitive 13
    components 124–6
    corporate image 6, 375, 376, 387–97
    cycle 245, 269, 278, 355, 449–50
    direct-response 6, 7, 27, 168, 170, 201, 271
    dollars 313
    double-duty 242
    elasticity 12–13
    elasticity coefficient 301
    email 206
    execution tactics 73
    internet 8
    likability by target audience 166–7
    local retail 241
    magazine 198–201
    mystery 192
    newspaper 194–7
    online 204–6
    outdoor 8, 203–4, 239
    pre-testing rough ads 212–30
    print 8
    processing 24, 25, 28–9
    processing measures 314–17
    and promotions 16–18, 25, 28–9, 271
    quality 14
    radio 192–4
    recognition 314–15, 330
    response modeling 228
    retail feature 7, 362–3
    and sales 11–16
    TV 8, 15–16, 188–92, 239, 377
    unit adjustments 269–74
    wearout 338, 341
    website 206
    Yellow Pages 201–3
advertising-to-sales ratio 298, 300
advertorials 382
aggregate tracking 35, 312, 327, 313, 332, 333
Aldi 56
ambush marketing 385
American Express 55, 131, 300, 301, 330, 340, 381
Anheuser-Busch 300, 352, 376, 388
anxiety 441–6
Apple Computer 50, 159, 161, 169, 203, 205, 334, 391, 393
approach behaviors 53, 416–18
approachability 175
approximate log-linear model 281
archetypal selling proposition (ASP) 54–5, 57, 65, 174
archetypes 54, 65–7, 180
arousal (emotional selling) 55, 360, 361–2
associate and repeat 157
AT&T 18, 299, 301
attention response 28, 29
attention tactics 34, 126, 188–208

Australian Tourist Commission 253
Aventis 394
average frequency 163–5
Avis 173
awareness advertising 6, 27, 170
awareness pattern 252–3, 255

bait and switch 362
Bank of America 302
Barnardos 457
Behavioral Sequence Model (BSM) 33, 95–7, 108, 109, 244, 450
benefit, inferior 56–7, 62
benefit claims 71, 76, 170
benefit positioning 50, 62–76
benefit presentation 418–22
beta binominal model 281
Birds Eye 18, 46, 67, 68, 73–4, 110, 214, 307
blitz pattern 245–6
BMW 161, 393
body organ donation and social marketing 437
Boeing 18
bonus packs 351–2
Booth Signs 156
brain-levels theory 51–3, 174
brand action intention 26, 34, 39, 114–16
brand advertising 6, 28
brand architecture 57–8
brand attitude 111, 433–4
brand awareness 14, 26, 29, 34, 39, 98, 107–8, 110, 126, 151, 152, 153–60, 225–7, 237, 261, 267, 317, 379, 385–6, 433–4
brand benefit beliefs 113–14, 228
brand benefit delivery 67
brand-building advertising 27
brand communication effects 25–8, 29, 30, 34, 313, 317
brand contact points 3, 4
brand delivery 64, 68
brand emotions 113–14, 126, 228, 391
brand equity 5, 11, 12, 18–20, 21, 31, 319
   corporate 18–19
brand identity 5, 42, 43, 109, 378, 379
brand-item alternatives 25
brand-item campaign 303
brand-item equity 19–20
brand loyals (BLs) 83–4, 266, 268
brand loyalty groups 87
brand loyalty segmentation 82–6, 432–4

brand marks 154
brand name 3
brand personality 72, 180
brand position statement 34
brand positioning 32–3, 36, 42, 44, 57–9, 391, 435–8
brand preference 14, 26, 29, 34, 39, 69, 70, 74, 88, 98, 106, 110–14, 151, 152, 153, 227, 238, 261, 378, 379, 386
brand preference score 64
brand preference strategy (BPREF) 267
brand preference strength 84
brand preference tactics 126, 160–77
brand-prompted ad recall (BPAR) 38, 314, 315–16
brand purchase intention 29, 261
brand recall 5, 107, 109–10, 151, 152, 157–9, 226, 240, 241, 267, 317, 339, 378, 379, 383
brand-recall-boosted brand recognition 107, 110, 159–60
brand recognition 107, 108–9, 151, 152, 153–6, 225, 240, 241, 267, 317, 339, 378, 379
brand reputation 67, 68, 69
brand switchers 83, 84–5, 88, 89, 266, 432
branding 57–8, 174
brands, follower 50
brands, store 367
Branson, Richard 55
budget 35, 93, 286, 330
Budweiser 50, 136, 383, 388
Burger King 173, 334

Camel 381
campaign budget-setting 303–9
campaign initiation 331–2
campaign-level targets 46
campaign management 35, 38–9, 329–31
campaign objectives 33–4, 36–7, 40
campaign position statement 98
campaign tracking 19, 31, 312–42
campaign wearout 333–41
Campbell's Soup 274, 300
Canadian Club & Cola 144, 145
canonical expansion model 281
card-based loyalty programs 367
carryover 269
category need 5, 26, 28, 29, 30, 43, 44, 45, 47, 102–7, 379, 380, 382
category need (C) positioning decision 46–9
category need explicit 156
category positioning 48–9

category-cued brand recall 385
category-prompted ad recall (CPAR) 314, 316–17
causal analysis 328
celebrity presenter 158, 177–8
central me-too positioning 51, 56
central positioning 50–1
CESLIP presenter model 177, 389–90
CHAID analysis 320, 329
Charmin 163
Chevrolet Monte Carlo 48, 49
choice 28
Chrysler Corporation 392
Chrysler Sebring 48, 49
Church of England 127
cinema advertising 239
Citibank Corporate Services 45, 57
Clorox 300, 381
Coca-Cola 18, 50, 55, 107, 142, 173, 301, 331–2, 335, 377, 383, 388, 392
Cole Haan 136
Colgate 55, 56, 159, 237, 300, 356
Colombia 204
color (retail environment) 360
Commonwealth Bank 109–10, 158
communication 6
communication objectives 33
company-branded generic-need advertising 376
company mission 387
company vision 387
Compaq 159
competitive advertising 13
competitive reactions 69–70
conformers (social marketing) 432, 438
consideration set 48
considered purchase 30
consumer values 335–6
contact coefficient 268, 385
content factors ratings 216
contests 355
continuous tracking 38, 320
continuous tracking research 269
conveyer(s) 55
    brainstorming (I-G-I method) 137
    properties 133–5
    remote conveyer model 131–43
    screening and selection 137–42
    types 135–7
    visual 135
Cornhill Insurance 387

corpographic proxies 93
corporate brand 375, 391
    awareness 389, 390
    emotions 391
    equity 18–19
corporate identity 387
corporate image 387
    advertising 6, 375, 376, 387–97
    communications, internal 392
corporate reputation 387, 389–90
cosmetic integration 72–3, 180
Cosmopolitan 167
coupons 353–4
creative brief 34, 35, 124, 126–30, 213
    remote conveyer model 131–43
creative idea 34, 55, 123–46
creative strategy 34, 37
creative tactics 34
creative target 46, 47, 81, 94–5
credence goods 176
credit card stickers 361
Crest toothpaste 55, 56, 336
cross-media duplications 277–8
curious disbelief 161
customer, target 43, 45, 47, 48–9, 81
customer behavior 357
customer benefit, importance or desirability 63–4
customer decision stages 24–5, 30, 313
customer franchise-building (CFB) 35, 347
customer response ad test (CRAT) 212, 221–30, 451–2
customer response steps 30–2
customer survey tracking 35
customer targeting
    using brand loyalty segmentation 82–6
    distinctions 47
customer tracking survey (CTS) 312–13
    analysis of results 327–9
    and campaign management 329–31
    interview methods 321–2
    measures 313–19
    methodologies 319–27, 329
    order of measures 322–7
    sample 318
customer values 335–6

DaimlerChrysler Corporation 26, 27
database marketing 7, 242
databasing 356

Decore 159
delivery (by each brand) 64, 68
Dell 18, 161, 299, 300, 381
Delta 394
Delvita 368
demographic proxy 93
de-resistance (sales exchange) 422
desirability, consumer 63–4
Deutsche Telekom 299, 301
DHL World Express 128–9
Diesel 145
differentiated positioning 50–1
direct extreme verbal claims 161
direct mail 8, 242
direct marketing 243
direct-marketing promotions 7
direct matching 93, 99, 244
direct price-offs 352, 354–5
direct-response advertising 6, 7, 27, 39, 168, 170,
    201, 242–3
direct selling 401
direct-to-customer trial promotions 7
Disney 18, 55, 94, 161, 387
disposition to purchase (or act) 261
Dorf 457
double-duty advertising 242
Dove 159
Dr. Pepper 50
durables 12, 14, 21
    advertising elasticity 13
    sales maintenance 88–9
Duracell 173, 355

Eastman Kodak 300
EBay 393
econometric modeling 329
effective frequency 259, 260–74
    maximum (MaxEF/c) 262–3, 271–4
    minimum (MEF/c) 262–3, 265–74
effective reach 330, 384
email advertising 206
emotion response 28, 29
emotion-shift 163
emotional authenticity 175
emotional benefit 62, 63, 74, 379
emotional selling proposition (ESP) 55, 57, 174
emotions, brand 113–14, 126, 228, 391
empowerment 175
end-customer target 45–6

Energizer 173, 355
entry-ticket benefits 33, 56, 62
equity
    brand-item 19–20
    uniqueness 19, 20, 21, 64, 84, 319
    value 19, 20, 21, 84, 319
Ericsson 18
Ernst & Young 394
Esso 386
ethical alternatives in social marcoms 440–1
ethics of marketing communication 53, 57, 361–2,
    363, 382, 452–9
event marketing 376
executional integration tactics 180–1
expenditure, marcoms 7–11
experimental favorable brand switchers
    (experimental FBSs) 84
expert, sincere presenter 172, 178
explicit comparison 172
exposure 260–1, 313–14, 376
exposure ratio 330
exposure-to-sales analysis 329
extreme positive emotion-shift 165
eyeball analysis 328

face-to-face interviews 321
face-to-face selling 7, 28, 420
fast-moving consumer goods (FMCG) 9, 12, 14, 16,
    21, 246
    advertising elasticity 12–13
    sales growth 89
    sales maintenance 88
    sampling 351
favorable brand switchers (FBSs) 83, 84–5, 88, 89,
    91, 98, 266, 432
favorable other-brand loyals (favorable OBLs) 86
favorable other-brand switchers (favorable
    OBSs) 85
Federal Express 55, 274
firmagraphic 93
Fishbein Extended Model 438, 440
Fisher-Price 53
flyers 241
focus groups 222
follower brands 50
follow-up (sales exchange) 423
Ford 18, 48, 49, 300
Four 'N' Twenty 18
free premium 353

free-standing inserts (FSIs) 9
frequency distributions 264
frequency rule 278, 279
functional benefits, I-D-U analysis for 67–8

General Electric 18, 169, 299, 300
General Motors 300
generic branding 367
generic-need ads 376
Gillette 161
GlaxoSmithKline 300
Goodyear 381
Gray's theory 441–6
Greenseas Tuna 454
Grey Goose 161
gross rating points (GRPs) 259, 313–14
guarantees 352
Gucci Rush 53
Guinness 131

Haagen-Daz 53
Hagar 94
Hallmark 48
handbills 241
Harley-Davidson 18
Head & Shoulders 18
Healthy Choice 159, 172
Heineken, Freddy 46
Heineken Beer 129–30
Heinz 67, 68, 110, 159
Herron Blue 173
Hershey 300
Hertz 173
Hewlett-Packard (H-P) 50, 300
high involvement 153
high-involvement/informational 153, 168–70, 197
high-involvement/transformational 153, 173–5
Hilton 299, 300
Hitachi 394
home shopping 368–9
Honda 145
HSBC 140, 141
Huggies 383
human evaluative conditioning (HEC) 167, 191, 453
Hyundai Motor Corporation 302

IBM 18, 46, 50, 53, 107, 144, 180, 300, 330

I-D-U benefit analysis 33, 42, 45, 62–8, 74, 451
I-D-U matrix 69
I-D-U model 63, 70, 390, 451
I-D-U strategy options 68–70
identification 175
imagery transfer 238
impact scheduling 11, 237, 249–52, 253, 255
implicit comparison 173
implied extreme verbal claims 161–2
implied extreme visual claims 162
importance, consumer 63–4
impulse purchase 30
impulsiveness 441–6
individual-group-individual (I-G-I) brainstorming 137
industry-specific positioning statement 417
inferior benefits 56–7, 62
informational advertising
    high-involvement 153, 168–70, 197
    low-involvement 160–1, 162, 340
informational brand preference 152, 153
informationally motivated products and services 71, 153
insertion 260–1
instinctual selling proposition (ISP) 53, 57, 174
in-store promotions 7
Intel 18, 300
intellectual stimulation 107, 161
internal corporate image communications 392
instrumental learning 190
Interbrand 18
internet advertising 8
introductory price allowance 349
involvement 114
Irish Spring soap 381

Jack Daniel's 382
John Hancock Insurance 381
Johnson & Johnson 300, 375
Jones' data on TV ad quality 15–16

Kao 375
Kellogg 300, 383, 386
key benefit 5, 33, 43, 45, 51, 62, 63, 74, 107, 379
key benefit claim 34, 124–5, 130–1, 153, 170–1
key benefit (B) positioning decision 49–57
key schema 5, 102, 103
Kinko's 393, 394
Kleenex 50, 51

Kmart 301, 353
Kodak 55, 300

Lacoste 178, 179
large-audience advertisers 239–41
Lean Cuisine 160–1, 172
learning response 28, 29
Lee Jeans 57
leverage calculations 89
Levi Strauss 204, 213, 302, 381
Levitt, Ted 46
Lexus cars 375
Linux 161
Listerine 173
local retail advertisers 241–2
long-form positioning statement 73
low involvement 152
low-involvement/informational 160–1, 162, 340
low-involvement/transformational 161, 162, 164–7, 340
Löwenbrau 136, 379
loyalty, store 358–9
loyalty programs 7
    card-based 368
Lufthansa 393

McDonald's 18, 53, 107, 131, 154, 157, 158, 173, 301, 355
Macintosh 144, 169
magazine advertising 198–201
Management Judgment Ad Test (MJAT) 34, 212–21, 230
manufacturers 7
manufacturer's coupons 354
manufacturer's repeat-purchase promotions to end-customers 354–7
manufacturer's trial promotions to end-customers 349–54
market leader 50
market share 318–19
marketing
    ambush 385
    audit 334
    event 376
    mix 334–5
    plan 334–6
marketing communications (marcoms) 3–5, 21
    advertising and promotions 11, 25, 28–9
    allocation, total 297–303
    brand communication effects 25–8, 30
    campaign planning 24, 32–6
    customer decision stages 24–5, 30
    customer response steps 30–2
    defined 6–7
    ethics 452–7
    expenditure 7–11, 376
    integrated 72–3
    media expenditures and use 7–11
    planning stages 32–5, 36, 39
    situation audit 44
    social 432, 438–47
    three levels of effects 24, 25, 29–30
Marks and Spencer 367
Marlboro 18, 165
Marriott 299, 300
Mars 383
masked ad recognition (MAR) 315
master brand 46, 57, 375
mathematical ability 403
Mattel 301
maximum effective frequency (MaxEF/c) 262–3, 271–4
Maxwell House 88
Mazda Motor Corporation 302
media
    budget 35, 286, 330
    cross-media duplications 277–8
    data 274–9
    expenditures and use 7–11
    mania 280–1, 282, 288, 306, 450
    models 280
    plan 330, 336–7
    primary 236–7
    schedule 35, 260, 280–8, 289
    secondary 236, 237–8
    strategy 35, 38, 235
    strategy in social marcoms campaigns 447–50
    target 46, 47, 81, 93–4
    vehicles 274–9, 450
media-type selection 35, 235–43
Mercedes 18
Merrill Lynch 18
Michelob beer 381
Microsoft 18, 300, 387
milk and social marketing 435–6
Miller beer 51, 335, 338
Millward Brown 38

minimum effective frequency (MEF/c) 35, 261, 262–3
   ad unit adjustments 269–74
   estimation formula 265–9
   per advertising cycle 449–50
mnemonic device 158–9
Mobil 158
mobile-viewed outdoor advertising 204, 239
moderately favorable prior attitude 169
Molson beer 167
monetary savings (point-of-purchase displays) 366
Moran's method of brand equity 19
Morgan Stanley Dean Witter 300
multiattribute model 62–3, 70
multi-brand loyals (multi-BLs) 83, 84
multi-purchase contest 355
multi-purchase premiums 355–6
multi-purchase sweepstakes 355
music (promotional stimulus) 360
Mustang 159
mystery advertising 192

Nabisco 274
Narhex Cross-Linked Elastin 169
national brands 367
Nature's Way 55
need arousal 25, 39, 105, 106
negative-attitude target audience 172
negative affect (emotional selling) 55
negative instinctive drives 53
negative new category users (negative NCUs) 86
negative prior attitude 169
Nestle 300
neuro-linguistic programming (NLP) 417–18
   matching 420–1
neutral other-brand loyals (neutral OBLs) 86
neutral other-brand switchers (neutral OBSs) 85
neutral prior attitude 169
Neutrogena 159
new category users (NCUs) 83, 86, 103, 254, 266
new line fee 349
new product campaigns 244
newspaper advertising 194–7
Nextel Communications 302
Nike 53, 131, 144, 154, 192, 301, 379, 388, 394
Nissan 393, 394

Nivea 18
Nokia 18
Nudie 391
Nurofen 173

off-invoice promotion 349
offenders (social marketing) 432, 438
Oldsmobile 381
olfactory cues 361–2
on consignment 349
online advertising 204–6
online home shopping 368
operant learning 190
opportunity to see (OTS) 261, 384
other-brand loyals (OBLs) 83, 86, 266
other-brand switchers (OBSs) 85
OTS (opportunity to see) 261
outdoor advertising 8, 203–4, 239
overclaim transformational benefit(s) 176
overweightness and social marketing 90, 436–7
own brand(s) 7

P&O 157–8
packaging 356–7
Palm Pilot 103
panel survey 319
paralogic 162
PC interactive shopping 7
Pennzoil 381
Pepsi 50, 144, 173, 301, 387
personal influence (PI) 248, 267–8
personal selling 7, 8, 28, 35, 90, 168, 401–26
personality profiles 65
personality segmentation and social marketing 434–5
personality traits 440, 441–7
personalization 157–8
persuasion in social marcoms 438–47
Philip Morris 391
Philips Electronics 302
piecemeal comparison 173
point-of-decision (P-O-D) media 243–4
point-of-purchase displays 363–7, 370
point-of-sale (POS) displays 7
positioning
   benefit 50, 62–76
   brand 32–3, 36, 42, 44, 58–9, 391
   and brand architecture 57–8
   category 48–9

positioning (*cont.*)
central 50–1
central me-too 51
differentiated 50–1
and integrated marcoms 72–3
research 44
statement 43, 44, 73–5, 93
three levels of 42
positive affect (emotional selling) 55
positive instinctive drives 53
positive new category users (positive NCUs) 86
postmodernism as the creative idea 143–5, 169
post-purchase behaviors 81
Powerade 381
pre-purchase behaviors 81, 90–1
premiums 353
presenter 177–80
celebrity 158, 177–8
expert, sincere 172, 178
ideal-similar 177
price-endings 366–7
price-off promotions 7, 363–4
price-off wording 365–6
price promotions 16
primary media 236–7
priming 238
print advertising 8
prior attitude 169
private label 367
Probe 159
problem removal 106
Procter & Gamble 18, 300, 302, 375
product containers 356
product pack-photo appeal 67
product placement 377, 378, 382–3, 384, 385
product sampling 350–1
profit measures 319
promotion processing 24, 25, 28–9
promotion strategy 35, 37
promotions 7
and advertising 16–18, 25, 28–9, 271
direct-marketing 7
direct-to-customer trial 7
price-off 7, 363–4
repeat-purchase 354
retailer's 357–8
sales 16–18, 347–71
short term tactical adjustments 272–3
prospecting 416

public relations (PR) 6, 375, 377, 378, 385
Puma 391
purchase
behaviors 81, 91
considered 30
facilitation 26, 30, 34, 116–17
impulse 30
intention 26

Qantas 379, 380
QBE Insurance 387
qualitative research 44
quasi-causal analysis 328–9

radio commercials 192–4
random duplication 278
rapport (sales exchange) 417
rational selling proposition (RSP) 55–6
Ray Ban 383
reach pattern 35, 235, 244, 384–5
combining 255–6
for established products 248–55
for new products 244–8
selection 449
reach rule 251, 278, 279
Reader's Digest 382
realism curved 153–4
rebates 351
recommendation (word-of-mouth) 92
Red Bull 53
Red Cross 53
Reebok 154, 381
Reece's Pieces 383
Reeves, Rosser 56
refutational approach 172
remote conveyer model 131–43
Renuzit 381
repeat purchase 89, 91, 305
promotion 354
research
positioning 44
social marketing 450–2
response advertising 27
retail
atmosphere 360
and credit cards 362
environment color 360–1
feature ads 7, 362–3
layout 359–60

music 361
    olfactory cues 361–2
    promotions 357–9
    support 272
retailers 7
returns 349
reverse-wedge/PI pattern 247–8
Revlon 46
Revson, Charles 46
rhetorical 'check' end-question 173
Rossiter-Percy-Bellman grid 151–3, 236
rough ads 214–16
routinized favorable brand switchers (routinized FBSs) 67, 84

S.C. Johnson 300
Safeway 301, 357–8
Sainsbury 367, 377
Saks 299, 301
sales
    and advertising 11–16
    and campaign tracking 318–19
    closing the sale 422–3
    effects 11–18
    growth 89
    maintenance 88–9
    modeling 329
    presentation 28
    promotions 16–18, 347–71
salesforce promotions 7
salespeople 403–14
Samsung 18
Saturn 393
Scholl 103, 104
Schroer's method 307–9, 330, 339
Scope 173
Sears 353, 394
seasonal priming pattern 254–5
secondary media 237–8
secondary point-of-decision (P-O-D) media 243–4
self-liquidating premium 353
selling
    face-to-face 7, 28, 420
    high-end retail 403, 411–13
    personal 7, 8, 28, 35, 90, 168, 401–26
    regular retail 402, 403–5
    small business 402, 406
    stages 414–23
    tactics, effective 415

    technical 403, 413–14
    trade 402, 406–7
    types of 402–14
sensory gratification 106, 107, 137, 165, 174
service sampling 350–1
service stickers 356
share of requirement (SOR) 84
share of voice (SOV) 13, 308
Sharper Image 171
Shell 131, 307, 379, 381
shifting reach pattern 253–4
shopping
    bags 356
    home 368–9
    interactive 7
short fad pattern 248
short positioning statement 73
Simplot 18
single-brand loyals (single-BLs) 83
six-step marcoms planning approach 4
Skoda U.K. 36–9
SKYY vodka 178
slogan 109, 393–5
slotting allowance 349
small-audience advertisers 242–3
Smirnoff vodka 4, 5
Smith's frozen dinners 162
social approval 107, 137, 165, 174
social marketing
    brand positioning 435–8
    defined 430
    media strategy 447–50
    and persuasion 438–47
    research 450–2
    target audience 432–5
social marketing campaigns 430–59
social skills 403
Sony 144, 299, 300, 381
Sorbent 51
Spam 48
spam email 206
speech rate convergence 417
speech sampling 418
sponsorships 6, 8, 375, 376, 378, 385
stakeholders 45, 90
Starbucks 18, 391
State Farm 55
stationary-viewed outdoor advertising 204, 239
status 175

Stingose 157, 158, 162, 163
store atmosphere 7 ·
store brands 51, 367
store loyalty 357–8
store layout 7, 359–62
subliminal affective priming 53
sweepstakes 355
synergy 238

tagline 109, 110, 380, 393–5
Target 299, 301
target audience 33, 46, 47, 81, 88–90, 93, 166–7,
   172–3, 266–7, 384–5
   action 317–18
   emotional authenticity 175
   reach 241
   in social marketing 432–5
target customer 43, 45, 47, 48–9, 81
target customer ideal-similarity 177
target customer (T) positioning decision 45–6
target customer reach 11
task matrix method 304
task method 303–6
T-C-B positioning model 33, 42, 43–59, 106
teaser campaigns 238
telemarketing 7, 8, 28, 35, 243, 401, 403, 407–11
telephone interviews 321
Telstra 386
terminology 70, 259
Tide 18
Toshiba 393
total marcoms allocation 297–303
Toyota 375
trade coupons 354
trade promotions 7
trade shows 8, 350
transformational advertising
   high-involvement 153, 173–5
   low-involvement 161, 162, 164–7, 3340
transformational brand preference 152, 153
transformational campaigns 240
transformationally motivated products and services
   71, 153
trial promotions to retailers 347–9
trust 175
turnover tables 328
TV advertising 8, 239, 377
   quality, Jones' data 15–16

TV commercials 188–92
TV interactive shopping 7
Tyson 394

Ultra Slim-Fast 159
unaware new category users (unaware NCUs) 86
unfavorable other-brand loyals (unfavorable
   OBLs) 86
unfavorable other-brand switchers (unfavorable
   OBSs) 85
Unilever 300, 375
unique execution 165
unique selling position (USP) 56
uniqueness (between brands) 64–5
uniqueness equity 19, 20, 21, 64, 84, 319
United Airlines 393
UPS 394
user-as-hero 176

vacillators (social marketing) 432–3, 438
value equity 19, 20, 21, 84, 319
values, consumer/customer 335–6
Verizon 299, 301
very positive opening visual 172
very short-term scheduling 273–4
Viagra 394
Video Storyboard Tests 163
Virgin 55
Visa 161
visual sensory gratification 240
Volkswagen 132, 133, 197, 198, 394
Volvo 56, 134, 135, 180, 379, 380, 387

warranties 352–3
wave method 319–20, 386
wearout 333–41
web banner advertising 206
web-based interviews 322
web TV advertising 206
websites 206
wedge pattern 246–7, 272
Wendy's 173, 301
Windex 274
Wisk 131, 163
word-of-mouth 92, 248

Yellow Pages advertising 201–3, 379